ALL ■ IN ■ ONE

CISA® Certified Information Systems Auditor

EXAM GUIDE

Second Edition

ALL·IN·ONE

CISA® Certified Information Systems Auditor

EXAM GUIDE

Second Edition

Peter H. Gregory

New York • Chicago • San Francisco • Lisbon
London • Madrid • Mexico City • Milan • New Delhi
San Juan • Seoul • Singapore • Sydney • Toronto

The McGraw-Hill Companies

Library of Congress Cataloging-in-Publication Data

Gregory, Peter H.
 All-in-one CISA certified information systems auditor exam guide /
Peter H. Gregory. -- 2nd ed.
   p. cm.
 Includes bibliographical references and index.
 ISBN 978-0-07-176910-5 (alk. paper)
 1. Information Systems Audit and Control
Association--Examinations--Study guides. 2. Electronic data processing
departments--Auditing--Examinations--Study guides. 3. Management
information systems--Auditing--Examinations--Study guides. 4.
Electronic data processing personnel--Certification--Study guides. I.
Title. II. Title: CISA certified information systems auditor exam guide.

 QA76.3.G7529 2012
 658.4'03--dc23

                              2011031506

CISA® Certified Information Systems Auditor All-in-One Exam Guide, Second Edition

234567890 DOC DOC 1098765432

ISBN: Book p/n 978-0-07-176911-2 and CD p/n 978-0-07-176912-9 of set 978-0-07-176910-5

MHID: Book p/n 0-07-176911-0 and CD p/n 0-07-176912-9 of set 0-07-176910-2

Sponsoring Editor Timothy Green	**Proofreader** Nancy Bell
Editorial Supervisor Janet Walden	**Indexer** Nancy Guenther
Project Editor Rachel Gunn	**Production Supervisor** James Kussow
Acquisitions Coordinator Stephanie Evans	**Composition** Apollo Publishing Services
Technical Editor Bobby Rogers	**Illustration** Lyssa Wald
Copy Editor Lisa McCoy	**Art Director, Cover** Jeff Weeks

To Rebekah and Shannon.

About the Author

Peter H. Gregory, CISA, CRISC, CISSP, DRCE, CCSK, is a 30-year career technologist and the manager of information security and risk management at Concur, a Redmond, Washington–based provider of integrated travel and expense management solutions. He has been deeply involved in the development of IT controls and internal IT audit since 2002, and has been leading the development and testing of secure IT environments since 1990. In addition, he has spent many years as a software engineer and architect, systems engineer, programmer, and systems operator. Throughout his career, he has written many articles, whitepapers, user manuals, processes, and procedures, and he has conducted numerous lectures and training classes.

Peter is the author of 24 books in information security and technology, including *Solaris Security*, *CISSP Guide to Security Essentials*, and *IT Disaster Recovery Planning for Dummies*. He is a columnist for *Software Magazine* and has spoken at numerous industry conferences including RSA, SecureWorld Expo, West Coast Security Forum, IP3, Society for Information Management, the Washington Technology Industry Association, and InfraGard.

Peter is an advisory board member at the University of Washington's certificate program in information security and risk management, the lead instructor and advisory board member for the University of Washington certificate program in information systems security, a board member of the Washington state chapter of InfraGard, and a founding member of the Pacific CISO Forum. He is a board member of InfraGard, a 2008 graduate of the FBI Citizens' Academy, and a member of the FBI Citizens' Academy Alumni Association.

Peter resides with his family in the Seattle, Washington, area and can be reached at www.peterhgregory.com.

About the Technical Editor

Bobby E. Rogers is a principal information security analyst with Dynetics, Inc., a national technology firm specializing in the certification and accreditation process for the U.S. government. He also serves as a penetration testing team lead for various government and commercial engagements. Bobby recently retired from the U.S. Air Force after almost 21 years, where he served as a computer networking and security specialist and designed and managed networks all over the world. His IT security experience includes several years working as an information assurance manager and a regular consultant to U.S. Air Force military units on various cybersecurity/computer abuse cases. He has held several positions of responsibility for network security in both the Department of Defense and private company networks. His duties have included perimeter security, client-side security, security policy development, security training, and computer crime investigations. As a trainer, he has taught a wide variety of IT-related subjects in both makeshift classrooms in desert tents and formal training centers. Bobby is also an accomplished author, having written numerous IT articles in various publications and training materials for the U.S. Air Force. He has also authored numerous security training videos.

He has a Bachelor of Science degree in computer information systems from Excelsior College and two Associates in Applied Science degrees from the Community College of the Air Force. Bobby's professional IT certifications include A+, Security+, ACP, CCNA, CCAI, CIW, CIWSA, MCP+I, MCSA (Windows 2000 and 2003), MCSE (Windows NT4, 2000, and 2003), MCSE: Security (Windows 2000 and 2003), CISSP, CIFI, CEH, CHFI, and CPTS. He is also a certified trainer.

CONTENTS AT A GLANCE

CONTENTS

Figure Credits

Figure 4-6 courtesy of Digital Aardvark, Inc.

Figure 4-9 courtesy of Oxford University Press, Inc.

Figure 5-2 courtesy of Fir0002/Flagstaffotos with permission granted under the terms of the GNU Free Documentation License, Version 1.2, http://commons.wikimedia.org/wiki/Commons:GNU_Free_Documentation_License,_version_1.2.

Figure 5-3 courtesy of Sassospicco with permission granted under the terms of the Creative Commons Attribution Share-Alike 2.5 License, http://creativecommons.org/licenses/by-sa/2.5/.

Figure 5-4, courtesy of Robert Jacek Tomczak, has been released into the public domain by its author at the Polish Wikipedia project.

Figure 5-5 courtesy of Robert Kloosterhuis with permission granted under the terms of the Creative Commons Attribution Share-Alike 2.5 License, http://creativecommons.org/licenses/by-sa/2.5/.

Figure 5-15 courtesy of Rebecca Steele.

Figure 5-16 courtesy of Harout S. Hhedeshian with permission granted under the terms of the Creative Commons Attribution 3.0 Unported License, http://creativecommons.org/licenses/by/3.0/.

Figure 5-17 courtesy of Stephanie Tsacas with permission granted under the terms of the Creative Commons Attribution Share-Alike 2.5 License, http://creativecommons.org/licenses/by-sa/2.5/.

Figure 5-18 courtesy of Fdominec with permission granted under the terms of the GNU Free Documentation License, Version 1.2, http://commons.wikimedia.org/wiki/Commons:GNU_Free_Documentation_License,_version_1.2.

Figure 6-3 courtesy Ingersoll Rand Security Technologies.

ACKNOWLEDGMENTS

I am especially grateful to Timothy Green for affirming the need to have this book published on a tight timeline. My readers deserve nothing less.

Heartfelt thanks to Stephanie Evans for proficiently managing this project, facilitating rapid turnaround, and equipping me with information I needed to produce the manuscript.

I would like to thank Bobby Rogers, who took on the task of tech reviewing the manuscript. Bobby carefully and thoughtfully read the entire draft manuscript and made many useful suggestions that have improved the book's quality.

Many thanks to contributors Tanya Scott, who wrote Chapter 1 and Appendix B of the first edition of this book and revised it for the second edition of this book, and Chris Tarnstrom, who wrote the original Appendix A and updated it for this edition. These important texts help readers better understand the CISA certification process and help IS auditors to be more effective in their work. Tanya's and Chris' professional auditing experience and insight add considerable value to this book, long after readers become CISA-certified. My vision for this book includes value for aspiring as well as practicing IS auditors; these contributions allow the book to fulfill this vision.

Many thanks to Lisa McCoy for her great copyediting and further improving readability. Much appreciation to Lyssa Wald, who expertly rendered my sketches into beautifully clear line art, and to Apollo Publishing Services for their page layout. Like Olympic athletes, they make hard work look easy.

Many thanks to my literary agent, Carole Jelen, for faithful assistance during this and other projects. Sincere thanks to Rebecca Steele, my business manager and publicist, for her long-term vision, for keeping me on track, and for photos that she obtained for the manuscript.

Despite having written 25 books, I have difficulty putting into words my gratitude for my wife Rebekah and daughter Shannon for tolerating my frequent absences (in the home office) while I revised and added content for this second edition. This project could not have been completed without their unfailing support. They both deserve the credit.

INTRODUCTION

The dizzying pace of information systems innovation has made vast expanses of information available to organizations and the public. Often, design flaws and technical vulnerabilities bring unintended consequences, often in the form of information theft and disclosure. The result: a patchwork of laws, regulations, and standards such as Sarbanes-Oxley, the European Privacy Directive, Gramm-Leach-Bliley, HIPAA, PCI-DSS, PIPEDA, and scores of U.S. state laws requiring public disclosure of security breaches involving private information. Through these, organizations are either required or incentivized to perform their own internal audits or undergo external audits that measure compliance in order to avoid penalties, sanctions, and embarrassing news headlines.

These developments have caused quite a surge in demand for IT security professionals and IS auditors. These highly sought professionals play a crucial role in the development of better compliance programs and reduced risk.

The Certified Information Systems Auditor (CISA) certification, established in 1978, is indisputably the leading certification for IS auditing. Demand for the CISA certification has grown so much that the once-per-year certification exam was changed to twice per year in 2005. That same year, the CISA certification was awarded accreditation by the American National Standards Institute (ANSI) under international standard ISO/IEC 17024. CISA is also one of the few certifications formally approved by the U.S. Department of Defense in its Information Assurance Technical category (DoD 8570.01-M). In 2009, *SC Magazine* named CISA the best professional certification program. In 2010, there were over 75,000 professionals holding the certification.

IS auditing is not a "bubble" or a flash in the pan. Rather, IS auditing is a permanent fixture in IS/IT organizations that have to contend with new technologies; new systems; new threats; and new data security and privacy laws, regulations, and standards. The CISA certification is the gold standard certification for professionals who work in this domain.

Purpose of This Book

Let's get the obvious out of the way: this is a comprehensive study guide for the IT or audit professional who needs a serious reference for individual or group-led study for the Certified Information Systems Auditor (CISA) certification. The majority of the content in this book contains the technical information that CISA candidates are required to know.

This book is also a reference for aspiring and practicing IS auditors. The content that is required to pass the CISA exam is the same content that practicing auditors need to be familiar with in their day-to-day work. This book is an ideal CISA exam study guide as well as a desk reference for those who have already earned their CISA certification.

This book is an excellent guide for someone exploring the IS audit profession. The study chapters explain all of the technologies and audit procedures, and the appendices explain process frameworks and the practical side of professional audits. This is useful for those readers who may wonder what the IS audit profession is all about.

How This Book Is Organized

This book is logically divided into four major sections:

- **Introduction** The "front matter" of the book plus Chapter 1 provide an overview of the CISA certification and the IS audit profession.

- **CISA study material** Chapters 2 through 6 contain everything a studying CISA candidate is responsible for. This same material is a handy desk reference for aspiring and practicing IS auditors.

- **IS auditor reference** Appendix A walks the reader through the entire process of a professional IS audit, from audit planning to delivery of the final report. Appendix B discusses control frameworks; this will help an IS auditor who needs to understand how control frameworks function, or who is providing guidance to an organization that needs to implement a control framework.

- **Practice exams** Appendix C explains the CISA practice exams and MasterExam software that accompany this book.

Notes on the Second Edition

ISACA has historically recalibrated the contents of its certifications every five years. In mid-2009, ISACA announced that it would update the CISA job practice, effective in the June 2011 examination. In order to keep this book up to date, I immediately contacted Tim Green at McGraw-Hill so that we might develop a plan for the second edition of this book as quickly as possible.

The new CISA job practice information was made available in late December 2010. We began work at that time to update the original manuscript. The result is this book, which has been updated to reflect all of the changes in the CISA job practice, as well as changes in audit practices and technology since the first edition was published.

Changes to the CISA Job Practice

Table 1 illustrates the old and new CISA job practices and their relation to chapters in this book.

The most significant change to the 2011 CISA job practice is the elimination of Business Continuity and Disaster Recovery (BCDR) as a major domain. The BCDR content was not eliminated, but instead it was integrated into two other domains: 2) Governance and Management of IT and 4) Information Systems Operations, Maintenance, and Support. The percentages among the domains have also changed slightly, due to the removal of BCDR as well as minor adjustments in the emphasis of one domain over another.

2006–2010 CISA Job Practice	2011–2015 CISA Job Practice	Book Chapter
1. The IS Audit Process (10%)	1. The Process of Auditing Information Systems (14%)	3. The Audit Process
2. IT Governance (15%)	2. Governance and Management of IT (14%)	2. IT Governance and Management
3. Systems and Infrastructure Life Cycle Management (16%)	3. Information Systems Acquisition, Development and Implementation (19%)	4. IT Life Cycle Management
4. IT Service Delivery and Support (14%)	4. Information Systems Operation, Maintenance, and Support (23%)	5. IT Service Delivery and Infrastructure
5. Protection of Information Assets (31%)	5. Protection of Information Assets (30%)	6. Information Asset Protection
6. Business Continuity and Disaster Recovery (14%)	(now a part of Domains 2 and 4)	Covered in Chapters 2 and 5 (was Chapter 7 in the first edition)

Table 1   Old and New CISA Job Practices

Another noteworthy change is the increase in weight of the IS Audit Process domain. In 2010 this was only 10 percent of the exam, but starting in 2011 the IS Audit Process is 14 percent of the exam.

 NOTE   Eliminating the BCDR domain is both an editorial statement and the result of a reality check. I think ISACA made this change because they realize that BCDR is more firmly embedded into IT governance, technology development, and operations. BCDR is not the silo it once was, but it has become a part of IT's DNA.

Within each domain, the CISA job practice contains many Task Statements and Knowledge Statements. These Task Statements and Knowledge Statements have undergone significant changes in their wording, but often the underlying meanings are similar to the old CISA job practice.

There are, however, several CISA job practice Knowledge Statements that are entirely new, listed here:

- **KS1.5**   Knowledge of fundamental business processes (e.g., purchasing, payroll, accounts payable, and accounts receivable), including relevant IT

- **KS1.6**   Knowledge of applicable laws and regulations that affect the scope, evidence collection and preservation, and frequency of audits

- **KS1.8**   Knowledge of different sample methodologies

- **KS1.10**   Knowledge of audit quality assurance systems and frameworks

- **KS2.7**   Knowledge of process optimization models

- **KS5.4** Knowledge of the security controls related to hardware and systems software (e.g., applications, operating systems, and database management systems)

- **KS5.5** Knowledge of risks and controls associated with virtualization of systems

- **KS5.6** Knowledge of the configuration, implementation, operation, and maintenance of network security controls

- **KS5.11** Knowledge of risks and controls associated with data leakage

- **KS5.14** Knowledge of risks and controls associated with peer-to-peer computing, instant messaging, and web-based technologies (e.g., social networking, message boards, and blogs)

- **KS5.15** Knowledge of controls and risks associated with the use of mobile and wireless devices

- **KS5.17** Knowledge of the evidence preservation techniques and processes followed in forensics investigations (e.g., IT, process, and chain of custody)

Some of these new Knowledge Statements represent additional emphasis on subjects that have been a part of the CISA job practice (e.g., applicable laws, forensics, and audit quality assurance systems), while others are evidence of the need for IS auditors to be familiar with emerging threats and trends (e.g., mobile and wireless devices, peer-to-peer computing, and instant messaging).

Becoming a CISA

This chapter discusses the following topics
- What it means to be a CISA-certified professional
- Getting to know ISACA, its code of ethics, and its standards
- The certification process
- Applying for the exam
- Maintaining your certification
- Getting the most from your CISA journey

Congratulations on choosing to become a Certified Information Systems Auditor (CISA). Whether you have worked for several years in the field of information systems auditing or have just recently been introduced to the world of controls, assurance, and security, don't underestimate the hard work and dedication required to obtain and maintain CISA certification. Although ambition and motivation are required, the rewards can far exceed the effort.

You probably never imagined you would find yourself working in the world of auditing or looking to obtain a professional auditing certification. Perhaps the increase in legislative or regulatory requirements for information system security led to your introduction to this field. Or possibly you have noticed that CISA-related career options are increasing exponentially and you have decided to get ahead of the curve. You aren't alone: 79,000 professionals worldwide reached the same conclusion and have earned the well-respected CISA certification. In 2009, *SC Magazine* named the CISA certification winner of the Best Professional Certification Program. Welcome to the journey and the amazing opportunities that await you.

I have put together this information to help you further understand the commitment needed, prepare for the exam, and maintain your certification. Not only is it my wish to see you pass the exam with flying colors, but I also provide you with the information and resources to maintain your certification and to proudly represent yourself and the professional world of information system (IS) auditing with your new credentials.

ISACA (formerly known as the Information Systems Audit and Control Association) is a recognized leader in the areas of control, assurance, and IT governance. Formed in 1967, this nonprofit organization represents more than 95,000 professionals in more than 160 countries. ISACA administers several exam certifications, including the CISA, the Certified Information Systems Manager (CISM), the Certified in Risk and Information

Systems Control (CRISC), and the Certified in the Governance of Enterprise IT (CGEIT) certifications. The certification program itself has been accredited by the American National Standards Institute (ANSI) under International Organization for Standardization and International Electrotechnical Commission standard ISO/IEC 17024:2003, which means that ISACA's procedures for accreditation meet international requirements for quality, continuous improvement, and accountability. If you're new to ISACA, I recommend that you tour the website and become familiar with the guides and resources available. In addition, if you're near one of the 180 local ISACA chapters in 75 countries, consider taking part in the activities and even reaching out to the chapter board for information on local meetings, training days, conferences, or study sessions. You may be able to meet other IS auditors who can give you additional insight into the CISA certification and the audit profession.

The CISA certification was established in 1978 and primarily focuses on audit, controls, assurance, and security. It certifies the individual's knowledge of testing and documenting IS controls and his or her ability to conduct formal IS audits. Organizations seek out qualified personnel for assistance with developing and maintaining strong control environments. A CISA-certified individual is a great candidate for this.

Benefits of CISA Certification

Obtaining the CISA certification offers several significant benefits.

- **Expands knowledge and skills; builds confidence**   Developing knowledge and skills in the areas of audit, controls, assurance, and security can prepare you for advancement or expand your scope of responsibilities. The personal and professional achievement can boost confidence that encourages you to move forward and seek new career opportunities.

- **Increases marketability and career options**   Because of various legal and regulatory requirements, such as Health Insurance Portability and Accountability Act (HIPAA), Payment Card Industry Data Security Standard (PCI-DSS), Sarbanes-Oxley, Gramm Leach Bliley Act (GLBA), Food and Drug Administration (FDA), Federal Energy Regulatory Commission/North American Electric Reliability Corporation (FERC/NERC), the European Privacy Directive (95/46/EC), along with the growing need for information systems and automation, controls, assurance, and audit experience, demand is growing for individuals with experience in documenting and testing controls. In addition, obtaining your CISA certification demonstrates to current and potential employers your willingness and commitment to improve your knowledge and skills in information systems auditing. Having a CISA can provide a competitive advantage and open up many doors of opportunity in various industries and countries.

- **To meet employment requirements**   Many government agencies and organizations are requiring CISA certifications for positions involving IS audit activities, for example, the United States Department of Defense (DoD). DoD Directive 8570 mandates that those personnel performing information assurance activities within the agency are certified with a commercial accreditation approved by the DoD. The DoD has approved the ANSI-accredited CISA certificate program because it meets ISO/IEC 17024:2003 requirements. All Information Assurance Technical (IAT) Level III personnel are mandated to obtain CISA certification, as are those who are contracted to perform similar activities.

- **Builds customer confidence and international credibility** Prospective customers needing control or audit work will have faith that the quality of the audits and controls documented or tested are in line with internationally recognized standards.

Regardless of your current position, demonstrating knowledge and experience in the areas of IS controls, audit, assurance, and security can expand your career options. The certification does not limit you to auditing; it can provide additional value and insight to those in or seeking the following positions:

- Executives such as chief executive officers (CEOs), chief financial officers (CFOs), and chief information officers (CIOs)
- Chief audit executives, audit partners, and audit directors
- Security and IT operations executives (Chief Technology Officers [CTO], Chief Information Security Officers [CISO], Chief Security Officers [CSO]), directors, managers, and staff
- Compliance executives and management
- Security and audit consultants

Becoming a CISA

To become a CISA, you are required to pay the exam fee, pass the exam, prove that you have the required experience and education, and agree to uphold ethics and standards. To keep your CISA certification, you are required to take at least 20 continuing education hours each year (120 hours in three years) and pay annual maintenance fees. This is depicted in Figure 1-1.

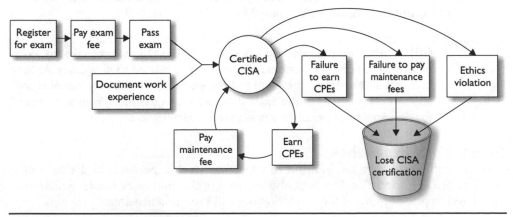

Figure 1-1 The CISA Certification Life Cycle

The following list outlines the major requirements for becoming certified:

- **Experience**   A CISA candidate must be able to submit verifiable evidence of at least five years' experience, with a minimum of two years' professional work experience in IS auditing, control, assurance, or security. Experience can be in any of the job content areas, but must be verified. For those with less than five years' experience, substitution and waiver options for up to three years' experience are available.

- **Ethics**   Candidates must commit to adhere to ISACA's Code of Professional Ethics, which guides the personal and professional conduct of those certified.

- **Standards**   Those certified agree to abide by IS auditing standards and minimum guidelines for performing IS audits.

- **Exam**   Candidates must receive a passing score on the CISA exam. A passing score is valid for up to five years, after which the score is void. This means that a CISA candidate who passes the exam has a maximum of five years to apply for CISA certification; candidates who pass the exam but fail to act after five years will have to take the exam again if they want to become CISA certified.

- **Education**   Those certified must adhere to the CISA Continuing Education Policy, which requires a minimum of 20 continuing professional education (CPE) hours each year, with a total requirement of 120 CPEs over the course of the certification period (three years).

- **Application**   After successfully passing the exam, meeting the experience requirements, and having read through the Code of Professional Ethics and Standards, a candidate is ready to apply for certification. An application must be received within five years of passing the exam.

Experience Requirements

To qualify for CISA certification, you must have completed the equivalent of five years' total work experience. These five years can take many forms, with several substitutions available. Additional details on the minimum certification requirements, substitution options, and various examples are discussed next.

 NOTE   Although it is not recommended, a CISA candidate can take the exam before completing any work experience directly related to IS auditing. As long as the candidate passes the exam and the work experience requirements are filled within five years of the exam date and within ten years from application for certification, the candidate is eligible for certification.

Direct Work Experience

You are required to have a minimum of two years' work experience in the field of IS audit, controls, or security. This is equivalent to 4,000 actual work hours, which must be related to one or more of the five following CISA job practice areas.

- **The Process of Auditing Information Systems**   Planning and conducting information systems audits in accordance with IS standards and best practices, communicating results, and advising on risk management and control practices.

- **Governance and Management of IT**   Ensuring that adequate organizational structures and processes are in place to align and support the organization's strategies and objectives.

- **Information Systems Acquisition, Development, and Implementation**   Ensuring that appropriate processes and controls are in place for the acquisition, development, testing, and implementation of information systems in order to provide reasonable assurance that the organization's strategies and objectives will be met.

- **Information Systems Operations, Maintenance, and Support**   Ensuring that systems and infrastructure have appropriate operations, maintenance, and support processes and controls in place to support meeting the organization's strategies and objectives.

- **Protection of Information Assets**   Ensuring that the organization's security policies, standards, procedures, and controls protect the confidentiality, integrity, and availability of information assets.

All work experience must be completed within the ten-year period before completing the certification application or within five years from the date of initially passing the CISA exam. You will need to complete a separate Verification of Work Experience form for each segment of experience.

There is only one exception to this minimum two-year direct work experience requirement: if you are a full-time instructor. This option is discussed in the next section.

Substitution of Experience

Up to a maximum of three years' direct work experience can be substituted with the following to meet the five-year experience requirement:

- One year of information systems or one year of non-IS auditing experience can be substituted for up to one year of direct work experience.

- Completion of a two- or four-year degree (60 to 120 completed university semester credit hours), regardless of when completed, can be substituted for one or two years of direct work experience, respectively. Transcripts or a letter confirming degree status must be sent from the university attended to obtain the experience waiver.

- If you have completed a bachelor's or master's degree from a university that enforces an ISACA-sponsored curriculum, it can be substituted for one or two years of direct work experience, respectively (for information on ISACA-sponsored curricula and participating universities, see www.isaca.org/modeluniversities). Transcripts or a letter confirming degree status will need to be sent from the university to obtain an experience waiver. This option cannot be used if you have already substituted or waived three years of direct work experience.

- Association of Chartered Certified Accountants (ACCA) members and Chartered Institute of Management Accountants (CIMA) members with full certification can apply for a two-year educational waiver.

- Those applying with a master's degree in information systems or information technology (IT) from an accredited university can apply for a one-year experience waiver.

As noted earlier, there is only one exception to the experience requirements. Should you have experience as a full-time university instructor in a related field (that is, information security, computer science, or accounting), each two years of your experience can be substituted for one year of required direct work experience, without limitation.

Here is an example CISA candidate whose experience and education are considered for CISA certification:

Jane Doe graduated in 1995 with a bachelor's degree in accounting. She spent five years working for an accounting firm conducting non-IS audits, and in January 2000, she began conducting IS audits full time. In January 2002, she took some time off work for personal reasons and rejoined the workforce in December 2008, working for a public company in their internal audit department documenting and testing financial controls. Jane passed the CISA exam in June 2009 and applied for CISA certification in January 2010. Does Jane have all of the experience required? What evidence will she need to submit?

- **Two-year substitution**   Jane obtained a bachelor's degree in accounting, which equates to two years' experience substitution.

- **Two years' direct experience**   She can count her two full years of IS audit experience in 2000 and 2001.

- **One-year substitution**   She cannot take into account one year of non-IS audit experience completed between January 1999 to January 2000, as it was not completed within ten years of application.

- **One-year substitution**   Jane would want to utilize her new internal audit financial controls experience for experience substitution rather than her earlier non-IS audit experience.

Jane would need to send the following with her application to prove experience requirements are met:

- Verification of Work Experience forms filled out and signed by her supervisors (or any superior) at the accounting firm, verifying both the IS and non-IS audit work conducted.

- Transcripts or letter confirming degree status sent from the university.

 NOTE   I recommend you also read the CISA certification qualifications on the ISACA website. From time to time ISACA does change the qualification rules, and I want you to have the most up-to-date information available.

ISACA Code of Professional Ethics

Becoming a CISA means that you agree to adhere to the ISACA Code of Professional Ethics. The code of ethics is a formal document outlining those things you will do to ensure the utmost integrity and that best support and represent the organization and certification.

The ISACA code of ethics requires ISACA members and certification holders to:

- Support the implementation of standards, procedures, and controls for IS.
- Encourage compliance with standards, procedures, and controls for IS.
- Conduct audits and related tasks with objectivity, due diligence, and professional care.
- Conduct audits in accordance with standards and best practices.
- Serve in the interest of stakeholders, lawfully and with integrity.
- Avoid engaging in acts that may be disreputable to the profession.
- Maintain privacy and confidentiality of information unless legally required to disclose it.
- Never disclose information for personal benefit or to inappropriate parties.
- Maintain competencies and agree to undertake only those activities that you can reasonably complete with professional competence.
- Inform appropriate parties of audit results, stating all significant facts known.
- Educate stakeholders and enhance their understanding of IS audit, security, control and risk management.

Failure to follow the code of ethics can result in investigation of the person's actions; potential disciplinary measures range from a written warning to the loss of certification and/or membership.

The full text and terms of enforcement of the ISACA Code of Ethics can be found at www.isaca.org/ethics.

ISACA IS Standards

An auditor can gather information from several credible resources to conduct an audit with integrity and confidence. ISACA has developed its own set of standards of mandatory requirements for IS auditing and reporting.

ISACA offers multiple levels of IS audit and assurance guidance: standards, guidance, and tools and techniques. Standards are higher-level *mandatory* requirements that inform IS audit and assurance professionals of minimal performance expectations. Guidelines provide guidance in applying the standards, while tools and techniques provide examples of procedures that audit and assurance professionals might follow.

As a CISA, you are required to abide by and promote the IS standards where applicable, encouraging compliance and supporting their implementation. As you prepare for certification and beyond, you will need to read through and become familiar with these standards. These standards were created to define the minimum level of acceptable performance needed to meet the professional requirements as defined by ISACA and to help set expectations. They have been established, vetted, and approved by ISACA.

IT Audit and Assurance Standards

The ISACA IT audit and assurance standards are mandatory—all ISACA-certified auditors are required to follow these standards in their professional work. The ISACA IT audit standards consist of sixteen sections covering topics including audit planning, evidence, IT controls, professional ethics, risk assessments, materiality, and auditor independence. These standards are described in detail in Chapter 3.

Standards for IS Control Professionals

Standards for IS Control Professionals, developed by ISACA, are extremely high-level and are specific to IT auditing. These basic standards include

- Professional and organizational independence
- Professional ethics and due professional care
- Skills, knowledge, and continuing professional education
- Appropriate planning of IT audit and assurance activities
- Work performance is appropriately supervised, evidenced, and effective
- Periodic reporting to management
- Monitoring of follow-up activities

While ISACA members and CISA certification holders are not required to follow the standards, you probably will find them useful in your work as an IS auditor.

ITAF: A Professional Practices Framework for IT Assurance

The Professional Practices Framework for IT Assurance (ITAF) has been developed and incorporates all of the ISACA IS standards and guidance. The framework provides guidance on design, conduct, and reporting of IT audit and assurance engagements. Terms and concepts are defined, and the framework also establishes three categories of standards that address IT audit and assurance professional roles and responsibilities, knowledge, skills and diligence, conduct, and reporting requirements.

General standards represent guiding principles by which the profession conducts IT audit and assurance activities. General standards include

- Independence and objectivity
- Reasonable expectation
- Management's acknowledgment

- Training and proficiency
- Knowledge of the subject matter
- Due professional care
- Suitable criteria
- Available criteria
- Selection of criteria

Performance standards focus on the IT audit or assurance professional's conduct of assurance activities—such as the design, evidence, findings, and conclusions. These standards include

- Planning and supervision
- Obtaining sufficient evidence
- Assignment performance
- Representations

Reporting standards cover the report produced by the IT audit or assurance professional, such as:

- Types of reports
- The means of communication
- Information to be communicated

I recommend that you check the ISACA website periodically for updates to the standards. As an ISACA member, you will automatically be notified when changes have been submitted and the documents are open for review (www.isaca.org/standards).

The Certification Exam

The certification is offered twice each year, in June and December. You have several ways to register; however, regardless of the method you choose, I highly recommend that you plan ahead and register early. Registering early and online reaps the most benefits, saving up to US$100 compared with late, mailed, or faxed registrations.

In 2011 the schedule of exam fees in U.S. dollars was:

- Early registration
  - $375 member/$515 nonmember—online
  - $425 member/$565 nonmember—fax/mail
- Regular registration
  - $425 member/$565 nonmember—online
  - $475 member/$615 nonmember—fax/mail

The test is administered by an ISACA-sponsored location. For additional details on the location nearest you, see the ISACA website.

Once registration is complete, you will immediately receive an e-mail acknowledging your registration, and within four weeks of processing you will receive a hard copy of the letter and a registration receipt in the mail. Two to three weeks prior to the test date you will receive an exam admission ticket via e-mail and regular mail. You will need the admission ticket to enter the test site—make sure to keep it unmarked and in a safe place until test time.

Each registrant has four hours to take the multiple-choice question exam. There are 200 questions on the exam representing the five job practice areas. The exam is not computerized but is provided via paper exam booklet. Each question has four answer choices; test-takers can select only one best answer by filling in the appropriate bubbles on the answer sheet provided, in pencil or pen. You will be scored for each job practice area and then provided one final score. All scores are scaled. Scores range from 200 to 800; however, a final score of 450 is required to pass.

Exam questions are derived from a job practice analysis study conducted by ISACA. The areas selected represent those tasks performed in a CISA's day-to-day activities and represent the background knowledge required to perform IS audit, control, assurance, or security tasks. More detailed descriptions of the task and knowledge statements can be found at www.isaca.org/cisajobpractice.

The CISA exam is quite broad in its scope. The exam covers five job practice areas, as shown in Table 1-1.

Independent committees have been developed to determine the best questions, review exam results, and statistically analyze the results for continuous improvement. Should you come across a horrifically difficult or strange question, do not panic. This question may have been written for another purpose. A few questions on the exam are included for research and analysis purposes and will not be counted against your score.

Domain	CISA Job Practice Area	Percentage of Exam
1	The Process of Auditing Information Systems	14
2	Governance and Management of IT	14
3	Information Systems Acquisition, Development, and Implementation	19
4	Information Systems Operations, Maintenance, and Support	23
5	Protection of Information Assets	30

Table 1-1 CISA Exam Practice Areas

NOTE Individuals who have been following the CISA practice areas will notice the absence of the Business Continuity and Disaster Recovery (BDCR) practice area starting in 2011. The contents of the Business Continuity and Disaster Recovery practice have been moved to two other domains; CISA candidates are still required to thoroughly understand BCDR.

Exam Preparation

The CISA certification requires a great deal of knowledge and experience from the CISA candidate. You need to map out a long-term study strategy in order to pass the exam. The following sections offer some tips and are intended to help guide you to, through, and beyond exam day.

Before the Exam

Consider the following list of tips on tasks and resources for exam preparation. They are listed in sequential order.

- **Obtain the Bulletin of Information (BOI)**   The BOI contains the most current information about exam requirements, additional information about the exam, registration instructions, test dates, score reporting, test center locations, and registration forms. The BOI can be found at www.isaca.org/cisaboi.

- **Read the Candidate's Guide**   For information on the certification exam and requirements for the current year, see www.isaca.org/cisaguide.

- **Register**   If you are able to, register early for the cost savings and to solidify your commitment to moving forward with this professional achievement.

- **Become familiar with the CISA job practice areas**   The job practice areas serve as the basis for the exam and requirements. Beginning with the June 2011 exam, the job practice areas have changed. Ensure your study materials align with the current list, shown at www.isaca.org/cisajobpractice.

- **Self-assess**   Run through practice exam questions, found on the CD at the back of this book. You may also go to the ISACA website for a free 50-question CISA self-assessment.

- **Iterative study**   Depending on how much work experience in IS auditing you have already, I suggest you plan your study program to take at least two months but as long as six months. During this time, periodically take practice exams and note your areas of strength and weakness. Once you have identified your weak areas, focus on those areas weekly by rereading the related sections in this book and retaking practice exams, and note your progress.

- **Avoid cramming**   We've all seen the books on the shelves with titles that involve last-minute cramming. Just one look on the Internet reveals a variety of websites that cater to teaching individuals how to most effectively cram for exams. There are also research sites claiming that exam cramming can lead to susceptibility to colds and flu, sleep disruptions, overeating, and digestive problems. One thing is certain: many people find that good, steady study habits result in less stress and greater clarity and focus during the exam. Due to the complexity of this exam, I highly recommend the long-term, steady-study option. Study the job practice areas thoroughly. There are many study options. If time permits, investigate the many resources available to you.

- **Find a study group**   Oftentimes ISACA chapters will have formed specific study groups or offer less expensive exam review courses. Contact your local chapter to see if these options are available to you. In addition, be sure to keep your eye on the ISACA website, as they are planning to launch exam preparation communities starting in 2011.

- **Admission ticket**   Approximately two to three weeks before the exam, you will receive the admission ticket. Do not write on or lose this ticket. Put it in a safe place, and take note of what time you will need to arrive at the site. Note this on your calendar.

- **Logistics check**   Check the Bulletin of Information and your admission ticket for the exact time you are required to report to the test site. Check the site a few days before the exam—become familiar with the location and tricks to getting there. If you are taking public transportation, be sure that you are looking at the schedule for the day of the exam: CISA exams are usually administered on a Saturday, when public transportation schedules may differ from weekday schedules. If you are driving, know the route and where to park your vehicle.

- **Pack**   Place your admissions ticket, several sharpened No. 2 pencils and erasers, and a photo ID in a safe place, ready to go. Your ID must be a current, government-issued photo ID that matches the name on the admission ticket and must not be handwritten. Examples of acceptable forms of ID are passports, driver's licenses, state IDs, green cards, and national IDs. Make sure you leave food, drinks, laptops, cell phones, and other electronic devices behind, as they are not permitted at the test site. For information on what can and cannot be brought to the exam site, see www.isaca.org/cisabelongings.

- **Notification decision**   Decide if you would like your test results e-mailed to you. You will have the opportunity to consent to an e-mail notification of the exam results. If you are fully paid (zero balance on exam fee) and have consented to the e-mail notification, you should receive a one-time e-mail approximately eight weeks from the date of the exam with the results.

- **Sleep**   Make sure you get a sound night's sleep before the exam. Research suggests that you steer clear of caffeine at least four hours before bedtime, keep a notepad and pen next to the bed to capture late-night thoughts that might keep you awake, eliminate as much noise and light as possible, and keep your room a good temperature for sleeping. In the morning, arise early so as not to rush and subject yourself to additional stress.

Day of the Exam

- **Arrive early**   Check the Bulletin of Information and your admission ticket for the exact time you are required to report to the test site. The ticket/ BOI explains that you must be at the test site *no later* than approximately 30 minutes *before* testing time. The examiner will begin reading the exam instructions at this time, and any latecomers will be disqualified from taking the test and will not receive a refund of fees.

- **Observe test center rules**   There may be rules about taking breaks. This will be discussed by the examiner along with exam instructions. If at any time during the exam you need something and are unsure as to the rules, be sure to ask first. For information on conduct during the exam, see www.isaca.org/cisabelongings.

- **Answering exam questions**   Read questions carefully, but do not try to overanalyze. Remember to select the *best* solution. There may be several reasonable answers, but one is *better* than the others.

After the Exam

Approximately eight weeks from the date of the exam, you will receive your exam results by e-mail or regular mail. Each job practice area score will be noted in addition to the overall final score. All scores are scaled. Should you receive a passing score, you will also receive the application for certification. Those unsuccessful in passing will receive a copy of the most current BOI. These individuals will want to take a close look at the job practice area scores to determine areas for further study. They may retake the exam as many times as needed on future exam dates, as long as they have registered and paid the applicable fees. Regardless of pass or fail, exam results will not be disclosed via telephone, fax, or e-mail (with the exception of the consented one-time e-mail notification).

Applying for CISA Certification

To apply for certification, you must be able to submit evidence of a passing score and related work experience. Keep in mind that once you receive a passing score, you have five years to use this score on a CISA application. After this time, you will need to take the exam again. In addition, all work experience submitted must have been within ten years of your new certification application.

To complete the application process, you need to submit the following information:

- **CISA application**   Note the Exam ID # as found in your exam results letter and list the information systems audit, control, security experience, and/or any experience substitutions, and identify which ISACA job practice area(s) the experience pertains to.

- **Verification of Work Experience form(s)**   These must be filled out and signed by your immediate supervisor or a person of higher rank in the organization to verify work experience noted on the application. You must fill out a complete set of Work Experience forms for each separate employer.

- **Transcript or letter**   If you are using an educational experience waiver, you must submit an original transcript or letter from the college or university confirming degree status.

As with the exam, after you've successfully mailed the application, you must wait approximately eight weeks for processing. If your application is approved, you will receive a package in the mail containing your letter of certification, certificate, and a copy of the Continuing Education Policy. You can then proudly display your certificate and use the designation ("CISA") on your résumé, e-mail profile, or business cards. Please note, however, that you cannot use the CISA logo.

Retaining Your CISA Certification

There is more to becoming a CISA than merely passing an exam, submitting an application, and receiving a paper certificate. Becoming a CISA is an ongoing journey. Those with CISA certification not only agree to abide by the code of ethics and adhere to the IS standards, but they must also meet ongoing education requirements and pay certification maintenance fees. Let's take a closer look at the education requirements and explain the fees involved in retaining certification.

Continuing Education

The goal of continuing professional education (CPE) requirements is to ensure that individuals maintain CISA-related knowledge so that they can better manage, assess, and design controls around IS. To maintain CISA certification, individuals must obtain 120 continuing education hours within three years, with a minimum requirement of 20 hours per year. Each CPE hour is to account for 50 minutes of active participation in educational activities.

What Counts as a Valid CPE Credit?

In order for training and activities to be utilized for CPEs, they must involve technical or managerial training that is directly applicable to IS assessments, audit, controls, or security. The following list of activities has been approved by the CISA certification committee and can count toward your CPE requirements:

- ISACA professional education activities and meetings.
- If you are an ISACA member, you can take Information Systems Control Journal CPE Quizzes online or participate in monthly webcasts. For each webcast, CPEs are rewarded after you pass a quiz.
- Non-ISACA professional education activities and meetings.
- Self-study courses.
- Vendor sales or marketing presentations (ten-hour annual limit).
- Teaching, lecturing, or presenting on subjects related to job practice areas.
- Publication of articles and books related to the profession.
- CISA exam question development and review.
- Passing related professional examinations.

- Participation in ISACA boards or committees (20-hour annual limit per ISACA certification).
- Contributions to the IS audit and control profession (ten-hour annual limit).
- Mentoring (ten-hour annual limit).

For more information on what is accepted as a valid CPE credit, see the Continuing Professional Education Policy (www.isaca.org/cisacpepolicy).

Tracking and Submitting CPEs

Not only are you required to submit a CPE tracking form for the annual renewal process, but you also should keep detailed records for each activity. Records associated with each activity should have

- Name of attendee
- Name of sponsoring organization
- Activity title
- Activity description
- Activity date
- Number of CPE hours awarded

It is in your best interest to track all CPE information in a single file. ISACA has developed a tracking form for your use, which can be found in the Continuing Professional Education Policy. To make it easy on yourself, consider keeping all related records such as receipts, brochures, and certificates in the same place. Documentation should be retained throughout the three-year certification period and for one additional year afterwards. This is especially important, as you may someday be audited. If this happens, you would be required to submit all paperwork. So why not be prepared? For new CISAs, the annual and three-year certification period begins January 1 of the year following certification. You are not required to report CPE hours for the first partial year after your certification; however, the hours earned from the time of certification to December 31 can be utilized in the first certification reporting period the following year. Therefore, should you get certified in January, you will have until the following January to accumulate CPEs and will not have to report them until you report the totals for the following year, which will be in October or November. This is known as the *renewal period*. During this time you will receive an e-mail directing you to the website to enter CPEs earned over the course of the year. Alternatively, the renewal will be mailed to you, and then CPEs can be recorded on the hard-copy invoice and sent with your maintenance fee payment. CPEs and maintenance fees must be received by January 15 to retain certification.

Notification of compliance from the certification department is sent after all of the information has been received and processed. Should ISACA have any questions about the information you have submitted, they will contact you directly.

Name_____John Jacob_____

Certification Number__67895787_____

Certification Period___1/1/2011_____to___12/31/2011____

Activity Title/Sponsor	Activity Description	Date	CPE Hours	Support Docs Included?
ISACA presentation/lunch	PCI compliance	2/12/2011	1 CPE	Yes (receipt)
ISACA presentation/lunch	Security in SDLC	3/12/2011	1 CPE	Yes (receipt)
Regional Conference, RIMS	Compliance, risk	1/15–17/2011	6 CPEs	Yes (CPE receipt)
BrightFly webinar	Governance, risk, & compliance	2/16/2011	3 CPEs	Yes (confirmation e-mail)
ISACA board meeting	Chapter board meeting	4/9/2011	2 CPEs	Yes (meeting minutes)
Presented at IIA meeting	IT audit presentation	6/21/2011	1 CPE	Yes (meeting notice)
Published an article in XYZ	Journal article on SOX ITGCs	4/12/2011	4 CPEs	Yes (article)
Vendor presentation	Learned about GRC tool capability	5/12/2011	2 CPEs	Yes
Employer-offered training	Change management course	3/26/2011	7 CPEs	Yes (certificate of course completion)

Table 1-2   Sample CPE Submission

Sample CPE Submission

Table 1-2 contains an example of a CPE submission.

CPE Maintenance Fees

To remain CISA-certified, you must pay CPE maintenance fees each year. These fees are (as of 2011) US$40 for members and $85 for nonmembers each year. These fees are in addition to ISACA membership and local chapter dues.

Revocation of Certification

A CISA-certified individual may have his or her certification revoked for the following reasons:

- Failure to complete the minimum number of CPEs during the period.
- Failure to document and provide evidence of CPEs in an audit.

- Failure to submit payment for maintenance fees.
- Failure to comply with the Code of Professional Ethics can result in investigation and ultimately can lead to revocation of certification.

If you have received a revocation notice, you will need to contact the ISACA Certification Department at certification@isaca.org for more information.

CISA Exam Preparation Pointers

- Register for the exam early and online to obtain the greatest financial savings.
- When studying for the exam, take as many practice exams as possible.
- Memorization will not work—for this exam, it is critical that you understand the concepts.
- If you have time while studying for the exam, begin gathering relevant Work Experience Verification forms from past employers and original transcripts from your college or university (if using the education experience waiver).
- Do not arrive late to the exam site. Latecomers are immediately disqualified and they forfeit exam fees.
- Begin keeping track of CPEs as soon as you obtain certification.
- Mark your calendar for CPE renewal time, which begins in October/November each year and ends January 15. Don't wait for the e-mail; set your own reminder.
- Become familiar with the code of ethics and IS standards.
- Become involved in your local ISACA chapter for networking and educational opportunities.

Summary

Becoming and being a CISA is a journey, not just a one-time event. It takes motivation, skill, good judgment, and proficiency to be a strong leader in the world of information systems auditing. The CISA was designed to help you navigate the IS auditing world with greater ease and confidence.

In the following chapters, each CISA job practice area will be discussed in detail, and additional reference material will be presented. Not only is this information useful for studying prior to the exam, but it is also meant to serve as a resource throughout your career as an audit professional.

IT Governance and Management

This chapter discusses the following topics
- IT governance structure
- Human resources management
- IT policies, standards, processes, and procedures
- Management practices
- IT resource investment, use, and allocation practices
- IT contracting and contract management strategies and practices
- Risk management practices
- Monitoring and assurance
- Business continuity planning

The topics in this chapter represent 14 percent of the CISA examination. This chapter discusses CISA job practice 2, "Governance and Management of IT."

IT governance should be the wellspring from which all other IT activities flow.

Properly implemented, *governance* is a *process* whereby senior management exerts strategic control over business functions through policies, objectives, delegation of authority, and monitoring. Governance is management's control over all other IT processes to ensure that IT processes continue to effectively meet the organization's business needs.

Organizations usually establish governance through an IT steering committee that is responsible for setting long-term IT strategy, and by making changes to ensure that IT processes continue to support IT strategy and the organization's needs. This is accomplished through the development and enforcement of IT policies, requirements, and standards.

IT governance typically focuses on several key processes, such as personnel management, sourcing, change management, financial management, quality management, security management, and performance optimization. Another key component is the establishment of an effective organization structure and clear statements of roles and responsibilities. An effective governance program will use a balanced scorecard or other means to monitor these and other key processes, and through a process of continuous improvement, IT processes will be changed to remain effective and to support ongoing business needs.

IT Governance Practices for Executives and Boards of Directors

Governance starts at the top.

Whether the organization has a board of directors, council members, commissioners, or some other top-level governing body, governance begins with the establishment of top-level objectives and policies that are translated into more actions, policies, processes, procedures, and other activities downward through each level in the organization.

This section describes governance practices recommended for IT organizations that include a strategy-developing committee, measurement via the balanced scorecard, security management, and enterprise architecture.

IT Governance

The purpose of IT governance is to align the IT organization with the needs of the business. The term *IT governance* refers to a collection of top-down activities intended to control the IT organization from a strategic perspective to ensure that the IT organization supports the business. Some of the products and activities that flow out of healthy IT governance include:

- **Policy** At its minimum, IT policy should directly reflect the mission, objectives, and goals of the overall organization.

- **Priorities** The priorities in the IT organization should flow directly from the organization's mission, objectives, and goals. Whatever is most important to the organization as a whole should be important to IT as well.

- **Standards** The technologies, protocols, and practices used by IT should be a reflection of the organization's needs. On their own, standards help to drive a consistent approach to solving business challenges; the choice of standards should facilitate solutions that meet the organization's needs in a cost-effective and secure manner.

- **Vendor management** The suppliers that IT selects should reflect IT priorities, standards, and practices.

- **Program and project management** IT programs and projects should be organized and performed in a consistent manner that reflects IT priorities and supports the business.

While IT governance contains the elements just described, strategic planning is also a key component of governance. Strategy is discussed in the next section.

IT Governance Frameworks

While every organization may have its unique missions, objectives, business models, tolerance for risk, and so on, organizations need not invent governance frameworks from scratch to manage their IT objectives. Several good frameworks can be adapted to meet organizations' needs, including:

- **COBIT** (Control Objectives for Information and related Technology)   This is an IT management framework developed by the IT Governance Institute and Information and Systems Audit and Control Association (ISACA). COBIT's four domains are Plan and Organize, Acquire and Implement, Deliver and Support, and Monitor and Evaluate.

- **ISO 27001**   This is the well-known international standard for top-down information security management.

- **ITIL**   Known as the *IT Infrastructure Library*, ITIL is a framework of processes for IT service delivery. ITIL was originally developed by the UK Office of Government Commerce in order to improve its IT management processes. The international standard, ISO 20000, is adapted from ITIL.

- **ISO 38500**   This is an international standard on corporate governance of information technology, suitable for small and large organizations in the public or private sector.

These and other frameworks are discussed in greater detail in Appendix B.

IT Strategy Committee

In organizations where IT provides significant value, the board of directors should have an IT strategy committee. This group will advise the board of directors on strategies to enable better IT support of the organization's overall strategy and objectives.

The IT strategy committee can meet with the organization's top IT executives to impart the board's wishes directly to them. This works best as a two-way conversation, where IT executives can inform the strategy committee of their status on major initiatives, as well as on challenges and risks. This ongoing dialogue can take place as often as needed, usually once or twice per year.

Readers should note that this suggestion of the IT strategy committee communicating with IT management is not an attempt to circumvent communications through intermediate layers of management. Those individuals should be included in this conversation as well.

The Balanced Scorecard

The balanced scorecard (BSC) is a management tool that is used to measure the performance and effectiveness of an organization. The balanced scorecard is used to determine how well an organization can fulfill its mission and strategic objectives, and how well it is aligned with overall organizational objectives.

In the balanced scorecard, management defines key measurements in each of four perspectives:

- **Financial**   Key financial items measured include the cost of strategic initiatives, support costs of key applications, and capital investment.

- **Customer**   Key measurements include the satisfaction rate with various customer-facing aspects of the organization.

- **Internal processes**   Measurements of key activities include the number of projects and the effectiveness of key internal workings of the organization.
- **Innovation and learning**   Human-oriented measurements include turnover, illness, internal promotions, and training.

Each organization's balanced scorecard will represent a unique set of measurements that reflects the organization's type of business, business model, and style of management.

The balanced scorecard methodology of greatest interest to readers of this book is the standard IT balanced scorecard, discussed in the next section.

The Standard IT Balanced Scorecard

The balanced scorecard should be used to measure overall organizational effectiveness and progress. A similar scorecard, the standard IT balanced scorecard (IT-BSC), can be used to specifically measure IT organization performance and results.

Like the balanced scorecard, the standard IT balanced scorecard has four perspectives:

- **Business contribution**   Key indicators here are the perception of IT department effectiveness and value as seen from other (non-IT) corporate executives.
- **User**   Key measurements include end-user satisfaction rate with IT systems and the IT support organization. Satisfaction rates of external users should be included if the IT department builds or supports externally facing applications or systems.
- **Operational excellence**   Key measurements include the number of support cases, amount of unscheduled downtime, and defects reported.
- **Innovation**   This includes the rate at which the IT organization utilizes newer technologies to increase IT value and the amount of training made available to IT staff.

The IT balanced scorecard should flow directly out of the organization's overall balanced scorecard. This will ensure that IT will align itself with corporate objectives. While the perspectives between the overall BSC and the IT-BSC vary, the approach for each is similar, and the results for the IT-BSC can "roll up" to the organization's overall BSC.

Information Security Governance

Security governance is the collection of management activities that establishes key roles and responsibilities, identifies and treats risks to key assets, and measures key security processes. Depending upon the structure of the organization and its business purpose, information security governance may be included in IT governance, or security governance may stand on its own (but if so, it should still be linked to IT governance so that these two activities are kept in sync).

The main roles and responsibilities for security should be:

- **Board of directors**   The board is responsible for establishing the tone for risk appetite and risk management in the organization. To the extent that the board of directors establishes business and IT security, so, too, should the board consider risk and security in that strategy.

- **Steering committee**   The security steering committee should establish the operational strategy for security and risk management in the organization. This includes setting strategic and tactical roles and responsibilities in more detail than was done by the board of directors. The security strategy should be in harmony with the strategy for IT and the business overall. The steering committee should also ratify security policy and other strategic policies and processes developed by the chief information security officer (CISO).

- **Chief information security officer (CISO)**   The CISO should be responsible for developing security policy; conducting risk assessments; developing processes for vulnerability management, incident management, identity and access management, security awareness and training, and compliance management; and informing the steering committee and board of directors of incidents and new or changed risks.

- **Management**   Every manager in the organization should be at least partially responsible for the conduct of their employees. This approach helps to establish a chain of accountability from the top of the organization, all the way down to individual employees.

- **All employees**   Every employee in the organization should be required to comply with the organization's security policy, as well as with security requirements and processes. All senior and executive management should demonstrably comply with these policies as an example for others.

Security governance should also make it clear that compliance with policies is a condition of employment; employees who fail to comply with policy are subject to discipline or termination of employment.

Reasons for Security Governance

Many organizations are dependent on their information systems. This has progressed to the point where organizations whose products or services are not information-related are completely dependent on the integrity and availability of their information systems to continue operations. Security governance, then, is needed to ensure that security-related incidents do not threaten the ongoing viability of the organization.

Security Governance Activities and Results

Within an effective security governance program, the organization's management will see to it that information systems necessary to support business operations will be adequately protected. Some of the activities that will take place include:

- **Risk management**   Management will make sure that risk assessments will be performed to identify risks in information systems. Follow-up actions will be carried out that will reduce the risk of system failure and compromise.

- **Process improvement**   Management will ensure that key changes will be made to business processes that will result in security improvements.

- **Incident response**   Management will put incident response procedures into place that will help to avoid incidents, reduce the impact and probability of incidents, and improve response to incidents so that their impact on the organization is minimized.

- **Improved compliance**   Management will be sure to identify all applicable laws, regulations, and standards and carry out activities to confirm that the organization is able to attain and maintain compliance.

- **Business continuity and disaster recovery planning**   Management will define objectives and allocate resources for the development of business continuity and disaster recovery plans.

- **Effectiveness measurement**   Management will establish processes to measure key security events such as incidents, policy changes and violations, audits, and training.

- **Resource management**   The allocation of manpower, budget, and other resources to meet security objectives is monitored by management.

- **Improved IT governance**   An effective security governance program will result in better strategic decisions in the IT organization that keep risks at an acceptably low level.

These and other governance activities are carried out through scripted interactions among key business and IT executives at regular intervals. Meetings will include a discussion of effectiveness measurements, recent incidents, recent audits, and risk assessments. Other discussions may include such things as changes to the business, recent business results, and any anticipated business events such as mergers or acquisitions.

Two key results of an effective security governance program are:

- **Increased trust**   Customers, suppliers, and partners trust the organization to a greater degree when they see that security is managed effectively.

- **Improved reputation**   The business community, including customers, investors, and regulators, will hold the organization in higher regard.

Enterprise Architecture

Enterprise architecture (EA) is both a business function and a technical model. In terms of a business function, the establishment of an enterprise architecture consists of activities that ensure that important business needs are met by IT systems. EA may also involve the construction of a model that is used to map business functions into the IT environment and IT systems in increasing levels of detail so that IT professionals can more easily understand the organization's technology architecture at any level.

The Zachman Model

The Zachman enterprise architecture framework, established in the late 1980s, continues to be the dominant EA standard today. Zachman likens IT enterprise architecture to the construction and maintenance of an office building: at a high (abstract, not number of floors) level, the office building performs functions such as containing office space. As we look into increasing levels of detail in the building, we encounter various trades (steel, concrete, drywall, electrical, plumbing, telephone, fire control, elevators, and so on), each of which has its own specifications, standards, regulations, construction and maintenance methods, and so on.

In the Zachman model, IT systems and environments are described at a high, functional level, and then in increasing detail, encompassing systems, databases, applications, networks, and so on. The Zachman framework is illustrated in Table 2-1.

While the Zachman model allows an organization to peer into cross-sections of an IT environment that supports business processes, the model does not convey the relationships between IT systems. *Data flow diagrams*, discussed in the next section, are used instead to depict information flows.

The U.S. federal government takes enterprise architecture quite seriously. All U.S. government agencies are required to develop enterprise architecture and use it in their strategic planning activities.

Data Flow Diagrams

Data flow diagrams (DFDs) are frequently used to illustrate the flow of information between IT applications. Like the Zachman model, a DFD can begin as a high-level diagram, where the labels of information flows are expressed in business terms. Written specifications about each flow can accompany the DFD; these specifications would describe the flow in increasing levels of detail, all the way to field lengths and communication protocol settings.

Similar to Zachman, DFDs permit nontechnical business executives to easily understand the various IT applications and the relationships between them. A typical DFD is shown in Figure 2-1.

	Data	Functional (Application)	Network (Technology)	People (Organization)	Time	Strategy
Scope	List of data sets important in the business	List of business processes	List of business locations	List of organizations	List of events	List of business goals and strategy
Enterprise Model	Conceptual data/object model	Business process model	Business logistics	Workflow	Master schedule	Business plan
Systems Model	Logical data model	System architecture	Detailed system architecture	Human interface architecture	Processing structure	Business rule model
Technology Model	Physical data/class model	Technology design	Technology architecture	Presentation architecture	Control structure	Rule design
Detailed Representation	Data definition	Program	Network architecture	Security architecture	Time definition	Rule speculation
Function Enterprise	Usable data	Working function	Usable network	Functioning organization	Implemented schedule	Working strategy

Table 2-1 Zachman Framework Shows IT Systems in Increasing Levels of Detail

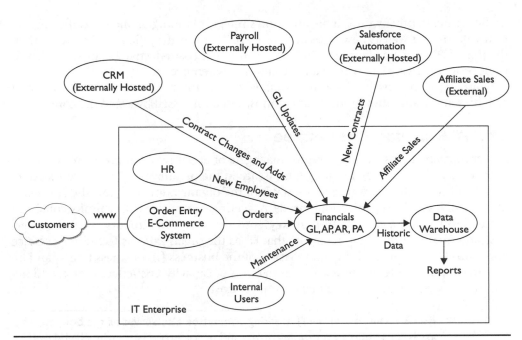

Figure 2-1 A typical DFD shows the relationship between IT applications.

IT Strategic Planning

In a methodical and organized way, a good strategic planning process answers the question of *what to do*, often in a way that takes longer to answer than it does to ask. While IT organizations require personnel who perform the day-to-day work of supporting systems and applications, some IT personnel need to spend at least part of their time developing plans for what the IT organization will be doing two, three, or more years in the future.

Strategic planning needs to be part of a formal, iterative planning process, not an ad hoc, chaotic activity. Specific roles and responsibilities for planning need to be established, and those individuals must carry out planning roles as they would any other responsibility. A part of the struggle with the process of planning stems from the fact that strategic planning is partly a creative endeavor that includes analysis of reliable information about future technologies and practices, as well as long-term strategic plans for the organization itself. In a nutshell, the key question is: *In five years, when the organization will be performing specific activities in a particular manner, how will IT systems support those activities?*

But it's more than just understanding how IT will support future business activities. Innovations in IT may help to shape what activities will take place, or at least how they will take place. On a more down-to-earth level, IT strategic planning is about the ability to provide the capability and capacity for IT services that will match the levels of and the types of business activities that the organization expects to achieve at certain points in the future. In other words, if organization strategic planning predicts specific transaction volumes (as well as new types of transactions) at specific points in the future, then the job of IT strategic planning will be to ensure that cost-effective IT systems of sufficient processing capacity will be up and running when needed.

Discussion of new business activities, as well as the projected volume of current activities at certain times in the future, is most often discussed by a steering committee.

The IT Steering Committee

A *steering committee* is a body of senior managers or executives that meets from time to time to discuss high-level and long-term issues in the organization. An *IT steering committee* will typically discuss the future states of the organization and how the IT organization will meet the organization's needs. A steering committee will typically consist of senior-level IT managers as well as key customers or constituents. This provider-customer dialogue will help to ensure that IT, as the organization's technology service arm, will fully understand the future vision of the business (in business terms) and be able to support future business activities in terms of capacity, cost-effectiveness, and the ability to support new activities that do not yet exist.

 NOTE The role of the IT steering committee also serves as the body for assessing results of recent initiatives and major projects to gain a high-level understanding of past performance in order to shape future activities. The committee also needs to consider industry trends and practices, risks as defined by internal risk assessments, and current IT capabilities.

The role of the IT steering committee is depicted in Figure 2-2.

Figure 2-2
The IT steering committee synthesizes a future strategy using several inputs.

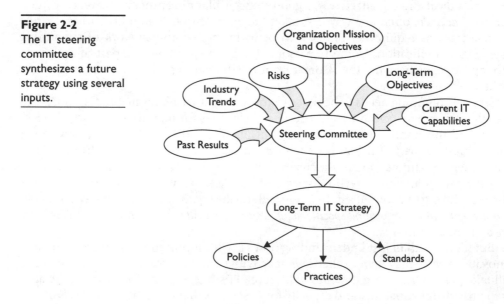

A steering committee's mission, objectives, roles, and responsibilities should be formally defined in a written charter. Steering committee meetings should be documented and published.

The steering committee needs to meet regularly to consider strategic issues and make decisions that translate into actions, tasks, and projects in IT and elsewhere.

Policies, Processes, Procedures, and Standards

Policies, processes, procedures, and standards define IT organizational behavior and uses of technology. They are part of the written record that defines how the IT organization performs the services that support the organization.

Policy documents should be developed and ratified by IT management. Policies state only *what* must be done (or not done) in an IT organization. They should not state *how* something must be done (or not done). That way, a policy document will be durable—meaning it may last many years with only minor edits from time to time.

IT policies typically cover many topics, including:

- **Roles and responsibilities**   This will range from general to specific, usually by describing each major role and responsibility in the IT department and then specifying which position is responsible for it. IT policies will also make general statements about responsibilities that all IT employees will share.

- **Development practices**   IT policy should define the processes used to develop and implement software for the organization. Typically, IT policy will require a formal development methodology that includes a number of specific ingredients, such as quality review and the inclusion of security requirements and testing.

- **Operational practices**   IT policy defines the high-level processes that constitute IT's operations. This will include service desk, backups, system monitoring, metrics, and other day-to-day IT activities.

- **IT processes, documents, and records**   IT policy will define other important IT processes, including incident management, project management, vulnerability management, and support operations. IT policy should also define how and where documents such as procedures and records will be managed and stored.

IT policy, like any other organization policy, is generally focused on what should be done and on what parties are responsible for different activities. However, policy generally steers clear of describing how these activities should be performed. That, instead, is the role of procedures and standards, discussed later in this section.

The relationship between policies, processes, procedures, and standards is shown in Figure 2-3.

Figure 2-3
Policies, processes,
procedures, and
standards

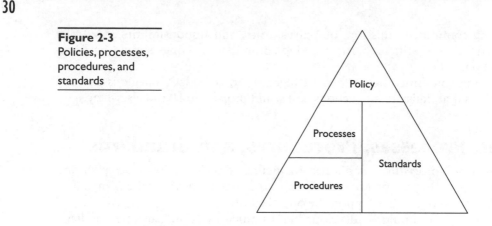

Information Security Policy

Security policy defines how an organization will protect its important assets. Like IT policy, information security policy defines several fundamental principles and activities:

- **Roles and responsibilities**   Security policy should define specific roles and responsibilities, including the roles of specific positions in the organization as well as the responsibilities of all staff members.

- **Risk management**   Security policy should define how the organization identifies and treats risks. An organization should perform periodic risk assessments and risk analysis, which will lead to decisions about risk treatment for specific risks that are identified.

- **Security processes**   Security policy should define important security processes, such as vulnerability management and incident management, and incorporate security in other business processes, such as software development and acquisition, vendor selection and management, and employee screening and hiring.

- **Acceptable use**   Security policy should define the types of activities that are acceptable and those that are not.

The best practice for information security policy is the definition of a top-down, management-driven information security program that performs periodic risk assessments to identify and focus on the most important risks in the organization. Roles and responsibilities define who is responsible for carrying out these activities. Executive management should have visibility and decision-making power, particularly in the areas of policy review and risk treatment.

It is generally accepted that security policy and security management should be separate from IT policy and IT management. This permits the security organization function to operate outside of IT, thereby permitting security to be objective and independent of IT. This puts security in a better position to be able to objectively assess IT systems and processes without fear of direct reprisal.

Privacy Policy

One of the most important policies an organization will develop that is related to information security is a privacy policy. A privacy policy describes how the organization will treat information that is considered private because it is related to a private citizen. A privacy policy defines two broad activities in this regard:

- **Protecting private information**   An organization that is required to collect, store, or transmit private information is duty-bound to protect this information so that it is not disclosed to unauthorized parties. This part of a privacy policy will describe what information is obtained and how it is protected.

- **Handling private information**   Aside from the actual protection of private information, some organizations may, in the course of their business activities, transmit some or all of this information to other parts of the organization or to other organizations. A privacy policy is typically forthright about this internal handling and the transmittals to other parties. Further, a privacy policy describes how the information is used by the organization and by other organizations to which it is transmitted. The privacy policy typically describes how a private citizen may confirm whether his or her private information is stored by the organization, whether it is accurate, and how the citizen can arrange for its removal if he or she wishes.

NOTE   Many countries have privacy laws that require an organization to have a privacy policy and to enact safeguards to protect private information.

Data Classification Policy

A data classification policy defines degrees of sensitivity for various types of information used in the organization. A typical data classification policy will define two or more (but rarely more than five) data classification levels. For example:

- Top Secret
- Secret
- Sensitive
- Public

Along with defining levels of classification, a data classification policy will define policies and procedures for handling of information in various settings at these levels. For instance, a data classification policy will state the conditions at each level in which sensitive information may be e-mailed, faxed, stored, transmitted, or shipped. Note that some methods for handling may be forbidden—such as e-mailing a top-secret document.

EXAM TIP While the CISO is responsible for establishing the organization's data classification policy, it is usually the responsibility of a document owner to correctly classify and mark a document. It is then the responsibility of any party that uses a document to handle it according to its classification level. All personnel who work with the document are responsible for handling it according to the classification policy.

System Classification Policy

A data classification policy may specify levels of security for systems storing classified information. A *system classification policy* will establish levels of system security that correspond to levels of data classification. Such a policy will help the organization to be more deliberate in its system hardening standards so that the most sensitive information will be stored only on systems with the highest levels of hardening (often, those higher levels of hardening are more costly and time consuming to manage; otherwise, an organization might just make all of its systems as secure).

Site Classification Policy

A site classification policy defines levels of security for an organization's worksites. This policy sets levels of physical security that corresponds to one or more factors:

- Criticality of staff that works at the site
- Criticality or value of business processes performed at the site
- Value of assets located at the site
- Sensitivity or value of data stored or processed at the site
- Siting risks associated with a site (man-made or natural hazards)

Based on the classification of a site, an organization may have additional security controls, such as video surveillance, guards, fences, visitor controls, and so on. Just as it does not make sense to protect all data at a single level, it also is sensible to have the right level of physical security at each site according to the information, equipment, or activity that takes place there.

Access Control Policy

An access control policy defines the need for specific processes and procedures related to the granting, review, and revocation of access to systems and work areas. This policy will state which roles are permitted to manage access controls, what levels of approval are required for access requests, how often access reviews will take place, and what access control records will be kept.

Often, there will be linkage between a data classification policy and an access control policy, since access controls protecting the most sensitive information may be stricter than access controls protecting less sensitive information.

Processes and Procedures

Process and procedure documents, sometimes called SOPs (standard operating procedures), describe in step-by-step detail how IT processes and tasks are performed. Formal procedure documents ensure that tasks are performed consistently and correctly, even when performed by different IT staff members.

In addition to the actual steps in support of a process or task, a procedure document needs to contain several pieces of metadata:

- **Document revision information**   The procedure document should contain the name of the person who wrote the document and who made the most recent changes to the document. The document should also include the name or location where the official copy of the document may be found.

- **Review and approval**   The document should include the name of the manager who last reviewed the procedure document, as well as the name of the manager (or higher) who approved the document.

- **Dependencies**   The document should specify which other procedures are related to this procedure. This includes those procedures that are dependent upon this procedure, and the procedures that this one depends on. For example, a document that describes the database backup process will depend on database management and maintenance documents; documents on media handling will depend on this document.

IT process and procedure documents are not meant to be a replacement for vendor task documentation. For instance, an IT department does not necessarily need to create a document that describes the steps for operating a tape backup device when the device vendor's instructions are available and sufficient. Also, IT procedure documents need not be remedial and include every specific keystroke and mouse click: they can usually assume that the reader has experience in the subject area and only needs to know how things are done in *this* organization. For example, a procedure document that includes a step that involves the modification of a configuration file does not need to include instructions on how to operate a text editor.

TIP   An IT department should maintain a catalog of its procedure documents to facilitate convenient document management. This will permit IT management to better understand which documents are in its catalog and when each was last reviewed and updated.

Standards

IT standards are official, management-approved statements that define the technologies, protocols, suppliers, and methods that are used by an IT organization. Standards help to drive consistency into the IT organization, which will make the organization more cost-efficient and cost-effective.

An IT organization will have different types of standards:

- **Technology standards** These standards specify what software and hardware technologies are used by the IT organization. Examples include operating system, database management system, application server, storage systems, backup media, and so on.

- **Protocol standards** These standards specify the protocols that are used by the organization. For instance, an IT organization may opt to use Transmission Control Protocol/Information Protocol (TCP/IP) v6 for its internal networks, Cisco gateway routing protocols (GRP), File Transfer Protocol Service (FTPS) for file transfer, Secure Shell (SSH) for device management, and so forth.

- **Supplier standards** This defines which suppliers and vendors are used for various types of supplies and services. Using established suppliers can help the IT organization through specially negotiated discounts and other arrangements.

- **Methodology standards** This refers to practices used in various processes, including software development, system administration, network engineering, and end-user support.

- **Configuration standards** This refers to specific detailed configurations that are to be applied to servers, database management systems, end-user workstations, network devices, and so on. This enables users, developers, and technical administrative personnel to be more comfortable with IT systems because the systems will be consistent with each other. This helps to reduce unscheduled downtime and to improve quality.

- **Architecture standards** This refers to technology architecture at the database, system, or network level. An organization may develop reference architectures for use in various standard settings. For instance, a large retail organization may develop specific network diagrams to be used in every retail location, down to the colors of wires to use and how equipment is situated on racks or shelves.

 TIP Standards enable the IT organization to be simpler, leaner, and more efficient. IT organizations with effective standards will have fewer types of hardware and software to support, which reduces the number of technologies that must be mastered by the organization. An organization that standardizes on one operating system, one database management system, and one server platform need only build expertise in those technologies. This enables the IT organization to manage and support the environment more effectively than if many different technologies were in use.

Applicable Laws, Regulations, and Standards

Organizations need to identify all of the laws, regulations, and standards that are applicable to their IT-based operations. As information technology has become more critical for organizations in many industry sectors, many nations and local governments have enacted new laws and regulations concerning the processing and protection of information.

The board of directors, strategy committee, or chief legal counsel should appoint an executive to be responsible for identifying all potentially applicable laws and regulations, who should then consult with inside or outside legal counsel to determine which are actually applicable.

Once applicable laws and regulations have been identified, the organization then needs to determine how they affect

- **Enterprise architecture** Laws and regulations may require that organizations put specific IT components into place that affect the organization's enterprise architecture.

- **Controls** Laws and regulations may require that additional controls be enacted or existing controls changed.

- **Processes** Laws and regulations may require that the organization perform certain tasks that may affect processes.

- **Personnel** Laws and regulations may require that certain personnel possess specific qualifications, certifications, or licenses.

Many factors will determine whether specific laws are applicable to an organization, including:

- Type of data that is stored, processed, or transmitted by the organization's systems

- Industry sector

- Location of stored, processed, or transmitted data

- Location of the owner(s) of stored, processed, or transmitted data

Organizations may also be required to comply with specific standards. For example, organizations that process, store, or transmit credit card numbers may be required to comply with the Payment Card Industry Data Security Standard (PCI DSS), even though there may be no laws requiring organizations to do so.

Risk Management

Organizations need to understand which activities, practices, and systems are introducing risk into its operations. The span of activities that seek, identify, and manage these risks is known as risk management. Like many other processes, risk management is a life cycle activity that has no beginning and no end. It's a continuous and phased set of activities that includes the examination of processes, records, and systems in order to identify risks. This is continued by an analysis that examines a range of solutions for reducing or eliminating risks, followed by formal decision-making that brings about a resolution to risks.

Risk management needs to support overall business objectives. This support will include the adoption of a risk appetite that reflects the organization's overall approach to risk. For instance, if the organization is a conservative financial institution, then that organization's risk management program will probably adopt a position of being risk averse. Similarly, a high-tech startup organization that, by its very nature, is comfortable with overall business risk will probably be less averse to risks identified in its risk management program.

Regardless of its overall position on risk, when an organization identifies risks, the organization can take one of four possible actions:

- **Accept**   The organization accepts the risk as-is.
- **Mitigate**   The organization takes action to reduce the level of risk.
- **Transfer**   The organization shares the risk with another entity, usually an insurance company.
- **Avoid**   The organization discontinues the activity associated with the risk.

These alternatives are known as risk treatments. Often, a particular risk will be treated with a blended solution that consists of two or more of the actions just listed.

This section dives into the details of risk management, risk analysis, and risk treatment.

The Risk Management Program

An organization that chooses to build a risk management program should establish some principles that will enable the program to succeed. These may include

- **Objectives**   The risk management program must have a specific purpose; otherwise, it will be difficult to determine whether the program is successful. Example objectives include: reduce number of industrial accidents, reduce the cost of insurance premiums, or reduce the number of stolen assets. If objectives are measurable and specific, then the individuals who are responsible for the risk management program can focus on its objectives in order to achieve the best possible outcome.

- **Scope**   Management must determine the scope of the risk management program. This is a fairly delicate undertaking because of the many interdependencies found in IT systems and business processes. However, in an organization with several distinct operations or business units (BUs), a risk management program could be isolated to one or more operational arms or BUs. In such a case, where there are dependencies on other services in the organization, those dependencies can be treated like an external service provider (or customer).

- **Authority** The risk management program is being started at the request of one or more executives in the organization. It is important to know who these individuals are and their level of commitment to the program.

- **Roles and responsibilities** This defines specific job titles, together with their respective roles and responsibilities in the risk management program. In a risk management program with several individuals, it should be clear which individuals or job titles are responsible for which activities in the program.

- **Resources** The risk management program, like other activities in the business, requires resources to operate. This will include a budget for salaries as well as for workstations, software licenses, and possibly travel.

- **Policies, processes, procedures, and records** The various risk management activities, such as asset identification, risk analysis, and risk treatment, along with some general activities like recordkeeping, should be written down.

 NOTE An organization's risk management program should be documented in a *charter*. A charter is a formal document that defines and describes a business program, and becomes a part of the organization's record.

The risk management life cycle is depicted in Figure 2-4.

The Risk Management Process

Risk management is a life cycle set of activities used to identify, analyze, and treat risks. These activities are methodical and, as mentioned in the previous section, should be documented so that they will be performed consistently and in support of the program's charter and objectives.

Figure 2-4
The risk management life cycle

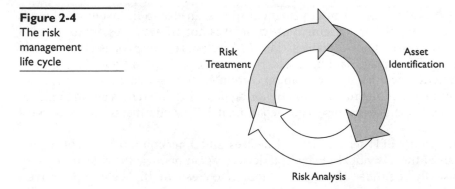

Asset Identification

The risk management program's main objective (whether formally stated or not) is the protection of the organization's assets. These assets may be tangible or intangible, physical, logical, or virtual. Some examples of assets include

- **Buildings and property**   These assets include structures and other improvements.

- **Equipment**   This can include machinery, vehicles, and office equipment such as copiers and fax machines.

- **IT equipment**   This includes computers, printers, scanners, tape libraries (the devices that create backup tapes, not the tapes themselves), storage systems, network devices, and phone systems.

- **Supplies and materials**   These can include office supplies as well as materials that are used in manufacturing.

- **Records**   These include business records, such as contracts, video surveillance tapes, visitor logs, and far more.

- **Information**   This includes data in software applications, documents, e-mail messages, and files of every kind on workstations and servers.

- **Intellectual property**   This includes an organization's designs, architectures, software source code, processes, and procedures.

- **Personnel**   In a real sense, an organization's personnel *are* the organization. Without its staff, the organization cannot perform or sustain its processes.

- **Reputation**   One of the intangible characteristics of an organization, reputation is the individual and collective opinion about an organization in the eyes of its customers, competitors, shareholders, and the community.

- **Brand equity**   Similar to reputation, this is the perceived or actual market value of an individual brand of product or service that is produced by the organization.

Grouping Assets   For risk management purposes, an electronic inventory of assets will be useful in the risk management life cycle. It is not always necessary to list each individual asset: often, it is acceptable to instead list *classes* or *groups* of assets as a single asset entity for risk management purposes. For instance, a single entry for laptop computers is preferred over listing every laptop computer; this is because the risks for all laptop computers are roughly the same (ignoring behavior differences among individual employees or employees in specific departments). This eliminates the need to list them individually.

Similarly, groups of IT servers, network devices, and other equipment can be named instead of all of the individual servers and devices, again because the risks for each of them will usually be similar. However, one reason to create multiple entries for servers might be their physical location or their purpose: servers in one location may have different risks than servers in another location, and servers containing high-value information will have different risks than servers that do not contain high-value information.

Sources of Asset Data   An organization that is undergoing its initial risk-management cycle has to build its asset database from scratch. Management will need to determine where this initial asset data will come from. Some choices include

- **Financial system asset inventory**   An organization that keeps all of its assets on the books will have a wealth of asset inventory information. However, it may not be entirely useful: asset lists often do not include the location or purpose of the asset and whether it is still in use. Correlating a financial asset inventory to assets in actual use may consume more effort than the other methods for creating the initial asset. However, for organizations that have a relatively small number of highly valued assets (for instance, a rock crusher in a gold mine or a mainframe computer), knowing the precise financial value of an asset is highly useful because the actual depreciated value of the asset is used in the risk analysis phase of risk management. Knowing the depreciated value of other assets is also useful, as this will figure into the risk treatment choices that will be identified later on.

> **TIP**   Financial records that indicate the value of an asset do not include the value of information stored on (or processed by) the asset.

- **Interviews**   Discussions with key personnel for purposes of identifying assets are usually the best approach. However, to be effective, several people usually need to be interviewed to be sure to include all relevant assets.
- **IT systems portfolio**   A well-managed IT organization will have formal documents and records for its major applications. While this information may not encompass every single IT asset in the organization, it can provide information on the assets supporting individual applications or geographic locations.
- **Online data**   An organization with a large number of IT assets (systems, network devices, and so on) can sometimes utilize the capability of local online data to identify those assets. For instance, a systems or network management system often includes a list of managed assets, which can be a good starting point when creating the initial asset list.
- **Asset management system**   Larger organizations may find it more cost effective to use an asset management application dedicated to this purpose, rather than rely on lists of assets from other sources.

Collecting and Organizing Asset Data   It is rarely possible to take (or create) a list of assets from a single source. Rather, more than one source of information is often needed to be sure that the risk management program has identified at least the important, in-scope assets that it needs to worry about.

Unless an organization has a short list of assets, it is usually useful to organize or classify assets. This will help to get the assets under study into smaller chunks that can be analyzed more effectively. There is no single way to organize assets, but a few ideas include

- **Geography** A widely dispersed organization may want to classify its assets according to their location. This will aid risk managers during the risk analysis phase, since many risks are geographic-centric, particularly natural hazards. Mitigation of risks is often geography based: for instance, it's easier to make sense of building a fence around one data center than putting up fences around buildings in every location.

- **Business process** Because most organizations rank the criticality of their individual business processes, it can be useful to group assets according to the business processes that they support. This helps the risk analysis and risk treatment phases, because assets supporting individual processes can be associated with business criticality and treated appropriately.

- **Organizational unit** In larger organizations, it may be easier to classify assets according to the organizational unit they support.

- **Sensitivity** Usually ascribed to information, sensitivity relates to the nature and content of that information. Sensitivity usually applies in two ways: to an individual, where the information is considered personal or private, and to an organization, where the information may be considered a trade secret. Sometimes sensitivity is somewhat subjective and arbitrary, but often it is defined in laws and regulations.

- **Regulation** For organizations that are required to follow government or private regulation regarding the processing and protection of information, it will be useful to include data points that indicate whether specific assets are considered in scope for specific regulations. This is important because some regulations specify how assets should be protected, so it's useful to be aware of this during risk analysis and risk treatment.

There is no need to choose which of these three methods will be used to classify assets. Instead, an IT analyst should collect several points of metadata about each asset (including location, process supported, and organizational unit supported). This will enable the risk manager to sort and filter the list of assets in various ways to better understand which assets are in a given location or which ones support a particular process or part of the business.

 TIP Organizations should consider managing information about assets in a fixed-assets application.

Risk Analysis

Risk analysis is the activity in a risk management program where individual risks are identified. A risk consists of the intersection of threats, vulnerabilities, and impact. In its simplest terms, risk is described in the following formula:

$$Risk = Probability \times Impact$$

This equation implies that risk is always used in quantitative terms, but risk is equally used in qualitative risk analysis.

Other definitions of risk include

- *The probable frequency and probable magnitude of future loss* (source: An Introduction to Factor Analysis of Information Risk (FAIR), Risk Management Insight, LLC)

- *The potential that a given threat will exploit vulnerabilities of an asset or group of assets and thereby cause harm to the organization* (source: ISO 27005)

These definitions convey essentially the same message: the amount of risk is directly proportional to the probability of occurrence and the impact that a risk would have if realized.

A risk analysis consists of identifying threats and their impact of realization against each asset. This usually also includes a vulnerability analysis, where assets are studied to determine whether they are vulnerable to identified threats. The sheer number of assets may make this task appear daunting; however, threat and vulnerability analyses can usually be performed against groups of assets. For instance, when identifying natural and human-made threats against assets, it often makes sense to perform a single threat analysis against all of the assets that reside in a given location. After all, the odds of a volcanic eruption are just as likely for any of the servers in the room—the threat need not be called out separately for each asset.

Threat Analysis   The usual first step in a risk analysis is to identify threats against an asset or group of assets. A *threat* is an event that, if realized, would bring harm to an asset and, hence, to the organization. A typical approach is to list all of the threats that have some realistic opportunity of occurrence; those threats that are highly unlikely to occur can be left out. For instance, the listing of meteorites, tsunamis in landlocked regions, and wars in typically peaceful regions will just add clutter to a risk analysis.

A more reasonable approach in a threat analysis is to identify all of the threats that a reasonable person would believe could occur, even if the probability is low. For example, include flooding when a facility is located near a river, hurricanes for an organization located along the southern and eastern coasts (and inland for some distance) of the United States, or a terrorist attack in practically every major city in the world. All of these would be considered reasonable in a threat analysis.

It is important to include the entire range of both natural and human-made threats. The full list could approach or even exceed 100 separate threats. The categories of possible threats include

- **Severe storms**   This may include tornadoes, hurricanes, windstorms, ice storms, and blizzards.

- **Earth movement**   This includes earthquakes, landslides, avalanches, volcanoes, and tsunamis.

- **Flooding**   This can include both natural and human-made situations.

- **Disease**   This includes sickness outbreaks and pandemics, as well as quarantines that result.

- **Fire**   This includes forest fires, range fires, and structure fires, all of which may be natural or human-caused.

- **Labor**   This includes work stoppages, sick-outs, protests, and strikes.

- **Violence**   This includes riots, looting, terrorism, and war.

- **Malware**   This includes all kinds of viruses, worms, Trojan horses, root kits, and associated malicious software.

- **Hacking attack**   This includes automated attacks (think of an Internet worm that is on the loose) as well as targeted attacks by employees, former employees, or criminals.

- **Hardware failures**   This includes any kind of failure of IT equipment or related environmental equipment failures, such as heating, ventilation, and air conditioning (HVAC).

- **Software failures**   This can include any software problem that precipitates a disaster. Examples are the software bug that caused a significant power blackout in the U.S. Northeast in 2003 and the AT&T long-distance network crash in 1990.

- **Utilities**   This includes electric power failures, water supply failures, and natural gas outages, as well as communications outages.

- **Transportation**   This may include airplane crashes, railroad derailments, ship collisions, and highway accidents.

- **Hazardous materials**   This includes chemical spills. The primary threat here is direct damage by hazardous substances, casualties, and forced evacuations.

- **Criminal**   This includes extortion, embezzlement, theft, vandalism, sabotage, and hacker intrusion. Note that company insiders can play a role in these activities.

- **Errors**   This includes mistakes made by personnel that result in disaster situations.

Alongside each threat that is identified, the risk analyst assigns a probability or frequency of occurrence. This may be a numeric value, expressed as a probability of one occurrence within a calendar year. For example, if the risk of a flood is 1 in 100, it would be expressed as 0.01, or 1 percent. Probability can also be expressed as a ranking; for example, Low, Medium, and High; or on a numeric probability scale from 1 to 5 (where 5 can be either highest or lowest probability).

An approach for completing a threat analysis is to

- **Perform a geographic threat analysis for each location**   This will provide an analysis on the probability of each type of threat against all assets in each location.

- **Perform a logical threat analysis for each type of asset**   This provides information on all of the logical (that is, not physical) threats that can occur to each asset type. For example, the risk of malware on all assets of one type is probably the same, regardless of their location.

Threat Forecasting Data Is Sparse

One of the biggest problems with information security-related risk management is the lack of reliable data on the probability of many types of threats. While the probability of some natural threats can sometimes be obtained from local disaster response agencies, the probabilities of most other threats are difficult to accurately predict.

The difficulty in predicting security events sits in stark contrast to volumes of available data related to automobile and airplane accidents, as well as human life expectancy. In these cases, insurance companies have been accumulating statistics on these events for decades, and the variables (for instance, tobacco and alcohol use) are well known. On the topic of cyber-related risk, there is a general lack of reliable data, and the factors that influence risk are not well known from a statistical perspective. It is for this reason that risk analysis still relies on educated guesses for the probabilities of most events.

- **Perform a threat analysis for each highly valued asset**   This will help to identify any unique threats that may have appeared in the geographic or logical threat analysis, but with different probabilities of occurrence.

Vulnerability Identification   A *vulnerability* is a weakness or absence of a protective control that makes the probability of one or more threats more likely. A *vulnerability analysis* is an examination of an asset in order to discover weaknesses that could lead to a higher-than-normal rate of occurrence or potency of a threat.

Examples of vulnerabilities include

- Missing or inoperative antivirus software
- Missing security patches
- Weak password settings
- Missing or incomplete audit logs
- Weak or defective application session management
- Mantraps (devices that are designed to permit the passage of persons one at a time) that permit tailgating

In a vulnerability analysis, the risk manager needs to examine the asset itself as well as all of the protective measures that are—or should be—in place to protect the asset from relevant threats.

Vulnerabilities can be ranked by severity. Vulnerabilities are indicators that show the effectiveness (or ineffectiveness) of protective measures. For example, an antivirus program on a server that updates its virus signatures once per week might be ranked as a medium vulnerability, whereas the complete absence (or malfunction) of an antivirus program on the same server might be ranked as a high vulnerability. Severity is an indication of the likelihood that a given threat might be realized. This is different from *impact*, which is discussed later in this section.

TIP A vulnerability, and its ranking, should not be influenced by the probability that a threat will be realized. Instead, a vulnerability ranking should depend on whether the threat will actually bring about harm to the asset. Also, the ranking of a vulnerability should not be influenced by the value of the asset or the impact of a realized threat. These factors are covered separately in risk management.

Probability Analysis   For any given threat and asset, the probability that the threat will actually be realized needs to be estimated. This is often easier said than done, as there is a lack of reliable data on security incidents. A risk manager still will need to perform some research and develop a best guess based on available data.

Impact Analysis   A threat, when actually realized, will have some effect on the organization. Impact analysis is the study of estimating the impact of specific threats on specific assets.

In impact analysis, it is necessary to understand the relationship between an asset and the business processes and activities that the asset supports. The purpose of impact analysis is to identify the impact on business operations or business processes. This is because risk management is not an abstract identification of abstract risks, but instead a search for risks that have real impact on business operations.

In an impact analysis, the impact can be expressed as a rating such as H-M-L (High-Medium-Low) or as a numeric scale, and it can also be expressed in financial terms. But what is also vitally important in an impact analysis is the inclusion of a *statement of impact* for each threat. Example statements of impact include "inability to process customer support calls" and "inability for customers to view payment history." Statements such as "inability to authenticate users" may be technically accurate, but they do not identify the business impact.

NOTE Because of the additional time required to quantify and develop statements of impact, impact analysis is usually performed only on the highest-ranked threats on the most critical assets.

Qualitative Risk Analysis   A qualitative risk analysis is an in-depth examination of in-scope assets with a detailed study of threats (and their probability of occurrence), vulnerabilities (and their severity), and statements of impact. The threats, vulnerabilities, and impact are all expressed in qualitative terms such as High-Medium-Low or in quasi-numeric terms such as a 1–5 numeric scale.

The purpose of qualitative risk analysis is to identify the most critical risks in the organization based on these rankings.

Qualitative risk analysis does not get to the issue of "how much does a given threat cost my business if it is realized?"—nor does it mean to. The value in a qualitative risk analysis is the ability to quickly identify the most critical risks without the additional burden of identifying precise financial impacts.

NOTE Organizations that do need to perform quantitative risk analysis often begin with qualitative risk analysis to determine the highest-ranked risks that warrant the additional effort of quantitative analysis.

Quantitative Risk Analysis   Quantitative risk analysis is a risk analysis approach that uses numeric methods to measure risk. The advantage of quantitative risk analysis is the statements of risk in terms that can be easily compared with the known value of their respective assets. In other words, risks are expressed in the same units of measure as most organizations' primary unit of measure: financial.

Despite this, quantitative risk analysis must still be regarded as an effort to develop estimates, not exact figures. Partly this is because risk analysis is a measure of events that may occur, not a measure of events that *do* occur.

Standard quantitative risk analysis involves the development of several figures:

- **Asset value (AV)**   This is the value of the asset, which is usually (but not necessarily) the asset's replacement value.

- **Exposure factor (EF)**   This is the financial loss that results from the realization of a threat, expressed as a percentage of the asset's total value. Most threats do not completely eliminate the asset's value; instead, they reduce its value. For example, if a construction company's $120,000 earth mover is destroyed in a fire, the equipment will still have salvage value, even if that is only 10 percent of the asset's value. In this case the EF would be 90 percent. Note that different threats will have different impacts on EF because the realization of different threats will cause varying amounts of damage to assets.

- **Single loss expectancy (SLE)**   This value represents the financial loss when a threat is realized one time. SLE is defined as AV × EF. Note that different threats have a varied impact on EF, so those threats will also have the same multiplicative effect on SLE.

- **Annualized rate of occurrence (ARO)**   This is an estimate of the number of times that a threat will occur per year. If the probability of the threat is 1 in 50, then ARO is expressed as 0.02. However, if the threat is estimated to occur four times per year, then ARO is 4.0. Like EF and SLE, ARO will vary by threat.

- **Annualized loss expectancy (ALE)**   This is the expected annualized loss of asset value due to threat realization. ALE is defined as SLE × ARO.

ALE is based upon the verifiable values AV, EF, and SLE, but because ARO is only an estimate, ALE is only as good as ARO. Depending upon the value of the asset, the risk manager may need to take extra care to develop the best possible estimate for ARO, based upon whatever data is available. Sources for estimates include

- History of event losses in the organization

- History of similar losses in other organizations

- History of dissimilar losses

- Best estimates based on available data

TIP When performing a quantitative risk analysis for a given asset, the ALE for all threats can be added together. The sum of all ALEs is the annualized loss expectancy for the total array of threats. A particularly high sum of ALEs would mean that a given asset is confronted with a lot of significant threats that are more likely to occur. But in terms of risk treatment, ALEs are better off left as separate and associated with their respective threats.

Developing Mitigation Strategies An important part of risk analysis is the investigation of potential solutions for reducing or eliminating risk. This involves understanding specific threats and their impact (EF) and likelihood of occurrence (ARO). Once a given asset and threat combination has been *baselined* (that is, the existing asset, threats, and controls have been analyzed to understand the threats as they exist *right now*), the risk analyst can then apply various hypothetical means for reducing risk, documenting each one in terms of its impact on EF and ARO.

For example, suppose a risk analysis identifies the threat of attack on a public web server. Specific EF and ARO figures have been identified for a range of individual threats. Now the risk analyst applies a range of fixes (on paper), such as an application firewall, an intrusion prevention system, and a patch management tool. Each solution will have a specific and unique impact on EF and ARO (these are all estimates, of course, just like the estimates of EF and ARO on the initial conditions); some will have better EF and ARO figures than others. Each solution should also be rated in terms of cost (financial or H-M-L) and effort to implement (financial or H-M-L).

NOTE Developing mitigation strategies is the first step in risk treatment, where various solutions are put forward, each with its cost and impact on risk.

While security analysts may have the responsibility for documenting vulnerabilities, threats, and risks, it is senior management's responsibility (through the security steering committee) to formally approve the treatment of risk. Risk treatment is discussed later in this chapter.

Risk Analysis and Disaster Recovery Planning Disaster recovery planning (DRP) and business continuity planning (BCP) utilize risk analysis to identify risks that are related to application resilience and the impact of disasters. The risk analysis performed for DRP and BCP is the same risk analysis that is discussed in this chapter—the methods and approach are the same, although the overall objectives are somewhat different.

Business continuity planning is discussed in depth later in this chapter. Disaster recovery planning is discussed in detail in Chapter 5.

High-Impact Events The risk manager is likely to identify one or more high-impact events during the risk analysis. These events, which may be significant enough to threaten the very viability of the organization, require risk treatment that belongs in the categories of business continuity planning and disaster recovery planning. These topics are discussed in detail later in this chapter.

Risk Treatment

When risks to assets have been identified through qualitative or quantitative risk analysis, the next step in risk management is to decide what to do about the identified risks. In the risk analysis, one or more potential solutions may have been examined, along with their cost to implement and their impact on risk. In risk treatment, a decision about whether to proceed with any of the proposed solutions (or others) is needed.

Risk treatment pits available resources against the need to reduce risk. In an enterprise environment, not all risks can be mitigated or eliminated because there are not enough resources to treat them all. Instead, a strategy for choosing the best combination of solutions that will reduce risk by the greatest possible margin is needed. For this reason, risk treatment is often more effective when all the risks and solutions are considered together, instead of each one separately. Then they can be compared and prioritized.

When risk treatment is performed at the enterprise level, risk analysts and technology architects can devise ways to bring about the greatest possible reduction in risk. This can be achieved through the implementation of solutions that will reduce many risks for many assets at once. For example, a firewall can reduce risks from many threats on many assets; this will be more effective than individual solutions for each asset.

So far I have been talking about risk mitigation as if it were the only option available when handling risk. Rather, you have four primary ways to treat risk: mitigation, transfer, avoidance, and acceptance. And there is almost always some leftover risk, called *residual risk*. These four approaches are discussed here.

Risk Mitigation

Risk mitigation involves the implementation of some solution that will reduce an identified risk. For instance, the risk of malware being introduced onto a server can be mitigated with antivirus software or a network-based intrusion prevention system. Either of these solutions would constitute mitigation of this risk on a given asset.

An organization usually makes a decision to implement some form of risk mitigation after performing some cost analysis to determine whether the reduction of risk is worth the expenditure of risk mitigation.

Risk Transfer

Risk transfer means that some or all of the risk is being transferred to some external entity, such as an insurance company or business partner. When an organization purchases an insurance policy to protect an asset against damage or loss, the insurance company is assuming part of the risk in exchange for payment of insurance premiums.

Risk Avoidance

In risk avoidance, the organization abandons the activity altogether, effectively taking the asset out of service so that the threat is no longer present.

NOTE Organizations do not often back away completely from an activity because of identified risks. Generally, this avenue is taken only when the risk of loss is great and when the perceived probability of occurrence is high.

Risk Acceptance

Risk acceptance occurs when management is willing to accept an identified risk as-is, with no effort taken to reduce it.

Residual Risk

Residual risk is the risk that is left over from the original risk after some of the risk has been removed through mitigation or transfer. For instance, if a particular threat had a probability of 10 percent before risk treatment and 1 percent after risk treatment, the residual risk is that 1 percent left over. This is best illustrated by the following formula:

$$Original\ Risk - Mitigated\ Risk - Transferred\ Risk = Residual\ Risk$$

It is unusual for risk treatment to eliminate risk altogether; rather, various controls are implemented that remove some of the risk. Often, management implicitly accepts the leftover risk; however, it's a good idea to make that acceptance of residual risk more formal by documenting the acceptance in a risk management log or a decision log.

Compliance Risk: The Risk Management Trump Card

Organizations that perform risk management are generally aware of the laws, regulations, and standards they are required to follow. For instance, U.S.-based banks, brokerages, and insurance companies are required to comply with the Gramm Leach Bliley Act (GLBA), and organizations that store, process, or transmit credit card numbers are required to comply with PCI-DSS (Payment Card Industry Data Security Standard).

GLBA, PCI-DSS, and other regulations often state in specific terms what controls are required in an organization's IT systems. This brings to light the matter of *compliance risk*. Sometimes, the risk associated with a specific control (or lack of a control) may be rated as a low risk, either because the probability of a risk event is low or because the impact of the event is low. However, if a given law, regulation, or standard requires that the control be enacted anyway, then the organization must consider the compliance risk. The risk of noncompliance may result in fines or other sanctions against the organization, which may (or may not) have consequences greater than the actual risk.

The end result of this is that organizations often implement specific security controls because they are required by laws, regulations, or standards—not because their risk analysis would otherwise compel them to.

IT Management Practices

The primary services in the IT organization typically are development, operations, and support. These primary activities require the support of a second layer of activities that together support the delivery of primary IT services to the organization. The second layer of IT management practices consists of

- Personnel management
- Sourcing
- Change management
- Financial management
- Quality management
- Security management
- Performance and capacity management

Some of these activities the IT organization undertakes itself, while some are usually performed by other parts of the organization. For instance, most of the personnel management functions are typically carried out by a human resources department. This is another essential reason for the existence of an organization-wide IT steering committee that is represented by other departments such as human resources. This enables the entire spectrum of IT management to be centrally controlled even when other departments perform some IT management functions.

Personnel Management

Personnel management encompasses many activities related to the status of employment, training, and the acceptance of policy. These personnel management activities ensure that the individuals who are hired into the organization are suitably vetted, trained, and equipped to perform their functions. It is important that they are provided with the organization's key policies so that their behavior and decisions will reflect the organization's needs.

Hiring

The purpose of the employee hiring process is to ensure that the organization hires persons who are qualified to perform their stated job duties and that their personal, professional, and educational histories are appropriate. The hiring process includes several activities necessary to ensure that candidates being considered are suitable.

Background Verification   Various studies suggest that 30 to 80 percent of employment candidates exaggerate their education and experience on their résumé, and some candidates commit outright fraud by providing false information about their education or prior positions. Because of this, employers need to perform their own background investigation on an employment candidate to obtain an independent assessment of the candidate's true background.

Employers should examine the following parts of a candidate's background prior to hiring:

- **Employment background**   An employer should check at least two years back, although five to seven years is needed for mid- or senior-level personnel.

- **Education background**   The employer should confirm whether the candidate has earned any of the degrees or diplomas listed on their résumé. There are many "diploma mills," enterprises that will print a fake college diploma for a fee.

- **Military service background**   If the candidate served in any branch of the military, then this must be verified to confirm whether the candidate served at all and whether they received relevant training and work experience.

- **Professional licenses and certifications**   If a position requires licenses or certifications, these need to be confirmed, including whether the candidate is in good standing with the organizations that manage those licenses and certifications.

- **Criminal background**   The employer needs to investigate whether the candidate has a criminal record. In countries with a national criminal registry like the National Crime Information Center (NCIC) in the United States, this is simpler than in countries like India that have no nationwide criminal records database.

- **Credit background**   The employer may wish to examine a candidate's credit and financial history. There are two principal reasons for this type of check: first, a good credit history indicates the candidate is responsible, while a poor credit history may be an indication of irresponsibility or poor choices (although in many cases a candidate's credit background is not entirely his or her own doing); second, a candidate with excessive debt and a poor credit history may be considered a risk for embezzlement, fraud, or theft.

- **Terrorist association**   Some employers wish to know whether a candidate has documented ties with terrorist organizations. In the United States, an employer can request verification of whether a candidate is on one of several lists of individuals and organizations with whom U.S. citizens are prohibited from doing business. Lists are maintained by the Office of Foreign Assets Control (OFAC), a department of the U.S. Treasury, and also by the U.S. Department of Commerce and the U.S. Bureau of Industry and Security.

- **References**   The employer may wish to contact two or more personal and professional references—people who know the candidate and will vouch for his or her background, work history, and character.

TIP In many jurisdictions, employment candidates are required to sign a consent form that will allow the employer (or a third-party agent acting on behalf of the employer) to perform the background check.

Background checks are a prudent business practice to identify and reduce risk. In many industries they are a common practice or even required by law. And in addition to performing a background check at the time of hire, many organizations perform them annually for employees in high-risk or high-value positions.

Employee Policy Manuals   Sometimes known as an *employee handbook*, an employee policy manual is a formal statement of the terms of employment, facts about the organization, benefits, compensation, conduct, and other policies.

Employee handbooks are often the cornerstone of corporate policy. A thorough employee handbook usually will cover a wide swath of territory, including the following topics:

- **Welcome**   This welcomes a new employee into the organization, often in an upbeat letter that makes the new employee glad to have joined the organization. This may also include a brief history of the organization.

- **Policies**   These are the most important policies in the organization, which include security, privacy, code of conduct (ethics), and acceptable use of resources. In the United States and other countries, the handbook may also include antiharassment and other workplace behavior policies.

- **Compensation**   This describes when and how employees are compensated.

- **Benefits**   This describes company benefit programs.

- **Work hours**   This discusses work hours and basic expectations for when employees are expected to report to work and how many hours per week they are expected to work.

- **Dress code**   This provides a description and guidelines for required attire in the workplace.

- **Performance review**   This describes the performance review policy and program that is used to periodically evaluate each employee's performance.

- **Promotions**   This describes the criteria used by the organization to consider promotions for employees.

- **Time off**   This describes compensated and uncompensated time off, including holidays, vacation, illness, disability, bereavement, sabbaticals, military duty, and leaves of absence.

- **Security**   This discusses basic expectations on the topics of physical security and information security, as well as expectations for how employees are expected to handle confidential and sensitive information.

- **Regulation**   If the organization is subject to regulation, this may be mentioned in the employee handbook so that employees will be aware of this and conduct themselves accordingly.

- **Safety**   This discusses workplace safety, which may cover evacuation procedures, emergency procedures, permitted and prohibited items and substances (for example, weapons, alcoholic beverages, other substances and items), procedures for working with hazardous substances, and procedures for operating equipment and machinery.

- **Conduct**   This covers basic expectations for workplace conduct, both with fellow employees and with customers, vendors, business partners, and other third parties.

- **Discipline**   Organizations that have a disciplinary process usually describe its highlights in the employee handbook.

NOTE   Employees are often required to sign a statement that affirms their understanding of and compliance with the employee handbook. Many organizations require that employees sign a new copy of the statement on an annual basis, even if the employee handbook has not changed. This helps to affirm for employees the importance of policies contained in the employee handbook.

Initial Access Provisioning   New employees may need access to office locations, computers, networks, and/or applications to perform their required duties. This will necessitate the provisioning of one or more building access and computer or network user accounts that they will use to perform their work-related tasks.

An access-provisioning process should be used to determine the access privileges that a new employee should be given. A template of job titles and access privileges should be set up in advance so that management can easily determine which access privileges any new employee will receive. But even with such a plan, each new employee's manager should still formally request these privileges be set up for new employees.

Job Descriptions   A job description is a formal document that describes the roles, responsibilities, and experience required. Each position in an organization, from chief executive officer to office clerk, should have a formal job description.

Job descriptions should also state that employees are required to support company policies, including but not limited to security and privacy, code of conduct, and acceptable use policies. By listing these in a job description, an employer is stating that all employees are expected to comply with these and other policies.

NOTE   Employers usually are required to include several boilerplate items or statements (such as equal opportunity clauses) in job descriptions to conform to local labor and workplace safety laws.

Employee Development

Once hired into the organization, employees will require training in the organization's policies and practices so that their contribution will be effective and further the organization's goals. Regular evaluation will help employees to focus their long-term efforts on personal and organization goals and objectives.

Training To be effective, employees need to receive periodic training. This includes

- **Skills training** This covers the need to learn how to use tools and equipment properly. In some cases, employees are required to receive training and prove competency before they are permitted to use some tools and equipment. Sometimes this is required by law.

- **Practices and techniques** Employees need to understand how the organization uses its tools and equipment for its specific use.

- **Policies** Organizations often impart information about their policies in the context of training. This helps the organization make sure that employees comprehend the material.

Performance Evaluation Many organizations utilize a performance evaluation process that is used to examine each employee's performance against a set of expectations and objectives. A performance evaluation program also helps to shape employees' behavior over the long term and helps them to reflect on how their effort contributes toward the organization's overall objectives. A performance evaluation is frequently used to determine whether (and by how much) an employee's compensation should be increased.

Career Path In many cultures, employees feel that they can be successful if they understand how they can advance within the organization. A career path program can achieve this by helping employees understand what skills are required for other positions in the organization and how they can strive toward positions that they desire in the future.

Mandatory Vacations

Some organizations, particularly those that deal with high-risk or high-value activities, enact mandatory vacations of one week or longer for some or all employees. This practice can accomplish three objectives:

- **Cross-training** An absence of one week or longer will force management to cross-train other employees so that the organization is less reliant upon specific individuals.

- **Audit** A minimum absence gives the organization an opportunity to audit the absent employee's work to make sure that the employee is not involved in any undesired behavior.

- **Reduced risk** Knowing that they will be away from their day-to-day activities for at least one or two contiguous weeks each year, employees are less apt to partake in prohibited activities that could be discovered by colleagues or auditors during their absence.

Termination

When an employee leaves an organization, several actions need to take place:

- Physical access to all work areas must be immediately revoked. Depending upon the sensitivity of work activities in the organization, the employee may also need to be escorted out of the work area and his or her personal belongings gathered by others and delivered to the departed employee's residence.

- Each of the employee's computer and network access accounts needs to be locked. The purpose of this is to protect the integrity of business information by permitting only authorized employees to access it. Locking computer accounts also prevents other employees from accessing information using the former employee's credentials.

 CAUTION The issue of whether a former employee's account should be removed or merely locked depends upon the nature of the application or system. In some cases, the record of actions taken by employees (such as an audit log) depends upon the existence of the employee's ID on the system; if a former employee's ID is removed, then those audit records may not properly reference who is associated with them.

If the organization chooses to lock rather than remove computer or network accounts for terminated employees, those accounts must be locked or restricted in a way that positively prohibits any further access. For instance, merely changing the passwords of terminated accounts to "locked" would be considered a highly *unsafe* practice in the event that anyone discovers the password. If changing the account's password is the only way to lock it, then a long and highly random password must be used and then forgotten so that even the account administrator cannot use it.

Transfers and Reassignments

In many organizations, employees will move from position to position over time. These position changes are not always upward through a career path, but are instead lateral moves from one type of work to another.

Unless an organization is very careful about its access management processes and procedures, employees who transfer and are promoted tend to accumulate access privileges. This happens because a transferring employee's old privileges are not revoked even though those privileges are no longer needed. Over a period of many years, an employee who is transferred or promoted every few years can accumulate many excessive privileges that can indicate significant risk should the individual choose to perform functions in the applications that they are no longer officially authorized to use. This phenomenon is sometimes known as "accumulation of privileges" or "privilege creep."

Privilege creep happens frequently in companies' accounting departments. An individual, for example, can move from role to role in the accounting department, all the while accumulating privileges that eventually result in the ability for that employee to defraud his or her employer by requesting, approving, and disbursing payments to themselves or their accomplices. Similarly, this can occur in an IT department when an employee transfers from the operations department to the software development department (which is a common career path). Unless the IT department deliberately removes the transferring employee's prior privileges, it will end up with an employee who is a developer with access to production systems—a red flag to auditors who examine roles and responsibilities.

Sourcing

The term *sourcing* refers to the choices that organizations make when selecting the personnel who will perform functions and where those functions will be performed.

The options include whose personnel will perform tasks:

- **Insourced**   The organization hires employees to perform work. These workers can be full time, part time, or temporary.

- **Outsourced**   The organization utilizes contractors or consultants to perform work.

- **Hybrid**   The organization can utilize a combination of insourced and outsourced workers.

Next, the options include where personnel will perform tasks:

- **On-site**   Personnel work in the organization's work site(s).

- **Off-site, local**   Personnel are not located on-site, but are near the organization's premises, usually in or near the same community.

- **Off-site, remote**   Personnel are in the same country, but not near the organization's premises.

- **Offshore**   Personnel are located in a different country.

 NOTE   Organizations are often able to work out different combinations of whether personnel are insourced or outsourced and where they perform their work. For instance, an organization can open its own office in a foreign country and hire employees to work there; this would be an example of offshore insourcing. Similarly, an organization can use contractors to perform work on-site; this is on-site outsourcing.

Insourcing

Insourcing, which is the practice of hiring employees for long-term work, is discussed earlier in this chapter in the "Personnel Management" section.

Outsourcing

Outsourcing is the practice of using contractors or consultants to perform work for the organization. An organization will make a decision to outsource a task, activity, or project for a wide variety of reasons:

- **Project duration**   An organization may require personnel only for a specific project, such as the development of or migration to a new application. Often, an organization will opt to use contractors or consultants when it cannot justify hiring permanent workers.

- **Skills** An organization may require personnel with certain hard-to-find skills but not need them on a full-time basis. Persons with certain skills may command a higher salary than the organization is willing to pay, and the organization may not have sufficient work to keep such a worker interested in permanent employment with the organization.

- **Variable demand** Organizations may experience seasonal increases and decreases of demand for certain workers. Organizations often cannot justify hiring full-time employees for peak demand capacity, when at other times those workers will not have enough work to keep them busy and productive. Instead, organizations will usually staff for average demand and augment staff with contractors for peak demand.

- **High turnover** Some positions, such as IT helpdesk and call center, are inherently high-turnover positions that are costly to replace and train. Instead, an organization may opt to outsource some or all of the personnel in these positions.

- **Focus on core activities** An organization may wish to concentrate on hiring for positions related to its core purpose and to outsource functions that are considered "overhead." For instance, an organization that produces computer hardware products may elect to outsource its IT computer support department so that it can focus on its product development and support.

- **Financial** A decision to outsource may be primarily financial. Usually an organization seeking to reduce costs of software development and other activities will outsource and off-shore these activities to service organizations located in other countries.

- **Complete time coverage** An organization that needs to have personnel available around the clock may choose to outsource part of that function to work centers in other time zones.

An organization that chooses to hire employees only in its core service areas can outsource many of its noncore functions, including these:

- **IT helpdesk and support** This is often a high-turnover function, as well as variable in demand, making this a good candidate for outsourcing.

- **Software development** An organization that lacks development and programming skills can elect to have contractors or consultants perform this work.

- **Software maintenance** An organization may wish to keep its developers and analysts focused on new software development projects and to leave maintenance of existing software to contractors.

- **Customer support** An organization may choose to outsource its telephone and online support to personnel or organizations in countries with lower labor costs.

TIP   Although outsourcing decisions appear, on the surface, to be economically motivated, some of the other reasons stated earlier may be even more important in some organizations. For example, the flexibility afforded by outsourcing may help to make an organization more agile, which may improve quality or increase efficiency over longer periods.

Outsourcing Benefits   Organizations that are considering outsourcing need to carefully weigh the benefits and the costs in order to determine whether the effort to outsource will result in measurable improvement in their processing, service delivery, or finances. In the 1990s, when many organizations rushed to outsource development and support functions to operations in other countries, they did so with unrealistic short-term gains in mind and without adequately considering all of the real costs of outsourcing. This is not to say that outsourcing is bad, but that many organizations made outsourcing decisions without fully understanding it.

Outsourcing can bring many benefits:

- **Available skills and experience**   Organizations that may have trouble attracting persons with specialized skills often turn to outsourcing firms whose highly skilled personnel can ply their trade in a variety of client organizations.

- **Economies of scale**   Often, specialized outsourcing firms can achieve better economies of scale through discipline and mature practices that organizations are unable to achieve.

- **Objectivity**   Some functions are better done by outsiders. Personnel in an organization may have trouble being objective about some activities such as process improvement and requirements definition. Also, auditors frequently must be from an outside firm in order to achieve sufficient objectivity and independence.

- **Reduced costs**   When outsourcing is done with offshore personnel, an organization may be able to lower its operating costs and improve its competitive market position, usually through currency exchange rates and differences in the standards of living in headquarters versus offshore countries.

When an organization is making an outsourcing decision, it needs to consider these advantages together with risks that are discussed in the next section.

Outsourcing Risks   While outsourcing can bring many tangible and intangible benefits to an organization, it is not without certain risks and disadvantages. Naturally, when an organization employs outsiders to perform some of its functions, it relinquishes some control. The risks of outsourcing include these:

- **Higher-than-expected costs**   Reduced costs were the main driver for offshore outsourcing in the 1990s. However, many organizations failed to fully anticipate the operational realities. For instance, when outsourcing to overseas operations, IT personnel back in U.S.-based organizations had to make many more expensive trips than expected. Also, changes in international currency exchange rates can transform this year's bargain into next year's high cost.

- **Poor quality**   The outsourced work product may be lower than was produced when the function was performed in-house.

- **Poor performance**   The outsourced service may not perform as expected. The capacity of networks or IT systems used by the outsourcing firm may cause processing delays or longer-than-acceptable response times.

- **Loss of control**   An organization that is accustomed to being in control of its workers may feel loss of control. Making small adjustments to processes and procedures may be more time-consuming or increase costs.

- **Employee integrity and background**   It may be decidedly more difficult to determine the integrity of employees in an outsourced situation, particularly when the outsourcing is taking place offshore. Some countries, even where outsourcing is popular, lack nationwide criminal background checks and other means for making a solid determination on an employee's background.

- **Loss of competitive advantage**   If the services performed by the outsourcing firm are not flexible enough to meet the organization's needs, this can result in the organization losing some of its competitive advantage. For example, an organization outsources its corporate messaging (e-mail and other messaging) to a service provider. Later, the organization wishes to enhance its customer communication by integrating its service application with e-mail. The e-mail service provider may be unable or unwilling to provide the necessary integration, which will result in the organization losing a competitive advantage.

- **Errors and omissions**   The organization performing outsourcing services may make serious errors or fail to perform essential tasks. For instance, an outsourcing service may suffer a data security breach that may result in the loss or disclosure of sensitive information. This can be a disastrous event when it occurs within an organization's four walls, but when it happens in an outsourced part of the business, the organization may find that the lack of control will make it difficult to take the proper steps to contain and remedy the incident. If an outsourcing firm has a security breach or other similar incident, it may be putting itself first and only secondarily watching out for the interests of its customers.

- **Vendor failure**   The failure of the organization to provide outsourcing services may result in increased costs and delays in service or product delivery.

- **Differing mission and goals**   An organization's employees are going to be loyal to its mission and objectives. However, the employees in an outsourced organization usually have little or no interest in the hiring organization's interests; instead, they will be loyal to the outsourcing provider's values, which may at times be in direct conflict. For example, an outsourcing organization may place emphasis on maximizing billable hours, while the hiring organization emphasizes efficiency. These two objectives conflict with each other.

- **Difficult recourse**   If an organization is dissatisfied with the performance or quality of its outsourced operation, contract provisions may not sufficiently facilitate any remedy. If the outsourced operation is in a foreign country, applying remediation in the court system may also be futile.

- **Lowered employee morale**   If part of an organization chooses to outsource, those employees who remain may be upset because some of their colleagues may have lost their jobs as a result of the outsourcing. Further, remaining employees may feel that their own jobs may soon be outsourced or eliminated. They may also feel that their organization is more interested in saving money than in taking care of its employees. Personnel who have lost their jobs may vent their anger at the organization through a variety of harmful actions that may threaten assets or other workers.

- **Audit and compliance**   An organization that outsources a part of its operation that is in-scope for applicable laws and regulation may find it more challenging to perform audits and achieve compliance. Audit costs may rise, as auditors need to visit the outsourced work centers. Requiring the outsourced organization to make changes to achieve compliance may be difficult or expensive.

- **Applicable laws**   Laws, regulations, and standards in headquarters and offshore countries may impose requirements on the protection of information that may complicate business operations or enterprise architecture.

- **Cross-border data transfer**   Governments around the world are paying attention to the flow of data, particularly the sensitive data of its citizens. Many countries have passed laws that attempt to exert control over data about its citizens when it is transferred out of their jurisdiction.

- **Time zone differences**   Communications will suffer when an organization outsources some of its operations to offshore organizations that are several time zones distant. It will be more difficult to schedule telephone conferences when there is very little overlap between workers in each time zone. It will take more time to communicate important issues and to make changes.

- **Language and cultural differences**   When outsourcing crosses language and cultural barriers, it can result in less-than-optimal communication and results. The outsourcing customer will express its needs through its own language and culture, but the outsourcing provider will hear those needs through its own language and culture. Both sides may be thinking or saying, "They don't understand what we want" and "We don't understand what they want." This can result in unexpected differences in work products produced by the outsourcing firm. Delays in project completion or delivery of goods and services can occur as a result.

CAUTION   Some of the risks associated with outsourcing are intangible or may lie outside the bounds of legal remedies. For instance, language and time zone differences may introduce delays in communication, adding friction to the business relationship in a way that may not be easily measurable.

Mitigating Outsourcing Risk The only means of exchange between an outsourcing provider and its customer organization are money and reputation. In other words, the only leverage that an organization has against its outsourcing provider is the withholding of payment and communicating the quality (or lack therein) of the outsourcing provider to other organizations. This is especially true if the outsourcing crosses national boundaries. Therefore, an organization that is considering outsourcing must carefully consider how it will enforce contract terms so that it receives the goods and services that it is expecting.

Many of the risks of outsourcing can be remedied through contract provisions. Some of the remedies are

- **Service level agreement (SLA)** The contract should provide details on every avenue of work performance and communication, including escalations and problem management.

- **Quality** Depending upon the product or service, this may translate into an error or defect rate, a customer satisfaction rate, or system performance.

- **Security policy and controls** Whether the outsourcing firm is safeguarding the organization's intellectual property, keeping business secrets, or protecting information about its employees or customers, the contract should spell out the details of the security controls that it expects the outsourcing firm to perform. The organization should also require periodic third-party audits and the results of those audits. The contract should contain a "right to audit" clause that allows the outsourcing organization to examine the work premises, records, and work papers on demand.

- **Business continuity** The contract should require the outsourcing firm to have reasonable measures and safeguards in place to ensure resilience of operations and the ability to continue operations with minimum disruption in the event of a disaster.

- **Employee integrity** The contract should define how the outsourcing firm will vet its employees' backgrounds so that it is not inadvertently hiring individuals with a criminal history and so employees' claimed education and work experience are genuine.

- **Ownership of intellectual property** If the outsourcing firm is producing software or other designs, the contract must define ownership of those work products and whether the outsourcing firm may reuse any of those work products for other engagements.

- **Roles and responsibilities** The contract should specify in detail the roles and responsibilities of each party so that each will know what is expected of them.

- **Schedule** The contract must specify when and how many items of work products should be produced.

- **Regulation** The contract should require both parties to conform to all applicable laws and regulations, including but not limited to intellectual property, data protection, and workplace safety.

- **Warranty**   The contract should specify terms of warranty for the workmanship and quality of all work products so that there can be no ambiguity regarding the quality of goods or services performed.

- **Dispute and resolution**   The contract should contain provisions that define the process for handling and resolving disputes.

- **Payment**   The contract should specify how and when the outsourcing provider will be paid. Compensation should be tied not only to the quantity but also to the quality of work performed. The contract should include incentive provisions for additional payment when specific schedule, quantity, or quality targets are exceeded. The contract should also contain financial penalties that are enacted when SLA, quality, security, audit, or schedule targets are missed.

The terms of an outsourcing contract should adequately reward the outsourcing firm for a job well done, which should include the prospect of earning additional contracts as well as referrals that will help it to earn outsourcing contracts from other customers.

Outsourcing Governance   You cannot outsource accountability.

Outsourcing is a convenient way to transfer some operations to an external organization, thereby allowing the outsourcing organization to be more agile and to improve focus on core competencies. While senior managers can transfer these activities to external organizations and even specify rewards for good performance and penalties for substandard performance, those senior managers are still ultimately accountable for the delivery of these services, whether they are outsourced or performed by internal staff.

In the context of outsourcing, the role of governance must be expanded to include the aggregation of activities that control the work performed by external organizations. Governance activities may include

- **Contracts**   The overall business relationship between the organization and its service providers should be defined in detailed legal agreements. The terms of legal agreements should define the work to be done (in general), the expectations of all parties, service levels, quality, the terms of compensation, and remedies in case expectations fail to be met. Appropriate levels of management must approve the content in contracts.

- **Work orders**   Sometimes called statements of work (SOWs), work orders describe in greater detail the work that is to be performed. While contracts are expected to change seldom, work orders operate in short-term intervals and are specific to currently delivered goods or services. Like contracts themselves, work orders should include precise statements regarding work output, timeliness, quality, and remedies.

- **Service level agreements**   These are documents that specify service levels in terms of the quantity of work, quality, timeliness, and remedies for shortfalls in quality or quantity.

- **Change management**   A formal method is needed so that changes in delivery specifications can be formally controlled.

- **Security** If the service provider has access to the organization's records or other intellectual property, the organization will require that specific security controls be in place.

- **Quality** Minimum standards for quality should be expressed in detail so that both service provider and customer have a common understanding of the quality of work to be performed.

- **Metrics** Often, the outsourcing organization will want to actively measure various aspects of the outsourced activity in order to have short-term visibility into work output as well as the ability to understand long-term trends.

- **Audits** The outsourcing organization may require that audits of the outsourced work be performed. These audits may be performed by a competent third party (such as a public accounting firm performing an SSAE16, ISAE3402, or SAS70 audit for financially related services) or by the customer. Often, an outsourcing organization will negotiate a "right to audit" clause in the contract, but will only exercise this if they suspect irregularities or issues related to the work performed.

Depending on the nature of specific outsourcing arrangements, the activities just listed may be combined or performed separately.

Benchmarking Benchmarking measures a process in order to compare its performance and quality with the same process in other organizations. The purpose is to discover opportunities for improvement that may result in lower cost, fewer resources, and higher quality.

In the context of outsourcing, benchmarking can be used to measure the performance of an outsourced process with the same process as performed by other outsourcing firms, as well as to compare it with the same process as performed internally by other organizations. The objective is the same: to learn whether a particular outsourcing solution is performing effectively and efficiently. Benchmarking is discussed in further detail in Chapter 4.

Third-Party Service Delivery Management

Service delivery management is the institution of controls and metrics to ensure that services are performed properly and with a minimum of incidents and defects. When activities are transferred to a service provider, service delivery management has some added dimensions and considerations.

When service delivery management is used to manage an external service provider, the service provider must be required to maintain detailed measurements of its work output. The organization utilizing an external service provider needs to also maintain detailed records of work received, as well as to perform its own defect management controls in order to ensure that the work performed by the service provider meets quality standards. Problems and incidents encountered by the organization should be documented and transmitted to the service provider in order to improve quality.

These activities should be included in the SLA or in the contract in order to ensure that the customer will be able to impose financial penalties or other leverage onto the service provider in order to improve quality while maintaining minimum work output.

Service delivery standards are defined in the international standard ISO 20000. Relevant controls from this standard can be used to impose a standard method for managing service delivery by the service provider.

Software as a Service Considerations

Software as a Service (SaaS) is an arrangement where an organization obtains a software application for use by its employees, where the software application is hosted by the software provider, as opposed to the customer organization. The primary advantages of using SaaS as opposed to self-hosting are

- **Capital savings** The SaaS provider hosts the application on its own servers, thereby eliminating the need to purchase servers and other equipment.

- **Labor savings** The SaaS provider performs all systems and database administration functions, including typical administrative tasks such as applying software or operating system patches, performance and capacity management, software upgrades, and troubleshooting.

 CAUTION An organization that is considering a SaaS provider for one of its applications will need to ensure that the SaaS provider has adequate controls in place to protect the organization's data. In particular, the SaaS provider should have controls in place that will prevent one SaaS customer from being able to view the data associated with a different customer.

An organization can consider a SaaS provider to be similar to other service providers. Generally, methods used to determine the integrity and quality of a SaaS provider would be the same as used with other service providers.

Change Management

Change management is a business process that is used to control changes made to an IT environment. A formal change management process consists of several steps that are carried out for each change:

- Request
- Review
- Approve
- Perform
- Verify
- Back out (when verification of a successful change fails)

Each step in change management includes recordkeeping. Change management is covered in detail in Chapter 4.

Financial Management

Sound financial management is critical in any organization. Because IT is a cost-intensive activity, it is imperative that the organization be well managed, with short-term and long-term budget planning, and that it track actual spending.

One area where senior management needs to make strategic financial decisions in IT is the manner in which it acquires software applications. At the steering committee level, IT organizations need to carefully weigh "make versus buy" with its primary applications. This typically falls into three alternatives:

- **Develop the application** The organization develops the application using in-house or contracted software developers, designers, and analysts.

- **Purchase the application** The organization licenses the application from a software vendor and installs it on servers that it leases or purchases.

- **Rent the application** This generally refers to the cloud computing or SaaS model, where the cloud/application service provider hosts the application on its own premises (or on an Internet data center) and the organization using the software pays either a fixed fee or an on-demand fee. The organization will have no capital cost for servers and little or no development cost (except, possibly, for interfaces to other applications).

The choice that an organization makes is not just about the finances, but is also concerned with the degree of control that the organization requires.

IT financial management is about not only applications, but also the other services that an IT organization provides. Other functions such as service desk, PC build and support, e-mail, and network services can likewise be insourced or outsourced, each with financial and other implications.

 NOTE Many larger organizations employ a "chargeback" feature for the delivery of IT services. This is a method where an IT organization charges (usually through budget transfers but occasionally through real funds) for the services that it provides. The advantage to chargeback is that the customers of the IT organization are required to budget for IT services and are less likely to make frivolous requests of IT, since every activity has a cost associated with it. Chargeback may also force an IT organization to be more competitive, as chargeback may invite IT's customers to acquire services from outside organizations and not from the internal IT organization. Chargeback can thus be viewed as outsourcing to the internal IT organization.

Quality Management

Quality management refers to the methods by which business processes are controlled, monitored, and managed to bring about continuous improvement. The scope of a quality management system in an IT organization may cover any or all of the following activities:

- Software development
- Software acquisition
- Service desk
- IT operations
- Security

The components that are required to build and operate a quality management system are

- **Documented processes**   Each process that is part of a quality management system must be fully documented. This means that all of the tasks, notifications, records, and data flows must be fully described in formal process documents that are themselves controlled.

- **Key measurements**   Each process under quality management must have some key measurement points so that management will be able to understand the frequency and effort expended for the process. Measurement goes beyond simply tallying and must include methods for recognizing; classifying; and measuring incidents, events, problems, and defects.

- **Management review of key measurements**   Key measurements need to be regularly analyzed and included in status reports that provide meaningful information to various levels of management. This enables management to understand how key processes are performing and whether they are meeting management's expectations.

- **Audits**   Processes in a quality management system should be periodically measured by internal or external auditors to ensure that they are being operated properly. These auditors need to be sufficiently independent of the processes and of management itself so that they can objectively evaluate processes.

- **Process changes**   When key measurements suggest that changes to a process are needed, a business or process analyst will make changes to the design of a process. Examples of process changes include the addition of data fields in a change request process, the addition of security requirements to the software development process, or a new method for communicating passwords to the users of newly created user accounts.

 TIP   An organization should document and measure its quality management processes, just as it does with all of the processes under its observation and control. This will help to confirm whether the quality management system itself is effective.

ISO 9000

Established in the 1980s, ISO 9000 remains the world's standard for quality management systems. The ISO 9001, 9002, 9003, and 9004 standards have been superseded by the single ISO 9001:2008 Quality Management System standard.

Organizations that implement the ISO 9001:2008 standard can voluntarily undergo regular external audits by an accredited firm to earn an ISO 9001:2008 certification. Over one million ISO 9001:2008 certificates have been issued to organizations around the world since 1978.

ISO 9000 began as a manufacturing product quality standard. While many manufacturing firms are certified to ISO 9000, the standard is growing in popularity among service providers and software development organizations.

ISO 20000

IT organizations have been adopting the IT Infrastructure Library (ITIL) of IT service management processes as a standard framework for IT processes. Organizations that desire a certification can be evaluated by an accredited external audit firm to the ISO 20000 IT Service Management standard. ISO 20000 supersedes the earlier BS 15000 standard.

The ITIL framework consists of 13 processes in five process groups:

- **Service Delivery Processes** The six processes in this group are capacity management, service continuity and availability management, service level management, service reporting, information security management, and budgeting and accounting. Capacity management is the practice of ensuring that IT systems have sufficient capacity to service business needs. Service continuity and availability management is the practice of guaranteeing that IT systems will function despite disruptive events such as equipment malfunctions and disasters. This is covered in detail later in this chapter. Security management is covered throughout this book. Service level management and service reporting are covered in Chapter 5.

- **Control Processes** The two processes in this group are configuration management and change management. Configuration management is the practice of recording configuration changes in IT systems; this is discussed in Chapter 5.

- **Release Processes** The process in this group is release management. This is the practice of promoting software and configuration changes onto production systems. This topic is discussed in Chapter 5.

- **Relationship Processes** The two processes in this group are business relationship management and supplier management. Business relationship management is beyond the scope of this book. Supplier management is discussed lightly in this chapter in the earlier section, "Sourcing."

- **Resolution Processes** The two processes in this group are incident management and problem management. An incident is any event that is not a part of the standard operation of an IT service and that causes an interruption to or reduction in quality of an IT service. A problem is the underlying cause of one or more incidents. These topics are discussed in Chapter 5.

All of these processes are interrelated and together constitute an effective framework for IT's primary function: delivering valuable services to enable key organization processes.

Security Management

Security management refers to several key activities that work together to identify risks and risk treatment for the organization's assets. In most organizations these activities should include

- **Security governance** Security governance is the practice of setting organization security policy and then taking steps to ensure that policy is followed. Security governance also is involved with the management and continuous improvement of other key security activities discussed in this section.

- **Risk assessment** This is the practice of identifying key assets in use by the organization and identifying vulnerabilities and threats against each asset. This is followed by the development of risk treatment strategies that attempt to mitigate, transfer, avoid, or accept identified risks.

- **Incident management** This practice is concerned with the planned response to security incidents when they occur in the organization. An incident is defined as a violation of security policy; such an incident may be minor (such as a user choosing an easily guessed password) or major (such as a hacking attack and theft of sensitive information). Some of the aspects of incident management include computer forensics (the preservation of evidence that could be used in later legal action) and the involvement of regulatory authorities and law enforcement.

- **Vulnerability management** This is the practice of proactively identifying vulnerabilities in IT systems, as well as in business processes, that could be exploited to the detriment of the organization. Activities that take place in vulnerability management include security scanning, patch management, and reviewing threat and risk advisories issued by software vendors and security organizations.

- **Access and identity management** These practices are used to control which persons and groups may have access to which organization assets, systems, and functions. Identity management is the activity of managing the identity of each employee, contractor, temporary worker, and, optionally, customer. These records are then used as the basis for controlling which buildings, IT systems, and business functions each person is permitted to use.

- **Compliance management** Security management should be responsible for knowing which laws, regulations, standards, requirements, and legal contracts the organization is required to comply with. Verification of compliance may involve internal or external audits and other activities to confirm that the organization is in compliance with all of these legal and other requirements.

- **Business continuity and disaster recovery planning** These practices allow the organization to develop response plans in the event that a disaster should occur that would otherwise threaten the ongoing viability of the organization. Business continuity and disaster recovery planning is covered in detail later in this chapter.

Optimizing Performance

Performance optimization is concerned with the continual improvement of IT processes and systems. This set of activities is concerned not only with financial efficiency, but also with the time and resources required to perform common IT functions. The primary objective of IT performance optimization is to ensure that the organization is getting the maximum benefit of IT services for the lowest possible expenditure of resources.

An organization that measures process performance is more able to recognize opportunities for making improvements to business processes. Organizations that reach a level of process maturity that includes measurement and feedback will be able to adopt a culture of continuous improvement. Management can track improvement opportunities and assign resources accordingly.

Performance optimization is considered a rather mature approach to the management of IT processes and systems. It requires mature processes with key controls and measurement points, and is one of the natural results of effective quality management. An organization that is not already monitoring and managing its processes is probably not ready to undertake performance optimization. See the earlier section "Quality Management" for more information on this perspective.

Performance optimization is a complicated undertaking because IT systems and processes usually change frequently over time; it can be difficult to attribute specific changes in systems or processes to changes in performance metrics.

Maturity models such as Software Engineering Institute Capability Maturity Model Integration (SEI CMMI) can be used to determine the level of an organization's processes. SEI CMMI focuses on whether an organization's processes have a level of maturity associated with measurement and continuous improvement.

The Control Objectives for Information and related Technology (COBIT) framework also contains facilities to identify and measure key performance indicators, with the aim of enabling continuous improvement to processes and technology. The COBIT framework contains 34 key IT processes, along with the means for any individual organization to determine how much (and what kind of) control is appropriate for each organization, based upon its business objectives and how IT supports them.

A typical organization will not have the same level of maturity across all of its departments and processes. Instead, some processes and departments will be more mature than others, often by a wide variance.

Benchmarking An organization may wish to benchmark its key processes. Benchmarking is a process of performing a detailed comparison of a business process (or system, or almost any other aspect of an organization) with that in other organizations. This will help an organization better understand how similar organizations are solving similar business problems, which could lead the organization to enact process improvements on its own.

Organization Structure and Responsibilities

Organizations require structure to distribute responsibility to groups of people with specific skills and knowledge. The structure of an organization is called an organization chart (org chart). Figure 2-5 shows a typical IT organization chart.

Organizing and maintaining an organization structure requires that many factors be taken into account. In most organizations, the org chart is a living structure that changes frequently, based upon several conditions, including

- **Short- and long-term objectives** Organizations sometimes move departments from one executive to another so that departments that were once far from each other (in terms of the org chart structure) will be near each other. This provides new opportunities for developing synergies and partnerships that did not exist before the reorganization. These organizational changes are usually performed to help an organization meet new objectives that were less important before and that require new partnerships and teamwork.

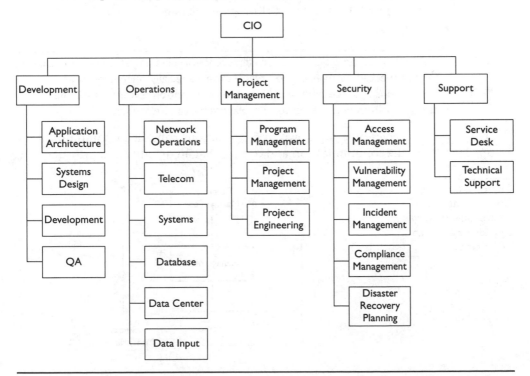

Figure 2-5 Typical IT organization chart

- **Market conditions**   Changes in market positions can cause an organization to realign its internal structure in order to strengthen itself. For example, if a competitor lowers its prices based on a new sourcing strategy, an organization may need to respond by changing its organizational structure in order to put experienced executives in charge of specific activities.

- **Regulations**   New laws, regulations, or standards may induce an organization to change its organizational structure. For instance, an organization that becomes highly regulated may elect to move its security and compliance group away from IT and place it under the legal department, since compliance has much more to do with legal compliance than industry standards.

- **Attrition and available talent**   When someone leaves the organization or moves to another position within the organization, particularly in positions of leadership, a space opens in the org chart that often cannot be filled right away. Instead, senior management will temporarily change the structure of the organization by moving the leaderless department under the control of someone else. Often, the decisions of how to change the organization will depend upon the talent and experience of existing leaders, in addition to each leader's workload and other factors. For example, if the director of IT program management leaves the organization, the existing department could temporarily be placed under the IT operations department, in this case, because the director of IT operations used to run IT program management. Senior management can see how that arrangement works out and later decide whether to replace the director of IT program management position or do something else.

 TIP   Many organizations use formal succession planning as a way of preparing for unexpected changes in the organization, especially terminations and resignations. A succession plan helps the organization to temporarily fill an absent position until a long-term replacement can be found.

This structure serves as a top-down and bottom-up conduit of communication. Figure 2-6 depicts the communication and control that an organization provides.

Figure 2-6
Communication and control flow upward and downward in an organization.

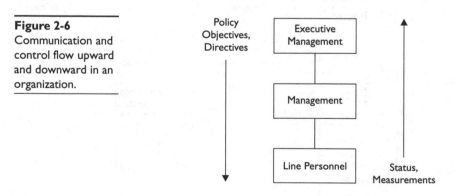

Roles and Responsibilities

The topic of roles and responsibilities is multidimensional: it encompasses positions and relationships on the organization chart, it defines specific job titles and duties, and it denotes generic expectations and responsibilities regarding the use and protection of assets.

Individual Roles and Responsibilities

Several roles and responsibilities fall upon all individuals throughout the organization:

- **Executive management**   The most senior managers and executives in an organization are responsible for developing the organization's mission, objectives, and goals, as well as policy. Executives are responsible for enacting security policy, which defines (among other things) the protection of assets.

- **Owner**   An owner is an individual (usually but not necessarily a manager) who is the designated owner-steward of an asset. Depending upon the organization's security policy, an owner may be responsible for the maintenance and integrity of the asset, as well as for deciding who is permitted to access the asset. If the asset is information, the owner may be responsible for determining who can access and make changes to the information.

- **Manager**   A manager is, in the general sense, responsible for obtaining policies and procedures and making them available to their staff members. They should also, to some extent, be responsible for their staff members' behavior.

- **User**   Users are individuals (at any level of the organization) who use assets in the performance of their job duties. Each user is responsible for how he or she uses the asset, and does not permit others to access the asset in his or her name. Users are responsible for performing their duties lawfully and for conforming to organization policies.

These generic roles and responsibilities should apply all across the org chart to include every person in the organization.

 TIP   The roles and responsibilities of executives, owners, managers, and users should be formally defined in an organization's security policy.

Job Titles and Job Descriptions

A *job title* is a label that is assigned to a *job description*. A job title denotes a position in the organization that has a given set of responsibilities and that requires a certain level and focus of education and prior experience. A job description is a list of those responsibilities and required education and experience.

EXAM TIP The CISA exam may present questions that address proper procedures for the audit of a specified job title. When considering your response, you should consider the job role assigned with the specific title rather than focusing on the title itself. Questions that address job titles are intended to examine understanding of their related roles—an example being the Network Management role associated with the Network Engineer title.

An organization that has a program of career advancement may have a set of career paths or career ladders that are models showing how employees may advance. For each job title, a career path will show the possible avenues of advancement to other job titles and the experience required to reach those other job titles.

Job titles in IT have matured and are quite consistent across organizations. This consistency helps organizations in several ways:

- **Recruiting** When the organization needs to find someone to fill an open position, the use of standard job titles will help prospective candidates more easily find positions that match their criteria.

- **Compensation baselining** Because of the chronic shortage of talented IT workers, organizations are forced to be more competitive when trying to attract new workers. To remain competitive, many organizations periodically undertake a regional compensation analysis to better understand the levels of compensation paid to IT workers in other organizations. The use of standard job titles makes the task of comparing compensation far easier.

- **Career advancement** When an organization uses job titles that are consistent in the industry, IT workers have a better understanding of the functions of positions within their own organizations and can more easily plan how they can advance.

The remainder of this section includes many IT job titles with a short description (not a full job description by any measure) of the function of that position.

Virtually all organizations also include titles that denote the level of experience, leadership, or span of control in an organization. These titles may include executive vice president, senior vice president, vice president, senior director, director, general manager, senior manager, manager, and supervisor. Larger organizations will use more of these, and possibly additional titles such as district manager, group manager, or area manager.

Executive Management Executive managers are the chief leaders and policy-makers in an organization. They set objectives and work directly with the organization's most senior management to help make decisions affecting the future strategy of the organization:

- **CIO (chief information officer)** This is the title of the topmost leader in a larger IT organization.

- **CTO (chief technical officer)**   This position is usually responsible for an organization's overall technology strategy. Depending upon the purpose of the organization, this position may be separate from IT.

- **CSO (chief security officer)**   This position is responsible for all aspects of security, including information security, physical security, and possibly executive protection (protecting the safety of senior executives).

- **CISO (chief information security officer)**   This position is responsible for all aspects of data-related security. This usually includes incident management, disaster recovery, vulnerability management, and compliance.

- **CPO (chief privacy officer)**   This position is responsible for the protection and use of personal information. This position is found in organizations that collect and store sensitive information for large numbers of persons.

Software Development   Positions in software development are involved in the design, development, and testing of software applications:

- **Systems architect**   This position is usually responsible for the overall information systems architecture in the organization. This may or may not include overall data architecture as well as interfaces to external organizations.

- **Systems analyst**   A systems analyst is involved with the design of applications, including changes in an application's original design. This position may develop technical requirements, program design, and software test plans. In cases where organizations license applications developed by other companies, systems analysts design interfaces to other applications.

- **Software developer/programmer**   This position develops application software. Depending upon the level of experience, persons in this position may also design programs or applications. In organizations that utilize purchased application software, developers often create custom interfaces, application customizations, and custom reports.

- **Software tester**   This position tests changes in programs made by software developers.

Data Management   Positions in data management are responsible for developing and implementing database designs and for maintaining databases:

- **Data manager**   This position is responsible for data architecture and data management in larger organizations.

- **Database architect**   This position develops logical and physical designs of data models for applications. With sufficient experience, this person may also design an organization's overall data architecture.

- **Database administrator (DBA)**   This position builds and maintains databases designed by the database architect and those databases that are included as a part of purchased applications. The DBA monitors databases, tunes them for performance and efficiency, and troubleshoots problems.

- **Database analyst**   This position performs tasks that are junior to the database administrator, carrying out routine data maintenance and monitoring tasks.

 EXAM TIP   The roles of data manager, database architect, database administrator, and database analyst are distinct from the data owner. The former are IT department roles for managing data technology, whereas the latter role governs the business use of data in information systems.

Network Management   Positions in network management are responsible for designing, building, monitoring, and maintaining voice and data communications networks, including connections to outside business partners and the Internet:

- **Network architect**   This position designs data and (increasingly) voice networks and designs changes and upgrades to the network as needed to meet new organization objectives.

- **Network engineer**   This position builds and maintains network devices such as routers, switches, firewalls, and gateways.

- **Network administrator**   This position performs routine tasks in the network such as making minor configuration changes and monitoring event logs.

- **Telecom engineer**   Positions in this role work with telecommunications technologies such as data circuits, phone systems, conferencing systems, and voicemail systems.

Systems Management   Positions in systems management are responsible for architecture, design, building, and maintenance of servers and operating systems. This may include desktop operating systems as well.

- **Systems architect**   This position is responsible for the overall architecture of systems (usually servers), both in terms of the internal architecture of a system and the relationship between systems. This position is usually also responsible for the design of services such as authentication, e-mail, and time synchronization.

- **Systems engineer**   This position is responsible for designing, building, and maintaining servers and server operating systems.

- **Storage engineer**   This position is responsible for designing, building, and maintaining storage subsystems.

- **Systems administrator**   This position is responsible for performing maintenance and configuration operations on systems.

Operations   Positions in operations are responsible for day-to-day operational tasks that may include networks, servers, databases, and applications:

- **Operations manager**   This position is responsible for overall operations that are carried out by others. Responsibilities will include establishing operations shift schedules.

- **Operations analyst**   This position may be responsible for the development of operational procedures; examining the health of networks, systems, and databases; setting and monitoring the operations schedule; and maintaining operations records.

- **Controls analyst**   This position is responsible for monitoring batch jobs, data entry work, and other tasks to make sure that they are operating correctly.

- **Systems operator**   This position is responsible for monitoring systems and networks, performing backup tasks, running batch jobs, printing reports, and other operational tasks.

- **Data entry**   This position is responsible for keying batches of data from hardcopy sources.

- **Media manager**   This position is responsible for maintaining and tracking the use and whereabouts of backup tapes and other media.

Security Operations   Positions in security operations are responsible for designing, building, and monitoring security systems and security controls to ensure the confidentiality, integrity, and availability of information systems:

- **Security architect**   This position is responsible for the design of security controls and systems such as authentication, audit logging, intrusion detection systems, intrusion prevention systems, and firewalls.

- **Security engineer**   This position is responsible for designing, building, and maintaining security services and systems that are designed by the security architect.

- **Security analyst**   This position is responsible for examining logs from firewalls, intrusion detection systems, and audit logs from systems and applications. This position may also be responsible for issuing security advisories to others in IT.

- **User account management**   This position is responsible for accepting approved requests for user access management changes and performing the necessary changes at the network, system, database, or application level. Often, this position is carried out by personnel in network and systems management functions; only in larger organizations is user account management performed in security or even in a separate user access department.

- **Security auditor**   This position is responsible for performing internal audits of IT controls to ensure that they are being operated properly.

 CAUTION   The security auditor position needs to be carefully placed in the organization so that persons in this role can be objective and independent from the departments they audit.

Service Desk   Positions at the service desk are responsible for providing frontline support services to IT and IT's customers:

- **Service desk manager**   This position serves as a liaison between end users and the IT service desk department.
- **Helpdesk analyst**   This position is responsible for providing frontline user support services to personnel in the organization.
- **Technical support analyst**   This position is responsible for providing technical support services to other IT personnel, and perhaps also to IT customers.

Quality Assurance   Positions in quality assurance are responsible for developing IT processes and standards and for measuring IT systems and processes to confirm their accuracy:

- **QA manager**   This position is responsible for facilitating quality improvement activities throughout the IT organization.
- **QC manager**   This position is responsible for testing IT systems and applications to confirm whether they are free of defects.

Other Roles   Other roles in IT organizations include

- **Vendor manager**   This position is responsible for maintaining business relationships with external vendors, measuring their performance, and handling business issues.
- **Project manager**   This position is responsible for creating project plans and managing IT projects.

Segregation of Duties

Information systems often process large volumes of information that is often highly valuable or sensitive. Measures need to be taken in IT organizations to ensure that individuals do not possess sufficient privileges to carry out potentially harmful actions on their own. Checks and balances are needed so that high-value and high-sensitivity activities involve the coordination of two or more authorized individuals. The concept of *segregation of duties* (SOD), also known as *separation of duties*, ensures that single individuals do not possess excess privileges that could result in unauthorized activities such as fraud or the manipulation or exposure of sensitive data.

The concept of segregation of duties has been long established in organization accounting departments where, for instance, separate individuals or groups are responsible for the creation of vendors, the request for payments, and the printing of checks. Since accounting personnel frequently handle checks and currency, the principles and practices of segregation of duties controls in accounting departments are the norm.

IT departments are lagging behind somewhat, since the functions in IT are less often involved in direct monetary activities, except in certain industries, such as banking. But thanks to financial scandals in the 1980s and 1990s that involved the illicit manipulation of financial records and the emergence of new laws such as Sarbanes-Oxley, the need for full and formal IT-level segregation of duties is now well recognized.

 CAUTION At its most basic form, the rule of segregation of duties specifies that no single individual should be permitted or be able to perform high-value, high-sensitivity, or high-risk actions. Instead, two or more parties must be required to perform these functions.

Segregation of Duties Controls

Preventive and detective controls should be put into place to manage segregation of duties matters. In most organizations, both the preventive and detective controls will be manual, particularly when it comes to unwanted combinations of access between different applications. However, in some transaction-related situations, controls can be automated, although they may still require intervention by others.

Some examples of segregation of duties controls include

- **Transaction authorization** Information systems can be programmed or configured to require two (or more) persons to approve certain transactions. Many of us see this in retail establishments where a manager is required to approve a large transaction or a refund. In IT applications, transactions meeting certain criteria (for example, exceeding normally accepted limits or conditions) may require a manager's approval to be able to proceed.

- **Split custody of high-value assets** Assets of high importance or value can be protected using various means of split custody. For example, a password to an encryption key that protects a highly valued asset can be split in two halves—one half assigned to two persons, and the other half assigned to two persons—so that no single individual knows the entire password. Banks do this for central vaults, where a vault combination is split into two or more pieces so that two or more are required to open it.

- **Workflow** Applications that are workflow-enabled can use a second (or third) level of approval before certain high-value or high-sensitivity activities can take place. For example, a workflow application that is used to provision user accounts can include extra management approval steps in requests for administrative privileges.

- **Periodic reviews** IT or internal audit personnel can periodically review user access rights to identify whether any segregation of duties issues exist. The access privileges for each worker can be compared against a segregation of duties control matrix. Table 2-2 shows an example matrix.

	Management	Systems Analyst	SW Developer	SW Test	DB Admin	Systems Admin	Network Admin	Security Admin	Systems Operator	Helpdesk
Management		OK	X	X	X	X	X	X	X	X
Systems Analyst	OK		OK	X	X	X	X	X	X	X
SW Developer	X	OK		X	X	X	X	X	X	X
SW Test	X	X	X		X	X	X	X	X	X
DB Admin	X	X	X	X		OK	X	X	X	X
Systems Admin	X	X	X	X	OK		OK	X	OK	OK
Network Admin	X	X	X	X	X	OK		X	X	X
Security Admin	X	X	X	X	X	X	X		X	X
Systems Operator	X	X	X	X	X	OK	X	X		OK
Helpdesk	X	X	X	X	X	OK	X	X	OK	

Table 2-2   Example Segregation of Duties Matrix Identifies Forbidden Combinations of Privileges

When SOD issues are encountered during a segregation of duties review, management will need to decide how to mitigate the matter. The choices for mitigating an SOD issue include

- **Reduce access privileges**   Management can reduce individual user privileges so that the conflict no longer exists.

- **Introduce a new mitigating control**   If management has determined that the person(s) need to retain privileges that are viewed as a conflict, then new preventive or detective controls need to be introduced that will prevent or detect unwanted activities. Examples of mitigating controls include increased logging to record the actions of personnel, improved exception reporting to identify possible issues, reconciliations of data sets, and external reviews of high-risk controls.

 TIP   An organization should periodically review its SOD matrix, particularly if new roles or high-value applications are added or changed.

Business Continuity Planning

Business continuity planning (BCP) is undertaken to reduce risks related to the onset of disasters and other disruptive events. BCP activities identify risks and mitigate those risks through changes or enhancements in technology or business processes so that the impact of disasters is reduced and the time to recovery is lessened. The primary objective of BCP is to improve the chances that the organization will survive a disaster without incurring costly or even fatal damage to its most critical activities.

The activities of BCP development scale for any size organization. BCP has the unfortunate reputation of existing only in the stratospheric, thin air of the largest and wealthiest organizations. This misunderstanding hurts the majority of organizations that are too timid to begin any kind of BCP efforts at all because they believe that these activities are too costly and disruptive. The fact is that any size organization, from a one-person home office to a multinational conglomerate, can successfully undertake BCP projects that will bring about immediate benefits as well as take some of the sting out of disruptive events that do occur.

Organizations can benefit from BCP projects, even if a disaster never occurs. The steps in the BCP development process usually bring immediate benefit in the form of process and technology improvements that increase the resilience, integrity, and efficiency of those processes and systems.

EXAM TIP Business continuity planning is closely related to disaster recovery planning—both are concerned with the recovery of business operations after a disaster. Business continuity planning is discussed in this chapter, while disaster recovery planning is discussed in Chapter 5.

Disasters

I always tried to turn every disaster into an opportunity. —John D. Rockefeller

In a business context, disasters are unexpected and unplanned events that result in the disruption of business operations. A disaster could be a regional event spread over a wide geographic area, or it could occur within the confines of a single room. The impact of a disaster will also vary, from a complete interruption of all company operations to merely a slowdown. (The question invariably comes up: when is a disaster a *disaster*? This is somewhat subjective, like asking, "When is a person sick?" Is it when he or she is too ill to report to work, or if he or she just has a sniffle and a scratchy throat? I'll discuss disaster declaration later in this chapter.)

Types of Disasters

BCP professionals broadly classify disasters as natural or man-made, although the origin of a disaster does not figure very much into how we respond to it. Let's examine the types of disasters.

Natural Disasters Natural disasters are those phenomena that occur in the natural world with little or no assistance from mankind. They are a result of the natural processes that occur in, on, and above the earth.

Examples of natural disasters include

- **Earthquakes** Sudden movements of the earth with the capacity to damage buildings, houses, roads, bridges, and dams; to precipitate landslides and avalanches; and to induce flooding and other secondary events.

- **Volcanoes** Eruptions of magma, pyroclastic flows, steam, ash, and flying rocks that can cause significant damage over wide geographic regions. Some volcanoes, such as Kilauea in Hawaii, produce a nearly continuous and predictable outpouring of lava in a limited area, whereas the Mount St. Helens eruption in 1980 caused an ash fall over thousands of square miles that brought many metropolitan areas to a standstill for days and also blocked rivers and damaged roads. Figure 2-7 shows a volcanic eruption as seen from space.

- **Landslides** Sudden downhill movements of earth, usually down steep slopes, can bury buildings, houses, roads, and public utilities and cause secondary (although still disastrous) effects such as the rerouting of rivers.

- **Avalanches** Sudden downward flows of snow, rocks, and debris on a mountainside. A *slab* avalanche consists of the movement of a large, stiff layer of compacted snow. A *loose snow* avalanche occurs when the accumulated snowpack exceeds its shear strength. A *power snow* avalanche is the largest type and can travel in excess of 200 mph and exceed 10 million tons of material. All types can damage buildings, houses, roads, and utilities, resulting in direct or indirect damage affecting businesses.

- **Wildfires** Fires in forests, chaparral, and grasslands are part of the natural order. However, fires can also damage buildings and equipment and cause injury and death.

Figure 2-7
Mount Etna
volcano in Sicily

- **Tropical cyclones**   The largest and most violent storms are known in various parts of the world as hurricanes, typhoons, tropical cyclones, tropical storms, and cyclones. Tropical cyclones consist of strong winds that can reach 190 mph, heavy rains, and storm surge that can raise the level of the ocean by as much as 20 feet, all of which can result in widespread coastal flooding and damage to buildings, houses, roads, and utilities and significant loss of life.

- **Tornadoes**   These violent rotating columns of air can cause catastrophic damage to buildings, houses, roads, and utilities when they reach the ground. Most tornadoes can have wind speeds from 40 to 110 mph and travel along the ground for a few miles. Some tornadoes can exceed 300 mph and travel for dozens of miles.

- **Windstorms**   While generally less intense than hurricanes and tornadoes, windstorms can nonetheless cause widespread damage, including damage to buildings, roads, and utilities. Widespread electric power outages are common, as windstorms can uproot trees that can fall into overhead power lines.

- **Lightning**   Atmospheric discharges of electricity that occur during thunderstorms, but also during dust storms and volcanic eruptions. Lightning can start fires and also damage buildings and power transmission systems, causing power outages.

- **Ice storms**   Ice storms occur when rain falls through a layer of colder air, causing raindrops to freeze onto whatever surface they strike. They can cause widespread power outages when ice forms on power lines and the resulting weight causes those power lines to collapse. A notable example is the Great Ice Storm of 1998 in eastern Canada, which resulted in millions being without power for as long as two weeks and in the virtual immobilization of the cities of Montreal and Ottawa.

- **Hail**   This form of precipitation consists of ice chunks ranging from 5mm to 150mm in diameter. An example of a damaging hailstorm is the April 1999 storm in Sydney, Australia, where hailstones up to 9.5cm in diameter damaged 40,000 vehicles, 20,000 properties, 25 airplanes, and caused one direct fatality. The storm caused $1.5 billion in damage.

- **Flooding**   Standing or moving water spills out of its banks and flows into and through buildings and causes significant damage to roads, buildings, and utilities. Flooding can be a result of locally heavy rains, heavy snow melt, a dam or levee break, tropical cyclone storm surge, or an avalanche or landslide that displaces lake or river water.

- **Tsunamis**   A series of waves that usually result from the sudden vertical displacement of a lake bed or ocean floor, but can also be caused by landslides or explosions. A tsunami wave can be barely noticeable in open, deep water, but as it approaches a shoreline, the wave can grow to a height of 50 feet or more. Recent notable examples are the 2004 Indian Ocean tsunami and the 2011 Japan tsunami. Coastline damage from the Japan tsunami is shown in Figure 2-8.

Figure 2-8
Damage to
structures caused
by the 2011 Japan
tsunami

- **Pandemic**   The spread of infectious disease over a wide geographic region, even worldwide. Pandemics have regularly occurred throughout history and are likely to continue occurring, despite advances in sanitation and immunology. A pandemic is the rapid spread of any type of disease, including typhoid, tuberculosis, bubonic plague, or influenza. Pandemics in the 20th century include the 1918–1920 Spanish flu, the 1956–1958 Asian flu, the 1968–1969 Hong Kong "swine" flu, and the 2009–2010 swine flu pandemic. Figure 2-9 shows an auditorium that was converted into a hospital during the 1918–1920 pandemic.

- **Extraterrestrial impacts**   This category includes meteorites and other objects that may fall from the sky from way, way up. Sure, these events are extremely rare, and most organizations don't even include these events in their risk analysis, but I've included it here for the sake of rounding out the types of natural events.

Figure 2-9
An auditorium was
used as a temporary
hospital during the
1918 flu pandemic.

Man-Made Disasters   Man-made disasters are those events that are directly or indirectly caused by human activity through action or inaction. The results of man-made disasters are similar to natural disasters: localized or widespread damage to businesses that results in potentially lengthy interruptions in operations.

Examples of man-made disasters include

- **Civil disturbances**   These can take on many forms, including protests; demonstrations; riots; strikes; work slowdowns and stoppages; looting; and resulting actions such as curfews, evacuations, or lockdowns.

- **Utility outages**   Failures in electric, natural gas, district heating, water, communications, and other utilities. These can be caused by equipment failures, sabotage, or natural events such as landslides or flooding.

- **Materials shortages**   Interruptions in the supply of food, fuel, supplies, and materials can have a ripple effect on businesses and the services that support them. Readers who are old enough to remember the petroleum shortages of the mid-1970s know what this is all about; Figure 2-10 shows a 1970s-era gasoline shortage. Shortages can result in spikes in the price of commodities, which is almost as damaging as not having any supply at all.

- **Fires**   As contrasted to wildfires, here I mean fires that originate in or involve buildings, equipment, and materials.

- **Hazardous materials spills**   Many created or refined substances can be dangerous if they escape their confines. Examples include petroleum substances, gases, pesticides and herbicides, medical substances, and radioactive substances.

Figure 2-10
Citizens wait in long lines to buy fuel during a gas shortage.

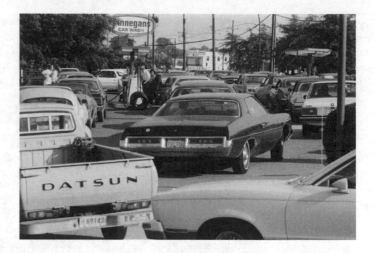

- **Transportation accidents** This broad category includes plane crashes, railroad derailment, bridge collapse, and the like.

- **Terrorism and war** Whether they are actions of a nation, nation-state, or group, terrorism and war can have devastating but usually localized effects in cities and regions. Often, terrorism and war precipitate secondary effects such as materials shortages and utility outages.

- **Security events** The actions of a lone hacker or a team of organized cybercriminals can bring down one system, one network, or many networks, which could result in widespread interruption in services. The hackers' activities can directly result in an outage, or an organization can voluntarily (although reluctantly) shut down an affected service or network in order to contain the incident.

NOTE It is important to remember that real disasters are usually complex events that involve more than just one type of damaging event. For instance, an earthquake directly damages buildings and equipment, but can also cause fires and utility outages. A hurricane also brings flooding, utility outages, and sometimes even hazardous materials events and civil disturbances such as looting.

How Disasters Affect Organizations

Disasters have a wide variety of effects on an organization that are discussed in this section. Many disasters have direct effects, but sometimes it is the secondary effects of a disaster event that are most significant from the perspective of ongoing business operations.

A risk analysis is a part of the BCP process (discussed in the next section in this chapter) that will identify the ways in which disasters are likely to affect a particular organization. It is during the risk analysis when the primary, secondary, and downstream effects of likely disaster scenarios need to be identified and considered. Whoever is performing this risk analysis will need to have a broad understanding of the ways in which a disaster will affect ongoing business operations. Similarly, those personnel who are developing contingency and recovery plans also need to be familiar with these effects so that those plans will adequately serve the organization's needs.

Disasters, by our definition, interrupt business operations in some measurable way. An event that has the *appearance* of a disaster may occur, but if it doesn't affect a particular organization, then we would say that no disaster occurred, at least for that particular organization.

It would be shortsighted to say that a disaster only affects *operations*. Rather, it is appropriate to understand the longer-term effects that a disaster has on the organization's *image*, *brand*, and *reputation*. The factors affecting image, brand, and reputation have as much to do with how the organization communicates to its customers, suppliers, and shareholders, as with how the organization actually handles a disaster in progress.

Some of the ways that a disaster affects an organization's operations include

- **Direct damage**   Events like earthquakes, floods, and fires directly damage an organization's buildings, equipment, or records. The damage may be severe enough that no salvageable items remain, or it may be less severe, where some equipment and buildings may be salvageable or repairable.

- **Utility interruption**   Even if an organization's buildings and equipment are undamaged, a disaster may affect utilities such as power, natural gas, or water, which can incapacitate some or all business operations. Significant delays in refuse collection can result in unsanitary conditions.

- **Transportation**   Similarly, a disaster may damage or render transportation systems such as roads, railroads, shipping, or air transport unusable for a period. Damaged transportation systems will interrupt supply lines and personnel.

- **Services and supplier shortage**   Even if a disaster does not have a direct effect on an organization, if any of its critical suppliers feel the effects of a disaster, that can have an undesirable effect on business operations. For instance, a regional baker that cannot produce and ship bread to its corporate customers will soon result in sandwich shops without a critical resource.

- **Staff availability**   A community-wide or regional disaster that affects businesses is likely to also affect homes and families. Depending upon the nature of a disaster, employees will place a higher priority on the safety and comfort of family members. Also, workers may not be able or willing to travel to work if transportation systems are affected or if there is a significant materials shortage. Employees may also be unwilling to travel to work if they fear for their personal safety or that of their families.

- **Customer availability**   Various types of disasters may force or dissuade customers from traveling to business locations to conduct business. Many of the factors that keep employees away may also keep customers away.

CAUTION The kinds of secondary and tertiary effects that a disaster has on a particular organization depend entirely upon its unique set of circumstances that constitute its specific critical needs. A risk analysis should be performed to identify these specific factors.

The Business Continuity Planning Process

The proper way to plan for disaster preparedness is to first know what kinds of disasters are likely and their possible effects on the organization. That is, *plan first, act later*.

The business continuity planning process is a life *cycle process*. In other words, business continuity planning (and disaster recovery planning) is not a one-time event or activity. It's a set of activities that result in the ongoing preparedness for disaster that continually adapts to changing business conditions and that continually improves.

The elements of the BCP process life cycle are

- Develop BCP policy.
- Conduct business impact analysis (BIA).
- Perform criticality analysis.
- Establish recovery targets.
- Develop recovery and continuity strategies and plans.
- Test recovery and continuity plans and procedures.
- Train personnel.
- Maintain strategies, plans, and procedures through periodic reviews and updates.

The BCP life cycle is shown in Figure 2-11. The details of this life cycle are described in detail in this chapter.

BCP Policy

A formal BCP effort must, like any strategic activity, flow from the existence of a formal policy and be included in the overall governance model that is the topic of this chapter. BCP should be an integral part of the IT control framework, not lie outside of it. Therefore, BCP policy should include or cite specific controls that ensure that key activities in the BCP life cycle are performed appropriately.

BCP policy should also define the scope of the BCP strategy. This means that the specific business processes (or departments or divisions within an organization) that are included in the BCP effort must be defined. Sometimes the scope will include a geographic boundary. In larger organizations, it is possible to "bite off more than you can chew" and define too large a scope for a BCP project, so limiting scope to a smaller, more manageable portion of the organization can be a good approach.

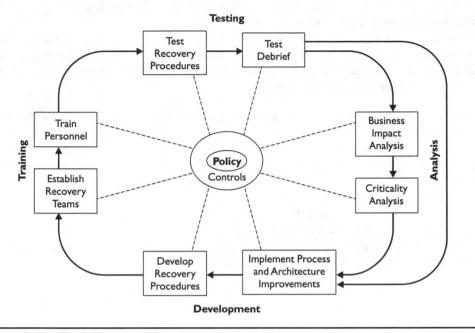

Figure 2-11   The BCP process life cycle

BCP and COBIT Controls   The specific COBIT controls that are involved with BCP are contained within *DS4—Ensure continuous service*. DS4 has 11 specific controls that constitute the entire BCP life cycle:

- Develop IT continuity framework.
- Conduct business impact analysis and risk assessment.
- Develop and maintain IT continuity plans.
- Identify and categorize IT resources based on recovery objectives.
- Define and execute change control procedures to ensure IT continuity plan is current.
- Regularly test IT continuity plan.
- Develop follow-up action plan from test results.
- Plan and conduct IT continuity training.
- Plan IT services recovery and resumption.
- Plan and implement backup storage and protection.
- Establish procedures for conducting post-resumption reviews.

These controls are discussed in this chapter and also in COBIT.

Business Impact Analysis

The objective of the business impact analysis (BIA) is to identify the impact that different scenarios will have on ongoing business operations. The BIA is one of several steps of critical, detailed analysis that must be carried out before the development of continuity or recovery plans and procedures.

Inventory Key Processes and Systems   The first step in a BIA is the collection of key business processes and IT systems. Within the overall scope of the BCP project, the objective here is to establish a detailed list of all identifiable processes and systems. The usual approach is the development of a questionnaire or intake form that would be circulated to key personnel in end-user departments and also within IT. A sample intake form is shown in Figure 2-12.

Typically, the information that is gathered on intake forms is transferred to a multi-columned spreadsheet, where information on all of the organization's in-scope processes can be viewed together. This will become even more useful in subsequent phases of the BCP project, such as the criticality analysis.

Process or system name	
Interviewee	
Title	
Department	
Contact info	
Date	
Process owner	
Process operator(s)	
Process description	
Customer facing (Y or N)	
IT system(s) used	
Key suppliers	
Communications needed	
Assets needed	
Process dependencies	
Other dependencies	
Documentation location	
Records location	

Figure 2-12   BIA sample intake form for gathering data about key processes

Planning Precedes Action

IT personnel are often eager to get to the fun and meaty part of a project. Developers are anxious to begin coding before design; system administrators are eager to build systems before they are scoped and designed; and BCP personnel fervently desire to begin designing more robust system architectures and to tinker with replication and backup capabilities before key facts are known. In the case of business continuity and disaster recovery planning, completion of the BIA and other analyses is critical, as the analyses help to define the systems and processes most needed before getting to the fun part.

TIP Use of an intake form is not the only accepted approach when gathering information about critical processes and systems. It's also acceptable to conduct one-on-one interviews or group interviews with key users and IT personnel to identify critical processes and systems. I recommend the use of an intake form (whether paper-based or electronic), even if the interviewer uses it him-/herself as a framework for note-taking.

Statements of Impact When processes and systems are being inventoried and cataloged, it is also vitally important to obtain one or more *statements of impact* for each process and system. A statement of impact is a qualitative or quantitative description of the impact if the process or system were incapacitated for a time.

For IT systems, you might capture the number of users and the names of departments or functions that are affected by the unavailability of a specific IT system. Include the geography of affected users and functions if that is appropriate. Example statements of impact for IT systems might include

- *Three thousand users in France and Italy will be unable to access customer records.*
- *All users in North America will be unable to read or send e-mail.*

Statements of impact for business processes might cite the business functions that would be affected. Some example statements of impact include

- *Accounts payable and accounts receivable functions will be unable to process.*
- *Legal department will be unable to access contracts and addendums.*

Statements of impact for revenue-generating and revenue-supporting business functions could quantify financial impact per unit of time (be sure to use the same units of time for all functions so that they can be easily compared with one another). Some examples include

- *Inability to place orders for appliances will cost at the rate of $1200 per hour.*
- *Delays in payments will cost $45,000 per day in interest charges.*

As statements of impact are gathered, it might make sense to create several columns in the main worksheet so that like units (names of functions, numbers of users, financial figures) can be sorted and ranked later on.

When the BIA is completed, you'll have the following information about each process and system:

- Name of the system or process
- Who is responsible for it
- A description of its function
- Dependencies on systems
- Dependencies on suppliers
- Dependencies on key employees
- Quantified statements of impact in terms of revenue, users affected, and/or functions impacted

You're almost home.

Criticality Analysis

When all of the BIA information has been collected and charted, the criticality analysis (CA) can be performed.

The *criticality analysis* is a study of each system and process, a consideration of the impact on the organization if it is incapacitated, the likelihood of incapacitation, and the estimated cost of mitigating the risk or impact of incapacitation. In other words, it's a somewhat special type of a risk analysis that focuses on key processes and systems.

The criticality analysis needs to include, or reference, a threat analysis. A threat analysis is a risk analysis that identifies every threat that has a reasonable probability of occurrence, plus mitigating controls or compensating controls, and new probabilities of occurrence with those mitigating/compensating controls in place. In case you're having a little trouble imagining what this looks like (I'm writing the book and I'm having trouble seeing this!), take a look at Table 2-3, which is a lightweight example of what I'm talking about.

In the preceding threat analysis, notice a couple of things:

- Multiple threats are listed for a single asset. In the preceding example, I mentioned just eight threats. For all the threats but one, I listed only a single mitigating control. For the extended power outage threat, I listed two mitigating controls.

- Cost of downtime wasn't listed. For systems or processes where you have a cost per unit of time for downtime, you'll need to include it here, along with some calculations to show the payback for each control.

- Some mitigating controls can benefit more than one system. That may not have been obvious in this example, but in the case of a UPS (uninterruptible power supply) and electric generator, many systems can benefit, so the cost for these mitigating controls can be allocated across many systems, thereby lowering the cost for each system. Another example is a high-availability

System	Threat	Probability	Mitigating Control	Cost	Mitigated Probability
Application Server	Denial of service	0.1%	High-performance filtering router	$60,000	0.01%
	Malware	1%	Antivirus	$200	0.1%
	Storage failure	2%	RAID-5	$20,000	0.01%
	Administrator error	15%	Configuration management tools	$10,000	1%
	Hardware CPU failure	5%	Server cluster	$15,000	1%
	Application software bug	5%	Source code reviews	$10,000	2%
	Extended power outage	25%	UPS Electric generator	$12,000 $40,000	2% 0.5%
	Flood	2%	Relocate data center	$200,000	0.1%

Table 2-3   Example Threat Analysis Identifies Threats and Controls for Critical Systems and Processes

storage area network (SAN) located in two different geographic areas; while initially expensive, many applications can use the SAN for storage, and all will benefit from replication to the counterpart storage system.

- Threat probabilities are arbitrary. In Table 2-3, the probabilities were for a single occurrence in an entire year, so, for example, 5 percent means the threat will be realized once every 20 years.

- The length of outage was not included. You may need to include this also, particularly if you are quantifying downtime per hour or other unit of time.

It is probably becoming obvious that a threat analysis, and the corresponding criticality analysis, can get complicated. The rule here should be this: the complexity of the threat and criticality analyses should be proportional to the value of the assets (or revenue, or both). For example, in a company where application downtime is measured in thousands of dollars per minute, it's probably worth taking a few weeks or even months to work out all of the likely scenarios and a variety of mitigating controls, and to work out which ones are the most cost-effective. On the other hand, for a system or business process where the impact of an outage is far less costly, a good deal less time can be spent on the supporting threat and criticality analysis.

EXAM TIP   Test-takers should ensure that any question dealing with BIA and CA places the business impact analysis first. Without this analysis, criticality analysis is impossible to evaluate in terms of likelihood or cost-effectiveness in mitigation strategies. The BIA identifies strategic resources and provides a value to their recovery and operation, which is, in turn, consumed in the criticality analysis phase. If presented with a question identifying BCP at a particular stage, make sure that any answers you select facilitate the BIA and then the CA before moving on toward objectives and strategies.

Establishing Key Recovery Targets

When the cost or impact of downtime has been established and the cost and benefit of mitigating controls has been considered, some key targets can be established for each critical process. The two key targets are recovery time objective and recovery point objective. These objectives determine how quickly key systems and processes are made available after the onset of a disaster and the maximum tolerable data loss that results from the disaster. The two key recovery targets are

- **Recovery time objective (RTO)** This refers to the maximum period that elapses from the onset of a disaster until the resumption of service.
- **Recovery point objective (RPO)** This refers to the maximum data loss from the onset of a disaster.

Once these objectives are known, the disaster recovery (DR) team can begin to build system recovery capabilities and procedures that will help the organization to economically realize these targets. This is discussed in detail in Chapter 5.

Developing Continuity Plans

In the previous section, I discussed the notion of establishing recovery targets and the development of architectures, processes, and procedures. The processes and procedures are related to the normal operation of those new technologies as they will be operated in normal day-to-day operations. When those processes and procedures have been completed, then the disaster recovery plans and procedures (those actions that will take place during and immediately after a disaster) can be developed.

For example, an organization has established RPO and RTO targets for its critical applications. These targets necessitated the development of server clusters and storage area networks with replication. While implementing those new technologies, the organization developed the operations processes and procedures in support of those new technologies that would be carried out every day during normal business operations. As a separate activity, the organization would then develop the procedures to be performed when a disaster strikes the primary operations center for those applications; those procedures would include all of the steps that must be taken so that the applications can continue operating in a warm site or hot site location.

The procedures for operating critical applications during a disaster are a small part of the entire body of procedures that must be developed. Several other sets of procedures must also be developed, including

- Personnel safety procedures
- Disaster declaration procedures
- Responsibilities
- Contact information
- Recovery procedures
- Continuing operations

All of these are required so that an organization will be adequately prepared in the event a disaster occurs.

Personnel Safety Procedures

When a disaster strikes, measures to ensure the safety of personnel need to be taken immediately. If the disaster has occurred or is about to occur to a building, personnel need to be evacuated as soon as possible. Arguably, however, in some situations evacuation is exactly the wrong thing to do; for example, if a hurricane or tornado is bearing down on a facility, then the building itself may be the best shelter for personnel, even if it incurs some damage. The point here is that personnel safety procedures need to be carefully developed, and possibly more than one set of procedures will be needed, depending on the event.

 TIP The highest priority in any disaster or emergency situation is the safety of human life.

Personnel safety procedures need to take many factors into account, including

- Ensuring that all personnel are familiar with evacuation and sheltering procedures
- Ensuring that visitors will know how to evacuate the premises and the location of sheltering areas
- Posting signs and placards that indicate emergency evacuation routes and gathering areas outside of the building
- Emergency lighting to aid in evacuation
- Fire extinguishment equipment (portable fire extinguishers and so on)
- The ability to communicate with public safety and law enforcement authorities, including in situations where communications and electric power have been cut off and when all personnel are outside of the building
- Care for injured personnel
- CPR and emergency first-aid training
- Safety personnel who can assist in the evacuation of injured and disabled persons
- The ability to account for visitors and other nonemployees
- Emergency shelter in extreme weather conditions
- Emergency food and drinking water
- Periodic tests to ensure that evacuation procedures will be adequate in the event of a real emergency

Local emergency management organizations may have additional information available that can assist an organization with its emergency personnel safety procedures.

Disaster Declaration Procedures

Disaster response procedures are initiated when a disaster is declared. However, there needs to be a procedure for the declaration itself so that there will be little doubt as to the conditions that must be present.

Why is a disaster declaration procedure required? Primarily because it's not always clear whether a situation is a real disaster. Sure, a 7.5 earthquake or a major fire is a disaster, but overcooking popcorn in the microwave that sets off a building's fire alarm system might not be. Many "in between" situations may or may not be disasters. A disaster declaration procedure must state some basic conditions that will help determine whether a disaster should be declared.

Further, who has the authority to declare a disaster? What if senior management personnel frequently travel and may not be around? Who else can declare a disaster? And, finally, what does it mean to declare a disaster—and what happens next? The following points constitute the primary items that organizations need to consider for their disaster declaration procedure.

Form a Core Team To be effective and workable, a core team of personnel needs to be established, all of whom will be familiar with the disaster declaration procedure, as well as the actions that must take place once a disaster has been declared. This core team should consist of middle and upper managers who are familiar with business operations, particularly those that are critical. This core team must be large enough so that a requisite few of them are on hand when a disaster strikes. In organizations that have second shifts, third shifts, and weekend work, some of the core team members should be those in supervisory positions during those off-hours times. However, some of the core team members can be personnel who work "business hours" and are not on-site all of the time.

Declaration Criteria The declaration procedure must contain some tangible criteria that a core team member can consult to guide him or her down the "is this a disaster" decision path.

The criteria for declaring a disaster should be related to the availability and viability of ongoing critical business operations. Some example criteria include any one or more of the following:

- Forced evacuation of a building containing or supporting critical operations that is likely to last for more than four hours

- Hardware, software, or network failures that result in a critical IT system being incapacitated or unavailable for more than four hours

- Any security incident that results in a critical IT system being incapacitated for more than four hours (security incidents could involve malware, break-in, attack, sabotage, and so on)

- Any event causing employee absenteeism or supplier shortages that, in turn, results in one or more critical business processes being incapacitated for more than eight hours

- Any event causing a communications failure that results in critical IT systems being unreachable for more than four hours

The preceding examples are a mostly complete list of criteria for many organizations. The periods will vary from organization to organization. For instance, a large, pure-online business such as Amazon.com would probably declare a disaster if its main websites were unavailable for more than a few minutes. But in an organization where computers are far less critical, an outage of four hours might *not* be considered a disaster.

Pulling the Trigger When disaster declaration criteria are met, the disaster should be declared. The procedure for disaster declaration could permit any single core team member to declare the disaster, but it may be better to have two or more core team members agree on whether a disaster should be declared. Whether an organization should use a single-person declaration or a group of two or more is each organization's choice.

All core team members empowered to declare a disaster should have the procedure on hand at all times. In most cases, the criteria should fit on a small, laminated wallet card that each team member can have with him or her or nearby at all times. For organizations that use the consensus method for declaring a disaster, the wallet card should include the names and contact numbers for other core team members so that each will have a way of contacting others.

Next Steps Declaring a disaster will trigger the start of one or more other response procedures, but not necessarily all of them. For instance, if a disaster is declared because of a serious computer or software malfunction, there is no need to evacuate the building. While this example may be obvious, not all instances will be this clear. Either the disaster declaration procedure itself or each of the subsequent response procedures should contain criteria that will help determine which response procedures should be enacted.

False Alarms Probably the most common cause of personnel not declaring a disaster is the fear that a real disaster is not taking place. Core team members empowered with declaring a disaster should not necessarily hesitate. Instead, core team members could convene with additional core team members to reach a firm decision, provided this can be done quickly.

If a disaster has been declared and later it is clear that a disaster has been averted (or did not exist in the first place), the disaster can simply be called off and declared to be over. Response personnel can be contacted and told to cease response activities and return to their normal activities.

TIP Depending on the level of effort that takes place in the opening minutes and hours of disaster response, the consequences of declaring a disaster when none exists may be significant, or not. In the spirit of continuous improvement, any organization that has had a few false alarms should seek to improve their disaster declaration criteria. Well-trained and experienced personnel can usually reduce the frequency of false alarms.

Responsibilities

During a disaster, many important tasks must be performed to evacuate or shelter personnel, assess damage, recover critical processes and systems, and carry out many other functions that are critical to the survival of the enterprise.

About 20 different responsibilities are described here. In a large organization, each responsibility may be staffed with a team of two, three, or many individuals. In small organizations, a few people may incur many responsibilities each, switching from role to role as the situation warrants.

All of these roles will be staffed by people who are available to fill them. It is important to remember that many of the "ideal" persons to fill each role will be unavailable during a disaster for several reasons, including

- **Injured, ill, or deceased** Some regional disasters will inflict widespread casualties that will include some proportion of response personnel. Those who are injured, ill (in the case of a pandemic, for instance, or who are recovering from a sickness or surgery when the disaster occurs), or who are killed by the disaster are clearly not going to be showing up to help out.

- **Caring for family members** Some types of disasters may cause widespread injury or require mass evacuation. In some of these situations, many personnel will be caring for family members whose immediate needs for safety will take priority over the needs of the workplace.

- **Unavailable transportation** Some types of disasters include localized or widespread damage to transportation infrastructure, which may result in many persons who are willing to be on-site to help with emergency operations being unable to travel to the work site.

- **Out of the area** Some disaster response personnel may be away on business travel or on vacation and be unable to respond. However, some persons being away may actually be opportunities in disguise; unaffected by the physical impact of the disaster, they may be able to help out in other ways, such as communications with suppliers, customers, or other personnel.

- **Communications** Some types of disasters, particularly those that are localized (versus widespread and obvious to an observer), require that disaster response personnel be contacted and asked to help. If a disaster strikes after hours, some personnel may be unreachable if they are engaged in any activity where they do not have a mobile phone with them or are out of range.

- **Fear** Some types of disasters (such as pandemic, terrorist attack, flood, and so on) may instill fear for safety on the part of response personnel who will disregard the call to help and stay away from the work site.

NOTE Response personnel in all disciplines and responsibilities will need to be able to piece together whatever functionality they are called on to do, using whatever resources are available—this is part art form and part science. While response and contingency plans may make certain assumptions, personnel may find themselves with fewer resources than planned, requiring them to do the best they can with the resources available.

Each function will be working with personnel in many other functions, often working with unfamiliar persons. An entire response and recovery operation may be operating almost like a brand-new organization in unfamiliar settings and with an entirely new set of playing rules. In typical organizations, teams work well when team members are familiar with, and trust, one another. In a response and recovery operation, the stress level is much higher because the stakes—company survival—are higher, and often the teams are composed of persons who have little experience with each other and these new roles. This will cause additional stress that will bring out the best and worst in people, as illustrated in Figure 2-13.

Emergency Response   These are the "first responders" during a disaster. Top priorities include evacuation or sheltering of personnel, first aid, triage of injured personnel, and possibly firefighting.

Command and Control (Emergency Management)   During disaster response operations, someone has to be in charge. In a disaster, resources may be scarce, and many matters vie for attention. Someone needs to fill the role of decision maker to keep disaster response activities moving and to handle situations that arise. This role may need to be rotated among various personnel, particularly in smaller organizations, to counteract fatigue.

TIP   Although the first person on the scene may be the person in charge *initially*, that will definitely change as qualified assigned personnel show up and take charge and as the nature of the disaster and response solidifies. The leadership roles may then be passed among key personnel already designated to be in charge.

Figure 2-13   Stress is compounded by the pressure of disaster recovery and the formation of new teams in times of chaos.

Scribe It's vital that one or more persons continually document the important events during disaster response operations. From decisions to discussions to status to roll call, these events must be written down so that the details of disaster response can be pieced together afterward. This will help the organization better understand how disaster response unfolded, how decisions were made, and who performed which actions, all of which will help the organization be better prepared for future events.

Internal Communications In many disaster scenarios, personnel may be stripped of many or all of their normal means of communication, such as desk phone, voicemail, e-mail, mobile phone, and instant messaging. Yet never are communications as vital as during a disaster, when nothing is going according to plan. Internal communications are needed so that status on various activities can be sent to command and control, and so that priorities and orders can be sent to disaster response personnel.

External Communications People outside of the organization need to know what's going on when a disaster strikes. There's a potentially long list of parties who want or need to know the status of business operations during and after a disaster, including

- Customers
- Suppliers
- Partners
- Shareholders
- Neighbors
- Regulators
- Media
- Law enforcement and public safety authorities

These different audiences need different messages, as well as messages in different forms.

Legal and Compliance Several needs may arise during a disaster that require the attention of inside or outside legal counsel. Disasters present unique situations that need legal assistance, such as:

- Interpretation of regulations
- Interpretation of contracts with suppliers and customers
- Management of matters of liability to other parties

TIP Typical legal matters need to be resolved before the onset of a disaster, with this information included in disaster response procedures, since legal staff members may be unavailable during the disaster.

Damage Assessment   Whether a disaster is a physically violent event, such as an earthquake or volcano, or instead involves no physical manifestation, such as a serious security incident, one or more experts are needed who can examine affected assets and accurately assess the damage. Because most organizations own many different types of assets (from buildings to equipment to information), qualified experts are needed to assess each asset type involved. It is not necessary to call upon all available experts, only those whose expertise matches the type of event that has occurred.

Some expertise may go well beyond the skills present in an organization, such as a building structural engineer who can assess potential earthquake damage. In such cases it may be sensible to retain the services of an outside engineer who will respond and provide an assessment on whether a building is safe to occupy after a disaster.

Salvage   Disasters destroy assets that the organization uses to make products or perform services. When a disaster occurs, someone (either a qualified employee or an outside expert) needs to examine assets to determine which are salvageable; then a salvage team needs to perform the actual salvage operation at a pace that meets the organization's needs.

In some cases, salvage may be a critical-path activity, where critical processes are paralyzed until salvage and repairs to critically needed machinery can be performed. In other cases, the salvage operation is performed on inventory of finished goods, raw materials, and other items so that business operations can be resumed. Occasionally, when it is obvious that damaged equipment or materials are a total loss, the salvage effort is one of selling the damaged items or materials to some organization that wants them.

Assessment of damage to assets may be a high priority when an organization will be filing an insurance claim. Insurance may be a primary source of funding for the organization's recovery effort.

 CAUTION   Salvage operations may be a critical-path activity or one that can be carried out well after the disaster. To the greatest extent possible, this should be decided in advance. Otherwise, the command-and-control function will need to decide the priority of salvage operations.

Physical Security   After a disaster, the organization's usual physical security controls may be compromised. For instance, fencing, walls, and barricades could be damaged, or video surveillance systems may be disabled or have no electric power. These and other failures could lead to increased risk of loss or damage to assets and personnel until those controls can be fixed. Also, security controls in temporary quarters such as hot/warm/cold sites and temporary work centers may be below those in primary locations.

Supplies   During emergency and recovery operations, personnel will require supplies of many kinds, from drinking water, writing tablets, and pens to cell phones, portable generators, and extension cords. This function may also be responsible for ordering replacement assets such as servers and network equipment for a cold site.

Transportation   When workers are operating from a temporary location and/or if regional or local transportation systems have been compromised, many arrangements for all kinds of transportation may be required to support emergency operations. These can include transportation of replacement workers, equipment, or supplies by truck, car, rail, sea, or air. This function could also be responsible for arranging for temporary lodging for personnel.

Network   This technology function is responsible for damage assessment to the organization's voice and data networks, building/configuring networks for emergency operations, or both. This function may require extensive coordination with external telecommunications service providers, who, by the way, may be suffering the effects of a local or regional disaster as well.

Network Services   This function is responsible for network-centric services such as domain name service (DNS), simple network management protocol (SNMP), and authentication.

Systems   This is the function that is responsible for building, loading, and configuring the servers and systems that support critical services, applications, databases, and other functions. Personnel may have other resources such as virtualization technology to enable additional flexibility.

Databases   For critical applications that rely upon databases, this function is responsible for building databases on recovery systems and for restoring or recovering data from backup media, replication volumes, or e-vaults onto recovery systems. Database personnel will need to work with systems, network, and applications personnel to ensure that databases are operating properly and are available as needed.

Data and Records   This function is responsible for access to and re-creation of electronic and paper business records. This is a business function that supports critical business processes and works with database management personnel and, if necessary, works with data-entry personnel to rekey lost data.

Applications   This function is responsible for recovering application functionality on application servers. This may include reloading application software; performing configuration; provisioning roles and user accounts; and connecting the application to databases, network services, and other application integration issues.

Access Management   This function is responsible for creating and managing user accounts for network, system, and application access. Personnel with this responsibility may be especially susceptible to social engineering and be tempted to create user accounts without proper authority or approval.

Information Security and Privacy   Personnel in this capacity are responsible for ensuring that proper security controls are being carried out during recovery and emergency operations. They will be expected to identify risks associated with emergency operations and to require remedies to reduce risks.

Security personnel will also be responsible for enforcing privacy controls so that employee and customer personal data will not be compromised, even as business operations are affected by the disaster.

Off-Site Storage   This function is responsible for managing the effort of retrieving backup media from off-site storage facilities and for protecting that media in transit to the scene of recovery operations. If recovery operations take place over an extended period (more than a couple of days), data at the recovery site will need to be backed up and sent to an off-site media storage facility to protect that information should a disaster occur at the hot/warm/cold site (and what bad luck that would be!).

User Hardware   In many organizations, little productive work gets done when employees don't have their workstations, printers, scanners, copiers, and other office equipment. Thus, a function is required to provide, configure, and support the variety of office equipment required by end users working in temporary or alternate locations. This function, like most others, will have to work with many others to ensure that workstations and other equipment are able to communicate with applications and services as needed to support critical processes.

Training   During emergency operations, when response personnel and users are working in new locations (and often on new or different equipment and software), some of these personnel may need training so that their productivity can be quickly restored. Training personnel will need to be familiar with many disaster response and recovery procedures so that they can help people in those roles understand what is expected of them. This function will also need to be able to dispense emergency operations procedures to these personnel.

Restoration   This function comes into play when IT is ready to migrate applications running on hot/warm/cold site systems back to the original (or replacement) processing center.

Contract Information   This function is responsible for understanding and interpreting legal contracts. Most organizations are a party to one or more legal contracts that require them to perform specific activities, provide specific services, and communicate status if service levels have changed. These contracts may or may not have provisions for activities and services during disasters, including communications regarding any changes in service levels.

This function is vital not only during the disaster planning stages but also during actual disaster response. Customers, suppliers, regulators, and other parties need to be informed according to specific contract terms.

Recovery Procedures

Recovery procedures are the instructions that key personnel use to bootstrap services (such as IT systems and other business-enabling technologies) that support the critical business functions identified in the BIA. The recovery procedures should work hand in hand with the technologies that may have been added to IT systems to make them more resilient.

An example would be useful here. A fictitious company, Acme Rocket Boots, determines that its order-entry business function is highly critical to the ongoing viability of the business and sets recovery objectives to ensure that order entry would be continued within no more than 48 hours after a disaster.

Acme determines that it needs to invest in storage, backup, and replication technologies to make a 48-hour recovery possible. Without these investments, IT systems supporting order-entry would be down for at least ten days until they could be rebuilt from scratch. Acme cannot justify the purchase of systems and software to facilitate an auto-failover of the order-entry application to hot-site DR servers; instead, the recovery procedure would require that the database be rebuilt from replicated data on warm-site servers. Other tasks, such as installing recent patches, would also be necessary to make recovery servers ready for production use. All of the tasks required to make the systems ready constitute the body of recovery procedures needed to support the business order-entry function.

This example is, of course, a gross oversimplification. Actual recovery procedures could take dozens of pages of documentation, and procedures would also be necessary for network components, end-user workstations, network services, and other supporting IT services required by the order-entry application. And those are the procedures needed just to get the application running again. More procedures would be needed to keep the applications running properly in the recovery environment.

Continuing Operations

Procedures for continuing operations have more to do with business processes than they do with IT systems. However, the two are related, since the procedures for continuing critical business processes have to fit hand in hand with the procedures for operating supporting IT systems that may also (but not necessarily) be operating in a recovery or emergency mode.

Let me clarify that last statement. It is entirely conceivable that a disaster could strike an organization with critical business processes that operate in one city but that are supported by IT systems located in another city. A disaster could strike the city with the critical business function, which means that personnel might have to continue operating that business function in another location, *on the original, fully featured IT application*. It is also possible that a disaster could strike the city with the IT application, forcing it into an emergency/recovery mode in an alternate location, while users of the application are operating in a business-as-usual mode. And, of course, a disaster could strike both locations (or a disaster could strike in one location where both the critical business function *and* its supporting IT applications are), throwing both the critical business function *and* its supporting IT applications into emergency mode. Any organization's reality could be even more complex than this: just add dependencies on external application service providers, applications with custom interfaces, or critical business functions that operate in multiple cities. If you wondered why disaster recovery and business continuity planning were so complicated, perhaps your appreciation has grown.

Restoration Procedures

When a disaster has occurred, IT operations need to temporarily take up residence in an alternate processing site while repairs are performed on the original processing site. Once those repairs are completed, IT operations would need to be transitioned back to the main (or replacement) processing facility. You should expect that the procedures for this transition would also be documented (and *tested*—testing is discussed later in this chapter).

NOTE Transitioning applications back to the original processing site is not necessarily just a second iteration of the initial move to the hot/warm/cold site. Far from it: the recovery site may have been a skeleton (in capacity, functionality, or both) of its original self. The objective is not necessarily to move the functionality at the recovery site back to the *original* site, but to restore the original functionality to the original site.

Let's look at an example. To continue the Acme Rocket Boots example: their order-entry application at the DR site had only basic, not extended, functions. For instance, customers could not look at order history, and they could not place custom orders; they could only order off-the-shelf products. But when the application is moved back to the primary processing facility, the history of orders accumulated on the DR application needs to be merged into the main order history database, *which was not a part of the DR plan*.

Considerations for Continuity and Recovery Plans

A considerable amount of detailed planning and logistics must go into continuity and recovery plans if they are to be effective.

Availability of Key Personnel An organization cannot depend upon every member of its regular expert workforce to be available in a disaster. As discussed earlier in this chapter in more detail, personnel may be unavailable for a number of reasons, including

- Injury, illness, or death
- Caring for family members
- Unavailable transportation
- Being out of the area
- Lack of communications
- Fear

TIP An organization must develop thorough and accurate recovery and continuity documentation as well as cross-training and plan testing. When a disaster strikes, an organization has one chance to survive, and it depends upon how well the available personnel are able to follow recovery and continuity procedures and to keep critical processes functioning properly.

Emergency Supplies   The onset of a disaster may cause personnel to be stranded at a work location, possibly for several days. This can be caused by a number of reasons, including inclement weather that makes travel dangerous or a transportation infrastructure that is damaged or blocked with debris.

Emergency supplies should be laid up at a work location and made available to personnel stranded there, regardless of whether they are supporting a recovery effort or not (it's also possible that severe weather or a natural or man-made event could make transportation dangerous or impossible).

A disaster can also prompt employees to report to a work location (at the primary location or at an alternate site) where they may remain for days at a time, even around the clock if necessary. A situation like this may make the need for emergency supplies less critical, but it still may be beneficial to the recovery effort to make supplies available to support recovery personnel.

An organization stocking emergency supplies at a work location should consider including

- Drinking water
- Food rations
- First-aid supplies
- Blankets
- Flashlights
- Battery or crank-powered radio

Local emergency response authorities may recommend other supplies be kept at a work location as well.

Communications   Communications within organizations, as well as with customers, suppliers, partners, shareholders, regulators, and others, is vital under normal business conditions. During a disaster and subsequent recovery and restoration operations, it's more important than ever, while many of the usual means for communications may be impaired.

Identifying Critical Personnel   A successful disaster recovery operation requires available personnel who are located near company operations centers. While the primary response personnel may consist of the individuals and teams responsible for day-to-day corporate operations, others need to be identified. In a disaster, some personnel will be unavailable for many reasons (discussed earlier in this chapter).

Key personnel, as well as their backup persons, need to be identified. Backup personnel can consist of other employees who have familiarity with specific technologies, such as operating system, database, and network administration, and who can cover for primary personnel if needed. Sure, it would be desirable for these backup personnel also to be trained in specific recovery operations, but at the very least, if these personnel have access to specific detailed recovery procedures, having them on a call list is probably better than having no available personnel during a disaster.

Identifying Critical Suppliers, Customers, and Other Parties   Besides employees, many other parties need to be notified in the event of a disaster. Outside parties need to be aware of the disaster, as well as of basic changes in business conditions.

In a regional disaster such as a hurricane or earthquake, nearby parties will certainly be aware of the disaster and that your organization is involved in it somehow. However, those parties may not be aware of the status of business operations immediately after the disaster: a regional event's effects can range from complete destruction of buildings and equipment to no damage at all and business-as-usual conditions. Unless key parties are notified of the status, they may have no other way to know for sure.

Parties that need to be contacted may include

- **Key suppliers**   This may include electric and gas utilities, fuel delivery, and materials delivery. In a disaster, an organization will often need to impart special instructions to one or more suppliers, requesting delivery of extra supplies or temporary cessation of deliveries.

- **Key customers**   Many organizations have key customers whose relationships are valued above most others. These customers may depend on a steady delivery of products and services that are critical to their own operations; in a disaster, those customers may have a dire need to know whether such deliveries will be able to continue or not and under what circumstances.

- **Public safety**   Police, fire, and other public safety authorities may need to be contacted, not only for emergency operations such as firefighting, but also for any required inspections or other services. It is important that "business office" telephone numbers for these agencies be included on contact lists, as 911 and other emergency lines may be flooded by calls from others.

- **Insurance adjusters**   Most organizations rely on insurance companies to protect their assets from damage or loss in a disaster. Because insurance adjustment funds are often a key part of continuing business operations in an emergency, it's important to be able to reach insurers as soon as possible after a disaster has occurred.

- **Regulators**   In some industries, organizations are required to notify regulators of certain types of disasters. While regulators obviously may be aware of noteworthy regional disasters, they may not immediately know an event's specific effects on an organization. Further, some types of disasters are highly localized and may not be newsworthy, even in a local city.

- **Media**   Media outlets such as newspapers and television stations may need to be notified as a means of quickly reaching the community or region with information about the effects of a disaster on organizations.

- **Shareholders**   Organizations are usually obliged to notify their shareholders of any disastrous event that affects business operations. This may be the case whether the organization is publicly or privately held.

The persons or teams responsible for communicating with these outside parties will need to have all of the individuals and organizations included in a list of parties to contact. This information should all be included in emergency response procedures.

Setting Up Call Trees   Disaster response procedures need to include a call tree. This is a method where the first personnel involved in a disaster begin notifying others in the organization, informing them of the developing disaster and enlisting their assistance.

Just as the branches of a tree originate at the trunk and are repeatedly subdivided, a call tree is most effective when each person in the tree can make just a few phone calls. Not only will the notification of important personnel proceed more quickly, but each person will not be overburdened with many calls.

Remember, in a disaster a significant portion of personnel may be unavailable or unreachable. Therefore, a call tree should be structured so that there is sufficient flexibility as well as assurance that all critical personnel will be contacted. Figure 2-14 shows an example call tree.

An organization can also use an automated outcalling system to notify critical personnel of a disaster. Such a system can play a prerecorded message or request that personnel call an information number to hear a prerecorded message. Most outcalling systems keep a log of which personnel have been successfully reached.

An automated calling system should not be located in the same geographic region. If it were, a regional disaster could damage the system or make it unavailable during a disaster. The system should be Internet accessible so that response personnel can access it to determine which personnel have been notified, and to make any needed changes before or during a disaster.

Wallet Cards   Wallet cards containing emergency contact information should be prepared for core team personnel for the organization, as well as for members in each department who would be actively involved in disaster response. Wallet cards are advantageous, because most personnel will have their wallet, pocketbook, or purse nearby at all times, even when away from home, running errands, traveling, or on vacation. Information on the wallet card should include contact information for fellow team members,

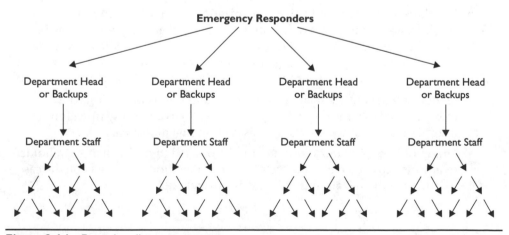

Figure 2-14   Example call tree structure

```
Emergency Contacts
Joe Phillips, VP Ops: 213-555-1212 h, 415-555-1212 m
Marie Peterson, CFO: 206-555-1212 h, 425-555-1212 m
Mark Woodward, IT Ops: 360-555-1212 h, 253-555-1212 m
Gary Doan, VP Facilities: 509-555-1212 h, 702-555-1212 m
Jeff Patterson, IT Networks: 760-555-1212 h, 310-555-1212 m
Documentation at briefcase.yahoo.com: Userid = wunderground, password = L0c43Dupt1te
Emergency conference bridge: 1-800-555-1212, host code 443322, PIN 0748
Disaster declaration criteria: 8-hr outage anticipated on critical systems, 2 core members vote,
then initiate call tree procedure to notify other response personnel

Off-site media storage vendor: 719-555-1212
Telecommunications and network service provider: 312-555-1212
Local emergency response authorities: 714-555-1212
Local health authorities: 702-555-1212
Local law enforcement authorities: 512-555-1212
Local hospitals: 808-555-1212, 913-555-1212
National weather service hotline: 602-555-1212
Regional transportation authority hotline: 312-555-1212
Local building inspectors: 414-555-1212
```

Figure 2-15   Example laminated wallet card for core team participants with emergency contact information and disaster declaration criteria

a few of the key disaster response personnel, and any conference bridges or emergency call-in numbers that are set up. An example wallet card is shown in Figure 2-15.

Transportation   Some types of disasters may make certain modes of transportation unavailable or unsafe. Widespread natural disasters, such as earthquakes, volcanoes, hurricanes, and floods, can immobilize virtually every form of transportation, including highways, railroads, boats, and airplanes. Other types of disasters may impede one or more types of transportation, which could result in overwhelming demand for the available modes. High volumes of emergency supplies may be needed during and after a disaster, but damaged transportation infrastructure often makes the delivery of those supplies difficult.

Components of a Business Continuity Plan
The complete set of business continuity plan documents will include the following:

- **Supporting project documents**   These will include the documents created at the beginning of the business continuity project, including the project charter, project plan, statement of scope, and statement of support from executives.
- **Analysis documents**   These include the
  - Business impact analysis (BIA)
  - Threat assessment and risk assessment
  - Criticality analysis
  - Documents defining recovery targets such as recovery time objective (RTO) and recovery point objective (RPO)

- **Response documents** These are all the documents that describe the required action of personnel when a disaster strikes, plus documents containing information required by those same personnel. Examples of these documents include

  - **Business recovery (or resumption) plan** This describes the activities required to recover and resume critical business processes and activities.

  - **Occupant emergency plan (OEP)** This describes activities required to safely care for occupants in a business location during a disaster. This will include both evacuation procedures and sheltering procedures, each of which might be required, depending upon the type of disaster that occurs.

  - **Emergency communications plan** This describes the types of communications imparted to many parties, including emergency response personnel, employees in general, customers, suppliers, regulators, public safety organizations, shareholders, and the public.

  - **Contact lists** These contain names and contact information for emergency response personnel as well as for critical suppliers, customers, and other parties.

  - **Disaster recovery plan** This describes the activities required to restore critical IT systems and other critical assets, whether in alternate or primary locations.

  - **Continuity of operations plan (COOP)** This describes the activities required to continue critical and strategic business functions at an alternate site.

  - **Security incident response plan (SIRP)** This describes the steps required to deal with a security incident that could reach disaster-like proportions.

- **Test and review documents** This is the entire collection of documents related to tests of all of the different types of business continuity plans, as well as reviews and revisions to documents.

Testing Recovery Plans

It's surprising what you can accomplish when no one is concerned about who gets the credit.
—Ronald Reagan

Business continuity and disaster recovery plans may look elegant and even ingenious on paper, but their true business value is unknown until their worth is proven through testing.

The process of testing DR and BC plans uncovers flaws not only in the plans, but also in the systems and processes that they are designed to protect. For example, testing a system recovery procedure might point out the absence of a critically needed hardware component, or a recovery procedure might contain a syntax or grammatical error that misleads the recovery team member and results in recovery delays. Testing is designed to uncover these types of issues.

Testing Recovery and Continuity Plans

Recovery and continuity plans need to be tested to prove their viability. Without testing, an organization has no way of really knowing whether its plans are effective. With ineffective plans, an organization has a far smaller chance of surviving a disaster.

Recovery and continuity plans have built-in obsolescence—not by design, but by virtue of the fact that technology and business processes in most organizations are undergoing constant change and improvement. Thus, it is imperative that newly developed or updated plans be tested as soon as possible to ensure their effectiveness.

Types of tests range from lightweight and unobtrusive to intense and disruptive. The types of tests are

- Document review
- Walkthrough
- Simulation
- Parallel test
- Cutover test

These tests are described in more detail in this section.

 TIP   Usually, an organization will perform the less intensive tests first to identify the most obvious flaws and follow with tests that require more effort.

Test Preparation

Each type of test requires advance preparation and recordkeeping. Preparation will consist of several activities, including

- **Participants**   The organization needs to identify personnel who will participate in an upcoming test. It is important to identify all relevant skill groups and department stakeholders so that the test will include a full slate of contributors.

- **Schedule**   The availability of each participant needs to be confirmed so that the test will include participation from all stakeholders.

- **Facilities**   For all but the document review test, proper facilities need to be identified and set up. This might consist of a large conference room or training room. If the test will take place over several hours, one or more meals and/or refreshments may be needed as well.

- **Scripting**   The simulation test requires some scripting, usually in the form of one or more documents that describe a developing scenario and related circumstances. Scenario scripting can make parallel and cutover tests more interesting and valuable, but this can be considered optional.

- **Recordkeeping** For all of the tests except the document review, one or more persons need to take good notes that can be collected and organized after the test is completed.

- **Contingency plan** The cutover test involves the cessation of processing on primary systems and the resumption of processing on recovery systems. This is the highest-risk plan, and things can go wrong. A contingency plan to get primary systems running again in case something goes wrong during the test needs to be developed.

These preparation activities are shown in Table 2-4.
The various types of tests are discussed next.

Document Review A *document review* test is a review of some or all disaster recovery and business continuity plans, procedures, and other documentation. Individuals typically review these documents on their own, at their own pace, but within whatever time constraints or deadlines that may have been established.

The purpose of a document review test is to review the accuracy and completeness of document content. Reviewers should read each document with a critical eye, point out any errors, and annotate the document with questions or comments that can be sent back to the document's author(s), who can make any necessary changes.

If significant changes are needed in one or more documents, the project team may want to include a second round of document review before moving on to more resource-intensive tests.

The owner or document manager for the organization's business continuity and disaster recovery planning project should document which persons review which documents, and perhaps even include the review copies or annotations. This practice will create a more complete record of the activities related to the development and testing of important BCP planning and response documents. It will also help to capture the true cost and effort of the development and testing of BCP capabilities in the organization.

Walkthrough A *walkthrough* is similar to a document review: it's a review of just the BCP documents. However, where a document review is carried out by individuals working on their own, a walkthrough is performed by an entire group of individuals in a live discussion.

	Document Review	Walkthrough	Simulation	Parallel Test	Cutover Test
Participants	Yes	Yes	Yes	Yes	Yes
Schedule	Yes	Yes	Yes	Yes	Yes
Facilities		Yes	Yes	Yes	Yes
Scripting			Yes	Optional	Optional
Recordkeeping	Yes	Yes	Yes	Yes	Yes
Contingency plan					Yes

Table 2-4 Preparation Activities Required for Each Type of DR/BC Test

A walkthrough is usually facilitated by a leader who guides the participants page by page through each document. The leader may read sections of the document aloud, describe various scenarios where information in a section might be relevant, and take comments and questions from participants.

A walkthrough is likely to take considerably more time than a document review. One participant's question on some minor point in the document could spark a worthwhile and lively discussion that could last a few minutes to an hour. The group leader or another person will need to take careful notes in the event that any deficiencies are found in any of the documents. The leader will also need to be able to control the pace of the review so that the group does not get unnecessarily hung up on minor points. Some discussions will need to be cut short or tabled for a later time or for an offline conversation among interested parties.

Even if major revisions are needed in recovery documents, it probably will be infeasible to conduct another walkthrough with updated documents. However, follow-up document reviews are probably warranted to ensure that they were updated appropriately, at least in the opinion of the walkthrough participants.

CAUTION Participants in the walkthrough should carefully consider that the potential audience for recovery procedures may be persons who are not as familiar as they are with systems and processes. They need to remember that the ideal personnel may not be available during a real disaster. Participants also need to realize that the skill level of recovery personnel might be a little below that of the experts who operate systems and processes in normal circumstances. Finally, walkthrough participants need to remember that systems and processes undergo almost continuous change, which could render some parts of the recovery documentation obsolete or incorrect all too soon.

Simulation   A *simulation* is a test of disaster recovery and business continuity procedures where the participants take part in a "mock disaster" to add some realism to the process of thinking their way through procedures in emergency response documents.

A simulation could be an elaborate and choreographed walkthrough test where a facilitator reads from a script and describes a series of unfolding events in a disaster such as a hurricane or an earthquake. This type of simulation might almost be viewed as "playacting," where the script is the set of emergency response documentation. By stimulating the imagination of simulation participants, it's possible for participants to really imagine that a disaster is taking place, which may help them to better understand what real disaster conditions might be like. It will help tremendously if the facilitator has actually experienced one or more disaster scenarios so that he or she can add more realism when describing events.

To make the simulation more credible and valuable, the scenario that is chosen should be one that has a reasonable chance of actually occurring in the local area. Good choices would include an earthquake in San Francisco or Los Angeles, a volcanic eruption in Seattle, or an avalanche in Switzerland. A poor choice would be a hurricane or tsunami in central Asia, because these events would not ever occur there.

A simulation can also go a few steps further. For instance, the simulation can take place at an established emergency operations center, the same place where emergency command and control would operate in a real disaster. Also, the facilitator could change some of the participants' roles to simulate the real absence of certain key personnel to see how remaining personnel might conduct themselves in a real emergency.

 TIP   The facilitator of a simulation is limited only by his or her own imagination when organizing a simulation. One important fact to remember, though, is that a simulation does not actually affect any live or DR systems— it's all as pretend as the make-believe cardboard television sets and computers found in furniture stores.

Parallel Test   A *parallel test* is an actual test of disaster recovery and/or business continuity response plans. The purpose of a parallel test is to evaluate the ability of personnel to follow directives in emergency response plans—to actually set up the DR business processing or data processing capability. In a parallel test, personnel are actually setting up the IT systems that would be used in an actual disaster and operating those IT systems with real business transactions to find out if the IT systems perform the processing correctly.

The outcome of a parallel test is threefold:

- It evaluates the accuracy of emergency response procedures.
- It evaluates the ability of personnel to correctly follow the emergency response procedures.
- It evaluates the ability of IT systems and other supporting apparatus to process real business transactions properly.

A parallel test is called a parallel test because live production systems continue to operate and the backup IT systems are processing business transactions *in parallel* to see if they process them the same as the live production systems do.

Setting up a valid parallel test is complicated in many cases. In effect, you need to insert a logical "Y cable" into the business process flow so that the information flow will split and flow both to production systems (without interfering with their operation) and to the backup systems. Results of transactions need to be compared. Personnel need to be able to determine whether the backup systems would be *able* to output correct data *without actually having them do so*. In many complex environments, you would not want the DR system to actually feed information back into a live environment, because that might cause duplicate events to occur someplace else in the organization (or with customers, suppliers, or other parties). For instance, in a travel reservations system, you would not want a DR system to actually book travel, because that would cost real money and consume available space on an airline or other mode of transportation. But it would be important to know whether the DR system would be able to perform those functions. Somewhere along the line, it will be necessary to "unplug" the DR system from the rest of the environment and manually examine results to see if they appear to be correct.

Organizations that do wish to see if their backup/DR systems can manage a *real* workload can perform a cutover test, which is discussed next.

Cutover Test   A *cutover test* is the most intrusive type of disaster recovery test. It will also provide the most reliable results in terms of answering the question of whether backup systems have the capacity to shoulder the real workload properly.

The consequences of a failed cutover test, however, might resemble an actual disaster: if any part of the cutover test fails, then real, live business processes will be going without the support of IT applications as though a real outage or disaster were in progress. But even a failure like this would show you that "no, the backup systems won't work in the event a real disaster were to happen later today."

In some respects, a cutover test is easier to perform than a parallel test. A parallel test is a little trickier, since business information is required to flow to the production system and to the backup system, which means that some artificial component has been somehow inserted into the environment. However, with a cutover test, business processing does take place on the backup systems only, which can often be achieved through a simple configuration someplace in the network or the systems layer of the environment.

TIP   Not all organizations perform cutover tests because they take a lot of resources to set up and are risky. Many organizations find that a parallel test is sufficient to tell whether backup systems are accurate, and the risk of an embarrassing incident is almost zero with a parallel test.

Documenting Test Results

Every type and every iteration of DR plan testing needs to be documented. It's not enough to say, "We did the test on September 10, 2009, and it worked." First of all, no test goes perfectly—opportunities for improvement are always identified. But the most important part of testing is to discover *what parts* of the test still need work so that those parts of the plan can be fixed before the next test (or a real disaster).

As with any well-organized project, success is in the details. The road to success is littered with big and little mistakes, and all of the things that are identified in every sort of DR test need to be detailed so that the next iteration of the test will give better results.

Recording and comparing detailed test results from one test to the next will also help the organization to measure progress. By this I mean that the quality of emergency response plans should steadily improve from year to year. Simple mistakes of the past should not be repeated, and the only failures in future tests should be in new and novel parts of the environment that weren't well thought out to begin with. And even these should diminish over time.

Improving Recovery and Continuity Plans

Every test of recovery and response plans should include a debrief or review so that participants can discuss the outcome of the test: what went well, what went wrong, and how things should be done differently next time. All of this information should be collected by someone who will be responsible for making changes to relevant documents. The updated documents should be circulated among the test participants who can confirm whether their discussion and ideas are properly reflected in the document.

Training Personnel

The value and usefulness of a high-quality set of disaster response and continuity plans and procedures will be greatly diminished if those responsible for carrying out the procedures are unfamiliar with them.

A person cannot learn to ride a bicycle by reading even the most detailed how-to instructions on the subject, so it's equally unrealistic to expect personnel to be able to properly carry out disaster response procedures if they are untrained in those procedures.

Several forms of training can be made available for the personnel who are expected to be available if a disaster strikes, including

- **Document review**   Personnel can carefully read through procedure documents to become familiar with the nature of the recovery procedures. But as mentioned earlier, this alone may be insufficient.

- **Participation in walkthroughs**   People who are familiar with specific processes and systems that are the subject of walkthroughs should participate in them. Exposing personnel to the walkthrough process will not only help to improve the walkthrough and recovery procedures, but will also be a learning experience for participants.

- **Participation in simulations**   Taking part in simulations will similarly benefit the participants by giving them the experience of thinking through a disaster.

- **Participation in parallel and cutover tests**   Other than experiencing an actual disaster and its recovery operations, no experience is quite like participating in parallel and cutover tests. Here, participants will gain actual hands-on experience with critical business processes and IT environments by performing the actual procedures that they would in the event of a disaster. When a disaster strikes, those participants can draw upon their memory of having performed those procedures in the past, instead of just the experience of having read the procedures.

You can see that all of the levels of tests that need to be performed to verify the quality of response plans are also training opportunities for personnel. The development and testing of disaster-related plans and procedures provide a continuous learning experience for all of the personnel involved.

Making Plans Available to Personnel When Needed

When a disaster strikes, often one of the effects is no access to even the most critical IT systems. Given a 40-hour workweek, there is roughly a 25 percent likelihood that critical personnel will be at the business location when a disaster strikes (at least the violent type of disaster that strikes with no warning, such as an earthquake—other types of disasters, such as hurricanes, may afford the organization a little bit of time to anticipate the disaster's impact). The point is that chances are very good that the personnel who are available to respond may be unable to access the procedures and other information that they will need, unless special measures are taken.

CAUTION   Complete BCP documentation often contains details of key systems, operating procedures, recovery strategies, and even vendor and model identification of in-place equipment. This information can be misused if available to unauthorized personnel, so the mechanism selected for ensuring availability must include planning to exclude inadvertent disclosure.

There are several ways that response and recovery procedures can be made available to personnel during a disaster, including

- **Hard copy**   While many have grown accustomed to the paperless office, disaster recovery and response documentation is one type of information that should be available in hardcopy form. Copies, even multiple copies, should be available for each responder, with a copy at the workplace and another at home, and possibly even a set in the responder's vehicle.

- **Soft copy**   Traditionally, softcopy documentation is kept on file servers, but as you might expect, those file servers might be unavailable in a disaster. Soft copies should be available on responders' portable devices (laptops, PDAs, and perhaps smart phones). An organization can also consider issuing documentation on memory sticks and cards. Depending upon the type of disaster, it can be difficult to know what resources will be available to access documentation, so making it available in more than one form will ensure that at least one copy of it will be available to the personnel who need access to it.

- **Alternate work/processing site**   Organizations that utilize a hot/warm/cold site for the recovery of critical operations can maintain hard copies and/or soft copies of recovery documentation there. This makes perfect sense; personnel working at an alternate processing or work site will need to know what to do, and having those procedures on-site will facilitate their work.

- **Online**   Soft copies of recovery documentation can be archived on an Internet-based site that includes the ability to store data. Almost any type of online service that includes authentication and the ability to upload documents could be suitable for this purpose.

- **Wallet cards**   It's unreasonable to expect to publish recovery documentation on a laminated wallet card, but those cards could be used to store the contact information for core response team members as well as a few other pieces of information, such as conference bridge codes, passwords to online repositories of documentation, and so on. An example wallet card appears earlier in this chapter, in Figure 2-15.

Maintaining Recovery and Continuity Plans

Business processes and technology undergo almost continuous change in most organizations. A business continuity plan that is developed and tested is liable to be outdated within months and obsolete within a year. If much more than a year passes, a DR plan in some organizations may approach uselessness. This section discusses how organizations need to keep their DR plans up-to-date and relevant.

A typical organization needs to establish a schedule whereby the principal DR documents will be reviewed. Depending on the rate of change, this could be as frequently as quarterly or as seldom as every two years.

Further, every change, however insignificant, in business processes and information systems should include a step to review and, possibly update, relevant DR documents. That is, a review of, and possibly changes to, relevant DR documents should be a required step in every business process engineering or information systems change process, and a key component of the organization's software development life cycle (SDLC). If this is done faithfully, then you would expect that the annual review of DR documents would conclude that few (if any) changes were required, although it is still a good practice to perform a periodic review, just to be sure.

Periodic testing of DR documents and plans, discussed in detail in the preceding section, is another vital activity. Testing validates the accuracy and relevance of DR documents, and any issues or exceptions in the testing process should precipitate updates to appropriate documents.

Sources for Best Practices

It is unnecessary to begin business continuity planning and disaster recovery planning by first inventing a practice or methodology. Business continuity planning and disaster recovery planning are advanced professions with several professional associations, professional certifications, international standards, and publications. Any or all of these are, or can lead to, sources of practices, processes, and methodologies:

- **U.S. National Institute of Standards and Technology (NIST)**   This is a branch of the U.S. Department of Commerce that is responsible for developing business and technology standards for the federal government. The standards developed by NIST are exceedingly high, and as a result many private organizations all over the world are adopting them. The NIST website is found at www.nist.gov.

- **Business Continuity Institute (BCI)**   This is a membership organization dedicated to the advancement of business continuity management. BCI has over 4,000 members in almost 100 countries. BCI holds several events around the world, prints a professional journal, and has developed several professional certifications, including

  - Associate of the Business Continuity Institute (ABCI)

  - Specialist of the Business Continuity Institute (SBCI)

  - Member of the Business Continuity Institute (MBCI)

  - Fellow of the Business Continuity Institute (FBCI)

    The BCI website can be found at www.thebci.org.

- **U.S. National Fire Protection Agency (NFPA)**   The NFPA has developed a pre-incident planning standard, NFPA 1620, which addresses the protection, construction, and features of buildings and other structures. It also requires the development of pre-incident plans that emergency responders can use to deal with fires and other emergencies. The NFPA website can be found at www.nfpa.org.

- **U.S. Federal Emergency Management Agency (FEMA)**   FEMA is a part of the Department of Homeland Security (DHS) and is responsible for emergency disaster relief planning information and services. FEMA's most visible activities are its relief operations in the wake of hurricanes and floods in the United States. Its website can be found at www.fema.gov.

- **Disaster Recovery Institute International (DRII)**   This is a professional membership organization that provides education and professional certifications for disaster recovery planning professionals. Its certifications include

  - Associate Business Continuity Professional (ABCP)

  - Certified Business Continuity Vendor (CBCV)

  - Certified Functional Continuity Professional (CFCP)

  - Certified Business Continuity Professional (CBCP)

  - Master Business Continuity Professional (MBCP)

- **Business Continuity Management Institute (BCMI)**   This is a professional association that specializes in education and professional certification. BCMI is a co-organizer of the World Continuity Congress, an annual conference that is dedicated to business continuity and disaster recovery planning. Its website can be found at www.bcm-institute.org. Certifications offered by BCMI include

  - Business Continuity Certified Expert (BCCE)

  - Business Continuity Certified Specialist (BCCS)

  - Business Continuity Certified Planner (BCCP)

  - Disaster Recovery Certified Expert (DRCE)

  - Disaster Recovery Certified Specialist (DRCS)

Auditing IT Governance

IT governance is more about business processes than it is about technology. This will make audits of IT governance rely more on interviews and documentation reviews than on inspections of information systems. Effective or ineffective IT governance is discernable in interviews of IT personnel as well as of business customers and end users.

 EXAM TIP   Governance questions on the exam will consider the ISACA's COBIT strategies as the standard, but will be generic enough in nature to ensure that an understanding of other common IT governance methods will remain applicable to the test-taker. Focus here on the measures and instruments used to validate the governance model.

Problems in IT governance will manifest themselves through a variety of symptoms:

- **Discontentment among staff or end users** Burned-out or overworked IT staff, low IT morale, high turnover, and malaise among end users about IT-supported systems can indicate an IT department that lacks maturity and is falling behind on its methodology or is applying Band-Aid fixes to systems.

- **Poor system performance** Excessive incidents of unscheduled downtime, a large backlog of support tasks, and long wait times indicate a lack of attention to the quality of applications.

- **Nonstandard hardware or software** A mix of hardware or software technologies among applications or end-user systems may indicate a lack of technology standards or the failure to enforce standards that are already in place.

- **Project dysfunction** An IT department suffering from late projects, aborted projects, and budget-busting projects indicates a lack of program and project management discipline.

- **Highly critical personnel** A disproportionate over-reliance on a few IT personnel indicates that responsibilities are not fairly apportioned over the entire IT staff. This may be a result of a lack of training, unqualified personnel, or high turnover.

Auditing Documentation and Records

The heart of an IT audit is the examination of documentation and records. They tell the story of IT control, planning, and day-to-day operations. When auditing IT governance, the IS (information systems) auditor will need to review many documents:

- **IT charter, strategy, and planning** These documents will indicate management's commitment to IT strategic planning as a formally required activity. Other documents that should be sought include IT steering committee meeting agendas, minutes, and decision logs.

- **IT organization chart and job descriptions** These documents give an indication of the organization's level of maturity regarding the classification of employees and their specific responsibilities. An org chart also depicts the hierarchy of management and control. Job description documents describe detailed responsibilities for each position in the IT organization. An IS auditor's interviews should include some inquiry into the actual skills and experience of IT personnel to see whether they correspond to their respective job descriptions.

- **HR/IT employee performance review process** The IS auditor should review the process and procedures used for employee performance reviews. In particular, the IS auditor should view actual performance goals and review documents to see how well individual employees' goals align with IT department objectives. Further, any performance problems identified in performance reviews can be compared with documents that describe the outcomes of key IT projects.

- **HR promotion policy** It will be helpful for the IS auditor to determine whether the organization has a policy (written or not) of promoting from within. In other words, when positions become available, does the organization first look within its ranks for potential candidates, or are new hires typically outsiders? This will influence both employee morale and the overall effectiveness of the IT organization.

- **HR manuals** Documents such as the employee handbook, corporate policies, and HR procedures related to hiring, performance evaluation, and termination should exist,; reflect regular management reviews; and reflect practices that meet the organization's business needs.

- **Life cycle processes and procedures** Processes such as the software development life cycle and change management should reflect the needs of IT governance. The IS auditor should request records from the software development life cycle (specifically, documents that describe specific changes to IT systems and supporting infrastructure) and change management process to see how changes mandated at the steering group level are carried out.

- **IT operations procedures** IT operations process documents for activities such as service desk, monitoring, and computer and network operations should exist. The IS auditor should request records for these activities to determine whether these processes are active.

- **IT procurement process** An IT organization needs to take a consistent and effective approach to the procurement process. The process should reflect management attention to requirements development, bidding, vendor selection, and due diligence so that any supplier risks are identified and mitigated in the procurement phase and reflected in the service agreement contract. The goods and services provided by suppliers should be required to adhere to the organization's IT policies, processes, and standards; exceptions should be handled in an exception process. Records should exist that reflect ongoing attention to this process.

- **Quality management documents** An IT organization that is committed to quality and improvement will have documents and records to support this objective.

- **Business continuity and disaster recovery documents** Documents such as the business impact assessment, critical assessment, and statements of impact, as well as evidence of periodic updates to recovery documentation and regular testing.

Like any other facets of an audit, the IS auditor needs to conduct several interviews and walkthroughs to gain a level of confidence that these documents reflect the actual management and operations of an IT organization. These interviews should include staff from all levels of management, as well as key end users who can also attest to IT's organization and commitment to its governance program and the maturity of its processes.

NOTE The IS auditor should also review the processes related to the regular review and update of IT governance documents. Regular reviews attest to active management involvement in IT governance. The lack of recent reviews might suggest that management began a governance program but has subsequently lost interest in it.

Auditing Contracts

The IS auditor who is examining IT governance needs to examine the service agreements between the organization and its key IT-related suppliers. Contracts should contain several items:

- **Service levels**   Contracts should contain a section on acceptable service levels and the process followed when service interruptions occur. Service outages should include an escalation path so that management can obtain information from appropriate levels of the supplier's management team.

- **Quality levels**   Contracts should contain specifications on the quality of goods or services delivered, as well as remedies when quality standards are not met.

- **Right to audit**   Contracts should include a right-to-audit clause that permits the organization to examine the supplier's premises and records upon reasonable notice.

- **Third-party audits**   Contracts should include provisions that require the supplier to undergo appropriate and regular audits. Audit reports from these audits should be available upon request, including remediation plans for any significant findings found in the audit reports.

- **Conformance to security policies**   Suppliers should be required to provide goods or services that can meet the organization's security policies. For instance, if the organization's security policy requires specific password-quality standards, then the goods or services from suppliers should be able to meet those standards.

- **Protection and use of sensitive information**   Contracts should include detailed statements that describe how the organization's sensitive information will be protected and used. This is primarily relevant in an online, SaaS (Software as a Service), or ASP (application service provider) model where some of the organization's data will reside on systems or networks that are under the control of a supplier. The contract should include details that describe how the supplier tests its controls to ensure that they are still effective. Third-party audits of these controls may also be warranted, depending upon the sensitivity of the information in question.

- **Compliance with laws and regulations**   Contracts should require that the supplier conform to all relevant laws and regulations. This should include laws and regulations that the organization itself is required to comply with; in other words, compliance with laws and regulations should flow to and include suppliers. For example, if a health-care organization is required to comply with HIPAA (Health Insurance Portability and Accountability Act, a U.S. law that requires specific protections of patient health-care information when in electronic form), any suppliers that store or manage the organization's health-care–related information must be required to also be in compliance with HIPAA regulations.

- **Incident notification** Contracts should contain specific language that describes how incidents are handled and how the organization is notified of incidents. This includes not only service changes and interruptions, but also security incidents. The supplier should be required to notify the organization within a specific period, and also provide periodic updates as needed.

- **Source code escrow** If the supplier is a software organization that uses proprietary software as a means for providing services, the supplier should be required to regularly deposit its software source code into a software escrow. A software escrow firm is a third-party organization that will place software into a vault and release it to customer organizations in the event of the failure of the supplier's business.

- **Liabilities** Contracts should clearly state which parties are liable for which actions and activities. They should further specify the remedies taken should any party fail to perform adequately.

- **Termination terms** Contracts should contain reasonable provisions that describe the actions taken if the business relationship is terminated.

 NOTE While the IS auditor may not be required to understand the nuances of legal contracts, the auditor should look for these sections in contracts with key suppliers. The IS auditor should also look for other contractual provisions in supplier contracts that are specific to any unique or highly critical needs that are provided by a supplier.

Auditing Outsourcing

When an auditor is auditing an organization's key processes and systems, those processes and systems that are outsourced require just as much (if not more) scrutiny than if they were performed by the organization's own staff using its own assets. However, it may be difficult to audit the services provided by a third-party supplier for several reasons:

- **Distance** The supplier may be located in a remote region, and travel to the supplier's location may be costly.

- **Lack of audit contract terms** The organization may not have a clause in its contract with the supplier that requires cooperation with auditors. While it may be said that the organization should have negotiated a right-to-audit clause, this point may be moot at the time of the audit.

- **Lack of cooperation** The supplier might not cooperate with the organization's auditors. Noncooperation takes many forms, including taking excessive time to return inquiries and providing incomplete or inadequate records. An audit report may include one or more findings (nonconformities) related to the lack of cooperation; this may provide sufficient leverage to force the supplier to improve its cooperation or for the organization to look for a new supplier.

An ideal situation is one where a supplier undergoes regular third-party audits that are relevant to the services provided and where the supplier makes those audit results available on request.

Auditing Business Continuity Planning

Audits of an organization's business continuity plan are especially difficult because it is impossible to prove whether the plans will work unless there is a real disaster.

The IT auditor has quite a task when it comes to auditing an organization's business continuity. The lion's share of the audit results hinges on the quality of documentation and walkthroughs with key personnel.

As is typical with most audit activities, an audit of an organization's BC program is a top-down analysis of key business objectives and a review of documentation and interviews to determine whether the BC strategy and program details support those key business objectives. This approach is depicted in Figure 2-16.

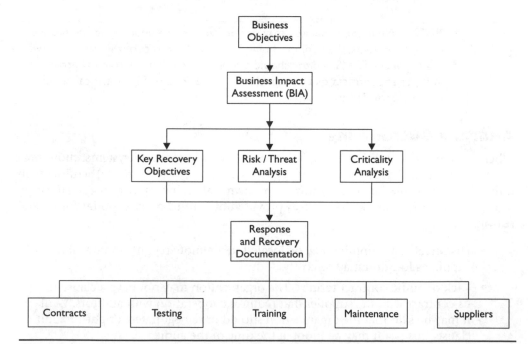

Figure 2-16 Top-down approach to an audit of business continuity

The objectives of an audit of business continuity planning should include the following activities:

- Obtain documentation that describes current business strategies and objectives. Obtain high-level documentation (for example, strategy, charter, objectives) for the BC program, and determine whether the BC program supports business strategies and objectives.

- Obtain the most recent BIA and accompanying threat analysis, risk analysis, and criticality analysis. Determine whether these documents are current, complete, and support the BC strategy. Also determine whether the scope of these documents covers those activities considered strategic according to high-level business objectives. Finally, determine whether the methods in these documents represent good practices for these activities.

- Determine whether key personnel are ready to respond during a disaster by reviewing test plans and training plans and results. Find out where emergency procedures are stored and whether key personnel have access to them.

- Verify whether there is a process for the regular review and update of BC documentation. Evaluate the process's effectiveness by reviewing records to see how frequently documents are being reviewed.

These activities are described in more detail in the following sections.

Auditing Business Continuity Plans

The bulk of an organization's business continuity plan lies in its documentation, so it should be of little surprise that the bulk of the audit effort will lie in the examination of this documentation. The following steps will help the auditor to determine the effectiveness of the organization's BC plans:

- Obtain a copy of business continuity documentation, including response procedures, contact lists, and communication plans.

- Examine samples of distributed copies of BC documentation, and determine whether they are up-to-date. These samples can be obtained during interviews of key response personnel, which are covered in this procedure.

- Determine whether all documents are clear and easy to understand, not just for primary responders, but for alternate personnel who may have specific relevant skills but less familiarity with the organization's critical applications.

- Examine documentation related to the declaration of a disaster and the initiation of disaster response. Determine whether the methods for declaration are likely to be effective in a disaster scenario.

- Obtain emergency contact information, and contact some of the personnel to see whether the contact information is accurate and up-to-date. Also determine whether all response personnel are still employed in the organization and that they are in the same or similar roles in support of disaster response efforts.

- Contact some or all of the response personnel who are listed in emergency contact lists. Interview them and see how well they understand their disaster response responsibilities and whether they are familiar with disaster response procedures. Ask each interviewee if they have a copy of these procedures. See if their copies are current.

- Determine whether a process exists for the formal review and update of business continuity documentation. Examine records to see how frequently, and how recently, documents have been reviewed and updated.

- Determine whether response personnel receive any formal or informal training on response and recovery procedures. Determine whether personnel are required to receive training and whether any records are kept that show which personnel received training and at what time.

Reviewing Prior Test Results and Action Plans

Effectiveness of business continuity plans relies, to a great degree, on the results and outcomes of tests. An IS auditor needs to carefully examine these tests to determine their effectiveness and to what degree they are used to improve procedures and to train personnel. The following procedure will help the IS auditor to determine the effectiveness of business continuity testing:

- Determine whether there is a strategy for testing business continuity procedures. Obtain records for past tests and a plan for future tests. Determine whether prior tests and planned tests are adequate for establishing the effectiveness of response and recovery procedures.

- Examine records for tests that have been performed over the past year or two. Determine the types of tests that were performed. Obtain a list of participants for each test. Compare the participants to lists of key recovery personnel. Examine test work papers to determine the level of participation by key recovery personnel.

- Determine whether there is a formal process for recording test results and for using those results to make improvements in plans and procedures. Examine work papers and records to determine the types of changes that were recommended in prior tests. Examine BC documents to see whether these changes were made as expected.

- Considering the types of tests that were performed, determine the adequacy of testing as an indicator of the effectiveness of the BC program. Did the organization only perform document reviews and walkthroughs, for example, or did the organization also perform parallel or cutover tests?

- If tests have been performed for two years or more, determine whether there's a trend showing continuous improvement in response and recovery procedures.

- If the organization performs parallel tests, determine whether tests are designed in a way that effectively determines the actual readiness of standby systems. Also determine whether parallel tests measure the capacity of standby systems or merely their ability to process correctly but at a lower level of performance.

Interviewing Key Personnel

The knowledge and experience of key personnel are vital to the success of any disaster response operation. Interviews will help the IT auditor determine whether key personnel are prepared and trained to respond during a disaster. The following procedure will guide the IT auditor in interviews:

- Obtain the name, title, tenure, and full contact information for each person interviewed.

- Ask the interviewee to summarize his or her professional experience and training and current responsibilities in the organization.

- Ask the interviewee whether he or she is familiar with the organization's business continuity and disaster recovery programs.

- Determine whether the interviewee is among the key response personnel expected to respond during a disaster.

- Ask the interviewee if he or she has been issued a copy of any response or recovery procedures. If so, ask to see those procedures; determine whether they are current versions. Ask if the interviewee has additional sets of procedures in any other locations (residence, for example).

- Ask the interviewee if he or she has received any training. Request evidence of this training (certificate, calendar entry, and so on).

- Ask the interviewee if he or she has participated in any tests or evaluations of recovery and response procedures. Ask the interviewee whether he or she felt the tests were effective, whether management takes the tests seriously, and whether any deficiencies in tests resulted in any improvements to test procedures or other documents.

Reviewing Service Provider Contracts

No organization is an island. Every organization has critical suppliers without which it could not carry out its critical functions. The ability to recover from a disaster also frequently requires the support of one or more service providers or suppliers. The IT auditor should examine contracts for all critical suppliers and consider the following guidelines:

- Does the contract support the organization's requirements for delivery of services and supplies, even in the event of a local or regional disaster?

- Determine whether the service provider has its own disaster recovery capabilities that will ensure its ability to deliver critical services during a disaster.

- Determine the recourse available should the supplier be unable to provide goods or services during a disaster.

Reviewing Insurance Coverage

The IT auditor should examine the organization's insurance policies related to the loss of property and assets supporting critical business processes. Insurance coverage should cover the actual cost of recovery, or a lesser amount if the organization's executive management has accepted a lower amount. The IT auditor should obtain documentation that includes cost estimates for various disaster recovery scenarios, including equipment replacement, business interruption, and the cost of performing business functions and operating IT systems in alternate sites. These cost estimates should be compared with the value of insurance policies.

Summary

IT governance is the top-down management and control of an IT organization. Governance is usually undertaken through a steering committee that consists of executives from throughout the organization. The steering committee is responsible for setting overall strategic direction and policy, ensuring that IT strategy is in alignment with the organization's strategy and objectives. The wishes of the steering committee are carried out through projects and tasks that steer the IT organization toward strategic objectives. The steering committee can monitor IT progress through a balanced scorecard.

Enterprise architecture provides a meaningful way to depict complex IT environments in functional terms. The Zachman framework is most often used to represent IT architecture in various layers of detail. Similarly, data flow diagrams illustrate the relationship between IT applications.

The IT steering committee is responsible for IT strategic planning. The IT steering committee will develop and approve IT policies, and appoint managers to develop and maintain processes, procedures, and standards, all of which should align with each other and with the organization's overall strategy.

Security governance is accomplished using the same means as IT governance: it begins with board-level involvement that sets the tone for risk appetite and is carried out through the chief information security officer (CISO), who develops security and privacy policies, as well as strategic security programs, including incident management, vulnerability management, and identity and access management.

Risk management is the practice of identifying key assets and the vulnerabilities they may possess and the threats that may harm them if permitted. This is accomplished through a risk assessment that identifies assets, threats, and vulnerabilities in detail, and is followed by specific risk treatment strategies used to mitigate, transfer, avoid, or accept risks. A risk assessment may be qualitative, where threats and risks are labeled on scales such as "high," "medium," and "low"; or it may be quantitative, where risks are expressed in financial terms.

Key management practices will help ensure that the IT organization will operate effectively. These practices include *personnel management*, which encompasses the hiring, development, and evaluation of employees, as well as onboarding and offboarding processes, and development of the employee handbook and other policies. Another key practice area is *sourcing*, which is the management of determining where and by whom key business processes will be performed; the basic choices are insourced or outsourced and on-site or off-site. The third key practice area is *change management*, the formal process whereby changes are applied to IT environments in a way that reduces risk and ensures highest reliability. The next practice area is *financial management*, a key area, given that IT organizations are cost-intensive and require planning and analysis to guarantee the best use of financial resources. Another practice area is *quality management*, where processes are carefully measured and managed so that they may be continuously improved over time. The next practice area is *security management*, which encompasses several activities, including risk assessments, incident management, vulnerability management, access and identity management, compliance management, and business continuity planning.

The IT organization should have a formal management and reporting structure, as well as established roles and responsibilities, and written job descriptions. Roles and responsibilities should address the need for segregation of duties to ensure that high-value and high-risk tasks are carried out by two or more persons and recorded.

Natural and man-made disasters can damage business facilities, assets, and information systems, thus threatening the viability of the organization by halting its critical processes. Even without direct effects, many secondary or indirect effects from a disaster such as crippled transportation systems, damaged communications systems, and damaged public utilities can seriously harm an organization. The development of business continuity plans helps an organization to be better prepared to act when a disaster strikes. A vital part of this preparation is the development of alternative means for continuing the most critical activities, usually in alternative locations that are not damaged by a disaster.

There is an accepted methodology to business continuity and disaster recovery planning, which begins with the development of a business continuity planning policy, a statement of the goals and objectives of a planning effort. This is followed by a BIA, a study of the organization's business processes to determine which are the most critical to the organization's ongoing viability. For each critical process, a statement of impact is developed, which is a brief description of the effect on the organization if the process is incapacitated for any significant period. The statement of impact can be qualitative or quantitative.

A criticality analysis is performed next, where all in-scope business processes are ranked in order of criticality. Ranking can be strictly quantitative, qualitative, or even subjective.

Next, recovery targets for each critical business process are developed. The key targets are RTO and RPO. These targets specify time to system restoration and maximum data loss, respectively. When these targets have been established, the project team can develop plans that include changes to technical architecture as well as business processes that will help achieve these established recovery objectives.

The effectiveness of business continuity plans can only be determined by testing. There are five types of tests: document review, walkthrough, simulation, parallel test, and cutover test. These five tests represent progressively more complex (and risky) means for testing procedures and IT systems to determine whether they will be able to actually support critical business processes in a real disaster. The parallel test involves the use of backup IT systems in a way that enables them to process real business transactions while primary systems continue to perform the organization's real work. The cutover test actually transitions business data processing to backup IT systems, where they will process actual business workload for a period.

Response personnel need to be carefully chosen from available staff to ensure that sufficient numbers of personnel will be available in a real disaster. Some personnel may be unable to respond for a variety of reasons that are related to the disaster itself. As a result, some of the personnel who respond in an actual disaster may not be as familiar with the systems and procedures required to recover and maintain them. This makes training and accurate procedures critical for effective disaster recovery.

The IS auditor who is auditing IT governance and risk management needs to examine organization policies, processes, and records that reflect active involvement by steering committees, management, and staff. The IS auditor must determine whether the IT organization is operating in alignment with overall organization objectives and according to the wishes of executive management.

Auditing an organization's business continuity capabilities involves the examination of BCP policies, plans, and procedures, as well as contracts and technical architectures. The IT auditor also needs to interview response personnel to gauge their readiness and to visit off-site media storage and alternate processing sites to identify risks present there.

Notes

- IT executives and the board of directors are responsible for imposing an IT governance model encompassing IT strategy, information security, and formal enterprise architectural mandates.

- Strategic planning is accomplished by the steering committee, addressing the near-term and long-term requirements aligning business objectives and technology strategies.

- Policies, procedures, and standards allow validation of business practices against acceptable measures of regulatory compliance, performance, and standard operational guidelines.

- Risk management involves the identification of potential risk and the appropriate response for each threat based on impact assessment using qualitative and/or quantitative measures for an enterprise-wide risk management strategy.

- Assigned IT management roles ensure that resource allocation, enterprise performance, and operational capabilities coordinate with business requirements by validating alignment with standards and procedures for change management and compliance with sourcing, financial, quality, and security controls.

- Formal organizational structure ensures alignment between operational roles and responsibilities within the enterprise, where a separation of duties ensures individual accountability and validation of policy alignment between coordinated team members.

- Business continuity planning ensures business recovery following a disaster. Business continuity focuses on maintaining service availability with the least disruption to standard operating parameters during an event, while disaster recovery focuses on post-event recovery and restoration of services.

- The BCP process encompasses a life cycle beginning with the initial BCP policy, followed by business impact and criticality analysis to evaluate risk and impact factors. Recovery targets facilitate the development of strategies for continuity and recovery, which then must be tested and conveyed to operation personnel through training and exercise. Post-implementation maintenance includes periodic reviews and updates as part of the enterprise continuous-improvement process.

- The business impact analysis (BIA) measures the impact on enterprise operation posed by various identified areas of risk. The output of the BIA is used in the criticality analysis (CA), which measures the impact of each risk against its likelihood and the cost of mitigation.

- The output of the BIA and CA is used when establishing recovery time objectives (RTOs) and recovery point objectives (RPOs), which can then be measured against relative cost scenarios for each identified risk and mitigation option.

- Recovery time objectives (RTOs) and recovery point objectives (RPOs) are fed into the disaster recovery process so that staff can develop resilient and recoverable IT architectures supporting critical business processes.

- BC plans must be tested to validate effectiveness through document review, walkthrough, simulation, parallel testing, or cutover testing practices. Regular testing must take place to ensure new objectives and procedures meet the requirements of a living enterprise environment. Participation in these tests provides familiarity and training for engaged operational staff members, raising understanding and awareness of requirements and responsibilities.

- Regular audit of the IT governance process ensures alignment with regulatory and business mandates in the evolving enterprise by ensuring all documentation, contracts, and sourcing policies are reviewed and updated to meet changes in the living enterprise.

Questions

1. IT governance is most concerned with:

   A. Security policy

   B. IT policy

   C. IT strategy

   D. IT executive compensation

2. One of the advantages of outsourcing is:

   A. It permits the organization to focus on core competencies.

   B. It provides reduced costs.

   C. It provides greater control over work performed by the outsourcing agency.

   D. It eliminates segregation of duties issues.

3. An external IS auditor has discovered a segregation of duties issue in a high-value process. What is the best action for the auditor to take?

   A. Implement a preventive control.

   B. Implement a detective control.

   C. Implement a compensating control.

   D. Document the matter in the audit report.

4. An organization has chosen to open a business office in another country where labor costs are lower and has hired workers to perform business functions there. This organization has:

   A. Outsourced the function

   B. Outsourced the function offshore

   C. Insourced the function on-site

   D. Insourced the function at a remote location

5. What is the purpose of a criticality analysis?

   A. Determine feasible recovery targets.

   B. Determine which staff members are the most critical.

   C. Determine which business processes are the most critical.

   D. Determine maximum tolerable downtime.

6. An organization needs to better understand whether one of its key business processes is effective. What action should the organization consider?

   A. Audit the process.

   B. Benchmark the process.

   C. Outsource the process.

   D. Offshore the process.

7. Annualized loss expectancy (ALE) is defined as:

    A. Single loss expectancy (SLE) times annualized rate of occurrence (ARO)

    B. Exposure factor (EF) times the annualized rate of occurrence (ARO)

    C. Single loss expectancy (SLE) times the exposure factor (EF)

    D. Asset value (AV) times the single loss expectancy (SLE)

8. A quantitative risk analysis is more difficult to perform because:

    A. It is difficult to get accurate figures on the impact of a realized threat.

    B. It is difficult to get accurate figures on the frequency of specific threats.

    C. It is difficult to get accurate figures on the value of assets.

    D. It is difficult to calculate the annualized loss expectancy of a specific threat.

9. A collection of servers that is designed to operate as a single logical server is known as a:

    A. Cluster

    B. Grid

    C. Cloud

    D. Replicant

10. The purpose of a balanced scorecard is to:

    A. Measure the efficiency of an IT organization

    B. Evaluate the performance of individual employees

    C. Benchmark a process in the organization against peer organizations

    D. Measure organizational performance and effectiveness against strategic goals

11. An organization has discovered that some of its employees have criminal records. What is the best course of action for the organization to take?

    A. Terminate the employees with criminal records.

    B. Immediately perform background checks, including criminal history, on all existing employees.

    C. Immediately perform background checks, including criminal history, on all new employees.

    D. Immediately perform background checks on those employees with criminal records.

12. The options for risk treatment are:

    A. Risk mitigation, risk reduction, and risk acceptance

    B. Risk mitigation, risk reduction, risk transfer, and risk acceptance

    C. Risk mitigation, risk avoidance, risk transfer, and risk acceptance

    D. Risk mitigation, risk avoidance, risk transfer, and risk conveyance

13. An IS auditor is examining the IT standards document for an organization that was last reviewed two years earlier. The best course of action for the IS auditor is:

   A. Locate the IT policy document and see how frequently IT standards should be reviewed.

   B. Compare the standards with current practices and make a determination of adequacy.

   C. Report that IT standards are not being reviewed often enough.

   D. Report that IT standards are adequate.

14. The most important step in the process of outsourcing a business function is:

   A. Developing a business case

   B. Measuring the cost savings

   C. Measuring the change in risk

   D. Performing due diligence on the external service provider

15. An organization has published a new security policy. What is the best course of action for the organization to undertake to ensure that all employees will support the policy?

   A. The company CEO should send an e-mail to all employees, instructing them to support the policy.

   B. The company should provide training on the new security policy.

   C. The company should publish the policy on an internal website.

   D. The company should require all employees to sign a statement agreeing to support the policy.

Answers

1. **C.** IT governance is the mechanism through which IT strategy is established, controlled, and monitored through the balanced scorecard. Long-term and other strategic decisions are made in the context of IT governance.

2. **A.** Outsourcing is an opportunity for the organization to focus on its core competencies. When an organization outsources a business function, it no longer needs to be concerned about training employees in that function. Outsourcing does not always reduce costs, because cost reduction is not always the primary purpose for outsourcing in the first place.

3. **D.** The external auditor can only document the finding in the audit report. An external auditor is not in a position to implement controls.

4. **D.** An organization that opens a business office in another country and staffs the office with its own employees is not outsourcing, but is insourcing. Outsourcing is the practice of using contract labor, which is clearly not the

case in this example. In this case, the insourcing is taking place at a remote location.

5. **C.** A criticality analysis is used to determine which business processes are the most critical by ranking them in order of criticality.

6. **B.** An organization that needs to better understand whether a key process is effective should consider benchmarking the process. This will help the organization better understand whether its approach is similar to that of other organizations.

7. **A.** Annualized loss expectancy (ALE) is the annual expected loss to an asset. It is calculated as the single loss expectancy (SLE—the financial loss experienced when the loss is realized one time) times the annualized rate of occurrence (ARO—the number of times that the organization expects the loss to occur).

8. **B.** The most difficult part of a quantitative risk analysis is determining the probability that a threat will actually be realized. It is relatively easy to determine the value of an asset and the impact of a threat event.

9. **A.** A server cluster is a collection of two or more servers that is designed to appear as a single server.

10. **D.** The balanced scorecard is a tool that is used to quantify the performance of an organization against strategic objectives. The focus of a balanced scorecard is financial, customer, internal processes, and innovation/learning.

11. **B.** An organization that has discovered that some employees have criminal records should have background checks performed on all existing employees, and also begin instituting background checks (which should include criminal history) for all new employees. It is not necessarily required to terminate these employees; the specific criminal offenses may not warrant termination.

12. **C.** The options for risk treatment are the actions that management will take when a risk has been identified. The options are risk mitigation (where the risk is reduced), risk avoidance (where the activity is discontinued), risk transfer (where the risk is transferred to an insurance company), and risk acceptance (where management agrees to accept the risk as-is).

13. **C.** IT standards that have not been reviewed for two years are out of date. If the IS auditor finds an IT policy that says that IT standards can be reviewed every two years, then there is a problem with IT policy as well; two years is far too long between reviews of IT standards.

14. **A.** Development of a business case is the most important step when considering the outsourcing of a business function. The other items (measuring cost savings and changes in risk, and performing due diligence on service providers) are parts of development of a business case.

15. **D.** All employees should be required to sign a statement agreeing to support the policy. The other actions are important but less effective.

The Audit Process

This chapter discusses the following topics
  • Audit management
  • ISACA auditing standards, procedures, and guidelines
  • Audit and risk analysis
  • Internal controls
  • Performing an audit

This chapter covers CISA Domain 1, "The Process of Auditing Information Systems." The topics in this chapter represent 14 percent of the CISA examination.

The IS audit process is the procedural structure used by auditors to assess and evaluate the effectiveness of the IT organization and how well it supports the organization's overall goals and objectives. The audit process is backed up by the framework that is the ISACA code of ethics, audit standards, guidelines, and audit procedures. This framework is used to ensure that auditors will take a consistent approach from one audit to the next throughout the entire industry. This will help to advance the entire audit profession and facilitate its gradual improvement over time.

Audit Management

An organization's audit function should be managed so that an audit charter, strategy, and program can be established; audits performed; recommendations enacted; and auditor independence assured throughout. The audit function should align with the organization's mission and goals, and work well alongside IT governance and operations.

The Audit Charter

As with any formal, managed function in the organization, the audit function should be defined and described in a charter document. The charter should clearly define roles and responsibilities that are consistent with ISACA audit standards and guidelines, including but not limited to ethics, integrity, and independence. The audit function should have sufficient authority that its recommendations will be respected and implemented, but not so much power that the audit tail will wag the IS dog.

The Audit Program

An *audit program* is the term used to describe the audit strategy and audit plans that include scope, objectives, resources, and procedures used to evaluate a set of controls and deliver an audit opinion. You could say that an audit program is the plan for conducting audits over a given period.

The term "program" in audit program is intended to evoke a similar "big picture" point of view as the term *program manager* does. A program manager is responsible for the performance of several related projects in an organization. Similarly, an audit program is the plan for conducting several audits in an organization.

Strategic Audit Planning

The purpose of audit planning is to determine the audit activities that need to take place in the future, including an estimate of the resources (budget and manpower) required to support those activities.

Factors That Affect an Audit

Like security planning, audit planning must take into account several factors:

- **Organization's strategic goals and objectives** The organization's overall goals and objectives should flow down to individual departments and their support of these goals and objectives. These goals and objectives will translate into business processes, technology to support business processes, controls for both the business processes and technologies, and audits of those controls. This is depicted in Figure 3-1.

Figure 3-1
The organization's goals and objectives translate down into audit activities.

- **New organization initiatives**   Closely related to goals and objectives, organizations often embark on new initiatives, whether new products, new services, or new ways of delivering existing products and services.

- **Market conditions**   Changes in the product or service market may have an impact on auditing. For instance, in a product or services market where security is becoming more important, market competitors could decide to voluntarily undergo audits in order to show that their products or services are safer or better than the competition's. Other market players may need to follow suit for competitive parity. Changes in the supply or demand of supply-chain goods or services can also affect auditing.

- **Changes in technology**   Enhancements in the technologies that support business processes may affect business or technical controls, which in turn may affect audit procedures for those controls.

- **Changes in regulatory requirements**   Changes in technologies, markets, or security-related events can result in new or changed regulations. Maintaining compliance may require changes to the audit program. In the 20-year period preceding the publication of this book, many new information security–related regulations have been passed or updated, including the Gramm-Leach-Bliley Act (GLBA), the Sarbanes-Oxley Act, and the Health Insurance Portability and Accountability Act (HIPAA), as well as national and state laws on privacy.

All of the changes listed here usually translate into new business processes or changes in existing business process. Often, this also involves changes to information systems and changes to the controls supporting systems and processes.

Changes in Audit Activities

These external factors may affect auditing in the following ways:

- **New internal audits**   Business and regulatory changes sometimes compel organizations to audit more systems or processes. For instance, after passage of the Sarbanes-Oxley Act of 2002, U.S. publicly traded companies had to begin conducting internal audits of those IT systems that support financial business processes.

- **New external audits**   New regulations or competitive pressures could introduce new external audits. For example, virtually all banks and many merchants had to begin undergoing external Payment Card Industry Data Security Standard (PCI-DSS) audits when that standard was established.

- **Increase in audit scope**   The scope of existing internal or external audits could increase to include more processes or systems.

- **Impacts on business processes**   This could take the form of additional steps in processes or procedures, or additions/changes in recordkeeping or record retention.

Resource Planning

At least once per year, management needs to consider all of the internal and external factors that affect auditing to determine the resources required to support these activities. Primarily, resources will consist of the budget for external audits and manpower for internal audits.

Additional external audits usually require additional man-hours to meet with external auditors; discuss scope; coordinate meetings with process owners and managers; discuss audits with process owners and managers; discuss audit findings with auditors, process owners, and managers; and organize remediation work.

Internal and external audits usually require information systems to track audit activities and store evidence. Taking on additional audit activities may require additional capacity on these systems.

Additional internal audits require all of the previously mentioned factors, plus time for performing the internal audits themselves. All of these details are discussed in this chapter, and in the rest of this book.

Audit and Technology

ISACA auditing standards require that the auditor retain technical competence. With the continuation of technology and business process innovation, auditors need to continue learning about new technologies, how they support business processes, and how they are controlled. Like many professions, IS auditing requires continuing education to stay current with changes in technology.

Some of the ways that an IS auditor can update their knowledge and skills include:

- **ISACA training and conferences**   As the developer of the CISA certification, ISACA offers many valuable training and conference events, including:
  - Computer Audit, Control, and Security Conference (CACS)
  - IT Governance, Risk, and Compliance Conference
  - Information Security and Risk Management Conference
  - ISACA Training Week
- **University courses**   This can include both for-credit and noncredit classes on new technologies. Some universities offer certificate programs on many new technologies; this can give an auditor a real boost of knowledge, skills, and confidence.
- **Vo-tech (vocational-technical) training**   Many organizations offer training in information technologies, including MIS Training Institute, SANS, Intense School, and ISACA.
- **Training webinars**   These events are usually focused on a single topic and last from one to three hours. ISACA and many other organizations offer

training webinars, which are especially convenient since they require no travel and many are offered at no cost.

- **ISACA chapter training**   Many ISACA chapters offer regular training events so that local members can acquire new knowledge and skills where they live.

- **Other security association training**   Many other security-related trade associations offer training, including ISSA (International Systems Security Association), SANS Institute (Systems Administrations, Audit, Network, Security), and CSI (Computer Security Institute). Training sessions are offered online, in classrooms, and at conferences.

- **Security conferences**   Several security-related conferences include lectures and training. These conferences include RSA, SANS, CSI, ISSA, and SecureWorld Expo. Many local ISACA and ISSA chapters organize local conferences that include training.

 EXAM TIP   ISACA requires CISA certification holders to undergo at least 40 hours of training per year in order to maintain their certification. Chapter 1 contains more information on this requirement.

Audit Laws and Regulations

Laws and regulations are one of the primary reasons why organizations perform internal and external audits. Regulations on industries generally translate into additional effort on the part of target companies to track their compliance. This tracking takes on the form of internal auditing, and new regulations sometimes also require external audits. And while other factors such as competitive pressures can compel an organization to begin or increase auditing activities, this section discusses laws and regulations that require auditing.

Automation Brings New Regulation

Automating business processes with information systems is still a relatively new phenomenon. Modern businesses have been around for the past two or three centuries, but information systems have been playing a *major* role in business process automation for only about the past 15 years. Prior to that time, most information systems supported business processes, but only in an ancillary way. Automation of entire business processes is still relatively young, and so many organizations have messed up in such colossal ways that legislators and regulators have responded with additional laws and regulations to make organizations more accountable for the security and integrity of their information systems.

Almost every industry sector is subject to laws and regulations that affect organizations' use of information systems. These laws are concerned primarily with one or more of the following characteristics and uses of information and information systems:

- **Security**   Some information in information systems is valuable and/or sensitive, such as financial and medical records. Many laws and regulations require such information to be protected so that it cannot be accessed by unauthorized parties and that information systems be free of defects, vulnerabilities, malware, and other threats.

- **Integrity**   Some regulations are focused on the integrity of information to ensure that it is correct and that the systems it resides on are free of vulnerabilities and defects that could make or allow improper changes.

- **Privacy**   Many information systems store information that is considered private. This includes financial records, medical records, and other information about people that they feel should be protected.

Computer Security and Privacy Regulations

This section contains several computer security and privacy laws in the United States, Canada, Europe, and elsewhere. The laws here fall into one or more of the following categories:

- **Computer trespass**   Some of these laws bring the concept of trespass forward into the realm of computers and networks, making it illegal to enter a computer or network unless there is explicit authorization.

- **Protection of sensitive information**   Many laws require that sensitive information be protected, and some include required public disclosures in the event of a breach of security.

- **Collection and use of information**   Several laws define the boundaries regarding the collection and acceptable use of information, particularly private information.

- **Offshore data flow**   Some security and privacy laws place restrictions or conditions on the flow of sensitive data (usually about citizens) out of a country.

- **Law enforcement investigative powers**   Some laws clarify and expand the search and investigative powers of law enforcement.

The consequences of the failure to comply with these laws vary. Some laws have penalties written in as a part of the law; however, the absence of an explicit penalty doesn't mean there aren't any! Some of the results of failing to comply include

- **Loss of reputation**   Failure to comply with some laws can make front-page news, with a resulting reduction in reputation and loss of business. For example, if an organization suffers a security breach and is forced to notify customers, word may spread quickly and be picked up by news media outlets, which will help spread the news further.

- **Loss of competitive advantage** An organization that has a reputation for sloppy security may begin to see its business diminish and move to its competitors. A record of noncompliance may also result in a failure to win new business contracts.

- **Government sanctions** Breaking many federal laws may result in sanctions from local, regional, or national governments, including losing the right to conduct business.

- **Lawsuits** Civil lawsuits from competitors, customers, suppliers, and government agencies may be the result of breaking some laws. Plaintiffs may file lawsuits against an organization even if there were other consequences.

- **Fines** Monetary consequences are frequently the result of breaking laws.

- **Prosecution** Many laws have criminalized behavior such as computer trespass, stealing information, or filing falsified reports to government agencies.

Knowledge of these consequences provides an incentive to organizations to develop management strategies to comply with the laws that apply to their business activities. These strategies often result in the development of controls that define required activities and events, plus analysis and internal audit to determine if the controls are effectively keeping the organization in compliance with those laws. While organizations often initially resist undertaking these additional activities, they usually accept them as a requirement for doing business and seek ways of making them more cost-efficient in the long term.

Determining Compliance with Regulations An organization should take a systematic approach to determine the applicability of regulations as well as the steps required to attain compliance and remain in this state.

Determination of applicability often requires the assistance of legal counsel who is an expert on government regulations, as well as experts in the organization who are familiar with the organization's practices.

Next, the language in the law or regulation needs to be analyzed and a list of compliant and noncompliant practices identified. These are then compared with the organization's practices to determine which practices are compliant and which are not. Those practices that are not compliant need to be corrected; one or more accountable individuals need to be appointed to determine what is required to achieve and maintain compliance.

PCI-DSS: A Highly Effective Non-Law

The Payment Card Industry Data Security Standard (PCI-DSS) is a data security standard that was developed by a consortium of the major credit card brands: VISA, MasterCard, American Express, Discover, and JCB. The major brands have the contractual right to levy fines and impose sanctions, such as the loss of the right to issue credit cards, process payments, or accept credit card payments. PCI-DSS has gotten a lot of attention, and by many accounts it has been more effective than many state and national laws.

Regulations Not Always Clear

Sometimes, the effort to determine what's needed to achieve compliance is substantial. For instance, when the Sarbanes-Oxley Act was signed into law, virtually no one knew exactly what companies had to do to achieve compliance. Guidance from the Public Company Accounting Oversight Board was not published for almost a year. It took another two years before audit firms and U.S. public companies were familiar and comfortable with the necessary approach to achieve compliance with the act.

Another approach is to outline the required (or forbidden) practices specified in the law or regulation and then "map" the organization's relevant existing activities into the outline. Where gaps are found, processes or procedures will need to be developed to bring the organization into compliance.

U.S. Regulations   Selected security and privacy laws and standards in the United States include

- Access Device Fraud, 1984
- Computer Fraud and Abuse Act of 1984
- Electronic Communications Act of 1986
- Electronic Communications Privacy Act (ECPA) of 1986
- Computer Security Act of 1987
- Computer Matching and Privacy Protection Act of 1988
- Communications Assistance for Law Enforcement Act (CALEA) of 1994
- Economic and Protection of Proprietary Information Act of 1996
- Health Insurance Portability and Accountability Act (HIPAA) of 1996
- Children's Online Privacy Protection Act (COPPA) of 1998
- Identity Theft and Assumption Deterrence Act of 1998
- Gramm-Leach-Bliley Act (GLBA) of 1999
- Federal Energy Regulatory Commission (FERC)
- Provide Appropriate Tools Required to Intercept and Obstruct Terrorism (PATRIOT) Act of 2001
- Sarbanes-Oxley Act of 2002
- Federal Information Security Management Act (FISMA) of 2002
- Controlling the Assault of Non-Solicited Pornography and Marketing (CAN-SPAM) Act of 2003
- California privacy law SB1386 of 2003
- Identity Theft and Assumption Deterrence Act of 2003

- Basel II, 2004

- Payment Card Industry Data Security Standard (PCI-DSS), 2004; updated 2010

- North American Electric Reliability Corporation (NERC), 1968/2006

- Massachusetts security breach law, 2007

Canadian Regulations   Selected security and privacy laws and standards in Canada include

- Interception of Communications (Section 184 of the Canada Criminal Code)

- Unauthorized Use of Computer (Section 342.1 of the Canada Criminal Code)

- Privacy Act, 1983

- Personal Information Protection and Electronic Documents Act (PIPEDA)

European Regulations   Selected security and privacy laws and standards from Europe include

- Convention for the Protection of Individuals with Regard to Automatic Processing of Personal Data, 1981, Council of Europe

- Computer Misuse Act (CMA), 1990, UK

- Directive on the Protection of Personal Data (95/46/EC), 2003, European Union (this law is expected to be updated or superseded in 2011)

- Data Protection Act (DPA) 1998, UK

- Regulation of Investigatory Powers Act 2000, UK

- Anti-Terrorism, Crime, and Security Act 2001, UK

- Privacy and Electronic Communications Regulations 2003, UK

- Fraud Act 2006, UK

- Police and Justice Act 2006, UK

Other Regulations   Selected security and privacy laws and standards from the rest of the world include

- Cybercrime Act, 2001, Australia

- Information Technology Act, 2000, India

ISACA Auditing Standards

The Information Systems Audit and Control Association (ISACA) has published a code of ethics, a set of IS auditing standards, audit guidelines to help understand the standards, and procedures that can be used when auditing information systems. These are discussed in this section. The relationship between these is illustrated in Figure 3-2.

Figure 3-2
Relationship
between ISACA
audit standards, audit
guidelines, audit
procedures, and
Code of Professional
Ethics

ISACA Code of Professional Ethics

Like many professional associations, ISACA has published a code of professional ethics. The purpose of the code is to define principles of professional behavior that are based on the support of standards, compliance with laws and standards, and the identification and defense of the truth.

Audit and IT professionals who earn the CISA certification are required to sign a statement that declares their support of the ISACA code of ethics. If someone who holds the CISA certification is found to be in violation of the code, he or she may be disciplined and possibly lose his or her certification. The full text of the ISACA code of ethics can be found at www.isaca.org/ethics.

 EXAM TIP   The CISA candidate is not expected to memorize the ISACA Code of Ethics, but is required to understand and be familiar with it.

ISACA Audit Standards

The ISACA audit standards framework defines minimum standards of performance related to security, audits, and the actions that result from audits. This section lists the standards and discusses each.

The full text of these standards is available at www.isaca.org/standards.

 EXAM TIP   ISACA does not require CISA candidates to memorize the risk-IT framework or audit standards, but they should understand its importance and purpose.

S1, Audit Charter
Audit activities in an organization should be formally defined in an audit charter. This should include statements of scope, responsibility, and authority for conducting audits. Senior management should support the audit charter through direct signature or by linking the audit charter to corporate policy.

S2, Independence

Behavior of the IS auditor should be independent of the auditee. The IS auditor should take care to avoid even the appearance of impropriety.

The IS auditor's placement in the command-and-control structure of the organization should ensure that the IS auditor can act independently.

S3, Professional Ethics and Standards

The IS auditor should adhere to the ISACA Code of Professional Ethics as well as other applicable standards. The IS auditor should conduct himself with professionalism and due care.

S4, Professional Competence

The IS auditor should possess all of the necessary skills and knowledge that are related to the processes and technologies being audited. The auditor should receive periodic training and continuing education in the practices and technologies that are related to her work.

S5, Planning

The IS auditor should perform audit planning work to ensure that the scope and breadth of auditing is sufficient to meet the organization's needs. She should develop and maintain documentation related to a risk-based audit process and audit procedures. The auditor should identify applicable laws and develop plans for any required audit activities to ensure compliance.

S6, Performance of Audit Work

IS auditors should be supervised to ensure that their work supports established audit objectives and meets applicable audit standards. IS auditors should obtain and retain appropriate evidence; auditors' findings should reflect analysis and the evidence obtained. The process followed for each audit should be documented and made a part of the audit report.

S7, Reporting

The IS auditor should develop an audit report that documents the process followed, inquiries, observations, evidence, findings, conclusions, and recommendations from the audit. The audit report should follow an established format that includes a statement of scope, period of coverage, recipient organization, controls or standards that were audited, and any limitations or qualifications. The report should contain sufficient evidence to support the findings of the audit.

S8, Follow-up Activities

After the completion of an audit, the IS auditor should follow up at a later time to determine if management has taken steps to make any recommended changes or apply remedies to any audit findings.

S9, Irregularities and Illegal Acts

IS auditors should have a healthy but balanced skepticism with regard to irregularities and illegal acts: The auditor should recognize that irregularities and/or illegal acts could be ongoing in one or more of the processes that he is auditing. He should recognize that management may or may not be aware of any irregularities or illegal acts.

The IS auditor should obtain written attestations from management that state management's responsibilities for the proper operation of controls. Management should disclose to the auditor any knowledge of irregularities or illegal acts.

If the IS auditor encounters material irregularities or illegal acts, he should document every conversation and retain all evidence of correspondence. The IS auditor should report any matter of material irregularities or illegal acts to management. If material findings or irregularities prevent the auditor from continuing the audit, the auditor should carefully weigh his options and consider withdrawing from the audit. The IS auditor should determine if he is required to report material findings to regulators or other outside authorities. If the auditor is unable to report material findings to management, he should consider withdrawing from the audit engagement.

S10, IT Governance

The IS auditor should determine if the IT organization supports the organization's mission, goals, objectives, and strategies. This should include whether the organization had clear expectations of performance from the IT department.

The auditor should determine if the IT organization is compliant with all applicable policies, laws, regulations, and contractual obligations. She should use a risk-based approach when evaluating the IT organization.

The IS auditor should determine if the control environment used in the IT organization is effective and should identify risks that may adversely affect IT department operations.

S11, Use of Risk Assessment in Audit Planning

The IS auditor should use a risk-based approach when making decisions about which controls and activities should be audited and the level of effort expended in each audit. These decisions should be documented in detail to avoid any appearance of partiality.

A risk-based approach does not look only at security risks, but overall business risk. This will probably include operational risk and may include aspects of financial risk.

S12, Audit Materiality

The IS auditor should consider materiality when prioritizing audit activities and allocating audit resources. During audit planning, the auditor should consider whether ineffective controls or an absence of controls could result in a significant deficiency or material weakness.

In addition to auditing individual controls, the auditor should consider the effectiveness of groups of controls and determine if a failure across a group of controls would constitute a significant deficiency or material weakness. For example, if an organization has several controls regarding the management and control of third-party service organizations, failures in many of those controls could represent a significant deficiency or material weakness overall.

S13, Use the Work of Other Experts

An IS auditor should consider using the work of other auditors when and where appropriate. Whether an auditor can use the work of other auditors depends on several factors, including

- The relevance of the other auditors' work

- The qualifications and independence of the other auditors

- Whether the other auditors' work is adequate (this will require an evaluation of at least some of the other auditors' work)

- Whether the IS auditor should develop additional test procedures to supplement the work of another auditor(s)

If an IS auditor uses another auditor's work, his report should document which portion of the audit work was performed by the other auditor, as well as an evaluation of that work.

S14, Audit Evidence

The IS auditor should gather sufficient evidence to develop reasonable conclusions about the effectiveness of controls and procedures. The sufficiency and integrity of audit evidence should be evaluated, and this evaluation should be included in the audit report.

Audit evidence includes the procedures performed by the auditor during the audit, the results of those procedures, source documents and records, and corroborating information. Audit evidence also includes the audit report.

S15, IT Controls

The IS auditor should evaluate and monitor those IT controls that are key to the organization's internal control environment. These controls are the policies, procedures, characteristics of information systems, and the organization's chain of command that work together to achieve the organization's business objectives.

The IS auditor should conduct risk assessments and develop audit plans to closely examine the organization's IT controls, and develop conclusions on whether each control is effective. Where the organization uses third parties to achieve controls, the auditor should evaluate the work of the third party, directly or through reliance on the work of other auditors.

The IS auditor should help the organization improve its controls by giving advice regarding the design, implementation, and operation of its controls.

S16, E-commerce

The IS auditor should evaluate all relevant controls in an organization's e-commerce environment to ensure that e-commerce transactions are controlled.

ISACA defines e-commerce as "the processes by which organizations conduct business electronically with their customers, suppliers, and other external business parties, using the Internet as an enabling technology." This includes both business-to-customer transactions as well as business-to-business transactions.

The IS auditor needs to thoroughly understand how an organization's e-commerce environment works, understand its controls, and evaluate those controls through internal audit testing.

ISACA Audit Guidelines

ISACA audit guidelines contain information that helps the auditor understand how to apply ISACA audit standards. These guidelines are a series of articles that clarify the meaning of the audit standards. They cite specific ISACA IS audit standards and COBIT controls, and provide specific guidance on various audit activities. ISACA audit guidelines also provide insight into why each guideline was developed and published.

The full text of these guidelines is available at www.isaca.org/standards.

G1, Using the Work of Other Auditors
Written June 1998, updated March 2008. Clarifies Standard S13, Using the Work of Other Experts; and Standard S6, Performance of Audit Work.

Explores details regarding using the work of other auditors, including assessing their qualifications, independence, relevance, and the level of review required.

G2, Audit Evidence Requirement
Written December 1998, updated May 2008. Clarifies Standard S6, Performance of Audit Work; Standard S9, Irregularities and Illegal Acts; Standard S13, Using the Work of Other Experts; and Standard S14, Audit Evidence.

Provides additional details regarding types of evidence, how evidence can be represented, and selecting and gathering evidence.

G3, Use of Computer-Assisted Audit Techniques (CAATs)
Written December 1998, updated March 2008. Clarifies Standard S6, Performance of Audit Work, Standard S5, Planning, Standard S3, Professional Ethics and Standards, Standard S7, Reporting, and Standard S14, Audit Evidence.

Provides details on the use of CAATs, whose use is increasing. In some information systems, CAATs provide the majority of available evidence. This guideline provides direction on the reliability of CAAT-based evidence, automated and customized test scripts, software tracing and mapping, expert systems, and continuous monitoring.

G4, Outsourcing of IS Activities to Other Organizations
Written September 1999, updated May 2008. Clarifies Standard S1, Audit Charter; Standard S5, Planning; and Standard S6, Performance of Audit Work.

Includes additional granularity for auditing outsourced IS activities, including examination of legal contracts and SLAs and service management.

G5, Audit Charter

Written September 1999, updated February 2008. Clarifies Standard S1, Audit Charter.

Guidance provides additional weight on the need for an audit mandate and additional details on the contents of an audit charter, including purpose, responsibilities, authority, accountability, communication with auditees, and quality assurance. Also includes details on the contents of an engagement letter.

G6, Materiality Concepts for Auditing Information Systems

Written September 1999, updated May 2008. Clarifies Standard S5, Planning; Standard S10, IT Governance; Standard S12, Audit Materiality; and Standard S9, Irregularities and Illegal Acts.

While financial audits can easily focus on materiality, IS audits focus on other topics, such as access controls and change management. This guidance includes information on how to determine materiality of audits of IS controls.

G7, Due Professional Care

Written September 1999, updated March 2008. Clarifies Standard S2, Independence; Standard S3, Professional Ethics and Standards; and Standard S4, Professional Competence.

This provides guidance to IS auditors for applying auditing standards and the ISACA Code of Professional Ethics on performance of duties with due diligence and professional care. This guidance helps the IS auditor better understand how to have good professional judgment in difficult situations.

G8, Audit Documentation

Written September 1999, updated March 2008. Clarifies Standard S5, Planning; Standard S6, Performance of Audit Work; Standard S7, Reporting; Standard S12, Audit Materiality; and Standard S13, Using the Work of Other Experts.

This guideline provides considerably more detail on the specific documentation needs for an IS audit. This includes providing additional information regarding the auditor's assessment methods and retention of audit documents.

G9, Audit Considerations for Irregularities and Illegal Acts

Written March 2000, updated September 2008. Clarifies Standard S3, Professional Ethics and Standards; Standard S5, Planning; Standard S6, Performance of Audit Work; Standard S7, Reporting; and Standard S9, Irregularities and Illegal Acts.

This guideline adds more color to ISACA audit standards for situations that the IS auditor may encounter, including nonfraudulent irregularities, fraud, and illegal acts. The guideline defines additional responsibilities of management and IS auditors when dealing with irregularities and illegal acts.

The guideline also describes the steps in a risk assessment that includes the identification of risks that are related to irregularities and illegal acts. Next, the guideline details the actions that an IS auditor should follow when encountering illegal acts, including internal and external reporting where required by law.

G10, Audit Sampling

Written March 2000, updated August 2008. Clarifies Standard S6, Performance of Audit Work.

This provides guidance on objective, statistically sound sampling techniques; sample design and selection; and evaluation of the sample selection.

G11, Effect of Pervasive IS Controls

Written March 2000, updated August 2008. Clarifies Standard S6, Performance of Audit Work.

Pervasive controls are those general controls that focus on the management and monitoring of information systems. Examples of pervasive controls are

- IS strategy
- Software development/acquisition life cycle
- Access management
- Security administration
- Capacity management
- Backup and recovery

This guideline helps the auditor understand the pervasive controls that should be a part of every organization's control framework. The IS auditor needs to determine the set of pervasive controls in her organization—they can be derived from the four COBIT domains: Plan and Organize (PO), Acquire and Implement (AI), Deliver and Support (DS), and Monitor and Evaluate (ME). It is no accident that these match up to the Deming Cycle process of Plan, Do, Check, Act.

G12, Organizational Relationship and Independence

Written September 2000, updated August 2008. Clarifies Standard S2, Independence; and Standard S3, Professional Ethics and Standards.

This guideline expands on the concept and practice of auditor independence so that the auditor can better understand how to apply audit standards and perform audits objectively and independently.

G13, Use of Risk Assessment in Audit Planning

Written September 2000, updated August 2008. Clarifies Standard S5, Planning; and Standard S6, Performance of Audit Work.

This guideline provides direction for the IS auditor to properly determine the risk associated with each control and related activity in the IS organization. Such guidance has been available for financial auditors, but was not readily available to IS auditors until publication of this guideline.

Rather than rely solely on judgment, IS auditors need to use a systematic and consistent approach to establishing the level of risk. The chosen approach should be used as a key input in audit planning.

G14, Application Systems Review

Written November 2001, updated October 2008. Clarifies Standard S6, Performance of Audit Work.

This guideline provides additional information for IS auditors who are performing an application systems review. The purpose of such a review is to identify application risks and evaluate an application's controls to determine how effectively the application supports the organization's overall controls and objectives.

G15, Planning

Written March 2002, updated May 2010. Clarifies Standard S5, Planning.

This guideline assists the IS auditor in the development of a plan for an audit project by providing additional information found in ISACA audit standard S5. An audit plan needs to take several matters into consideration, including overall business requirements, the objectives of the audit, and knowledge about the organization's processes and information systems. Levels of materiality should be established and a risk assessment performed, if necessary.

G16, Effect of Third Parties on an Organization's IT Controls

Written March 2002, updated March 2009. Clarifies Standard S5, Planning; and Standard S6, Performance of Audit Work.

Third-party organizations can become a key component in one or more controls. In situations where an organization outsources key business applications, the third party's controls for practical purposes supplement the organization's own controls.

The IS auditor needs to understand how a third-party organization supports the organization's business objectives. This may require a review of contracts, service level agreements, and other business documents that describe the services that the third-party organization provides.

The auditor will need to review the third party's controls through reviews of independent audits of another third-party organization. The IS auditor also needs to understand the effects and the risks associated with the use of the third party, and be able to identify countermeasures or compensating controls that will minimize risk.

G17, Effect of Nonaudit Role on the IS Auditor's Independence

Written July 2002, updated June 2009, May 2010. Clarifies Standard S2, Independence; and Standard S3, Professional Ethics and Standards.

In many organizations, IS auditors are involved in many nonaudit activities, including security strategy development, implementation of information technologies, software design, development and integration, process development, and implementation of security controls. These activities provide additional knowledge and experience, which help the IS auditor better understand how security and technology support the organization. However, some of these activities may adversely affect the IS auditor's independence and objectivity.

G18, IT Governance

Written July 2002, updated May 2010. Clarifies Standard S6, Performance of Audit Work.

Organizations have created a critical dependency upon information technology to conduct business transactions. The role of IT systems is critical to an organization's goals and objectives. This trend has made IT governance all the more critical to an organization's success. IS auditors need to have a clear understanding of the role of IT governance when planning and carrying out an audit.

G19, Irregularities and Illegal Acts

This guideline was replaced in September 2008 by Guideline G9, Audit Considerations for Irregularities and Illegal Acts.

G20, Reporting

Written January 2003. Clarifies Standard S7, Reporting.

This guideline describes how an IS auditor should comply with ISACA auditing standards on the development of audit findings, audit opinion, and audit report.

G21, Enterprise Resource Planning (ERP) Systems Review

Written August 2003.

This guideline provides additional information for the IS auditor who is performing a review or audit of enterprise resource planning (ERP) applications and systems. The guideline describes ERP systems and business process reengineering (BPR), and provides considerable detail of audit procedures.

G22, Business-to-Consumer (B2C) E-commerce Review

Written August 2003, updated October 2008. Clarifies Standard S6, Performance of Audit Work.

This guideline provides additional information for the IS auditor who may be performing a review or audit of a business-to-consumer e-commerce application or system. The guideline defines and describes e-commerce systems and describes several areas that should be the focus of an audit. The guideline includes a detailed audit plan and areas of possible risk.

G23, System Development Life Cycle (SDLC) Review

Written August 2003. Clarifies Standard S6, Performance of Audit Work.

This guideline provides IS auditors with additional information regarding audits of the process of defining, acquiring, and implementing applications. This process is commonly known as the systems development life cycle (SDLC).

G24, Internet Banking

Written August 2003. Clarifies Standard S2, Independence; Standard S4, Professional Competence; Standard S5, Planning; and Standard S6, Performance of Audit Work.

This guideline provides IS auditors with detailed information regarding the review and audit of Internet banking applications. The guideline describes Internet banking and includes detailed audit procedures.

G25, Review of Virtual Private Networks

Written July 2004. Clarifies S6, Performance of Audit Work.

This guideline describes virtual private network (VPN) technology and architecture, and provides detailed audit procedures. The guideline includes a description of VPN-related risks.

G26, Business Process Reengineering (BPR) Project Reviews

Written July 2004. Clarifies S6, Performance of Audit Work.

This guideline describes the process of BPR and the potentially profound effect it can have on organizational effectiveness. The guideline describes operational risks associated with BPR and includes audit guidelines for BPR projects and their impact on business processes, information systems, and corporate structures.

G27, Mobile Computing

Written September 2004. Clarifies Standard S1, Audit Charter; Standard S4, Professional Competence; Standard S5, Planning; and Standard S6, Performance of Audit Work.

This guideline describes the phenomenon of mobile computing in business operations, the technologies that support mobile computing, the risks associated with mobile computing, and guidance on applying audit standards on mobile computing infrastructures.

 TIP   Because of many advances in mobile computing, I recommend that readers watch for an update to this guideline in 2011 or 2012.

G28, Computer Forensics

Written September 2004. Clarifies Standard S3, Professional Ethics and Standards; Standard S4, Professional Competence; Standard S5, Planning; and Standard S6, Performance of Audit Work.

Because of their expertise in security and controls, IS auditors are subject to being asked to assist with investigations of irregularities, fraud, and criminal acts. This guideline defines forensic terms and includes forensic procedures that should be followed in such proceedings.

 TIP   Because of recent advancements in forensic tools and techniques, I recommend that readers watch for an update in 2011 or 2012.

G29, Post-implementation Review

Written January 2005. Clarifies Standard S6, Performance of Audit Work; and Standard S8, Follow-up Activities.

This guideline includes recommended practices for carrying out a post-implementation review of a new or updated information system. The purpose of a post-implementation review is to measure the effectiveness of the new system.

G30, Competence

Written June 2005. Clarifies Standard S4, Professional Competence.

This guideline provides additional details on the need for an IS auditor to attain and maintain knowledge and skills that are relevant to IS auditing and information technologies in use.

G31, Privacy

Written June 2005. Clarifies Standard S1, Audit Charter; Standard S5, Planning; and Standard S6, Performance of Audit Work.

This guideline provides additional information about privacy so that the IS auditor can properly consider privacy requirements, concerns, and laws during IS audits. The guideline includes details on the approach for personal data protection.

G32, Business Continuity Plan (BCP) Review from IT Perspective

Written September 2005. Clarifies Standard S6, Performance of Audit Work.

This guideline provides recommended practices for the review of business continuity plans and testing of BCP controls. It includes a description of business continuity planning, disaster recovery planning (DRP), and business impact analysis (BIA).

G33, General Considerations on the Use of the Internet

Written March 2006. Clarifies Standard S4, Professional Competence; Standard S5, Planning; and Standard S6, Performance of Audit Work.

This guideline provides detailed information for the IS auditor regarding the use of the Internet in support of business information systems. It includes a description of risks and audit procedures for evaluating controls that include the use of Internet-based resources.

G34, Responsibility, Authority, and Accountability

Written March 2006. Clarifies Standard S1, Audit Charter.

This guideline updates the responsibility, authority, and accountability of IS auditors in light of the advancements in technology and the pervasive use of information technology in support of critical business processes in the time since Standard S1 was originally written.

G35, Follow-up Activities

Written March 2006. Clarifies Standard S8, Follow-up Activities.

This guideline provides additional direction to IS auditors with regard to follow-up activities after an IS audit.

G36, Biometric Controls

Written February 2007. Clarifies Standard S6, Performance of Audit Work; and Standard S10, IT Governance.

This guideline provides additional information about biometric technology, including guidance on reviewing and auditing such technology.

G37, Configuration Management
Written November 2007. Clarifies Standard S6, Performance of Audit Work.

This guideline provides information about auditing configuration management tools and processes, and whether they are effective at making an organization's IT environment more efficient and stable.

G38, Access Controls
Written February 2008. Clarifies Standard S1, Audit Charter; and Standard S3, Professional Ethics and Standards.

This guideline provides additional direction on the audit of access controls and how they protect an organization's assets from disclosure and abuse.

G39, IT Organization
Written May 2008. Clarifies Standard S10, IT Governance.

This guideline provides additional information to the IS auditor regarding the audit and review of IT governance. It describes the common themes that exist among most IT organizations, as well as the typical differences between them. This information can assist an IS auditor by describing the common attributes of IT organizations.

G40, Review of Security Management Practices
Written October 2008. Clarifies Standard S1, Audit Charter; and Standard S3, Professional Ethics and Standards.

This guideline provides additional direction to IS auditors who are reviewing and auditing an organization's security management practices. Information is a key asset in many organizations, and the protection of that information is vital to the organization's survival. Security management provides the framework for that protection.

G41, Return on Security Investment (ROSI)
Written May 2010. Clarifies Standard S10, IT Governance.

This guideline provides information to IS auditors who are reviewing security and IT governance. Organizations need to consider return on security investment in new projects and develop key metrics to measure ROSI. Management needs to apply the principles of continuous improvement and strive to improve ROSI over time.

G42, Continuous Assurance
Written May 2010. Clarifies Standard S5, Planning; Standard S6, Performance of Audit Work; Standard S7, Reporting; and Standard S14, Audit Evidence.

This guideline provides information to IS auditors on new methods for collecting evidence and reporting on control effectiveness so that results can be delivered to control owners quickly. This will help control owners learn about deficiencies sooner, which will give them more time to remediate controls.

ISACA Audit Procedures

ISACA audit procedures contain information that helps the auditor understand how to audit different types of technologies and processes. While auditors are not required to follow these procedures, they provide insight into how technologies and processes can be audited effectively.

The full text of these procedures is available at www.isaca.org/standards.

P1, Risk Assessment

Written July 2002.

This procedure defines the IS audit risk assessment as a methodology used to optimize the allocation of IS audit resources through an understanding of the organization's IS environment and the risks associated with each aspect or component in the environment. In other words, it is a method for identifying where the highest risks are so that IS auditors can concentrate their audit activities on those areas.

The procedure describes a detailed scoring-based methodology that can be used to objectively identify areas of highest risk. It includes several example risk assessments to illustrate the methodology in action. The examples include listings of risk factors, weighting, and scoring to arrive at a total risk ranking for components in the environment.

P2, Digital Signature and Key Management

Written July 2002.

This procedure describes the evaluation of a certificate authority (CA) business function. It defines key terms and includes detailed checklists on the key characteristics of a CA that must be examined in an audit. The procedure considers business attributes, technology and its management, and whether the CA has had any prior audits. The areas examined are organizational management, certification and accreditation, technology architecture, and operations management. Each area includes a checklist of procedures to be completed by the auditor.

P3, Intrusion Detection Systems (IDS) Review Procedure

Written August 2003.

This procedure describes the function of an intrusion detection system, its purpose, and benefits. Both host-based and network-based IDS systems are described in detail. The procedure includes a detailed list of attributes to examine during an audit.

P4, Viruses and Other Malicious Code

Written August 2003.

This is a detailed procedure for assessing an organization's antivirus and anti-malware business and technical controls. Also included is a procedure for end users to follow if they suspect a malware infection on their workstation.

P5, Control Risk Self-Assessment

Written August 2003.

This is a detailed control risk self-assessment (CRSA) procedure. This is a process that is used to identify risks and mitigate them through the implementation of controls. While a CRSA is not a substitute for an external audit, it does help the organization focus inward, identify risk areas, and develop solutions to reduce risk. This helps an organization take responsibility for identifying and mitigating areas of risk.

P6, Firewalls
Written August 2003.

This procedure includes a detailed description of the types of firewalls, how they function, and how they are configured. Also covered are detailed descriptions of network address translation (NAT), virtual private networks (VPNs), and network architecture that is related to firewalls. The procedure also includes detailed steps to audit a firewall, including its configuration and its operation.

P7, Irregularities and Illegal Acts
Written November 2003.

This audit procedure helps the IS auditor assess the likelihood that irregularities could occur in business processes. Irregularities could include errors, illegal acts, and fraud. This procedure contains a detailed list of analytical procedures and computer-assisted audit procedures that can detect irregularities. It contains examples of irregularities and procedures for reporting irregularities, or conditions that could permit them.

P8, Security Assessment—Penetration Testing and Vulnerability Analysis
Written September 2004.

This procedure document contains detailed information for IS auditors and other security professionals who are responsible for performing penetration tests and vulnerability analyses. The procedure includes detailed discussions and checklists for external penetration testing, internal penetration testing, tests of physical access controls, social engineering, wireless network assessments, war dialing, manual and automated scans of web-based applications, and vulnerability assessments. The procedure also contains guidance on report preparation.

P9, Evaluation of Management Controls over Encryption Methodologies
Written January 2005.

This procedure contains a thorough description of encryption technology, including discussions of symmetric key cryptography, public key cryptography, and one-way hashing. The procedure includes risk assessment on the use of encryption, a discussion on the common uses and applications of encryption, laws and regulations on the use of encryption, and a detailed audit procedure.

P10, Business Application Change Control
Written October 2006.

This procedure describes and details the purpose and phases of the SDLC and includes detailed procedures for auditing change control procedures.

P11, Electronic Funds Transfer
Written May 2007.

This procedure describes the electronic funds transfer (EFT) system in detail and includes an EFT risk assessment and detailed audit procedures.

Information Technology Assurance Framework (ITAF)

Developed by ISACA and the IT Governance Institute, the Information Technology Assurance Framework (ITAF) is an end-to-end framework that was developed to guide organizations in developing and managing IT assurance and IT audit. The ITAF can be thought of as an actionable manual on the implementation of IT assurance and IT audit. With many cross-references to COBIT and ISACA audit standards, guidelines, and procedures, ITAF might be thought of as a sort of Rosetta Stone that ties COBIT and ISACA audit standards together.

ITAF is composed of 14 main sections, described here:

- **Section 1000: Introducing the IT Assurance Framework**

  - **Section 1100: ITAF overview**   Describes ITAF as a framework for the design, performance, and reporting of IT audit; concepts for IT assurance; and establishes roles, responsibilities, skills, conduct and reporting requirements for IT audit.

  - **Section 1500: Organization of the IT Assurance Framework**   Describes the organization of the ITAF framework as shown in Figure 3-3. The main components are found within sections 2000, 3000, and 4000.

  - **Section 1700: Use of the IT Assurance Framework**   ITAF standards (in section 2000) are mandatory, while guidelines (section 3000) and tools (section 4000) are optional. This section also discusses IT assurance, audit scoping, and risk assessment.

  - **Section 1800: Important Terms and Definitions**   This section includes several terms that are used throughout the document.

  - **Section 1900: How the ITAF Is Organized**   Another section that describes the organization of the entire ITAF framework. The ITAF version analyzed for this book was the initial version, and I expect that sections 1500 and 1900 will be combined in future versions.

- **Section 2000: IT Assurance Standards: Defining a Common Reference Point**

  - **Section 2100: IT Assurance Standards: Overview and Use**   This is a short introductory section that describes the three main sections here (2200: general standards; 2400, performance standards; and 2600, reporting standards), and reminds the reader that these standards are all mandatory for an organization that adopts this framework. This section also includes a copy of the ISACA Code of Ethics.

- **Section 2200: General Standards**   These are the IT assurance general standards: IT audit independence and objectivity; a reasonable expectation that these standards are achievable; management acknowledgment of support for IT assurance and IT audit; training, subject matter knowledge, and proficiency of IT audit staff; the establishment of due professional care when implementing IT assurance and performing IT audit; and IT audits' evaluation IT environments against suitably selected and available criteria.

- **Section 2400: Performance Standards**   These standards address the performance of IT audits in the categories of planning and supervision, collection of sufficient evidence, timeliness of audits, and documentation of audit representation.

- **Section 2600: Reporting Standards**   These standards address types of reports, means of communications, and the information communicated in audit reports.

- **Section 3000: IT Assurance Guidelines: Putting the Standards into Practice**

  - **Section 3100: IT Assurance Guidelines: Overview and Use**   This is a short introductory section that describes the three main sections here (3200, enterprise topics; 3400, IT management processes; 3600, IT audit and assurance processes; 3800, IT audit and assurance management).

  - **Section 3200: Enterprise Topics**   The guidelines in this section address enterprise-wide topics, including IT policies, practices, and standards; and assurance initiatives in IT and IT assurance.

  - **Section 3400: IT Management Processes**   The guidelines in this section describe the many processes that an IT organization should have in place. There are many cross-references to COBIT and ISACA audit standards in this section.

  - **Section 3600: IT Audit and Assurance Processes**   The guidelines in this section describe common practices for IT audit and assurance, as well as discussions on issues and concerns in these practices. There are several cross-references to COBIT controls and ISACA audit standards and procedures in this section.

  - **Section 3800: IT Audit and Assurance Management**   The guidelines in this section contain the information necessary to manage IT audits. Like the other sections in this part of ITAF, there are several references to COBIT and ISACA audit standards, procedures, and guidelines.

- **Section 4000: IT Assurance Tools and Techniques (reserved for future development)**

- **Glossary**

- **References**

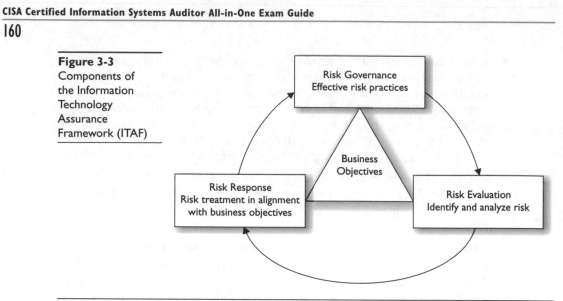

Figure 3-3
Components of
the Information
Technology
Assurance
Framework (ITAF)

EXAM TIP   ISACA does not require CISA candidates to memorize the ITAF, but they should understand its importance and purpose.

Risk Analysis

In the context of an audit, *risk analysis* is the activity that is used to determine the areas that warrant additional examination and analysis.

In the absence of a risk analysis, an IS auditor is likely to follow his or her "gut instinct" and apply additional scrutiny in areas where they *feel* risks are higher. Or, an IS auditor might give all areas of an audit equal weighting, putting equal resources into low-risk areas and high-risk areas. Either way, the result is that an IS auditor's focus is not necessarily on the areas where risks really are higher.

Relationship Between Standards, Guidelines, and Procedures

The ISACA audit standards, guidelines, and procedures have all been written to assist IS auditors with audit- and risk-related activities. They are related to each other in this way:

- *Standards* are statements that all IS auditors are expected to follow, and they can be considered a rule of law for auditors.

- *Guidelines* are statements that help IS auditors better understand how ISACA standards can be implemented.

- *Procedures* are examples of steps that can be followed when auditing specific business processes or technology systems.

The ISACA Code of Ethics encompasses the standards, guidelines, and procedures through the requirement of proper professional behavior.

Auditors' Risk Analysis and the Corporate Risk Management Program

A risk analysis that is carried out by IS auditors is distinct and separate from risk analysis that is performed as part of the IS risk management program. Often, these risk analyses are carried out by different personnel and for somewhat differing reasons. A comparison of IS auditor and IS management risk analysis is shown in Table 3-1.

In Table 3-1, I am not attempting to show a *polarity* of focus and results, but instead a *tendency* for focus based on the differing missions and objectives of IS audit and IS management.

The ISACA Risk-IT Framework

Auditors' risk analysis and corporate risk management can both be performed using the ISACA Risk-IT Framework. This framework, which is depicted in Figure 3-4, approaches risk from the enterprise perspective, encompassing all types of business risk, including IT risk.

The Risk-IT Framework consists of three major activities:

- **Risk Governance**   The purpose of risk governance is to ensure that IT risk is integrated into the organization's enterprise risk management (ERM) program.

- **Risk Evaluation**   The purpose of risk evaluation is to provide a framework of processes for performing risk assessments against business assets and explained in business terms.

- **Risk Response**   The purpose of risk response is to provide a framework of processes for responding to identified risks through reporting and risk treatment.

Activity	IS Audit Focus Tendency	IS Management Focus Tendency
Perspective	Objective	Subjective
Focus of risk assessment	All areas of potential risk	Existing controls
Identify a high risk in an existing control	Additional audit scrutiny on the control during the audit	Continue operating control
Identify a high risk; no existing control	Additional audit scrutiny on the activity as though control exists; recommend creation of control	Create and operate control

Table 3-1   Comparison of IS Audit and IS Management Risk Analysis

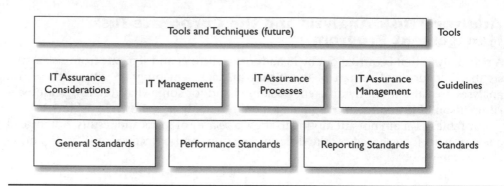

Figure 3-4 The ISACA Risk-IT Framework high-level components

Like other business frameworks, the Risk-IT Framework contains detailed top-down explanations of business processes and includes references to COBIT, ISACA audit standards, and Val-IT—another IT Governance Institute framework concerned with achieving business value from IT investments.

 EXAM TIP ISACA does not require CISA candidates to memorize the Risk-IT Framework, but they should understand its importance and purpose.

Evaluating Business Processes

The first phase of a risk analysis is an evaluation of business processes. The purpose of evaluating business processes is to determine the purpose and importance of business activities. While parts of a risk analysis may focus on technology, remember that technology exists to support business processes, not the other way around.

When a risk analysis starts with a focus on business processes, it is possible to consider the entire process and not just the technology that supports it. When examining business processes, it is important to obtain all available business process documentation, including

- **Charter or mission statement**   Often, an organization will develop and publish a high-level document that describes the process in its most basic terms. This usually includes the reason that the process exists and how it contributes to the organization's overall goals and objectives.

- **Process architecture**   A complex process may have several procedures, flows of information (whether in electronic form or otherwise), internal and external parties that perform functions, assets that support the process, and the locations and nature of records. In a strictly IT-centric perspective, this would be a data flow diagram or an entity-relationship diagram, but starting with either of those would be too narrow a focus. Instead, it is necessary to look at the entire process, with the widest view of its functions and connections with other processes and parties.

- **Procedures**   Looking closer at the process will reveal individual procedures—documents that describe the individual steps taken to perform activities that are part of the overall process. Procedure documents usually describe who (if not by name, then by title or department) performs what functions with what tools or systems. Procedures will cite business records that might be faxes, reports, databases, phone records, application transactions, and so on.

- **Records**   Business records contain the events that take place within a business process. Records will take many forms, including faxes, computer reports, electronic worksheets, database transactions, receipts, canceled checks, and e-mail messages.

- **Information system support**   When processes are supported by information systems, it is necessary to examine all available documents that describe information systems that support business processes. Examples of documentation are architecture diagrams, requirements documents (which were used to build, acquire, or configure the system), computer-run procedures, network diagrams, database schemas, and so on.

Once the IS auditor has obtained business documents and records, she can begin to identify and understand any risk areas that may exist in the process.

NOTE   The risk analysis method described here is no different from the risk analysis that takes place during the business impact assessment phase in a disaster recovery project, covered in Chapter 2.

Identifying Business Risks

The process of identifying business risks is partly analytical and partly based on the auditor's experience and judgment. An auditor will usually consider both within the single activity of risk identification.

An auditor will usually perform a *threat analysis* to identify and catalog risks. A threat analysis is an activity whereby the auditor considers a large body of possible threats and selects those that have some reasonable possibility of occurrence, however small. In a threat analysis, the auditor will consider each threat and document a number of facts about each, including

- **Probability of occurrence**   This may be expressed in qualitative (high, medium, low) or quantitative (percentage or number of times per year) terms. The probability should be as realistic as possible, recognizing the fact that actuarial data on business risk is difficult to obtain and more difficult to interpret. Here, an auditor's judgment is required to establish a reasonable probability.

- **Impact**   This is a short description of the results if the threat is actually realized. This is usually a short description, from a few words to a couple of sentences.

- **Loss**   This is usually a quantified and estimated loss should the threat actually occur. This figure might be a loss of revenue per day (or week or month) or the replacement cost for an asset, for example.

- **Possible mitigating controls**   This is a list of one or more countermeasures that can reduce the probability or the impact of a threat, or both.

- **Countermeasure cost and effort**   The cost and effort to implement each countermeasure should be identified, either with a high-medium-low qualitative figure or a quantitative estimate.

- **Updated probability of occurrence**   With each mitigating control, a new probability of occurrence should be cited. A different probability, one for each mitigating control, should be specified.

- **Updated impact**   With each mitigating control, a new impact of occurrence should be described. For certain threats and countermeasures, the impact may be the same, but for some threats, it may be different. For example, for a threat of fire, a mitigating control may be an inert gas fire suppression system. The new impact (probably just downtime and cleanup) will be much different from the original impact (probably water damage from a sprinkler system).

The auditor will put all of this information into a chart (or electronic spreadsheet) to permit further analysis and the establishment of conclusions—primarily, which threats are most likely to occur and which ones have the greatest potential impact on the organization.

 TIP   The establishment of a list of threats, along with their probability of occurrence and impact, depends heavily on the experience of the IS auditor and the resources available to him.

Risk Mitigation

The actual mitigation of risks identified in the risk assessment is the implementation of one or more of the countermeasures found in the risk assessment. In simple terms, mitigation could be as easy as a small adjustment in a process or procedure, or a major project to introduce new controls in the form of system upgrades, new components, or new procedures.

When the IS auditor is conducting a risk analysis prior to an audit, risk mitigation may take the form of additional audit scrutiny on certain activities during the audit. An area that the auditor identified as high risk could end up performing well, while other lower-risk areas could actually be the cause of control failures.

Additional audit scrutiny could take several forms, including one or more of the following:

- More time spent in inquiry and observation
- More personnel interviews

- Higher sampling rates
- Additional tests
- Re-performance of some control activities to confirm accuracy or completeness
- Corroboration interviews

Countermeasures Assessment

Depending upon the severity of the risk, mitigation could also take the form of additional (or improved) controls, even prior to (or despite the results of) the audit itself. The new or changed control may be major or minor, and the time and effort required to implement it could range from almost trivial to a major project.

The cost and effort required to implement a new control (or whatever the countermeasure is that is designed to reduce the probability or impact of a threat) should be determined before it is implemented. It probably does not make sense to spend $10,000 to protect an asset worth $100 —unless, of course, there was considerable reputation also associated with that $100 asset.

NOTE The effort required to implement a control countermeasure should be commensurate with the level of risk reduction expected from the countermeasure. A quantified risk analysis may be needed if the cost and effort seem high, especially when compared to the value of the asset being protected.

Monitoring

After countermeasures are implemented, the IS auditor will need to reassess the controls through additional testing. If the control includes any self-monitoring or measuring, the IS auditor should examine those records to see if there is any visible effect of the countermeasures.

The auditor may need to re-perform audit activities to determine the effectiveness of countermeasures. For example, additional samples selected after the countermeasure is implemented can be examined and the rate of exceptions compared to periods prior to the countermeasure's implementation.

Internal Controls

The policies, procedures, mechanisms, systems, and other measures designed to reduce risk are known as internal controls. An organization develops controls to ensure that its business objectives will be met, risks will be reduced, and errors will be prevented or corrected.

Controls are used in two primary ways in an organization: They are created to achieve desired events, and they are created to avoid unwanted events.

Control Classification

Several types, classes, and categories of controls are discussed in this section. Figure 3-5 depicts this control classification.

Types of Controls

The three types of controls are physical, technical, and administrative:

- **Physical**   These types of controls exist in the tangible, physical world. Examples of physical controls are video surveillance, bollards, and fences.

- **Technical**   These controls are implemented in the form of information systems and are usually intangible. Examples of technical controls include encryption, computer access controls, and audit logs.

- **Administrative**   These controls are the policies and procedures that require or forbid certain activities. An example administrative control is a policy that forbids personal use of information systems.

 EXAM TIP   ISACA does not expressly use the terms "type," "class," or "category" to describe and distinguish the variety of controls and their basic characteristics. Rather, these terms are used to highlight the multidimensional nature of controls and how they can be classified. Like other constructs, these are models that enable us to better imagine how controls operate and are used.

Classes of Controls

There are six classes of controls:

- **Preventive**   This type of control is used to prevent an unwanted event. Examples of preventive controls are computer login screens (which prevent unauthorized persons from accessing information), keycard systems (which prevent unauthorized persons from entering a building or workspace), and encryption (which prevent persons lacking an encryption key from reading encrypted data).

Figure 3-5
Control classification shows types, classes, and categories of controls.

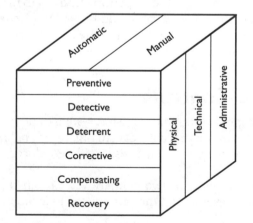

- **Detective** This type of control is used to record both wanted and unwanted events. A detective control cannot enforce an activity (whether it is desired or undesired), but instead it can only make sure that it is known that the event occurred. Examples of detective controls include video surveillance and audit logs.

- **Deterrent** This type of control exists in order to convince someone that they should not perform some unwanted activity. Examples of deterrent controls include guard dogs, warning signs, and visible video surveillance cameras and monitors.

 NOTE Auditors and security professionals usually prefer preventive controls over detective controls because preventive controls actually *block* unwanted events. Likewise, auditors prefer detective controls to deterrent controls because detective controls record events while deterrent controls do not. However, there are often circumstances where cost, resource, or technical limitations force an organization to accept a detective control when it would prefer a preventive one. For example, there is no practical way to build a control that would prevent criminals from entering a bank, but a detective control (security cameras) would record what they did after they arrived.

- **Corrective** This type of control occurs after some unwanted event has occurred. An example corrective control is the act of improving a process when it was found to be defective.

- **Compensating** This type of control is enacted because some other direct control cannot be used. For example, a video surveillance system can be a compensating control when it is implemented to compensate for the lack of a stronger detective control, such as a keycard access system.

- **Recovery** This type of control is used to restore the state of a system or asset to its pre-incident state. An example recovery control is the use of a tool to remove a virus from a computer.

 NOTE Many controls can be classified in more than one class. For example, a video surveillance camera can be thought of as both a detective control (because it is part of a system that records events) and a deterrent control (because its visibility is designed to discourage persons from committing unwanted acts). Also, an audit log can be thought of as both a detective and a compensating control—detective because it records events and compensating because it may compensate for a lack of a stronger, preventive control, such as a user IDs and password access control. The organization of controls described in this section is not according to any published standard.

Categories of Controls

There are two categories of controls:

- **Automatic** This type of control performs its function with little or no human judgment or decision-making. Examples of automatic controls include a login page on an application that cannot be circumvented and a security door that automatically locks after someone walks through the doorway.

- **Manual** This type of control requires a human to operate it. A manual control may be subject to a higher rate of errors than an automatic control. An example of a manual control is a monthly review of computer users.

 NOTE IS auditors and security professionals often prefer automatic controls to manual ones, as they are typically less prone to error. However, there are often circumstances where an organization must settle for a manual control because of cost or other factor.

Internal Control Objectives

Internal control objectives are statements of desired states or outcomes from business operations. Example control objectives include

- Protection of IT assets
- Accuracy of transactions
- Confidentiality and privacy
- Availability of IT systems
- Controlled changes to IT systems
- Compliance with corporate policies

Control objectives are the foundation for controls. For each control objective, one or more controls will exist to ensure the realization of the control objective. For example, the "Availability of IT Systems" control objective will be met with several controls, including

- IT systems will be continuously monitored, and any interruptions in availability will result in alerts sent to appropriate personnel.
- IT systems will have resource-measuring capabilities.
- IT management will review capacity reports monthly and adjust resources accordingly.
- IT systems will have anti-malware controls that are monitored by appropriate staff.

Together, these four (or more) controls contribute to the overall control objective on IT system availability. Similarly, the other control objectives will have one or more controls that will ensure their realization.

TIP   Control objectives should be established prior to the controls themselves.

IS Control Objectives

IS control objectives resemble ordinary control objectives but are set in the context of information systems. Examples of IS control objectives include

- Protection of information from unauthorized personnel
- Protection of information from unauthorized modification
- Integrity of operating systems
- Controlled and managed changes to information systems
- Controlled and managed development of application software

An organization will probably have several additional IS control objectives on other basic topics such as malware, availability, and resource management.

Like ordinary control objectives, IS control objectives will be supported by one or more controls.

EXAM TIP   CISA candidates are not required to memorize COBIT or other frameworks, but familiarity with them will help the CISA candidate to better understand how they contribute to effective IT governance and control.

The COBIT Controls Framework

To ensure that IT is aligned with business objectives, the COBIT (Control Objectives for Information and related Technology) controls framework of four domains and 34 processes is an industry-wide standard. The four domains are Plan and Organize, Acquire and Implement, Deliver and Support, and Monitor and Evaluate.

COBIT contains more than 200 detailed control objectives to support these domains and processes.

Established in 1996 by ISACA and the IT Governance Institute, COBIT is the result of industry-wide consensus by managers, auditors, and IT users. Today, COBIT is accepted as a best-practices IT process and control framework.

General Computing Controls

An IS organization supporting many applications and services will generally have some controls that are specific to each individual application. However, IS will also have a set of controls that apply across all applications and services. These are usually called its general computing controls, or GCCs.

An organization's GCCs are general in nature and are often implemented in different ways on different information systems, based upon their individual capabilities and limitations. Examples of GCCs include

- Applications require unique user IDs and strong passwords.

- Passwords are encrypted while stored and transmitted, and are not displayed.

- Highly sensitive information, such as bank account numbers, is encrypted when stored and transmitted.

- All administrative actions are logged, and logs are protected from tampering.

Readers who are familiar with information systems technology will quickly realize that these GCCs will be implemented differently across different types of information systems. Specific capabilities and limitations, for example, will result in somewhat different capabilities for password complexity and data encryption. Unless an organization is using really old information systems, the four GCCs shown here can probably be implemented everywhere in an IS environment. *How* they are implemented is the subject of the next section.

IS Controls

The GCCs discussed in the previous section are implemented across a variety of information technologies. Each general computing control is mapped to a specific IS control on each system type, where it is implemented. In other words, IS controls describe the implementation details for GCCs.

For example, a GCC for password management can be implemented through several IS controls—one for each type of technology platform in use in the organization: one for Windows servers, one for Linux servers, and one for each application that performs its own access management. Those specific IS controls would describe implementation details that reflect the capabilities and limitations of each respective platform.

Performing an Audit

An audit is a systematic and repeatable process whereby a competent and independent professional evaluates one or more controls, interviews personnel, obtains and analyzes evidence, and develops a written opinion on the effectiveness of the controls.

An IS audit, then, is an audit of information systems and the processes that support them. An IS auditor interviews personnel, gathers and analyzes evidence, and delivers a written opinion on the effectiveness of controls implemented in information systems.

An auditor cannot just begin an audit. Rather, audits need to be planned events. Formal planning is required that includes

- **Purpose**   The IS auditor and the auditee must establish a *reason* why an audit is to be performed. The purpose for a particular audit could be to determine the level of compliance to a particular law, regulation, standard, or contract. Another reason could be to determine whether specific control deficiencies identified in past audits have been remediated. Still another reason is to determine the level of compliance to a new law or standard that the organization may be subject to in the future.

- **Scope**   The auditor and the auditee must also establish the scope of the audit. Often, the audit's purpose will make the scope evident, but not always. Scope may be multidimensional: It could be a given period, meaning records spanning a start date and end date may comprise the body of evidence, geography (systems in a particular region or locale), technology (systems using a specific operating system, database, application, or other aspect), business process (systems that support specific processes such as accounting, order entry, or customer support), or segment of the organization.

- **Risk analysis**   To know which areas require the greatest amount of attention, the IS auditor needs to be familiar with the levels of risk associated with the domain being audited. Two different perspectives of risk may be needed: First, the IS auditor needs to know the relative levels of risk among the different aspects of the domain being audited so that audit resources can be allocated accordingly. For example, if the audit is on an ERP system and the auditor knows that the accounts receivable function has been problematic in the past, the IS auditor will probably want to devote more resources and time on the accounts receivable function than on others. Second, the IS auditor needs to know about the absolute level of risk across the entire domain being audited. For example, if this is an audit to determine compliance to new legislation, the overall risk could be very high if the consequences of noncompliance are high. Both aspects of risk enable the IS auditor to plan accordingly.

- **Audit procedures**   The purpose and scope of the audit may help to define the procedures that will be required to perform the audit. For a compliance audit, for example, there may be specific rules on sample sizes and sampling techniques, or it may require the auditors with specific qualifications to perform the audit. A compliance audit may also specify criteria for determining if a particular finding constitutes a deficiency or not. There may also be rules for materiality.

- **Resources**   The IS auditor must determine what resources are needed and available for the audit. In an external audit, the auditee (which is a client organization) may have a maximum budget figure available. For an external or internal audit, the IS auditor needs to determine the number of man-hours that will be required in the audit and the various skills required. Other resources that may be needed include specialized tools to gather or analyze information obtained from information systems—for example, an analysis program to process the roles and permissions in a database management system in order to identify high-risk areas. To a great degree, the purpose and scope of the audit will determine which resources are required to complete it.

- **Schedule** The IS auditor needs to develop an audit schedule that will give enough time for interviews, data collection and analysis, and report generation. However, the schedule could also come in the form of a constraint, meaning the audit must be complete by a certain date. If the IS auditor is given a deadline, he will need to see how the audit activities can be made to fit within that period. If the date is too aggressive, the IS auditor will need to discuss the matter with the auditee to make required adjustments in scope, resources, or schedule.

Appendix A is devoted to a pragmatic approach to conducting audits.

Audit Objectives

The term *audit objectives* refers to the specific goals for an audit. Generally, the objective of an audit is to determine if controls exist and are effective in some specific aspect of business operations in an organization.

Depending on the subject and nature of the audit, the auditor may examine the controls and related evidence herself, or the auditor may instead focus on the business content that is processed by the controls. In other words, if the focus of an audit is an organization's accounting system, the auditor may focus on financial transactions in the system to see how they affect financial bookkeeping. Or, the auditor could focus on the IS processes that support the operation of the financial accounting system. Formal audit objectives should make such a distinction so that the auditor has a sound understanding of the objectives. This tells the auditor what to look at during the audit. Of course, the type of audit being undertaken helps too; this is covered in the next section.

Types of Audits

The scope, purpose, and objectives of an audit will determine the type of audit that will be performed. IS auditors need to understand each type of audit, including the procedures that are used for each:

- **Operational audit** This type of audit is an examination of IS controls, security controls, or business controls to determine control existence and effectiveness. The focus of an operational audit is usually the operation of one or more controls, and it could concentrate on the IS management of a business process or on the business process itself. The scope of an operational audit is shaped to meet audit objectives.

- **Financial audit** This type of audit is an examination of the organization's accounting system, including accounting department processes and procedures. The objective of a financial audit is to determine if business controls are sufficient to ensure the integrity of financial statements.

- **Integrated audit**   This type of audit combines an operational audit and a financial audit in order for the auditor to gain a complete understanding of the entire environment's integrity. Such an audit will closely examine accounting department processes, procedures, and records, as well as the IS applications that support the accounting department. Virtually every organization uses a computerized accounting system for management of its financial records; the computerized accounting system and all of the supporting infrastructure (database management system, operating system, networks, workstations, and so on) will be examined to see if the IS department has the entire environment under adequate control.

- **IS audit**   This type of audit is a detailed examination of most or all of an IS department's operations. An IS audit looks at IT governance to determine if IS is aligned with overall organization goals and objectives. The audit also looks closely at all of the major IS processes, including service delivery, change and configuration management, security management, systems development life cycle, business relationship and supplier management, and incident and problem management. This audit will determine if each control objective and control is effective and operating properly.

- **Administrative audit**   This type of audit is an examination of operational efficiency within some segment of the organization.

- **Compliance audit**   This type of audit is performed to determine the level and degree of compliance to a law, regulation, standard, or internal control. If a particular law or standard requires an external audit, the compliance audit may have to be performed by approved or licensed external auditors; for example, a U.S. public company financial audit must be performed by a public accounting firm, and a PCI audit must be performed by a licensed QSA (qualified security assessor). If, however, the law or standard does not explicitly require audits, the organization may still wish to perform one-time or regular audits to determine the level of compliance to the law or standard. This type of audit may be performed by internal or external auditors, and typically is performed so that management has a better understanding of the level of compliance risk.

- **Forensic audit**   This type of audit is usually performed by an IS auditor or a forensic specialist in support of an anticipated or active legal proceeding. In order to withstand cross-examination and to avoid having evidence being ruled inadmissible, strict procedures must be followed in a forensic audit, including the preservation of evidence and a chain of custody of evidence.

- **Service provider audit**   Because many organizations outsource critical activities to third parties, often these third-party service organizations will undergo one or more external audits in order to increase customer confidence in the integrity of the third-party organization's services. In the United States, a Statement on Standards for Attestation Engagements No. 16, *Reporting on Controls at a Service Organization* (SSAE 16) can be performed on a service provider's operations and the audit report transmitted to customers of the service provider. SSAE16 superseded the Statement of Accounting Standards No. 70 (SAS 70) audit in 2011. The SSAE 16 standard was developed by the American Institute of Certified Public Accountants (AICPA) for the purpose of auditing third-party service organizations that perform financial services on behalf of their customers.

 TIP SSAE 16 is closely aligned with the global standard, International Auditing and Assurance Standards Board (IAASB) International Standard on *Assurance Engagement 3402, Assurance Reports on Controls at a Service Organization* (ISAE 3402).

- **Pre-audit** While not technically an audit, a pre-audit is an examination of business processes, IS systems, and business records in anticipation of an upcoming external audit. Usually, an organization will undergo a pre-audit in order to get a better idea of its compliance to a law, regulation, or standard prior to an actual compliance audit. An organization can use the results of a pre-audit to implement corrective measures, thereby improving the outcome of the real audit.

Compliance vs. Substantive Testing

It is important for IS auditors to understand the distinction between compliance testing and substantive testing. These two types of testing are defined here:

- **Compliance testing** This type of testing is used to determine if control procedures have been properly designed and implemented, and that they are operating properly. For example, an IS auditor might examine business processes, such as the systems development life cycle, change management, or configuration management, to determine if information systems environments are properly managed.

- **Substantive testing** This type of testing is used to determine the accuracy and integrity of transactions that flow through processes and information systems. For instance, an IS auditor may create test transactions and trace them through the environment, examining them at each stage until their completion.

IS audits sometimes involve both compliance testing and substantive testing. The audit objectives that are established will determine if compliance testing, substantive testing, or both will be required.

Audit Methodology

An *audit methodology* is the set of audit procedures that are used to accomplish a set of audit objectives. An organization that regularly performs audits should develop formal methodologies so that those audits are performed consistently, even when carried out by different personnel.

The phases of a typical audit methodology are described in the remainder of this section.

Audit Subject

Determine the business process, information system, or other domain to be audited.

Audit Objective

Identify the purpose of the audit. For example, this may be an audit that is required by a law, regulation, standard, or business contract. Or this may be an audit to determine compliance with internal control objectives to measure control effectiveness.

Type of Audit

Identify the type of audit that is to be performed. This may be an operational audit, financial audit, integrated audit, administrative audit, compliance audit, forensic audit, or a security provider audit.

Audit Scope

The business process, department, or application that is the subject of the audit needs to be identified. Usually, a span of time needs to be identified as well so that activities or transactions during that period can be examined.

NOTE The *subject* of an audit is a broad definition, whereas the *scope* further defines exactly which processes, locations, and systems will be audited.

Pre-Audit Planning

Here, the auditor needs to obtain information about the audit that will enable her to establish the audit plan. Information needed includes

- Location(s) that need to be visited
- A list of the applications to be examined
- The technologies supporting each application
- Policies, standards, and diagrams that describe the environment

This and other information will enable the IS auditor to determine the skills required to examine and evaluate processes and information systems. The IS auditor will be able to establish an audit schedule and will have a good idea of the types of evidence that are needed. The IS audit may be able to make advance requests for certain other types of evidence even before the on-site phase of the audit begins.

Audit Statement of Work

For an external audit, the IS auditor may need to develop a statement of work or engagement letter that describes the audit purpose, scope, duration, and costs. The auditor may require a written approval from the client before audit work can officially begin.

Establish Audit Procedures

Using information obtained regarding audit objectives and scope, the IS auditor can now develop procedures for this audit. For each objective and control to be tested, the IS auditor can specify

- A list of people to interview
- Inquiries to make during each interview
- Documentation (policies, procedures, and other documents) to request during each interview
- Audit tools to use
- Sampling rates and methodologies
- How and where evidence will be archived
- How evidence will be evaluated

Communication Plan

The IS auditor will develop a communication plan in order to keep the IS auditor's management, as well as the auditee's management, informed throughout the audit project. The communication plan may contain one or more of the following:

- A list of evidence requested, usually in the form of a PBC (provided by client) list, which is typically a worksheet that lists specific documents or records and the names of personnel who can provide them (or who provided them in a prior audit).
- Regular written status reports that include activities performed since the last status report, upcoming activities, and any significant findings that may require immediate attention.
- Regular status meetings where audit progress, issues, and other matters may be discussed in person or via conference call.
- Contact information for both IS auditor and auditee so that both parties can contact each other quickly if needed.

Report Preparation

The IS auditor needs to develop a plan that describes how the audit report will be prepared. This will include the format and the content of the report, as well as the manner in which findings will be established and documented.

The IS auditor will need to make sure that the audit report complies with all applicable audit standards, including ISACA IS audit standards.

If the audit report requires internal review, the IS auditor will need to identify the parties that will perform the review, and make sure that they will be available at the time when the IS auditor expects to complete the final draft of the audit report.

Wrap-up

The IS auditor needs to perform a number of tasks at the conclusion of the audit, including the following:

- Deliver the report to the auditee.
- Schedule a closing meeting so that the results of the audit can be discussed with the auditee and so that the IS auditor can collect feedback.
- For external audits, send an invoice to the auditee.
- Collect and archive all work papers.
- Update PBC documents if the IS auditor anticipates that the audit will be performed again in the future.
- Collect feedback from the auditee and convey to any audit staff as needed.

Post-audit Follow-up

After a given period (which could range from days to months), the IS auditor should contact the auditee to determine what progress the auditee has made on the remediation of any audit findings. There are several good reasons for doing this:

- It establishes a tone of concern for the auditee organization (and an interest in its success) and demonstrates that the auditee is taking the audit process seriously.
- It helps to establish a dialogue whereby the auditor can help auditee management work through any needed process or technology changes as a result of the audit.
- It helps the auditor better understand management's commitment to the audit process and to continuous improvement.
- For an external auditor, it improves goodwill and the prospect for repeat business.

 NOTE An audit methodology is a process. Like any process, it should have a documented end-to-end and process document that is reviewed from time to time.

Audit Evidence

Evidence is the information collected by the auditor during the course of the audit project. The contents and reliability of the evidence obtained are used by the IS auditor to reach conclusions on the effectiveness of controls and control objectives. The IS auditor needs to understand how to evaluate various types of evidence and how (and if) it can be used to support audit findings.

The auditor will collect many kinds of evidence during an audit, including

- Observations
- Written notes
- Correspondence
- Internal process and procedure documentation
- Business records

When the IS auditor examines evidence, he needs to consider several characteristics about the evidence, which will contribute to its weight and reliability. These characteristics include the following:

- **Independence of the evidence provider** The IS auditor needs to determine the independence of the party providing evidence. She will place more weight on evidence provided by an independent party than upon evidence provided by the party being audited. For instance, phone and banking records obtained directly from those respective organizations will be given more credence than an organization's own records (unless original statements are also provided).

- **Qualifications of the evidence provider** The IS auditor needs to take into account the qualifications of the person providing evidence. This is particularly true when evidence is in the form of highly technical information, such as source code or database extracts. The quality of the evidence will rest partly upon the evidence provider's ability to explain the source of the evidence and how it was produced. Similarly, the qualifications of the auditor come into play, as he will similarly need to be able to thoroughly understand the nature of the evidence and be familiar enough with the technology to be able to determine its veracity.

- **Objectivity** Objective evidence may be considerably more reliable than subjective evidence. An audit log, for instance, is quite objective, whereas an auditee's or auditor's opinion of the audit log is less objective.

- **Timing** The IS auditor needs to understand the availability of evidence in the systems being audited. Certain log files, extract files, debug files, and temporary files that may be of value during the examination of the system may be available only for short periods before they are recycled or removed. Often, intermediate files are not backed up or retained for long periods. When an IS auditor is tracing transactions through a system during substantive testing, she will need to understand early on what files or intermediate data should be retrieved so that she can later analyze the data after those intermediate files have been cycled out.

 NOTE The IS auditor needs to gain a thorough understanding of the sufficiency of evidence gathered using ISACA audit standards S6, Performance of Audit Work; and S14, Audit Evidence.

Gathering Evidence

The IS auditor must understand and be experienced in the methods and techniques used to gather evidence during an audit. The methods and techniques used most often in audits include

- **Organization chart review**   The IS auditor should request a current org chart, as well as the job descriptions of key personnel. This will help the auditor to understand management, control, and reporting structures within the organization.

- **Review of department and project charters**   These documents describe the roles and responsibilities of the IS organization overall, as well as specific departments within IS. The charters for any recent major projects should be requested as well in order to understand newer objectives that could represent adjustments in organizational behavior. If the audit is going to focus on applications used by other departments, the auditor should request those departments' charters and descriptions, which will help him better understand those departments' functions, roles, and responsibilities.

- **Review of third-party contracts and service level agreements (SLAs)**   Even if they are not a focus of the audit, certain third-party contracts and SLAs may provide additional insight into the workings and culture of the IS organization.

- **Review of IS policies and procedures**   The auditor should obtain and review IS policies as well as process and procedure documents that are related to the audit. This will help the auditor to better understand the tone and direction set by management, as well as give the auditor a better idea of how well organized the IS organization really is.

- **Review of IS standards**   The auditor should obtain any IS standards documents to understand current policy on the vendors, products, methods, languages, and protocols in use. She should review process and documentation standards as well to see how consistently the organization follows them; this will give the auditor valuable insight into the discipline in the organization.

 NOTE   The IS auditor should pay attention to what IS charters, policies, and procedure documents do say, as well as what they don't say. He should perform corroborative interviews to determine if these documents really define the organization's behavior or if they're just window dressing. This will help the auditor to understand the maturity of the organization, a valuable insight that will be helpful when writing the audit report.

- **Review of IS system documentation**   If the subject of the audit (directly or indirectly) is an IS application, the auditor should obtain much of the project documentation that chronicles the development or acquisition of the system. This may include the following:
  - Feasibility study
  - Functional, technical, and security requirements

- Responses from vendors (at least the one chosen)
- Evaluation of vendor responses
- System design documentation, including data flow diagrams, entity-relationship diagrams, database schema, and so on
- Test plans and results
- Implementation guides and results
- User manuals
- Operations manuals
- Business continuity plans
- Changes made since initial release
- Reports of system stability, capacity, and availability

 NOTE　The IS auditor should examine the organization's SDLC process and determine how closely system documentation follows it.

- **Personnel interviews**　The IS auditor should conduct walkthrough interviews with key personnel who can describe the function, design, use, and operation of the system. Rather than assume that all acquired documentation is absolutely complete and accurate, the auditor should ask open-ended questions to gain additional insight into how well the system really operates. He should develop questions in advance in order to keep the interview on track and to make sure that all topics are covered. The auditor should carefully select key questions and ask them of more than one individual to compare answers, which will give him more insight.

 NOTE　Some organizations may coach their personnel so that they do not provide any more than the minimum amount of information. An experienced auditor should recognize this, and may need to get creative (without compromising ethics standards!) in order to get to key facts and circumstances. The IS auditor must always be polite, friendly, and request cooperation of each interviewee. She must always be truthful and never threaten any interviewee.

- **Passive observation**　When an IS auditor is embedded in an organization, people will "let their guard down" after they are accustomed to his presence. The auditor may be able to observe people being themselves and possibly will hear or see clues that will give better insight into the culture and tone of the organization.

Observing Personnel

It is rarely sufficient for an auditor to obtain and understand process documentation and be able to make judgments about the effectiveness of the process. Usually, the auditor will need to collect evidence in the form of observations to see how consistently a system's process documentation is actually followed. Some of the techniques in observing personnel include

- **Real tasks** The auditor should request to see some IS functions actually being carried out. For example, if an auditor is examining user access management processes, he should be able to observe the persons who manage user accounts to see how they perform their tasks. The auditor should compare the steps taken against procedure documentation; he can also observe the configuration settings that the interviewee has made to see if they are being done according to procedure documents.

- **Skills and experience** The auditor should ask each interviewee about his or her career background to determine the interviewee's level of experience and career maturity. This will help the auditor to understand whether key responsibilities are in the hands of personnel who can really handle them.

- **Security awareness** The IS auditor should observe personnel to see if they are following security policies and procedures. She can casually ask the interviewee what they know about security procedures to see if the security awareness program is effective. This should implicitly be a part of every audit, even if not explicitly included in scope. Major deviations from policy or common sense could well constitute deficiencies.

- **Segregation of duties** The IS auditor should observe personnel to see if adequate segregation of duties (SOD) is in place. Lapses could include a user account administrator creating or changing a user account without official approval, or a systems engineer making a quick change on a system without going through the change management process.

An experienced IS auditor will have a well-developed "sixth sense," an intuition about people that can be used to better understand the people who execute procedures.

Sampling

Sampling refers to the technique that is used when it is not feasible to test an entire population of transactions. The objective of sampling is to select a portion of a population so that the characteristics observed will reflect the characteristics of the entire population.

There are several methods for sampling:

- **Statistical sampling** Here, a technique of random selection is used that will statistically reflect the entire population. The auditor will need to determine the size of the sample (usually expressed as a percentage of the entire population) so that the results obtained through testing will statistically reflect the entire population, where each event in the population has an equal chance of being selected.

- **Judgmental sampling** (also known as nonstatistical sampling)   Here, the IS auditor judgmentally and subjectively selects samples based on established criteria such as risk or materiality. For instance, when reviewing a list of user accounts to examine, the auditor can purposely select those users whose accounts represent higher risk than the others in the population.

- **Attribute sampling**   This technique is used to study the characteristics of a given population to answer the question "how many?". After the auditor has selected a statistical sample, she then examines the samples. A specific attribute is chosen, and the samples examined to see how many items have the characteristic and how many do not. For example, an auditor is testing a list of terminated user accounts to see how many were terminated within 24 hours and how many were not. This is used to statistically determine the rate at which terminations are performed within 24 hours among the entire population.

- **Variable sampling**   This technique is used to statistically determine the characteristic of a given population to answer the question "how much?". For example, an auditor who wishes to know the total value of an inventory can select a sample and then statistically determine the total value in the entire population based on the total value of the sample.

- **Stop-or-go sampling**   This technique is used to permit sampling to stop at the earliest possible time. The IS auditor will use this technique when he feels that there are a low risk and rate of exceptions in the overall population.

- **Discovery sampling**   This technique is used when an IS auditor is trying to find at least one exception in a population. When he is examining a population where even a single exception would represent a high-risk situation (such as embezzlement or fraud), the auditor will recommend a more intensive investigation to determine if additional exceptions exist.

- **Stratified sampling**   Here, the event population will be divided into classes, or strata, based upon the value of one of the attributes. Then, samples are selected from each class, and results are developed from each class or combined into a single result. An example of where this could be used is a selection of purchase orders (POs), where the IS auditor wants to make sure that some of the extremely high-value and low-value POs will be selected to see if there is any statistical difference in the results in different classes.

When performing sampling, the IS auditor needs to understand several aspects of statistical sampling techniques, including

- **Confidence coefficient** Sometimes known as the reliability factor or confidence level, this is expressed as a percentage, as the probability that the sample selected actually represents the entire population. A confidence coefficient of 95 percent is considered high.

- **Sampling risk** This is equal to one minus the confidence coefficient percentage. For example, if a given sample has a 93 percent confidence coefficient, the risk level is 7 percent (100 percent minus 93 percent equals 7 percent).

- **Precision** This represents how closely the sample represents the entire population. A low precision figure means high accuracy, and a high precision figure means low accuracy. A smaller sample makes the precision higher, and the risk of exceptions in the entire population is higher.

- **Expected error rate** This is an estimate that expresses the percentage of errors that may exist in the entire population. When the expected error rate is higher, the sample needs to be higher (because a population with a high rate of errors requires greater scrutiny). If the expected error rate is low, the sample can be smaller.

- **Sample mean** This is the sum of all samples divided by the number of samples. This equals the average value of the sample.

- **Sample standard deviation** This is a computation of the variance of sample values from the sample mean. This is a measurement of the "spread" of values in the sample.

- **Population standard deviation** Within the entire evidence population, this is a computation of the variance of values from the mean. All other factors being equal, a larger population standard deviation means the auditor should select a larger set of samples.

- **Tolerable error rate** This is the highest number of errors that can exist without a result being materially misstated.

 NOTE Part of the body of evidence in an audit is a description of how a sample was selected and why the particular sampling technique was used.

Reliance Upon the Work of Other Auditors

Audit departments and external auditors, like other IT service organizations, are challenged to find qualified audit professionals who understand all aspects of organizations' technologies in use. Increased specialization in IT is resulting in auditors with increased technical knowledge in certain areas, but fewer auditors with all of the knowledge required to perform an audit. This and other factors are putting increasing pressure on organizations to outsource some auditing tasks (or entire audits) to third-party organizations.

When considering reliance upon other auditors, many potential issues must be examined, including

- Laws, regulations, standards, or contracts that may place restrictions on the use of third-party auditors
- Impact on risk
- Costs and the overhead required to manage external auditors
- Impact on audit schedule and reporting
- Impact on general and professional liability
- Audit standards and methodologies used by the third-party auditor
- Competence and experience of the third-party auditor
- Independence and objectivity of internal versus external auditors
- Methods for communication of audit issues and results
- Access by third-party auditor to internal records and systems
- Protection and privacy of information made available to external auditors
- Background checks, nondisclosure, and other agreements for third-party audit personnel
- Audit management controls used to manage external audit activities

 NOTE IS auditors should be familiar with ISACA audit guideline G1, Using the Work of Other Auditors; and standard S6, Performance of Audit Work, in order to properly manage the work performed by external auditors.

Computer-Assisted Audit and Automated Work Papers

When auditing complex information systems, IS auditors often need to obtain sample data from systems with a variety of operating systems, database management systems, record layouts, and processing methods. Auditors are turning to computer-assisted audit techniques (CAATs) to help them examine and evaluate data across these complex environments.

Reliance on Third Party Audit Reports

Another common setting for the reliance of other auditors is the case where an organization may choose to rely upon audit reports for an external service provider rather than audit the external service provider directly. A typical example is a case where an organization hires a payroll services provider and the payroll services provider has its own SSAE16 audit that is performed on qualified audit firms. The organization's own auditors will likely choose to rely on the payroll service provider's SSAE16 audit rather than audit the payroll service provider directly.

Protecting Automated Work Papers

CAATs help IS auditors by making sampling easier and by capturing data that has varying degrees of persistence in an organization's application environment. That captured data will often be considered part of the body of work papers. Controls need to be enacted to protect automated work papers, including

- **Access control**   Only authorized persons (ideally only the auditor) should have read access to automated work papers.
- **Protection from damage**   Automated work papers must be protected so that no person is able to change or remove them.
- **Backup**   Automated work papers should be included in data backups.
- **Encryption**   Automated work papers should be encrypted if they contain sensitive information. Effective key management procedures and controls must be in place.

When using CAATs, auditors need to document the evidence they obtain from systems and be able to link it to business transactions. Often, auditors will have to obtain several other items, including

- Application source code
- Online reports that correlate captured data to transactions and results
- Database schemas
- Data flow diagrams and flow charts
- Sample reports
- Operations procedures

Generalized Audit Software

IS auditors can use generalized audit software (GAS) to directly read and access data from database platforms and flat files. They can independently and directly acquire sample data from databases, which they can then analyze on a separate system. Generalized audit software has the ability to select samples, select data, and perform analysis on data. This can help the auditor better understand key data sets in a system, enabling him to determine the integrity and accuracy of a system.

Continuous Auditing

CAATs can also be used as part of a continuous audit approach, where samples are obtained automatically over long periods instead of just during audit engagements. This represents a paradigm shift from the traditional model of periodic sampling and reporting. To be truly effective, continuous auditing should include the following:

- Frequent notifications to auditors and control owners on audit results
- Triggers to notify auditors and control owners of control failures and other exceptions

Additional guidance on the use of CAATs and continuous auditing is found in ISACA auditing guidelines G3, Guideline on Computer-Assisted Audit Techniques; and G42, Continuous Assurance.

NOTE IS auditors need to take care that the effort to set up the CAAT environment doesn't expend more effort than other methods for sampling and analysis.

Reporting Audit Results

The work product of an audit project is the audit report, a written report that describes the entire audit project, including audit objectives, scope, controls evaluated, opinions on the effectiveness and integrity of those controls, and recommendations for improvement.

While an IS auditor or audit firm will generally use a standard format for an audit report, some laws and standards require that an audit report regarding those laws or standards contain specific information or be presented in a particular format. Still, there will be some variance in the structure and appearance of audit reports created by different audit organizations.

The auditor is typically asked to present findings in a closing meeting, where he can explain the audit and its results and be available to answer questions about the audit. The auditor may include an electronic presentation to guide discussion of the audit.

Structure and Contents

While there are often different styles for presenting audit findings, as well as regulations and standards that require specific content, an audit report will generally include several elements:

- **Cover letter** Audit reports frequently include a cover letter that describes the audit, its scope and purpose, and findings. Often, this letter is used as evidence to other organizations that the audit took place.

- **Introduction** The report should contain an introduction that describes the contents of the audit report.

- **Summary** The report should include an executive summary that briefly describes the audit, its purpose and scope, and findings and recommendations.

- **Description of the audit** The report should include a high-level description of the audit, its purpose, and its objectives.

- **Listing of systems and processes examined** The report should contain a list of systems, applications, and business processes that were examined.

- **Listing of interviewees** The audit report should contain a complete list of interviewees, when they were interviewed, and topics discussed.

- **Listing of evidence obtained**   The report should contain a detailed list of all evidence obtained, from whom, and when it was obtained. Electronic evidence should be described, including the time it was acquired, the system it was obtained from, and the method used to obtain it. The names of any staff members who assisted should be included.

- **Explanation of sampling techniques**   Each time the auditor performed any sampling, the techniques used should be described.

- **Description of findings and recommendations**   Here, detailed explanations describe the effectiveness of each control, based on evidence and the auditor's judgment. Exceptions are described in detail to demonstrate that they actually occurred. Information in this section may be organized according to criticality, technology in use, or business function, or more than one of these.

When the IS auditor is creating the report, he must make sure that it is balanced, reasonable, and fair. The report should not just be a list of everything that was bad; it should also include a list of controls that were found to be operating effectively.

The IS auditor also needs to take care when describing recommendations, realizing that any organization is capable of only so much change in a given period. If the audit report contains many findings, the auditor needs to realize that the organization may not be able to remediate all of them in an elegant manner. Instead, the organization will need to understand which findings should be remediated first—the audit report should provide this guidance.

Evaluating Control Effectiveness

When developing an audit report, the auditor needs to communicate the effectiveness of controls to the auditee. Often, this reporting is needed at several layers; for instance, the auditor may provide more detailed findings and recommendations to control owners, while the report for senior management may contain only the significant findings.

One method that auditors frequently use is the development of a matrix of all audit findings, where each audit finding is scored on a criticality scale. This helps the auditor to illustrate the audit findings that are the most important and those that are less important. The auditor can also report on cases where an ineffective control is mitigated (fully or partially) by one or more compensating controls. For example, a system may not have the ability to enforce password complexity (e.g., requiring upper- and lower-case letters, plus numbers and special characters), but this can be compensated through the use of longer-than-usual passwords and perhaps even more frequent expiration.

NOTE   The IS auditor should review ISACA auditing standard S7, Reporting, and guideline G20, Reporting, when developing the audit report to ensure that the report is complete and accurate.

Other Audit Topics

This section includes important discussions related to IS audits.

Detecting Fraud

Fraud is defined as the intentional deception made for personal gain or damage to an-other party. In the context of corporate information systems and IS auditing, fraud is an act whereby a person discovers and exploits a weakness in a process or system for per-sonal gain.

Management is responsible for implementing controls designed to prevent, deter, and detect fraud. However, no system or process is without weaknesses—worse yet, if two or more employees agree to a conspiracy to defraud the organization, it is possible for the conspirators to, at least temporarily, steal from the organization.

While detecting fraud is certainly not the IS auditor's primary responsibility, an IS auditor surely has many opportunities to discover exploitable weaknesses in processes and systems that could be used to defraud the organization. Occasionally, the IS audi-tor will discover evidence of fraud while examining transaction samples during sub-stantive testing.

When the auditor detects signs of fraud, he should carefully evaluate what he has found and then communicate his findings to the appropriate authorities. Precisely whom he contacts will depend on the nature and structure of the organization and whether there is regulatory oversight of the organization. The auditor needs to be ex-tremely careful when reporting his findings within the organization because the person he reports his findings to could be the perpetrator—or associated with the perpetrator. This logic may prompt the auditor to report this finding directly to the audit commit-tee, thereby bypassing all potential perpetrators in the organization (usually, members of the audit committee are not employees in the organization, have no role in the orga-nization's operations, and hence are probably not among the culprits).

If the organization has no audit committee or similar overseeing body, the auditor may be compelled to report his findings to industry regulators or law enforcement.

When the auditor is representing an external audit organization, often the auditor will discuss the weakness or actual fraud with selected members of the audit organiza-tion in order to confirm his observations and agree on a plan for notifying the auditee or outside authorities.

Communication of the weakness or actual fraud typically begins with a phone call or face-to-face conversation, which will be followed up by a formal written letter. This will satisfy the need to inform the auditee quickly (via the phone call) and formally (via the written letter).

Audit Risk and Materiality

What if there are material errors in business processes that remain undetected by the IS auditor? There are a number of ways in which this can occur, including

- **Control risk** This is the risk that a material error exists that will not be prevented or detected by the organization's control framework. For example, a manual control that is designed to detect unauthorized changes in an information system may fail if the personnel who review logs overlook significant errors or fraud.

- **Detection risk**   This is the risk that an IS auditor will overlook errors or exceptions during an audit. Detection risk should be a part of the IS auditor's risk assessment that is carried out at the beginning of an audit; this would help the auditor focus on those controls that require additional scrutiny (meaning higher sampling rates) and thereby improve the chances of detecting errors.

- **Inherent risk**   This is the risk that there are material weaknesses in existing business processes and there are no compensating controls to aid in their detection or prevention. Inherent risks exist independent of the audit.

- **Overall audit risk**   This is the summation of all of the residual risks discussed in this section.

- **Sampling risk**   This is the risk that the sampling technique used will not detect transactions that are not in compliance with controls.

Materiality   In financial audits, materiality is established as a dollar amount threshold that is calculated in one of several possible ways, including a percentage of pretax income, a percentage of gross profit, a percentage of total assets, a percentage of total revenue, a percentage of equity, or blended methods using two or more of these.

Then, when an auditor is examining transactions and controls during an audit, a finding can be classified as a material weakness if the dollar amount of the exceptions exceeds the materiality threshold. There is, however, some latitude (more in some cases and less in others) in the auditor's judgment as to whether a finding is material.

In an IS audit, the controls being examined usually do not have dollar figures associated with them and deficiencies are not measured against materiality thresholds in the same way. Instead, materiality in an IS audit occurs when a control deficiency (or combination of related control deficiencies) makes it possible for serious errors, omissions, irregularities, or illegal acts to occur as a result of the deficiency(ies). Here more than in a financial audit, the judgment of the IS auditor is very important in determining if a finding is material.

Auditing and Risk Assessment

When assessing the effectiveness of controls in an organization, the IS auditor should take the time to understand how the organization approaches risk assessment and risk treatment.

Risk Assessment   Organizations should periodically undertake risk assessments in order to identify areas of risk that warrant remediation. A risk assessment should identify, prioritize, and rank risks. The subject of risk assessment should be those business processes and supporting information systems and infrastructures that are central to the organization's mission.

After identifying risks, the risk assessment should include one or more potential remedies, each with an analysis of the cost and effort to implement and the estimated reduction in risk. When these remedies and their impact (in terms of risk reduction) are then ranked, the result should be a list of the most effective initiatives for reducing risk in the organization.

There are two types of risk assessment: qualitative and quantitative. A qualitative risk assessment rates risks as high-medium-low, whereas a quantitative risk analysis rates risks in terms of actual probabilities and costs. A quantitative risk assessment is considerably more difficult and time-consuming to perform, since it can be difficult to ascertain reasonable probabilities of threats and their financial impact. However, when seriously considering measures to reduce risk on the highest-risk areas in the assessment, sometimes it makes sense to perform some quantitative risk assessment in order to verify which investments are the ones that will make the most difference.

Risk Treatment   Once risks have been identified, *risk treatment* is the term that describes the action taken to address them. There are four possible avenues for risk treatment:

- **Risk reduction**   This involves making changes to processes, procedures, systems, or controls that will reduce either the probability of a threat or its impact. For example, if the risk assessment identifies a threat of a SQL injection attack on an application, the organization can reduce risk by implementing an application firewall that will block such attacks.

- **Risk transfer**   This typically involves the use of insurance, which is used to compensate the organization for the financial losses or damages that will occur if the threat were realized. For example, the organization can transfer the risk of a denial of service attack by purchasing a cyberinsurance policy that would compensate the organization if such an attack were to occur.

- **Risk avoidance**   Here, the organization will cease the activity associated with the risk. For instance, if the risk assessment identifies risks associated with the implementation of an e-commerce capability, the organization might choose to abandon this idea, thereby avoiding e-commerce–related risk.

- **Risk acceptance**   In this case, the organization feels that the risk is acceptable and that no measures need to be taken to reduce the risk further.

Rarely does an organization make a decision that fits entirely within a single risk treatment category. Rather, risk treatment is usually a blended approach, where, for instance, measures are taken to reduce risk; however, even a combination of measures rarely eliminates all risk—there is usually some risk left over after some risk treatment is performed. This leftover risk is known as *residual risk*. And like the dirt that can't be picked up with a broom and dustpan, the leftover risk is usually accepted.

Control Self-Assessment

Control self-assessment (CSA) is a methodology used by an organization to review key business objectives, risks related to achieving these objectives, and the key controls designed to manage those risks. The primary characteristic of a CSA is that the organization takes initiative to self-regulate rather than engage outsiders, who may be experts in auditing but not in the organization's mission, goals, and culture.

Advantages and Disadvantages

Like almost any business activity, control self-assessments have a number of advantages and disadvantages that the IS auditor and others should be familiar with. This will help the organization make the most of this process and avoid some common problems.

The advantages of control self-assessments include

- Risks can be detected earlier, since subject matter experts are involved earlier
- Improvement of internal controls
- Ownership of controls through involvement in their improvement
- Improved employee awareness of controls through involvement in their improvement
- Improved relationship between departments and auditors

Some of the disadvantages of control self-assessments include the following:

- It could be mistaken as a substitute for an internal audit.
- It may be considered extra work and dismissed as unnecessary.
- It may be considered an attempt by the auditor to shrug off responsibilities.
- Lack of employee involvement would translate to little or no process improvement.

The Control Self-Assessment Life Cycle

Like most continuous-improvement processes, the control self-assessment process is an iterative life cycle. The phases in the control self-assessment are

- **Identify and assess risks**   Here, operational risks are identified and analyzed.
- **Identify and assess controls**   Controls to manage risks are identified and assessed. If any controls are missing, new controls are designed.
- **Develop questionnaire or conduct workshop**   Here, an interactive session is conducted, if possible, for discussion of risks and controls. If personnel are distributed across several locations, a questionnaire is developed and sent to them.
- **Analyze completed questionnaires or assess workshop**   If a workshop was held, the workshop results are assessed to see what good ideas for remediation emerged. If a questionnaire was distributed, the results are analyzed to see what good ideas for risk remediation were identified.
- **Control remediation**   Using the best ideas from the workshop or questionnaire, controls are designed or altered to better manage risk.
- **Awareness training**   This activity is carried out through every phase of the life cycle to keep personnel informed about the activities in the various phases.

The control self-assessment life cycle is illustrated in Figure 3-6.

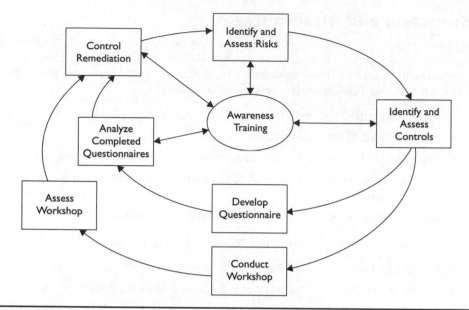

Figure 3-6 The control self-assessment life cycle

Self-Assessment Objectives

The primary objective of a control self-assessment is to transfer some of the responsibility for oversight of control performance and monitoring to the control owners. The IS auditor's role is not diminished, as the IS audit still needs to periodically test control effectiveness, but control owners will play a more active role in the audit of their controls.

Another objective of control self-assessment is the long-term reduction in exceptions. As control owners assume more responsibility for the performance of their controls, they will strive to avoid situations where IS auditors identify exceptions. The control self-assessment gives control owners an opportunity and a process for cleaning house and improving audit results.

 NOTE The IS auditor should be involved in control self-assessments to ensure that the CSA process is not hijacked by efficiency zealots who try to remove the controls from processes because they do not understand their significance.

Auditors and Self-Assessment

IS auditors should be involved in control self-assessments that various departments conduct. The role of IS auditors should be that of an objective subject matter expert who can guide discussions in the right direction so that controls will receive the right kind of development over time.

IS auditors should resist too large a role in control self-assessments. Responsibility for control development and maturation should lie within the department that owns the control self-assessment. However, if a department is new at CSA, it may take some time before they are confident and competent enough to take full ownership and responsibility for the process.

Implementation of Audit Recommendations

The purpose of internal and external audits is to identify potential opportunities for making improvements in control objectives and control activities. The handoff point between the completion of the audit and the auditee's assumption of control is in the portion of the audit report that contains findings and recommendations. These recommendations are the imperatives that the auditor recommends the auditee perform to improve the control environment.

Implementation of audit recommendations is the responsibility of the auditee. However, there is some sense of shared responsibility with the auditor, as the auditor seeks to understand the auditee's business so that she can develop recommendations that can reasonably be undertaken and completed. In a productive auditor-auditee relationship, the auditor will develop recommendations using the fullest possible understanding of the auditee's business environment, capabilities, and limitations—in essence saying, "Here are my recommendations to you for reducing risk and improving controls." And the auditee, having worked with the auditor to understand his methodology and conclusions, and who has been understood by the auditor, will accept the recommendations and take full responsibility for them—in essence saying, "I accept your recommendations and will implement them." This is the spirit and intent of the auditor-auditee partnership.

Summary

The audit function in an organization should be defined and described in a charter. The audit program and audit strategy should support the organization's mission and objectives and facilitate business development and growth.

Auditors need to establish and maintain technical competence so that they can effectively evaluate technical controls and identify technical control risks. They will need to attend periodic training in the technologies in use by the organization, as well as in emerging technologies that the organization may use in the future.

The ISACA Code of Ethics defines the standards of behavior and conduct for IS auditors. The ISACA auditing standards framework defines mandatory audit standards, guidelines that contain suggestions for implementing the standards, and procedures that can be used to audit information systems. All persons who hold the CISA designation are required to uphold the ISACA Code of Ethics; violations will result in investigations and possible disciplinary actions, including expulsion.

ISACA audit standards, guidelines, and procedures provide a framework that can be used to guide the development of an IT assurance program. The Information Technology Assurance Framework (ITAF) is a complete IT assurance and audit framework that borrows elements from COBIT and ISACA audit standards, guidelines, and procedures.

IS auditors need to perform a risk analysis as an integral part of an audit project in order to identify risk areas that require additional audit resources. The result of the risk analysis will help the auditor to build a complete audit plan that includes the right level of activities to be carried out during the audit.

The ISACA Risk-IT Framework provides a set of processes for performing risk governance, risk evaluation, and risk response.

Internal controls are the policies, procedures, mechanisms, systems, and other means designed to reduce risk and facilitate the achievement of business objectives. Controls are classified in several different ways that describe how they are designed to control behaviors and outcomes.

Internal control objectives are statements of desired states and outcomes in the organization. They are supported by one or more controls that ensure the realization of control objectives. Controls are measurable and can be defined and enforced with processes, procedures, or automatic mechanisms within information systems. IS control objectives resemble internal control objectives, but are focused on the desired states and outcomes within the context of information systems.

General computing controls are controls that are applied across an entire IS environment. An organization will likely have additional controls that are applied to individual applications or components in the environment.

An audit is the planned, methodical evaluation of controls and control objectives. A key activity in an audit is the identification and acquisition of evidence that supports the operation of controls and helps the auditor reach a conclusion about the effectiveness of a control.

IS auditors generally develop and follow an audit methodology, which is a process that ensures consistent audits from start to finish.

Evidence is the information collected by the auditor during the course of the audit. The reliability and relevance of evidence helps the auditor reach sound conclusions on the effectiveness of controls and control objectives.

Sampling is the technique used when it is not feasible to test an entire population of transactions. Sampling techniques need to be carefully considered so that they accurately represent the entire population.

Computer-assisted audit techniques (CAATs) are used to automate sampling and analysis of information in complex application environments. CAATs can help to analyze and correlate data that would be too difficult to perform manually. Continuous auditing consists of samples that are automatically gathered over long periods.

The audit report is the work product of the audit project. It contains a summary, a description of evidence gathered, and findings and conclusions.

In IS audits, materiality is the threshold where control deficiencies make it possible for serious errors, omissions, irregularities, or illegal acts to occur.

A control self-assessment is an activity used by an organization to take ownership of controls and make improvements in the implementation of its controls through workshops and other activities.

Notes

- An audit program is the audit strategy and the plans that include scope, objectives, resources, and procedures used to evaluate controls and processes.

- IS auditors need to stay current with technology through training courses, webinars, ISACA chapter training events, and industry conferences.

- Several laws, regulations, and standards require internal or external audits to ensure that organizations achieve and maintain compliance.

- The types of controls are physical, technical, and administrative.

- The classes of controls are preventive, detective, deterrent, corrective, compensating, and recovery.

- The categories of controls are automatic and manual.

- The types of audits are operational audits, financial audits, integrated audits, IS audits, administrative audits, compliance audits, forensic audits, and service provider audits. Pre-audits can be performed to help an organization prepare for an upcoming audit.

- Compliance testing is used to determine if control procedures have proper design and are operating properly. Substantive testing is used to verify the accuracy and integrity of transactions as they flow through a system.

- Audit methodologies define an audit subject, audit objective, type of audit, audit scope, pre-audit planning, audit statement of work, audit procedures, communication plan, report preparation, wrap-up, and post-audit follow-up.

- The types of evidence that the auditor will collect during an audit include observations, written notes, correspondence, process and procedure documentation, and business records.

- During an audit, the auditor should obtain org charts, department charters, third-party contracts, policies and procedures, standards, and system documentation. She should conduct several interviews with pre-written questions and carefully observe personnel to better understand their discipline, as well as organizational culture and maturity.

- The types of sampling include statistical sampling, judgmental sampling, attribute sampling, variable sampling, stop-or-go sampling, discovery sampling, and stratified sampling. The IS auditor needs to understand the meaning of confidence coefficient, sampling risk, precision, expected error rate, sample mean, sample standard deviation, and tolerable error rate.

- An audit report usually includes a cover letter, introduction, summary, audit description, list of systems examined, interviewees, evidence, explanation of sampling techniques, findings, and recommendations.

- The types of risks that are related to audits include control risk, detection risk, inherent risk, overall audit risk, and sampling risk.

- Computer-assisted audit techniques, generalized audit software, and continuous auditing present many challenges and opportunities that may result in more frequent and rapid reporting, which can help to reduce the time needed to mitigate control failures and exceptions.

- External auditors may be needed when the organization lacks specific expertise or resources to conduct an internal audit. However, some regulations and standards require external, independent audits.

Questions

1. An IS auditor is planning an audit project and needs to know which areas are the highest risk. What is the best approach for identifying these risk areas?

   A. Perform the audit; control failures will identify the areas of highest risk.

   B. Perform the audit and then perform a risk assessment.

   C. Perform a risk assessment first and then concentrate control tests in high-risk areas identified in the risk assessment.

   D. Increase sampling rates in high-risk areas.

2. An auditor has detected potential fraud while testing a control objective. What should the auditor do next?

   A. Notify the audit committee.

   B. Conduct a formal investigation.

   C. Report the fraud to law enforcement.

   D. Report the suspected fraud to management.

3. The possibility that a process or procedure will be unable to prevent or detect serious errors and wrongdoing is known as:

   A. Detection risk

   B. Inherent risk

   C. Sampling risk

   D. Control risk

4. The categories of risk treatment are:

   A. Risk avoidance, risk transfer, risk mitigation, and risk acceptance

   B. Risk avoidance, risk transfer, and risk mitigation

   C. Risk avoidance, risk reduction, risk transfer, risk mitigation, and risk acceptance

   D. Risk avoidance, risk treatment, risk mitigation, and risk acceptance

5. An IS auditor needs to perform an audit of a financial system and needs to trace individual transactions through the system. What type of testing should the auditor perform?

A. Discovery testing

B. Statistical testing

C. Compliance testing

D. Substantive testing

6. An IS auditor is auditing the change management process for a financial application. The auditor has two primary pieces of evidence: change logs and a written analysis of the change logs performed by a business analyst. Which evidence is best and why?

A. The change log is best because it is subjective.

B. The written analysis is best because it interprets the change log.

C. The change log is best because it is objective and unbiased.

D. The written analysis is best because it is objective.

7. Under which circumstances should an auditor use subjective sampling?

A. When the population size is low

B. When the auditor feels that specific transactions represent higher risk than most others

C. When the risk of exceptions is low

D. When statistical sampling cannot be performed

8. An IS auditor has discovered a high-risk exception during control testing. What is the best course of action for the IS auditor to take?

A. Immediately perform mitigation.

B. Include the exception in the report and mark the test as a control failure.

C. Immediately inform the auditee of the situation.

D. Immediately inform the audit committee of the situation.

9. What is the appropriate role of an IS auditor in a control self-assessment?

A. The IS auditor should participate as a subject matter expert.

B. The IS auditor should act as facilitator.

C. The IS auditor should not be involved.

D. The IS auditor should design the control self-assessment.

10. Which of the following would NOT be useful evidence in an IS audit?

A. Personnel handbook

B. Organization mission statement and objectives

C. Organization chart

D. Organization history

11. An auditor has discovered that automated work papers were configured with read/write permissions for database administrators. What actions should the auditor take?

    A. Simply continue to rely on the automated work papers.

    B. Note an exception and continue to rely on these automated work papers.

    C. Recommend that permissions on automated work papers be changed so that no personnel have write access so that this data may be relied upon in the future.

    D. Notify the board of directors or the audit committee.

12. During an audit, an auditor has discovered a process that is being performed consistently and effectively, but the process lacks procedure documentation. What action should the auditor take?

    A. Document the process.

    B. Find that the process is effective but recommend that it be documented.

    C. Write the procedure document for the auditee and include it in audit evidence.

    D. Find that the process is ineffective.

13. During audit planning, an auditor has discovered that a key business process in the auditee organization has been outsourced to an external service provider. Which options should the auditor consider?

    A. Audit the external service provider or rely on a SSAE16 audit report if one is available.

    B. Audit the external service provider.

    C. Determine that the business process is not effective.

    D. Request that the external service provider submit its internal audit work papers.

14. Why should an auditor prefer bank statements over a department's own business records that list bank transactions?

    A. Bank statements can be provided in electronic format.

    B. Bank statements contain data not found in internal records.

    C. Bank statements are usually easier to obtain.

    D. Bank statements are independent and objective.

15. Which of the following statements is true about ISACA audit standards, guidelines, and procedures?

    A. ISACA audit standards are mandatory, while ISACA audit guidelines and procedures are optional.

    B. ISACA audit standards and guidelines are optional, while ISACA audit procedures are mandatory.

C. ISACA audit standards, guidelines, and procedures are all mandatory.

D. ISACA audit standards, guidelines and procedures are all optional.

Answers

1. **C.** The IS auditor should conduct a risk assessment first to determine which areas have highest risk. She should devote more testing resources to those high-risk areas.

2. **A.** When the IS auditor suspects fraud, he should conduct a careful evaluation of the matter and notify the audit committee. Because audit committee members are generally not involved in business operations, they will be sufficiently removed from the matter, and they will have the authority to involve others as needed.

3. **D.** Control risk is the term that signifies the possibility that a control will fail to prevent or detect unwanted actions.

4. **A.** The four categories of risk treatment are risk mitigation (where risks are reduced through a control or process change), risk transfer (where risks are transferred to an external party such as an insurance company), risk avoidance (where the risk-bearing activity is discontinued), and risk acceptance (where management chooses to accept the risk).

5. **D.** The auditor should perform substantive testing, which is a test of transaction integrity.

6. **C.** The change log is the best evidence because it is objective and not subject to human judgment.

7. **B.** Subjective sampling is used when the auditor wants to concentrate on samples known to represent higher risk.

8. **C.** The IS auditor should immediately inform the auditee when any high-risk situation is discovered.

9. **B.** The IS auditor should act as a facilitator of a control self-assessment, but allow management to make any decisions regarding changes to controls.

10. **D.** Of the choices given, the organization history would be the least useful. The others will provide insight into the organization's mission and goals, and how it sets out to achieve them.

11. **C.** If an auditor has discovered that automated work papers could be updated by any personnel, then they should not be trusted to contain complete and accurate information. Once this is fixed, the auditor can rely on this data going forward, but should not rely on the information prior to that point in time.

12. **B.** The auditor should determine that the process is effective and recommend that it be documented. However, some regulations may find that such a process is ineffective based on the principle that it lacks documentation.

13. **A.** An auditor who has determined that a key business process has been outsourced needs to determine effectiveness of that process by auditing that process or by relying on a separate audit report of that process.

14. **D.** An auditor would prefer bank statements over internal records because bank statements are produced by a bank, which is independent and objective. A bank is unlikely to alter its records to improve the audit outcome of one of its customers.

15. **A.** ISACA audit standards are mandatory for all ISACA certification holders, including CISA. ISACA audit standards and procedures are optional.

IT Life Cycle Management

This chapter discusses the following topics
- Program and project management
- The software development life cycle (SDLC)
- Infrastructure development and implementation
- Maintaining information systems
- Business processes and business process reengineering
- Application controls
- Auditing the software development life cycle
- Auditing business and application controls

This chapter covers CISA domain 3, "Information Systems Acquisition, Development and Implementation," representing 19 percent of the CISA examination.

Organizations employ business processes to organize the tasks related to the development and maintenance of application software and the underlying IT infrastructure. Business processes provide constraint and management control for high-value activities such as software development and maintenance and infrastructure development and maintenance, as well as the structure for projects and project management.

Many organizations recognize that business processes themselves have the same intricacies as software, and that life cycle management is appropriate for, and similar to, the life cycle for software development. They also realize that business processes and application software are often tightly coupled and must often be managed as complex single entities.

IS auditors should pay particular attention to an organization's methodologies and practices for the development and management of software, infrastructure, and business processes. This will give the auditor valuable information on the effectiveness of an organization's life cycle management and how well the organization develops requirements and can transform them into applications and infrastructure that support key business processes.

In addition to auditing the organization's development processes, auditors must audit software applications. Areas of particular interest include controls that govern input, processing, and output, as much as the application's ability to perform calculations correctly and maintain the integrity of data that is being accessed by many users simultaneously.

Business Realization

Business realization is the result of strategic planning, process development, and systems development, which all contribute toward a launch of business operations to reach a set of business objectives. This chapter focuses on process and systems development, which are used to build the engine of business operations. Audits of these activities provide an objective view of their effectiveness. Business realization is depicted in Figure 4-1.

Portfolio and Program Management

A *program* is an organization of many large, complex activities and can be thought of as *a set of projects that work to fulfill one or more key business objectives or goals*. A program is generally a multiyear effort that is made up of many complex projects, each with its own project managers, project schedule, budget, and participants.

A program is usually run by a *program manager* who has oversight over all of the projects in the program. Figure 4-2 shows the relationship between a program manager and the projects that he or she manages.

Like a single project, a program has a defined scope, budget, resources, and a schedule.

A program also helps to organize and coordinate the operation of its projects, identify dependencies between them, manage conflicts and issues, and manage common and shared resources used by project teams.

Starting a Program

When an organization sets objectives and goals that will be realized through a program, a number of activities usually take place:

- **Development of a program charter** A *charter* is a formal document that defines the objectives of a program, its main timelines, sources of funding, the names of its principal leaders and managers, and the names of the business executive(s) who are sponsoring the program.

Figure 4-1 Business realization

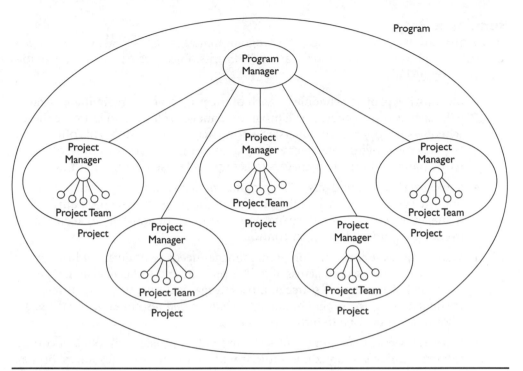

Figure 4-2   A program and several projects under its management

- **Identification of available resources**   Senior management must identify the resources that will be used by the program. These will include funding, personnel, and business assets such as information systems and other equipment.

The charter and resources provide the direction and the means to begin a program that will get the business closer to realizing its objectives.

What's in a Title?

Many middle and senior managers are program managers, even if they don't have "program manager" in their title or job description. Any manager who is responsible for the execution of multiple concurrent projects, particularly if those projects are helping the organization get closer to common objectives, is a program manager.

Running a Program

After a program has been launched, the program manager needs to actively manage it to ensure that the program is on track and fulfilling its objectives. Some of the activities required may include

- **Monitoring project schedules**   Each of the projects running in the program will have its own schedule. The program manager will need to examine these schedules periodically to understand how each is progressing. This often requires the program manager to frequently communicate with program participants and project managers to get up-to-date status on project tasks.

- **Managing project budgets**   The program manager needs to monitor and manage spending by each of the projects in the program. The program manager may need to make spending adjustments periodically to keep the overall program budget under control.

- **Managing resources**   The program manager needs to understand how resources are being used across all of the projects and to make changes as needed. Resources are scarce in most IT organizations, so this requires creativity: often, the program manager needs to *find* resources before those resources can be used to further program goals.

- **Identifying and managing conflicts**   Individual projects will often encounter resource conflicts—sometimes projects will vie for the same resources, or they may require resources in use outside of the program.

- **Creating program status reports for senior management**   As executive sponsors for the program, senior management need to be kept informed of program status, in whatever level of detail they require. Often, these status reports will describe issues and conflicts and how they are being resolved. Sometimes, however, status reports will describe unresolved conflicts that require senior management intervention in the form of resource prioritization in order to keep vital programs moving ahead.

These activities enable management to measure progress and to make adjustments to resources and priorities to keep the program running smoothly.

Project Portfolio Management

The project portfolio is the organization's entire set of active projects at any given time. Unlike a program, where projects are related and support a common objective, a portfolio of projects is simply *all* of the active projects, which may support many different and even unrelated objectives and be part of different programs.

An organization needs to maintain a collection of information about all of its projects in a central location. Having this information will help a senior manager or executive quickly view high-level information about all of the active projects in the organization. Often, this information will be stored electronically in a form that will allow an executive to sort and filter company projects in various ways. Some of the information that may be maintained in this portfolio of projects includes

- Executive sponsor
- Program manager
- Project manager
- Start and end dates
- Names of participants
- Objectives or goals that the project supports
- Budget
- Resources used
- Dependencies

NOTE Ease of access to project and program portfolios helps management better understand what activities are taking place and the resources that each is consuming.

Business Case Development

The prevalent point of view is that IT exists in support of business objectives. Given this assumption, every IT project should directly or indirectly result in tangible business benefits.

Before any IT project is permitted to begin, a *business case* for the project is developed. The purpose of a business case is to explain the benefits to the business that will be realized as a result of the project.

The development of a business case will normally follow a feasibility study. A feasibility study defines the business problem and describes a number of potential solutions. However, it is possible that none of the solutions will result in a benefit for the business. For example, each may be too costly or incur excessive risk. However, the business case should go beyond the feasibility study in terms of business benefits and include actual figures for costs and benefits.

A typical business case is a written document that includes

- **Business problem** This is a description of the business problem in qualitative and quantitative terms.
- **Feasibility study results** The business case should include results of the feasibility study if one was performed.
- **High-level project plan** This should include a timeline and number of persons required.
- **Budget** This should include the cost to execute the project as well as costs associated with the solution.
- **Metrics** The business case should include information on how business benefit will be measured, as well as expected before-and-after measurements.

Estimates should be backed up by examples of the benefits of similar projects in the organization or in other organizations.

- **Risks**   The business case should include risks that may occur, as well as how those risks can be mitigated. These risks may be market risks or financial risks.

 NOTE   Some organizations make the development of a business case the first phase in the actual project; however, this arrangement may be self-serving, as the project team may be taking the point of view of justifying the continuation of the project instead of focusing on whether the project will actually benefit the business. The development of a business case should be performed in an objective manner by persons who do not benefit from the result.

The start of a project is not the only time to assess the project's business case and decide whether to undertake the project. At key milestones throughout the project, the business case should be reevaluated. As a project unfolds, often situations develop that could not be anticipated earlier, and these situations sometimes result in added costs or other changes. For this reason, the business case should be reconsidered throughout the project so that senior management can determine whether the project should continue or not.

 NOTE   Decisions on whether to continue a project should not be made only by those people who benefit from the project, but by other stakeholders who can be more objective. Otherwise, there is a risk that projects will be continued for their own sake instead of for the good of the business.

Measuring Business Benefits

In the mid-to-late 20th century, information technology was primarily used to automate tasks, and in that era it was fairly easy to measure the benefits derived from IT. Often, measuring the benefits was a matter of comparing the cost and time spent to perform tasks manually versus the cost and time spent to automate those tasks. Information technology's role today is business transformation, which provides benefits that are not so easily measured and are often not short-term in nature.

For example, an organization that invests in a new customer relationship management (CRM) application may do so to improve its customer service in measurable ways. Shortly after implementing a CRM system, productivity may even decrease until individuals and teams understand how to operate and fully leverage the new system. But customer satisfaction may improve in future quarters. A year or more may be required to see whether customer satisfaction is a blip or an actual upward trend attributable to the new CRM. The new system can also help the organization to improve its products and services; the benefits from these improvements may not be felt for years after implementation of the new CRM.

Measuring business benefits requires that the organization select key performance indicators and measure them formally and accurately over the long term. When new projects and programs are considered, business benefits should be estimated and measurements should be taken before and after the project has completed in order to validate whether the project's predictions were valid. The nature of the project may require months or even years of measurements to validate project results.

 NOTE Major projects should include post-implementation reviews that take place long after the project's completion (as long as 24 months or even longer) to determine whether trends in key metrics changed as predicted.

Business case development should include a description of the business benefits that are expected from the completed project, including how those benefits will be measured. These key metrics should be decided before the project begins. If key metrics are not being measured, those measurements should begin as soon as possible so that the organization will have enough "before and after" metrics to more easily tell whether the project has benefited the organization or not.

NOTE An organization that does not agree on key metrics is in danger of setting self-fulfilling metrics later on as a way of justifying the project, regardless of whether it actually benefited the organization.

In the spirit of continuous improvement, careful analysis of key metrics long after a project has been completed should lead the organization to consider additional changes in its processes and technologies.

Project Management

The preceding section on business realization is concerned with the high-level view across many projects. This section on project management takes a closer look at the management of individual projects.

A *project* is a coordinated and managed sequence of tasks that results in the realization of an objective or goal. The effort may be performed by a single individual or many. A project's duration may be a few days or as much as two years or longer.

Organizing Projects

Projects should be organized in a methodical way that supports the organization's objectives. Management should formally approve projects, and they should be documented in a consistent manner.

In addition to being a collection of organized activities, a project has a social context and culture. A project consists of a project team, which consists of the people who perform tasks for the project. The relationships among these people fall into four models:

- **Direct report**   A department manager serves as the project manager. Project team members report directly to the manager and are obliged to carry out the directives from the manager. In a slight variation, the department manager could be a project team member, and the project manager is someone who reports to the department manager.

- **Influencer** The project manager has no direct management influence over project team members. The project manager must practice the art of influence and persuasion over the project team members to keep the project moving.

- **Pure project** The project manager is given authority over the project team members, even though the team members do not report to the project manager.

- **Matrix** The project manager and project team manager have authority over each project team member.

NOTE While a project may have a formal plan and schedule, it's the people on the project team who help a project reach its objectives. Paying attention to the human side of projects is just as important as the project objectives themselves.

Initiating a Project

Formal project launch occurs when the project has been approved by the IT steering committee or similar oversight body. Management needs to appoint a project manager as well as all project team members.

Unless project team members have no other responsibilities, management also needs to establish priorities for the team and for each team member. Because most or all project team members will probably have other responsibilities, management needs to be very clear on where project activities fall on the priority list.

Management also needs to express its support for the project schedule and important project milestones so that all project team members are aware of management's objectives for timely project completion. This will help to motivate project team members to start and complete tasks on time.

NOTE A project kickoff meeting is an effective way to convey these messages: management can gauge project team members' interest by studying their body language. A meeting is also an effective way to discuss issues and answer questions in real time.

Developing Project Objectives

The specific objectives of a project must be established and documented before the project begins. In fact, project objectives should be a part of the project's description when the project is being considered for approval by the IT steering committee. Project objectives should be specific, measurable, achievable, relevant, and time-bound (SMART). They should support and relate to business objectives and to the organization's key performance indicators.

Example project objectives are

- Reduce customer service call wait time by 70 percent.
- Reduce implementation time for new customers by five days.
- Reduce annual storage system costs by $70,000.

Additional objectives may also be developed that are not a project's key objectives, but may clarify a project's purpose or the manner in which it will be performed.

Object Breakdown Structure

As a part of the project objectives, a project manager may develop an object breakdown structure (OBS), which represents the components of the project in graphical or tabular form. An object breakdown structure can help management and project team members better visualize the scope and objectives of the project. An example OBS appears in Figure 4-3.

An OBS is a visual or structural representation of the system, software, or application, in a hierarchical form, from high level to fine detail. An OBS is not a schematic, architecture, or data flow diagram, although one or more of these may also need to be developed, either as a part of the design or as a tool to help project participants better understand the overall system.

Work Breakdown Structure

Another common method for depicting a project is the work breakdown structure (WBS). This is a logical representation of the high-level and detailed tasks that must be performed to complete the project. A WBS used for this purpose can also be used as the basis for the creation of the project schedule. An example WBS is shown in Figure 4-4.

The WBS created in this phase will be simpler than the full-fledged project plan, which will include the resources required to perform each task, task dependencies, and schedules.

Figure 4-3   An object breakdown structure (OBS) helps participants understand project scope and objectives.

Figure 4-4 A work breakdown structure (WBS) depicts a project's tasks.

In simpler projects, the WBS and the project plan are the same thing. Or, put another way, the WBS can be the *start* of the project plan, in terms of its containing all of the tasks that need to be included in the project plan. With tools like Planner, the WBS is the list of tasks in the left column, and the project plan is that same list when it also contains dependencies, dates, resources, and other details. Project planning is discussed in more detail later in this section.

Managing Projects

Projects should be managed by a project manager. The project manager is responsible for performing several activities:

- **Building and managing the project schedule** The project manager may have developed the original project schedule, and he or she will be responsible for maintaining the schedule throughout the life of the project. As tasks are completed early, on time, or late, this will impact the rest of the project schedule, and the project manager will need to make adjustments to take into account these scheduling variations. Besides changes in timing, other types of changes in the schedule will be required, including new tasks, new dependencies, and other unforeseen matters.

- **Recording task completion**   As tasks progress and are completed, the project manager must keep the project schedule up-to-date. The project schedule must accurately reflect the status of each task.

- **Running project meetings**   The project manager organizes regular meetings of project participants where status and issues are discussed. The project manager facilitates project meetings to make sure that the meeting agenda is followed. The project manager is also responsible for sending meeting agendas, meeting minutes, and other updates to the project team.

- **Tracking project expenditures**   The project manager is responsible for tracking and reporting on project costs.

- **Communicating project status**   The project manager is responsible for communicating project status to project team members and also to management. A project status report will include details on the status of tasks, whether the project is still on schedule and on budget, and a list of open and closed issues.

 NOTE   The project manager needs to be a highly organized, methodical individual who is detail oriented and a good communicator and negotiator. While knowledge of the technologies in a project is useful, of utmost importance are the project manager's people skills, without which he or she will be unable to work with project team members and to be an effective facilitator and problem solver.

Project Roles and Responsibilities

Formal roles and responsibilities need to be established so that projects will be well organized and have the greatest possible chance of success. Defined roles and responsibilities ensure that important tasks are known to all project participants. Typical roles and responsibilities include

- **Senior management**   Support the approval of the project, its funding, and resource allocation.

- **IT steering committee**   Commission the feasibility study, approve the project, assign IT resources to the project, and approve the project schedule. Periodically review project status and progress. Take corrective action when necessary—for example, when priorities conflict.

- **Project manager**   Develop the detailed project plan, identify and indicate dependencies, estimate the time required to complete each task. Track progress at the task level. Call regular project meetings where project status and issues are discussed among project team members. Track spending and other resource allocation. Publish status reports to project team members and to senior management.

- **Project team members**   Participate in all project team meetings; complete tasks on time; identify issues and communicate them to the project manager; look for opportunities to optimize tasks, reduce necessary resources, and improve the project.

- **End-user management**   Assign staff to the project team, support the development of business requirements, test cases, test data, and system testing.

- **End users**   Develop business requirements, test cases, use cases, test data, test systems, and report test results to the project manager. Participate in acceptance testing and provide accurate, timely results.

- **Project sponsor**   Define project objectives, provide budget and other resources, and work with project manager and other management stakeholders to ensure that the project delivers the desired outcomes.

- **Systems development management**   Provide adequate hardware, software, tools, and resources to facilitate development. Assign competent, trained developers to the project, and support their participation in the project.

- **Systems developers**   Develop software and systems that conform to functional requirements, good coding practices, and organization IT standards. Perform unit, program, and system testing as required. Ensure that software and systems are free of software bugs, vulnerabilities, and security issues that could result in undesired activities such as a break-in or disclosure of sensitive information. Develop operational procedures.

- **Quality assurance**   Review the results and deliverables throughout the project to determine whether the project deliverables are in compliance with project and regulatory compliance.

- **Security manager**   Provide security requirements, privacy requirements, regulatory requirements, audit requirements, test plans, and test cases. Ensure system meets organizational controls and audit requirements. Perform security testing. Report test results to project manager.

- **IT operations**   Provide operational requirements, review operational procedures, and participate in acceptance testing. Participate in system implementation, and operate system after implementation. Report post-implementation problems to project manager and developers.

- **Auditor**   The IS auditor or audit team that will later audit the systems and processes built or changed in the project should act in an advisory role and as a controls expert. The auditor should not otherwise act as a decision maker on the project team.

 NOTE   In smaller organizations, one person may have two or more project roles. In large organizations (or large projects in any size organization), each role may be assigned to one person, a group, or even an entire team.

Project Planning

The term *project planning* refers to the activities related to the development and management of a project. The project manager is responsible for identifying all of the activities required for the project, the sequence in which they must be performed, dependencies between tasks, the resources required, and the priorities of tasks and resources. The project manager will also be expected to determine how the project can make the most efficient use of resources and the shortest time period in which the entire project can be completed.

Project planning encompasses many detailed activities:

- **Task identification**   One of the first steps in the development of a project plan is identifying all of the tasks that must be performed to complete the project. This is often accomplished using a project management tool that can be used to build a detailed work breakdown structure (WBS). When completed, a WBS is a structural decomposition of all of the work necessary to complete the entire project, task by task, bit by bit.

- **Task estimation**   Once the project planner has identified all of the tasks required to complete the project, the next step is determining how much time and effort each task requires. There are a couple of different ways to measure this: actual effort and elapsed time. For example, it may take a painter one hour to paint a room, but it may take four hours for the paint to dry. Often, it is necessary to know how many hours or days of work are required for one or more persons to perform a task, but knowing elapsed time is critical also.

- **Task resources**   It is necessary to know what resources are required to perform a task. Resources include people (and not just any people—often a given task must be performed by specific people), equipment, consumable resources, outside professional services, materials, software licenses, and so on.

- **Task dependencies**   Often in a project there will be tasks that cannot be started until other tasks have been completed. Project managers must discern all of the dependencies between projects so that project teams don't run into unexpected obstacles.

- **Milestone tracking**   In larger projects it is a good idea to identify milestones. Milestones are significant events in the project when major phases have been completed. Example milestones are completion of design, completion of software development, completion of network wiring, and completion of software testing. Often management will wish to schedule a project review meeting when these milestones have been completed; such reviews give management an opportunity to make go/no-go decisions on whether the project should be permitted to continue, or to see whether any lingering issues should first be addressed before the project is continued.

- **Task tracking**   When a project is in progress, the project manager must accurately track the status and progress of every task. He or she also must look toward the short-term and long-term future, anticipate future resource needs, and make sure that tasks that have not started yet will be able to start without undue delay.

NOTE One of the most common pitfalls in project planning is the failure to properly identify task resources and dependencies. Sometimes a project planner will have "optimized" a project plan, only to find out that many tasks that could be done at the same time must be done one at a time. This happens when several tasks that are slated to be done in parallel must all be performed by the same individual. For example, five tasks that take one day each were scheduled to all take place on the same day, but it turns out that the same person is required to perform all of those tasks; this results in those tasks being completed one day after another, requiring five days in all.

Estimating and Sizing Software Projects

Several tools and methods can be used to estimate the amount of effort required to complete tasks in a project. Tools and methodologies can make the task of estimating work more accurate, because they rely on techniques that have been proven over the long run. Also, tools and methodologies can reduce the time required to perform the estimating work.

Object Breakdown Structure (OBS) The object breakdown structure (OBS) can be useful to visually depict the system and its components, particularly in complex projects where the tasks, costs, and other aspects of the project are not immediately evident. Object breakdown structures are described in more detail earlier in this chapter.

Work Breakdown Structure (WBS) The work breakdown structure (WBS), described in detail earlier in this chapter, is a great way to get to the tasks in a complex project. A project manager or planner can decompose large efforts into smaller and smaller pieces, down to the task level.

Source Lines of Code (SLOC) Sizing for software projects has traditionally relied upon source lines of code (SLOC) estimates. Experienced systems analysts could make rough estimates on the numbers of lines of code required for a given software project. Then, using results from past projects, the analyst could make an accurate estimate for the time required to develop a program based on its length. A similar measuring unit is kilo lines of code (KLOC).

The advantage of SLOC and KLOC is that they are quantitative and somewhat repeatable for a given computer language such as COBOL, FORTRAN, or BASIC. However, these methods are falling out of favor because many of the languages in use today are not textual in nature.

The most direct replacement for SLOC/KLOC are methods that estimate the effort required to program a form, page, window, report, cell, widget, file, or calculation. For example, programming effort for a web application would be tied to the number of forms, pages, and windows in a web application and the number of fields and variables in each.

An analogy between the older and newer methods for estimating source code is to estimate the time required to develop engineering drawings for an automobile. Old methods would rely on the weight (number of pounds, akin to number of lines of code) of the car. Newer methods rely on the number of individual features (engine size, number of doors, seats, lights, accessories, and so on).

COCOMO The Constructive Cost Model (COCOMO) method for estimating software development projects was developed in the aerospace industry in the 1970s and represented an advancement in the ability to estimate the effort required to develop software. Three levels of COCOMO were developed, called Basic COCOMO, Intermediate COCOMO, and Detailed COCOMO. Only Basic COCOMO is described here.

Basic COCOMO uses a minimal number of inputs:

- **KLOC**   The number of lines of code (in thousands)
- **Complexity rating**   This rating for the project, expressed as "organic" (a smaller project with experienced software engineers and less-than-rigid requirements), "semi-detached" (a larger project with a mix of rigid and semi-rigid requirements), and "embedded" (a large project with highly specific and restrictive requirements)

Equations in Basic COCOMO are

$$E = a(KLOC)^b$$
$$D = c(E)^d$$
$$P = E/D$$

where:

E = Effort required in man-months
D = Development time in months
P = Number of people required

The values a, b, c, and d are taken from Table 4-1.

Let's look at two examples. First, a software project has 32,000 lines of code and is classified as organic. Using the COCOMO estimating model, this effort will require 91.3 man-months, 13.9 months of elapsed time, and seven people.

In a second example, a software project requires 186,000 lines of code and is classified as embedded. Using the formulas here, this project will require 1,904 man-months, 28 months of elapsed time, and 68 people. This is a large project!

Function Point Analysis (FPA)   *Function point analysis* (FPA) is a time-proven estimation technique for larger software projects. Developed in the 1970s, it looks at the number of application functions and their complexity. FPA is not hindered by specific technologies or measuring techniques (such as lines of code), so it is more adaptable for today's graphical user interface (GUI)–based software.

Table 4-1 COCOMO Weighting Factors	Project Type	a	b	c	d
	Organic	2.4	1.05	2.5	0.38
	Semi-detached	3.0	1.12	2.5	0.35
	Embedded	3.6	1.20	2.5	0.32

In FPA, the analyst studies the detailed design specifications for an application program and counts the number of user inputs, user outputs, user queries, files, and external interfaces. The analyst then selects a complexity weighting factor for each of those five points. The number of inputs, outputs, queries, files, and interfaces are multiplied by their respective complexity weights, and those products are added together. The sum is called the number of unadjusted *function points* (FPs) for the program.

A *value adjustment factor* (VAF) is then determined for the application; this factor will raise or lower the function points based upon 14 criteria that address various aspects of application complexity. The total number of unadjusted function points is multiplied by the VAF to yield the total adjusted function points.

A sample FPA calculation table appears in Table 4-2.

The only disadvantage of function point analysis is that the value of an FP for a program does not directly specify the time required to develop it. However, an organization that has used function point analysis in the past will probably have a pretty good idea of the number of man-hours or man-months each FP requires.

Other Costs In addition to man-months, other costs will need to be considered in a software project, including

- **Development, modeling, and testing tools** The project may require new tools for developers or additional licenses if there are more developers working on the project than the number of available licenses.

- **Workstations** Developers, testers, or users may require additional (or more powerful) workstations.

- **Servers** The project may require additional servers or upgrades to existing servers. Servers may be needed for production and for development and testing purposes.

Parameter	Count	Weighting			Results
		Simple	Average	Complex	
# of user inputs	_____	× 3	× 4	× 6	= _____
# of user outputs	_____	× 4	× 5	× 7	= _____
# of user queries	_____	× 3	× 4	× 6	= _____
# of files opened	_____	× 7	× 10	× 15	= _____
# of external interfaces	_____	× 5	× 7	× 10	= _____
				Total Unadjusted Function Points	= _____
				Multiplied by Value Adjustment Factor	× _____
				Total Adjusted Function Points	= _____

Table 4-2 Using FPA to Estimate Effort Required to Develop Complex Applications

- **Software licenses**   This includes operating systems, database management systems, application software, and possibly more.

- **Network devices**   The project may require additional network devices such as switches, routers, or firewalls to tie everything together.

- **Training**   Developers or testers may need training on the use of their tools, and users may need training regarding the use of new software.

- **Equipment**   This could include office equipment such as copiers, and just about anything else.

Additional costs associated with a project may be specific to certain industries, regulations, or locales.

Scheduling Project Tasks

When the project manager or planner has established the complete breakdown of tasks and has determined resources, dependencies, and levels of effort for each, he or she can create the actual project schedule. Tools such as Trac, Planner, and Microsoft Project will automatically assign dates to tasks once their duration, dependencies, and resources are identified.

After the planner has entered all of the tasks into a project planning tool, he or she will probably discover that the end date of the project (as calculated by the tool) is long after the date that senior management has defined as the end of the project.

This is where a good project planner/manager begins to earn his or her compensation.

This is a critical phase in the project, when the project manager begins to analyze the project plan and look for ways to shorten the overall duration. Methods for optimizing project duration and squeezing the project into management-supplied constraints include

- **Shorten task duration**   The project manager should consult with subject matter experts who provided time estimates for each task and see whether those estimates were high. A good project manager may make the expert uncomfortable as he or she asks the expert to justify the time frames on the plan.

- **Reduce dependencies**   The project manager can consult with subject matter experts to find ways to reduce dependencies, which can enable more tasks to run in parallel (which is okay as long as there aren't multiple tasks stacking up on individual resources or teams).

- **Identify critical paths**   The project manager can perform critical path analysis (discussed in more detail later in this section). This will help to point out which parts of the project may need additional scrutiny.

Gantt Chart   A Gantt chart is a visual representation of a project where individual tasks occupy rows on a worksheet and horizontal time bars depict the time required to complete each task relative to other tasks in the project. A Gantt chart can also show schedule dependencies and percent completion of each task. A sample Gantt chart is shown in Figure 4-5.

Program (or Project) Evaluation and Review Technique (PERT)   *A program (or project) evaluation and review technique* (which is nearly always known just as PERT) chart provides a visual representation of project tasks, timelines, and dependencies. A PERT chart shows project tasks left-to-right in time sequence, with connectors signifying dependencies. An example PERT chart is shown in Figure 4-6.

Critical Path Methodology (CPM)   A PERT chart helps to illustrate how a project is a "network" of related and sequenced tasks. In this network it is possible to draw "paths" through ordered tasks from the beginning to the end of the project.

When a PERT chart includes notation regarding the elapsed time required for each task, you can follow each path through the network and add the elapsed time to get a total time for each path.

A project's *critical path* is that path through the PERT chart with the highest total elapsed time.

Figure 4-5   A Gantt chart illustrates task duration, schedule dependencies, and percent completion.

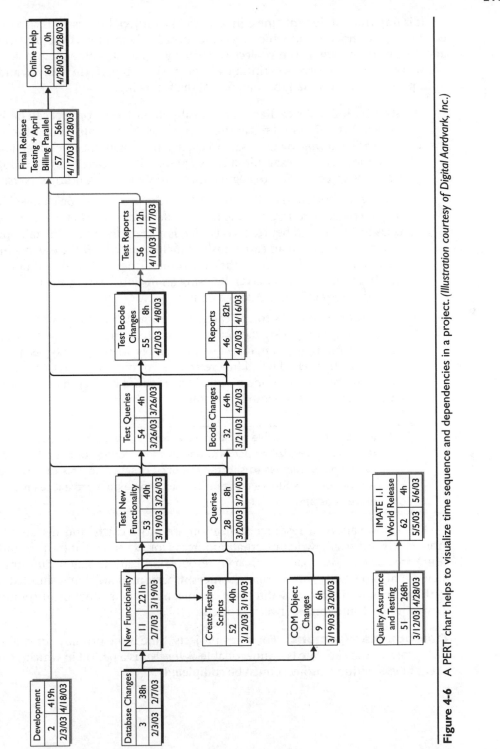

Figure 4-6 A PERT chart helps to visualize time sequence and dependencies in a project. *(Illustration courtesy of Digital Aardvark, Inc.)*

It is important to identify the critical path in a project, because this allows the project manager to understand which tasks are most likely to impact the project schedule and to determine when the project will finally conclude. When a project manager knows which tasks are on the critical path, he or she can perform analysis and attempt to improve the project plan through one of the following:

- **Start critical tasks earlier** If a critical-path task on a project can be started earlier, then this will directly affect the project's end date. To be able to start a task earlier, it may be necessary to change the way that earlier dependent tasks are performed. For example, a Unix system administrator can be brought into a project a week earlier to begin critical tasks such as building servers.

- **Reduce dependencies** If earlier tasks in the project can be changed, then it may be possible to remove one or more dependencies that will allow critical tasks to begin (and hence, end) earlier. For example, a task "Install operating system" depends on an earlier task, "Purchase server." If the organization has an available server in-house, then the project does not need to wait to order, purchase, and receive a server. By using an in-house server, the task "Install operating system" can be started earlier.

- **Apply more resources to critical tasks** Some labor-intensive tasks can be completed more quickly if more resources are available to assist with them. An experienced project manager will be able to identify the types of tasks that can be shortened by adding resources. An old adage says, "Nine women cannot make a baby in one month." Experienced project managers are keenly aware of the concept behind this truth.

NOTE It is impossible to rid a project of critical paths. It is, however, possible (and even essential) to perform one or more rounds of critical-path analysis to find opportunities to shorten the project schedule. This can also help to smooth out resource utilization so that people on a project team are used more constantly.

Peaks and valleys of resource utilization are more costly and disruptive. They're more costly, especially when external resources (for example, contractors and consultants) are used, since on-again off-again resource utilization may incur extra fees. But they can also be costly for internal resources if personnel are being shuttled back and forth between projects. Starts and stops can mean that personnel incur startup time as they move back and forth between projects.

Timebox Management For many projects, time is the primary constraint, and in such projects, the end date is nonnegotiable. A *timebox* is a period in which a project (or a set of tasks within a project) must be completed.

Squeeze to Fit

Left to their own accord, most projects would greatly overrun the period and budget intended by their sponsors and customers. An initial project plan for a simple software development project, for example, may span nine months—but management, being astute with the timing of software projects, wants it done in three.

Most project managers are capable of creating project plans whose schedules extend practically to infinity. However, management should (and does) apply pressure to shorten a project's schedule, often by a significant proportion.

What separates expert project managers from the rest is their ability to optimize a project plan by relentlessly seeking opportunities to compress the schedule by removing dependencies. They achieve this by becoming familiar with the details of every task and by asking tough questions of the experts on the team.

Timeboxing can increase the chances that a large project can be completed, by splitting it into several periods (each usually a few weeks long). Each timebox has its own budget, which is fixed. The deliverable for each timebox, however, can be adjusted somewhat, provided that the customer (or primary end user) agrees with any changes.

NOTE The main problems that timeboxing overcomes are procrastination and projects whose timelines slip. One characteristic of software developers is a tendency to strive for perfection on a project. The result of this tendency is that developers will complete a task and then repeatedly "preen" the output, which takes considerable extra time with little tangible benefit.

Good, Cheap, Fast: Pick Any Two

Experienced project managers are—consciously or unconsciously—aware of the Good-Cheap-Fast triangle in project management. For any project, for the characteristics Good, Cheap, and Fast, management may choose which two characteristics are the most desirable. Whichever two they select, the third characteristic will take an inverse trend.

These are the three principles:

- If a project is Good and Cheap, it will not be Fast.
- If a project is Good and Fast, it will not be Cheap.
- If a project is Cheap and Fast, it will not be Good.

While these statements are not absolute, they are reasonable principles to keep in mind when managing issues that affect budget, schedule, and the quality of the project's outcome.

Project Records

Projects need to have a written record of their proceedings, from project inception to shutdown. The purpose of these records is to help project managers and other project team members keep track of the details related to the project during its lifetime and beyond.

The types of records that most often need to be kept for a project include

- **Project plans**   Initial project plans as well as the records used to track task scheduling and completion.

- **Project changes**   Proposed and approved (as well as rejected) changes to the project schedule, deliverables, budget, and so on need to be recorded.

- **Meeting agendas and minutes**   Issues, decisions, and other matters encountered and discussed from week to week.

- **Resource consumption**   Purchase orders, invoices, and receipts for equipment, supplies, and services. This may also include time sheets and invoices for contractors, consultants, and other service providers.

- **Task information**   Details associated with the performance and/or completion of project tasks.

Project Documentation

Virtually every IT project needs to include documentation that describes the software or application that is built or modified. Documentation helps a wide audience with many aspects of an application, including

- **Users**   End users of applications need to understand how these products are supposed to be used. This includes the operation of all user interfaces, the business meaning of application controls, and how to solve typical problems and issues.

- **Support**   If end-user support is provided, these individuals need to know how to guide users through typical and not-so-typical problems and how to fix common problems.

- **IT operations**   System operators who monitor and operate applications need to know what they are supposed to do. This can include application, database, and operating system monitoring; problem identification and resolution; backups; system recovery; and daily or weekly tasks.

- **Developers**   Detailed descriptions of the application will help current and future developers understand how the software application works. Descriptions of the inner workings of individual programs and tools, internal and external data flows, interfaces, and state diagrams will help developers understand an application so that they can more easily support problems and make future changes.

- **Auditors**   IT and business auditors who audit the application or the business process(es) supported by the application need to know how the application works. This includes business controls such as access controls and the enforcement of business rules, as well as the manner in which business information is stored and processed.

- **Configuration management**   This includes information on the methods to be used to manage and record configuration changes in the application and in the supporting infrastructure and services.

- **Disaster recovery and business continuity planning**   If the application supports a business process that is in-scope for business continuity planning or disaster recovery planning, then a complete set of documentation is required that describes system recovery and emergency operations.

- **Management**   Company management needs to understand how applications support critical business functions, as well as information about the internal and external resources required to build and support the application.

 NOTE   For software projects where existing applications are being updated, all of the existing documents associated with the application need to be reviewed and updated.

Project Change Management

When a project is launched, company management has agreed to sponsor and allocate resources to the project, based upon the objectives of the project at its onset. As a project is launched and as it progresses week by week, the project manager and team will meet regularly to discuss the schedule and any issues that arise that were unanticipated at the start of the project.

While managing the project schedule, a project manager could be tempted to adjust the end date on a task that is running late to adjust affected downstream tasks. However, doing so may affect the budget or the final project deliverable. Management might not appreciate the project manager making arbitrary changes to the project schedule without asking for permission. If management permits this degree of latitude from the project manager, it is likely that the schedule will continue to slip here and there, significantly affecting the final completion date as well as the budget and resource utilization. This type of change cannot be permitted to take place.

Issues that affect the overall project schedule, deliverables, resources, and budget need to be formally identified and submitted for approval through a formal change process. Management needs to establish parameters for changes to budget, schedule, deliverables, and resources. For example, any proposed project change that results in a change of budget or final delivery date would need to be approved by management. The procedure for making changes to the project should be done in two basic steps:

1. The project team, together with the project manager, should identify the specific issue, its impact on the project, and their proposed remedy. This information should be packaged into a formal request.

2. This change request should be presented to management, either in one of the regular project meetings or in a separate meeting that includes the project manager, any relevant project team members (experts in the specific matter to be discussed), and members of senior management—preferably those who are sponsoring the project. The proposed change and its impact on the project should be discussed, and management should make a decision on whether to approve the change.

It should be evident that not every small change needs to go through this process. A spending increase of $10 is hardly a reason to call a management review, and an increase of $10,000 done without any review may make management fuming mad. Management needs to set some parameters so that change reviews will only take place when changes exceed arbitrarily set thresholds.

Smaller changes in schedule and budget can be made a part of a regular project status report that should be sent to management and project sponsors. Smaller issues of changes to budget, schedule, and resources can be highlighted so that management is aware of these less significant changes.

 NOTE Tracking changes in a project is as important as tracking the project's activities. Only through tracking of project changes such as schedule, resource, and cost adjustments can the project manager and senior management understand the status of a project at any given time.

Project Closure

When the developed or updated application is completed, the application will be handed over to users and support staff. Before the project team disbands, some project closure activities need to take place:

- **Project debrief** Here, project team members conduct an honest assessment of the performance of the project. Every aspect of the project is considered: project management, management support, team member participation, user participation, tools and technologies, issues and how they were managed, and turnover. Lessons on what went well and what did not are included.

- **Project documentation archival** All of the records associated with the project are archived for future reference. This includes project plans, memorandums, meeting agendas and minutes, budgets, drawings, specifications, requirements, documentation, and practically everything else.

- **Management review** This is similar to the project debrief and may be the same or a different activity than the project debrief. Management provides the same kind of feedback on the performance of the project that project team members do themselves.

- **Training** Users, operators, support, and analysts need to be trained on the new or changed system. In some cases this should be handled prior to project closure, particularly if users will be using the system before that time.

- **Formal turnover to users, operations, and support** When the project is completed, the project team formally relinquishes control of all the elements of the project. Responsibility for managing and operating the application is transferred to IT operations and support. Responsibility for using the application is transitioned to business owners and end users.

Project Management Methodologies

Planning, initiating, and managing a project is a complex undertaking, and there are many different types of projects, even within an individual organization. Several project management methodologies are in use. These methodologies differ in approach, documentation, and management techniques.

Project Management Body of Knowledge (PMBOK)

The PMBOK guide is an international standard (IEEE Std 1490-2003) that defines the essentials of project management. The PMBOK is process-based; processes are described as

- Inputs (documentation, plans, designs, and so on)
- Tools and techniques (mechanisms applied to inputs)
- Outputs (documentation, products, or services)

In the PMBOK model, processes in most projects are arranged in five process groups and nine knowledge areas. The process groups for running a project are

1. Initiating
2. Planning
3. Executing
4. Controlling and Monitoring
5. Closing

The knowledge areas are

1. Project Integration Management
2. Project Scope Management
3. Project Time Management
4. Project Cost Management
5. Project Quality Management
6. Project Human Resource Management
7. Project Communications Management
8. Project Risk Management
9. Project Procurement Management

The process groups and knowledge areas form a matrix, where every process within project management falls into one knowledge area and one group.

NOTE The PMBOK is described in a publication called *A Guide to the Project Management Body of Knowledge,* published by the Project Management Institute (PMI).

PRojects IN Controlled Environments (PRINCE2)

The PRojects IN Controlled Environments (PRINCE2) is a project management framework that was developed by the UK Office of Government Commerce. Like PMBOK, PRINCE2 is a process-driven framework. The elements of the framework consist of 45 subprocesses that are organized into eight top-level processes:

1. Starting Up a Project (SU)
2. Planning (PL)
3. Initiating a Project (IP)
4. Directing a Project (DP)
5. Controlling a Stage (CS)
6. Managing Product Delivery (MP)
7. Managing Stage Boundaries (SB)
8. Closing a Project (CP)

Each of these processes has its own structure and additional detail that describe steps and required activities. The structure and information flow in PRINCE2 is illustrated in Figure 4-7.

Figure 4-7 The PRINCE2 process structure and information flow

NOTE PRINCE2 is the de facto project management framework in the United Kingdom and several other countries.

Scrum

Scrum is an iterative and incremental process most commonly used to manage an Agile software development effort. Scrum defines several roles:

- **ScrumMaster**   This is the project manager or team leader.
- **Product owner**   This is the customer, or the customer's representative who speaks for the customer.
- **Team**   These are the project team members who do the actual project work.
- **Users**   These are the people who will be using the software once it has been developed or updated.
- **Stakeholders**   These are other parties who contribute in some way to the project, such as customers, vendors, and suppliers.
- **Managers**   These individuals provide resources to the project.

These roles belong to two major groups: *pigs* and *chickens* (I am serious, please stay with me here), after a semifamous pig and chicken joke. The pigs are the ScrumMaster, product owner, and team members. Like the pig in the joke, these persons are totally committed to the project and their jobs are on the line.

A typical Scrum team is just five to nine members. Larger projects are organized into a Scrum of Scrums that scales upward to include hundreds of programmers.

The chickens are those persons who are not a part of the actual project team, but are involved in the project to a somewhat lesser extent. The chicken roles are the users, stakeholders, and managers. While interested in the outcome of the project, their jobs are probably not on the line.

A typical Scrum project consists of a *sprint*, a focused effort to produce some portion of the total project deliverable. A sprint usually lasts from two to four weeks.

The project team meets every day in a meeting called the *daily standup* (or the *Daily Scrum*) that lasts no more than 15 minutes. It is called a *standup* because participants

The Pig and the Chicken

A pig and a chicken are walking down a road. The chicken looks at the pig and says, "Hey, why don't we open a restaurant?" The pig looks back at the chicken and says, "Good idea. What would you like to call it?" The chicken thinks about it and says, "Why don't we call it 'Ham and Eggs'?" "I don't think so," says the pig, "I'd be totally committed but you'd only be involved."

usually stand (it helps the meeting go faster). The ScrumMaster leads the meeting and asks three questions of each team member:

1. What have you done since yesterday?
2. What are you planning to do by tomorrow?
3. What obstacles are preventing you from completing your work?

While chickens are welcome to join the daily standup, only pigs are permitted to speak.

At the end of each sprint, a *sprint retrospective* is held, a meeting that is a reflection of the just-completed sprint. A retrospective is usually limited to four hours.

The documents that are created and maintained in a Scrum project are

- **Product backlog** This is a list of required features that describes deliverables for the entire project (not just the current sprint).
- **Sprint backlog** This is a detailed document that describes how the project team will implement requirements for the current sprint.
- **Burn down chart** This is a document that shows the number of remaining tasks for the current sprint or the count of items on the sprint backlog.

The Scrum process is illustrated in Figure 4-8.

 NOTE Despite the humor in its terminology, Scrum is taken seriously and is used by several large software product firms such as IBM and Microsoft.

Figure 4-8 The Scrum process consists of one or more sprints that produce project deliverables every two to four weeks.

The Software Development Life Cycle (SDLC)

Developing and maintaining software is a complex undertaking that requires a great deal of structure, organization, and discipline. Application software is used to automate or support key business processes. Organizations rely heavily on applications to be operating properly, on demand, and with sufficient capacity.

Designing, developing, and using software requires a diverse array of skills that are typically located in several parts of an organization. These diverse skills are carried out by persons with different levels and styles of education, and in the workplace, these different groups of people are sometimes suspicious of one another and believe that the others do not really understand the way things ought to be.

Software development projects are expensive. Given the cost of developers, project managers, software tools, and computer hardware, even a "small" project can easily run many tens of thousands of dollars, and large projects can cost several million.

Management wants the project to finish on time and on budget, and users want the software to operate as promised. Shareholders want the entire development process to be efficient and effective.

 NOTE The CISA exam may include multiple questions related to the SDLC or its business process equivalent, the BPLC, covered later in this chapter. Familiarity with the phases of the SDLC is key to success in these questions.

These factors are among those that demand that the software development process be highly organized and structured so that all activities are performed according to a plan. The SDLC is a framework for deciding what software should do, building it accordingly, performing testing to verify features, placing it in production, providing support, and maintaining it after initial implementation.

SDLC Phases

The *software development life cycle* (SDLC) is the term used to describe the "end-to-end" process for developing and maintaining software. A common structure for SDLC is a *waterfall*-style framework that consists of distinct phases:

- Feasibility study
- Requirements definition
- Design
- Development
- Testing
- Implementation
- Post-implementation

Organizations often employ a "gate process" approach to their SDLC by requiring that a formal review be held at the conclusion of each phase before the next phase is permitted to begin. The review is usually a formal meeting where project managers and other participants describe the status of the project; management, if satisfied that the current phase of the project has been completed successfully and that all requirements have been met, will permit the project to proceed to the next phase.

In addition to the waterfall SDLC model, iterative and spiral models are used in SDLC processes. The iterative and spiral models both operate in (visually) circular modes, as opposed to the linear waterfall model.

The *spiral* model consists of the development of requirements, design, and one or more prototypes, followed by additional requirements and design phases until the entire design is complete. Similarly, the development in the *iterative* model goes through one or more loops of planning, requirements, design, coding, and testing until development and implementation are considered complete.

SDLC in this section is described from the waterfall model's perspective. The activities discussed in this section in the waterfall model are quite similar to those in the iterative and spiral models.

Software and Business Capabilities Imagined

The first phase of the SDLC is the feasibility study. But how does the feasibility study get started? It does not create itself; instead, the feasibility study is started as a result of some pre-SDLC event.

An instantiation of the SDLC is created when management has decided that some new software application is needed, or when significant changes are needed in an existing application. By "instantiation" I mean that management has made a decision to initiate the process to develop or update a software application. Management makes such a decision as a response to an event, which could be any of the following:

- **Changes in market conditions** For example, the entrance of a new competitor or the development of a new product or service feature by a competitor may spur management to respond by matching the competitor's capabilities. A competitor can also create a new market through an innovation in products or services; this kind of a move sometimes needs to be answered by making a change to maintain parity with the competitor. Or, *your* organization may be the one that creates a new market through some groundbreaking innovation in the way that it does business or in what it delivers to its customers.

- **Changes in costs or expenses** Dramatic shifts in capital or expense costs may force an organization to make changes. For instance, higher fuel costs may prompt the organization to reduce field service calls, but doing so might require better remote diagnostic and self-healing capabilities. In the 1990s, the shift to software development outsourcing required transformations in development methodologies that prompted organizations to make or buy better defect-management applications. And dropping telecommunications costs and higher bandwidth meant that online service providers began to ratchet up their offerings, most of which required enhancements to existing online service applications, and sometimes brand-new ones.

- **Changes in regulation**   The rise in dependence on technology has resulted in some negative events, which in turn resulted in new legislation or changes in existing legislation. Examples of new and updated regulation include Sarbanes-Oxley, GLBA (Gramm Leach Bliley Act), HIPAA (Health Insurance Portability and Accountability Act), FERC/NERC (regulations from the Federal Energy Regulatory Commission and the North American Electric Reliability Corporation), USA PATRIOT Act (Uniting and Strengthening America by Providing Appropriate Tools Required to Intercept and Obstruct Terrorism Act of 2001), PCI DSS (Payment Card Industry Data Security Standard), and many others. Many of these regulations require organizations to implement additional safeguards, controls, and recordkeeping to information systems. Sometimes this results in an organization opting to discontinue use of an older information system in favor of making or buying a newer application that can more effectively comply with applicable laws.

- **Changes in risk**   New types of vulnerabilities are discovered with regularity, and new threats are developed in response to vulnerabilities as well as changes in economic conditions and organizational business models. In other words, hackers find new ways to try and attack systems for profit within the growing cyber-criminal enterprises of the world. Applications that were considered safe just a few years ago are now known to be too vulnerable to operate. Reducing risk sometimes means making changes to application logic, and sometimes it requires that an application be discontinued altogether.

- **Changes in customer requirements**   Similarly, changes like those just discussed will often prompt customer organizations to ask for new features or for changes in existing features in the products and services they buy. Often this requires changes in processes and applications to meet these customers' needs.

 NOTE   Internal and external events prompt management to action by initiating changes in business processes, product designs, service models, and, frequently, the software applications that are used to support and manage them. What begins as an informal discussion turns to more formal actions and, finally, to the initiation of a project to make changes.

Feasibility Study

The feasibility study is the first formal phase in the SDLC. The feasibility study is an intellectual effort that seeks to determine whether a specific change or set of changes in business processes and underlying applications is practical to undertake.

Capital and money are the fuel and lubricant for an organization. Often the purpose of a feasibility study is not to answer the question, "Can a specific type of change be made to the business?" but rather, "Is a specific type of change to the business feasible from a cost and benefit perspective?" In other words, the feasibility study is an analysis of proposed changes to business processes and supporting applications, including the costs associated with making those changes and the benefits that are expected as a result of those changes. While there is often a qualitative aspect in the feasibility study, there is almost always a quantitative aspect that states, "These specific changes will cost XXX to build, YYY to maintain, and are anticipated to make a ZZZ impact on revenue."

Organizations don't always make changes to business processes to increase revenue or reduce costs. However, revenue and costs are nearly always the quantitative elements that receive attention. For example, if an organization is enacting changes to processes and systems to remain compliant with regulations, management is still going to be interested in the cost and revenue impact that the changes will bring about.

A feasibility study often will propose two or more approaches to a particular challenge. For instance, if a project has been initiated as a result of changes in market conditions, the purpose of the feasibility study may be to explore various ways to respond to those market conditions; for each way to respond, there may be two, three, or more ways to implement the change by using a variety of technologies or approaches. For example, when the online video rental market became crowded and margins diminished (a market condition), companies in this market space responded by offering new ways for its customers to view movies—in particular by downloading them directly and thereby eliminating the need to ship DVDs through the mail. The companies in the online video rental market may well have considered other ways of expanding or differentiating their services, such as rent-to-own, surprise movies (an extra movie in addition to the one ordered), a rewards program, or incentives for discounts by having customers create written reviews for movies viewed.

Considerations that the feasibility study should also include are

- Time required to develop or acquire software (or to make changes) and whether the solution can be developed or acquired within that time frame
- A comparison between the cost of developing the application versus buying one
- Whether an existing system can meet the business need
- Whether the application supports strategic business objectives
- Whether a solution can be developed (or acquired) that is compatible with other IT systems
- The cost of building interfaces between the new system and other existing systems
- The impact of the proposed changes to the business on regulatory compliance
- Whether future requirements can be met by the system

A feasibility study should seek to uncover every reasonable issue and risk that will be associated with the new system. The study should have the appearance and form of impartiality, and should not reflect the biases and preferences on the part of those who are taking part in the feasibility study or its outcome.

A feasibility study may also include or reference a formal business plan for the proposed new activity. A business plan is a formal document that describes the new business activity, its contribution and impact to the organization, resources required to operate the activity, benefits from operating the activity, and risks associated with the activity.

 NOTE When the feasibility study has been completed, a formal management review should take place so that senior management fully understands the results and recommendations of the study and whether the project should proceed or whether any changes to the plan should take place.

Requirements Definition

Requirements describe necessary characteristics of a new application or of changes being made to an existing application. They will describe how the application should work, as well as the technologies that it should support. The types of requirements used in software projects are

- Business functional requirements
- Technical requirements and standards
- Security and regulatory requirements
- Disaster recovery and business continuity requirements
- Privacy requirements

These types of requirements are described in detail in the remainder of this section.

Business Functional Requirements   Nearly every software project will include functional requirements. These are statements that describe required characteristics that the software must have to support business needs. This includes both the way that the software accepts, processes, and produces information, and how users interact with the software in terms of technology, appearance, and user interface function.

Functional requirements should be a part of new software acquisitions as well as modifications or updates to software.

Example functional requirements resemble the following:

- Application supports payroll tax calculations for U.S. federal, states, counties, and cities.
- Application supports payment by credit card and electronic check.
- Application encrypts credit card numbers, Social Security numbers, and driver's license numbers in storage and when transmitted.

Notice that the preceding examples do not specify *how* the application is to accomplish these things. Business requirements are interested in *what* the application does; the application designer will determine *how* the application will support those requirements.

There are a few circumstances where new business requirements are not needed for a software modification. For example, if a software interface is being upgraded, an existing software program may need to be modified to work with the new interface. A change like this should be transparent to users, and the software should not differ in the way that it supports existing business requirements. So, in a way, it can be argued that business requirements apply even in this case: the program will still be required to adhere to existing business functional requirements.

 NOTE It is not unusual for a formal requirements document to span many hundreds of pages. This will be the case especially for larger and more complex applications such as customer relationship management (CRM), enterprise resource planning (ERP), manufacturing resource planning (MRP), or service management systems.

Technical Requirements and Standards To help the organization remain efficient, any new application or system should use the same basic technologies that are already in use (or that are planned on being used in the long term). The details related to maintaining the consistency that is required constitute the majority of technical requirements and standards.

An organization of any appreciable size should have formal technical standards in place. These standards are policy statements that cite the technologies, protocols, vendors, and services that make up the organization's core IT infrastructure. The purpose of standards is to increase technological consistency throughout the entire IT infrastructure, which helps to simplify the environment and reduce costs. Standards should include the following:

- Server hardware, operating system, and operating system configuration
- Server tools and services
- Interfaces
- Database and storage management system
- Network architecture, communications protocols, and services
- Authentication and authorization models and protocols
- Security architecture, hardening, configuration, and algorithms
- Software development methodologies, tools, languages, and processes
- User applications and tools

In addition, an organization may have other standards that describe methodologies, technologies, or practices.

When an organization is considering the acquisition of a new system, the requirements for the new system should include the organization's IT standards. This will help the organization select a system that will have the lowest possible impact on capital and operational costs over the lifetime of the system.

Besides IT standards, many additional technical requirements will define the desired new system. These requirements will describe several characteristics of the system, including

- How the system will accept, process, and output data
- Specific data layouts for interfaces to other systems
- Support of specific modules or tools that will supplement or support application functions (for example, the type of tax table that will be used in an invoicing or payroll system)
- Language support
- Specific middleware support
- Client platform support

 NOTE The entire body of technical requirements should accomplish two sweeping objectives: first, to ensure that the new system will blend harmoniously with the existing environment; and second, that the new system will operate as required at the technical level.

Security and Regulatory Requirements Security and regulatory requirements must be developed to ensure that the new application will contain appropriate controls and characteristics that will protect sensitive information and comply with applicable regulations.

Security and regulation are sometimes strange bedfellows, and sometimes they are symbiotic. It is often better to split security and regulatory requirements into two separate sections. However, security and regulation are often mashed together, since it seems that the majority of recent applicable regulations are security-related. I have kept these two topics in a single section because I suspect that most readers expect to find security and compliance together, but I recommend you separate them, since many security requirements are not associated with regulations, and because many regulations are not security-related. In the remainder of this subsection I will keep them separated.

Organizations should have an existing security requirements document that can be readily applied to any software development or acquisition project. These requirements should describe the business and technical controls that address several security topics, including

- **Authentication** This broad category includes many specific requirements related to the manner in which application users authenticate onto the system. For systems that perform autonomous authentication, this will include all of the password quality requirements (minimum length, expiration, complexity, and so on), account lockout settings, password reset procedures, user account provisioning, and user ID standards. Authentication standards may also include requirements for machine and system accounts in support of automated functions in the application. For applications that use a network-based authentication service such as LDAP (Lightweight Directory Access Protocol), Kerberos, or a single-sign-on (SSO) solution, security requirements should describe how the application must interface with a network authentication service.

- **Authorization**   This category includes requirements related to the manner in which different users are granted access to different functions and data in the application. Authorization requirements may include the way in which roles are established, maintained, and audited. An organization may require that the application support a number of "roles," which are templates that contain authorization details that can be applied to a user account.

- **Access control**   This category has to do with how the application is configured to permit access to users and/or roles. Unlike authorization, which is about assigning roles to users, access control is concerned with assigning access permissions to objects such as application functions and data. Depending upon the way in which an application is designed, permissions assignment may be user-centric, object-centric, or both.

- **Encryption**   Really another form of access control, encryption is used to hide data that, for whatever reason, may exist in "plain sight" and yet must still be protected from those who do not have authorization to access it. Encryption standards will fall into two broad categories: (1) data requiring encryption in certain settings and contexts, and with certain encryption algorithms and key lengths; and (2) key management to be handled in specific ways that will permit the application to be operated similarly to other applications in the IT environment.

- **Data validation**   Applications should not blindly trust all input data to be properly formed and formatted. Instead, an application should perform validation checks against input data, whether a user types in input data on an application input form, or if the application receives the data via a batch feed from a trusted source. Data validation includes not only input data, but also the results of intermediate calculations and output data. Requirements should also specify what the application should do when it encounters data that fails a validation check.

- **Audit logging**   This is the characteristic whereby the application creates an electronic record of events. These events include application configuration changes, adding and deleting users, changing user roles and permissions, resetting user login credentials, changing access control settings, and, of course, the actions and transactions that the application is designed to handle. Requirements about audit logging will be concerned with the configuration that is used to control the types of events that are written to an audit log, as well as the controls used to protect the audit log from tampering (which, if permitted, could enable someone to "erase their tracks").

- **Security operational requirements**   Management of passwords, encryption keys, event logs, patching, and other activities is required to maintain an application's confidentiality, integrity, and availability.

Disaster Recovery and Business Continuity Requirements Applications that do—or may in the future—support critical business functions included in an organization's disaster recovery plans need to have certain characteristics. Depending upon specific recovery targets specified for the business process supported by the application, these requirements may include the ability for the application to run on a server cluster, support data replication, facilitate rapid recovery from backup tape or database redo logs, run in a load-balanced mode, or be installed on a cold recovery server without complicated, expensive, or time-consuming software licensing issues. Requirements could also dictate the ability for the application to be easily recovered from a server image on a storage area network (SAN), operate correctly in a virtual server environment, and operate correctly in an environment with a vastly different infrastructure, like that kind that may be found in a recovery environment such as a hot site. An application might also be expected to work with a different brand or version of database management system, or to coexist with other applications, even though it may usually be configured to run on a server by itself.

Privacy Requirements In the broadest sense, privacy is about two distinctly different issues. First, privacy has to do with the protection of personally sensitive information so that it cannot be accessed by unauthorized parties. This aspect of privacy neatly falls into the umbrella of security: security requirements can be developed that require access controls or encryption of personal information.

The other aspect of privacy is the prevention of proliferation of personally sensitive information. This has a lot less to do with security and more to do with how the organization treats sensitive information and whether it permits this information to be passed on to other organizations for their own purposes. In this regard, privacy is about business functionality that is specifically related to how the application handles personal information.

For example, if an application includes canned reports about customers that are sent to third parties, those reports should be configurable so that they can contain (or omit) certain fields. For instance, date of birth might be omitted from a report that is sent to a third-party organization in order to reduce the possibility of the third party using or abusing information to the detriment of individual customers. The rule in this case is "you can't abuse or misuse information you do not possess."

Privacy is often addressed by regulation, so an organization may choose to classify privacy requirements in a privacy section or in a regulations section.

Organizing and Reviewing Requirements In a software project where many individuals are contributing requirements, the project manager should track each requirement back to a specific individual so that person can justify or explain those requirements if needed.

When all requirements have been collected and categorized, the project manager should check with each contributor to make sure that each requirement is actually a *requirement* and not merely a nice-to-have feature. Perhaps each requirement can be weighted or ranked in order of importance. This will help, especially in a request for proposal (RFP) situation where analysts need to evaluate suppliers' conformance to individual requirements. This helps project personnel to better determine which vendors are able to meet the requirements that matter most.

 TIP The teams that develop requirements need to make sure that requirements are measurable. The reason for this is that the requirements developed in this phase of the project should flow directly into user acceptance testing plans (for functional requirements) and system testing plans (for technical requirements).

The RFP Process The vast majority of mainstream business functions, such as accounting, customer relationship management, incident management, sales force management, and enterprise resource planning, can be handled exceedingly well using common off-the-shelf (COTS) software. Advances in COTS software have resulted in most IT organizations only needing to develop custom interfaces between COTS applications and specialized programs that cannot be readily obtained. Thus, the SDLC process can be morphed somewhat to accommodate the fact that most big software projects are a matter of buying, not making:

- **Requirements** This trend makes the development of good requirements much more important, since the matching of different vendors' software products with business and technical requirements depends mostly on requirements. The software that is obtained is configurable only to a point, and it probably will not be able to perform other functions so easily. In an environment where a business analyst or project manager realizes that some requirements were omitted, if the organization wrote its own software, then it might be fairly easy to change the application. If, on the other hand, some important requirements were omitted and a product selection was made in the absence of those requirements, the organization may have to live without the functionality related to those requirements. It's kind of like specifying a four-passenger automobile because you forgot about that fifth family member; now that you've got the car, it's difficult to make a change.

- **Vendor financial stability** When an organization is considering purchasing or licensing software from a software vendor, the organization should examine the financial stability of the vendor. This is done as a way of determining whether the vendor is likely to be in business in the future. If the vendor's financial fundamentals are unhealthy, then purchasing software from this vendor is a risky proposition, since the vendor may not be in business in the future. This would probably require the organization to change its software in another expensive application migration that could have been avoided.

- **Product roadmap** While the software vendor may be healthy, it's also important to understand the vendor's long-term vision for its product. This includes not only business functionality but also the technical platforms that will be supported in the future. In this regard it is also useful to know whether any of the vendors being considered can be deemed to be market leaders or market followers. If the organization shopping for software is likewise a market leader, it may make more sense to select a market-leading company that will be able to keep up with the organization's own vision and market leadership.

- **Experience**   It's important to understand how much experience a prospective vendor has. A suitable vendor should have many years of experience developing software for the solution that the organization is trying to solve. This will help to clarify whether the vendor has been in the business of developing this particular type of software for a long time, or whether it has only recently entered the market. Deep experience will give confidence that the vendor has experience helping its customers solve the types of business problems that its software is designed to solve, whereas a company with little experience will probably have more difficulty helping its customers solve even simpler business problems, not to mention unusual or complex problems. You do not want to be in the position of calling the software vendor to ask, "Hi, we have a new kind of problem that we need to solve," only to receive the answer, "Well, we won't be able to be of much help because we're new at this ourselves."

- **Vision**   Even for a software product as mundane as accounting, it is important to know each vendor's vision for how it aims to innovate and to approach business problems in the future. If a vendor's vision varies widely from your organization's vision, perhaps that particular vendor is not the best choice. However, a difference in vision should almost never disqualify a vendor entirely, but it should be just one more variable in the long equation of vendor selection.

- **References**   When an organization is considering purchasing software from an outside vendor, it is wise to discuss the vendor with at least two or three reference customers. I suggest that a standard questionnaire be developed before any vendor contacts are made. A questionnaire will help the project manager or business analyst to collect the same information from each reference customer. This will help the organization more easily compare reference information that has been collected from several reference clients.

Questions asked of reference clients fall into several areas:

- **Satisfaction with installation**   If the software vendor will be helping with software installation and setup, ask reference clients about the quality of this effort. Find out what kinds of specific issues came up and how the vendor managed them.

- **Satisfaction with migration**   If the software vendor is going to be assisting with migrating business functionality to the new software application, ask each reference client about the quality of this effort. Whether it went well or not so well, get the names of specific personnel so that your organization can (if feasible) ask that certain vendor staff be there to support migration.

- **Satisfaction with support**   Find out from each reference client whether they are satisfied with each vendor's support organization. See if the support organization provides timely, high-quality, and consistently good service.

- **Satisfaction with long-term roadmap**   Ask the reference client if they are satisfied with each vendor's long-term product roadmap. Ask what strengths and weaknesses are in the roadmap.

- **What went well**   Find out each vendor's strengths and try to determine if those strengths are associated with individual vendor employees or with the vendor overall. Ask if the reference client would choose the vendor again and why (or why not).

- **What did not go so well**   Ask the reference client what parts of their software project did not go so well. Find out if the reference client believes their experience to be associated with one specific vendor employee or whether their problems were with the entire company as a whole.

Finally, ask each vendor's reference client what other questions should have been asked. Sometimes you'll find out about a completely different set of activities that were associated with the vendor's migration.

- **Evaluation**   When you have received RFP responses from each vendor, you can begin to chart the responses in a multicolumn spreadsheet with each vendor's responses in a separate column. You can even score each response with a Low-Medium-High rating, and use that to see how the vendors rank in terms of requirements and references. If the field of potential vendors can be reduced to the top two or three vendors, you may wish to evaluate their products in your IT environment for a time.

  Evaluation means having the software in your organization to install and try out with some users. The evaluation should be highly scripted—not to "win" or "lose," but to systematically verify that the software performs as claimed, and that the vendor's responses to your functional requirements are credible. If the software operates differently than their claims in the RFP responses, it's time to either ask hard questions or disqualify them for stretching the truth and move on.

- **Vendor support**   Success with a given vendor's software product can rest on vendor support alone. Specifically, if there are problems and support is of insufficient quality, the project can stall or even fail. Support quality has a few dimensions to it, including timeliness, quality, and speed to escalation. If a vendor falls short in any of these areas, then that choice may have more risk.

- **Source code escrow**   When an organization develops its own software, of course the software is already in the organization's custody. However, when a third-party vendor develops the software, the customer probably does not have a copy of it. Under ordinary business conditions, this is acceptable. However, should the vendor fail, the vendor will be unable to maintain the software and the organization would be stuck with a software package without source code or programmers to support it.

Source code escrow is a viable solution to this problem, and it works like this. The software vendor sends an electronic copy of its source code to a third-party software escrow firm, which keeps control of the software. If, however, the software vendor goes out of business, then the organization will be able to obtain a copy of the vendor's software for support purposes. This is a bad-case scenario but it's better than the worst-case scenario, where the software vendor goes out of business and the organization has no source code at all.

- **Selection**   After the organization has narrowed the search down to two or three vendors, it's time to do more critical thinking, discussing, and identifying of the primary strengths, weaknesses, and differentiators between the vendor finalists. The RFP team should make a recommendation to management on its choice, explaining why this particular vendor should be chosen over the others.

  The final decision on a software vendor should be made by management, with the RFP team being a consultative body. Remember, senior management will be making a business decision that partly considers the technology and partly considers the value proposition (the value derived from a given expenditure).

- **Contract negotiation**   When the selection is made, the contract between the organization and the software vendor needs to be negotiated. There are plenty of ways that the software vendor can be held accountable in terms of delivering and supporting software that meets the business's needs. However, the organization purchasing the software will also likely have obligations of its own.

  I recommend that you *not* tell the other vendor finalists that they are out of the game too soon. If contract negotiations with the first-choice vendor do not proceed well, it may be smart to begin negotiations with one of the other finalists (management should decide which vendor).

  Contract negotiation should be left to the lawyers. However, lawyers on each side will often consult with IT experts or management to make sure that sections of contract language accurately describe systems, controls, security, and any other matters that lawyers may not have expertise in.

- **Closing the RFP**   When the RFP process has concluded, the project team can begin preparations for testing and implementing the software. For obvious reasons, the design and development phases of the SDLC process are usually skipped altogether, unless the organization needs to build some custom interfaces or other programs that will enable the acquired software to work in the environment.

Design

When all functional, technology, security, privacy, regulatory, and other requirements have been finalized, design of the application can begin. It is assumed that a high-level design was developed in the feasibility study, since an elementary design is necessary to estimate costs in order to compute the financial viability of the application, but if not, the high-level design should be developed first.

The design effort should be a top-down process, starting with the major components of the application and then decomposing each module into increasingly detailed pieces.

It's difficult to say whether a data flow diagram, entity relationship diagram (ERD), or some other high-level depiction of the application should be developed first. This will depend partly upon the nature of the application, and partly on the experience of the programmers, analysts, and designers. Regardless, design should start out at a high level and graduate to levels of increasing complexity, to the point where database designers and developers have sufficient detail to begin development.

Project team members who represent business owners/operators/customers should review the application design to confirm that the analysts' and designers' concept of the application agrees with that of business owners. Reviews should be done at each level of design, not just at the top level. Business experts should be able to read and understand both a high-level design and a detailed design and to confirm whether the design is appropriate or not.

NOTE Design review by customers can be a step in the process where business customers and designers do not see eye to eye and where they might disagree on the design and attribute that disagreement either to differences in the understanding of technology or to practical versus abstract thinking. To prematurely end the design review could have costly consequences.

The potential consequences of failing to come to an agreement on design are vividly illustrated in the classic illustration shown in Figure 4-9.

As proposed by the project sponsor.

As specified in the project request.

As designed by the senior analyst.

As produced by the programmers.

As installed at the user's site.

What the user wanted.

Figure 4-9 Alexander et al., *The Oregon Experiment*, 1975, p. 44. Used by Permission of Oxford University Press, Inc.

Key activities in the software design phase include

- The use of a structured software design tool or methodology that records details of data flow and processing flow from high levels to detail levels
- Generalized and detailed database design at the logical and physical levels
- "Storyboards" showing user interaction with the application
- Details on reports that can be generated by the application

The application design effort should also include the development of test plans that will be used during the development and test phases of the project. Test plans need to be developed no later than the design phase, because programmers will need to perform unit testing during development as a way of verifying that they have coded software modules properly. If test plans are not developed until the test phase, then programmers will have to figure out tests on their own, or they might not perform enough testing, which will result in many more defects being discovered during the formal testing phase of the project.

When design reviews have concluded that the design is complete, a "design freeze" should be instituted, whereby no further changes to any level of design will be permitted. With a design freeze in effect, both designers and users are more apt to really think through all of the details of the design and do a better job of confirming whether the design is correct.

An organization that does not institute a design freeze will find the design changing throughout the development phase, which will result in different parts of the application conforming to different "versions" of the ever-changing design. This will result in chaos during the development and testing phases, and is sure to result in many more reported defects during user acceptance testing. Management should strongly assert a design freeze, since changing the design during the development phase will drive up development costs when developers are forced to rework code that was written in conformance to earlier versions of the design.

NOTE Organizations that have internal IT auditors on staff should include them in design reviews so that they can confirm whether the application design will result in an application whose integrity can be confirmed through auditing. Organizations that incur external audits may wish to invite external auditors to review the design documents for this same purpose.

Development

They have been waiting all this time, and finally the developers can have their fun. Developers take the detailed design documents that were developed in the design phase and begin building the application. The activities in the development phase include

- **Coding the application** Using tools selected for the project, developers will build the application code. Newer development tools may include design elements, code generators, debuggers, or testing tools that will make developers more productive.

- **Developing program- and system-level documents**   During development, developers document technical details such as program logic, data flows, and interfaces. This aids other developers later on when modifications to the application are needed.

- **Developing user procedures**   As they develop user interfaces, developers can write the procedure documents and help text that application users will read. In a larger, formal environment, developers may write the essential core of these documents, which will be completed by tech writers. But an even better idea may be this: end-user documentation is written by tech writers who derive procedures from requirements; then the software developers will use technical requirements and the completed end-user documentation to guide them on development of end-user software.

- **Working with users**   As they develop the parts of the application that interface with users, developers will need to work with them to ensure that the forms, screens, and reports that they build will meet users' needs.

Application Programming Languages   An organization that is considering an application development project has to make several strategic decisions regarding the technologies and techniques that will be used to perform the development and to operate the completed application.

Among those choices is the programming language(s) that will be used to write the application. Rarely does an organization have a wide-open choice of languages; rather, its choices will be constrained by several factors, including

- **Standards**   The organization's preferences for specific brands of computer hardware, operating systems, and databases will limit available languages to those that are available on its chosen application platform.

- **Available expertise**   Preferences will be further limited by available programming experience on its staff, or on the part of contracted developers. After the application has been developed and placed in use, the organization will need to make periodic changes; an experienced developer will be needed for that task as well.

- **Practicality**   For a given hardware and software environment, the nature of the application will make some of the available languages more desirable and others less so. For instance, an organization wants to write a professional-services invoicing application in a Unix environment where assembler, C, and C++ are the available languages. Chances are good that assembler will be eliminated, because assembler is a poor choice for application development. Instead, either C or C++ will be chosen.

Another factor that will influence language selection is the availability of development and testing tools. With nearly as much scrutiny as for the application features themselves, the organization should carefully select an application development environment if it does not already have one (or if it has determined that its present capabilities are insufficient).

Requirements for a development environment must include functions that will permit developers to write software code that can meet functional requirements for the application itself. If, for example, functional requirements specify a high degree of accuracy in a way that requires a high volume of test cases, a development environment that can help to automate testing will enable developers to more easily perform this rigorous testing.

Development in a Software Acquisition Setting In a software acquisition situation where an organization is purchasing software instead of developing it themselves, development activities may still be required. In a software acquisition project, software development is often needed to facilitate several needs:

- **Customizations** Larger off-the-shelf applications make accommodations for customizations that must be developed. These customizations can take many forms, including application code modules, XML documents, and configurations.

- **Interfaces to other systems** Applications rarely stand alone. Instead, they accept data from various sources and, in turn, provide data to other systems. Often "bridge programs" need to be written that serve to move and transform data from one environment to another.

- **Authentication** In an effort to improve security or make application adoption easier, organizations often desire that new applications use a system- or network-based authentication service. The primary advantage to this approach is that users do not need to remember yet another user ID and password. An application's authentication can often be tied to LDAP or Microsoft Active Directory.

- **Reports** Complex applications may have a report writer module that is used to create custom reports. Depending upon the underlying technology, a developer may be needed to develop these reports. Even if a report authoring tool is intuitive and easy to use, a developer may still be needed to help users design reports.

 NOTE An organization that is considering acquiring software should develop and enforce policies regarding the extent to which customizations will be permitted. Customizations can be costly when off-the-shelf software upgrades take place, because they may need to be rewritten to work with the upgraded software. The cost savings of using off-the-shelf software can be negated by the additional time required to manage and upgrade customizations.

Debugging The first and most important part of software testing is performed by the developers themselves during development. *Debugging* is the process of testing software code to make sure that it operates properly and is free of defects. The testing that a developer performs is called *unit testing;* this means that the individual modules that developers create are tested on their own. Wider-scale testing is usually performed by others later on in the development cycle.

The objectives of debugging include the following:

- **Correct operations** Software developers need to make sure that software modules are manipulating data and performing calculations correctly.

- **Proper input validation** All input fields and input records should perform detailed checks on all input data to prevent errors and tampering. Manipulation of input data is one of the principal forms of application abuse and one of the greatest causes of security incidents.

- **Proper output validation** Modules must perform output validation to ensure that output data is within bounds. Output validation is one way to detect malfunctions that occur in an application module.

- **Proper resource usage** Modules should be tested to make sure that they utilize resources such as memory correctly. Modules should properly request and relinquish resources so that malfunctions such as memory leaks do not occur.

 NOTE While it is tempting to gloss over debugging and unit testing, the effort usually pays big dividends by streamlining the integration effort and reducing the number of defects in system testing. Defects that could have been found during debugging usually take longer to find during system testing, because a defect must first be isolated to a specific section of code before it can be debugged and corrected.

Source Code Management In any size development effort, whether the development team is 1 or 50 programmers, an organization should use a source code repository tool. Such a tool has several purposes:

- **Protection** A source code management tool often includes access controls so that only authorized personnel are permitted to access application source code. This helps to protect the organization's intellectual property and to prevent other persons from learning the secrets of the application's inner workings, which could lead to fraud or misuse of the application later on.

- **Control** A source code management system utilizes "check out" and "check in" functions so that only one developer at a time may work on a specific part of the application. This helps to ensure the integrity of the application's source code.

- **Version control** A source code management system tracks each version of the code as it is checked in by developers. The system tracks the changes made from version to version, and can show the differences in code between versions, and also permit the reversion to an older version if application problems arise later on.

- **Recordkeeping** A source code management system maintains records related to check-out, check-in, and modifications to source code. This makes it possible for management to know what changes are being made to source code and who is making those changes.

NOTE Source code management is not an activity that is limited to the period when the application is first developed; on the contrary, source code management is a vital activity that must continue throughout the life span of the application.

Testing

During the requirements, design, and even development phases of a software project, various project team members develop specific facts and behavioral characteristics about the application. Each of those characteristics must be verified before the application is approved for production use. This concept is depicted in a V-model in Figure 4-10. The V-model is sometimes used to depict the increasing levels of detail and complexity in the SDLC.

The stages of testing in a software development project are unit testing, system testing, functional testing, and user acceptance testing.

Unit Testing Unit testing is usually performed by developers during the coding phase of the software development project. When each developer is assigned the task of building a section of an application, the specifications that are given to the developer should include test plans or test cases that the developer will use to verify that the code works properly. This is true, whether the part of the application that the user is working on is seen and used by end users, or whether it is buried deep within the bowels of the application and never seen by anyone.

In a formal development environment, the unit test plans should be very specific and list each test that the developer should undertake. The developer then performs each of the tests and records the results (usually the actual output) of the test. Those test results are then archived so that they can be referred to later if needed.

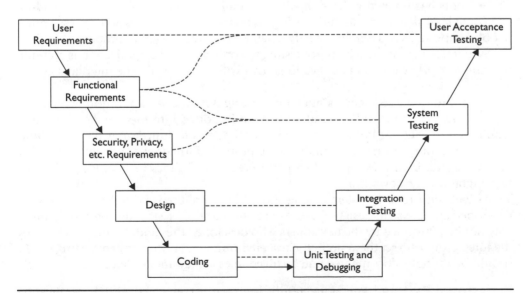

Figure 4-10 Requirements and design characteristics must all be verified through testing.

The archiving of unit testing records sometimes proves valuable when later phases of testing are taking place and some problem is found. Developers trying to isolate the cause of later testing problems can refer back to test plans and results at the unit testing phase to see whether the test plans and results of various unit-testing activities were performed correctly, or whether they contained appropriate test cases. This evidence can save the project team a lot of time by eliminating the need for unit testing to be repeated.

Unit testing should be a part of the development of each module in the application. When a developer is assigned a programming task in a software development project, unit testing should be performed immediately after coding and debugging have taken place. In some organizations, developers work in pairs—the senior developer writes code, and the junior developer performs testing. This gives junior programmers an opportunity to learn more about advanced programming by observing the senior developer and by testing his or her code.

 NOTE It can be easily argued that unit testing for a software module should not be performed by the developer who wrote the module. The developer may be under time pressure to complete development and testing, and may overlook test cases or gloss over errors as irrelevant. Also, a developer can be said to be too familiar with his or her code to be capable of objectively testing it. The methodology of "written by one and tested by another" has the advantage of objective testing, but can be more difficult to carry out in smaller organizations where there may only be a single developer writing all of the code.

System Testing As various parts of the application are developed and unit-tested, they will be installed into a test environment. When a sufficient number of modules or components has been completed, it will eventually become possible to begin end-to-end (or at least partial end-to-end) testing. In this way, it will be possible to test a number of components as a whole to verify whether they work together properly.

System testing includes interface testing to confirm that the application is communicating properly with other applications. This will include real-time interfaces as well as batch processing.

System testing also includes migration testing. When one application is replacing another, data from the old application is often imported into the new application to eliminate the need for both old and new applications to function at the same time. Migration testing ensures that data is being properly formatted and inserted into the new application. This testing is often performed several times in advance of the real, live migration at cutover time.

As with unit testing, system testing should have pre-prepared test plans that were developed at the system design phase. As with unit testing, system testing should probably not be performed by the developers who developed the modules under test, or by the integrators who set them up in the test environment. Further, system testing results should be formally documented and archived in case they are needed later.

Functional Testing Functional testing is primarily concerned with the verification of functional requirements that were developed earlier in the application project.

Each functional requirement must be expressed in a way that makes it inherently verifiable. When each functional requirement is developed, one or more tests should also be developed, which are tested during the functional testing phase of the project.

Functional tests should be formally recorded, including test input and test results. All of this should be archived in case it's needed if the application is suspected of malfunctioning. Often functional test results can verify whether the malfunction was present during the functional testing before the application went live.

User Acceptance Testing (UAT)   Before business users will formally approve and begin using a new (or updated) application, often a formal phase called *user acceptance testing* (UAT) is performed. UAT should consist of a formal, written body of specific tests that permits application users to determine whether the application will operate properly.

The detailed output of user acceptance testing should be archived, as it may be needed in the future.

UAT is often a stage in the acceptance of purchased software, as well as in software that is developed by a third-party organization. User acceptance testing is the formal test that determines whether the customer organization will accept (and pay for, as the case may be) the application and begin formal use of it.

 NOTE   Acceptance criteria for UAT should be developed by end users and not by developers or designers; otherwise, internal or external customers are liable to end up with software that does not function as desired.

Quality Assurance Testing (QAT)   Quality assurance testing (QAT) is a formal verification of system specifications and technologies. Users are usually not involved in QAT; instead, this testing is typically performed by IT or IS departments.

Like user acceptance testing, QAT should be a "gatekeeper" test in any situation where the organization is purchasing off-the-shelf software or if the application software is being developed by an external organization. The results of QAT should also determine whether the organization will formally accept and pay for the application.

Implementation

Implementation is the phase of the project where the completed application software is placed into the production environment and started.

Implementation must be started before UAT and QAT begin. UAT and QAT should be performed on the production environment that is anticipated to become the in-use production environment once approvals to use the application are obtained.

From the very day that construction of the implementation environment begins, that environment should be as controlled as a production environment. This means that all changes to the environment should go through a change management process. Also, administrative access to the production environment should be restricted to those personnel who will be supporting the environment after it goes live. The implementation timeline, in relation to other phases of the software development project, is depicted in Figure 4-11.

Figure 4-11 Implementation involves preparing the production environment prior to user acceptance testing and quality assurance testing.

 NOTE Because the production environment is the environment where UAT and QAT testing usually takes place, this environment must be absolutely pristine and free from the possibility of tampering by developers and other personnel.

Implementation Planning Implementation is a complicated undertaking that requires advance planning. Some activities may have a long lead time associated with them, requiring some implementation activities to begin during development or earlier.

- **Prepare physical space for production systems** An existing data center may be used for an application's servers and other equipment. But if there isn't room, or if an existing data center's available space is insufficient, then the organization may need to consider expanding an existing data center or consider a collocation center.

- **Build production systems** The actual servers that the application will use must be built and configured. If the organization does not have the necessary servers available, then they must be leased or purchased; depending upon the type of hardware, considerable lead time may be required. Once the hardware is available, personnel will need to install and configure operating systems and possibly other subsystems such as database management systems or application management systems.

- **Install application software** Once the systems are ready for the application software, it can be installed and configured.

- **Migrate data** For environments where an existing application will be retired, data from the former environment usually needs to be transferred to the new environment. Often this procedure requires the development of one or more custom programs to extract, convert, and insert the data into the new environment. This procedure is usually performed more than once: it must be rehearsed at least one time to make sure that it works properly. Also, migrated data is often needed for testing and training prior to the actual cutover.

NOTE As each phase of implementation is completed, the newly completed component should be locked down immediately and treated as though it is already in production. Usually this is the only way to ensure the integrity of the environment.

Training The success of the entire software development project hinges on the knowledge and skills of several different people in the organization. Among those who may need training:

- **End users** Personnel who will be using the application need to be trained so that they will know how to operate it properly.

- **Customers** If outside customers will be using the new application, they will need an appropriate amount of information so that they will understand how to use it. In other cases, customers will not be using the application directly, but a new application can still influence how they interact with the organization. If customer service or sales personnel are using a new application for taking orders or looking up customer data, they may be asking different questions or presenting different information to the customer.

- **Support staff** Personnel who provide customer service to users and customers need to be trained in the workings of the application, as well as on administrative "back office" tools that they may use to assist users.

- **Trainers** Organizations that employ a training organization will need to "train the trainers" so that, in turn, they will be able to train users and customers correctly.

The purpose of an application may require that others also receive training. This could include internal or external auditors, or regulators who have oversight over the organization.

Data Migration In the context of the SDLC, the purpose of a data migration is to transfer data from an older, soon-to-be-retired system to a new system. Depending upon the nature of the old and new applications, the purpose of the data migration might be to make historical records that originated in the older system available in the newer system.

In some cases, an organization will continue to keep the older application running to facilitate access to historical data. In some circumstances, it may require fewer resources to keep the old application running than to migrate the historical data to the new application.

Data migration often requires the development of programs that extract data from the old application, perform required transformations, and then format the data and import it into the new application. This is frequently a complex task, as there may be differences so significant between the data models of the old and new applications that the meaning of stored data differs between them. In some cases it will be necessary to create some parts of the database in the new application by extracting data from the old application and then performing calculations to create the data necessary in the new. Careful analysis must be done in all cases to make sure that the *meaning* of data in each application is known so that the migration will be done properly. Some techniques and considerations that ensure a successful migration:

- **Record counts**   Programs or utilities should be used to count the number of records in counterpart tables in the old and new environments. This will confirm the completeness of the migration programs that move data from the old environment to the new one.

- **Batch totals**   Data records with numeric values can be added together in the old and new databases. This will help to confirm the integrity of key data elements in the old and new environments.

- **Checksums**   Programs that compute checksums can be run against old and new databases to ensure the accuracy of migrated data. Programmers do need to be aware of the methods used to store data, which could lead to differences in checksums. For instance, an address field in one application may pad the field with spaces, but in the other it may be padded with nulls. Also, the way that dates are stored can vary between applications. While using checksums can be valuable, programmers and analysts must be familiar with any differences in data representation between the old and new environments.

 NOTE   Like other software projects, the migration programs themselves must be carefully designed and tested, and results of tests analyzed to make sure that they are working properly. Often it is necessary to perform a test migration—well in advance of the scheduled cutover date—to give enough time to make sure that the migration programs have been properly written.

Cutover   When the production system has been constructed, applications loaded, data migrated, and all testing performed and verified, the project team has reached the cutover milestone. Often, management review and approval are required to verify that all necessary steps have been completed correctly.

Depending upon the nature of the application, as well as external influences such as regulation or business requirements, an organization may transfer processing to the new environment in one of several ways:

- **Parallel cutover**   The organization may operate both the old and new applications in parallel for a time, making careful comparisons between old and new to ensure that the new application is working properly.

- **Geographic cutover**   In an environment used in large geographic regions such as a retail point-of-sale application, the organization may migrate individual locations to the new application instead of moving all locations at one time.

- **Module-by-module cutover**   The organization may migrate different parts of the application at different times. In a financial management application, for instance, the organization could move accounts receivable to the new environment, later move accounts payable, and still later move general ledger. During and between each of these phases, the organization must keep track of exactly which business information resides in which system.

- **All-at-once cutover**   An organization may elect to migrate the entire
  environment at one time.

The project team must analyze all available methods for a cutover, and choose the
method that will balance risk, efficiency, and cost-effectiveness.

Analysts may discover problems in data in the old environment that necessitate a
cleanup be performed prior to the migration, or as a part of the migration. Examples of
the types of problems that can be found include duplicate records, incomplete records,
or records that contain values that violate one or more business rules. Analysts who
discover data inconsistencies such as these need to alert the project team to the matter
and then help the project team decide how to remedy the situation.

Rollback Planning   Sometimes an organization will migrate an application from
an old environment to a new one, and shortly afterward will discover a serious problem
in the new environment that requires a return to the old environment. Rollback planning is a safety net that provides a last-resort path away from a situation where the organization cannot continue using the new environment.

A rollback is a serious undertaking and would be considered only when there is a
problem in the new environment that is so serious that it cannot be easily remedied.
Still, rollback planning is recommended in environments where the availability and
integrity of an application is critical to the organization.

Post-implementation

The software project is not completed when the application cutover has taken place.
Several activities still must take place before the project is closed. This section describes
these final tasks.

Post-implementation Review   After the implementation of a new application,
a formal review needs to take place. The purpose of the review is to collect all known
open issues and to identify and discuss the performance of the project. Because the
organization is likely to undertake similar projects in the future, it is a valuable use of
time to identify what parts of the project went well and which could have been done
better. The implementation review should consider

- **System adequacy**   The project team should work with the users of the new
  system and collect issues and comments, which are then discussed in the
  implementation review. Any issues requiring further attention should be
  identified.

- **Security review**   The system's access controls and other security controls
  should be discussed, and any issues or problems identified.

- **Issues**   All known problems regarding the new environment should be
  identified. This should include user feedback, operations feedback, and the
  accuracy and completeness of documentation and records. The project team
  needs to discuss each issue and assign it to one or more individuals who will
  address and remedy it.

- **Return on investment**   If the purpose for implementing the application was to establish or improve return on investment (ROI) or efficiency, then initial measurements need to be taken. The project team needs to recognize that several business cycles may be required before an accurate ROI can be determined.

More than one post-implementation review may be needed. To hold a single post-implementation review shortly after going live and then calling it good is probably inadequate for most organizations. Instead, a series of reviews may be needed, perhaps stretching over years.

 NOTE   IS auditors should be involved in every phase of the SDLC, including post-implementation reviews, to ensure that the application is functioning according to whatever control or regulatory requirements are attended to by auditors. Auditor feedback must be included in the body of issues and comments that is reviewed in the initial and subsequent reviews.

Software Maintenance   Immediately after implementation, the application enters the maintenance phase. From this point forward, all changes to the environment must be performed under formal processes, including incident management, problem management, defect management, change management, and configuration management. All of these processes should have been modified as necessary to accommodate the new application when cutover was completed.

Software Development Risks

Software development is not a risk-free endeavor. Even when management provides adequate resources for a software development project and supports a viable methodology, there are still many more paths to failure than to success.

Some of the specific risks that are associated with software development projects include

- **Application inadequacy**   The application may fail to support all business requirements. During the requirements and specifications phases of a software development project, some business requirements may have been overlooked, disregarded, or unappreciated. Whatever the reason, an application that falls short of meeting all business requirements may, as a result, be underutilized or even abandoned.

- **Project risk**   If the application development (or acquisition) project is not well run, the project may exceed spending budgets, time budgets, or both. This may result in large delays and even abandonment of the project altogether if management has considered the project a failure.

- **Business inefficiency**   The application may fail to meet business efficiency expectations. In other words, the application itself may be difficult to use, it may be exceedingly slow, or business procedures may require additional manual work to meet business needs. This can result in critical business tasks taking too long or requiring additional resources to complete.

- **Market changes** Between the time that a software development project is approved and when it is completed, sudden and unexpected changes in market conditions can spell disaster for the project. For instance, drastic supply or price shocks in a macroenvironment can have an adverse effect on costs that may make a new business activity no longer viable. Changes in the market can also result in reduced margins on products and services, which can turn the ROI of a project upside-down.

 NOTE Management is responsible for the business decisions that it makes; in ideal situations they make these decisions with sufficient information at hand. Usually, however, there are some unknowns.

Alternative Software Development Approaches and Techniques

For decades, the waterfall approach to software development was the de facto model used by most organizations. Breakthroughs and changes in technology in the 1970s and 1980s have led to new approaches in software development that can be every bit as effective and, in many cases, more efficient and faster.

Agile Development

Agile development is a relatively new software development model and is referred to as an alternate methodology that is appropriate for some organizations. The Agile methodology utilizes the "Scrum" project methodology that is discussed in detail earlier in this chapter. In an agile development project, a larger development team is broken up into smaller teams of five to nine developers and a leader, and the project deliverables are broken up into smaller pieces that can each be attained in just a few weeks.

Prototyping

Application prototyping is a methodology whereby rapidly developed application prototypes are developed with user input and continuous involvement. In this method, users work closely with developers who build specific components in short periods and solicit frequent user feedback.

The primary advantage of prototyping is that the risks of the application turning out all wrong are reduced because users are constantly involved and can head off an incorrect approach before more time is wasted.

The main disadvantage of prototyping is that the system is developed based only on what the user sees and knows; other functional requirements that users may be unaware of may go unaddressed, resulting in a system with inadequate controls and resilience.

Rapid Application Development

Rapid application development (RAD) is a response to the slower and more structured application development methodologies (such as waterfall) that were developed in the 1970s. RAD is characterized by the following activities and features:

- Small development teams consisting of highly experienced developers and analysts
- The development of prototypes
- Development tools that integrate data design, data flow, user interface, and prototyping
- A central repository for software components with an emphasis on code reusability
- Design and prototype analysis sessions with end users
- Tight time frames

RAD can almost be thought of as a 1960s-era protest of the political and business establishment. In most cases, it takes the opposite approach to software development from the then-traditional and time-proven (but also inefficient and time-consuming) development models created in the decades before.

Data-Oriented System Development

Data-oriented system development (DOSD) is, as the name suggests, a data-centric software development methodology. In DOSD, data is the central focus, the "hub of the wheel" as it were, and the other development activities occur as a result of data analysis and design.

Data-oriented system development is found in some of the larger information processing environments that are interconnected by many organizations. For instance, airline reservations systems, merchant and payment processing systems, securities trading systems, and medical records processing systems all have well-defined data and transaction interfaces. Organizations that wish to participate in these larger systems will build their own applications that are focused on the published data interfaces on the systems they wish to connect to.

DOSD can be applied to environments that utilize batches of transactions that are (for example) transmitted via File Transfer Protocol (FTP) and processed in bulk, as well as transactions that are performed in real time, such as airline reservations or securities trading.

Object-Oriented System Development

Object-oriented (OO) system development is a world unto itself that contains an entire vocabulary to describe objects and many other software components. It is so different from traditional structured programming (such as FORTRAN and C) that it has its own languages and even databases if you wish to implement one.

There are entire books (and even series of books) written on OO development and technology. I will summarize the basic vocabulary and activities here.

The basic unit of OO technology is the **class**. A class describes the characteristics of an object, including its attributes, properties, fields, and the *methods* it can perform.

The instantiation of a class is called an **object**. You could think of a class as stored code and configuration, and when it's running, the part that is running is the object.

A **method** refers to the actions that an object can perform. If, for instance, an object is written to calculate the interest on a loan, the method is the software code in the object that performs the calculation. In other programming languages, subroutines and functions are basically the same thing as a method in OO.

Objects routinely employ another technique known as **encapsulation**. This is a common practice whereby any particular method may call other methods to perform its work. This is similar to a function calling another function. The point of encapsulation in OO is that the software developer does not need to know anything about the implementation details of a method, including whether it calls other methods.

At the beginning of this narrative I mentioned a class. OO frequently has a hierarchy of classes. A class can belong to a parent class, and in turn, a class can contain subclasses. But parent classes and subclasses are not just ways of arranging or storing classes. Rather, the relationship of classes is functional. The attributes of a parent class are passed downward through **inheritance**.

Earlier I stated that when a class is instantiated, it becomes an object. Depending on the data that is passed on to the object, it may behave in different ways. This characteristic is known as **polymorphism**. For example, a class that computes shipping charges will behave in different ways, depending upon the source and destination addresses, as well as on special circumstances such as customers. In this case, polymorphism is not just about the rate that is chosen for shipping, but possibly other objects will be called, such as objects to handle customs, taxes, or hazardous materials declarations.

OO programming and operational environments will have one or more **class libraries**. These take many forms, depending upon the operating system, languages, and subsystems that are in use. For instance, in the Java language, class libraries are stored in JAR (Java ARchive) files that are located on the system where programs can refer to them when needed.

Component-Based Development

Component-based development is an approach that reflects the software architecture of an application. Here, an application environment will be made up of several independent components, often located on different physical systems, which work together.

For example, a large application environment might consist of a group of centrally located servers that process primary transactions. These servers contain interfaces, using standard interface technologies such as CORBA (Common Object Request Broker Architecture), DCOM (Distributed Component Object Model), or SOA (Service-Oriented Architecture), that other parts of the overall application environment may communicate with. For instance, auxiliary components such as batch input and output, data warehouses, static table updates (such as tax or shipping rates), and client programs may all be independent applications that communicate with the core system.

NOTE In a component-based environment, some components may be systems that are owned and operated by other organizations. This is especially true of web-based mash-ups, where applications may include components from external applications.

Web-Based Application Development

The creation of the HTML content-display standard and the HTTP communications protocol has revolutionized application development. The web browser is ubiquitous and has become the universal client platform that is not unlike an intelligent terminal from earlier eras.

The Web, as it is popularized now, came along just in time: two-tier and three-tier client-server computing, the great new application development paradigm that was developed in the 1990s, was not living up to its promise, particularly in the areas of performance and upkeep of client software. Web software has greatly simplified software development from the perspective of the user interface (UI); while the developer has a little less control over what and how data will be displayed on a user workstation, the trade-off in not having to maintain client-side software is seen as acceptable.

From a development methodology perspective, web application development can be performed within virtually all of the development frameworks, including waterfall, agile, RAD, DOSD, and OO (all discussed in this chapter). Primarily it's the technology that differentiates web-based application development from its alternatives.

Two important standards have been developed that facilitate communications between web-based applications; they are SOAP and WSDL. SOAP, or Simple Object Access Protocol, is an XML-based application programming interface (API) specification that facilitates real-time communications between applications using the HTTP and HTTPS protocols. Functionally, SOAP operates similarly to RPC (Remote Procedure Call), wherein one application transmits a query to another application, and the other application responds with a query result. SOAP messages are based in the XML (eXtensible Markup Language) standard.

WSDL, or Web Services Description Language, is another service that serves as a specification repository for the SOAP services available in a particular environment. This permits an application to discover what services are available on an application server.

Reverse Engineering

Reverse engineering is the process of analyzing a system to see how it functions, usually as a means for developing a similar system. Reverse engineering usually requires tools that examine computer binary code and that build a programming language equivalent.

The practice can help to speed up a development project, where an organization needs to build an application that is similar to another in its possession that exists in binary format only. Without reverse engineering, the organization would have to spend additional time in the software design and development phases of the project.

This practice is usually forbidden in software license agreements, because using it would reveal protected intellectual property that could damage the software maker.

System Development Tools

Application developers can create source code using tools ranging from text editors to advanced tools such as computer-aided software engineering and 4GLs. While there's little reason to discuss Notepad or Emacs, advanced development tools are worth attention and are discussed in this section.

Computer-Aided Software Engineering

Computer-aided software engineering, or CASE, represents a broad variety of tools that are used to automate various aspects of application software development. CASE tools cover three basic realms of development:

- **Upper CASE** This includes activities ranging from requirements gathering to the development of data models, data flow diagrams (DFDs), and interfaces.
- **Middle CASE** This involves the development of detailed designs, including screen layouts, report definitions, data design, and data flows.
- **Lower CASE** This involves the creation of program source code and data schemas.

These terms are primarily used to loosely classify various CASE tools. Some CASE tools are strictly Upper CASE, while others include Middle CASE and/or Lower CASE, but many cover the entire range of functionality and can be used to capture specifications, create data structure and flow diagrams, define program functions, and generate source code.

CASE tools do not usually create source code that is ready for implementation and testing. Rather, they are used to create the majority (in the best cases) of code for a given program; then the developer(s) would add details and specific items that the CASE tool did not cover. CASE tools are not used to replace the work of a developer, but to help make the coding part of a development project take less time, improve consistency, and enhance program quality.

CASE tools often contain *code generators* that create the actual program source code.

 NOTE CASE tools do not eliminate the need for any of the essential phases of the SDLC. With or without CASE tools, it is still necessary for a project team to create requirements, specifications, and design. CASE does help to automate some of these activities, however.

Fourth-Generation Languages

The term *fourth-generation languages*, or 4GLs, refers to a variety of tools that are used in the development of applications, or that are parts of the applications themselves.

There is no universally accepted definition for fourth-generation languages, unlike with first-, second-, and third-generation languages. Fourth-generation languages were developed independently by many different organizations and researchers, and they carry a diversity of concepts that contributes to the inability to describe all of them in a single definition. Common among nearly all of the fourth-generation languages and tools is that they are event-driven rather than procedure-driven, and they are less detailed than procedural languages.

4GLs are most often used as adjuncts to applications rather than for their core functionality. For instance, 4GLs are useful for report generators, query generators, and other higher-level functions. 4GLs are typically designed for use by nontechnical users who have few or no programming skills. 4GLs can also be used by developers as code generators.

Acquiring Cloud-Based Infrastructure and Applications

Organizations often choose to acquire a business application that is hosted in a cloud or SaaS (Software as a Service) environment, as opposed to hosting the application on their own systems. This section discusses issues that organizations should understand when considering this option.

The common options available for cloud-based application environments are

- **Software as a Service (SaaS)** Here, an application service provider is hosting its application software on its own infrastructure, often located in a data center and used by several customers. Users access the application in much the same way that they would if the application was hosted within the organization's own IT environment.

- **Infrastructure as a Service** Here, a cloud service provider is providing only servers and supporting network components. While the organization is relieved of the burden of purchasing application servers and storage systems, it still needs to install and manage applications on those servers, which are typically located in some distant data center. In this model, the cloud service provider may or may not support the server operating systems; these are among the choices available to organizations considering cloud-based services.

Regardless of the basic cloud model that is chosen, the organization needs to understand many details that are related to the manner in which the cloud provider provides its services to the organization. Some of these details are

- **Access control** The cloud service provider must have an effective access control plan to ensure that only authorized personnel have access to infrastructure, applications, and data. Often, the organization using cloud services will manage access control in upper layers (e.g., in applications it may install and maintain on cloud servers), while the cloud provider will manage access control in lower levels (e.g., in virtual machine hypervisors).

- **Environment segregation**   The cloud service provider must effectively separate systems and data between customers so that no cloud customer is able to access systems and data for other cloud customers.

- **Physical security**   The cloud services provider must provide adequate physical security so that only authorized personnel will have physical access to all cloud environment infrastructure and facilities.

- **Regulation**   The cloud service provider must provide controls that will meet all applicable regulatory needs for its customers.

- **Privacy**   The cloud service provider (and, indeed, the organization using cloud services) must implement safeguards to ensure appropriate protection and handling of personally identifiable information (PII) stored in cloud environments.

- **Legal jurisdiction**   The cloud service provider and its customers must have a firm understanding regarding the physical location of stored data, relative to the location of the owner(s) of that data. This will enable legal counsel to understand the applicability of security and privacy laws governing the use of stored data.

- **Availability**   The cloud services provider must deliver availability of services to customers at a level to meet customers' expectations. This applies not only to the steady availability of services, but also to on-demand availability.

- **Audit**   Many standards, regulations, and legal agreements require some level of auditing of systems, applications, and their supporting controls. The cloud environment must be verifiable in this regard.

Infrastructure Development and Implementation

Infrastructure is used to connect applications to users and to each other. They are the networks, servers, storage systems, and other facilities that support the use of applications.

While an organization may be able to acquire off-the-shelf software for many of its core business activities, infrastructure is almost always custom-built for the organization. Whereas software applications are like the tools in the hand of an astronaut, infrastructure is like the astronaut's glove, which must be tailor-made to fit each astronaut's hand. Infrastructure needs to conform to the organization's geography, business model, security requirements, regulatory requirements, and culture.

Formal processes are required to design and develop infrastructure that is sure to meet the organization's needs. This section describes the detailed process of the infrastructure development life cycle that is needed to ensure that the infrastructure will properly support the use of applications and other IT facilities and tools.

Infrastructure

In the context of business applications and information systems, infrastructure is the collection of networks, network services, devices, facilities, and system software that facilitate access to, communications with, and protection of those business applications.

For instance, a user who wishes to access a business application uses a workstation that is connected to a local area network (LAN). To access the business application, the workstation communicates over networks formed with routers, switches, firewalls, and cabling. All of that "in between" equipment and cabling constitutes infrastructure.

Infrastructure facilitates the communication and use of applications. Without infrastructure, applications cannot function or be accessed by users. Since infrastructure is so vital, its construction and maintenance requires the same level of formality and process as the business applications that it supports.

Review of Existing Architecture

When an organization is considering an upgrade to some component or aspect of infrastructure, it must first review what infrastructure already exists. Changes or additions to infrastructure will be most effective when existing infrastructure is carefully analyzed. This permits the organization to make necessary additions and changes that will be most effective at the lowest possible cost. Characteristics of existing architecture that need to be considered include

- Physical security
- Size and weight
- Power requirements
- Compatibility with existing infrastructure as well as infrastructure that will be acquired in the future
- Operations and support

Requirements

The next step in any upgrade of infrastructure is the development of requirements. As with the SDLC, it is important to know exactly what is expected of the infrastructure in terms of specific features and capabilities. An analyst or project team should develop specific requirements in a number of categories:

- **Business functional requirements**   These specify what the addition or change to infrastructure is expected to do. For instance, networks or network services will be expected to support new or improved communications between users and applications, remote access, or services between applications.

- **Technical requirements and standards**   These specify what technologies and standards must be followed for the new infrastructure. Additions or changes to infrastructure should support existing protocol and services standards such as TCP/IP, LDAP (used for authentication), product standards for devices such as routers and switches, and other standards that will permit the new infrastructure to work harmoniously with existing infrastructure with the smallest possible increases in support costs. Technical requirements for infrastructure should also include performance requirements such as availability, latency, and throughput so that the infrastructure will have the capacity to support all needed business functions.

- **Security and regulatory requirements**   These requirements specify how information is protected from unauthorized third parties. Examples include firewalls to limit access, intrusion detection systems to create alerts of possible tampering, and encryption to protect information from eavesdropping and interception.

- **Privacy requirements**   These requirements specify how information is protected and handled in order to limit the use of personal information to officially sanctioned purposes.

Design

Additions and changes to existing infrastructure (or even to brand-new infrastructure) must be designed, and that design validated by other subject matter experts. An infrastructure design may also include the use of specific protocols or services for authentication, routing, encryption, device management, and administrative support. When an infrastructure is being expanded or upgraded, generally the new components will need to work with the same support and management methods that are used for existing infrastructure, except when the infrastructure change has to do with a change in these features.

The design should be detailed enough so that a network or systems engineer can determine the logical and physical components that are needed and can configure them to support business needs. If software or hardware vendors will be asked to make suggestions on the components required for the infrastructure, then the design must be detailed enough so that they can make appropriate recommendations that will meet business needs.

Procurement

More often than not, additions or changes to infrastructure involve the procurement of infrastructure hardware and/or software.

Request for Proposal (RFP)   Any significant expansion or upgrade to infrastructure may require the use of an RFP (request for proposal). This is a formal process whereby the organization gathers all business and technical requirements and forwards them to several qualified vendors, who produce formal written proposals that include detailed information on the equipment and services required to perform the upgrade. Some organizations require the RFP process be used for any purchases that exceed an arbitrarily set figure.

When the project team receives RFP responses, the responses must be evaluated to determine which vendors are capable of meeting the organization's business and technical needs. The project team may also need to evaluate one or more of the vendors' solutions to "see for themselves" whether each vendor's proposed solution will successfully meet the organization's needs.

Evaluation   If the project team will be evaluating potential solutions, the team will need to provide whatever facilities are required to house the equipment or software. The project team will also need to take whatever time is required to test the components to see whether they can support business needs. This may require the team to provide other equipment to set up an end-to-end test.

Each of the business and technical requirements needs to be verified. This will require that one or more project team members work with the equipment being evaluated to see how that equipment works. A test checklist should be developed that has a one-to-one correspondence to each business and technical requirement. This will permit project team members to objectively rate each feature from each vendor.

Testing

Before new infrastructure—and significant changes to existing infrastructure—can be made available for production users, the infrastructure should first be formally and thoroughly tested. This helps to confirm that the infrastructure was built correctly and that it will be reliable and secure.

Each of the functional and technical requirements that were developed earlier needs to be systematically verified. This means that a detailed test plan needs to be developed that uses functional and technical requirements as a source. For instance, if a technical standard requires a specific routing protocol configuration setting, then a network engineer on the project team needs to verify whether network devices support that feature.

Most organizations do not have a test network environment that completely mirrors their production network. This means that some of the testing needs to be creative, and some testing and verification can't be done until implementation time. The project team will need to discuss the hard-to-test characteristics of the new infrastructure and decide the best course of action that facilitates the greatest amount of testing and the lowest risk of project failure. In other words, the results of some testing won't be known until the new infrastructure goes live.

Proof of Concept

Because integration issues are often so complicated, organizations are turning to the *proof of concept* in order to evaluate a proposed new technology or system. In a proof of concept, the organization will ask an infrastructure vendor to set up components in the organization's environment and perform some simple integrations with existing systems. This helps the organization to better understand the likely answer to the question, "Will this new technology work in *our* environment?" before committing to a particular solution.

The project team should carefully plan the proof of concept so that key features can be demonstrated. A proof of concept is usually performed over a relatively short period, and only a small proportion of integration will be performed. Also remember that the vendor is providing the proof-of-concept hardware and resources without compensation (but with the hope that its solution will be chosen); there is only so much that a vendor will be willing to do for free. This is why it is important to identify the key, measurable objectives before the proof of concept is carried out.

Those tests that cannot be done until implementation will become part of the verification that implementation was performed correctly.

Implementation

When evaluation and testing are complete, and all obstacles and issues have been satisfied, the new infrastructure (or changes to existing infrastructure) can be implemented. This may involve the physical installation of cabling, devices, and other components, as well as the use of common carrier facilities such as communications circuits. In implementation, the infrastructure is all assembled, tested, and placed into production use.

Maintenance

Infrastructure requires periodic maintenance, usually in the form of software and hardware upgrades and configuration changes to accommodate changes in the business and technical environment. These changes should be controlled through change management and configuration management processes that are described in detail earlier in this chapter.

Maintaining Information Systems

The job is only half done when an application has been written. Like any system with moving parts (whether real or virtual), applications and the environments that support them require frequent maintenance. There are dual aspects to system maintenance: process and technology.

The Change Management Process

Change management is a formal process whereby every change that is made to an environment is required to be formally requested, reviewed, and approved first. The purpose of change management—which is also known as *change control*—is to identify and reduce risks associated with changes to an IT environment. Change management also helps to reduce unscheduled downtime in an environment. The typical components in a change management process are

- **Change request** Here, the requestor describes, in structured detail, the desired change. The change request should include a procedure for making the change, who will make the change, and who will verify the change (this should be two different individuals or groups); include a procedure for verifying that the change was made properly, when the change will be made, and a plan for backing out of the change if it is unsuccessful; and include results from test implementations in a testing environment. The request should be distributed to all stakeholders to give them time to read and understand the change.
- **Change review** A quorum of stakeholders meets to discuss the requested change. The person or group proposing the change should describe the change and why it is being made, and should be able to answer questions from others about the change and its impact. If the stakeholders agree that the change may proceed, then the change is approved.

- **Perform the change**   The person or team slated to perform the change does so at the agreed-upon date and time, using instructions that were agreed upon in the review phase of the change. Results from the change are recorded and archived.

- **Verify the change**   Any necessary tests are performed to verify that the change was done properly and that it has produced the desired result. If the change takes too long, or if the change cannot be successfully verified, the change must be backed out of according to the agreed-upon procedure.

- **Emergency changes**   When the performance of a change cannot wait until the next scheduled change review, organizations usually provide a process whereby developers or engineers are permitted to make an emergency change. Typically some management approval is still required; personnel should never be permitted to just make changes and then inform others after the fact. Emergency changes still need to be formally reviewed in a change review to ensure that all stakeholders understand what change was made to the environment. A long-term goal that should be realized from managing emergency changes is the reduction in the need to make emergency changes, but instead to be able to anticipate situations and manage them proactively.

NOTE   The change management process should be formalized and include a documented process, procedures, forms, and recordkeeping.

Unauthorized Changes

Organizations need to have tools and methods in place to detect unauthorized changes that are made to systems, and to respond to those changes. Two avenues of action need to take place: first, there is the behavioral aspect, where management needs to discuss the unauthorized changes with the person(s) who made them; second, the impact of those unauthorized changes needs to be understood, and appropriate actions taken as a result.

Controls should be in place to prevent unauthorized changes from occurring. Some of these controls include

- **Segregation of duties**   Critical activities like application software changes should be apportioned among a group of individuals so that no single individual is able to make key changes. For instance, only developers should have access to source code and be able to make changes to a staging area. Next, only authorized personnel should be able to read changes from a staging area and place those changes into production. No one should be able to do all of these things.

- **Application code review**   Before checking in any change to application code, an independent review should be performed to make sure that only approved changes are being made.

- **Least privilege access**   Only those personnel who have a need to access and make changes to a system should be able to do so. For example, developers should not be able to make changes to production systems.

- **File integrity checking**   Production systems should be equipped with file integrity checking software that automatically detects and reports changes to files on a system. This will help to detect changes that may have been made without formal approval.

Configuration Management

Configuration management (CM) is the combination of a business recordkeeping process and automated tool(s) where the configuration of components in an IT environment is independently recorded. This activity has many potential benefits:

- **Recovery**   When configuration information for IT systems is stored independent of the systems themselves, configuration management information can be used to recover a system or device in the event of a malfunction or failure.

- **Consistency**   Often, automated tools are used to manage systems and devices in an environment. A configuration management tool can help an organization drive consistency into the configuration of its systems and devices. This consistency will simplify administration, reduce mistakes, and result in less unscheduled downtime.

Configuration management and change management processes together can help to reduce errors by requiring approval for changes and then by recording them when they are completed.

Controlling and Recording Configuration Changes

While CM is usually considered a means for recording changes made to a system, it can also be used to control those changes. Typically this is achieved through the use of tools that control system configuration and through system access controls that prohibit changes that circumvent those tools.

Automated tools are almost always used for configuration management. These tools include a configuration management database (CMDB) that serves as a repository for every component in an environment and that contains information on every configuration change made on those components. The more sophisticated configuration management tools also permit their operator to revert a given component to a configuration that existed at any time in the past.

Configuration Management and Change Control

While controlling and recording changes in an environment is highly valuable for some organizations, CM is not a substitute for change management. Instead, CM is the means by which change management–approved changes are carried out on systems. Change management is the review and approval of changes, while configuration management is used to perform and record changes.

Business Processes

Organizations that are mature in their thinking will treat their business processes almost like they do their software: both are carefully designed, constructed, and operated, and any changes that are made for either one should be formally considered.

Both software and processes should be considered as structured and procedural. The primary difference between the two is that software directs the processing of information in computers, while processes direct the activities of personnel.

Organizations that understand this type of approach to processes will control their processes like they control their software: through a life cycle.

The Business Process Life Cycle (BPLC) and Business Process Reengineering (BPR)

Like software, business processes should not be constructed on a whim, but instead be carefully planned, designed, and constructed, with the involvement of all concerned parties in the organization. These activities are a part of the *business process life cycle* (BPLC).

The most important component in the business process life cycle is *business process reengineering* (BPR), which is the set of activities related to the process of making changes to business processes.

A *process* is a set of procedures that achieves some purpose or objective. These procedures must be formally documented and usually will require recordkeeping of the activities controlled by the process. The procedures will help ensure that the activities are carried out correctly and consistently. The records produced help to document the activities that occurred as the process was carried out over and over. Depending upon the nature of the process, the records serve as tangible evidence that each activity occurred at specific dates and times, by specific personnel, using specific resources. Records will also record details about activities such as money spent, products or services processed or sold, and names of customers or others. Records are also used to create statistics about the process that helps management to understand how well the process is performing and how it is contributing to overall business goals.

There should be a process to control the creation of new processes as well as changes to existing processes. This process is remarkably similar to the SDLC (since software and processes are so similar, this should be of little surprise) and consists of the following major steps:

- **Feasibility study** This is an effort to determine the viability of a new process or of a change in an existing process. The amount of rigor needed here is proportional to the impact of the new or changed process.
- **Requirements definition** This is a formal record of the details of the process that must be included in the new or changed process. All stakeholders should contribute to the requirements definition process and review to ensure that everyone understands the details of the process.

- **Design** When requirements are completed, the process can be designed. Depending upon the nature of the process, this may include descriptions of activities performed by various personnel; the business equipment, assets, or materials used; and the specific involvement of customers, partners, and suppliers.

- **Development** Here, the details of the process are developed, using all of the requirements and design as a guide. This will include detailed procedures, templates for recordkeeping, and whatever other details are required.

- **Testing** When procedures have been developed, they are then tested to ensure their accuracy and suitability. Detailed test plans need to be developed that have a one-to-one correspondence to each of the requirements developed in that earlier phase.

- **Implementation** When the process has been perfected through testing, it is ready to be implemented. This means using the process in actual business operations with real equipment, people, materials, and money.

- **Monitoring** The process needs to be continually monitored (primarily through its recordkeeping) so that management can manage resource allocation in support of process operations, and to determine whether the process is performing against stated goals.

- **Post-implementation** After the process has been implemented, one or more formal reviews need to take place to review the development process itself as well as the new (or changed) process. Depending upon the size, impact, and scope of the process, several reviews may need to be held, possibly over years, to measure the effectiveness of the process and its results.

The reality in business today is that information systems and applications are used to support most business processes. This means that software development and process development often occur side by side and must be coordinated so that software applications meet the needs of the business processes that they support.

As organizations began to understand that business processes can be designed, developed, and improved like software, the term *business process reengineering* (BPR) as a beneficial activity came into being in 1990. BPR became popular almost overnight as U.S. companies struggled to stay competitive with foreign companies who were intruding into their market spaces.

Business process management (BPM) is more often the term that is used to describe ongoing process improvement. A formal discipline of its own, BPM is a "Plan-Do-Check-Act" continuous improvement cycle described in the preceding paragraphs and illustrated in Figure 4-12.

Benchmarking a Process

Benchmarking is the term used to describe the activity of continuous process improvement. The purpose of benchmarking is to compare key measurements in a business

Figure 4-12
The business process
management life
cycle

process to the same measurements performed by other organizations, particularly those that are considered to be top performers.

Typically the steps in process benchmarking are

- **Plan** A critical process is selected and measurement techniques identified. If the process has been through at least one improvement cycle, metrics may be available; otherwise, the team will need to figure out how the process is measured in terms of throughput, cost, and quality.

- **Research** The team collects information about the target process over time. The team also identifies other organizations whose similar processes can be monitored and measured.

- **Measure and observe** The benchmarking team collects actual measurements on other organizations' processes. In "friendly" situations, the team will be able to visit the organization and be permitted to collect measurements openly. In "unfriendly" situations, the team will need to make indirect measurements using whatever information is readily and legally available. The team will also need to collect qualitative data about the processes that it is measuring in the other organizations so that it can understand how the other organizations' processes are performed.

- **Analyze** The team compares measurements of its own processes against those of the other organizations. Often the team will need to adjust measurements to account for known differences. Then the team will identify differences in metrics between its organization and those of the other organizations.

- **Adapt** Here the team needs to understand the fundamental reasons why other organizations' measurements are better than its own. The team will need to understand not only the quantitative differences, but also the qualitative differences, between its organization's processes and the other organizations' processes in order to see how the other organizations achieve their metrics.

- **Improve** Finally, the team recommends process improvements in its own organization. Management makes commitments to improve its process in specific ways to help its process to become more effective and efficient.

Benchmarking is relatively straightforward when other organizations are cooperative with regard to observation and measurement.

But in a competitive situation, market rivals are unlikely to cooperate, and in some situations, cooperation may even be considered illegal.

Capability Maturity Models

Capability maturity models are another way to understand the effectiveness of an organization's business processes, particularly its software development processes. Three software development maturity models are discussed in this section.

Software Engineering Institute Capability Maturity Model (SEI CMM)

Developed at Carnegie Mellon University, the Software Engineering Institute Capability Maturity Model (SEI CMM) is a conceptual model that helps an organization better understand its own process maturity. This is a necessary step if an organization wishes to improve its processes, particularly if the organization is not precisely sure how to begin this improvement.

The SEI CMM defines five levels of maturity:

1. **Initial**   This level has no process, no procedures, and no consistency. Success, when it is attained, is achieved through brute force and luck.

2. **Repeatable**   At this level of maturity, there is some consistency in the ways that individuals perform tasks from one time to the next, as well as some management planning and direction to ensure that tasks and projects are performed consistently.

3. **Defined**   The organization has developed a site-wide, documented software development process that is used for all development projects.

4. **Managed**   At this level, the documented software development process includes key measurement points used to measure effectiveness, efficiency, and defects. These measurements are performed and reported to management as a part of the life cycle.

5. **Optimizing**   At this highest level of maturity, the organization has instituted metrics-driven process improvement techniques to bring about continuous improvement in its SDLC.

Considerable effort is required for an organization to ascend from one level to the next. This model helps an organization to better understand its current level of maturity and the process changes needed to improve its maturity over time.

Capability Maturity Model Integration (CMMI)

Following the success of the SEI CMM, many other maturity models were developed for other software-related activities. The capability maturity model integration (CMMI) is an aggregation of these other models into an overall maturity model. Like the SEI

CMM, the CMMI has five levels of maturity, although its labels differ. The CMMI has been designed with consideration for other software development methodologies, such as agile development, component-based development, and iterative development.

ISO 9126, Software Engineering

International standard ISO 9126 is used to evaluate the quality of software. This standard classifies software quality within a set of characteristics that includes

- Functionality
- Reliability
- Usability
- Efficiency
- Maintainability
- Portability

Each of these characteristics has subcharacteristics that are further divided into attributes. Each attribute is objectively measured; these measurements contribute to measured software quality results.

ISO 15504, Software Process Improvement and Capability Determination

International standard ISO 15504 is also known as the Software Process Improvement and Capability dEtermination (SPICE) model. This is a maturity model that is based on SEI CMM and another model called Bootstrap.

SPICE defines six levels of software development maturity:

- Level 0 Incomplete
- Level 1 Performed
- Level 2 Managed
- Level 3 Established
- Level 4 Predictable
- Level 5 Optimizing

Several reference models for SPICE have been developed, including software and system life cycle processes, component-based development, IT service management, quality management, automotive embedded software, and medical device software.

Application Controls

Software applications accept, process, store, and transmit information. Unless specifically programmed and configured, software applications lack the ability to properly distinguish valid and reasonable data from that which is not. Controls are necessary to ensure that information at each stage of processing retains its required integrity.

NOTE Exam questions may present a more complex situation than simple input, process, and output controls. Few business processes exist in a vacuum, so many process controls will also need to have the full set of internal input, process, and output controls for each subprocess. Test takers should watch for questions that address application controls that may deal with subprocess requirements, or in which the output of one process is presented as the input for the process under review (affecting which set of controls is appropriate to the question).

While there are marked differences in the architecture of software applications, the typical approach to controls is to apply these controls at the point of entry, processing, and exit. In other words, controls around input data, processing, and output data are needed.

Input Controls

Data that is presented to an application as input data must be validated for authorization, reasonableness, completeness, and integrity. Several controls must be implemented to ensure these points.

Input Authorization

All data that is input into a system must be authorized by management. The method of authorization or approval takes many forms:

- **User access controls**   Only approved personnel, such as system operators, input clerks, business analysts, and customer service representatives, are permitted to log in and use applications.

- **Workstation identification**   Only approved terminals and workstations are permitted to be used to input transactions. Identification can take many forms, including electronic serial number, network address, or digital certificate.

- **Approved transactions and batches**   Through manual signature, online approval, and other means, management and other approved personnel perform necessary checks and verifications before individual transactions and batches of transactions are permitted to be input and processed.

- **Source documents**   In some settings, data can be input only from existing source documents. This can include mailed invoices, checks, receipts, or forms filled in by customers. Source documents themselves should be controlled so that they cannot be altered, misplaced, or removed.

NOTE Well-designed applications will include audit logs that record when specific data was input, how it was input, and who authorized its input. This will permit an organization to research matters where there is a question on the source of specific input data after the fact.

Input Validation

The process of input validation is used to make sure that the type and values of information are appropriate and reasonable. The types of input validation include

- **Type checking**   Each input field should be programmed to accept only the type of data that is appropriate for the field. For instance, a numeric field should contain only numeric digits, and a name field should contain only alphabetic characters.

- **Range and value checking**   Input fields need to validate the range and value of characters. For instance, the day field in a date should only accept figures 1 through 31, and the month field 1 through 12. Even more intelligent checking is often warranted; for example, a date field often should be a date that is only in the past, or the future, or even a specific range of the past or future. Other examples include only valid ZIP or postal codes, only valid telephone numbers, and only valid IP addresses. In some cases, input data must match values in a table of data stored in the application; for instance, only valid city, state, or country codes; telephone area codes; or valid Universal Product Code (UPC) codes.

- **Existence**   This is a simple check to confirm that each input field actually contains data.

- **Consistency**   This is a check that compares related data from different input fields. For instance, a ZIP code value in an input field can be validated by comparing it to the range of allowed ZIP codes for the city and state values.

- **Length**   Programs must validate the length of input data in an input field. Fields like names and addresses are often limited to, say, 30 characters. This is especially important on interactive programs where intruders may attempt buffer overflow attacks in an attempt to cause the program to malfunction.

- **Check digits**   Numeric values such as bank account numbers can be verified for integrity by recalculating their check digits.

- **Spelling**   Input fields that are supposed to contain common words can be spell-checked.

- **Unwanted characters**   Input fields should filter out unwanted characters that could be a result of mistyping. However, unwanted characters can also be a sign of a software malfunction (on a system that is the source of input data) or of an attempted security break-in.

- **Batch controls**   Batches of data should include calculations and counts to ensure the integrity and completeness of a batch of data. Some available methods include transaction counts, control totals (the numeric sum of one or more numeric fields in all of the batch records), and hash totals (a computed "sum" of all of the input fields, regardless of their actual type).

Input validation is certainly necessary on user input forms in applications where users are filling in online forms. However, input validation is just as necessary on batch input and other automated functions; errors in other systems can occur that can cause input data to be input into the wrong fields; failure to validate data can result in inappropriate data being input and stored in a system, which can lead to other problems later.

Error Handling

As software programs perform all of the input validation checking described earlier, these programs must be programmed or configured to take specific action when any of the input validations fail. There are many possible responses, depending upon the type of data being input as well as the method of input:

- **Batch rejection** For input batches, if the transaction count, control totals, or hash totals of a batch do not agree with expected values, the entire batch should be rejected. Usually the application software will have no way to determine what exactly is wrong with the batch, so the only reasonable course of action is to reject the entire batch, which will require data control analysts to examine the batches to see what went wrong.

- **Transaction rejection** For individual input transactions, whether automated or user input, the software application can reject the transaction.

- **Request re-input** An interactive user program can request that the user re-input the entire form, or just the individual field that appears to be incorrect.

When an application rejects input, in most cases the application will need to create a log entry, error report, or other record of the rejected input so that data analysts will know that an error occurred and take steps to correct it. If the application does not create a record of the error, then analysts are apt to believe that all data was input successfully, which could lead to problems later on when those invalid transactions cannot be found anywhere in the system.

Processing Controls

It is necessary to ensure that data in a system retains its integrity. All new data that is created—for instance, as a result of calculations—must be checked for reasonableness to make sure that calculations are working properly and that bad information or program code is not creeping in through some other means. The controls to make sure that data in the system retains its integrity are discussed in this section.

Editing

In many types of applications, data that is initially input into the system will be changed from time to time. For example, a subscriber's e-mail or mailing address may change, or a bank account number or license plate number may change. Often these changes are performed either directly by customers or by a customer service representative during a telephone conversation.

Whenever values are changed, the new values must be validated before they are accepted and stored; otherwise, problems may ensue later on. The types of validation checks performed during editing are similar to those performed during initial input, described earlier in this section.

Calculations

When application programs are performing calculations, the results of those calculations need to be validated for accuracy and reasonableness to verify that the application is performing calculations properly. Several techniques are used to validate calculations:

- **Run-to-run totals** This validates that specific stored or calculated data values retain their values throughout the steps in a transaction. This helps to ensure that no errors, tampering, or software malfunctions have occurred.

- **Limit checking** Results of specific calculations can be checked for upper and lower limits. Calculation results that exceed predetermined limits can be rejected.

- **Batch totals** When data is processed in batches, batch totals that are calculated at the beginning of the batch can be recalculated at the end of processing for the batch to ensure the integrity of the batch data.

- **Manual recalculation** An analyst or clerk can recalculate certain transaction calculations manually, and those manual calculation results can be verified or keyed into the application.

- **Reconciliation** When a set of records is processed that results in the creation of a second set of records—or the next stage of calculation results—totals from the old to new batches may need to be calculated to ensure that processing was done correctly and that no data corruption or calculation errors occurred.

- **Hash values** The values in selected sets of numeric or text fields can be rehashed at various stages of calculations to verify that they have not been altered or tampered with.

Data File Controls

When processing is performed on data stored in data files, several types of controls are needed to ensure the security and integrity of those data files. Some of the controls available include

- **Data file security** Access controls can be configured so that only authorized users or processes are permitted to access data files.

- **Error handling** Erroneous transactions that need to be corrected or re-input should be checked by personnel other than those who originally keyed them.

- **Internal and external labeling** Labeling on removable storage media is vital to ensure that the correct volume (whether tape, disc, or other storage medium) has been loaded.

- **Data file version**   The version of a data file should be independently verified to ensure that the proper file is being processed. This would, for example, help to prevent processing yesterday's file twice.
- **Source files**   Data input at the beginning of a processing run should be retained for a minimum period in case a batch needs to be rerun many days or weeks later.
- **Transaction logs**   Log files containing transactions should be retained for a minimum period in support of later troubleshooting or the investigation of data errors weeks or months later.

Processing Errors

Errors that occur during processing must be recorded in a logfile or other output medium that will be examined by personnel. All errors need to be addressed, whether through rekeying of errant data, rerunning failed batch runs, correcting data transmission errors, or other means.

Processing errors that occur in interactive programs may display an error message to the user. Depending upon the type of program, the user may have an opportunity to correct or rekey information.

Output Controls

Applications accept input data, perform calculations, and produce output data. The results of final calculations and transformations need to be checked for reasonableness and validity. Several types of output controls are available, depending upon the type of activity and data.

Controlling Special Forms

Some calculation outputs are printed on special physical forms such as checks, warrants, and certificates. These forms should be serialized and kept in a locking cabinet. In high-value situations, these forms should be kept in dual custody, where two individuals are required in order to access them.

A forms log should be maintained to account for the use of forms. This log should be examined frequently to ensure that forms are used only for their stated purpose and that all are accounted for.

Checks and other negotiable instruments must be secured at all times to ensure that all are accounted for and properly handled. Just as with electronic data, physical forms must be inventoried and accounted for at each stage of processing and handling.

Signature devices and stamps, when used, must be secured at all times. They should be stored in locations separate from checks and certificates, and under the control of separate individuals.

Report Distribution and Receipt

Application processing often results in the creation of reports that are sent to authorized personnel in paper or electronic form. Often these reports will contain sensitive information, which requires that the reports be safeguarded at all times in any form.

Forms that are printed and later delivered may need to be placed in tamper-proof or tamper-evident envelopes. Forms that remain in electronic form may need to be encrypted or password-protected. Reports that are transmitted over public networks need to be encrypted. If recipients send electronic reports to printers, special safeguards may be required so that sensitive data is not left on printers for others to view.

Reconciliation

Numeric and financial data on reports may need to be reconciled to input data, data from intermediate calculations, or control totals. This activity, when required, should be documented and logged.

Retention

Reports are sometimes the only human-readable data available during each business cycle. Whether for research, reference, or statutory requirement, it is often necessary to retain reports for a minimum period of up to several years. Reports containing sensitive data will need to be physically safeguarded to prevent access by unauthorized personnel.

NOTE Output controls are just as vital as input controls, because the outputs from one system do not necessarily become the inputs to another system that the organization has control over. Sometimes, one system's output will become another system's inputs where little or no input validation takes place.

Auditing the Software Development Life Cycle

Audits of the processes used to create and maintain software will assist the organization in knowing how effective these processes are. This provides the organization with valuable information that can be used to make its processes more effective. If the IS auditor examines only an organization's applications and controls but not the processes used to create them, then the root cause of endemic problems in applications and processes may be unknowable.

NOTE The exam will expect a general understanding of the details for each type of audit practice. Focus on the type of documentation and the mechanism for validation of each as you review this section. Watch for exam questions that may begin with phrases such as "During the design phase…" or similar terminology to guide your response.

Auditing Project Management

The IS auditor who is auditing an organization's project management is verifying whether the organization's projects are adequately controlled. Controls in project management ensure the integrity of the organization's projects so that the systems and processes that are built actually support the requirements that are supported and agreed to by management.

The activities that the IS auditor should review when auditing project management include

- Oversight by senior management and any steering committee(s)
- Risk management techniques used in the project
- Processes and methodologies used to build project plans
- Methods for dealing with issues
- Management of costs
- Status reporting to management
- Project change control
- Project recordkeeping, including decisions, approvals, resource utilization, and costs

Auditing the Feasibility Study

IS auditors should audit any feasibility studies that occur at the beginning of major projects. The activities that IS auditors should review include

- Budgets and cost justifications, and whether they can be independently verified
- Criticality of the project and/or the criticality of the business process supported by the project
- Alternatives that were considered, including the feasibility that existing systems could be used in support of the business need
- Reasonableness of the solution that was chosen and implemented

Auditing Requirements

An IS auditor should audit a project's requirements and the process that was used to develop them. The IS auditor needs to review several aspects of requirements:

- Identify all of the personnel who contributed requirements and determine whether this body of personnel actually represents all true stakeholders.
- Interview several of the requirements contributors to better understand whether contributors' requirements were included, and whether they were altered without their knowledge.
- Identify any ranking or alteration of requirements that may have occurred without the knowledge of those who contributed them.
- Perform some reasonableness checking of requirements to see if they support the project described in the feasibility stage.
- Determine whether the body of requirements was approved by management.

Auditing Design

The IS auditor should audit the design and specifications that were developed during a project. During the audit the IS auditor should consider whether

- The design actually reflects and supports requirements and the feasibility study
- The design contains sufficient detail that application developers can produce software that will unambiguously meet the organization's requirements and business needs
- The design was adequately reviewed and whether it was approved by management
- The design will reasonably result in a successful implementation that meets the users' needs
- Testing and UAT (user acceptance testing) plans and criteria were developed by this phase in the project

Auditing Software Acquisition

For software development projects where the organization acquires software from an outside vendor, an IS auditor should audit several aspects and activities in the acquisition stage of the project. The IS auditor should consider whether

- The organization performed a formal RFP process
- All requirements were transferred to the RFP document
- Suitable vendors were considered their responses were properly analyzed against each of the requirements
- The vendor that was selected could support a majority of the requirements
- The organization did any reference checking, evaluation, or pilot prior to purchase
- The contract contains clauses that reasonably protect the organization in the event the software or the vendor fail to perform adequately
- The contract was reviewed by the organization's legal department before being signed

Auditing Development

For software development projects where the organization develops software on its own, the IS auditor should consider whether

- The developers were adequately trained and experienced in the languages and tools used in the project
- The chosen design and development tools were adequate for the project
- The chosen computer language and other related technologies were adequate for the project

- The application contains adequate controls to ensure proper operation, recordkeeping, and support of business processes
- The application was written in support of stated requirements
- The application has adequate input, processing, and output controls
- The application performs calculations correctly
- The application produces adequate transaction and audit logs

Auditing Testing

Software that is developed within the organization or acquired from an outside vendor needs to be tested to ensure that it meets the organization's requirements. When auditing software testing, the IS auditor should consider whether

- All test plans were developed during the requirements and design phases
- Test plans reflect the entirety of requirements and design elements
- All tests were performed and verified successfully
- Actual test results are available for review as well as who performed the testing
- Test results have been archived for later research if needed
- Parallel tests were needed were performed
- UAT was performed, and the results of those tests are available

Auditing Implementation

Implementation should be performed only after all testing has been successful and all issues identified during testing have been resolved. When auditing implementation, the IS auditor should consider whether

- The system was implemented using established change control procedures
- The system was administratively locked down before implementation, thereby preventing tampering by any developer or other persons who do not have authorization to access production systems
- Data conversions were performed in a controlled manner, including controls to ensure correct conversion processing

Auditing Post-implementation

The IS auditor should audit all post-implementation activities, considering whether

- Any post-implementation review took place and, if so, whether the review was documented and actions taken
- The application supports the entire body of requirements established during the project
- The application is being measured to verify whether it is meeting established performance and ROI targets

- Excessive changes were made to the system after implementation, which could be an indicator of inadequate requirements or testing
- Excessive unscheduled downtime or errors occurred, which could be an indicator of inadequate requirements or testing
- Control balances indicate that the application is performing properly

Auditing Change Management

Change management is the management process where all changes to an environment are controlled. The IS auditor should consider whether

- A change management policy and process exists and is followed in practice
- Adequate records exist that indicate how much the change management process is followed
- The number of emergency changes indicates inadequate requirements or testing
- Proposed changes contain implementation procedures, back-out procedures, and test results
- Minutes are kept of change management meetings
- Emergency changes are adequately reviewed

Auditing Configuration Management

Configuration management involves controlling, configuring, and recording configuration changes to information systems. When auditing configuration management, the IS auditor should consider whether

- Configuration management policies and controls exist and are followed
- Configuration management tools are used to control and/or record changes made to systems
- Changes are approved through the change management process
- Configuration management tools are able to verify the integrity of systems and whether discrepancies are resolved

Auditing Business Controls

Business controls are those points in business processes where key activities occur. The IS auditor needs to identify the key processes in an organization and to understand the controls that are in place—or that should be in place—that govern the integrity of those processes.

While many business controls are supported by IT applications, the auditor also needs to take a business process perspective and understand the control points from a strictly process viewpoint. This is necessary because, while controls may be automated by applications, personnel are still in control and responsible for the correct operation of business processes. Further, processes, even when partly or entirely automated, must still be monitored and managed by staff or management. And, these processes must be documented—itself an important control.

 NOTE For the IS auditor to overlook business controls and focus only on IT applications would be a disservice to the organization, for the auditor could miss the obvious control points in key business processes. Remember, the IT system is not the process; instead, the IT system *supports* the process.

Auditing Application Controls

Application controls ensure that only valid data enters a system through input controls, that calculations yield only valid results, and that output data is valid. The IS auditor needs to examine system documentation to understand internal and external data flows and calculations. The IS auditor also needs to examine system records to ensure that all changes made to the system were authorized. Several aspects of application activity need to be examined; these are described in the remainder of this section.

Transaction Flow

The IS auditor should audit an application and follow transactions from end to end. The IS auditor should consider whether

- Any data flow diagrams or flowcharts exist that describe data flow in the transaction, and whether such diagrams or flowcharts correctly identify the flow of data
- Any data items in the transaction were altered in the data flow, and where alterations occurred, whether audit log entries recorded those changes, including who made them

Observations

During an audit of information systems, the IS auditor should make several observations, including whether

- Any segregations of duties (SODs) are established in terms of the entire transaction process flow
- Input data is authorized, and how the authorization is documented
- Any balancing or reconciliation is performed to ensure data integrity
- Errors occur, how they are detected, and how they are handled
- Reports and other outputs are generated, controlled, protected, examined, and acted upon

Data Integrity Testing

Data integrity testing is used to confirm whether an application properly accepts, processes, and stores information. Data integrity tests will determine whether there are any failures or errors in input, processing, or output controls in an application. The IS auditor should perform several tests on the application, in each case attempting to input data that is invalid or unreasonable to see whether the application properly rejects such data. The auditor should also attempt to have the application perform calculations that should result in errors or exceptions—for example, a calculation result that should be rejected.

The IS auditor not only should test the stated input, calculation, and output rules for data integrity, but also should assess the efficacy of the rules themselves. For example, an auditor should determine whether the absence of a rule forbidding the entry of negative hours in a time-reporting system constitutes a deficiency in the application's rules.

Testing Online Processing Systems

Online processing systems are characterized by their ability to process transactions for many users simultaneously. An online application must be able to compartmentalize each user's work so that the users do not interfere with each other, even if two or more users are attempting to read or update the same records. A typical database management system (DBMS) will be able to enforce record locking, and an application must have logic to deal with locked records gracefully.

Business records and transactions in database management systems are usually made up of rows in several different tables. *Referential integrity* is the characteristic that requires that the database management system maintain the parent-child relationships between records in different tables and prohibit activities such as deleting parent records and transforming child records into orphans. Application logic must be designed to prevent these situations and other types of "collisions" and deadlocks that can occur when many users are performing different tasks in an application. The characteristic of *atomicity* states that a complex transaction, which could consist of simultaneous actions on many records in many different tables, is performed as a single unit of work: either it will all be completed properly or none of it will be completed. This helps to ensure the integrity of all data in the database management system.

The IS auditor will need to fully understand the inner workings of an application, including the actions of different transactions on the underlying DBMS. Then the auditor will need to stage a number of different tests to see how the application handles situations that may challenge the integrity of business information. Some examples include

- Having two different users try to open the same transaction to update them
- Having two different users try to open the same transaction, where one will remove the transaction while the other is trying to update it
- Having two different users open related records in a database while one of the users attempts to remove records that the other is viewing

These are simple examples, but they should serve to illustrate the need for the IS auditor to see whether the application properly manages business records.

Auditing Applications

Applications must never be assumed to perform all of their input, processing, and output perfectly. This must be the mind-set of the IS auditor: that every important function of applications must be verified to be operating correctly and completely.

Many techniques are available for auditing IT applications, including

- **Transaction tracing**   Here, auditors enter specific transactions and then carefully examine the application, data, and reports to see how the transaction is represented and processed in the application.
- **Test batches**   The IS auditor creates a batch of test transactions with expected outcomes and directs that they be processed by the system and their results compared against what is expected.
- **Software mapping**   This is a process whereby the application software is traced during execution to determine whether there are any unused sections of code. Unused code could signify faulty program logic, obsolete code, or backdoors.
- **Baselining**   This process uses sets of input data (batch- or key-processed by the system) with known results. After system changes, the same sets of data are processed again to see whether the expected results have changed.
- **Parallel testing**   Programs that simulate the application's function are used to process real data to see whether results vary from the production system.

It is not suggested that an IS auditor employ all of these methods, but instead select those that will be most effective at verifying correct and complete processing.

Continuous Auditing

Continuous auditing permits the IS auditor to conduct audits of an online environment in a way that is less disruptive on business operations. Instead of more costly and invasive audits, IS auditors can test systems while they are running and with minimum or no involvement from IT staff. Continuous auditing techniques, also known as *computer-assisted audit testing* (CAAT), are especially useful in applications such as an e-commerce operation where there is no paper audit trail. Several techniques are available to perform online auditing:

- **Audit hooks**   Special audit modules are placed in key points in an application and are designed to trigger if a specific audit exception or special condition occurs. This can alert auditors to the situation, permitting them to decide whether additional action is required.

- **System Control Audit Review File and Embedded Audit Modules (SCARF/ EAM)**   Here, special audit software modules are embedded in the application; these modules perform continuous auditing and create an independent log of audit results.

- **Integrated test facility (ITF)**   This permits test transactions to be processed in a live application environment. A separate test entity is required, however, so that test data does not alter financial or business results (because the test data does not present actual transactions).

- **Continuous and intermittent simulation (CIS)**   Here, the application will contain an audit software module that examines online transactions. When a transaction meets audit criteria, the transaction is processed by the application and is also processed by a parallel simulation routine, and the results of the two are compared. These results are logged so that an auditor may examine them at a later time and decide whether any action is required based upon the results.

- **Snapshots**   This technique involves the use of special audit modules embedded in an online application that samples specific transactions. The modules make copies of key parts of transactions, often by copying database records and storing them independently. This allows an auditor to trace specific transactions through an application to view the state of transactions as they flow through the application.

- **Online inquiry**   Here, an auditor has the ability to query the application and/or its database to retrieve detailed information on specific transactions or groups of transactions. The auditor must often have an intimate knowledge of transaction and data structures to make use of this technique.

Summary

Organizations should have processes and procedures in place to manage the development, acquisition, and maintenance of software applications and supporting infrastructure. These processes ensure that all of the activities related to additions and changes to software applications are performed consistently, and that all necessary considerations are included and documented.

Program management is the oversight of several projects and project teams. A program manager oversees project managers who manage individual projects in a program that contributes to an organization's objective. The program manager's oversight includes monitoring project schedules, budgets, resource allocation, conflicts, and the preparation of status reports for senior management. Another form of program management involves the management of a *project portfolio,* which is a collection of all of the active projects, regardless of whether they contribute to a single corporate objective or to many.

Management should approve any new project only after a valid business case has been developed, reviewed, and approved. A *business case* describes the business problem, the results of any feasibility studies, a project plan, budget, and related risks. The project will be approved only if there is a reasonable expectation of business benefits; a business case should include one or more ways in which the outcome of the project can be measured so that management can tell whether the project resulted in actual business benefit.

Projects require formal planning that includes the development of a project schedule, methods for estimating the time required for individual tasks, management of budgets and resources, identifying and resolving issues and conflicts, management of project records, and the creation of status reports for management. Changes to projects should be managed through a formal review and approval process. Project debriefs or reviews should take place when projects conclude so that the organization can identify lessons learned that will help improve future projects.

Software development and acquisition should be managed through an SDLC or similar process. The SDLC is a rigorous set of activities to make sure that new applications will meet the organization's business needs. The phases of the software development life cycle are feasibility study, requirements definition, design, development, testing, implementation, and post-implementation. These phases are all formally documented, reviewed, and measured.

The feasibility study and requirements definition phases help a project team develop a highly detailed set of specifications that developers can use to build the application. An organization that is purchasing off-the-shelf software can use requirements to make sure that the right software product will be selected.

The testing phase ensures that the application that was developed or acquired will actually perform as required. A test plan should be formally developed; this plan should be a direct derivation from formal requirements that were developed earlier in the project; essentially, every requirement must be measurable and confirmed during testing. Other critical activities in a software development project include data migration (where data is transferred from an older application to the new application), training (for users, operations, and technical support staff), and implementation of the new software application.

Some alternatives to the traditional SDLC process include agile development, prototyping, rapid application development (RAD), data-oriented system development (DOSD), object-oriented (OO) system development, component-based development, web-based development, and reverse engineering.

Software developers often use system development tools to aid in software development. These tools include computer-aided software engineering (CASE) and fourth-generation languages (4GLs) that can make developers more productive.

Acquiring cloud-based applications requires the same steps as software acquisition, although there are additional considerations that need to be managed, including access control, environment segregation, and legal jurisdiction.

Change management and configuration management processes are used to manage changes to existing applications and infrastructure. Change management is a formal process where desired changes are planned, tested, and reviewed prior to implementation. Configuration management is a process (usually supported by automated tools) of recording configuration information in operating systems, software environments, and applications.

Like software applications and infrastructure, business processes should also be managed by a life cycle process that includes feasibility studies, requirements definition, business process engineering, testing, and implementation. Often, business processes are tightly coupled to software applications; frequently, changes to one will necessitate changes in the other.

Software applications should be equipped with controls that ensure the integrity of information and the integrity of processing and applications. These controls include input validation, processing validation, and output validation, all of which make sure that the data in the application is of the proper type and within required numeric ranges.

IS auditors who audit life cycle management activities need to obtain and examine documents that describe program and project management processes, charters, and records. They need to understand the processes that are used to develop and acquire software applications and supporting infrastructure, as well as the processes used to maintain them. IS auditors need to understand the processes that are in place and to examine records to help determine whether the processes are followed and effective.

Notes

- Business realization operates at the strategic level developing portfolio programs, coordinated by formal business case modeling against business benefit.

- Project management strategies guide program execution through organization of resources and development of clear project objectives. Management of the project schedule, roles, change management, and subsequent completion or closure criteria determine the outcome of each project. Many project management methodologies exist to guide project expectations, requirements, and completion criteria.

- The software development life cycle (SDLC) defines a subset of project management focusing on the requirements for the creation, implementation, and maintenance of application software. The SDLC relies on a sequence of events that may occur one time or cyclically as part of a formal continual improvement process. The SDLC phases include a feasibility study, definition of requirements, design, development, testing, implementation, and post-implementation phases.

- Application access is facilitated by the enterprise infrastructure, which is in turn developed, implemented, and maintained through a process similar to the SDLC. Infrastructural development begins with a review of existing infrastructure elements, matching each to identified requirements to produce the initial design. After procurement to meet design requirements, the activities of testing, implementation, and post-implementation follow similarly to the SDLC.

- Post-implementation maintenance of information systems includes both change and configuration management strategies to ensure the enterprise remains aligned with business requirements and practices.

- The business process life cycle (BPLC) and business process reengineering (BPR) aid in coordinating business processes using a sequence of events identical to that of the SDLC focused on business process creation, implementation, and maintenance. Benchmarking facilitates continuous improvement within the BPLC, while capability maturity models can allow point-in-time assessment of business process and information system capability alignment.

- Application controls limit information system access at the point of entry (input controls), during consumption (process controls), and at the point of expression (output controls).

- Auditing each element of the enterprise's development life cycle validates alignment between business and regulatory controls against process and functional control strategies and standards. The auditor should be familiar with the project management strategy in place within an enterprise to ensure that both the elements and the process used to develop each are properly aligned with business process requirements.

- Auditing application controls validates the proper operation of input, process, and output controls by following transaction flow from initiation through conclusion and performing data integrity testing appropriate to the application design. Computer-aided audit testing (CAAT) systems are particularly useful for continuous audit of application controls.

Questions

1. What testing activities should developers perform during the development phase?

   A. Security testing

   B. Integration testing

   C. Unit testing

   D. Developers should not perform any testing

2. The purpose of function point analysis (FPA) is to:

   A. Estimate the effort required to develop a software program

   B. Identify risks in a software program

   C. Estimate task dependencies in a project plan

   D. Inventory inputs and outputs in a software program

3. A project manager needs to identify the tasks that are responsible for project delays. What approach should the project manager use?

   A. Function point analysis

   B. Gantt analysis

   C. Project evaluation and review technique

   D. Critical path methodology

4. A software developer has informed the project manager that a portion of the application development is going to take five additional days to complete. The project manager should:

   A. Inform the other project participants of the schedule change

   B. Change the project schedule to reflect the new completion time

   C. Create a project change request

   D. Adjust the resource budget to account for the schedule change

5. The phases and their order in the software development life cycle are:

   A. Requirements, feasibility, design, development, testing, implementation, post-implementation

   B. Feasibility, requirements, design, development, testing, implementation, post-implementation

   C. Feasibility, requirements, design, development, testing, implementation

   D. Requirements, feasibility, development, testing, implementation, post-implementation

6. What personnel should be involved in the requirements phase of a software development project?

   A. Systems administrators, network administrators, and software developers

   B. Developers, analysts, architects, and users

   C. Security, privacy, and legal analysts

   D. Representatives from each software vendor

7. The primary source for test plans in a software development project is:

   A. Requirements

   B. Developers

   C. End users

   D. Vendors

8. The primary purpose for a change management process is to:

   A. Record changes made to systems and infrastructure

   B. Review and approve proposed changes to systems and infrastructure

   C. Review and approve changes to a project schedule

   D. Review and approve changes to application source code

9. What is the purpose of a capability maturity model?

   A. To assess the experience of software developers

   B. To assess the experience of project managers

   C. To assess the integrity of application software

   D. To assess the maturity of business processes

10. The purpose of input validation checking is:

    A. To ensure that input values are within acceptable ranges

    B. To ensure that input data contains the correct type of characters

    C. To ensure that input data is free of hostile or harmful content

    D. All of these

11. An organization is considering the acquisition of enterprise software that will be hosted by a cloud services provider. What additional requirements need to be considered for the cloud environment?

    A. Logging

    B. Access control

    C. Data segregation

    D. Performance

12. System operators had to make an emergency change in order to keep an application server running. To satisfy change management requirements, the systems operators should:

    A. Document the steps taken

    B. Fill out an emergency change request form

    C. Seek approval from management before making the change

    D. All of these

13. A global organization is planning the migration of a business process to a new application. What cutover methods can be considered?

    A. Parallel, geographic, module by module, or all at once

    B. Parallel, geographic, or module by module

    C. Parallel, module by module, or all at once

    D. Parallel, geographic, or all at once

14. The purpose of rollback planning is:

    A. Complete backup media migration

    B. Satisfy regulatory requirements

    C. Provide the ability to revert to the old environment in case something goes wrong

    D. Make sure that personnel understand how a migration is supposed to be performed

15. The reason that functional requirements need to be measureable is

    A. Developers need to know how to test functional requirements

    B. Functional tests are derived directly from functional requirements

    C. To verify correct system operation

    D. To measure system performance

Answers

1. **C.** Developers should only be performing unit testing to verify that the individual sections of code they have written are performing properly.

2. **A.** Function point analysis (FPA) is used to estimate the effort required to develop a software program.

3. **D.** Critical path methodology helps a project manager determine which activities are on a project's "critical path."

4. **C.** When any significant change needs to occur in a project plan, a project change request should be created to document the reason for the change.

5. **B.** The phases of the software development life cycle are feasibility, requirements, design, development, testing, implementation, and post-implementation.

6. **B.** Requirements need to be developed by several parties, including developers, analysts, architects, and users.

7. **A.** The requirements that are developed for a project should be the primary source for detailed tests.

8. **B.** The main purpose for change management is to review and approve proposed changes to systems and infrastructure. This helps to reduce the risk of unintended events and unplanned downtime.

9. **D.** A capability maturity model helps an organization to assess the maturity of its business processes, which is an important first step to any large-scale process improvement efforts.

10. **D.** Input validation checking is used to ensure that input values are within established ranges, of the correct character types, and free of harmful content.

11. **C.** In addition to business, functional, security, and privacy requirements, an organization considering cloud-based services needs to understand how the cloud services provider segregates the organization's data apart from its other customers.

12. **D.** When making an emergency change, personnel should first seek management approval, document the details of the change, and initiate an emergency change management procedure.

13. **A.** The migration to a new application can be done in several ways: parallel (running old and new systems side by side); geographic (migrating users in each geographic region separately); module by module (migrating individual modules of the application), or migrate all users, locations, and modules at the same time.

14. **C.** Rollback planning is needed so that the organization can revert to the old system in case something in a data migration goes wrong.

15. **B.** Functional requirements should be measurable, because test cases should be developed directly from functional requirements. The same can be said about security and privacy requirements—all must be measurable because all should be tested.

IT Service Delivery and Infrastructure

This chapter discusses the following topics
- Information systems operations
- Information systems hardware
- Information systems architecture and software
- Network infrastructure, technologies, models, and protocols
- Disaster recovery planning
- Auditing infrastructure, operations, and disaster recovery planning

---

The topics in this chapter represent 23 percent of the CISA examination. This chapter discusses CISA job practice 4, "IT Service Delivery and Support."

IT organizations are effective if their operations are effective. Management needs to be in control of IT operations, which means that all aspects of operations need to be measured, those measurements and reports reviewed, and management-directed changes carried out.

IT organizations are service organizations—their existence is to serve the organization and support its business processes. IT's service management operations need to be well designed, adequately measured, and reviewed by management.

IS auditors need to have a keen understanding of the workings of computer hardware, operating systems, and network communications technology. This knowledge will help the auditor to better understand many aspects of service management and operations.

Information Systems Operations

- IS operations is term that encompasses the day-to-day control of the information systems, applications, and infrastructure that support organizational objectives and processes. IS operations is composed of several sets of activities, which include management and control of operations.

- IT service management

- Infrastructure operations

- Monitoring
- Software program library management
- Quality management
- Security management
- Media control

These activities are discussed in detail in the remainder of this section.

Management and Control of Operations

All of the activities that take place in an IS department should be managed and controlled. This means that all actions and activities performed by operations personnel should be a part of a procedure, process, or project that has been approved by management. Processes, procedures, and projects should have enough recordkeeping so that management can understand the status of these activities.

Management is ultimately responsible for all activities that take place in an IS operations department. The primary high-level management activities that govern IS operations are

- **Development of processes and procedures**   Every repetitive activity performed by any operations personnel should be documented in the form of a process or procedure. This means that documents that describe each step of every process and procedure need to be developed, reviewed, approved by management, and made available to operations staff.

- **Development of standards**   From the way that operations performs tasks to the brands and technologies used, standards drive consistency in everything that IS operations does.

- **Resource allocation**   Management is responsible for allocating resources that support IS operations, including manpower, technology, and budget. Resource allocation should align with the organization's mission, goals, and objectives.

- **Process management**   All IS operations processes should be measured and managed. This will ensure that processes are being performed properly, accurately, and within time and budget targets.

IT Service Management

IT service management (ITSM) is the set of activities that ensures the delivery of IT services is efficient and effective, through active management and the continuous improvement of processes.

ITSM consists of several distinct activities:

- Service desk
- Incident management
- Problem management
- Change management

- Configuration management
- Release management
- Service-level management
- Financial management
- Capacity management
- Service continuity management
- Availability management

Each of these activities is described in detail in this section.

ITSM is defined in the IT Infrastructure Library (ITIL) process framework, a well-recognized standard. The content of ITIL is managed by the UK-based Office of Government Commerce. IT service management processes can be audited and registered to the ISO 20000 standard, the first international standard for ITSM.

Service Desk

Often known as the helpdesk or call center, the *IT service desk* function handles incidents and service requests on behalf of customers by acting as a single point of contact. The service desk will perform end-to-end management of incidents and service requests (at least from the perspective of the customer) and also be responsible for communicating status reports to the customer.

The service desk can also serve as a collection point for other ITSM processes, such as change management, configuration management, service-level management, availability management, and other ITSM functions.

Incident Management

ITIL defines an *incident* as *"any event* which is not part of the standard operation of a service and which causes, or may cause, an interruption to, or a reduction in, the quality of that service. The stated ITIL objective is to restore normal operations as quickly as possible with the least possible impact on either the business or the user, at a cost-effective price."

Thus, an incident may be any of the following:

- Service outage
- Service slowdown
- Software bug

IT Infrastructure Library, Not Just for the UK

While the IT Infrastructure Library (ITIL) may have its roots in the UK, it has very much become an international standard. Partly this is due to ITIL being adopted by the International Standards Organization in the ISO 20000 standard, and partly because IT management practices are becoming more standardized and mature.

Regardless of the cause, incidents are a result of failures or errors in any component or layer in IT infrastructure.

In ITIL terminology, if the incident has been seen before and its root cause is known, this is a *known error*. If the service desk is able to access the catalog of known errors, this may result in more rapid resolution of incidents, resulting in less downtime and inconvenience. The change management and configuration management processes are used to make modifications to the system in order to fix it temporarily or permanently.

If the root cause of the incident is not known, the incident may be escalated to a *problem*, which is discussed in the next section.

Problem Management

When several incidents have occurred that appear to have the same or a similar root cause, a *problem* is occurring. ITIL defines a *problem* as "a condition often identified as a result of multiple incidents that exhibit common symptoms. Problems can also be identified from a single significant incident, indicative of a single error, for which the cause is unknown, but for which the impact is significant."

The overall objective of problem management is the reduction in the number and severity of incidents.

Problem management can also include some proactive measures, including system monitoring to measure system health and capacity management that will help management to forestall capacity-related incidents.

Examples of problems include

- A server that has exhausted available resources that result in similar, multiple errors (which, in ITSM terms, are known as incidents)
- A software bug in a service that is noticed by and affecting many users
- A chronically congested network that causes the communications between many IT components to fail

Similar to incidents, when the root cause of a problem has been identified, the change management and configuration management processes will be enacted to make temporary and permanent fixes.

Change Management

Change management is the set of processes that ensures all changes performed in an IT environment are controlled and performed consistently. ITIL defines change management as the "process to ensure that standardized methods and procedures are used for efficient and prompt handling of all changes, in order to minimize the impact of change-related incidents upon service quality, and consequently improve the day-to-day operations of the organization."

The main purpose of change management is to ensure that all proposed changes to an IT environment are vetted for suitability and risk, and to ensure that changes will not interfere with each other or with other planned or unplanned activities. In order to be effective, each stakeholder should review all changes so that every perspective of each change is properly reviewed.

A typical change management process is a formal "waterfall" process that includes the following steps:

- **Proposal or request** Here, the person or group performing the change announces the proposed change. Typically, a change proposal will contain a description of the change, the change procedure, the IT components that are expected to be affected by the change, a verification procedure to ensure that the change was applied properly, a back-out procedure in the event the change cannot be applied (or failed verification), and the results of tests that were performed in a test environment. The proposal should be distributed to all stakeholders several days prior to review.

- **Review** This is typically a meeting or discussion about the change, where the personnel who will be performing the change can discuss the change and answer any of the stakeholders' questions. Since the change proposal was sent out earlier, each stakeholder should have had an opportunity to read about the change in advance of the review. Stakeholders can discuss any aspect of the change during the review. The stakeholders may agree to approve the change, or they may request that it be deferred or that some aspect of the proposed change be altered.

- **Approval** When a change has been formally approved in the review step, the person or group responsible for change management recordkeeping will record the approval, including the names of the individuals who consented to the change. If, however, a change has been deferred or denied, the person or group that proposed the change will need to make alterations to the proposed change so that it will be acceptable, or they can withdraw the change altogether.

- **Implementation** The actual change is implemented per the procedure described in the change proposal. Here, the person(s) identified as the change implementers perform the actual change to the IT system(s) identified in the approved change procedure.

- **Verification** After the implementers have completed the change, they will perform the verification procedure to make sure that the change was implemented correctly and that it produces the desired result. Generally, the verification procedure will include one or more steps that include the gathering of evidence that shows the change is correct. This evidence will be filed with other records related to the change, and may be useful in the future if there is any problem with the system where this change is suspected as a part of the root cause.

- **Post-change review** Some or all changes in an IT organization will be reviewed after the change is implemented. In this activity, the person(s) who made the change discuss the change with other stakeholders in order to learn more about the change and whether any updates to future changes may be needed.

These activities should be part of a change control board, a group of stakeholders from IT and every group that is affected by changes in IT applications and supporting infrastructure.

NOTE The change management process is similar to the software development life cycle in that it consists of activities that systematically enact changes to an IT environment.

Change Management Records   Most or all of the activities related to a change should include updates to business records so that all of the facts related to each change are captured for future reference. In even the smallest IT organization, there are too many changes taking place over time to expect that anyone will be able to recall facts about each change later on. Records that are related to each change serve as a permanent record.

Emergency Changes   While most changes can be planned in advance using the change management process described here, there are times when IT systems need to be changed right away. Most change management processes include a process for emergency changes that details most of the steps in the nonemergency change management process, but they are performed out of order. The steps for emergency changes are

- **Emergency approval**   When an emergency situation arises, the staff members attending to the emergency should still seek management approval for the proposed change. This approval may be done by phone, in person, or in writing (typically e-mail). If the approval was by phone or in person, e-mail or other follow-up is usually performed. Certain members of management should be designated in advance who can approve these emergency changes.

- **Implementation**   The staff members perform the change.

- **Verification**   Staff members verify that the change produced the expected result. This may involve other staff members from other departments or end users.

- **Review**   The emergency change is formally reviewed. This review may be performed alongside nonemergency changes with the same group of individuals who discuss nonemergency changes.

Like nonemergency changes, emergency changes will have the full set of records that are available for future reference.

Linkage to Problem and Incident Management   Often, changes are made as a result of an incident or problem. Emergency and nonemergency changes should reference specific incidents or problems so that those incidents and problems may be properly closed once verification of their resolution has been completed.

Configuration Management
Configuration management (CM) is the process of recording the configuration of IT systems. Each configuration setting is known in ITSM parlance as a *configuration item* (CI). CIs usually include the following:

- **Hardware complement**   The hardware specifications of each system (e.g., CPU speed, amount of memory, firmware version, adaptors, and peripherals).

- **Hardware configuration**   Settings at the hardware level may include boot settings, adaptor configuration, and firmware settings.

- **Operating system version and configuration**   This includes versions, patches, and many operating system configuration items that have an impact on system performance and functionality.

- **Software versions and configuration**   Software components such as database management systems, application servers, and integration interfaces often have many configuration settings of their own.

Organizations that have many IT systems may automate the CM function with tools that are used to automatically record and change configuration settings. These tools help to streamline IT operations and make it easier for IT systems to be more consistent with one another. The database of system configurations is called a configuration management database (CMDB).

Linkage to Problem and Incident Management   An intelligent problem and incident management system is able to access the CMDB to help IT personnel determine whether incidents and problems are related to specific configurations. This can be an invaluable aid to those who are seeking to determine a problem's root cause.

Linkage to Change Management   Many configuration management tools are able to automatically detect configuration changes that are made to a system. With some change and configuration management systems, it is possible to correlate changes detected by a configuration management system with changes approved in the change management process. Further, many changes that are approved by the change management process can be performed by configuration management tools, which can be used to push changes out to managed systems.

Release Management
Release management is the ITIL term used to describe the portion of the SDLC where changes in applications are made available to end users. Release management is used to control the changes that are made to software programs, applications, and environments.

The release process is used for several types of changes to a system, including

- **Incidents and problem resolution**   Casually known as bug fixes, these types of changes are done in response to an incident or problem, where it has been determined that a change to application software is the appropriate remedy.

- **Enhancements**   This is where new functions in an application are created and implemented. These enhancements may have been requested by customers, or they may be a part of the long-range vision on the part of the designers of the software program.

- **Subsystem patches and changes**   Changes in lower layers in an application environment may require a level of testing that is similar to what is used when changes are made to the application itself. Examples of changes are patches, service packs, and version upgrades to operating systems, database management systems, application servers, and middleware.

The release process is a sequential process. That is, each change that is proposed to a software program will be taken through each step in the release management process. In many applications, changes are usually assembled into a "package" for process efficiency purposes: it is more effective to discuss and manage groups of changes than it would be to manage individual changes.

The steps in a typical release process are

- **Requirements**   Here, each software change is described in terms of a feature description and requirements. The feature description is a high-level description of a change to software that may explain the change in business terms. Requirements are the detailed statements that describe a change in enough detail for a developer to make changes and additions to application code that will provide the desired functionality. Often, end users will be involved in the development of requirements so that they may verify that the proposed software change is really what they desire.

- **Design**   After requirements have been developed, a programmer/analyst or application designer will create a formal design. For an existing software application, this will usually involve changes to existing design documents and diagrams, but for new applications, these will need to be created from scratch or copied from similar designs and modified. Regardless, the design will have a sufficient level of detail to permit a programmer or software engineer to complete development without having to discern the meaning of requirements or design.

- **Development**   When requirements and design have been completed, reviewed, and approved, programmers or software engineers begin development. This involves actual coding in the chosen computer language with approved development tools, as well as the creation or update to ancillary components, such as a database design or application programming interface (API). Developers will often perform their own *unit testing*, where they test individual modules and sections of the application code to make sure that it works properly.

- **Testing**   When the developer(s) have finished coding and unit testing, a more formal and comprehensive test phase is performed. Here, analysts, dedicated software testers, and perhaps end users will test all of the new and changed functionality to confirm whether it is performing according to requirements. Depending on the nature of the changes, some amount of *regression testing* is also performed; this means that functions that were confirmed to be working properly in prior releases are tested again to make sure that they continue to work as expected. Testing is performed according to formal, written test plans that are designed to confirm that every requirement is fulfilled. Formal test scripts are used, and the results of all tests should be recorded and archived. The testing that users perform is usually called user acceptance testing (UAT). Often, automated test tools are used, which can make testing more accurate and efficient. After testing is completed, a formal review and approval are required before the process is allowed to continue.

- **Release preparation**   When UAT and regression testing have been completed, reviewed, and approved, a release management team will begin to prepare the new or changed software for release. Depending upon the complexity of the application and of the change itself, release preparation may involve not only software installation but also the installation or change to database design, and perhaps even changes to customer data. Hence, the software release may involve the development and testing of data conversion tools and other programs that are required so that the new or changed software will operate properly. As with testing and other phases, full records of testing and implementation of release preparation details need to be captured and archived.

- **Release deployment**   When release preparation is completed (and perhaps reviewed and approved), the release is installed on the target system(s). Personnel deploying the release will follow the release procedure, which may involve the use of tools that will make changes to the target system at the operating system, database, or other levels; any required data manipulation or migration; and the installation of the actual software. The release procedure will also include verification steps that will be used to confirm the correct installation of all components.

Utilizing a Gate Process   Many organizations utilize a "gate process" approach in their release management process. This means that each step of the process undergoes formal review and approval before the next step is allowed to begin. For example, a formal design review will be performed and attended by end users, personnel who created requirements and feature description documents, developers, and management. If the design is approved, development may begin. But if there are questions or concerns in the design review, the design may need to be modified and reviewed again before development is allowed to begin.

Service-Level Management
Service-level management is composed of the set of activities that confirm whether IS operations is providing adequate service to its customers. This is achieved through continuous monitoring and periodic review of IT service delivery.

An IS department often plays two different roles in service-level management. As a provider of service to its own customers, the IS department will measure and manage the services that it provides directly. Also, many IS departments directly or indirectly manage services that are provided by external service providers. Thus, many IS departments are both service provider and customer, and often the two are interrelated. This is depicted in Figure 5-1.

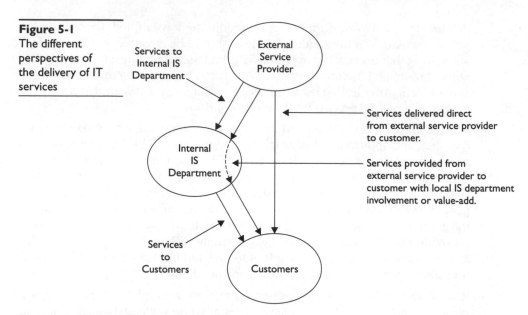

Figure 5-1
The different perspectives of the delivery of IT services

Financial Management

Financial management for IT services consists of several activities, including

- Budgeting
- Capital investment
- Expense management
- Project accounting and project return on investment (ROI)

IT financial management is the portion of IT management that takes into account the financial value of IT services that support organizational objectives.

Capacity Management

Capacity management is a set of activities that confirm there is sufficient capacity in IT systems and IT processes to meet service needs. Primarily, an IT system or process has sufficient capacity if its performance falls within an acceptable range, as specified in service-level agreements (SLAs).

Capacity management is not just a concern for current needs; capacity management must also be concerned about meeting future needs. This is attained through several activities, including

- **Periodic measurements**   Systems and processes need to be regularly measured so that trends in usage can be used to predict future capacity needs.
- **Considering planned changes**   Planned changes to processes and IT systems may have an impact on predicted workload.
- **Understanding long-term strategies**   Changes in the organization, including IT systems, business processes, and organizational objectives, may have

an impact on workloads, requiring more (or less) capacity than would be extrapolated through simpler trend analysis.

- **Changes in technology**   Several factors may influence capacity plans, including the expectation that computing and network technologies will deliver better performance in the future and that trends in the usage of technology may influence how end users use technology.

Linkage to Financial Management   One of the work products of capacity management is a projection for the acquisition of additional computer or network hardware to meet future capacity needs. This information needs to be made a part of budgeting and spending management processes.

Linkage to Service-Level Management   If there are insufficient resources to handle workloads, capacity issues may result in violations to SLAs. Systems and processes that are overburdened will take longer to respond. In some cases, systems may stop responding altogether.

Linkage to Incident and Problem Management   Systems with severe capacity issues may take excessive time to respond to user requests. In some cases, systems may malfunction or users may give up. Often, users will call the service desk, resulting in the logging of incidents and problems.

Service Continuity Management

Service continuity management is the set of activities that is concerned with the ability of the organization to continue providing services, primarily in the event that a natural or manmade disaster has occurred. Service continuity management is ITIL parlance for the more common terms *business continuity planning* and *disaster recovery planning*.

Business continuity is discussed later in this chapter. Disaster recovery planning is discussed in Chapter 2.

Availability Management

The goal of availability management is to sustain IT service availability in support of organizational objectives and processes. The availability of IT systems is governed by:

- **Effective change management**   When changes to systems and infrastructure are properly vetted through a change management process, changes are less likely to result in unanticipated downtime.

- **Effective application testing**   When changes to applications are made according to a set of formal requirements, review, and testing, the application is less likely to fail and become unavailable.

- **Resilient architecture**   When the overall architecture of an application environment is designed from the beginning to be highly reliable, it will be more resilient and more tolerant of individual faults and component failures.

- **Serviceable components**   When the individual components of an application environment can be effectively serviced by third-party service organizations, those components will be less likely to fail unexpectedly.

NOTE Organizations typically measure availability as a percentage of uptime of an application or service.

Infrastructure Operations

Infrastructure operations is the entire set of activities performed by network, system, and application operators, facilitating the continued operation of business applications. The tasks that may be required in infrastructure operations include

- Running jobs according to the job schedule
- Monitoring jobs and allocating resources to jobs based on priority
- Restarting failed jobs and processes
- Facilitating backup jobs by loading or changing backup media
- Monitoring systems, applications, and networks for availability and adequate performance
- Performing after-hours maintenance activities such as equipment cleaning and system restarts

All routine and incident handling procedures in infrastructure operations should be formally documented.

Monitoring

Information systems, applications, and supporting infrastructure must be monitored to ensure that they continue to operate as required.

Monitoring tools and programs enables IT operations staff to detect when software or hardware components are not operating as planned. The IT operations staff must also make direct observations in order to detect some problems. The types of errors that should be detected and reported include

- System errors
- Program errors
- Communications errors
- Operator errors

Simply put, any event that represents unexpected or abnormal activity should be recorded so that management and customers may become aware of them. This requires that incident and problem management processes be developed. Incident and problem management are discussed in detail in the earlier section, "IT Service Management."

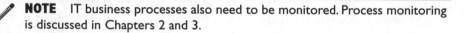

NOTE IT business processes also need to be monitored. Process monitoring is discussed in Chapters 2 and 3.

Software Program Library Management

The *software program library* is the facility that is used to store and manage access to an organization's application source and object code.

In most organizations, application source code is highly sensitive. It may be considered intellectual property, and it may contain information such as algorithms, encryption keys, and other sensitive information that should be accessed by as few persons as possible. In a very real sense, application source code should be considered information and be treated as such through the organization's security policy and data classification policy.

A software program library often exists as an information system with a user interface and several functions, including

- **Access and authorization controls** The program library should uniquely identify all individuals who attempt to access the program library and authenticate them with means that are commensurate with the sensitivity of the application. The program library should be able to manage different roles or levels of access so that each person is able to perform only the functions that they are authorized to perform. Also, the program library should be able to restrict access to different modules or applications stored within it; for example, source code that is more sensitive (such as the code related to access control or data encryption) should be accessible by fewer personnel than less sensitive source code.

- **Program checkout** This means that an authorized user is able to access some portion of application source code, presumably to make a modification or perform analysis. Checkout permits the user to make a copy of the source code module that might be stored elsewhere on the program library or on another computer. Often, checkout is only permitted upon management approval, or it may be integrated with a defect tracking system so that a developer is able to check out a piece of source code only if there is a defect in that program that has been assigned to her. When source code is checked out, the program library may be able to "lock" that section of source code so that another developer is not able to also check it out—this could result in a "collision" where two developers are making changes to the same section of code at the same time.

- **Program check-in** This function allows an authorized user to return a section of application source code to the program library. A program library will usually only permit the person who checked out a section of code to check it back in. If the user who is checking in the code section made modifications to it, the program library will process those changes and may perform a number of additional functions, including version control and code scanning. If the section of code being checked in was locked, the program library will either automatically unlock it or ask the user whether it should remain locked.

- **Version control**   This function allows the program library to manage changes to the source code by tracking the changes that are made to it each time it is checked in. Each time a source code module is modified, a "version number" is incremented. This gives the program library the ability to recall any prior version of a source code module at any time in the future. This can be useful during program troubleshooting or investigations into a particular programmer's actions.

- **Code analysis**   Some program library systems are able to perform different types of code analysis when source code is checked in. This may include a security scan that will examine the code to look for vulnerabilities or a scan that will determine whether the checked-in module complies with local coding policies and standards.

These controls enable an organization to have a high degree of control over the integrity and, hence, quality and security, of its software applications.

Quality Assurance

The purpose of quality assurance is to ensure that changes to software applications, operating system configuration, network device configuration, and other types of changes to information systems are performed properly. Primarily, this is carried out through independent verification of work.

 NOTE   The implementation step in most development and change processes can be divided into two parts: one person who implements a change and another person who verifies its accuracy.

Security Management

Information security management is the collection of high-level activities that ensure that an organization's information security program is adequate and operating properly. An information security management program usually consists of several activities:

- Development of security policy, processes, procedures, and standards
- Risk assessment
- Impact analysis
- Vulnerability management

These topics are discussed in detail in Chapter 6.

Media Control

Security standards and privacy laws have highlighted the need for formal processes to ensure the proper management of digital media, including its protection, as well as destruction of data that is no longer needed. These processes are usually a part of data retention and data purging procedures so that data that is needed is adequately protected with physical and logical security controls, and data that is no longer needed is effectively erased. Procedures related to the disposal of media that is no longer needed now include steps to erase data on that media or make the data on that media irretrievable in some other way.

Media that should be considered in scope for media management and destruction policies and procedures includes

- Backup media
- Virtual tape libraries
- Optical media
- Hard drives and solid-state drives
- Flash memory in computers, network devices, disk drives, workstations, mobile devices, and portable USB storage devices
- Hard drives in printers, copiers, and scanners
- Hard copy

Policies and procedures for media sanitization need to be included in service provider contracts, as well as recordkeeping to track the destruction of media over time.

Information Systems Hardware

Hardware is the elemental basis of information systems. It consists of circuit boards containing microprocessors and memory, and circuitry connecting other components, such as hard disk drives, and peripherals, such as printers, monitors, and network connections.

IS auditors need to understand at least the basic concepts of computer hardware architecture, maintenance, and monitoring so that an organization's use and care of information systems hardware can be properly assessed. A lack of knowledge in this area could result in the auditor overlooking or failing to understand important aspects of an organization's operations.

Computer Usage

Computers are manufactured for a variety of purposes and contexts, and are used for many different purposes. They can be classified by their capacity, throughput, size, use, or the operating system or software that they use.

Types of Computers

From a business perspective, computers are classified according to their size and portability. In this regard, the types of computers are

- **Supercomputer**   These are the largest computers in terms of the number and/or power of their central processing units (CPUs). Supercomputers are generally employed for scientific applications such as weather and climate forecasting, seismology, and other computer-intensive applications.

- **Mainframe** These are the business workhorse computers that are designed to run large, complex applications that operate on enormous databases or support vast numbers of users. When computing began, mainframes were the *only* kind of computer; most of the other types were derived from the mainframe.

- **Midrange** These computers are not as large and powerful as mainframe computers, but are larger or more powerful than small servers. There are no hard distinctions between these sizes of computers, but only vague, rough guidelines.

- **Server** If mainframe computers are the largest business servers, then the ordinary *server* is the smallest. In terms of its hardware complement and physical appearance, a server can be indistinguishable from a user's desktop computer.

- **Blade server** This is a style of hardware design where servers are modules that plug in to a cabinet. Each module contains all of the internal components of a stand-alone computer. The cabinet itself will contain power supplies and network connectors.

- **Appliance** This is a type of computer that typically comes with one or more tools or applications preinstalled. The term "appliance" is used to connote the fact that little or no maintenance is required on the system.

- **Desktop** This is a computer that is used by an individual worker. Its size makes it fairly easy to move from place to place, but it is not considered portable. The desktop computers of today are more powerful in many ways than the mainframe computers of a few decades ago. Desktop computers used to be called *microcomputers,* but the term is seldom used now.

- **Laptop/notebook** This computer is portable in every sense of the word. It is self-contained, is equipped with a battery, and folds for storage and transport. Functionally, desktop and laptop computers are nearly identical: they may run the same operating system and programs.

- **Mobile** These computers come in the form of smart phones, tablet computers, and netbook computers.

Uses for Computers

Aside from the sizes and types of computers discussed in the previous section, computers may also be used for several reasons, including

- **Application server** This is a computer—usually a mainframe, midrange, or server—that runs application-server software. An application server contains one or more application programs that run on behalf of users. Data used by an application server may be stored on a database server.

- **Web server** This is a server that runs a web server program to make web pages available to users. A web server will usually contain both the web server software and the content ("pages") that are requested by and sent to users' web browser programs. A web server can also be linked to an application

Mobile Devices, the New and Disruptive Endpoint

Much is said about endpoints being the weak link in IS infrastructure. But historically speaking, these proclamations are more about laptop computers, which, for the most part, can be well managed by enterprises.

Mobile devices are a different matter entirely. They are turning all of the rules about endpoint computing on their head. Principally:

- End users choose which models to purchase and own them outright.

- End users can install any application they choose.

- Mobile devices can be easily connected to corporate e-mail without any help from the IT department.

- There are few, if any, anti-malware or other anti-tampering tools available.

- There are few, if any, enterprise management tools available to effectively manage these devices.

- Mobile devices are easily lost and more easily broken into than laptop computers.

- Mobile device manufacturers have published application interfaces, thereby enabling the creation of malware that can steal data and alter operation of the device.

IS auditors need to understand how organizations are addressing the mobile device dilemma.

server or database server to permit the display of business information, such as filling out order forms, viewing reports, and so on.

- **Database server** Also a mainframe, midrange, or small server, a database server runs specialized database management software that controls the storage and processing of large amounts of data that reside in one or more databases.

- **File server** This computer is used to provide a central location for the storage of commonly used files. File servers may be used by application servers or by a user community.

- **Print server** In an environment that uses shared printers, a print server is typically used to receive print requests from users or applications and store them temporarily until they are ready to be printed.

- **Production server/test server** The terms *production server* and *test server* denote whether a server supports actual business use (a production server) or whether it is a separate server that can be used to test new programs or configurations (a test server). Most organizations will have at least one test server for every type of production server so that any new programs, configurations, patches, or settings can be tested on a test server, where there will be little or no risk of disrupting actual business operations.

- **Thick client**   A thick client is a user's computer (of the desktop or laptop variety) that contains a fully functional operating system and application programs. Purists will argue that a thick client is *only* a thick client if the system contains one or more software application client programs. This is a reasonable distinction between a thick client and a workstation, described later.

- **Thin client**   A thin client is a user's workstation that contains a minimal operating system and little or no data storage. Thin-client computers are often used in businesses where users run only application programs that can be executed on central servers and display data shown on the thin client's screen. A thin client may be a desktop or laptop computer with thin-client software, or it may be a specialized computer with no local storage other than flash memory.

- **Workstation**   A user's laptop or desktop computer. For example, a PC running the Windows operating system and using Star Office word processor and spreadsheet programs, a Firefox browser, and Winamp media player would be considered a workstation.

- **Mobile device** A user's smart phone, tablet computer, or netbook computer.

 NOTE   For the most part, computers are designed for general use in mind so that they may perform any of the functions listed here.

Computer Hardware Architecture

Computers made since the 1960s share common characteristics in their hardware architecture. They have one or more central processing units, a bus (or more than one), main memory, and secondary storage. They also have some means for communicating with other computers or with humans, usually through communications adaptors.

This section describes computer hardware in detail.

Central Processing Unit

The central processing unit, or CPU, is the main hardware component of a computer system. The CPU is the component that executes instructions in computer programs.

Each CPU has an *arithmetic logic unit* (ALU), a control unit, and a small amount of memory. The memory in a CPU is usually in the form of *registers*, which are memory locations where arithmetic values are stored.

The CPU in modern computers is wholly contained in a single large-scale integration integrated circuit (LSI IC), more commonly known as a *microprocessor*. A CPU is attached to a computer circuit board (often called a motherboard on a personal computer) by soldering or a plug-in socket. A CPU on a motherboard is shown in Figure 5-2.

Figure 5-2
A CPU that is
plugged into a
computer circuit
board (Image
courtesy Fir0002/
Flagstaffotos)

CPU Architectures A number of architectures dominate the design of CPUs. Two primary architectures that are widely used commercially are

- **CISC (complex instruction set computer)** This CPU design has a comprehensive instruction set, and many instructions can be performed in a single cycle. This design philosophy claims superior performance over RISC. Well-known CISC CPUs include Intel x86, VAX, PDP-11, Motorola 68000, and System/360.

- **RISC (reduced instruction set computer)** This CPU design uses a smaller instruction set (meaning fewer instructions in its "vocabulary"), with the idea that a small instruction set will lead to a simpler microprocessor design and better computer performance. Well-known RISC CPUs include Alpha, MIPS, PowerPC, and SPARC.

Another aspect of CPUs that is often discussed is the power requirements. Typically the CPUs that are used for laptop computers and mobile devices are known as low-power CPUs, while other CPUs are used in desktop, server, and mainframe systems, where performance and speed are more important considerations than power consumption.

Computer Architectures Early computers had a single CPU. However, it became clear that many computing tasks could be performed more efficiently if computers had more than one CPU to perform them. Some of the ways that computers have implemented CPUs are

- **Single CPU** In this design, the computer has a single CPU. This simplest design is still prevalent, particularly among small servers and personal computers.

- **Multiple CPUs** A computer design can accommodate multiple CPUs, from as few as 2 to as many as 128 or more. There are two designs for multi-CPU computers: symmetric and asymmetric. In the symmetric design, all CPUs are equal in terms of how the overall computer's architecture uses them. In the asymmetric design, one CPU is the "master." Virtually all multi-CPU computers made today are symmetric.

- **Multicore CPUs** A change in the design of CPUs themselves has led to multicore CPUs, in which two or more central processors occupy a single CPU chip. The benefit of multicore design is the ability for software code to be executed in parallel, leading to improved performance. Many newer servers and personal computers are equipped with multicore CPUs, and some are equipped with multiple multicore CPUs.

Bus

A *bus* is an internal component in a computer that provides the means for the computer's other components to communicate with each other. A computer's bus connects the CPU with its main and secondary storage, as well as to external devices.

Most computers also utilize electrical connectors that permit the addition of small circuit boards that may contain additional memory, a communications device or adaptor (for example, a network adaptor or a modem), a storage controller (for example, a SCSI or ATA disk controller), or an additional CPU.

Several industry standards for computer buses have been developed. Notable standards include

- **SBus** This standard was developed by Sun Microsystems. It uses a 32-bit data path and has a transfer rate up to 100 Mbit/sec.

- **MBus** This standard was developed by Sun Microsystems and employs a 64-bit data path and a transfer rate of 80 Mbit/sec.

- **PCI Local Bus** This bus standard was developed by Intel and is popular in Intel-based desktop PCs. It has a transfer rate of 133 Mbit/sec.

- **PC Card** Formerly known as *PCMCIA*, the PC Card bus is prevalent in laptop computers, and is commonly used for the addition of specialized communication devices or disk controllers.

It is not uncommon for a computer to have more than one bus. For instance, many PCs have an additional bus that is known as a front-side bus (FSB), which connects the CPU to a memory controller hub, as well as a high-speed graphics bus, a memory bus, and the low pin count (LPC) bus that is used for low-speed peripherals such as parallel and serial ports, keyboard, and mouse.

Main Storage

A computer's main storage is used for short-term storage of information. Main storage is usually implemented with electronic components such as *random access memory* (RAM), which is relatively expensive but also relatively fast in terms of accessibility and transfer rate.

A computer uses its main storage for several purposes:

- **Operating system**   The computer's running operating system uses main storage to store information about running programs, open files, logged-in users, in-use devices, active processes, and so on.

- **Buffers**   Operating systems and programs will set aside a portion of memory as a "scratch pad" that can be used to temporarily store information retrieved from hard disks or information that is being sent to a printer or other device. Buffers are also used by network adaptors to temporarily store incoming and outgoing information.

- **Storage of program code**   Any program that the computer is currently executing will be stored in main storage so that the CPU can quickly access and read any portion of the program as needed. Note that the program in main storage is only a *working copy* of the program, used by the computer to quickly reference instructions in the program.

- **Storage of program variables**   When a program is being run, it will store intermediate results of calculations and other temporary data. This information is stored in main storage, where the program can quickly reference portions of it as needed.

Main storage is typically volatile. This means that the information stored in main storage should be considered temporary. If electric power were suddenly removed from the computer, the contents of main storage would vanish and would not be easily recovered, if at all.

Different technologies are used in computers for main storage:

- **DRAM (Dynamic RAM)**   The most common form of semiconductor memory, data is stored in capacitors that require periodic refreshing to keep them charged—hence the term *dynamic*.

- **SRAM (Static RAM)**   Another form of semiconductor memory that does not require periodic refresh cycles like DRAM.

A typical semiconductor memory module is shown in Figure 5-3.

Secondary Storage

Secondary storage is the permanent storage used by a computer system. Unlike primary storage (which is usually implemented in volatile RAM modules), secondary storage is persistent and can last many years.

Figure 5-3
Typical RAM module
for a workstation
or server
(Image courtesy
Sassospicco)

This type of storage is usually implemented using hard disk drives or solid-state drives ranging in capacity from megabytes to terabytes.

Secondary storage represents an economic and performance tradeoff from primary storage. It is usually far slower than primary storage, but the unit cost for storage is far less costly. At the time of this writing, the price paid for about 12GB of RAM could also purchase a 1.5TB hard disk drive, which makes RAM (primary) storage more than 1,000 times more expensive than hard disk (secondary) storage. A hard disk drive from a desktop computer is shown in Figure 5-4.

A computer uses secondary storage for several purposes:

- **Program storage**   The programs that the computer executes are contained in secondary storage. When a computer begins to execute a program, it makes a working copy of the program in primary storage.

- **Data storage**   Information read into, created by, or used by computer programs is often stored in secondary storage. Secondary storage is usually used when information is needed for use at a later time.

- **Computer operating system**   The set of programs and device drivers that are used to control and manage the use of the computer is stored in secondary storage.

- **Temporary files**   Many computer programs need to store information for temporary use that may exceed the capacity of main memory. Secondary storage is often used for this purpose. For example, a user wishes to print a data file onto a nearby laser printer; software on the computer will transform the stored data file into a format that is used by the laser printer to make a readable copy of the file; this "print file" is stored in secondary storage temporarily until the printer has completed printing the file for the user, and then the file is deleted.

- **Virtual memory**   This is a technique for creating a main memory space that is physically larger than the actual available main memory. Virtual memory (which should not be confused with virtualization) is discussed in detail later in this chapter in the section, "Computer Operating Systems."

Figure 5-4
Typical computer
hard disk drive
(Image courtesy
Robert Jacek
Tomczak)

While secondary storage is usually implemented with hard disk drives, some systems use semiconductor flash memory in devices called solid-state drives. Flash is a nonvolatile semiconductor memory that can be rewritten and requires no electric power to preserve stored data.

While secondary storage technology is persistent and highly reliable, hard disk drives and even solid-state drives are known to fail from time to time. For this reason, important data in secondary storage is often copied to other storage devices, either on the same computer or on a different computer, or it is copied onto computer backup tapes that are designed to store large amounts of data for long periods at low cost. This practice of data backup is discussed at length in the section "Information Systems Operations" earlier in this chapter.

Firmware

Firmware is special-purpose storage that is used to store the instructions needed to start a computer system. Typically, firmware consists of low-level computer instructions that are used to control the various hardware components in a computer system and to load and execute components of the operating system from secondary storage. This process of system initialization is known as an initial program load (IPL) or bootstrap (or just "boot").

Read-only memory (ROM) technology is often used to store a computer's firmware. Several available ROM technologies are in use, including

- **ROM (read-only memory)**   The earliest forms of ROM are considered permanent and can never be modified. The permanency of ROM makes it secure, but it can be difficult to carry out field upgrades. For this reason ROM is not often used.

- **PROM (programmable read-only memory)**   This is also a permanent and unchangeable form of storage. A PROM chip can be programmed only once, and must be replaced if the firmware needs to be updated.

- **EPROM (erasable programmable read-only memory)**   This type of memory can be written to with a special programming device and then erased and rewritten at a later time. EPROM chips are erased by shining ultraviolet (UV) light through a quartz window on the chip; the quartz window is usually covered with a foil label, although sometimes an EPROM chip does not have a window at all, which effectively makes it a PROM device.

- **EEPROM (electrically erasable programmable read-only memory)**   This is similar to EPROM, except that no UV light source is required to erase and reprogram the EEPROM chip; instead, signals from the computer in which the EEPROM chip is stored can be used to reprogram or update the EEPROM. Thus, EEPROM was one of the first types of firmware that could be updated by the computer on which it was installed.

- **Flash**   This memory is erasable, reprogrammable, and functionally similar to EEPROM, in that the contents of flash memory can be altered by the computer that it is installed in. Flash memory is the technology used in popular portable storage devices such as USB memory devices, Secure Digital (SD) cards, Compact Flash, and Memory Stick.

A well-known use for firmware is the ROM-based BIOS (basic input/output system) on IBM and Intel-based personal computers.

I/O and Networking

Regardless of their specific purpose, computers nearly always must have some means for accepting input data from some external source, as well as for sending output data to some external destination. Whether this input and output are continuous or infrequent, computers usually have one or more methods for transferring data. These methods include

- **Input/output (I/O) devices**   Most computers have external connectors to permit the attachment of devices such as keyboards, mice, monitors, scanners, printers, and cameras. The electrical signal and connector-type standards include PS/2 (for keyboards and mice), USB, parallel, serial, and FireWire. Some types of computers lack these external connectors; instead, special adaptor cards can be plugged into a computer's bus connector. Early computers required reprogramming and/or reconfiguration when external devices were connected, but newer computers are designed to automatically recognize when an external device is connected or disconnected, and will adjust automatically.

- **Networking**   A computer can be connected to a local or wide area data network. Then, one of a multitude of means for inbound and outbound data transfer can be configured that will use the networking capability. Some computers will have built-in connectors or adaptors, but others will require the addition of internal or external adaptors that plug into bus connectors such as SBus, MBus, PC Card, or PCI.

Multicomputer Architectures

Organizations that use several computers have a lot of available choices. Not so long ago, organizations that required several servers would purchase individual server computers. Now there are choices that can help to improve performance and reduce capital, including

- **Blade computers**   This architecture consists of a main chassis component that is equipped with a central power supply, cooling, network, and console connectors, with several slots that are fitted with individual CPU modules. The advantage of blade architecture is the lower-than-usual unit cost for each server module, since it consists of only a circuit board. The costs of power supply, cooling, and so on, are amortized among all of the blades. A typical blade system is shown in Figure 5-5.

Figure 5-5
Blade computer
architecture (Image
courtesy Robert
Kloosterhuis)

- **Grid computing** The term *grid computing* is used to describe a large number of loosely coupled computers that are used to solve a common task. Computers in a grid may be in close proximity to each other or scattered over a wide geographic area. Grid computing is a viable alternative to supercomputers for solving computationally intensive problems.

- **Server clusters** A *cluster* is a tightly coupled collection of computers that are used to solve a common task. In a cluster, one or more servers actively perform tasks, while zero or more computers may be in a "standby" state, ready to assume active duty should the need arise. Clusters usually give the appearance of a single computer to the perspective of outside systems. Clusters usually operate in one of two modes: *active-active* and *active-passive.* In active-active mode, all servers perform tasks; in active-passive mode, some servers are in a standby state, waiting to become active in an event called a failover, which usually occurs when one of the active servers has become incapacitated.

These options give organizations the freedom to develop a computer architecture that will meet their needs in terms of performance, availability, flexibility, and cost.

Virtualization Architectures
Virtualization refers to the set of technologies that permits two or more running operating systems to reside on a single physical computer. Virtualization technology permits organizations to use its computing resources more efficiently.

Before I explain the benefits of virtualization, I should first state one of the principles of computer infrastructure management. It is a sound practice to use a server for one single purpose. Using a single server for multiple purposes can introduce a number of problems, including

- Tools or applications that reside on a single computer may interfere with one another.
- Tools or applications that reside on a single computer may interact with each other or compete for common resources.
- A tool or application on a server could, although rarely, cause the entire server to stop running; on a server with multiple tools or applications, this could cause the other tools and applications to stop functioning.

Prior to virtualization, the most stable configuration for running many applications and tools was to run each on a separate server. This would, however, result in a highly inefficient use of computers and of capital.

Virtualization permits IT departments to run many applications or tools on a single server, each within its own respective operating system, thereby making more efficient use of computers (not to mention electric power and data center space). Virtualization software emulates computer hardware so that an operating system running in a virtualized environment does not know that it is actually a virtual machine. Virtualization software, known as a *hypervisor*, includes resource allocation configuration settings so that each *guest* (a running operating system, also known as a *virtual machine*) will have so much memory, hard disk space, and other peripherals available for its use. Virtualization also facilitates the sharing of peripheral devices such as network connectors so that many guests can use an individual network connector, although each will have its own unique IP address.

Virtualization software provides security by isolating each running operating system and preventing it from interfering with others. This is similar to the concept of *process isolation* within a running operating system, where a process is not permitted to access resources used by other processes.

A server with running virtual machines is depicted in Figure 5-6.

Figure 5-6 Virtualization

Many security issues need to be considered in a virtualization environment, including

- **Access control**   Access to virtualization management and monitoring functions should be restricted to those personnel who require it.

- **Resource allocation**   A virtualization environment needs to be carefully configured so that each virtual machine is given the resources that it requires to function correctly and perform adequately.

- **Logging and monitoring**   Virtual environments need to be carefully monitored so that any sign of security compromise will be quickly recognized and acted on.

- **Hardening**   Virtual environments need to be configured so that only necessary services and features are enabled, and all unnecessary services and features are either disabled or removed.

- **Vulnerability management**   Virtualization environments need to be monitored as closely as operating systems and other software so that the IT organization is aware of newly discovered security vulnerabilities and available patches.

Hardware Maintenance

In comparison to computer hardware systems that were manufactured through the 1980s, today's computer hardware requires little or no preventive or periodic maintenance.

Computer hardware maintenance is limited to periodic checks to ensure that the computer is free of dirt and moisture. From time to time, a systems engineer will need to open a computer system cabinet and inspect it for accumulation of dust and dirt, and she may need to remove this debris with a vacuum cleaner or filtered compressed air. Depending on the cleanliness of the surrounding environment, inspection and cleaning may be needed as often as every few months or as seldom as every few years.

Maintenance may also be carried out by third-party service organizations that specialize in computer maintenance.

Hardware maintenance is an activity that should be monitored. Qualified service organizations should be hired to perform maintenance at appropriate intervals. If periodic maintenance is required, management should establish a service availability plan that includes planned downtime when such operations take place.

Automated hardware monitoring tools can provide information that will help determine whether maintenance is needed. Automated monitoring is discussed in the next section.

Hardware Monitoring

Automated hardware monitoring tools can be used to keep a continuous watch on the health and utilization of server and network hardware. In an environment with many servers, this capability can be centralized so that the health of many servers and network devices can be monitored using a single monitoring program.

Hardware monitoring capabilities may vary among different makes of computer systems, but can include any or all of the following:

- **CPU**   Monitoring will indicate whether the system's CPU is operating properly and whether its temperature is within normal range.

- **Power supply**   Monitoring will show whether the power supply is operating properly, including input voltage, output voltage and current, cooling fans, and temperature.

- **Internal components**   Monitoring will specify whether other internal components such as storage devices, memory, chipsets, controllers, adaptors, and cooling fans are operating properly and within normal temperature ranges.

- **Resource utilization**   Monitoring will measure the amount of resources in use, including CPU, memory, disk storage, and network utilization.

- **Asset management**   Many monitoring systems can track the assets that are present in the environment, giving management an electronic asset inventory capability.

- **External environment**   Monitoring is usually considered incomplete unless the surrounding environment is also monitored. This usually includes temperature, humidity, the presence of water, and vibration in locales where earthquakes are common. Monitoring can also include video surveillance and access door alarms.

Centralized monitoring environments typically utilize the local area network for transmitting information from systems to a central console. Many monitoring consoles have the ability to send alert messages to the personnel who manage the systems being monitored. Often, reports can show monitoring statistics over time so that personnel can identify trends that could be indications of impending failure.

Information Systems Architecture and Software

This section discusses computer operating systems, data communications, file systems, database management systems, media management systems, and utility software.

Computer Operating Systems

Computer operating systems (which are generally known as operating systems, or OSs) are large, general-purpose programs that are used to control computer hardware and facilitate the use of software applications. Operating systems perform the following functions:

- **Access to peripheral devices**   The operating system controls and manages access to all devices and adaptors that are connected to the computer. This includes storage devices, display devices, and communications adaptors.

- **Storage management**   The operating system provides for the orderly storage of information on storage hardware. For example, operating systems provide file system management for the storage of files and directories on hard drives.

- **Process management** Operating systems facilitate the existence of multiple processes, some of which will be computer applications and tools. Operating systems ensure that each process has private memory space and is protected from interference by other processes.

- **Resource allocation** Operating systems facilitate the sharing of resources on a computer such as memory, communications, and display devices.

- **Communication** Operating systems facilitate communications with users and also with other computers through networking. Operating systems typically have drivers and tools to facilitate network communications.

- **Security** Operating systems restrict access to protected resources through user and device authentication.

Examples of popular operating systems include AIX, Solaris, Linux, Mac OSX, and Microsoft Windows.

The traditional context of the relationship between operating systems and computer hardware is this: One copy of a computer operating system runs on a computer at any given time. Virtualization, however, is changing all of that. Virtualization is discussed earlier in this chapter.

Server Clustering

Using special software, a group of two or more computers can be configured to operate as a *cluster*. This means that the group of computers will appear as a single computer for the purpose of providing services. Within the cluster, one computer will be active and the other computer(s) will be in passive mode; if the active computer should experience a hardware or software failure and crash, the passive computer(s) will transition to active mode and continue to provide service. This is known as *active-passive* mode. The transition is called a *failover*.

Clusters can also operate in *active-active* mode, where all computers in the cluster provide service; in the event of the failure of one computer in the cluster, the remaining computer(s) will continue providing service.

Grid Computing

Grid computing is a technique used to distribute a problem or task to several computers at the same time, taking advantage of the processing power of each, in order to solve the problem or complete the task in less time. Grid computing is a form of distributed computing, but in grid computing, the computers are coupled more loosely and the number of computers participating in the solution of a problem can be dynamically expanded or contracted at will.

Cloud Computing

Cloud computing refers to dynamically scalable and usually virtualized computing resources that are provided as a service. Cloud computing services may be rented or leased so that an organization can have a scalable application without the need for supporting hardware. Or, cloud computing may include networking, computing, and even application services in a Software as a Service (SaaS) model. Cloud computing is discussed in more detail in Chapter 4.

Data Communications Software

The prevalence of network-centric computing has resulted in networking capabilities being included with virtually every computer and being built in to virtually every computer operating system. Almost without exception, computer operating systems include the ability for the computer to connect with networks based on the TCP/IP suite of protocols, enabling the computer to communicate on a home network, enterprise business network, or the global Internet.

Data communications is discussed in greater detail later in this chapter in the section, "Network Infrastructure."

File Systems

A *file system* is a logical structure that facilitates the storage of data on a digital storage medium such as a hard drive, CD/DVD-ROM, or flash memory device. The structure of the file system facilitates the creation, modification, expansion and contraction, and deletion of data files. A file system may also be used to enforce access controls to regulate which users or processes are permitted to access or alter files in a file system.

It can also be said that a file system is a special-purpose database designed for the storage and management of files.

Modern file systems employ a storage hierarchy that consists of two main elements:

- **Directories**   A *directory* is a structure that is used to store files. A file system may contain one or more directories, each of which may contain files and subdirectories. The topmost directory in a file system is usually called the "root" directory. A file system may exist as a hierarchy of information, in the same way that a building can contain several file rooms, each of which contains several file cabinets, which contain drawers that contain dividers, folders, and documents. Directories are sometimes called *folders* in some computing environments.

- **Files**   A *file* is a sequence of zero or more characters that are stored as a whole. A file may be a document, spreadsheet, image, sound file, computer program, or data that is used by a program. A file can be small as zero characters in length (an empty file) or as large as many gigabytes (trillions of characters). A file occupies units of storage on storage media (which could be a hard disk or flash memory device, for example) that may be called blocks or sectors; however, the file system hides these underlying details from the user so that the file may be known simply by its name and the directory in which it resides.

Well-known file systems in use today include

- **FAT (File Allocation Table)**   This file system has been used in MS-DOS and early versions of Microsoft Windows. Versions of FAT include FAT12, FAT16, and FAT32. FAT is often used as the file system on portable media devices such as flash drives. FAT does not support security access controls, including specifying access permissions to files and directories.

- **NTFS (NT File System)** This is used in newer versions of Windows, including desktop and server editions. NTFS supports file- and directory-based access control and file system journaling.

- **HFS (Hierarchical File System)** This is the file system used on computers running the Mac OSX operating system.

- **ISO 9660** This is a file system used by CD-ROM and DVD-ROM media.

- **UDF (Universal Disk Format)** This is an optical media file system that is considered a replacement for ISO 9660. UDF is widely used on rewritable optical media.

Database Management Systems

A database management system, or DBMS, is a software program that facilitates the storage and retrieval of potentially large amounts of information. A DBMS contains methods for inserting, updating, and removing data; these functions can be used by computer programs and software applications. A DBMS also usually contains authentication and access control, thereby permitting the control over which users may access what data.

Database Management System Organization

Most database management systems employ a data definition language (DDL) that is used to define the structure of the data contained in a database. The DDL will define the types of data stored in the database, as well as relationships between different portions of that data.

Database management systems employ some sort of a data dictionary (DD) or directory system (DS) that is used to store information about the internal structure of databases stored in the DBMS.

To better understand how they relate to each other, the DDL can be thought of as the instructions for building a database's structure and data relationships; the DD or DS is where the database's structure and relationships are stored and used by the DBMS.

Database management systems also employ a data manipulation language (DML) that is used to insert, delete, and update data in a database. SQL is a popular data manipulation language that is used in the Oracle and SQL Server database management systems.

Database Management System Structure

There are three principal types of DBMSs in use today: relational, object, and hierarchical. Each is described in this section.

Relational Database Management Systems
Relational database management systems (rDBMSs) represent the most popular model used for database management systems. A relational database permits the design of a structured, logical representation of information.

Many relational databases are accessed and updated through the *SQL* (Structured Query Language) computer language. Standardized in ISO and ANSI standards, SQL is used in many popular relational database management system products.

RDBMS Basic Concepts   A relational database consists of one or more *tables*. A table can be thought of as a simple list of records, like lines in a data file. The records in a table are often called *rows*. The different data items that appear in each row are usually called *fields*.

A table often has a *primary key*. This is simply one of the table's fields, whose values are unique. For example, a table of healthcare patient names can include each patient's Social Security number, which can be made the primary key for the table.

One or more *indexes* can be built for a table. An index facilitates rapid searching for specific records in a table based upon the value of one of the fields other than the primary key. For instance, a table that contains a list of assets that includes their serial numbers can have an index of the table's serial numbers. This will permit a rapid search for a record containing a specific serial number; without the index, rDBMS software would have to sequentially examine every record in the table until the desired record was found.

One of the most powerful features of a relational database is the use of *foreign keys*. Here, a foreign key is a field in a record in one table that can reference a primary key in another table. For example, a table that lists sales orders includes fields that are foreign keys, each of which references records in other tables. This is shown in Figure 5-7.

Figure 5-7   Fields in a sales order table point to records in other tables.

Relational databases enforce *referential integrity*. This means that the database will not permit a program (or user) to delete rows from a table if there are records in other tables whose foreign keys reference the row to be deleted. The database instead will return an error code that will signal that there are rows in other tables that would be "stranded" if the row was deleted. Using the example in Figure 5-7, a relational database will not permit a program to delete salesperson #2 or #4 since there are records in the sales order table that reference those rows.

The power of relational databases comes from their design and from the SQL language. Queries are used to find one or more records from a table using the SELECT statement. An example statement is

```
SELECT * FROM Orders WHERE Price > 100 ORDER BY Customer
```

One powerful feature in relational databases is a special query called a *join*, where records from two or more tables are searched in a single query. An example join query is

```
SELECT Salesperson.Name, count(*) AS Orders FROM Salesperson JOIN Salesperson_
Number ON Salesperson.Number = Orders.Salesperson GROUP BY Salesperson.Name
```

This query will produce a list of salespersons and the number of orders they have sold.

Relational Database Security   Relational databases in commercial applications need to have some security features. Three primary security features are

- **Access controls**   Most relational databases have access controls at the table and field levels. This means that a database can permit or deny a user the ability to read data from a specific table or even a specific field. In order to enforce access controls, the database needs to authenticate users so that it knows the identity of each user making access requests. Database management systems employ a DCL to control access to data in a database.

- **Encryption**   Sensitive data such as financial or medical records may need to be encrypted. Some relational databases provide field-level database encryption that permits a user or application to specify certain fields that should be encrypted.

- **Audit logging**   Database management systems provide audit logging features that permit an administrator or auditor to view some or all activities that take place in a database. Audit logging can show precisely the activities that take place, including details of database changes and the person who made those changes. The audit logs themselves can be protected so that they resist tampering, which can make it difficult for someone to make changes to data and erase their tracks.

Database administrators can also create *views*, which are stored queries accessible as virtual tables. Views can simplify viewing data by aggregating or filtering data. They can improve security by exposing only certain records or fields to users.

Object Database Management Systems An *object database* (or object database management system, ODBMS) is a database where information is represented as objects that are used in object-oriented programming languages. Object-oriented databases are used for data that does not require static or predefined attributes, such as a fixed-length field or defined data structure. The data can even be of varying types. The data that is contained in an object-oriented database is unpredictable in nature.

Unlike the clean separation between programs and data in the relational database model, object databases make database objects appear as programming language objects. Both the data and the programming method are contained in an object. Object databases are really just the mechanisms used to store data that is inherently part of the basic object-oriented programming model. Thus, when a data object is accessed, the data object itself will contain functions (methods), negating the requirement for a query language like SQL.

Object databases are not widely used commercially. They are limited to a few applications requiring high-performance processing on complex data.

Relational databases are starting to look a little more like object databases through the addition of object-oriented interfaces and functions; object-oriented databases are starting to look a little more like relational databases through query languages such as Object Query Language (OQL).

Hierarchical Database Management Systems A *hierarchical database* is so named because its data model is a top-down hierarchy, with parent records and one or more child records in its design. The dominant hierarchical database management system product in use today is IBM's IMS (Information Management System) that runs on mainframes in nearly all of the larger organizations in the world.

A *network database* is similar to a hierarchical database, extended somewhat to permit lateral data relationships (like the addition of "cousins" to the parent and child records). Figure 5-8 illustrates hierarchical and network databases.

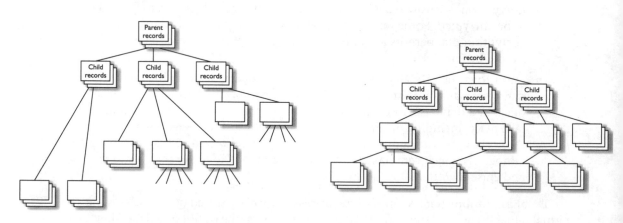

Hierarchical Database Structure

Network Database Structure

Figure 5-8   Hierarchical and network databases

Media Management Systems

Information systems may employ automated tape management systems (TMSs) or disk management systems (DMSs) that track the tape and disk volumes that are needed for application processing.

Disk and tape management systems instruct system operators to mount specific media volumes when they are needed. These systems reduce operator error by requesting specific volumes and rejecting incorrect volumes that do not contain the required data.

TMSs and DMSs are most often found as a component of a computer backup system. Most commercial backup systems track which tape or disk volumes contain which backed-up files and databases. Coupled with automatic volume recognition (usually through barcode readers), backup systems maintain an extensive catalog of the entire collection of backup media and their contents. When data needs to be restored, the backup software (or the TMS or DMS) will specify which media volume should be mounted, verify that the correct media is available, and then restore the desired data as directed.

Utility Software

Utility software is a term that represents the broad class of programs that support the development or use of networks, systems, and applications. Utility software is most often used by IT specialists whose responsibilities include some aspect of system development, support, or operations. End users, on the other hand, most often use software applications instead of utilities.

Utility software can be classified into the following categories:

- **Software and data design** This includes program and data modeling tools that are used to design new applications or to model existing applications.

- **Software development** These programs are used to facilitate the actual coding of an application (or another utility). Development tools can provide a wide variety of functions, including program language syntax checking, compilation, debugging, and testing.

- **Software testing** Apart from unit testing that may be present in a development environment, dedicated software testing tools perform extensive testing of software functions. Automated testing tools can contain entire suites of test cases that are run against an application program, with the results stored for future reference.

- **Security testing** This refers to several different types of software tools that are used to determine the security of software applications, operating systems, database management systems, and networks. One type of security testing tool examines an application's source code, looking for potential security vulnerabilities. Another type of security testing tool will run the application program and input different forms of data to see if the application contains vulnerabilities in the way that it handles this data. Other security testing tools examine operating system and database management system settings. Still others will send specially crafted network messages to a target system to see what types of vulnerabilities might exist that could be exploited by an intruder or hacker.

- **Data management** These utilities are used to manipulate, list, transform, query, compare, encrypt, decrypt, import, or export data. They may also test the integrity of data (for instance, examining an index in a relational database or the integrity of a file system) and possibly make repairs.

- **System health** These utilities are used to assess the health of an operating system by examining configuration settings; verifying the versions of the kernel, drivers, and utilities; and making performance measurements and tuning changes.

- **Network** These utilities are used to examine the network in order to discover other systems on it, determine network configuration, and listen to network traffic.

Utilities and Security

Because some utilities are used to observe or make changes to access controls or security, organizations should limit the use of utilities to those personnel whose responsibilities include their use. All other personnel should not be permitted to use them.

Because many utilities are readily available, simply posting a policy will not prevent their use. Instead, strict access controls should be established so that unauthorized users who do obtain utilities would derive little use from them.

Software Licensing

The majority of organizations purchase many software components in support of their software applications. For example, organizations often purchase operating systems, software development tools, database management systems, web servers, network management tools, office automation systems, and security tools. Organizations need to be aware of the licensing terms and conditions for each of the software products that they lease or purchase.

To be effective, an organization should centralize its records and expertise in software licensing to avoid licensing issues that could lead to unwanted and potentially embarrassing legal actions. Some of the ways that an organization can organize and control its software usage include

- **Develop policy** The organization should develop policies that define acceptable uses of software.

- **Centralize procurement** This can help to funnel purchasing through a group or department that can help to manage and control software use.

- **Implement software metering** Automated tools that are installed on each computer (including user workstations) can alert IT of every software program that is run in the organization. This can help to raise awareness of any new software programs that are being used, as well as the numbers of copies of programs installed and in use.

- **Implement concurrent licensing** The organization can use dynamic license management that controls the number of persons who are able to use a program simultaneously. This can help reduce costs for expensive programs used infrequently by many employees.

- **Review software contracts**   The person or group with responsibility for managing software licensing should be aware of the terms and conditions of use.

Digital Rights Management

The Internet has provided a means for easily distributing content to large numbers of people. This ability, however, runs afoul of legal copyright protection afforded to the owners of copyrighted work. This encompasses software programs as well as documents and media.

Organizations also are faced with the problem of limiting the distribution of documents for privacy or intellectual property protection. For example, an organization may publish a technical whitepaper describing its services, and desires that only its current customers be able to view the whitepaper.

Digital rights management (DRM) is a set of emerging technologies that permits the owner of digital information (such as documents) to control their access, even after those documents are no longer contained in their environment. In some instances, these technologies are implemented in system hardware (such as electronic book readers), and in other cases they are implemented in software.

Whether implemented in hardware or software, the program or device displaying information will first examine the file being displayed to determine whether the information should be displayed or not. Some of the characteristics that the owner of a file may be able to set include

- **Expiration**   The owner of a file may be able to set an expiration date, after which time the file cannot be viewed or used.

- **Registration**   The owner of a file may be able to require anyone viewing the file to register themselves in a reliable way (such as through e-mail address verification).

- **Authentication**   The owner of a file may be able to require that persons viewing a file first authenticate themselves.

Network Infrastructure

Networks are used to transport data from one computer to another, either within an organization or between them. Network infrastructure is the collection of devices and cabling that facilitates network communications among an organization's systems, as well as between the organization's systems and those belonging to other organizations. This section describes network infrastructure in the following 10 sections:

- Network architecture
- Network-based services
- Network models

- Network technologies
- Local area networks
- Wide area networks
- The TCP/IP suite of protocols
- The global Internet
- Network management
- Networked applications

Network Architecture

The term *network architecture* has several meanings, all of which comprise the overall design of an organization's network communications. An organization's network architecture, like other aspects of its information technology, should support the organization's mission, goals, and objectives.

The facets of network architecture include

- **Physical network architecture**   This part of network architecture is concerned with the physical locations of network equipment and media. This includes, for instance, the design of a network cable plant (also known by the term *structured cabling*), as well as the locations and types of network devices. An organization's physical network architecture may be expressed in several layers. A high-level architecture may depict global physical locations or regions and their interconnectivity, while an in-building architecture will be highly specific regarding the types of cabling and locations of equipment.

- **Logical network architecture**   This part of network architecture is concerned with the depiction of network communications at a local, campus, regional, and global level. Here, the network architecture will include several related layers, including representations of network protocols, addressing, routing, security zones, and the utilization of carrier services.

- **Data flow architecture**   This part of network architecture is closely related to application and data architecture. Here, the flow of data is shown as connections among applications, users, partners, and suppliers. Data flow can be depicted in nongeographic terms, although representations of data flow at local, campus, regional, and global levels are also needed, since geographic distance is often inversely proportional to capacity and throughput.

- **Network standards and services**   This part of network architecture is more involved with the services that are used on the network and less with the geographic and spatial characteristics of the network. Services and standards need to be established in several layers, including cable types, addressing standards, routing protocols, network management protocols, utility protocols (such as domain name service [DNS], network time protocol [NTP], file sharing, printing, e-mail, remote access, and many more), and application data interchange protocols, such as SOA (Service-Oriented Architecture), SOAP (Simple Object Access Protocol), and XML (Extensible Markup Language).

Types of Networks

Computer networks can be classified in a number of different ways. The primary method of classification is based on the size of a network. By *size*, we refer not necessarily to the number of nodes or stations on the network, but to its physical or geographic size. These types are (from smallest to largest)

- **Personal area network (PAN)**   Arguably the newest type of network, a personal area network is generally used by a single individual. Its reach ranges from a few centimeters up to three meters, and is used to connect peripherals and communication devices for use by an individual.

- **Local area network (LAN)**   The original type of network, a local area network connects computers and devices together in a small building or a residence. The typical maximum size of a LAN is 100 meters, which is the maximum cable length for popular network technologies such as Ethernet.

- **Campus area network (CAN)**   A campus area network is a term that connotes the interconnection of LANs for an organization that has buildings in close proximity.

- **Metropolitan area network (MAN)**   A network that spans a city or regional area is sometimes known as a metropolitan area network. Usually, this type of network consists of two or more in-building LANs in multiple locations that are connected by telecommunications circuits (e.g., MPLS, T-1, Frame Relay, or dark fiber) or private network connections over the global Internet.

- **Wide area network (WAN)**   A wide area network is a network whose size ranges from regional to international. An organization with multiple locations across vast distances will connect its locations together with dedicated telecommunications connections or protected connections over the Internet. It is noted that an organization will also call a single point-to-point connection between two distant locations a "WAN connection."

The classifications discussed here are not rigid, nor do they impose restrictions on the use of any specific technology from one to the next. Instead, they are simply a set of terms that allow professionals to speak easily about the geographic extent of their networks with easily understood terms.

The relative scale of these network terms is depicted in Figure 5-9.

Network-Based Services

Network-based services are the protocols and utilities that facilitate system- and network-based resource utilization. In a literal sense, many of these services operate on servers; they are called network-based services because they facilitate or utilize various kinds of network communication.

Figure 5-9
A comparison of
network sizes

Some of these services are

- **E-mail**   E-mail servers collect, store, and transmit e-mail messages from person to person. They accept incoming e-mail messages from other users on the Internet, and likewise send e-mail messages over the Internet to e-mail servers that accept and store e-mail messages for distant recipients.

- **Print**   Print servers act as aggregation points for network-based printers in an organization. When users print a document, their workstation sends it to a specific printer queue on a print server. If other users are also sending documents to the same printer, the print server will store them temporarily until the printer is able to print them.

- **File storage**   File servers provide centralized storage of files for use among groups of users. Often, centralized file storage is configured so that files stored on remote servers almost appear to be stored locally on user workstations.

- **Directory**   These services provide centralized management of resource information. Examples include DNS, which provides translation between resource name and IP address, and Lightweight Directory Access Protocol (LDAP), which provides directory information for users and resources, and is often used as a central database of user IDs and passwords. An example of an LDAP-based directory service is Active Directory, which is the Microsoft implementation of and extensions to LDAP.

- **Remote access**   Network- and server-based services within an organization's network are protected from Internet access by firewalls and other means. This makes them available only to users whose workstations are physically connected to the enterprise network. Remote access permits an authorized employee to remotely access network-based services from anywhere on the Internet via an encrypted "tunnel" that logically connects them to the enterprise network as though they were physically there.

- **Terminal emulation** In many organizations with mainframe computers, PCs have replaced "green screen" and other types of mainframe-centric terminals. Terminal emulation software on PCs allows them to function like those older mainframe terminals.

- **Time synchronization** It is a well-known fact among systems engineers that the time clocks built in to most computers are not very accurate (some are, in fact, notoriously *inaccurate*). Distributed applications and network services have made accurate "timestamping" increasingly important. Time synchronization protocols allow an organization's time server system to make sure that all other servers and workstation time clocks are synchronized. And the time server itself will synchronize with one of several reliable Internet-based time servers, GPS-equipped time servers, or time servers that are attached to international standard atomic clocks.

- **Network connectivity and authentication** Many organizations have adopted one of several available methods that authenticate users and workstations before logically connecting them to the enterprise network. This helps to prevent nonorganization-owned or noncompliant workstations from being able to connect to an internal network, which is a potential security threat. Users or workstations that are unable to authenticate are connected to a "quarantine" network where users can obtain information about the steps they need to take to get connected to enterprise resources. Network-based authentication can even quickly examine an organization workstation, checking it for proper security settings (antivirus, firewall, security patches, and so on), and allow it to connect logically only if the workstation is configured properly. Various protocols that are used to connect, verify, and authenticate devices to a network include dynamic host configuration protocol (DHCP), 802.1X, and network access control (NAC).

- **Web security** Most organizations have a vested interest in having some level of control over the choice of Internet websites that their employees choose to visit. Websites that serve no business purpose (for example, online gambling, porn, and online games) can be blocked so that employees cannot access them. Further, many Internet websites (even legitimate ones) host malware that can be automatically downloaded to user workstations. Web security appliances can examine incoming content for malware, in much the same way that a workstation checks incoming files for viruses.

- **Anti-malware** Malware (viruses, worms, Trojan horses, and so on) remains a significant threat to organizations. Antivirus software (and now, increasingly, anti-spyware and anti-rootkit software) on each workstation is still an important line of defense. Because of the complexity of anti-malware, many organizations have opted to implement centralized management and control. Using a central anti-malware console, security engineers can quickly spot workstations whose anti-malware is not functioning, and they can force new anti-malware updates to all user workstations. They can even force user workstations to commence an immediate whole-disk scan for malware if an outbreak has started. Centralized anti-malware consoles can also receive virus infection alerts from workstations and keep centralized statistics on virus updates and outbreaks, giving security engineers a vital "big picture" status.

- **Network management** Larger organizations with too many servers and network devices to administer manually often turn to network management systems. These systems serve as a collection point for all alerts and error messages from vital servers and network devices. They can also be used to centrally configure network devices, making wide-scale configuration changes possible by a small team of engineers. Network management systems also measure network performance, throughput, latency, and outages, giving network engineers vital information on the health of the enterprise network.

Network Models

Network models are the archetype of the actual designs of network protocols. While a model is often a simplistic depiction of a more complicated reality, the OSI and TCP/IP network models accurately illustrate what is actually happening in the network. It is fairly difficult to actually *see* the components of the network in action; the models help us to understand how they work.

The purpose of developing these models was to build consensus among the various manufacturers of network components (from programs to software drivers to network devices and cabling) in order to improve interoperability between different types of computers. In essence, it was a move toward networks with "interchangeable parts" that would facilitate data communications on a broad scale.

The two dominant network models that are used to illustrate networks are OSI and TCP/IP. Both are described in this section.

The OSI Network Model

The first widely accepted network model is the *Open Standards Interconnection* model, known as the OSI model. The OSI model was developed by the International Organization for Standardization (ISO) and the International Telecommunications Union (ITU). The working groups that developed the OSI model ignored the existence of the TCP/IP model, which was gaining in popularity around the world and has become the de facto world standard.

The OSI model consists of seven layers. Messages that are sent on an OSI network are encapsulated; a message that is constructed at layer 7 is placed inside of layer 6, which is then placed inside of layer 5, and so on. This is not figurative—this encapsulation literally takes place and can be viewed using tools that show the detailed contents of packets on a network. Encapsulation is illustrated in Figure 5-10.

The layers of the OSI model are, from bottom to top

- Physical
- Data link

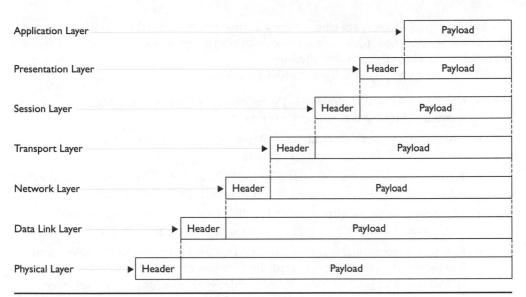

Figure 5-10 Encapsulation of packets in the OSI network model

- Network
- Transport
- Session
- Presentation
- Application

Because it is difficult for many people to memorize a list such as this, there are some memory aids to help remember the sequence of these layers. Some of these aids are

- Please Do Not Throw Sausage Pizza Away
- Please Do Not Touch Steve's Pet Alligator
- All People Seem To Need Data Processing
- All People Standing Totally Naked Don't Perspire

The layers of the OSI model are explained in more detail in the remainder of this section.

OSI Layer 1: Physical The *physical layer* in the OSI model is concerned with electrical and physical specifications for devices. This includes communications cabling, voltage levels, and connectors, as well as some of the basic specifications for devices that would connect to networks. At the physical layer, networks are little more than electric signals flowing in wires or radio frequency airwaves.

At the physical layer, data exists merely as bits; there are no frames or packets here. The physical layer also addresses the modulation of digital information into voltage and current levels in the physical medium.

Examples of OSI physical layer standards include

- **Cabling**   10BASE-T, 100BASE-TX, twinax, and fiber optics, which are standards for physical network cabling.

- **Communications**   RS-232, RS-449, and V.35, which are standards for sending serial data between computers.

- **Telecommunications**   T1, E1, SONET, DSL, and POTS, which are standards for common carrier communications networks for voice and data.

- **Wireless communications**   802.11a PHY (meaning the physical layer component of 802.11) and other wireless local area network airlink standards.

- **Wireless telecommunications**   W-CDMA, CDMA, CDMA2000, TDMA, and UMTS, which are airlink standards for wireless communications between cell phones and base stations (these standards also include some OSI layer 2 features).

OSI Layer 2: Data Link   The *data link layer* in the OSI model focuses on the method of transferring data from one station on a network to another. In the data link layer, information is arranged into frames and transported across the medium. Error correction is usually implemented as collision detection, as well as the confirmation that a frame has arrived intact at its destination, usually through the use of a checksum.

The data link layer is concerned only with communications on a local area network. At the data link layer, there are no routers (or routing protocols). Instead, the data link layer should be thought of as a collection of locally connected computers to a single physical medium. Data link layer standards and protocols are only concerned with getting a frame from one computer to another on that local network.

Examples of data link layer standards include

- **LAN protocols**   Ethernet, Token Ring, ATM, FDDI, and Fibre Channel are protocols that are used to assemble a stream of data into frames for transport over a physical medium (the physical layer) from one station to another on a local area network. These protocols include error correction, primarily through collision detection; collision avoidance; synchronous timing; or tokens.

- **802.11 MAC/LLC**   This is the data link portion of the well-known Wi-Fi (wireless LAN) protocols.

- **Common carrier packet networks**   MPLS (Multiprotocol Label Switching), Frame Relay, and X.25 are packet-oriented standards for network services provided by telecommunications carriers. Organizations that required point-to-point communications with various locations would often obtain a Frame Relay or X.25 connection from a local telecommunications provider. X.25 has been all but replaced by Frame Relay, and now Frame Relay is being replaced by MPLS.

- **ARP (Address Resolution Protocol)**   This protocol is used when one station needs to communicate with another and the initiating station does not know the receiving station's network link layer (hardware) address. ARP is prevalent in TCP/IP networks, but is used in other network types as well.

- **PPP and SLIP**   These are protocols that are used to transport TCP/IP packets over point-to-point serial connections (usually RS-232). SLIP is now obsolete, and PPP is generally seen only in remote access connections that utilize dial-up services.

- **Tunneling**   PPTP (Point to Point Tunneling Protocol), L2TP (Layer 2 Tunneling Protocol), and other tunneling protocols were developed as a way to extend TCP/IP (among others) from a centralized network to a branch network or a remote workstation, usually over a dial-up connection.

In the data link layer, stations on the network must have an address. Ethernet and Token Ring, for instance, use MAC (Media Access Control) addressing. Most other multistation protocols also utilize some form of addressing for each device on the network.

OSI Layer 3: Network   The purpose of the OSI *network layer* is the delivery of messages from one station to another via one or more networks. The network layer can process messages of any length, and will "fragment" messages so that they are able to fit into packets that the network is able to transport.

The network layer is the layer that is concerned with the interconnection of networks and of packet *routing* between networks. Network devices called *routers* are used to connect networks together. Routers are physically connected to two or more networks, and are configured with (or have some ability to learn) the network settings for each network. Using this information, routers are able to make routing decisions that will enable them to forward packets to the correct network, moving them closer to their ultimate destination.

Examples of protocols at the network layer include

- **IP (Internet Protocol)**   This is the network layer protocol used in the TCP/IP suite of protocols. IP is concerned with the delivery of packets from one station to another, whether the stations are on the same network or on different networks. IP has the *IP address* scheme for assigning addresses to stations on a network; this is entirely separate from link layer addressing such as Ethernet's MAC addressing. IP is the basis for the global Internet.

- **ICMP (Internet Control Message Protocol)**   This is a communications diagnostics protocol that is also a part of the TCP/IP suite of protocols. Its primary use is the transmission of error messages from one station to another; these error messages are usually related to problems encountered when attempting to send packets from one station to another.

- **RRC (Radio Resource Control)**   This is a part of the Universal Mobile Telecommunications System, Wideband Code Division Multiple Access (UMTS WDCMA) wireless telecommunications protocol that is used to facilitate the allocation of connections between user devices (usually cell phones and other mobile data devices) and the telecommunications network (usually via cellular *base stations*).

- **AppleTalk**   This is the original suite of protocols developed by Apple Computer for networking the Apple brand of computers. The suite of protocols includes the transmission of messages from one computer over interconnected networks, as well as routing protocols. AppleTalk has since been deprecated in favor of TCP/IP.

OSI Layer 4: Transport   The *transport layer* in the OSI model is primarily concerned with the *reliability* of data transfer between systems. The transport layer manages the following characteristics of data communications:

- **Connection orientation**   At the transport layer, communications between two stations can take place in the context of a *connection*. Here, two stations will initiate a unique, logical context under which they can exchange messages until at a later time the stations agree to end the connection. Stations can have two or more unique connections established concurrently; each is uniquely identified.

- **Guaranteed delivery**   Protocols at the transport layer can track individual packets in order to guarantee delivery. For example, the TCP protocol uses something like a return receipt for each transported packet to confirm that each sent packet was successfully received by the destination.

- **Order of delivery**   The transport layer includes protocols that are able to track the order in which packets are delivered. Typically, each transported packet will have a serialized number that the receiving system will use to make sure that packets on the receiving system are delivered to higher layers in proper order. When coupled with guaranteed delivery, a receiving system can request retransmission of any missing packets, ensuring that none are lost.

The protocols at the transport layer are doing the heavy lifting by ensuring the integrity of messages that flow from system to system. The ability for data communications to take place over the vast worldwide network that is the global Internet is made possible by the characteristics of protocols in the transport layer.

Examples of transport layer protocols include

- **TCP (Transmission Control Protocol)**   This is the "TCP" in the TCP/IP protocol suite. The TCP protocol is connection-oriented through the use of numbered "ports." When a system sends a TCP packet to another system on a specific port, that port number helps the operating system direct the message to a specific program. For example, port 25 is used for inbound e-mail, ports 20 and 21 are used for FTP (File Transfer Protocol), and port 80 is used for HTTP (Hypertext Transfer Protocol). Hundreds of preassigned port numbers are the subject of Internet standards. TCP employs guaranteed delivery and guaranteed order of delivery.

- **UDP (User Datagram Protocol)**   This is the other principal protocol used by TCP/IP in the OSI transport layer. Unlike TCP, UDP is a lighter-weight protocol that lacks connection orientation, order of delivery, and guaranteed delivery. UDP consequently has less computing and network overhead, which makes it ideal for some protocols that are less sensitive to occasional packet loss. Examples of protocols that use UDP are DNS (Domain Name System), TFTP (Trivial File Transfer Protocol), and VoIP (Voice over IP). Like TCP, UDP does employ port numbers so that incoming packets on a computer can be delivered to the right program or process. Sometimes UDP is called "unreliable data protocol," a memory aid that is a reference to the protocol's lack of guaranteed delivery.

The TCP/IP suite of protocols is described in more detail later in this chapter.

OSI Layer 5: Session   The *session layer* in the OSI model is used to control connections that are established between systems. This involves connection establishment, termination, and recovery.

In the OSI model, connection control takes place in the session layer. This means that the concept of the establishment of a logical connection between systems is a session layer function. However, the TCP protocol—which is generally thought of as a transport layer protocol—handles this on its own. So it could be said that the portion of the TCP protocol that handles connection setup and teardown is mapped to the OSI session layer, while the transport portion of TCP maps to the OSI transport layer.

Examples of session layer protocols include

- **TCP (Transmission Control Protocol)**   The portion of TCP that initiates and terminates a logical connection is considered an OSI session layer function.

- **Interprocess communications**   Sockets and named pipes are some of the ways that processes on a system (or on different systems) exchange information.

- **SIP (Session Initiation Protocol)**   SIP is the protocol used to set up and tear down VoIP and other communications connections.

- **RPC (Remote Procedure Call)**   This is another interprocess communication technology that permits an application to execute a subroutine or procedure on another computer.

- **NetBIOS (Network Basic Input/Output System)**   This permits applications to communicate with one another using the legacy NetBIOS API.

OSI Layer 6: Presentation   The *presentation layer* in the OSI model is used to translate or transform data from lower layers (session, transport, and so on) into formats that the application layer can work with. Examples of presentation layer functions include

- **Character set translation**   Programs or filters are sometimes needed to translate character sets between ASCII and EBCDIC, for instance.

- **Encryption/decryption**   Communications may be encrypted if data is to be transported across unsecure networks. Example protocols are SSL (Secure

Sockets Layer), TLS (Transport Layer Security), and MIME (Multipurpose Internet Mail Extensions).

- **Codecs**   Protocols such as MPEG (Moving Picture Experts Group) use *codecs* to encode/decode or to compress/decompress audio and video data streams.

OSI Layer 7: Application   The *application layer* in the OSI model contains programs that communicate directly with the end user. This includes utilities that are packaged with operating systems, as well as tools and software applications.

Examples of application layer protocols include

- **Utility protocols**   DNS, SNMP (Simple Network Management Protocol), DHCP (Dynamic Host Configuration Protocol), and NTP (Network Time Protocol)

- **Messaging protocols**   SMTP (Simple Mail Transfer Protocol), NNTP (Network News Transfer Protocol), Gopher, HTTP, X.400, and X.500

- **Data transfer protocols**   NFS (Network File System) and FTP

- **Interactive protocols**   TELNET, SSH (secure shell)

End-user applications that communicate over networks are often considered OSI layer 7 programs. However, applications may include layer 6 functions as well and communicate with each other using layer 5 protocols such as TCP and UDP.

The TCP/IP Network Model

The TCP/IP network model is one of the basic design characteristics of the TCP/IP suite of protocols. The network model consists of four "layers," where each layer is used to manage some aspect of the transmission, routing, or delivery of data over a network. In a layered model, a layer receives services from the next lowest layer and provides services to the next higher layer.

OSI: A Model That Has Never Been Implemented

The OSI network model is a distinguished tool for teaching the concepts of network encapsulation and the functions taking place at each layer. However, the problem is that no actual, living network protocol environments have ever been built that contain all of the layers of the OSI model, and it is becoming increasingly apparent that none ever will. The world's dominant network standard, TCP/IP, is a layered model that consists of four layers, and it's not likely that TCP/IP's model will ever be increased to seven layers.

As the OSI model was being developed and socialized by the ISO, the rival TCP/IP model was quickly becoming the world's standard for data network communications. OSI has been relegated to a teaching tool, and the model itself is more of an interesting museum piece that represents an idea that never came to fruition.

The TCP/IP network model utilizes *encapsulation*. This means that a message created by an application program is encapsulated within a transport layer message, which in turn is encapsulated within an Internet layer message, which is encapsulated in a link layer message, which is delivered to a network adaptor for delivery across a physical network medium. This encapsulation is depicted in Figure 5-11.

The layers of the TCP/IP model, from bottom to top, are

- Link
- Internet
- Transport
- Application

These layers are discussed in detail in this section.

One of the primary purposes of the layered model (in both the OSI and TCP/IP models) is to permit *abstraction*. This means that each layer need be concerned only with its own delivery characteristics, while permitting other layers to manage their own matters. For instance, order of delivery is managed by the transport layer; at the Internet and link layers, order of delivery is irrelevant. Also, the link layer is concerned with just getting a message from one station to another and with collisions and the basic integrity of the message as it is transported from one device to another; but the link layer has no concept of a logical connection or with order of delivery, which are addressed by higher layers.

TCP/IP Link Layer The *link layer* is the lowest layer in the TCP/IP model. Its purpose is the delivery of messages (usually called *frames*) from one station to another on a local network. Being the lowest layer of the TCP/IP model, the link layer provides services to the transport layer.

The link layer is the physical layer of the network, and is usually implemented in the form of hardware network adaptors. TCP/IP can be implemented on top of any viable

Figure 5-11 Encapsulation in the TCP/IP network model

physical medium that has the capacity to transmit frames from one station to another. Examples of physical media used for TCP/IP include Ethernet, Asynchronous Transfer Mode (ATM), Universal Serial Bus (USB), Wi-Fi, General Packet Radio Service (GPRS), Digital Subscriber Line (DSL), Integrated Services Digital Network (ISDN), and fiber optics.

The link layer is only concerned with the delivery of messages from one station to another on a local network. At this layer, there is no concept of neighboring networks or of routing; these are handled at higher layers in the model.

TCP/IP Internet Layer   The *Internet layer* of the TCP/IP model is the foundation layer of TCP/IP. The purpose of this layer is the delivery of messages (called packets) from one station to another on the same network or on different networks. The Internet layer receives services from the link layer and provides services to the transport layer.

At this layer, the delivery of messages from one station to another is not guaranteed. Instead, the Internet layer makes only a best effort to deliver messages. The Internet layer also does not concern itself with the order of delivery of messages. Concerns such as these are addressed at the transport layer.

The primary protocol that has been implemented in the Internet layer is known as IP (Internet Protocol). IP is the building block for nearly all other protocols and message types in TCP/IP. One other protocol is common in the Internet layer: ICMP (Internet Control Message Protocol), a diagnostic protocol that is used to send error messages and other diagnostic messages over networks.

At the Internet layer, there are two types of devices: hosts and routers. Hosts are computers that could be functioning as servers or workstations. They communicate by creating messages that they send on the network. Routers are computers that forward packets from one network to another. In the early Internet, routers really *were* computers like others, with some additional configurations that they used to forward packets between networks.

The relationship between hosts and routers is depicted in Figure 5-12.

TCP/IP Transport Layer   The *transport layer* in the TCP/IP model consists of two main packet transport protocols, TCP and UDP, as well as a few other protocols that were developed after the initial design of TCP/IP. The transport layer receives services from the Internet layer and provides services to the application layer.

Several features are available at the transport layer for packet delivery, including

- **Reliable delivery**   This involves two characteristics: integrity of the packet contents and guaranteed delivery. The TCP protocol includes these two features that ensure confirmation that a packet sent from one station will be delivered to its destination and that the contents of the packet will not be altered along the way.

- **Connection orientation**   This involves the establishment of a persistent logical "connection" between two stations. This is particularly useful when a station is communicating on many simultaneous "conversations" from one or more source stations. When a connection is established, the two stations will negotiate and agree on arbitrary high-numbered ports (channels) that will make each established connection unique.

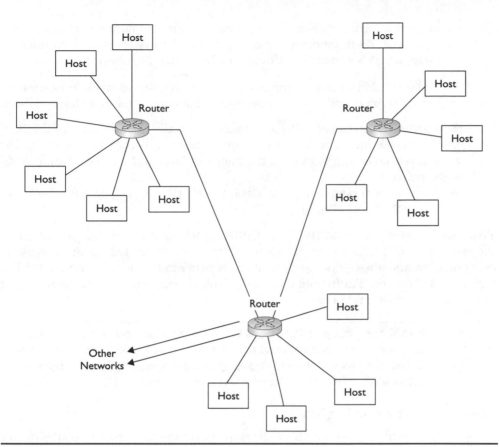

Figure 5-12   Hosts and routers at the Internet layer

- **Order of delivery**   Here, the order of delivery of packets is guaranteed to match the order in which they were sent. While the order of delivery may be a bygone conclusion in a small local area network, this is important in large internetworks, especially where there may be more than one active route between two stations.

- **Flow control**   This means that the delivery of packets from one station to another will not overrun the destination station. For example, the transfer of a large file from a faster system to a slower system could overrun the slower system, unless it had a way to periodically pause the transfer so that it could keep up with the inbound messages.

- **Port number**   Here, a message on one station may be sent to a specific port number on a destination station. A port number essentially signifies the type of message that is being sent. A "listener" program can be set up on a destination system to listen on a preassigned port, and then will process messages received on that port number. The primary advantage of port numbers is that a destination system does not need to examine the contents of a message in order to discern its type; instead, the port number defines the purpose. There are many standard port numbers established, including 23 = telnet, 25 = e-mail, 53 = domain name service, 80 = http, and so on.

It should be noted that not all transport layer protocols utilize all of these features. For instance, the UDP protocol utilizes only flow control but none of the other features listed.

TCP/IP Application Layer   The *application layer* is the topmost layer of the TCP/IP model. This layer interfaces directly with applications and application services. The application layer receives services from the transport layer and may communicate directly with end users.

Application layer programs include DNS, SNMP, DHCP, NTP, SMTP, NNTP, Gopher, HTTP, X.400, X.500, NFS, FTP, and TELNET.

The TCP/IP and OSI Models   The TCP/IP model was not designed to conform to the seven-layer OSI network model. However, the models are similar in their use of encapsulation and abstraction, and some layers between the two models are similar. Figure 5-13 shows the TCP/IP and OSI models side by side and how the layers in one model correspond to the other.

EXAM TIP   Mapping TCP/IP and OSI models to each other has no practical purpose except to understand their similarities and differences. There is not unanimous agreement on the mapping of the models. It is easy to argue for some small differences in the way that they are conjoined.

Network Technologies

Many network technologies have been developed over the past several decades. Some, like Ethernet, DSL, and TCP/IP, are found practically everywhere, while other technologies, such as ISDN, Frame Relay, and AppleTalk, have had shorter lifespans.

The IS auditor needs to be familiar with network technologies, architectures, protocols, and media so that he may examine an organization's network architecture and

Figure 5-13
The TCP/IP and
OSI network models
side by side

OSI	TCP/IP
Application Presentation Session	Application
Transport	Transport
Network	Internet
Data Link Physical	Link

operation. The following sections describe network technologies at a level of detail that should be sufficient for most auditing needs:

- **Local area networks**   This section discusses local area network topologies, cabling, and transport protocols (including Ethernet, ATM, Token Ring, USB, and FDDI).

- **Wide area networks**   This section discusses wide area networks, including transport protocols MPLS, SONET, T-Carrier, Frame Relay, ISDN, and X.25.

- **Wireless networks**   This section discusses wireless network standards Wi-Fi, Bluetooth, Wireless USB, NFC, and IrDA.

- **TCP/IP suite of protocols**   This section discusses TCP/IP protocols in the link layer, Internet layer, transport layer, and application layer.

- **The global Internet**   This section discusses global Internet addressing, DNS, routing, and applications.

- **Network management**   This section discusses the business function, plus the tools and protocols used to manage networks.

- **Networked applications**   This section discusses the techniques used to build network-based applications.

Local Area Networks

Local area networks (LANs) are networks that exist within a small area, such as a floor in a building, a lab, storefront, office, or residence. Because of signaling limitations, a LAN is usually several hundred feet in length or less. A LAN will usually have, at most, a few hundred computers connected to it.

Physical Network Topology

Wired LANs are transported over network cabling that runs throughout a building. Network cabling is set up in one of three physical topologies:

- **Star**   In a star topology, a separate cable is run from a central location to each computer. This is the way that most networks are wired today. The central location might be a wiring closet or a computer room, where all of the cables from each computer would converge at one location and be connected to network equipment such as a switch or hub.

- **Ring**   A ring topology consists of cabling that runs from one computer to the next. Early Token Ring and Ethernet networks were often wired this way. Where the network cable was attached to a computer, a "T" connector was used: one part connected to the computer itself, and the other two connectors were attached to the network cabling.

- **Bus**   A bus topology consists of a central cable, with connectors along its length that would facilitate "branch" cables that would be connected to individual computers. Like the ring topology, this was used in early networks but is seldom used today.

These three topologies are depicted in Figure 5-14.

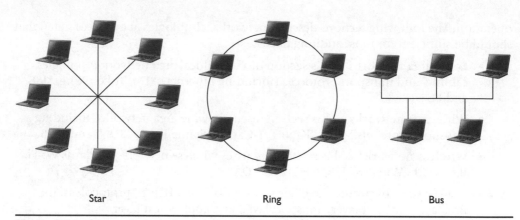

Star   Ring   Bus

Figure 5-14   Network physical topologies: star, ring, and bus

It should be noted that the logical function and physical topology of a network might vary. For instance, a Token Ring network may resemble a physical star, but it will function logically as a ring. An Ethernet network functions as a bus, but may be wired as a star, bus, or ring, depending on the type of cabling used (and, as indicated earlier, star topology is prevalent). The point is that logical function and physical topology often differ from each other.

Cabling Types
Several types of cables have been used in local area networks over the past several decades. This section will focus on the types in use today, but will mention those that have been used in the past, which may still be in use in some organizations.

Twisted-Pair Cable   Twisted-pair cabling is a thin cable that contains four pairs of insulated copper conductors, all surrounded by a protective jacket. Several varieties of twisted-pair cabling are suitable for various physical environments and provide various network bandwidth capabilities.

Because network transmissions can be subject to interference, network cabling may include shielding that protects the conductors from interference. Some of these types are

- **Shielded twisted pair (U/FTP or STP)**   This type of cable includes a thin metal shield that protects each pair of conductors from electromagnetic interference (EMI), making it more resistant to interference.

- **Screened unshielded twisted pair (S/UTP)**   Also known as foiled twisted pair (FTP), this type of cable has a thin metal shield that protects the conductors from EMI.

- **Screened shielded twisted pair (S/STP or S/FTP)**   This type of cable includes a thin layer of metal shielding surrounding each twisted pair of conductors, plus an outer shield that protects all of the conductors together. This is all covered by a protective jacket.

- **Unshielded twisted pair (UTP)**   This type of cable has no shielding and consists only of the four pairs of twisted conductors and the outer protective jacket.

The abbreviations for twisted-pair cable have recently changed in compliance with international standard ISO/IEC 11801, "Information technology — Generic cabling for customer premises." The new standard takes the form *X/YTP*, where *X* denotes whether the entire cable has shielding, and *Y* indicates whether individual pairs in the cable are shielded. Table 5-1 shows the old and new names and their meanings. The old names are likely going to be in common use for many years, as office buildings and residences around the world are wired with twisted-pair cabling that is labeled with the old names; this wiring is likely going to last for decades in many locations.

Twisted-pair network cabling is also available with different capacity ratings to meet various bandwidth requirements. The common ratings include

- **Category 3**   This is the oldest still-recognized twisted-pair cabling standard, capable of transporting 10Mbit Ethernet up to 100 m (328 ft). The 100BASE-T4 standard permitted up to 100Mbit Ethernet over Cat-3 cable by using all four pairs of conductors. Category 3 cable is no longer installed, but is still found in older networks.

- **Category 5**   Known as "Cat-5," this cabling grade has been in common use since the mid-1990s, and is suitable for 10Mbit, 100Mbit, and 1000Mbit (1Gbit) Ethernet over distances up to 100 m (328 ft.). Category 5 cable is typically made from 24-gauge copper wire with three twists per inch. A newer grade called **Category 5e** has better performance for Gigabit Ethernet networks.

- **Category 6**   This is the cabling standard for Gigabit Ethernet networks. Cat-6 cabling greatly resembles Cat-5 cabling, but Cat-6 has more stringent specifications for crosstalk and noise. Cat-6 cable is typically made from 23-gauge copper. Category 6 cabling is "backward compatible" with Category 5 and 5e cabling, which means that Cat-6 cables can be used for 10Mbit and 100Mbit Ethernet networks as well as 1000Mbit (1Gbit).

Old Name	New Name	Cable Shielding	Pair Shielding
UTP	U/UTP	None	None
FTP	F/UTP	Foil	None
STP	U/FTP	None	Foil
S-FTP	SF/UTP	Foil, braiding	None
S-STP	S/FTP	Braiding	Foil

Table 5-1   Old and New Twisted-Pair Cabling Abbreviations and Meaning

- **Category 7**   This cable standard has been developed to permit 10Gbit Ethernet over 100 m of cabling. Cat-7 cabling is almost always made from S/FTP cabling to provide maximum resistance to EMI. A newer grade known as **Category 7a** is designed to have telephone, cable TV, and 1GB networking in the same cable. This newer grade is still under development.

- **Category 8**   This is a new cable standard that is still under development, designed for high-speed networking.

Twisted-pair cable ratings are usually printed on the outer jacket of the cable. Figure 5-15 shows a short length of Category 5 cable with the rating and other information stamped on it.

Fiber Optic Cable   Fiber optic cable is the transmission medium for fiber optic communications, which is the method of transmitting information using pulses of light instead of electric signals through metal cabling. The advantages of fiber optic cable are its much higher bandwidth, lower loss, and compact size. Because communications over fiber optic cable are based on light instead of electric current, they are immune from EMI.

In local area networks, multimode-type fiber optic cable can carry signals up to 10 Gbit/sec up to 600 m (and distances up to a few kilometers at lower bandwidths), sufficient for interconnecting buildings in a campus-type environment. For longer distances, single-mode–type fiber optic cable is used, usually by telecommunications carriers for interconnecting cities for voice and data communications.

Compared to twisted-pair and other network cable types, fiber optic cable is relatively fragile and must be treated with care. It can never be pinched, bent, or twisted— doing so will break the internal fibers. For this reason, fiber optic cabling is usually

Figure 5-15
Category 5 twisted-
pair cable (Image
courtesy Rebecca
Steele)

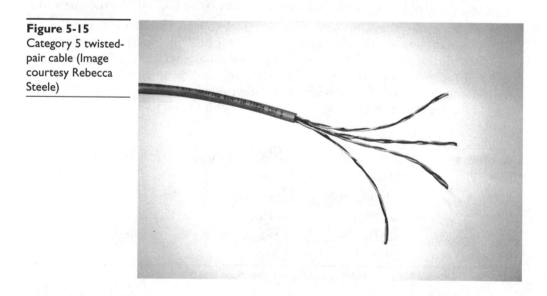

Figure 5-16
Fiber optic cable with its connector removed to reveal its interior (Image courtesy Harout S. Hedeshian)

limited to data centers requiring high bandwidths between systems, where network engineers will carefully route fiber optic cabling from device to device, using guides and channels that will prevent the cable from being damaged. But the advantage of fiber optic cabling is its high capacity and freedom from EMI.

Figures 5-16 and 5-17 show fiber optic cable and connectors.

Other Types of Network Cable Twisted-pair and fiber optic cable are the primary local area network cable types. However, older types of cable have been used and are still found in many installations, including

- **Coaxial** Coaxial cable consists of a solid inner conductor that is surrounded by an insulating jacket, surrounded by a metallic shield. A plastic jacket protects the shield. Coaxial cables were used in early Ethernet networks with cable types such as *10base5* and *10base2*. Twist-lock or threaded connectors were used to connect coaxial cable to computers or network devices. A typical coaxial cable is shown in Figure 5-18.

Figure 5-17
Connectors link fiber optic cable to network equipment. (Image courtesy Stephane Tsacas)

Figure 5-18
Coaxial cable (Image
courtesy Fdominec)

- **Serial** Point-to-point network connections can be established over USB or RS-232 serial cables. In the case of serial lines, in the 1980s, many organizations used central computers and user terminals that communicated over RS-232 serial cabling. At that time these existing cable plants made the adoption of SLIP (Serial Line Internet Protocol) popular for connecting workstations and minicomputers to central computers using existing cabling. SLIP is all but obsolete now, although USB is still growing in popularity.

Network Transport Protocols

Many protocols, or standards, have been developed to facilitate data communications over network cabling. Ethernet, ATM, Token Ring, USB, and FDDI protocols are described in detail in the following sections.

Ethernet

Ethernet is the dominant protocol used in LANs. It is a frame-based protocol, which means that data transmitted over an Ethernet-based network is placed into a "frame" that has places for source and destination addresses as well as contents.

Shared Medium Ethernet is a "broadcast" or "shared medium" type of protocol. This means that a frame that is sent from one station on a network to another station may be physically received by all stations that are connected to the network medium. When each station receives the frame, the station will examine the destination address of the frame to determine whether the frame is intended for that or another station. If the frame is destined for another station, the station will simply ignore the frame and do nothing. The destination station will accept the frame and deliver it to the operating system for processing.

Collision Avoidance Ethernet networks are asynchronous—a station that needs to transmit a frame may do so at any time. However, Ethernet also employs a "collision avoidance" mechanism whereby a station that wishes to broadcast a frame will first listen to the network to see if any other stations are transmitting. If another station is transmitting, the station that wishes to transmit will "back off" and wait for a short interval and then try again (in a 10Mbit Ethernet, the station will wait for 9.6 microseconds). If a collision (two stations transmitting at the same time) does occur, both transmitting stations will stop, wait a short interval (the length of the interval is based on a randomly generated number), and then try again. The use of a random number as a part of the "back off" algorithm ensures that each station has a statistically equal chance to transmit its frames on the network.

Ethernet Addressing On an Ethernet network, each station on the network has a unique address called a Media Access Control (MAC) address, expressed as a six-byte hexadecimal value. A typical address is displayed in a notation separated by colons or dashes, such as F0:E3:67:AB:98:02.

The Ethernet standard dictates that no two devices in the entire world will have the same MAC address; this is established through the issuance of ranges of MAC addresses that are allocated to each manufacturer of Ethernet devices. Typically, each manufacturer will be issued a range, which consists of the first three bytes of the MAC address; the manufacturer will then assign consecutive values for the last three bytes to each device that it produces.

For example, a company is issued the value A0-66-01 (called its Organizationally Unique Identifier, or OUI). The devices that the company produces will have that value as the first three bytes of its MAC address and assign three additional bytes to each device that it produces, giving addresses such as A0-66-01-FF-01-01, A0-66-01-FF-01-02, A0-66-01-FF-01-03, and so on. This will guarantee that no two devices in the world will have the same address.

Ethernet Frame Format An Ethernet frame consists of a header segment, a data segment, and a checksum. The header segment contains the destination MAC address, the source MAC address, and a two-byte Ethernet type field. The data segment ranges from 46 to 1,500 bytes in length. The checksum field is four bytes in length and is a CRC (cyclical redundancy check) checksum of the entire frame. An Ethernet frame is shown in Figure 5-19.

Figure 5-19 An Ethernet frame consists of a header, data, and checksum.

Ethernet Devices   Network devices are required to facilitate the transmission of frames on an Ethernet network. These devices include

- **Network adaptor**   A network adaptor, commonly known as a network interface card (NIC), is a device that is directly connected to a computer's bus and contains one or more connectors to which an Ethernet network cable may be connected. Often, a computer's NIC is integrated with the computer's motherboard, but a NIC may also be a separate circuit card that is plugged into a bus connector.

- **Repeater**   A repeater is a device that receives and retransmits the signal on an Ethernet network. Repeaters are useful for situations in which cable lengths exceed 100 m, or to interconnect two or more Ethernet networks. A disadvantage of repeaters is that they propagate collisions and other network anomalies onto all parts of the network. Repeaters are seldom used today.

- **Bridge**   A bridge is a device that is used to interconnect Ethernet networks. For example, an organization may have an Ethernet network on each floor of a multistory building; an Ethernet bridge can be used to interconnect each of the separate Ethernet networks. A bridge is similar to a repeater, except that a bridge does not propagate errors such as collisions, but instead only propagates well-formed packets.

- **Hub**   Organizations came to realize that ring and bus topology networks were problematic with regard to cable failures. This gave rise to the star topology as a preferred network architecture, because a cable problem would affect only one station instead of many or all. A multiport repeater would be used to connect all of the devices to the network. Over time, this device became known as a hub. Like repeaters, Ethernet hubs propagate packets to all stations on the network.

- **Gateway**   A device that acts as protocol converter, or which performs some other type of transformation of messages.

- **Switch**   An Ethernet switch is similar to a hub, but with one important difference: a switch will listen to traffic and learn the MAC address(es) associated with each port (connector) and will send packets only to destination ports. The result is potentially greater network throughput, because each station on the network will be receiving only the frames that are specifically addressed to it. When only one station is connected to each port on an Ethernet switch, theoretically, collisions will never occur.

Devices such as routers, layer 3 switches, layer 4 switches, and layer 4-7 switches are discussed in the section, "TCP/IP Protocols and Devices," later this chapter.

ATM

ATM, or Asynchronous Transfer Mode, is a link-layer network protocol developed in the 1980s in response to the need for high-speed networks that delivered better performance than 10Mbit Ethernet networks. ATM is a dominant protocol in the core networks of telecommunications carriers. The speeds of ATM networks are tied to the speed of the SONET transport layer, which begins at 155 Mbit/sec.

Unlike Ethernet, ATM is a *synchronous* network, which means that messages (called *cells*) on an ATM network are transmitted in synchronization with a network-based time clock. Stations on an Ethernet, on the other hand, transmit whenever they feel like it, provided the network is quiet at the moment.

ATM cells are fixed at a length of 53 bytes (5-byte header and 48-byte payload). This small frame size improves performance by reducing jitter, which is a key characteristic of networks that are carrying streaming media.

ATM is a connection-oriented link-layer protocol. This means that two devices on an ATM network that wish to communicate with each other will establish a connection through a *virtual circuit*. A connection also establishes a Quality of Service (QoS) setting for the connection that defines the priority and sensitivity of the connection.

Cells that are transmitted from one station to another are transported through one or more ATM switches. The path that a cell takes is established at the time that the virtual circuit is established. An ATM switch is used even when two stations on the same local area network are communicating with each other.

Like Ethernet, ATM can be used to transport TCP/IP messages. TCP/IP packets that are larger than 48 bytes in length are transmitted over ATM in pieces and reassembled at the destination.

Token Ring

Token Ring is a local area network protocol that was developed by IBM in the 1980s. Historically, Token Ring was prevalent in organizations that had IBM mainframe or midrange computer systems. However, as TCP/IP and Ethernet grew in popularity, Token Ring declined and it is rarely found today.

Token Ring networks operate through the passage of a three-byte token frame from station to station on the network. If a station has information that it needs to send to another station on the network, it must first receive the token; then it can place a frame on the network that includes the token and the message for the destination station. When the token frame reaches the destination station, the destination station will remove the message from the token frame and then pass an empty token (or a frame containing the token and a message for another station) to the next station on the network.

Token Ring Devices   The principal Token Ring device is the multistation access unit, or MAU. A MAU is a device that contains several Token Ring cable connectors and connects network cables from the MAU to each station on the network. A typical MAU contains as many as eight connectors; if a Token Ring network is to contain more than eight stations, MAUs can be connected together using their ring in/ring out connectors. Figure 5-20 shows small and large Token Ring networks.

Token Ring Design Considerations   The design of Token Ring technology makes collisions impossible, since no station can transmit unless it possesses the token. A disadvantage of this design occurs if the station with the token encounters a malfunction that causes it to not propagate the token. This results in a momentary pause until the network goes into a recovery mode and regenerates a token.

Figure 5-20   Token Ring network topologies

Universal Serial Bus

Universal Serial Bus, or USB, is not typically considered a network technology, but rather a workstation bus technology. This is primarily because USB is used to connect peripherals such as mice, keyboards, storage devices, printers, scanners, cameras, and network adaptors. However, the USB specification indeed contains full networking capabilities, which makes use of those small USB hubs possible.

USB data rates are shown in Table 5-2.

Cable length for USB is restricted to five meters. The maximum number of devices on a USB network is 127.

One of the valuable characteristics of USB technology is the ability to "hot plug" devices. This means that USB devices can be connected and disconnected without the need to power down the workstation they are connected to. This is achieved primarily through the design specification for devices and device drivers that tolerate plugging and unplugging. This does not mean, however, that all types of USB devices may be plugged and unplugged at will. USB mass storage devices, for instance, should be logically "dismounted" in order to ensure the integrity of the file system on the device.

Table 5-2 USB Data Rates	USB Version	Data Rate
	1.0	12 Mbit/sec
	2.0	480 Mbit/sec
	3.0	5.0 Gbit/sec

FDDI

Fiber distributed data interface, or FDDI, is a local area network technology whose range can extend up to 200 km over optical fiber. FDDI is a "dual ring" technology that utilizes redundant network cabling and counter-rotating tokens, which together make FDDI highly resilient. Each ring has a 100 Mbit/sec data rate, making the entire network capable of 200 Mbit/sec.

FDDI has been largely superseded by 100 Mbit/sec and 1 Gbit/sec Ethernet, and is not often seen in commercial networks.

Wide Area Networks

Wide area networks, commonly known as WANs, are those networks that extend for miles to thousands of miles between stations. The term WAN is generally used in two ways: to connote an organization's entire regional or global data network and as the label for the long-distance network connections used to join individual networks together. In the second usage, the terms "WAN link" and "WAN connection" are used.

Wide Area Transmission Modes

Before discussing specific WAN protocols, it is important to understand the basics of message transmission techniques used in wide area networks.

The basic problem of wide area communications is the need to efficiently route communications from many different endpoints to many destinations, without constructing dedicated connections between all possible communication sources and destinations. Instead, some scheme for sharing a common communication medium is needed. These methods are

- **Circuit-switched**   Here, a dedicated, end-to-end communications channel is established that lasts for the duration of a connection. The best-known example of circuit-switched technology is the old public-switched telephone network, where a telephone call from one telephone to another occupied a dedicated circuit that was assigned at the onset of the call and used until the call was finished.

- **Packet-switched**   Communications between endpoints takes place over a stream of packets, which are routed through switches until they reach their destination. Frame Relay and the TCP/IP Internet are good examples of packet-switched networks. And while landline telephone calls still have the appearance of being circuit-switched, telephone conversations are actually converted into packets for transmission through the core of a telecommunications network.

- **Message-switched**   Each message is switched to its destination when a communications path is available. An example of message switching is the transmission of individual e-mail messages between servers on the Internet.

- **Virtual circuit**   A logical communications channel is established between two endpoints on a packet-switched network. This communications channel may be known as a permanent virtual circuit (PVC) or a switched virtual circuit (SVC). Virtual circuits are used in Frame Relay networks. Virtual private networks (VPNs) can also be thought of as virtual circuits.

Wide Area Network Protocols

This section describes several well-known protocols used in wide area networks.

MPLS   *Multiprotocol Label Switching,* or MPLS, is a variable-length, packet-switched network technology. In an MPLS network, each packet has one or more *labels* affixed to it that contain information that helps MPLS routers to make packet-forwarding decisions, without having to examine the contents of the packet itself (for an IP address, for instance).

MPLS can be used to carry many types of traffic, including Ethernet, ATM, SONET, and IP. It is often used to trunk voice and data networks over WAN connections between business locations in an enterprise network. One of the strengths of MPLS is its QoS properties, which facilitate the rapid transfer of packets using time-sensitive protocols such as VoIP and H.323.

MPLS employs two types of devices: label edge routers (LERs) and label switch routers (LSRs). Label edge routers are used at the boundaries of an MPLS network; LERs push a label onto incoming packets that enter the network. LSRs make packet-forwarding decisions based upon the value of the label. When a packet leaves the MPLS network, another LER pops the label off the packet and forwards it out of the MPLS network.

SONET   *Synchronous Optical Networking,* or SONET, is a class of telecommunications network transport technologies transmitted over fiber optic networks. It is a multiplexed network technology that can be used to transport voice and data communications at very high speeds over long distances.

SONET networks are almost exclusively built and operated by telecommunications network providers, who sell voice and data connectivity services to businesses. Often, the endpoint equipment for SONET networks provides connectivity using a native technology such as MPLS, Ethernet, or T-1.

Telecommunications service providers often encapsulate older services, such as DS0, DS-1, T-1, and Frame Relay, over SONET networks.

The data rates available in SONET networks are shown in Table 5-3. Rates are expressed using the term Optical Carrier Level, abbreviated OC.

Table 5-3 SONET OC Levels	SONET OC Level	Data Rate
	OC-1	51,840 Kbit/sec
	OC-3	155,520 Kbit/sec
	OC-12	622,080 Kbit/sec
	OC-24	1,244,160 Kbit/sec
	OC-48	2,488,320 Kbit/sec
	OC-192	9,9539280 Kbit/sec
	OC-3072	159,252,240 Kbit/sec

T-Carrier   The term *T-Carrier* refers to a class of multiplexed telecommunications carrier network technologies developed to transport voice and data communications over long distances using copper cabling.

The basic service in T-Carrier technology is known as DS-0, which is used to transport a single voice circuit. The data rate for a DS-0 is 64 Kbit/sec. Another basic T-Carrier service is the DS-1, also known as T-1. DS-1 contains 24 channels, each a DS-0. The total speed of a DS-1 is 1,544 Kbit/sec. There are additional services, all of which are shown, together with their respective data rates and channels, in Table 5-4. These services are unique to North America.

In Europe, T-Carrier circuits are known instead as E-1 and E-3, which multiplex 32 and 512 64 Kbit/sec circuits, respectively. The European T-Carrier standards are based on multiples of 32 circuits, whereas North American standards are based on multiples of 24 circuits. Otherwise, there isn't much practical difference between them.

T-Carrier protocols are *synchronous*, which means that packets transported on a T-Carrier network are transmitted according to the pulses of a centralized clock that is usually controlled by the telecommunications carrier. This is contrasted with Ethernet, which is asynchronous, meaning a station on an Ethernet may transmit a frame at any time of its choosing (provided the network is not busy at that exact moment).

Organizations that use T-Carrier services to carry data can utilize individual DS-0 channels (which are the same speed as a dial-up connection) or an entire T-1 circuit without multiplexing. This enables use of the entire 1,544 Kbit/sec as a single resource.

Frame Relay   Frame Relay is a carrier-based, packet-switched network technology. It is most often used to connect remote data networks to a centralized network; for example, a retail store chain might use Frame Relay to connect each of its retail store LANs to the corporate LAN.

Frame Relay is often more economical than dedicated DS-0 or DS-1/T-1 circuits. By their nature, Frame Relay backbone networks are shared, in the sense that they transport packets for many customers.

Connections between locations using Frame Relay are made via a permanent virtual circuit (PVC), which is not unlike a VPN, except that the payload is not encrypted. For purposes of security and privacy, PVCs are generally considered private, like a T-1 circuit.

Frame Relay has all but superseded the older X.25 services. However, MPLS is rapidly overtaking Frame Relay.

T-Carrier Class	Data Rate	Number of DS-0 Channels
DS-0	64 Kbit/sec	1
DS-1 (T-1)	1,544 Kbit/sec	24
DS-2	6,312 Kbit/sec	96
DS-3 (T-3)	44,736 Kbit/sec	672
DS-4	274,176 Kbit/sec	4,032
DS-5	400,352 Kbit/sec	5,760

Table 5-4   T-Carrier Data Rates and Channels in North America

ISDN   ISDN, or Integrated Services Digital Network, is best described as a digital version of the public-switched telephone network. In many regions of the United States, ISDN was the first "high-speed" Internet access available for residential and small business subscribers.

A subscriber with ISDN service will have a digital modem with one connection to a digital ISDN voice telephone and one connection (typically Ethernet) to a computer. The speed of the computer connection in this configuration is 64 Kbits/sec. Alternatively, the ISDN modem could be configured in a "bonded" state with no voice telephone and only a computer connection at 128 Kbits/sec. Both of these configurations use a BRI (basic rate interface) type of connection.

Higher speeds were also available, up to 1,544 Kbits/sec, and are known as a PRI (primary rate interface) type of connection.

ISDN utilizes a separate, but similar, environment where an ISDN modem "dials" a phone number, similar to dial-up Internet service.

X.25   X.25 is an early packet network technology used for long-distance data communications, typically between business locations. It usually connects slow-speed serial communications devices such as terminals. At each location, an X.25 PAD (packet assembler-disassembler) device connects local devices to the X.25 network. The PAD would be configured to send outgoing packets to specific destinations over the X.25 network.

X.25 contained no authentication or encryption, and has been largely replaced by the newer Frame Relay and MPLS technologies discussed earlier in this section.

Wide Area Network Devices

This section describes devices used to connect wide area network components to each other and to an organization's internal network.

Modem   A modulator-demodulator unit, also known as a modem, is a device used to connect a telecommunications carrier network to a computer or a local area network. Early modems consisted of an analog telephone connector for connecting to the public telephone network, and a serial port for connecting to a computer. Later versions connect to ISDN, cable, and DSL networks and an Ethernet port for connecting to a single computer or a LAN.

Multiplexor   A multiplexor is a device that connects several separate signals and combines them into a single data stream. There are four basic types of multiplexing, which are

- **Time division**   Separate signals are combined into a pattern where each individual signal occupies a separate dedicated timeslot.

- **Asynchronous time division multiplexing**   Separate signals are allocated into timeslots of varying sizes depending on need.

- **Frequency division multiplexing**   Separate signals are combined into a single stream where each separate signal occupies a nonoverlapping frequency.

- **Statistical multiplexing**   Separate signals are inserted into available timeslots. This is different from time division multiplexing, where input signals are assigned to timeslots. In statistical multiplexing, input signals are dynamically assigned to available timeslots.

Channel Service Unit/Digital Service Unit   Also known as a CSU/DSU, a channel service unit/digital service unit is a device that is used to connect a telecommunications circuit (typically a T-1 line) to a device such as a router.

WAN Switch   A WAN switch is a general term that encompasses several types of wide area network switching devices, including ATM switches, Frame Relay switches, MPLS switches, and ISDN switches. See respective sections on these technologies earlier in this chapter.

Router   A router is a device used to connect two or more networks together. In the context of wide area networks, a router would be used to connect two or more wide area networks to each other.

See also the discussion of routers in the "TCP/IP Protocols and Devices" section later in this chapter.

Wireless Networks

Several types of wireless technologies are available to organizations that wish to implement data communications without constructing or maintaining a wiring plant. Furthermore, wireless networks permit devices to move from place to place, even outside of buildings, facilitating highly flexible and convenient means for high-speed communications.

The technologies discussed in this section are the type that an organization would set up on its own, without any services required from a telecommunications service provider.

Wi-Fi

Wi-Fi is the popular term used to describe several similar standards developed around the IEEE 802.11i/a/b/n standards. Wi-Fi, or WLAN, permits computers to communicate with each other wirelessly at high speeds over moderate distances from each other. The term "Wi-Fi" is a trademark of the Wi-Fi Alliance for certifying products as compatible with IEEE 802.11 standards. The usual term describing networks based on IEEE 802.11 standards is Wireless LAN, or WLAN, although this term is not often used.

Wi-Fi Standards   The various Wi-Fi standards are illustrated in Table 5-5.

Table 5-5 A Comparison of Wi-Fi Standards	Standard	Year Introduced	Maximum Data Rate	Indoor Range
	802.11a	1999	54 Mbit/sec	35 m
	802.11b	1999	11 Mbit/sec	38 m
	802.11g	2003	54 Mbit/sec	38 m
	802.11n	2009	150 Mbit/sec	70 m

Wi-Fi Security   Wi-Fi networks can be configured with several security features that protect the privacy as well as the availability of the Wi-Fi network. Available features include

- **Authentication**   Individual stations that wish to connect with a Wi-Fi network can be required to provide an encryption key. Furthermore, the user may be required to provide a user ID and password. Without this information, a station is unable to connect to the Wi-Fi network and communicate with it. Wi-Fi access points can contain a list of user IDs and passwords, or they can be configured to utilize a network-based authentication service such as RADIUS, LDAP, or Active Directory. Use of the latter generally makes more sense for organizations that wish to centralize user authentication information; this also makes access simpler for employees who do not need to remember yet another user ID and password.

- **Access control**   A Wi-Fi network can be configured to permit only stations with known MAC addresses to connect to it. Any station without a permitted address will not be able to connect.

- **Encryption**   A Wi-Fi network can use encryption to protect traffic from interception through over-the-air eavesdropping. It can encrypt with the WEP (Wired Equivalent Privacy), WPA (Wi-Fi Protected Access), or WPA2 method. A Wi-Fi network can also be configured to not use encryption, in which case another station may be able to eavesdrop on any communications on the wireless network. When a Wi-Fi network uses encryption, only the airlink communications are encrypted; network traffic from the Wi-Fi access point to other networks will not be encrypted.

- **Network identifier**   A Wi-Fi access point is configured with a service set identifier (SSID) that identifies the network. For organizations that provide network access only for their own personnel, it is recommended that the SSID *not* be set to a value that makes the ownership or identity of the access point obvious. Using a company name, for instance, is not a good idea. Instead, a word—even a random set of characters—that does not relate to the organization's identity should be used. The reason for this is that the SSID will not itself identify the owner of the network, which could, in some circumstances, invite outsiders to attempt to access it. An exception to this is a "public hotspot" used to provide free network access, where the SSID will clearly identify the establishment providing access.

- **Broadcast**   A Wi-Fi access point can be configured to broadcast its SSID, making it easier for users to discover and connect to the network. However, broadcasting SSIDs also alerts outsiders to the presence of the network, which can compromise network security by encouraging someone to attempt to connect to it. However, turning off the SSID broadcast does not make the network absolutely secure: a determined intruder can obtain tools that will allow him to discover the presence of a Wi-Fi network that does not broadcast its SSID.

- **Signal strength**   The transmit signal strength of a Wi-Fi access point can be configured so that radio signals from the access point do not significantly exceed the service area. Often, signal strength of access points will be set to maximum, which provides persons outside the physical premises with a strong signal. Instead, transmit signal strength should be turned down so that as little signal as possible leaves the physical premises. This is a challenge in shared-space office buildings, however, and thus cannot be used as a Wi-Fi network's *only* security control.

CAUTION   Because a Wi-Fi network utilizes radio signals, an untrusted outsider is able to intercept those signals, which could provide enough information for that outsider to penetrate the network. It is for this reason that all of the controls discussed in this section should be utilized in order to provide an effective defense-in-depth security protection.

Bluetooth

Bluetooth is a short-range airlink standard for data communications between computer peripherals and low power consumption devices. Designed as a replacement for short-range cabling, Bluetooth also provides security via authentication and encryption.

Applications using Bluetooth include

- Mobile phone earsets
- In-car audio for smart phones
- Data transfer between smart phones and computers
- Music player headphones
- Computer mice, keyboards, and other low-power and low-speed peripherals
- Printers and scanners

Bluetooth is a lower-power standard, which supports the use of very small devices, such as mobile phone earsets. The standard includes one-time authentication of devices using a process called "pairing." Communications over Bluetooth can also be encrypted so that any eavesdropping is made ineffective. Data rates range from 1 to 3 Mbit/sec.

Wireless USB

Wireless USB (WUSB) is a short-range, high-bandwidth wireless protocol used for personal area networks (PANs). Data rates range from 110 to 480 Mbit/sec. WUSB is typically used to connect computer peripherals that would otherwise be connected with cables.

WUSB can be thought of as a competitor to Bluetooth. In the long term, only one of these protocols is likely to succeed.

NFC

Near-Field Communications, or NFC, is a standard of extremely short-distance radio frequencies that are commonly used for merchant payment applications. The typical maximum range for NFC is 10 cm (4 in).

NFC supports two types of communications: active-active and active-passive. In active-active mode, the base station and the wireless node electronically transmit messages over the NFC airlink. In active-passive mode, the wireless node has no active power supply and instead behaves more like an RFID (radio frequency identification) card. Throughput rates range from 106 to 848 kbit/sec.

Common applications of NFC include merchant payments using a mobile phone or credit card–sized card, and advanced building access control systems.

IrDA

IrDA stands for Infrared Data Association, which is the organization that has developed technical standards for point-to-point data communications using infrared light. IrDA has been used for communications between devices such as laptop computers, PDAs, and printers.

IrDA is not considered a secure protocol: there is no authentication or encryption of IrDA-based communications.

Bluetooth and USB have largely replaced IrDA, and few IrDA-capable devices are now sold.

TCP/IP Protocols and Devices

TCP/IP, the technology that the Internet is built upon, contains many protocols. This section discusses many of the well-known protocols, layer by layer. First, link layer protocols are discussed, followed by Internet layer protocols, then transport layer protocols, and finally application layer protocols. This is followed by a discussion of network devices that are used to build TCP/IP networks.

Link Layer Protocols

The link layer (sometimes referred to as the network access layer) is the lowest logical layer in the TCP/IP protocol suite. Several protocols have been implemented as link layer protocols, including

- **ARP (Address Resolution Protocol)** This protocol is used when a station on a network needs to find another station's MAC when it knows its Internet layer (IP) address. Basically, a station sends a broadcast on a local network, asking, in effect, "What station on this network has IP address xx.xx.xx.xx?" If any station on the network does have this IP address, it responds to the sender. When the sending station receives the reply, the receiving station's MAC address is contained in the reply, and the sending station can now send messages to the destination station since it knows its MAC address. Another type of ARP message is known as a *gratuitous ARP* message that informs other stations on the network of the station's IP and MAC addresses.

- **RARP (Reverse Address Resolution Protocol)**   This protocol is used by a station that needs to know its own Internet layer (IP) address. A station sends a broadcast on a local network, asking, "This is my MAC address (xx.xx.xx. xx.xx.xx). What is my IP address supposed to be?" If a station configured to respond to RARP requests exists on the network, it will respond to the querying station with an assigned IP address. RARP has been superseded by BOOTP (Bootstrap Protocol) and later by DHCP (Dynamic Host Configuration Protocol).

- **OSPF (Open Shortest Path First)**   This is a routing protocol that is implemented in the TCP/IP link layer. The purpose and function of routing protocols are discussed in detail later in this section.

- **L2TP (Layer 2 Tunneling Protocol)**   This is a tunneling protocol that is implemented in the link layer. The purpose and function of tunneling protocols are discussed later in this section.

- **PPP (Point-to-Point Protocol)**   This packet-oriented protocol is used mainly over point-to-point physical connections such as RS-232 or HSSI (High-Speed Serial Interface) between computers.

- **Media Access Control (MAC)**   This framing protocol is the underlying protocol used by various media such as Ethernet, DSL, MPLS, and ISDN.

Internet Layer Protocols

Internet layer protocols are the fundamental building blocks of TCP/IP. The Internet layer is the bottom-most layer where a frame or packet is uniquely TCP/IP.

Protocols in the TCP/IP Internet layer include

- IP
- ICMP
- IGMP
- IPsec

IP Protocol   IP is the principal protocol used by TCP/IP at the Internet layer. The main transport layer protocols (discussed in the next section), TCP and UDP, are built on the IP protocol.

The purpose of the IP protocol is to transport messages over internetworked networks. IP is the workhorse of the TCP/IP protocol suite: most communications used on the Internet are built on it.

Characteristics of the IP protocol include

- **IP addressing**   At the IP layer, nodes on networks have unique addresses. IP addressing is discussed in detail later in this section.

- **Best-effort delivery**   IP does not guarantee that a packet will reach its intended destination.

- **Connectionless** Each packet is individual and not related to any other packet.
- **Out-of-order packet delivery** No assurances for order of delivery are addressed by IP. Packets may arrive out of order at their destination.

Higher-layer protocols such as TCP address reliability, connections, and order of delivery.

ICMP Protocol ICMP is used by systems for diagnostic purposes. Primarily, ICMP messages are automatically issued whenever there are problems with IP communications between two stations. For example, one station attempts to send a message to another station, and a router on the network knows that there is no existing route to the destination station. In this case, the router will send an ICMP Type 3, Code 1 "No route to host" diagnostic packet back to the sending station to inform it that the destination station is not reachable.

ICMP message types are shown in Table 5-6.

ICMP Message Type	Definition
0	Echo reply
1	(reserved)
2	(reserved)
3	Destination unreachable (contains 14 subcodes that describe the reason in detail)
4	Source quench
5	Redirect message (with 4 subcodes)
6	Alternate host address
7	(reserved)
8	Echo request
9	Router advertisement
10	Router solicitation
11	Time exceeded (with 2 reason subcodes)
12	Parameter problem: bad IP header (with 3 reason subcodes)
13	Timestamp
14	Timestamp reply
15	Information request
16	Information reply
17	Address mask request
18	Address mask reply
19–29	(reserved)
30	Traceroute
31–255	(seldom used or reserved for future use)

Table 5-6 ICMP Message Types

The well-known "ping" command uses the ICMP 8 Echo Request packet type. If the target station is reachable, it will respond with ICMP 1 Echo Reply packets. The ping command is used to determine whether a particular system is reachable from another system over a TCP/IP network.

IGMP Protocol   IGMP is used to manage a type of communications called *multicast.*

IPsec Protocol   Internet Protocol Security, usually known as IPsec, is a suite of protocols that is used to secure IP-based communication. The security that IPsec provides is in the form of authentication and encryption.

IPsec authentication is used to confirm the identity of a station on a network. This is used to prevent a rogue system from easily masquerading as another, real system. Authentication is achieved through the establishment of a security association (SA) between two nodes, which permits the transmission of data from the originating node to the destination node. If the two nodes need to send messages in both directions, two SAs need to be established. The Internet Key Exchange (IKE) protocol is used to set up associations.

IPsec has two primary modes of operation:

- **Transport mode**   Here, only the payload of an incoming packet is authenticated or encrypted. The original IP header is left intact. The original headers are protected with hashes; if the headers are altered, the hashes will fail and an error will occur.

- **Tunnel mode**   Here, each entire incoming packet is encapsulated within an IPsec packet. The entire incoming packet can be encrypted, which protects the packet against eavesdropping. This mode is often used for protecting network traffic that traverses the Internet, thereby creating a VPN between two nodes, between two networks, or between a remote node and a network. IPsec tunnel mode is shown in Figure 5-21.

Internet Layer Node Addressing

In order to specify the source and destination of messages, TCP/IP utilizes a numeric address scheme. In the TCP/IP protocol, a station's address is known as an "IP address." On a given network, no two stations will have the same IP address; this uniqueness permits any station to communicate directly with any other station.

The TCP/IP IP address scheme also includes something called a *subnet mask*, which permits a station to determine whether any particular IP address resides on the same subnetwork. Furthermore, an IP address plan usually includes a *default gateway*, a station on the network that is able to forward messages to stations on other networks.

Figure 5-21   IPsec tunnel mode protects all traffic between two remote networks.

IP Addresses and Subnets   The notation of an IP address is four sets of integers, separated by periods ("."). The value of each integer may range from 0 through 255; hence, each integer is an eight-bit value. A typical IP address is 141.204.13.240. The entire IP address is 32 bits in length.

Each station on a network is assigned a unique IP address. Uniqueness permits any station to send messages to any other station; the station only needs to know the IP address of a destination station.

A larger organization may have hundreds, thousands, or even tens of thousands of stations on many networks. Typically, a network is the interconnection of computers within a single building, or even one part of a building. Within a larger building or collection of buildings, the individual networks are called subnetworks, or subnets. Those subnets are joined together by network devices such as routers or switches; they function as gateways between networks.

Subnet Mask   A subnet mask is a numeric value that determines which portion of an IP address is used to identify the network and which portion is used to identify a station on the network.

For example, an organization has the network 141.204.13. On this network the organization can have up to 256 stations, numbered 0 through 255. Example station IP addresses on the network are 141.204.13.5, 141.204.13.15, and 141.204.13.200.

A subnet mask actually works at the bit level. A "1" signifies that a bit in the same position in an IP address is the *network identifier*, while a "0" signifies that a bit in the same position is part of the station's address. In the previous example, where the first three numbers in the IP address signify the network, the subnet mask would be 255.255.255.0. This is illustrated in Figure 5-22.

Default Gateway   Networks are usually interconnected so that a station on one network is able to communicate with a station on any other connected network (subject to any security restrictions). When a station wishes to send a packet to another station, the sending station will examine its own network ID (by comparing its IP address to the subnet mask) and compare that to the IP address of the destination. If the destination station is on the same network, the station may simply send the packet directly to the destination station.

Station IP Address	141.204.13.15	10001101.11001100.00001101.00001111
Subnet Mask	255.255.255.0	11111111.11111111.11111111.00000000
Network Portion	141.204.13.0	10001101.11001100.00001101.00000000
Station Portion	0.0.0.15	00000000.00000000.00000000.00001111

Network Address   Station Address

Figure 5-22   A subnet mask denotes which part of an IP address signifies a network and which part signifies a station on the network.

If, however, the destination station is on a different network, the sending station cannot send the packet to it directly. Instead, the sending station will send the packet to a node called the *default gateway*—usually a router that has knowledge of neighboring and distant networks and is capable of forwarding packets to their destination. Any network that is interconnected to other networks will have a default gateway, which is where all packets for "other" networks are sent. The default gateway will forward the packet closer to its ultimate destination.

For example, a station at IP address 141.204.13.15 wishes to send a packet to a station at IP address 141.204.21.110. The sending station's subnet mask is 255.255.255.0, which means it is on network 141.204.13. This is a different network from 141.204.21.110, so the sending station will send the packet instead to the default gateway at 141.204.13.1, a router that can forward the packet to 141.204.21.110.

When the packet reaches a router that is connected to the 141.204.21 network, that router can send the packet directly to the destination station, which is on the same network as the router.

Classful Networks   The original plan for subnets and subnet masks allowed for the network/node address boundary to align with the decimals in IP addresses. This was expressed in several classes of networks, shown in Table 5-7.

The matter of the shortage of usable IP addresses in the global Internet is related to classful networks. This is discussed later in this chapter in the section, "The Global Internet."

Classless Networks   It became clear that the rigidity of Class A, Class B, and Class C networks as the only ways to create subnets was wasteful. For instance, the smallest subnet available was a Class C network with its 256 available addresses. If a given subnet had only one station on it, the other 255 addresses were wasted and unused. This situation gave rise to classless networks, where subnet masks could divide networks at any arbitrary boundary.

Classless networks don't have names like the classful networks' Class A, Class B, and Class C. Instead, they just have subnet masks that help to serve the purpose of preserving IP addresses and allocating them more efficiently.

Table 5-8 shows some example subnet masks that can be used to allocate IP addresses to smaller networks.

A more rapid way of expressing an IP address with its accompanying subnet mask has been developed, where the number of bits in the subnet mask follows the IP address after a slash. For example, the IP address 141.204.13.15/26 means the subnet mask is the first 26 bits (in binary) of the IP address, or 255.255.255.192. This is easier than expressing the IP address and subnet mask separately.

Class	Subnet Mask	Number of Stations Per Network
A	255.0.0.0	16,777,216
B	255.255.0.0	65,536
C	255.255.255.0	256

Table 5-7   Classes of Networks

Subnet Mask (Decimal)	Subnet Mask (Binary)	CIDR Notation	Number of Nodes
255.255.255.254	11111111.11111111.11111111.11111110	/31	2
255.255.255.252	11111111.11111111.11111111.11111100	/30	4
255.255.255.248	11111111.11111111.11111111.11111000	/29	8
255.255.255.240	11111111.11111111.11111111.11110000	/28	16
255.255.255.224	11111111.11111111.11111111.11100000	/27	32
255.255.255.192	11111111.11111111.11111111.11000000	/26	64
255.255.255.128	11111111.11111111.11111111.10000000	/25	128
255.255.255.0	11111111.11111111.11111111.00000000	/24	256

Table 5-8 Classless Network Subnet Masks

Virtual Networks (VLANs) In the preceding discussions of IP addresses and subnets, the classic design of TCP/IP LANs specifies that LANs are physically separate. Each LAN will have its own physical cabling and devices.

Virtual networks, known as VLANs, are logically separate networks that occupy the same physical network. VLANs are made possible through advanced configuration of network devices, including switches and routers.

The primary advantage of VLAN technology is the cost savings realized through the use of fewer network cables and devices. Another advantage of VLAN technology is the ability to device a single network into logically separate networks, thereby creating smaller broadcast domains and reducing the potential for information leakage.

The main disadvantage is that, while they are logically separate, VLANs occupy a single physical medium: traffic on one VLAN has the potential to disrupt traffic on other VLANs, since they must share the physical network.

Special IP Addresses Other IP addresses are used in the IP protocol that have not been discussed thus far. These other addresses and their functions are

- **Loopback** The IP address 127.0.0.1 (or any other address in the entire 127 address block) is a special "loopback" address that is analogous to earlier technologies where a physical loopback plug would be connected to a network connector in order to confirm communications within a system or device. The 127.0.0.1 loopback address serves the same function. If a system attempts to connect to a system at IP address 127.0.0.1, it is essentially communicating with itself. A system that is able to connect to itself through its loopback address is testing its IP protocol drivers within the operating system; during network troubleshooting, it is common to issue a "ping 127.0.0.1" or similar command to verify whether the computer's IP software is functioning correctly.

- **Broadcast** The highest numeric IP address in an IP subnet is called its broadcast address. When a packet is sent to a network's broadcast address, all active stations on the network will logically receive and potentially act on the incoming message. For example, in the network 141.204.13/24, the broadcast address is 141.204.13.255. Any packet sent to that address would be sent to all stations. A ping command sent to a network's broadcast address will cause all stations to respond with an echo reply.

Transport Layer Protocols

The two principal protocols in TCP/IP's transport layer are TCP and UDP. The majority of Internet communications are based on these. This section explores TCP and UDP in detail.

TCP and UDP support the two primary types of Internet-based communication: that which requires highly reliable and ordered message delivery, and that which has a high tolerance for lost messages. TCP and UDP are uniquely designed for these two scenarios.

TCP TCP is a highly reliable messaging protocol that is used in situations where high-integrity messaging is required. The main characteristics of TCP-based network traffic are

- **Unique connections** The TCP protocol utilizes what is known as a *connection* between two stations. TCP supports several concurrent connections between any two stations.

- **Guaranteed message integrity** The TCP protocol performs checks on the sent and received packets to ensure that the packet arrived at its destination fully intact. If the checksum indicates that the packet was altered in transit, the TCP protocol will handle retransmission.

- **Guaranteed delivery** The TCP protocol guarantees message delivery. This means that if an application sends a message to another application over an established TCP connection and the function sending the message receives a "success" code from the operating system, then the message was successfully delivered to the destination system. This is contrasted with the message delivery used by UDP that is discussed later in this section.

- **Guaranteed delivery sequence** Packets sent using the TCP protocol include sequence numbers so that the destination system can assemble arriving packets into the correct order. This guarantees that an application receiving packets from a sending application over TCP can be confident that packets are arriving in the same order in which they were sent.

UDP UDP is a lightweight messaging protocol used in situations where speed and low overhead are more important than guaranteed delivery and delivery sequence.

Unlike the connection-oriented TCP protocol, UDP is "connectionless." This means that UDP does not need to set up a connection between sending and receiving systems before messages can be sent; instead, the sending system just sends its messages to the destination system. Like TCP, messages can be sent to a specific port number on a destination system.

UDP does nothing to assure order of delivery. Hence, it is entirely possible that packets may arrive at the destination system out of order. In practice, this is a rarity, but the point is that UDP does not make any effort to reassemble packets into their original order upon arrival.

Furthermore, not only does UDP not guarantee the sequence of delivery, but it also does not even guarantee that the destination system will receive a packet. In UDP, when an application sends a message to a target system, the "success" error code returned by the operating system only means that the packet was sent. The sending system receives no confirmation that the packet was received by the destination system.

Application Layer Protocols

Scores of protocols have been developed for the TCP/IP application layer. Several are discussed in this section; they are grouped by the type of service that they provide.

File Transfer Protocols

- **FTP (File Transfer Protocol)**   An early and still widely used protocol for batch transfer of files or entire directories from one system to another. FTP is supported by most modern operating systems, including Unix and Windows. One drawback of FTP is that the login credentials (and all data) are transmitted unencrypted, which means that anyone eavesdropping on network communications can easily intercept them and use them later.

- **FTPS (File Transfer Protocol Secure, or FTP-SSL)**   This is an extension to the FTP protocol where authentication and file transfer are encrypted using SSL or TLS.

- **SFTP (SSH File Transfer Protocol)**   This is an extension to the FTP protocol where authentication and file transfer are encrypted using SSH.

- **SCP (Secure Copy)**   This is a file transfer protocol that is similar to rcp (remote copy) but which is protected using SSH.

- **rcp (remote copy)**   This is an early Unix-based file transfer protocol that is used to copy files or directories from system to system. The main drawback with rcp is the lack of encryption of credentials or transferred data.

Messaging Protocols

- **SMTP (Simple Mail Transfer Protocol)**   This is the protocol used to transport virtually all e-mail over the Internet. SMTP is used to route e-mail messages from their source over the Internet to a destination e-mail server. It is an early protocol that lacks authentication and encryption. It is partly for this reason that people should consider their e-mail to be nonprivate.

- **POP (Post Office Protocol)**   This is a protocol used by an end-user e-mail program to retrieve messages from an e-mail server. POP is not particularly secure because user credentials and messages are transported without encryption.

- **IMAP (Internet Message Access Protocol)**   Like POP, this is a protocol used by an end-user program to retrieve e-mail messages from an e-mail server.

- **NNTP (Network News Transport Protocol)**   This is the protocol used to transport Usenet news throughout the Internet, and from news servers to end users using news-reading programs. Usenet news has been largely deprecated by web-based applications.

File and Directory Sharing Protocols

- **NFS (Network File System)**   This protocol was developed in order to make a disk-based resource on another computer appear as a logical volume on a local computer. The NFS protocol transmitted the disk requests and replies over the network.

- **RPC (Remote Procedure Call)**   This protocol is used to permit a running process to make a procedure call to a process running on another computer. RPC supports a variety of functions that permit various types of client-server computing.

Session Protocols

- **TELNET**   This is an early protocol that is used to establish a command-line session on a remote computer. TELNET does not encrypt user credentials as they are transmitted over the network.

- **rlogin**   This is an early Unix-based protocol used to establish a command-line session on a remote system. Like TELNET, rlogin does not encrypt authentication or session contents.

- **SSH (secure shell)**   This protocol provides a secure channel between two computers whereby all communications between them are encrypted. SSH can also be used as a tunnel to encapsulate and thereby protect other protocols.

- **HTTP (Hypertext Transfer Protocol)**   This protocol is used to transmit webpage contents from web servers to users who are using web browsers.

- **HTTPS (Hypertext Transfer Protocol Secure)**   This is similar to HTTP in its use for transporting data between web servers and browsers. HTTPS is not a separate protocol, but instead is the instance where HTTP is encrypted with SSL or TLS.

- **RDP (Remote Desktop Protocol)**   This proprietary protocol from Microsoft is used to establish a graphical console interface to another computer.

Management Protocols

- **SNMP (Simple Network Management Protocol)**   This protocol is used by network devices and systems to transmit management messages indicating a need for administrative attention. SNMP is used to monitor networks and their components; SNMP messages are generated when events warrant attention by network engineers or system engineers. In larger organizations, SNMP messages are collected by a network management system that displays the network topology and devices that require attention.

- **NTP (Network Time Protocol)** This protocol is used to synchronize the time-of-day clocks on systems with time-reference standards. The use of NTP is vital because the time clocks in computers often drift (run too fast or too slow), and it is important for all computers' time clocks in an organization to be precisely the same so that complex events can be more easily correlated.

Directory Services Protocols

- **DNS (domain name service)** This is a vital Internet-based service that is used to translate domain names (such as www.isecbooks.com) into IP addresses. A call to a DNS server is a prerequisite for system-to-system communications where one system wishes to establish a communications session with another system and where it only knows the domain name for the target system.

- **LDAP (Lightweight Directory Access Protocol)** This protocol is used as a directory service for people and computing resources. LDAP is frequently used as an enterprise authentication and computing resource service. Microsoft Active Directory is an adaptation of LDAP.

- **X.500** This protocol is a functional predecessor to LDAP that provides directory services.

TCP/IP Network Devices

Network devices are required to facilitate the transmission of packets among TCP/IP networks. These devices include

- **Router** This device is used to connect two or more separate TCP/IP networks to each other. A router typically has two or more network interface connectors, each of which is connected to a separate network. A router that is used to connect LANs is typically equipped with Ethernet interfaces, while a router used to connect LANs with WANs will have one or more Ethernet connectors and one or more connectors for WAN protocols such as T-1 or MPLS. A router may also have an access control list (ACL) that the router uses to determine whether packets passing through it should be permitted to proceed to their destination.

- **Firewall** This device is used to control which network packets are permitted to cross network boundaries. Typically, a firewall will block or permit packets to pass based on their source IP address, destination IP address, and protocol. Firewalls are typically used at an organization's network boundary to protect it from unwanted network traffic from the Internet, but still permitting traffic to the organization's e-mail servers, for instance.

- **Application firewall** This device is used to control packets being sent to an application server, blocking those that contain unwanted or malicious content. An application firewall can help to protect a web server from attacks such as SQL injection or buffer overflow.

- **Proxy server** This device is typically used to control end-user access to websites on the Internet. A proxy server typically controls access according to policy.

- **Layer 3 switch** This device routes packets between different TCP/IP networks. Functionally, this is the same as a router; a router performs network routing using software running on a microprocessor, while a layer 3 switch performs this routing using a dedicated application-specific integrated circuit (ASIC), giving it much better performance than a router.

- **Layer 4 switch** This device is used to route packets to destinations based on TCP and UDP port numbers.

- **Layer 4-7 switch** Also known as a content switch, web switch, or application switch, this device is used to route packets to destinations based on their internal content. Layer 4-7 switches can be used to intelligently route incoming network traffic to various servers based on policy, performance, or availability.

Ironically, the names of layer 3, layer 4, and layer 4-7 switches are based on their OSI network model layers even though these are TCP network devices.

Other network devices such as hubs, switches, and gateways are discussed in the section, "Ethernet Devices," earlier in this chapter.

The Global Internet

The TCP/IP networks owned by businesses, government, military, and educational institutions are interconnected; collectively this is known as the global Internet—or just the Internet. It is in the context of the global Internet that TCP/IP topics such as node addressing, routing, domain naming, and other matters are most relevant.

IP Addressing

The allocation of routable IP addresses is coordinated through a central governing body known as the Internet Assigned Numbers Authority (IANA). This coordination is necessary so that duplicate addresses are not allocated, which would cause confusion and unreachable systems.

The original IP address allocation scheme appears in Table 5-9.

Addresses	Name	Total Number of Networks Available	Addresses per Network
1.0.0.0–126.255.255.255	Class A networks	126	16,777,124
128.0.0.0–191.255.255.255	Class B networks	16,384	65,532
192.0.0.0–223.255.255.255	Class C networks	2,097,152	254

Table 5-9 Internet IP Address Allocation

When the TCP/IP protocol was established, the entire IP address space (that is, the entire range of possible addresses from 1.1.1.1 through 255.255.255.255) appeared to be far more than would ever be needed. However, it soon became apparent that the original IP address allocation scheme was woefully inadequate. This led to the establishment of ranges for private networks and rules for their use. Private address ranges are listed in Table 5-9.

> **NOTE** The number of available addresses does not take network IDs and broadcast addresses into account, which will make the number of actual addresses lower. This will vary, based upon how networks are subnetted.

The private addresses listed in Table 5-10 are not "routable." This means that no router on the Internet is permitted to forward a packet with any IP address within any of the private address ranges. These IP addresses are intended for use wholly within organizations to facilitate communication among internal systems. When any system with a private address needs to communicate with a system on the Internet, its communication is required to pass through a gateway that will translate the internal IP address to a public routable IP address. The NAT (Network Address Translation) protocol is often used for this purpose.

Domain Name System

The Internet utilizes a centrally coordinated domain name registration system. Several independent *domain registrars* are licensed to issue new domain names to individuals and corporations in exchange for modest fees. These domain registrars often also provide DNS services on behalf of each domain name's owner.

New and changed domain names are periodically uploaded to the Internet's "root" DNS servers, enabling users to access services by referring to domain names such as www.newsite.com.

Network Routing

Routers used by Internet service providers (ISPs) receive and forward IP traffic to and from any of the millions of systems that are connected to the Internet. These big routers exchange information on the whereabouts of all publicly reachable networks in large "routing tables" that contain rules about the topology of the Internet and the addresses and locations of networks. Internet routers exchange this information through the use

Table 5-10 Private Address Ranges	Address Range	Available Addresses
	10.0.0.0–10.255.255.255	16,777,214
	172.16.0.0–172.31.255.255	1,048,576
	192.168.0.0–192.168.255.255	131,072

of routing protocols, which are "out of band" messages that contain updates to the topology and IP addressing of the Internet. Some of these protocols are

- BGP (Border Gateway Protocol)
- OSPF (Open Shortest Path First)
- IGRP (Interior Gateway Routing Protocol)
- EIGRP (Enhanced Interior Gateway Routing Protocol)
- IS-IS (Intermediate System to Intermediate System)
- RIP (Routing Information Protocol; this is one of the earliest protocols and no longer used for Internet routing)

Organizations with several internal networks also use one or more of these routing protocols so that their routers can keep track of the changing topology and addressing of its network.

Global Internet Applications

Applications are what make the Internet popular. From electronic banking to e-commerce, entertainment, news, television, and movies, applications on the Internet have made it possible for people anywhere to view or receive virtually any kind of information and content.

The World Wide Web   The World Wide Web is the term that encompasses all of the world's web servers, which are accessible from workstations of many types that use web browser programs. Requests to web servers, and content returned to browsers, are issued using HTTP and HTTPS. Content sent to browsers consists primarily of text written in HTML, as well as rich text, including images and dynamic content.

The World Wide Web rapidly gained in popularity because information and applications could be accessed from anywhere without any special software. Readily available tools simplified the publication of many types of data to the Web.

The most critical service that supports the World Wide Web is DNS. This service translates server domain names into IP addresses. For example, if a user wants to visit www.widgets.com, the operating system running the user's browser will make a request to a local DNS server for the IP address corresponding to www.widgets.com. After the DNS server responds with the server's IP address, the user's browser can issue a request to the server (at www.widgets.com) and then receive content from the server.

Web servers can act as application servers. Authenticated users can receive menus, data entry screens and forms, query results, and reports, all written in HTML, all with only web browser software.

E-mail   Electronic mail was one of the Internet's first applications. E-mail existed before the Internet, but it was implemented on the Internet as a way to send messages not only *within* organizations, but also *between* them. The SMTP and POP protocols were developed and adopted early on, and are still widely used today. SMTP remains the backbone of Internet e-mail transport.

Instant Messaging   It makes good sense that e-mail, while far more rapid than postal-delivered letters, can still be slow if a person's inbox is overflowing. Instant messaging (IM), originally developed on DEC PDP-11 computers in the 1970s and on Unix in the early 1980s, was adapted to the Internet in the early 1990s. Instant messaging, like all other Internet applications, is based on the TCP/IP protocol suite and enables people all over the world to communicate in real-time via text, voice, and video.

Network Tunneling   Tunneling refers to a number of protocols that permit communications between two endpoints to be encapsulated in a logical "tunnel." Often, a tunnel is used to protect communications containing sensitive data that is transported over public networks such as the Internet. Packets in a tunnel can be encrypted, which hides the true endpoint IP addresses as well as the message contents from any intermediate system that may eavesdrop on those communications. Tunnels are frequently called virtual private networks (VPNs), both because of the security (through encryption and authentication) as well as the abstraction that a VPN provides by hiding the details of the path between systems.

VPNs are frequently used for end-user remote access into an organization's network. When an end user wishes to connect to an organization's internal network, the network will establish a session with a VPN server and provide authentication credentials. An encrypted tunnel will then be established that gives the end user the appearance of being connected to the internal network.

Network Management

Network management is the function of ensuring that a data network continues to support business objectives. The activities that take place include monitoring network devices, identifying problems, and applying remedies as needed to restore network operations.

The purpose of network management is the continued reliable operation of an organization's data network. A properly functioning data network, in turn, supports business applications that support critical business processes.

Network Management Tools

Network management requires tools that are used to monitor, troubleshoot, and maintain data networks. This permits an IT organization to ensure the continuous operation of its data network so that it has sufficient capacity and capability to support applications and services vital to the organization's ongoing business operations.

The tools that are used to fulfill this mission include

- **Network management systems**   These are software applications that collect network management messages that are sent from network devices and systems. These messages alert the management system that certain conditions exist on the device, some of which may require intervention. Some network management systems also contain the means for network administrators and engineers to diagnose and correct conditions that require attention.

- **Network management reports**   Network management systems generally have the ability to generate reports showing key metrics such as network availability, utilization, response time, and downtime. Reports from helpdesk systems or incident management systems also help to better understand the health of an organization's networks.

- **Network management agents**   Agents are small software modules that reside on managed network devices and other systems. These agents monitor operations on the device or system and transmit messages to a centralized network management system when needed.

- **Incident management systems**   These systems are general-purpose ticketing engines that capture and track individual incidents and report on an organization's timely response to them. Often, network management systems and incident management systems can be integrated together so that conditions requiring attention in the network can automatically create a ticket that will be used to track the course of the incident until it is closed.

- **Protocol analyzers**   A protocol analyzer is a device that is connected to a network in order to view network communications at a detailed level. A protocol analyzer can capture selected types of network traffic (for instance, communications to or from a specific system, or communications of a specific type) and save it for later analysis.

- **Sniffers**   A sniffer is a software program that can be installed on a network-attached system to capture network traffic being transmitted to and/or from the system. This is similar to a protocol analyzer, but is not a separate device.

Networked Applications

Other than simple end-user tools on a business workstation, business applications are rarely installed and used within the context of an individual computer. Instead, many applications are centrally installed and used by people in many locations. Data networks facilitate the communications between central servers and business workstations. The two types of applications discussed in this section are client-server and web-based.

Client-Server

Client-server applications are a prior-generation technology used to build high-performance business applications. They consist of one or more central application servers, database servers, and business workstations. The central application servers contain some business logic, primarily the instructions to receive and respond to requests sent from workstations. The remainder of the business logic will reside on each business workstation; primarily this is the logic used to display forms and reports for the user.

When a user is using a client-server application, he or she is typically selecting functions to input, view, or change information. When inputting information, application logic on the business workstation will request, analyze, and accept the information and then transmit it to the central application server for further processing and storage.

When viewing information, a user will typically select a viewing function with, perhaps, criteria specifying which information they wish to view. Business logic on the workstation will validate this information and then send a request to the central application server, which, in turn, will respond with information that is then sent back to the workstation and transformed for easy viewing.

The promise of client-server applications was improved performance by removing all application display logic from the central computer and placing that logic on each individual workstation. This scheme succeeded in principle but failed in practice for two principal reasons:

- **Network performance** Client-server applications often overburdened the organization's data network, and application performance failed when many people were using it at once. A typical example is a database query issued by a workstation that results in thousands of records being returned to the workstation over the network.

- **Workstation software updates** Keeping the central application software and the software modules on each workstation in sync proved to be problematic. Often, updates required that all workstations be upgraded at the same time. Invariably, some workstations are down (powered down by end users or taken home if they are laptop computers) and unavailable for updates.

Organizations that did implement full-scale client-server applications were often dissatisfied with the results. And at nearly the same time, the World Wide Web was invented and soon proved to be a promising alternative.

Web-Based Applications

With client-server applications declining in favor, web-based applications were the only way forward. The primary characteristics of web-based applications that made them highly favorable included

- **Centralized business logic** All business logic resides on one or more centralized servers. There are no longer issues related to pushing software updates to workstations since they run web browsers that rarely require updating.

- **Lightweight and universal display logic** Display logic, such as forms, lists, and other application controls, is easily written in HTML, a simple markup language that displays well on workstations without any application logic on the workstation.

- **Low network requirements** Unlike client-server applications that would often send large amounts of data from the centralized server to the workstation, web applications send only display data to workstations.

- **Workstations requiring few, if any, updates** Workstations require only browser software.

- **Fewer compatibility issues** Instead of requiring a narrow choice of workstations, web-based applications can run on nearly every kind of workstation, including Unix, Windows, Mac OS, or Linux.

Middleware

Middleware is a component used in some client-server or web-based application environments to control the processing of communications or transactions. Middleware manages the interaction between major components in larger application environments.

Some of the common types of middleware include

- **Transaction processing (TP) monitors**   A TP monitor manages transactions between application servers and database servers in order to ensure the integrity of business transactions and a collection of database servers.

- **RPC gateways**   These systems facilitate communications through the suite of RPC protocols between various components of an application environment.

- **Object request broker (ORB) gateways**   An ORB gateway facilitates the execution of transactions across complex, multiserver application environments that use CORBA (Common Object Request Broker Architecture) or Microsoft COM/DCOM technologies.

- **Message servers**   These systems store and forward transactions between systems and ensure the eventual delivery of transactions to the right systems.

Middleware is typically used in a large, complex application environment, particularly when there are multiple technologies (operating systems, databases, and languages) in use. Middleware can be thought of as "glue" that helps the application environment operate more smoothly.

Disaster Recovery Planning

Disaster recovery planning (DRP) is undertaken to reduce risks related to the onset of disasters and other events.

Disaster recovery planning is closely related to business continuity planning (BCP). The groundwork for DRP begins in BCP activities such as the business impact analysis, criticality analysis, establishment of recovery objectives, and testing. The outputs from these activities are the key inputs to DRP:

- The business impact analysis and criticality analysis help to prioritize which business processes (and, therefore, which IT systems) are the most important.

- Key recovery targets specify how quickly specific IT applications are to be recovered. This guides DRP personnel as they develop new IT architectures that make IT systems compliant with those objectives.

- Testing of DRP plans can be performed in coordination with tests of BCP plans to more accurately simulate real disasters and disaster response.

Business continuity planning is discussed in detail in Chapter 2.

Disaster Response Teams' Roles and Responsibilities

Disaster recovery plans need to specify the teams that are required for disaster response, as well as each team's roles and responsibilities. Table 5-11 describes several teams and their roles.

Team	Responsibilities
Emergency Management	Coordinates activities of all other response teams.
First Responders	These are usually outside personnel such as police, fire, and rescue who help to extinguish fires, evacuate personnel, and provide emergency medical aid.
Communications	Coordinates communication among teams, as well as between teams and outside entities.
Damage Assessment	Examines equipment, supplies, furnishing, and assets to determine what can be used immediately in support of critical processes and what will need to be handed off to salvage teams.
Salvage	Examines equipment, supplies, furnishings, and other assets to determine what can be salvaged for immediate or long-term reuse.
Network Engineering	Establishes and maintains electronic (voice and data) communications in support of critical services during a disaster.
Systems Engineering	Establishes and maintains systems as needed to support critical applications and services.
Database Engineering	Establishes and maintains database management systems as needed to support critical applications. Performs data recovery, using local or remotely stored media as needed.
Application Support	Establishes and maintains critical applications in support of critical business processes.
Application Development	Makes changes to critical applications as needed during the recovery effort.
End-User Computing	Establishes and maintains end-user computing facilities (desktop computers, laptop computers, mobile devices, etc.) as needed in support of critical applications and services.
Systems Operations	Performs routine and nonroutine tasks such as backups to keep critical applications running.
Transportation	Coordinates transportation of personnel to recovery sites.
Relocation	Acquires housing and other resources needed by personnel who are working at remote operations centers.
Security	Coordinates physical and logical security activities to ensure the continuous protection of staff, assets, and information.
Finance	Facilitates the availability of financial resources as needed to commence and continue emergency response operations.

Table 5-11 Disaster Response Teams' Roles and Responsibilities

NOTE Some of the roles in Table 5-11 may overlap with responsibilities defined in the organization's business continuity plan. DR and BC planners will need to work together to ensure that the organization's overall response to disaster is appropriate and does not overlook vital functions.

Because of variations in organizations' disaster response plans, some of these teams will not be needed in some organizations.

Recovery Objectives

During the business impact analysis and criticality analysis phases of a BCDR project, the speed with which each business activity (with its underlying IT systems) needs to be restored after a disaster is determined.

Recovery Time Objective (RTO)

Recovery time objective (RTO) is the period from the onset of an outage until the resumption of service. RTO is usually measured in hours or days. Each process and system in the BIA should have an RTO value.

RTO does not mean that the system (or process) has been recovered to 100 percent of its former capacity. Far from it—in an emergency situation, management may determine that a DR (disaster recovery) server in another city with, say, 60 percent of the capacity of the original server is adequate. That said, an organization could establish two RTO targets, one for partial capacity and one for full capacity.

NOTE For a given organization, it's probably best to use one unit of measure for all systems. That will help to avoid any errors that would occur during a rank-ordering of systems so that two days does not appear to be a shorter period than four hours.

Further, a system that has been recovered in a disaster situation might not have 100 percent of its functionality. For instance, an application that lets users view transactions that are more than two years old may, in a recovery situation, only contain 30 days' worth of data. Again, such a decision is usually the result of a careful analysis of the cost of recovering different features and functions in an application environment. In a larger, complex environment, some features might be considered critical, while others are less so.

CAUTION Senior management should be involved in any discussion related to recovery system specifications in terms of capacity or functionality.

Recovery Point Objective (RPO)

A recovery point objective (RPO) is the period for which recent data will be irretrievably lost in a disaster. Like RTO, RPO is usually measured in hours or days. However, for critical transaction systems, RPO could even be measured in minutes.

RPO is usually expressed as a worst-case figure; for instance, the transaction processing system RPO will be two hours or less.

The value of a system's RPO is usually a direct result of the frequency of data backup or replication. For example, if an application server is backed up once per day, the RPO is going to be at least 24 hours (or one day, whichever way you like to express it). Maybe it will take three days to rebuild the server, but once data is restored from backup tape, no more than the last 24 hours of transactions are lost. In this case, the RTO is three days and the RPO is one day.

Publishing RTO and RPO Figures

If the storage system for an application takes a snapshot every hour, the RPO could be one hour, unless the storage system itself was damaged in a disaster. If the snapshot is replicated to another storage system four times per day, then the RPO might be better expressed as six to eight hours.

The last example brings up an interesting point. There might not be one golden RPO figure for a given system. Instead, the severity of a disrupting event or a disaster will dictate the time to get systems running again (RTO) with a certain amount of data loss (RPO). Here are some examples:

- A server's CPU or memory fails and is replaced and restarted in two hours. No data is lost. The RTO is two hours and the RPO is zero.

- The storage system supporting an application suffers a hardware failure that results in the loss of all data. Data is recovered from a snapshot on another server taken every six hours. The RPO is six hours in this case.

- The database in a transaction application is corrupted and must be recovered. Backups are taken twice per day. The RPO is 12 hours. However, it takes 10 hours to rebuild indexes on the database, so the RTO is closer to 22 to 24 hours, since the application cannot be returned to service until indexes are available.

 NOTE When publishing RTO and RPO figures to customers, it's best to publish the worst-case figures: "If our data center burns to the ground, our RTO is X hours and the RPO is Y hours." Saying it that way would be simpler than publishing a chart that shows RPO and RTO figures for various types of disasters.

Pricing RTO and RPO Capabilities

Generally speaking, the shorter the RTO or RPO for a given system, the more expensive it will be to achieve the target. Table 5-12 depicts a range of RTOs along with the technologies needed to achieve them and their relative cost.

The BCP project team needs to understand the relationship between the time required to recover an application and the cost required to recover the application within that time. A shorter recovery time is more expensive, and this relationship is not linear.

RTO/RPO	Technologies Needed	Cost
2 weeks	Backup tapes; buy a server when the original server has burned or floated away	$
I week	Backup tapes; replacement server on hand	$$
2 days	Backup tapes; application software installed on replacement server	$$
12 hours	Backup tapes or replication; application server installed and running on replacement server	$$$
I hour	Server cluster with auto or manual failover; near-real-time replication	$$$$
5 minutes	Load balancing or rapid failover server cluster; real-time replication	$$$$$

Table 5-12 The Lower the Recovery Time Objective (RTO), the Higher the Cost to Achieve It

This means that reducing RPO from three days to six hours may mean that the equipment and software investment might double, or it might increase eightfold. There are so many factors involved in the supporting infrastructure for a given application that the BCP project team has to just knuckle down and develop the cost for a few different RTO and RPO figures.

The business value of the application itself is the primary driver in determining the amount of investment that senior management is willing to make to reach any arbitrary RTO and RPO figures. This business value may be measured in local currency if the application supports revenue. However, the loss of an application during a disaster may harm the organization's reputation. Again, management will have to make a decision on how much it will be willing to invest in DR capabilities that bring RTO and RPO figures down to a certain level. Figure 5-23 illustrates these relationships.

Developing Recovery Strategies

When management has chosen specific RPO and RTO targets for a given system or process, the BCP project team can now roll up its sleeves and devise some ways to meet these targets. This section discusses the technologies and logistics associated with various recovery strategies. This will help the project team to decide which types of strategies are best suited for their organization.

Figure 5-23
Aim for the
sweet spot.

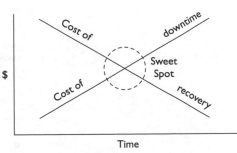

> **NOTE** Developing recovery strategies to meet specific recovery targets is an iterative process. The project team will develop a strategy to reach specific targets for a specific cost; senior management could well decide that the cost is too high and that they are willing to increase RPO and/or RTO targets accordingly. Similarly, the project team could also discover that it is less costly to achieve specific RPO and RTO targets, and management could respond by lowering those targets. This is illustrated in Figure 5-24.

Site Recovery Options

In a worst-case disaster scenario, the site where information systems reside is partially or completely destroyed. In most cases, the organization cannot afford to wait for the damaged or destroyed facility to be restored, as this could take weeks or months. If an organization can take *that* long to recover an application, you'd have to wonder whether it is needed at all. The assumption has got to be that in a disaster scenario, critical applications will be recovered in another location. This other location is called a *recovery site*. There are two dimensions to the process of choosing a recovery site: the first is the speed at which the application will be recovered at the recovery site; the second is the location of the recovery site itself. Both are discussed here.

As you might expect, speed costs. If a system is to be recovered within a few minutes or hours, the costs will be much higher than if the system can be recovered in five days.

Figure 5-24
Recovery objective
development
flowchart

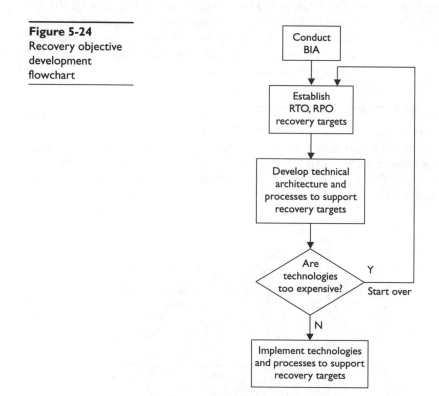

Various types of facilities are available for rapid or not-too-rapid recovery. These facilities are called hot sites, warm sites, and cold sites. As the names might suggest, hot sites permit rapid recovery, while cold sites provide a much slower recovery. The costs associated with these are somewhat proportional as well, as illustrated in Table 5-13.

The details about each type of site are discussed in the remainder of this section.

Hot Sites A *hot site* is an alternate processing center where backup systems are already running and in some state of near-readiness to assume production workload. The systems at a hot site most likely have application software and database management software already loaded and running, perhaps even at the same patch levels as the systems in the primary processing center.

A hot site is the best choice for systems whose RTO targets range from zero to several hours, perhaps as long as 24 hours.

A hot site may consist of leased rack space (or even a cage for larger installations) at a colocation center. If the organization has its own processing centers, then a hot site for a given system would consist of the required rack space to house the recovery systems. Recovery servers will be installed and running, with the same version and patch level for the operating system, database management system (if used), and application software.

Systems at a hot site require the same level of administration and maintenance as the primary systems. When patches or configuration changes are made to primary systems, they should be made to hot-site systems at the same time or very shortly afterward.

Because systems at a hot site need to be at or very near a state of readiness, a strategy needs to be developed regarding a method for keeping the data on hot standby systems current. This is discussed in detail in the later section, "Recovery and Resilience Technologies."

Systems at a hot site should have full network connectivity. A method for quickly directing network traffic toward the recovery servers needs to be worked out in advance so that a switchover can be accomplished. This is also discussed in the "Recovery and Resilience Technologies" section.

When setting up a hot site, the organization will need to send one or more technical staff members to the site to set up systems. But once the systems are operating, much or all of the system- and database-level administration can be performed remotely. However, in a disaster scenario, the organization may need to send the administrative staff to the site for day-to-day management of the systems. This means that workspace for these personnel needs to be identified so that they can perform their duties during the recovery operation.

Table 5-13 Relative Costs of Recovery Sites	Site Type	Speed to Recovery	Cost
	Hot	0–24 hours	$$$$
	Warm	24 hours–7 days	$$$
	Cold	Over 7 days	$$
	Mobile	2–7 days	$$$–$$$$

NOTE Hot-site planning needs to consider work (desk) space for on-site personnel. Some colocation centers provide limited work areas, but these areas are often shared and often have little privacy for phone discussions. Also, transportation, hotel, and dining accommodations need to be arranged, possibly in advance, if the hot site is in a different city from the primary site.

Warm Sites A *warm site* is an alternate processing center where recovery systems are present, but at a lower state of readiness than recovery systems at a hot site. For example, while the same version of the operating system may be running on the warm site system, it may be a few patch levels behind primary systems. The same could be said about the versions and patch levels of database management systems (if used) and application software: they may be present, but they're not as up-to-date.

A warm site is appropriate for an organization whose RTO figures range from roughly one to seven days. In a disaster scenario, recovery teams would travel to the warm site and work to get the recovery systems to a state of production readiness and to get systems up-to-date with patches and configuration changes to bring the systems into a state of complete readiness.

A warm site is also used when the organization is willing to take the time necessary to recover data from tape or other backup media. Depending upon the size of the database(s), this recovery task can take several hours to a few days.

The primary advantage of a warm site is that its costs are lower than for a hot site, particularly in the effort required to keep the recovery system up-to-date. The site may not require expensive data replication technology, but instead data can be recovered from backup media.

Cold Sites A *cold site* is an alternate processing center where the degree of readiness for recovery systems is low. At the very least, a cold site is nothing more than an empty rack, or just allocated space on a computer room floor. It's just an address in someone's data center or colocation site where computers can be set up and used at some future date.

Often, there is little or no equipment at a cold site. When a disaster or other highly disruptive event occurs in which the outage is expected to exceed 7 to 14 days, the organization will order computers from a manufacturer, or perhaps have computers shipped from some other business location, so that they can arrive at the cold site soon after the disaster event has begun. Then personnel would travel to the site and set up the computers, operating systems, databases, network equipment, and so on, and get applications running within several days.

The advantage of a cold site is its low cost. The main disadvantage is the cost, time, and effort required to bring it to operational readiness in a short period. But for some organizations, a cold site is exactly what is needed.

Table 5-14 shows a comparison of hot, warm, and cold recovery sites and a few characteristics of each.

	Cold	Warm	Hot
Computers	Ship to site	On site	Running
Application Software	To be installed	Installed	Running
Data	To be recovered	To be recovered	Continuously updated
Connectivity	To be established	Ready to go	Already connected
Support Staff	Travel to site	Travel to site	On site or remotely managed
Cost	Lowest	Moderate	Highest

Table 5-14   Detailed Comparison of Cold, Warm, and Hot Sites

Mobile Sites   A *mobile site* is a portable recovery center that can be delivered to almost any location in the world. A viable alternative to a fixed location recovery site, a mobile site can be transported by semi truck, and may even have its own generator, communications, and cooling capabilities.

APC and SunGuard have mobile sites installed in semi truck trailers. Oracle has mobile sites that can include a configurable selection of servers and workstations, all housed in shipping containers that can be shipped by truck, rail, ship, or air to any location in the world.

Reciprocal Sites   A *reciprocal recovery site* is a data center that is operated by another company. Two or more organizations with similar processing needs will draw up a legal contract that obligates one or more of the organizations to temporarily house another party's systems in the event of a disaster.

Often, a reciprocal agreement pledges not only floor space in a data center, but also the use of the reciprocal partner's computer system. This type of arrangement is less common, but is still used by organizations that use mainframe computers and other high-cost systems.

NOTE   With the wide use of Internet colocation centers, reciprocal sites have fallen out of favor. Still, they may be ideal for organizations with mainframe computers that are otherwise too expensive to deploy to a cold or warm site.

Geographic Site Selection   An important factor in the process of recovery site selection is the location of the recovery site. The distance between the main processing site and the recovery site is vital and may figure heavily into the viability and success of a recovery operation.

A recovery site should not be located in the same geographic region as the primary site. A recovery site in the same region may be involved in the same regional disaster as the primary site and may be unavailable for use or be suffering from the same problems present at the primary site.

By "geographic region" I mean a location that will likely experience the effects of the same regional disaster that affects the primary site. No arbitrarily chosen distance (such as 100 miles) guarantees sufficient separation. In some locales, 50 miles is plenty of distance; in other places, 300 miles is too close—it all depends on the nature of disasters that are likely to occur in these areas. Information on regional disasters should be available from local disaster preparedness authorities or from local disaster recovery experts.

Considerations When Using Third-Party Disaster Recovery Sites

Since most organizations cannot afford to implement their own secondary processing site, the only other option is to use a disaster recovery site that is owned by a third party. This could be a colocation center or a disaster services center. An organization considering such a site needs to ensure that its services contract addresses the following:

- **Disaster definition**   The definition of disaster needs to be broad enough to meet the organization's requirements.
- **Equipment configuration**   IT equipment must be configured as needed to support critical applications during a disaster.
- **Availability of equipment during a disaster**   IT equipment needs to actually be available during a disaster. The organization needs to know how the disaster service provider will allocate equipment if many of its customers suffer a disaster simultaneously.
- **Customer priorities**   The organization needs to know whether the disaster services provider has any customers (government or military, for example) whose priorities may exceed their own.
- **Data communications**   There must be sufficient bandwidth and capacity for the organization plus other customers who may be operating at the disaster provider's center at the same time.
- **Testing**   The organization needs to know what testing it is permitted to perform on the service provider's systems so that the ability to recover from a disaster can be tested in advance.
- **Right to audit**   The organization should have a "right to audit" clause in its contract so that it can verity the presence and effectiveness of all key controls in place at the recovery facility.
- **Security and environmental controls**   The organization needs to know what security and environmental controls are in place at the disaster recovery facility.

Acquiring Additional Hardware

Many organizations elect to acquire their own server, storage, and network hardware for disaster recovery purposes. The way that an organization will need to go about acquiring hardware will depend on its high-level recovery strategy:

- **Cold site** An organization will need to be able to purchase hardware as soon as the disaster occurs.

- **Warm site** An organization will need to purchase hardware in advance of the disaster, or it may be able to purchase hardware when the disaster occurs. The choice taken will depend on the recovery time objective.

- **Hot site** An organization will need to purchase its recovery hardware in advance of the disaster.

Pros and cons to these strategies are listed in Table 5-15. Warm site strategy is not listed, since an organization could purchase hardware either in advance of the disaster or when it occurs. But because cold and hot sites are deterministic, they are included in the table.

The primary business reason for not choosing a hot site is the high capital cost required to purchase disaster recovery equipment that may never be used. One way around this obstacle is to put those recovery systems to work every day. For example, recovery systems could be used for development or testing of the same applications that are used in production. This way, systems that are purchased for recovery purposes are being well utilized for other purposes, and they'll be ready in case a disaster occurs.

When a disaster occurs, the organization will be less concerned about development and testing, and more concerned about keeping critical production applications running. It will be a small sacrifice to forgo development or testing (or whatever low-criticality functions are using the DR hardware) during a disaster.

Recovery and Resilience Technologies

Once recovery targets have been established, the next major task is the survey and selection of technologies to enable recovery time and recovery point objectives to be met. The important factors when considering each technology are

- Does the technology help the information system achieve the RTO and RPO targets?

- Does the cost of the technology meet or exceed budget constraints?

- Can the technology be used to benefit other information systems (thereby lowering the cost for each system)?

Strategy	Advantages	Disadvantages
Hot	Hardware already purchased and ready for use.	Capital is tied up in equipment that may never be used. Higher cost to continue maintaining recovery systems.
Cold	Capital is spent only if needed. Lower costs (until a disaster occurs).	The right equipment may be difficult to find and purchase. Difficult to test recovery strategy unless hardware is purchased, leased, or borrowed.

Table 5-15 Hardware Acquisition Pros and Cons for Cold and Hot Recovery Sites

- Does the technology fit well into the organization's current IT operations?

- Will operations staff require specialized training on the technology used for recovery?

- Does the technology contribute to the simplicity of the overall IT architecture, or does it complicate it unnecessarily?

These questions are designed to help determine whether a specific technology is a good fit, from a technology as well as from process and operational perspectives.

RAID   Redundant Array of Independent Disks (RAID) is a family of technologies that is used to improve the reliability, performance, or size of disk-based storage systems. From a disaster recovery or systems resilience perspective, the feature of RAID that is of particular interest is the reliability. RAID is used to create virtual disk volumes over an array (pun intended) of disk storage devices and can be configured so that the failure of any individual disk drive in the array will not affect the availability of data on the disk array.

RAID is usually implemented on a hardware device called a *disk array*, which is a chassis in which several hard disks can be installed and connected to a server. The individual disk drives can usually be "hot swapped" in the chassis while the array is still operating. When the array is configured with RAID, a failure of a single disk drive will have no effect on the disk array's availability to the server to which it is connected. A system operator can be alerted to the disk's failure, and the defective disk drive can be removed and replaced while the array is still fully operational.

There are several options for RAID configuration, called *levels*:

- **RAID-0**   This is known as a *striped volume*, where a disk volume splits data evenly across two or more disks in order to improve performance.

- **RAID-1**   This creates a *mirror*, where data written to one disk in the array is also written to a second disk in the array. RAID-1 makes the volume more reliable, through the preservation of data, even when one disk in the array fails.

- **RAID-4**   This level of RAID employs data striping at the block level by adding a dedicated parity disk. The parity disk permits the rebuilding of data in the event one of the other disks fails.

- **RAID-5**   This is similar to RAID-4 block-level striping, except that the parity data is distributed evenly across all of the disks instead of dedicated on one disk. Like RAID-4, RAID-5 allows for the failure of one disk without losing information.

- **RAID-6**   This is an extension of RAID-5, where two parity blocks are used instead of a single parity block. The advantage of RAID-6 is that it can withstand the failure of any two disk drives in the array, instead of a single disk, as is the case with RAID-5.

 NOTE   Several nonstandard RAID levels have been developed by various hardware and software companies. Some of these are extensions of RAID standards, while others are entirely different.

Storage systems are hardware devices that are entirely separate from servers—their only purpose is to store a large amount of data and to be highly reliable through the use of redundant components and the use of one or more RAID levels. Storage systems generally come in two forms:

- **Storage area network (SAN)**   This is a stand-alone storage system that can be configured to contain several virtual volumes and connected to several servers through fiber optic cables. The servers' operating systems will often consider this storage to be "local," as though it consisted of one or more hard disks present in the server's own chassis.
- **Network attached storage (NAS)**   This is a stand-alone storage system that contains one or more virtual volumes. Servers access these volumes over the network using the Network File System (NFS) or Server Message Block/Common Internet File System (SMB/CIFS) protocols, common on Unix and Windows operating systems, respectively.

Replication   Replication is an activity where data that is written to a storage system is also copied over a network to another storage system. The result is the presence of up-to-date data that exists on two or more storage systems, each of which could be located in a different geographic region.

Replication can be handled in several ways and at different levels in the technology stack:

- **Disk storage system**   Data-write operations that take place in a disk storage system (such as a SAN or NAS) can be transmitted over a network to another disk storage system, where the same data will be written to the other disk storage system.
- **Operating system**   The operating system can control replication so that updates to a particular file system can be transmitted to another server where those updates will be applied locally on that other server.
- **Database management system**   The database management system (DBMS) can manage replication by sending transactions to a DBMS on another server.
- **Transaction management system**   The transaction management system (TMS) can manage replication by sending transactions to a counterpart TMS located elsewhere.
- **Application**   The application can write its transactions to two different storage systems. This method is not often used.

Replication can take place from one system to another system, called *primary-backup* replication. This is the typical setup when data on an application server is sent to a distant storage system for data recovery or disaster recovery purposes.

Replication can also be bidirectional, between two active servers, called *multiprimary* or *multimaster*. This method is more complicated, because simultaneous transactions on different servers could conflict with one another (such as two reservation agents trying to book a passenger in the same seat on an airline flight). Some form of concurrent transaction control would be required, such as a *distributed lock manager*.

In terms of the speed and integrity of replicated information, there are two types of replication:

- **Synchronous replication**   Here, writing data to a local and to a remote storage system are performed as a single operation, guaranteeing that data on the remote storage system is identical to data on the local storage system. Synchronous replication incurs a performance penalty, as the speed of the entire transaction is slowed to the rate of the remote transaction.

- **Asynchronous replication**   Writing data to the remote storage system is not kept in sync with updates on the local storage system. Instead, there may be a time lag, and you have no guarantee that data on the remote system is identical to that on the local storage system. However, performance is improved, because transactions are considered complete when they have been written to the local storage system only. Bursts of local updates to data will take a finite period to replicate to the remote server, subject to the available bandwidth of the network connection between the local and remote storage systems.

NOTE   Replication is often used for applications where the RTO is smaller than the time necessary to recover data from backup media. For example, if a critical application's RTO is established to be two hours, then recovery from backup tape is probably not a viable option, unless backups are performed every two hours. While more expensive than recovery from backup media, replication ensures that up-to-date information is present on a remote storage system that can be put online in a short period.

Server Clusters   A *cluster* is a collection of two or more servers that appear as a single server resource. Clusters are often the technology of choice for applications that require a high degree of availability and a very small RTO, measured in minutes.

When an application is implemented on a cluster, even if one of the servers in the cluster fails, the other server (or servers) in the cluster will continue to run the application, usually with no user awareness that such a failure occurred.

There are two typical configurations for clusters, *active/active* and *active/passive*. In active/active mode, all servers in the cluster are running and servicing application requests. This is often used in high-volume applications where many servers are required to service the application workload.

In active/passive mode, one or more servers in the cluster are active and servicing application requests, while one or more servers in the cluster are in a "standby" mode; they can service application requests, but won't do so unless one of the active servers fails or goes offline for any reason. When an active server goes offline and a standby server takes over, this event is called a *failover*.

A typical server cluster architecture is shown in Figure 5-25.

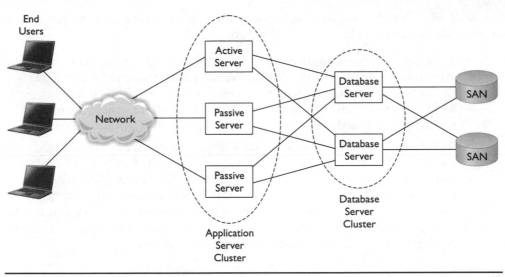

Figure 5-25 Application and database server clusters

A server cluster is typically implemented in a single physical location such as a data center. However, a cluster can also be implemented where great distances separate the servers in the cluster. This type of cluster is called a *geographic cluster*, or geo-cluster. Servers in a geo-cluster are connected through a WAN connection. A typical geographic cluster architecture is shown in Figure 5-26.

Network Connectivity and Services An overall application environment that is required to be resilient and have recoverability must have those characteristics present within the network that supports it. A highly resilient application architecture that includes clustering and replication would be of little value if it had only a single network connection that was a single point of failure.

Figure 5-26 Geographic cluster with data replication

An application that requires high availability and resilience may require one or more of the following in the supporting network:

- **Redundant network connections**   These may include multiple network adapters on a server, but also a fully redundant network architecture with multiple switches, routers, load balancers, and firewalls. This could also include physically diverse network provider connections, where network service provider feeds enter the building from two different directions.

- **Redundant network services**   Certain network services are vital to the continued operation of applications, such as DNS (the function of translating server names like www.mcgraw-hill.com into an IP address), NTP (used to synchronize computer time clocks), SMTP, SNMP, authentication services, and perhaps others. These services are usually operated on servers, which may require clustering and/or replication of their own, so that the application will be able to continue functioning in the event of a disaster.

Developing Recovery Plans

A disaster recovery planning effort starts with the initial phases of the business continuity planning (BCP) project: the business impact analysis (BIA) and criticality analysis (CA) lead to the establishment of recovery objectives that determine how quickly critical business processes need to be back up and running.

With this information, the DR team can determine what additional data processing equipment is needed (if any) and establish a roadmap for acquiring that equipment.

The other major component in the DR project is the development of recovery plans. These are the process and procedure documents that will be triggered when a disaster has been declared. These processes and procedures will instruct response personnel how to establish and operate business processes and IT systems after a disaster has occurred. It's not enough to have all of the technology ready if personnel don't know what to do.

Most DR plans are going to have common components, which are

- **Disaster declaration procedure**   This needs to include criteria for how a disaster is determined and who has the authority to declare a disaster.

- **Roles and responsibilities**   DR plans need to specify what activities need to be performed and specify which persons or teams are best equipped to perform them.

- **Emergency contact lists**   Response personnel need contact information for other personnel so that they may establish and maintain communications as the disaster unfolds and recovery operations begin. These contact lists should contain several different ways of contacting personnel, since some disasters have an adverse impact on regional telecommunications infrastructure.

- **System recovery procedures**   These are the detailed steps for getting recovery systems up and running. These procedures will include a lot of detail describing obtaining data, configuring servers and network equipment, confirming that the application and business information is healthy, and starting business applications.

- **System operations procedures**   These are detailed steps for operating critical IT systems while they are in recovery mode. These detailed procedures are needed because the systems in recovery mode may need to be operated differently than their production counterparts; further, they may need to be operated by personnel who have not been doing this before.

- **System restoration procedures**   These are the detailed steps to restore IT operations back to the original production systems.

NOTE   Business continuity and disaster recovery plans work together to get critical business functions operating again after a disaster. Because of this, BC and DR teams need to work closely when developing their respective response procedures to make sure that all activities are covered, but without unnecessary overlap.

DR plans need to take into account the likely disaster scenarios that may occur to an organization. Understanding these scenarios can help the DR team take a more pragmatic approach when creating response procedures. The added benefit is that not all disasters result in the entire loss of a computing facility. Most are more limited in their scope, although all of them can still result in a complete inability to continue operations. Some of these scenarios are

- Complete loss of network connectivity
- Sustained electric power outage
- Loss of a key system (this could be a server, storage system, or network device)
- Extensive data corruption or data loss

These scenarios are probably more likely to occur than a catastrophe such as a major earthquake or hurricane (depending on where your data center is located).

Data Backup and Recovery

Disasters and other disruptive events can damage information and information systems. It's essential that fresh copies of this information exist elsewhere and in a form that enables IT personnel to easily load this information into alternative systems so that processing can resume as quickly as possible.

CAUTION   Testing backups is important; testing recoverability is critical. In other words, performing backups is only valuable to the extent that backed-up data can be recovered at a future time.

Backup to Tape and Other Media

Tape backup is just about as ubiquitous as power cords. From a disaster recovery perspective, however, the issue probably is not whether the organization *has* tape backup, but whether its current backup capabilities are adequate in the context of disaster recovery. An organization's backup capability may need to be upgraded if

- The current backup system is difficult to manage.
- Whole-system restoration takes too long.
- The system lacks flexibility with regard to disaster recovery (for instance, how difficult it would be to recover information onto a different type of system).
- The technology is old or outdated.
- Confidence in the backup technology is low.

Many organizations may consider tape backup as a means for restoring files or databases when errors have occurred, and they may have confidence in their backup system for that purpose. However, the organization may have somewhat less confidence in their backup system and its ability to recover all of their critical systems accurately and in a timely manner.

Tape is not the only medium for backups. While tape has been the default medium since the 1960s, using a hard disk as a backup medium is growing in popularity: hard disk transfer rates are far higher, and disk is a random-access medium, whereas tape is a sequential-access medium. A virtual tape library (VTL) is a type of data storage technology that sets up a disk-based storage system with the appearance of tape storage, permitting existing backup software to continue to back data up to "tape," which is really just more disk storage.

E-vaulting is another viable option for system backup. E-vaulting permits organizations to back up their systems and data to an off-site location, which could be a storage system in another data center or a third-party service provider. This accomplishes two important objectives: reliable backup and off-site storage of backup data.

Backup Schemes

There are three main schemes for backing up data; they are the full, incremental, and differential backups. Each is explained here.

- **Full backup**   This is a complete copy of a data set.
- **Incremental backup**   This is a copy of all data that has changed since the last full or incremental backup.
- **Differential backup**   This is a copy of all data that has changed since the last full backup.

The precise nature of the data to be backed up will determine which combination of backup schemes is appropriate for the organization. Some of the considerations for choosing an overall scheme include

- Criticality of the data set
- Size of the data set
- Frequency of change of the data set
- Performance requirements and the impact of backup jobs
- Recovery requirements

An organization that is creating a backup scheme usually starts with the most common scheme, which is a full backup once per week and an incremental or differential backup every day. However, as stated previously, various factors will influence the design of the final backup scheme. Some examples include

- A small data set could be backed up more than once a week, while an especially large data set might be backed up less often.
- A more rapid recovery requirement may induce the organization to perform differential backups instead of incremental backups.
- If a full backup takes a long time to complete, it should probably be performed during times of lower demand or system utilization.

Backup Media Rotation

Organizations will typically want to retain backup media for as long as possible in order to provide a greater array of choices for data recovery. However, the desire to maintain a large library of backup media will be countered by the high cost of media and the space required to store it. And while legal or statutory requirements may dictate that backup media be kept for some minimum period, the organization may be able to creatively find ways to comply with such requirements without retaining several generations of such media.

Some example backup media rotation schemes are discussed here.

First In First Out (FIFO)   In this scheme, there is no specific requirement for retaining any backup media for long periods (e.g., one year or more). The method in the FIFO rotation scheme specifies that the oldest available backup tape is the next one to be used.

The advantage of this scheme is its simplicity. However, there is a significant disadvantage: any corruption of backed-up data needs to be discovered quickly (within the period of media rotation), or else no valid set of data can be recovered. Hence, only low-criticality data without any lengthy retention requirements should be backed up using this scheme.

Grandfather-Father-Son   The most common backup media rotation scheme, grandfather-father-son creates a hierarchical set of backup media that provides for greater retention of backed-up data that is still economically feasible.

In the most common form of this scheme, full backups are performed once per week and incremental or differential backups are performed daily.

Daily backup tapes used on Monday are not used again until the following Monday. Backup tapes used on Tuesday, Wednesday, Thursday, Friday, and Saturday are handled in the same way.

Full backup tapes created on Sunday are kept longer. Tapes used on the first Sunday of the month are not used again until the first Sunday of the following month. Similarly, tapes used on the second Sunday are not reused until the second Sunday of the following month, and so on for each week's tapes for Sunday.

For even longer retention, for example, tapes created on the first Sunday of the first month of each calendar quarter can be retained until the first Sunday of the first month of the next quarter. Backup media can be kept for even longer if needed.

Towers of Hanoi   The Towers of Hanoi backup media retention scheme is complex but results in a more efficient scheme for producing a more lengthy retention of some backups. Patterned after the Towers of Hanoi puzzle, the scheme is most easily understood visually, as in Figure 5-27 in a five-level scheme.

Backup Media Storage

Backup media that remains in the same location as backed-up systems is adequate for data recovery purposes, but completely inadequate for disaster recovery purposes: any event that physically damages information systems (such as fire, flood, hazardous chemical spill, and so on) is likely to also damage backup media. To provide disaster recovery protection, backup media must be stored off-site in a secure location. Selection of this storage location is as important as the selection of a primary business location: in the event of a disaster, the survival of the organization may depend upon the protection measures in place at the off-site storage location.

 EXAM TIP   CISA exam questions relating to off-site backups may include details for safeguarding data during transport and storage, mechanisms for access during restoration procedures, media aging and retention, or other details that may aid you during the exam. Watch for question details involving the type of media, geo-locality (distance, shared disaster spectrum [such as a shared coastline], and so on) of the off-site storage area and the primary site, or access controls during transport and at the storage site, including environmental controls and security safeguards.

Day of Cycle

	1	2	3	4	5	6	7	8	9	10	11	12	13	14	15	16	17	18	19	20
Backup Set to Use		A		A		A		A		A		A		A		A		A		A
			B				B				B				B				B	
					C								C							
									D									D		
	E																			

Figure 5-27   Towers of Hanoi backup rotation scheme

The criteria for selection of an off-site media storage facility are similar to the criteria for selection of a hot/warm/cold recovery site discussed earlier in this chapter. If a media storage location is too close to the primary processing site, then it is more likely to be involved in the same regional disaster, which could result in damage to backup media. However, if the media storage location is too far away, then it might take too long for a delivery of backup media, which would result in a recovery operation that runs unacceptably long.

Another location consideration is the proximity of the media storage location and the hot/warm/cold recovery site. If a hot site is being used, then chances are there is some other near-real-time means (such as replication) for data to get to the hot site. But a warm or cold site may be relying on the arrival of backup media from the off-site media storage facility, so it might make sense for the off-site facility to be near the recovery site.

An important factor when considering off-site media storage is the method of delivery to and from the storage location. Chances are that the backup media is being transported by a courier or a shipping company. It is vital that the backup media arrive safely and intact, and that the opportunities for interception or loss be reduced as much as possible. Not only can a lost backup tape make recovery more difficult, but it can also cause an embarrassing security incident if knowledge of the loss were to become public. From a confidentiality/integrity perspective, encryption of backup tapes is a good idea, although this digresses somewhat from disaster recovery (concerned primarily with availability). Backup tape encryption is discussed in Chapter 6.

 NOTE The requirements for off-site storage are a little less critical than for a hot/warm/cold recovery site. All you have to do is be able to get your backup media out of that facility. This can occur even if there is a regional power outage, for instance.

Backup media that must be kept on-site should be stored in locked cabinets or storerooms that are separate from the rooms where backups are performed. This will help to preserve backup media if a relatively small fire breaks out in the room containing computers that are backed up.

Backup Media Records and Destruction

To ensure the ability of restoring data from backup media, organizations need to have meticulous records that list all backup volumes in place, where they are located, and which data elements are backed up on them. Without these records, it may prove impossible for an organization to recover data from its backup media library.

Protecting Sensitive Data with Encryption

Information security and data privacy laws are expanding data protection requirements by requiring encryption of backup media in many cases. This is a sensible safeguard, especially for organizations that utilize off-site backup media storage. There is a risk of loss of backup media when it is being transported back and forth from an organization's primary data center and the backup media off-site storage facility.

Laws and regulations may specify maximum periods that specific information may be retained. Organizations need to have good records management that helps them track which business records are on which backup media volumes. When it is time for an organization to stop retaining a specific set of data, those responsible for the backup media library need to identify the backup volumes that can be recycled. If the data on the backup media is sensitive, the backup volume may need to be erased prior to use. Any backup media that is being discarded needs to be destroyed so that no other party can possibly recover data on the volume. Records of this destruction need to be kept.

Testing DR Plans

Disaster response plans need to be accurate and complete if they are going to result in a successful recovery. It is recommended that recovery and response plans be thoroughly tested.

The types of recovery tests are

- Document review
- Walkthrough
- Simulation
- Parallel test
- Cutover test

These test methods are described in detail in Chapter 2.

Auditing IS Infrastructure and Operations

Auditing infrastructure and operations requires considerable technical expertise in order for the auditor to fully understand the technology that she is examining. Lacking technical knowledge, interviewed subjects may offer explanations that can evade vital facts that the auditor should be aware of.

Auditing Information Systems Hardware

Auditing hardware requires attention to several key factors and activities, including

- **Standards**   The auditor should examine hardware procurement standards that specify the types of systems that the organization uses. These standards should be periodically reviewed and updated. A sample of recent purchases should be examined to see whether standards are being followed. The scope of this activity should include servers, workstations, network devices, and other hardware used by IS.

- **Maintenance**   Maintenance requirements and records should be examined to see whether any required maintenance is being performed. If service contracts are used, these should be examined to ensure that all critical systems are covered.

- **Capacity**   The auditor should examine capacity management and planning processes, procedures, and records. This will help the auditor to understand whether the organization monitors its systems' capacity and does any planning for future expansion.

- **Change management**   Change management processes and records should be examined to see whether hardware changes are being performed in a life cycle process. All changes that are made should be requested and reviewed in advance, approved by management, and recorded.

- **Configuration management**   The auditor should examine configuration management records to see whether the IS organization is tracking the configuration of its systems in a centralized and systematic manner.

Auditing Operating Systems

Auditing operating systems requires attention to many different details, including

- **Standards**   The auditor should examine written standards to see if they are complete and up-to-date. He or she should then examine a sampling of servers and workstations to see whether they comply with the organization's written standards.

- **Maintenance and support**   Business records should be examined to see whether the operating systems running on servers or workstations are covered by maintenance or support contracts.

- **Change management**   The auditor should examine operating system change management processes and records to see whether changes are being performed in a systematic manner. All changes that are made should be requested and reviewed in advance, approved by management, and recorded.

- **Configuration management**   Operating systems are enormously complex; in all but the smallest organizations, configuration management tools should be used to ensure consistency of configuration among systems. The auditor should examine configuration management processes, tools, and recordkeeping.

- **Security management**   The auditor should examine security configurations on a sample of servers and workstations, and determine whether they are "hardened" or resemble manufacturer default configurations. This determination should be made in light of the relative risk of various selected systems. An examination should include patch management and administrative access.

Auditing File Systems

File systems containing business information must be examined to ensure that they are properly configured. An examination should include

- **Capacity**   File systems must have adequate capacity to store all of the currently required information, plus room for future growth. The auditor should examine any file storage capacity management tools, processes, and records.

- **Access control**   Files and directories should be accessible only by personnel with a business need. Records of access requests should be examined to see if they correspond to the access permissions observed.

Auditing Database Management Systems

Database management systems (DBMSs) are as complex as operating systems. This complexity requires considerable auditor scrutiny in several areas, including

- **Configuration management**   The configuration of DBMSs should be centrally controlled and tracked in larger organizations to ensure consistency among systems. Individual DBMSs and configuration management records should be compared.

- **Change management**   Databases are used to store not only information, but also software in many cases. The auditor should examine DBMS change management processes and records to see whether changes are being performed in a consistent, systematic manner. All changes that are made should be requested and reviewed in advance, approved by management, tested, implemented, and recorded. Changes to software should be examined in coordination with an audit of the organization's software development life cycle.

- **Capacity management**   The availability and integrity of supported business processes requires sufficient capacity in all underlying databases. The auditor should examine procedures and records related to capacity management to see whether management ensures sufficient capacity for business data.

- **Security management**   Access controls determine which users and systems are able to access and update data. The auditor should examine access control configurations, access requests, and access logs.

Auditing Network Infrastructure

The IS auditor needs to perform a detailed study of the organization's network infrastructure and underlying management processes. An auditor's scrutiny should include

- **Network architecture**   The auditor should examine network architecture documents. These should include schematics, topology and design, data flow, routing, and addressing.

- **Security architecture**   Security architecture documents should be examined, including critical and sensitive data flows, network security zones, access control devices and systems, security countermeasures, intrusion detection systems, firewalls, screening routers, gateways, anti-malware, and security monitoring.

- **Standards**   The auditor should examine standards documents and determine whether they are reasonable and current. Selected devices and equipment should be examined to see whether they conform to these standards.

- **Change management**   All changes to network devices and services should be governed by a change management process. The auditor should review change management procedures and records, and examine a sample of devices and systems to ensure that changes are being performed within change management policy.

- **Capacity management**   The auditor should determine how the organization measures network capacity, whether capacity management procedures and records exist, and how capacity management affects network operations.

- **Configuration management**   The auditor should determine whether any configuration management standards, procedures, and records exist and are used. He or she should examine the configuration of a sampling of devices to see whether configurations are consistent from device to device.

- **Administrative access management**   Access management procedures, records, and configurations should be examined to see whether only authorized persons are able to access and manage network devices and services.

- **Network components**   The auditor should examine several components and their configuration to determine how well the organization has constructed its network infrastructure to support business objectives.

- **Log management**   The auditor should determine whether administrative activities performed on network devices and services are logged. He should examine the configuration of logs to see if they can be altered. The logs themselves should be examined to determine whether any unauthorized activities are taking place.

- **User access management**   Often, network-based services provide organization-wide user access controls. The auditor should examine these centralized services to see whether they conform to written security standards. Examination should include user ID convention, password controls, inactivity locking, user account provisioning, user account termination, and password reset procedures.

Auditing Network Operating Controls

The IS auditor needs to examine network operations in order to determine whether the organization is operating its network effectively. Examinations should include

- **Network operating procedures**   The auditor should examine procedures for normal activities for all network devices and services. These activities will include login, startup, shutdown, upgrade, and configuration changes.

- **Restart procedures**   Procedures for restarting the entire network (and portions of it for larger organizations) should exist and be tested periodically. A network restart would be needed in the event of a massive power failure, network failure, or significant upgrade.

- **Troubleshooting procedures**   The auditor should examine network troubleshooting procedures for all significant network components. Procedures that are specific to the organization's network help network engineers and analysts quickly locate problems and reduce downtime.

- **Security controls**   Operational security controls should be examined, including administrator authentication, administrator access control, logging of administrator actions, protection of device configuration data, security configuration reviews, and protection of audit logs.

- **Change management**   All changes to network components and services should follow a formal change management life cycle, including request, review, approval by management, testing in a separate environment, implementation, verification, and complete recordkeeping. The auditor should examine change management policy, procedures, and records.

Auditing IS Operations

Auditing IS operations involves examining the processes used to build, maintain, update, and repair computing hardware, operating systems, and network devices. Audits will cover processes, procedures, and records, as well as examinations of information systems.

Auditing Computer Operations

The auditor should examine computer operational processes, including

- **System configuration standards**   The auditor should examine configuration standards that specify the detailed configuration settings for each type of system that is used in the organization.

- **System build procedures**   The auditor should examine the procedures used to install and configure the operating system.

- **System recovery procedures**   The procedures that are used to recover systems from various types of failures should be examined. Usually, this will include reinstalling and configuring the operating system, restoring software and data from backup, and verifying system recovery.

- **System update procedures**   The auditor should examine procedures used for making changes to systems, including configuration changes and component upgrades.

- **Patch management**   The auditor should examine the procedures for receiving security advisories, risk analysis, and decisions regarding when new security patches should be implemented. Procedures should also include testing, implementation, and verification.

- **Daily tasks**   Daily and weekly operating procedures for systems should be examined, which may include data backup, log review, log file cycling, review of performance logs, and system capacity checks.

- **Backup**   The auditor should examine procedures and records for file and database backup, backup verification, recovery testing, backup media control and inventory, and off-site media storage.

- **Media control**   Media control procedures should be examined, which includes backup media retirement procedures, disk media retirement procedures, media custody, and off-site storage.

- **Monitoring**   Computer monitoring is discussed in detail later in this section.

Auditing File Management

The IS auditor should examine file management policies and procedures, including

- **File system standards**   The auditor should examine file system standards that specify file system architecture, directory naming standards, and technical settings that govern disk utilization and performance.

- **Access controls**   The auditor should examine file system access control policy and procedures, the configuration settings that control which users and processes are able to access directories and files, and log files that record access control events such as permission changes and attempted file accesses.

- **Capacity management**   The settings and controls used to manage the capacity of file systems should be examined. This should include logs that show file system utilization, procedures for adding capacity, and records of capacity-related events.

- **Version control**   In file systems and data repositories that contain documents under version control, the auditor should examine version control configuration settings, file update procedures, and file recovery procedures and records.

Auditing Data Entry

The IS auditor should examine data entry standards and operations, including

- **Data entry procedures**   This may include document control, input procedures, and error recovery procedures.

- **Input verification**   This may include automatic and manual controls used to ensure that data has been entered properly into forms.

- **Batch verification**   This may include automatic and manual controls used to calculate and verify batches of records that are input.

- **Correction procedures**   This may include controls and procedures used to correct individual forms and batches when errors occur.

Auditing Lights-Out Operations

A *lights-out operation* is any production IT environment, such as computers in a data center, that runs without on-site operator intervention. The term "lights out" means that the computers can be in a room with the lights out since no personnel are present to attend to them.

Audit activities of a lights-out operation will primarily fall into the other categories of audits discussed in this chapter, plus a few specific activities, including

- Remote administration procedures
- Remote monitoring procedures

Auditing Problem Management Operations

The auditor should examine the organization's problem management operations, including

- **Problem management policy and processes**   The auditor should examine policy and procedure documents that describe how problem management is supposed to be performed.
- **Problem management records**   A sampling of problems and incidents should be examined to see whether problems are being properly managed.
- **Problem management timelines**   The time spent on each problem should be examined to see whether resolution falls within the SLA.
- **Problem management reports**   The auditor should examine management reports to ensure that management is aware of all problems.
- **Problem resolution**   The auditor should examine a sample of problems to see which ones required changes in other processes. The other process documents should be examined to see if they were changed. The auditor also should examine records to see if fixes were verified by another party.
- **Problem recurrence**   The auditor should examine problem records to make sure that the same problems are not coming up over and over again.

Auditing Monitoring Operations

The IS auditor needs to audit system monitoring operations to ensure that it is effective, including

- **Monitoring plan**   The auditor should review any monitoring plan documents that describe the organization's monitoring program, tools, and processes.
- **Problem log**   Monitoring problem logs should be reviewed to see what kinds of problems are being recorded. The auditor should see whether all devices and systems are represented in problem logs.
- **Preventive maintenance**   The auditor should examine monitoring results, monitoring plan, and preventive maintenance records, and determine whether the level of preventive maintenance is adequate and effective.
- **Management review and action**   Any monitoring reports, meeting minutes, and decision logs should be examined to see whether management is reviewing monitoring reports and whether management actions are being carried out.

Auditing Procurement

The auditor should examine hardware and software procurement processes, procedures, and records to determine whether any of the following activities are being performed:

- **Requirements definition**   All stakeholders (both technical and business, as appropriate) need to develop functional, technical, and security requirements. Each requirement needs to be approved and used to apply scrutiny to candidate products and services. Each candidate supplier's responses need to be scored on their merits regarding their ability to meet requirements. This entire process needs to be transparent and documented. Auditors will need to examine procurement policies, procedures, and records from selected procurement projects.

- **Feasibility studies**   Many requests for service will require an objective feasibility study that will be designed to identify the economic and business benefits that may be derived from the requested service. Auditors need to examine selected feasibility study documents as well as policy and procedure documents for performing feasibility projects.

Auditing Disaster Recovery Planning

The objectives of an audit of disaster recovery planning should include the following activities:

- Determine the effectiveness of planning and recovery documentation by examining previous test results.

- Evaluate the methods used to store critical information off-site (which may consist of off-site storage, alternate data centers, or e-vaulting). Examine environmental and physical security controls in any off-site or alternate sites and determine their effectiveness. Note whether off-site or alternate site locations are within the same geographic region—which could mean that both the primary and alternate sites may be involved in common disaster scenarios.

Auditing Disaster Recovery Plans

The following steps will help the auditor to determine the effectiveness of the organization's disaster recovery plans:

- Obtain a copy of disaster recovery documentation, including response procedures, contact lists, and communication plans.

- Examine samples of distributed copies of DR documentation, and determine whether they are up-to-date. These samples can be obtained during interviews of key response personnel, which are covered in this procedure.

- Determine whether all documents are clear and easy to understand, not just for primary responders, but for alternate personnel who may have specific relevant skills but less familiarity with the organization's critical applications.

- Obtain contact information for off-site storage providers, hot-site facilities, and critical suppliers. Determine whether these organizations are still providing services to the organization. Call some of the contacts to determine the accuracy of the documented contact information.

- Obtain logical and physical architecture diagrams for key IT applications that support critical business processes. Determine whether BC documentation includes recovery procedures for all components that support those IT applications. See whether documentation includes recovery for end users and administrators for the applications.

- If the organization uses a hot site, examine one or more systems to determine whether they have the proper versions of software, patches, and configurations. Examine procedures and records related to the tasks in support of keeping standby systems current. Determine whether these procedures are effective.

- If the organization has a warm site, examine the procedures used to bring standby systems into operational readiness. Examine warm-site systems to see whether they are in a state where readiness procedures will likely be successful.

- If the organization has a cold site, examine all documentation related to the acquisition of replacement systems and other components. Determine whether the procedures and documentation are likely to result in systems capable of hosting critical IT applications and within the period required to meet key recovery objectives.

- Determine whether any documentation exists regarding the relocation of key personnel to the hot/warm/cold processing site. See whether the documentation specifies which personnel are to be relocated and what accommodations and supporting logistics are provided. Determine the effectiveness of these relocation plans.

- Determine whether backup and off-site (or e-vaulting) storage procedures are being followed. Examine systems to ensure that critical IT applications are being backed up and that proper media are being stored off-site (or that the proper data is being e-vaulted). Determine whether data recovery tests are ever performed and whether results of those tests are documented and problems are properly dealt with.

- Evaluate procedures for transitioning processing from the alternate processing facility back to the primary processing facility. Determine whether these procedures are complete and effective.

- Determine whether a process exists for the formal review and update of business continuity documentation. Examine records to see how frequently, and how recently, documents have been reviewed and updated. Determine whether this is sufficient and effective by interviewing key personnel to understand whether significant changes to applications, systems, networks, or processes are reflected in recovery and response documentation.

- Determine whether response personnel receive any formal or informal training on response and recovery procedures. Determine whether personnel are required to receive training, and whether any records are kept that show which personnel received training and at what time.

- Examine the organization's change control process. Determine whether the process includes any steps or procedures that require personnel to determine whether any change has an impact on disaster recovery documentation or procedures.

Reviewing Prior Test Results and Action Plans

The effectiveness of disaster recovery plans relies on the results and outcomes of tests. The IS auditor needs to examine these plans and activities to determine their effectiveness. The following will help the IS auditor audit disaster recovery testing:

- Determine whether there is a strategy for testing business continuity procedures. Obtain records for past tests and a plan for future tests.

- Examine records for tests that have been performed over the past year or two. Determine the types of tests that were performed. Obtain a list of participants for each test. Compare the participants to lists of key recovery personnel. Examine test work papers to determine the level of participation by key recovery personnel.

- Determine whether there is a formal process for recording test results and for using those results to make improvements in plans and procedures. Examine work papers and records to determine the types of changes that were recommended in prior tests. Examine BC documents to see whether these changes were made as expected.

- Considering the types of tests that were performed, determine the adequacy of testing as an indicator of the effectiveness of the DR program. Did the organization only perform document reviews and walkthroughs, for example, or did the organization also perform parallel or cutover tests?

- If tests have been performed for two years or more, determine whether there's a trend showing continuous improvement in response and recovery procedures.

- If the organization performs parallel tests, determine whether tests are designed in a way that effectively determines the actual readiness of standby systems. Also determine whether parallel tests measure the capacity of standby systems or merely their ability to process correctly but at a lower level of performance.

- Determine whether any tests included the retrieval of backup data from off-site storage or e-vaulting facilities.

Evaluating Off-Site Storage

Storage of critical data and other supporting information is a key component in any organization's business continuity plan. Because some types of disasters can completely destroy a business location, including its vital records, it is imperative that all critical information is backed up and copies moved to an off-site storage facility. The following procedure will help the IT auditor determine the effectiveness of off-site storage:

- Obtain the location of the off-site storage or e-vaulting facility. Determine whether the facility is located in the same geographic region as the organization's primary processing facility.

- Visit the off-site storage facility. Examine its physical security controls as well as its safeguards to prevent damage to stored information in a disaster. Consider the entire spectrum of physical and logical access controls. Examine procedures and records related to the storage and return of backup media, and of other information that the organization may store there.

- Take an inventory of backup media and other information stored at the facility. Compare this inventory with a list of critical business processes and supporting IT systems to determine whether all relevant information is, in fact, stored at the off-site storage facility.

- Determine how often the organization performs its own inventory of the off-site facility, and whether steps to correct deficiencies are documented and remedied.

- Examine contracts, terms, and conditions for off-site storage providers or e-vaulting facilities, if applicable. Determine whether data can be recovered to the original processing center and to alternate processing centers within a period that will ensure that disaster recovery can be completed within recovery time objectives.

- Determine whether the appropriate personnel have current access codes for off-site storage or e-vaulting facilities, and whether they have the ability to recover data from those facilities.

- Determine what information, in addition to backup data, exists at the off-site storage facility. Information stored off-site should include architecture diagrams, design documentation, operations procedures, and configuration information for all logical and physical layers of technology and facilities supporting critical IT applications, operations documentation, and application source code.

- Obtain information related to the manner in which backup media and copies of records are transported to and from the off-site storage or e-vaulting facility. Determine whether controls protecting transported information are adequate.

- Obtain records supporting the transport of backup media and records to and from the off-site storage facility. Examine samples of records and determine whether they match other records such as backup logs.

Evaluating Alternative Processing Facilities

The IT auditor needs to examine alternate processing facilities to determine whether they are sufficient to support the organization's business continuity and disaster recovery plans. The following procedure will help the IT auditor determine whether an alternate processing facility will be effective:

- Obtain addresses and other location information for alternate processing facilities. These will include hot sites, warm sites, cold sites, and alternate processing centers owned or operated by the organization.

- Determine whether alternate facilities are located within the same geographic region as the primary processing facility and the probability that the alternate facility will be adversely affected by a disaster that strikes the primary facility.

- Perform a threat analysis on the alternate processing site. Determine which threats and hazards pose a significant risk to the organization and its ability to effectively carry out operations during a disaster.

- Determine the types of natural and man-made events likely to take place at the alternate processing facility. Determine whether there are adequate controls to mitigate the effect of these events.

- Examine all environmental controls and determine their adequacy. This should include environmental controls (HVAC), power supply, uninterruptible power supply (UPS), power distribution units (PDUs), and electric generators. Also examine fire detection and suppression systems, including smoke detectors, pull stations, fire extinguishers, sprinklers, and inert gas suppression systems.

- If the alternate processing facility is a separate organization, obtain the legal contract and all exhibits. Examine these documents and determine whether the contract and exhibits support the organization's recovery and testing requirements.

Summary

All activities in the IS department should be managed, controlled, and monitored. Activities performed by operations personnel should be a part of a procedure or process that is approved by management. Processes, procedures, and projects should have sufficient recordkeeping to facilitate measurements.

IT operations should be structured in a service management model that is aligned with the IT Infrastructure Library (ITIL) or the Control Objectives for Information and related Technology (COBIT) framework of processes. These frameworks ensure that comprehensive coverage of activities is likely to be taking place in most IS organizations.

IS auditors need to have a thorough understanding of information systems hardware and software and how they work to support business objectives. This includes knowing how computer hardware functions; how operating systems are installed, configured, and operated; how end users' workstations are provisioned, managed, and used; and how software applications operate. Because they are not always implemented properly at first, IS auditors need to understand newer technologies such as virtualization, virtual desktops, and mobile devices to ensure that the organization is not incurring unnecessary risk through their use.

Network management tools and systems help management understand a network's utilization, capacity, and problems. Network management should be a part of a larger infrastructure monitoring strategy.

During a disaster recovery planning project, once acceptable architectures and process changes have been determined, the organization sets out to make investments in these areas to bring its systems and processes closer to the recovery objectives. Procedures for recovering systems and processes are also developed at this time, as well as procedures for other aspects of disaster response, such as emergency communications plans and evacuation plans.

Some of the investment in IT system resilience may involve the establishment of an alternate processing site, where IT systems can be resumed in support of critical business processes. There are several types of alternate sites, including a hot site, where IT systems are in a continual state of near-readiness and can assume production workload within an hour or two; a warm site, where IT systems are present but require several hours to a day of preparation; and a cold site, where no systems are present but must be acquired, which may require several days of preparation before those replacement systems are ready to support business processes.

Some of the technologies that may be introduced in IT systems to improve recovery targets include RAID, a technology that improves the reliability of disk storage systems; replication, a technique for copying data in near–real time to an alternate (and usually distant) storage system; and clustering, a technology where several servers (including some that can be located in another region) act as one logical server, enabling processing to continue even if one or more servers are incapacitated or unreachable.

Notes

- All IT activities should be a part of a documented process, procedure, or project.

- Key systems, applications, and infrastructure should be monitored to ensure that they continue to operate properly in their support of key business processes.

- Software program libraries should be controlled with access and authorization controls, check out and check in, version control, and code analysis.

- Media sanitization procedures ensure that data leakage will not result from discarded data storage media.

- Mobile devices such as tablet computers and smart phones are the new endpoints. Lacking mature enterprise management controls and anti-malware tools, and being small enough to easily lose, mobile devices are the attack vector of the future. The IS auditor needs to understand how the organization addresses these matters.

- It is as important to understand the internal architecture of computers as it is to understand how computers can be combined together to form clusters and multi-tier application environments.

- Automated monitoring of computing and network infrastructure includes monitoring of internal components such as CPU, power supply, memory, and storage. Monitoring also includes resource utilization such as CPU, memory, disk storage, and network. The external environment, including temperature, humidity, water, and vibration, should also be monitored.

- Software license management ensures that the organization will remain in compliance with its software license agreements and avoid costly and embarrassing legal trouble. Automated tools can help monitor the installation and use of licensed software.

- While it has never been implemented in its pure form, it is still important to understand the concepts of the seven-layer OSI data model. Terms from the model are used by IT specialists; for instance, layer 4 switches are a type of network device that routes packets based on their OSI layer 4 characteristics.

- IS auditors need to understand the TCP/IP model and TCP/IP's common protocols enough to be able to identify risks and control weaknesses.

- A network's logical architecture (star, ring, and bus) often does not match its physical architecture (star, ring, bus).

- A key place to examine on a network is its boundary. Edge devices such as firewalls, routers, wireless access points, and gateways contain configurations that control inbound and outbound traffic. Mistakes here can be costly.

- Most of the older and less secure TCP/IP protocols such as TELNET, FTP, and RCP have been superseded by newer protocols such as SSH, SFTP, and FTPS.

- Business continuity planning ensures business recovery following a disaster. Business continuity focuses on maintaining service availability with the least disruption to standard operating parameters during an event, while disaster recovery focuses on post-event recovery and restoration of services.

- Once recovery objectives have been identified, strategies can be developed to meet each objective. Many solutions may include redundant (hot, warm, or cold) alternate sites, redundant service operation or storage in high-availability or distributed-cluster environments, alternative network access strategies, and backup/recovery strategies structured to meet identified recovery time and recovery point requirements.

Questions

1. A web application is displaying information incorrectly and many users have contacted the IT service desk. This matter should be considered a(n):

   A. Incident

   B. Problem

   C. Bug

   D. Outage

2. An IT organization is experiencing many cases of unexpected downtime that are caused by unauthorized changes to application code and operating system configuration. Which process should the IT organization implement to reduce downtime?

   A. Configuration management

   B. Incident management

   C. Change management

   D. Problem management

3. An IT organization manages hundreds of servers, databases, and applications, and is having difficulty tracking changes to the configuration of these systems. What process should be implemented to remedy this?

   A. Configuration management

   B. Change management

   C. Problem management

   D. Incident management

4. A computer's CPU, memory, and peripherals are connected to each other through a(n):

   A. Kernel

   B. FireWire

   C. Pipeline

   D. Bus

5. A database administrator has been asked to configure a database management system so that it records all changes made by users. What should the database administrator implement?

   A. Audit logging

   B. Triggers

   C. Stored procedures

   D. Journaling

6. The layers of the TCP/IP reference model are:

   A. Link, Internet, transport, application

B. Physical, link, Internet, transport, application

C. Link, transport, Internet, application

D. Physical, data link, network, transport, session, presentation, application

7. The purpose of the Internet layer in the TCP/IP model is:

A. Encapsulation

B. Packet delivery on a local network

C. Packet delivery on a local or remote network

D. Order of delivery and flow control

8. The purpose of the DHCP protocol is:

A. Control flow on a congested network

B. Query a station to discover its IP address

C. Assign an IP address to a station

D. Assign an Ethernet MAC address to a station

9. An IS auditor is examining a wireless (Wi-Fi) network and has determined that the network uses WEP encryption. What action should the auditor take?

A. Recommend that encryption be changed to WPA

B. Recommend that encryption be changed to EAP

C. Request documentation for the key management process

D. Request documentation for the authentication process

10. 126.0.0.1 is an example of a:

A. MAC address

B. Loopback address

C. Class A address

D. Subnet mask

11. What is the most important consideration when selecting a hot site?

A. Time zone

B. Geographic location in relation to the primary site

C. Proximity to major transportation

D. Natural hazards

12. An organization has established a recovery point objective of 14 days for its most critical business applications. Which recovery strategy would be the best choice?

A. Mobile site

B. Warm site

C. Hot site

D. Cold site

13. What technology should an organization use for its application servers to provide continuous service to users?

   A. Dual power supplies

   B. Server clustering

   C. Dual network feeds

   D. Transaction monitoring

14. An organization currently stores its backup media in a cabinet next to the computers being backed up. A consultant told the organization to store backup tapes at an offsite storage facility. What risk did the consultant most likely have in mind when he made this recommendation?

   A. A disaster that damages computer systems can also damage backup media.

   B. Backup media rotation may result in loss of data backed up several weeks in the past.

   C. Corruption of online data will require rapid data recovery from off-site storage.

   D. Physical controls at the data processing site are insufficient.

15. Which of the following statements about virtual server hardening is true?

   A. The configuration of the host operating system will automatically flow to each guest operating system.

   B. Each guest virtual machine needs to be hardened separately.

   C. Guest operating systems do not need to be hardened because they are protected by the hypervisor.

   D. Virtual servers do not need to be hardened because they do not run directly on computer hardware.

Answers

1. **B.** A problem is defined as a condition that is the result of multiple incidents that exhibit common symptoms. In this example, many users are experiencing the effects of the application error.

2. **C.** Change management is the process of managing change through a life cycle process that consists of request, review, approve, implement, and verify.

3. **A.** Configuration management is the process (often supplemented with automated tools) of tracking configuration changes to systems and system components such as databases and applications.

4. **D.** A computer's bus connects all of the computer's internal components together, including its CPU, main memory, secondary memory, and peripheral devices.

5. **A.** The database administrator should implement audit logging. This will cause the database to record every change that is made to it.

6. **A.** The layers of the TCP/IP model are (from lowest to highest) link, Internet, transport, and application.

7. **C.** The purpose of the Internet layer in the TCP/IP model is the delivery of packets from one station to another, on the same network or on a different network.

8. **C.** The DHCP protocol is used to assign IP addresses to computers on a network.

9. **A.** The WEP protocol has been seriously compromised and should be replaced with WPA or WPA2 encryption.

10. **C.** Class A addresses are in the range 0.0.0.0 to 127.255.255.255. The address 126.0.0.1 falls into this range.

11. **B.** An important selection criterion for a hot site is the geographic location in relation to the primary site. If they are too close together, then a single disaster event may involve both locations.

12. **D.** An organization that has a 14-day recovery time objective (RTO) can use a cold site for its recovery strategy. Fourteen days is enough time for most organizations to acquire hardware and recover applications.

13. **B.** An organization that wishes its application servers to be continuously available to its users needs to employ server clustering. This enables at least one server to always be available to service user requests.

14. **A.** The primary reason for employing off-site backup media storage is to mitigate the effects of a disaster that could otherwise destroy computer systems and their backup media.

15. **B.** In a virtualization environment, each guest operating system needs to be hardened, no different from operating systems running directly on server (or workstation) hardware.

Information Asset Protection

This chapter discusses the following topics
- Information security management
- Logical access controls
- Network security
- Environmental security
- Physical security

This chapter discusses CISA job practice 5, "Protection of Information Assets." The topics in this chapter represent 30 percent of the CISA examination.

Information assets consist of information and information systems. *Information* includes software, tools, and data. *Information system* is an inclusive term that encompasses servers, workstations, mobile devices, network devices, gateways, appliances, and almost every other kind of IT hardware that is used.

Information Security Management

Information security management is the collection of policies, processes, and procedures that ensure an organization's security policy is effective. Security management is composed of a number of distinct and interrelated processes, including policy development and enforcement, security awareness training, user access management, security incident management, vulnerability management, service provider management, encryption, network access management, environmental controls, and physical access controls. Ongoing executive support is key to the success of a security management program.

These and other processes should be periodically audited to confirm their effectiveness. Control failures and exceptions should be documented, and action plans developed to improve processes and systems.

Aspects of Information Security Management

The protection of information-related assets is the cornerstone of information security management. Flowing out of IT governance and risk management, information security management is a top-down set of coordinated activities whose key objective is the protection of information systems and other information-related assets.

An organization with sound IT governance and risk management programs will develop strategies, policies, and processes that align with the organization's overall objectives. Through a number of strategic processes, such as business impact assessment (BIA), management will have a clear idea of which information-related assets are the most vital to the organization. Through a risk management program, management will take appropriate measures to protect those assets.

 NOTE Rather than a separate activity, information security management should be hand-in-glove with IT governance and risk management, which is the focus of Chapter 2.

Executive Support

Information security management will be effective only when it has an appropriate level of executive-level support. A level of visible commitment to security management is required, including the ratification of security policies, delegation of key roles and responsibilities, allocation of resources, and leadership by example. Without executive support as a foundation, an organization's information security program cannot hope to succeed and be effective.

Policies and Procedures

An effective information security program depends upon a clear rule of law in the form of an information security policy. A complete information security policy should contain the following elements:

- **Statement of executive support**   The policy document must clearly state that the information security policy has the full and unwavering support of the organization's executives. The policy should include a signature block that shows their support in writing.

- **Roles and responsibilities**   Information security policy should define security-related roles and responsibilities, including who is responsible for policy development and enforcement. It should also include who is responsible for performing risk assessments and making risk-based decisions. The policy should also describe how the structure of asset ownership works and clearly state how asset owners have some responsibilities in protecting the assets that they control. Finally, the policy should state the responsibilities that all employees have.

- **Value of information-related assets**   The information security policy should include the idea that the organization's information system and information are valued assets that deserve protection. While the tangibility of some assets may be difficult to value monetarily, they are valuable nonetheless and must be protected.

- **Protection of information assets**   Since the organization's information-related assets have value, they must be protected. The policy should describe the ways that information assets are protected through controls to protect their confidentiality, integrity, and availability.

- **Acceptable behavior**   Information security policy must clearly state what is expected of the organization's employees by defining the types of behavior and activities that are required, permitted, and forbidden.

- **Risk management**   The information security policy should describe the manner through which risks are measured and treated. This should include a policy for handling exceptions (circumstances where security policy and organization objectives are at odds with one another).

- **Support of laws and regulations**   Information security policy should clearly state the organization's support of applicable laws and regulations. For instance, policy should include statements of support for intellectual property laws through the use of copyrighted and trademarked works.

- **Enforcement and consequences**   The policy should state how it is to be enforced and by whom, and a statement of the consequences of willful or negligent violation of security policy should be included. Generally, a policy should state that "violations may result in disciplinary action including termination of employment."

An organization's security policy should be easily found and understood. The policy can be published on the organization's internal website or portal. It should be written in a style that makes it easily understood by all personnel.

Security Awareness

People do not have particularly good instincts when it comes to the protection of information systems and information-related assets. But people are generally teachable, and they can be trained in the methods used to safeguard the organization's information and systems. A formal security awareness program should include activities that will help employees better understand how information protection measures work and how they should be used. Most employees will agree that organization assets are valuable and should be protected—they just need to know *how* it is done.

The designers of a comprehensive security awareness program need to understand that people have a variety of learning styles, which means that reliance on a single method for disseminating security information is not going to work for everyone. Some of the elements of a security awareness program include

- **Signed acknowledgment of security policy**   In order to drive home the point of the seriousness of the company's security policy, all employees should be required to sign a statement that says they have read, understood, and will conform to the entire security policy. This should be done at the time of hire, but increasingly, organizations are requiring employees to sign this once each year.

- **Security awareness training upon hire**   Each new employee should receive a dose of formal training at the time of hire. This training should serve as an orientation to the organization's security policy and programs of asset protection. This will help the employee know his or her responsibilities, where to find the policy and additional information, how they are expected to participate in asset protection, and the consequences for failing to do so.

- **Annual security awareness training**   Many organizations are extending their security awareness training from the time of hire to annually for all employees. This gives employees opportunities for "refresher" materials as well as updated information that is based on new practices, threats, and policies. The state of the art of security controls is ever-changing, and security awareness training should be updated accordingly.

- **Internal website**   An internal website (or other manner through which the organization makes information available to its employees on demand) should include content on security awareness, controls, policies, and other information that employees can access. Like security policy, the information should be easy to understand and use—and employees should be able to easily understand *how* to use the information there to better protect the organization's assets.

- **Periodic messages**   From time to time, it may be necessary to send e-mails to groups of employees (or the entire organization) to make them aware of things that they need to know. Periodic messages also help distribute information to employees who won't bother to visit an internal website—some rely on the company to "push" information to them that they will read.

- **Posters and flyers**   Sometimes, it may be advantageous to make employees aware of security matters in ways other than websites and e-mail messages. Posters can be put up where people congregate: kitchens, break rooms, meeting rooms, and auditoriums. Like websites and e-mail, an organization should not rely on just one method for communications; posters and flyers are another effective way to get the message to employees.

- **Rewards for desired behavior**   Management should reward its employees for making contributions toward the protection of organization assets. For example, employees who notice and report security threats or vulnerabilities, or who find a better way to protect assets, could be rewarded with recognition awards or gift certificates.

 NOTE   An effective security awareness program should help to create a culture of participation in the protection of the organization's information assets.

Security Monitoring and Auditing

The only things that can be managed are those that are measured. In an organization's information security program, several key areas need to be monitored and audited.

This will help management better understand whether its security policies and controls are effective.

Security analysts and auditors should periodically test the organization's controls (including but not limited to security controls) to see if they are working properly. Indeed, this is the topic of this entire book. Only through monitoring and auditing can an organization really know whether the policies, procedures, and controls that it has established are doing a good job of protecting the organization's information and information systems.

Monitoring is also discussed in Chapter 2, and is covered in more detail in Chapter 5.

Incident Response

A security incident is an event where the confidentiality, integrity, or availability of information (or an information system) has been or is in danger of being compromised. An organization should have an incident response plan in place that will define how the organization should respond when an incident occurs. Some of the common types of incidents that should be included in a response plan include

- **Information exposure or theft** Information that is protected by one or more controls may still be exposed to unauthorized persons through a weakness in controls or by deliberate acts.

- **Information system theft** Laptop computers, mobile devices, and other information-processing equipment can be stolen, which may directly or indirectly lead to further compromises. If the stolen device contains retrievable sensitive information or the means to access sensitive information stored elsewhere, then what has started out as a theft of a tangible asset may expand to become a compromise of sensitive information as well.

- **Information corruption** A human intruder or automated malware such as a worm or virus may damage information stored on a system. This damage may or may not be readily noticed.

- **Malware** Viruses, Trojan horses, worms, and rootkits can penetrate a system and result in consumption of resources or corruption or compromise of information.

Most organizations periodically test their incident response plans to make sure that they will be effective when a real security incident occurs.

Corrective and Preventive Actions

Any organization that is intent on reducing risk through security-related processes and activities needs to consider using corrective and preventive actions processes. The purpose of these processes is to formally track corrective and preventive actions so that they will be completed on time and not forgotten.

A corrective and preventive actions process may be as simple as a list of actions tracked on a spreadsheet or as complex as an incident tracking system (sometimes known as a ticketing system or a helpdesk application). The level of complexity should meet the organization's needs for tracking, reporting, follow-up, and escalation of actions.

Roles and Responsibilities

An effective information security management program requires several key roles and responsibilities, which are held by individuals or groups. These roles and responsibilities should be formally defined in the organization's information security policy. They can also be defined in a charter document that describes the mission, objectives, roles, and responsibilities in the organization's information security program. Either way, this information must be readily available to all employees.

Security-related roles and responsibilities include these core elements:

- **Executive management**   Responsible for ratification and support of information security policy and overall responsibility for asset protection.

- **Security steering committee**   A committee of senior-level officials from every department in the organization for approval of security policies, discussion of risk-related matters, and allocation of resources to carry out asset protection.

- **Chief information security officer (CISO)**   The senior-level official who is responsible for development and enforcement of security policy and the protection of information assets.

- **Chief privacy officer (CPO)**   The senior-level official who is responsible for the proper handling of personally sensitive information belonging to employees and customers to protect their privacy rights.

- **Security auditors**   Responsible for monitoring and testing security controls and delivering written opinions on the effectiveness of those controls.

- **Security administrators**   Responsible for operating or monitoring specific security controls such as user access controls, firewalls, or intrusion detection systems.

- **Security analyst**   Responsible for implementing security policy by designing, improving, and/or monitoring security processes and security controls.

- **Systems analysts**   Responsible for implementing security policy by designing application software that includes adequate controls to protect the application as well as the information that it manages and stores.

- **Software developers**   Responsible for coding application software that includes controls to prevent application misuse or bypass of controls to protect the integrity and confidentiality of information.

- **Managers**   Responsible for the actions of the employees whom they supervise.

- **Asset owners**   Responsible for protection and integrity of assets, and for approving requests to access the assets they control.

- **Employees**   Responsible for supporting security policy by using information systems and handling information assets properly, and for reporting incidents and other security matters to management.

EXAM TIP The roles and responsibilities here are considered common practice. There will be minor variations in the roles and responsibilities described here in many organizations.

Asset Inventory and Classification

Information assets fall into two basic categories: information and information systems. *Information* consists of software, tools, and every type of data. *Information system* is an inclusive term that encompasses servers, workstations, mobile devices, network devices, gateways, appliances, and almost every other kind of IT hardware that is used.

Information and information systems both need to be inventoried. This helps management continue to be aware of their existence so that they can be properly managed over time.

Information and information systems also need to be classified. This will ensure that they will be properly handled according to their sensitivity, importance, and other classification criteria.

Hardware Asset Inventory

An IS organization that is responsible for the management of information and information systems must have a means for knowing what all of those assets are. More than that, IS needs to acquire and track several characteristics about every hardware asset, including

- **Identification** This includes make, model, serial number, asset tag number, and any other means for identifying the asset.

- **Value** Initially, this may signify the purchased value, but may also include its depreciated value if an IS asset management program is associated with the organization's financial asset management program.

- **Location** The asset's location needs to be specified so that its existence may be verified in a periodic inventory.

- **Security classification** Security management programs almost always include a plan for classifying the sensitivity of information and/or information systems. Example classifications include top secret, secret, restricted, confidential, and public.

- **Asset group** IS assets may be classified into a hierarchy of asset groups. For example, any of the servers in a data center that support a large application may be assigned to an asset group known as "Application X Servers."

- **Owner** This is usually the person or group responsible for the operation of the asset.

- **Custodian** Occasionally, the ownership and operations of assets will be divided into two bodies, where the owner owns them but a custodian operates or maintains them.

Because hardware assets are installed, moved, and eventually retired, it is important to periodically verify the information in the asset inventory by physically verifying the existence of the physical assets. Depending upon the value and sensitivity of systems and data, this inventory "true-up" may be performed as often as monthly or as seldom as once per year. Discrepancies in actual inventory must be investigated in order to verify that assets have not been moved without authorization or stolen.

Information Assets

Sometimes overlooked because it is intangible, the information that is stored in systems should be treated as an asset. In almost all cases, information such as software and databases has tangible value and should be included in the list of IS assets.

Information Classification Overview   In most organizations, various types and sets of information will have varying degrees of sensitivity. These levels of sensitivity will implicitly dictate that information in different levels should be handled somewhat differently. For instance, the most sensitive information should be encrypted whenever stored or transmitted and should be accessible to only those individuals who have a justified need to use it.

Would it be easier to simply handle all information the same way as the most sensitive information in the organization? While it would be easier to remember how to handle and dispose of all information, it would also be onerous. Encrypting everything and shredding everything would be a wasteful use of resources. That said, it is incumbent on an organization to build a simple information classification program that is easy to understand and follow. Too many levels of classification would be as burdensome as a single level.

Information Classification Details   In most organizations, an information classification program can be defined in detail in less than a dozen pages, and the practical portions of it could almost fit on a single page. For many organizations, a simple four-level classification program is a good place to start. The four levels could be: secret, restricted, confidential, and public. Any information in the organization would be classified into one of these four levels.

Handling procedures for each of these levels is found in Table 6-1.

The foregoing classification and handling guidelines are meant as an example to illustrate the differences in various forms of data handling for various classification levels. However, the contents of Table 6-1 can serve as a starting point for an actual data classification and handling procedure.

Access Controls

Access controls are the technology-based methods of controlling access to an information-based resource. Access controls must be actively managed by staff members who are authorized to perform this function and trained to perform it properly.

	Secret	Restricted	Confidential	Public
Example information types	Passwords; merger and acquisition plans and terms	Credit card numbers; bank account numbers; Social Security numbers; detailed financial records; detailed system configuration; vulnerability scan reports	System documentation; end-user documentation; internal memos; network diagrams	Brochures; press releases
Storage on server	Must be encrypted; store only on servers labeled sensitive	Must be encrypted	Access controls required	No restrictions
Storage on mobile device	Must never be stored on mobile device	Must be encrypted	Access controls required	No restrictions
E-mail	Must never be e-mailed	Must be encrypted	Authorized recipients only	No restrictions
Website	Must never be stored on any web server	Must be encrypted	Access controls required	No restrictions
Fax	Encrypted, manned fax only	Manned fax only; no e-mail–based fax	Manned fax only	No restrictions
Courier	Double wrapped; signature and secure storage required	Signature and secure storage required	Signature required	No restrictions
Hardcopy storage	Double locked in authorized locations only	Double locked	Locked	No restrictions
Hardcopy distribution	Only with owner permission; must be registered	To authorized parties only; only with owner permission	To authorized parties only	No restrictions
Hardcopy destruction	Cross-cut shred; make record of destruction	Cross-cut shred	Cross-cut shred or secure waste bin	No restrictions
Softcopy destruction	Erase with DoD 5220.22-M spec tool	Erase with DoD 5220.22-M spec tool	Delete and empty recycle bin	No restriction

Table 6-1 Example Information Handling Guidelines

The workings of access controls are discussed later in this chapter in the section "Logical Access Controls."

Access controls also exist in the physical world, and are discussed later in this chapter in the section "Physical Security Controls."

Access Control Management

The management of access controls requires that processes and business rules be established that govern how access controls are managed. These processes and rules are used to decide which persons will be permitted to access which data and functions in the organization.

The processes to manage access controls are

- **Access control request** Any new request for access must be formally made via an established request procedure. The request should be approved by the subject's manager, as well as by the owner of the resource to which access is being requested.

- **Access control review** A periodic review of all users' access to systems must be performed to verify that everyone who has access is still entitled to that access and to verify that all access for terminated employees has been removed.

- **Segregation of duties review** A periodic review of each user's access rights in all systems must be performed to verify that each employee does not have a combination of access privileges that would constitute a violation of segregation of duties.

- **Employee transfer** When an employee is transferred from one position to another, the access rights associated with the departed position must be removed and any new access rights for the new position established.

- **Employee termination** When an employee is no longer employed by the organization, all access rights for that employee must be terminated immediately.

All of these processes must have a robust recordkeeping plan so that all requests, reviews, transfers, and terminations are well documented. These records must themselves be restricted so that only authorized persons may view them. These records also must be protected against tampering.

In addition to these processes, there are several audit and monitoring procedures to verify correct operation of these procedures; auditing is discussed later in this chapter.

Access Control Logs

The preceding section discussed business processes and the records that are associated with them. In addition to those records, the information systems that persons are given permission to access must have automatic records of their own. These systems must record all accesses made by persons. And like the records associated with business processes, these records must also be protected from alteration. This topic is discussed in more detail later in this chapter in the section, "Logical Access Controls."

Privacy

Privacy is the protection of personal information from unauthorized disclosure, use, and distribution. *Personal information* refers to a variety of elements about a private citizen, some of which are not well known, including their name in combination with one or more of the following:

- Date and place of birth
- Place of residence
- Fixed and mobile telephone numbers
- Social insurance (e.g., Social Security) number
- Driver's license number
- Passport number
- Financial account (e.g., credit card, bank account, retirement account) numbers

Historically, the concern about privacy stemmed from organizations that collected, aggregated, and then distributed databases containing private citizens' information, which was then used for targeted marketing and other purposes.

More recently, the worry about privacy has concerned the rise in identity theft, which is made possible from the proliferation of private information and the failure to adequately secure that information. Cybercriminals have had an easy time discovering and stealing this information in order to conduct wide-scale identity theft.

Organizations that collect any of the previously mentioned items on behalf of customers or other constituents need to develop policies that define what the organization is permitted to do with this information. Organizations also need to be aware of applicable privacy laws and regulations, and ensure they are fully compliant with them. For each item of potentially sensitive information, an organization should be able to specify

- Why it collects the information
- How it uses the information
- How long it retains the information
- How the information can be corrected by its owners
- To what other organizations the information is distributed and why
- Who is responsible for protecting the information
- How an owner can opt out (causing the cessation of storage of that information)

Business processes, procedures, and records should exist for all of these associated uses and actions, which can then be monitored and audited by others as needed.

Third-Party Management

Nearly every IS organization relies on one or more third-party organizations in the development, support, or operations of its information systems. There are so many specialties and subspecialties in information technology that even the largest organizations need to utilize third-party organizations to build, support, or manage their IT environment.

Third Parties and Risk

The use of any third-party organization should not be permitted to increase overall security risk to an organization. When considering outsourcing a service to a third party, a risk assessment should be performed to identify and characterize risks associated with this.

Some of the types of services that third-party service organizations provide include

- Internet service providers (ISPs)
- Internet hosting providers
- Application service providers (for e-mail, CRM [customer relationship management], ERP [enterprise resource planning], MRP [materials resource planning], payroll, and expense reporting)
- Managed security services
- Software development and testing
- Call centers
- Collection services
- Management and business consultants
- Auditors and security assessors
- Vendors that support hardware and software solutions
- Janitorial and other cleaning
- Shipping and receiving
- Building and equipment maintenance
- Temporary employee services

The primary risk with a third-party service provider is that the service provider will have access to some of the organization's sensitive information. Whether the service provider will have access to the organization's applications and data, or whether the organization will be sending data to the service provider, this overall risk needs to be broken down into each component and analyzed.

For each risk identified, one or more compensating controls need to be identified, ideally so that the risk can be reduced to the same level as though the organization were performing the service on its own.

Types of Third-Party Access

Depending upon the type of service, third-party service providers will have access to the organization's information in a variety of ways, including

- Physical access to hardcopy business records
- Physical access to information systems
- Physical access to media such as hard drives, backup tapes, and CD/DVD-ROM
- Login to application as end user
- Login to application as administrative user
- Login to database
- Login to operating system
- Login to network device

 NOTE A third-party service provider does not necessarily need access to sensitive business records to pose a risk. A service provider that is familiar with the organization's business practices can cause harm to the organization by interfering with business operations or disclosing business practices to outsiders such as customers or competitors.

Risks Associated with Third-Party Access

Knowing the type of access that a third-party service provider will have to an organization's information, the types of risks can be identified. Some of these risks are

- Theft of business records
- Exposure of business records to unauthorized parties
- Alteration of business records
- Damage (both deliberate and accidental) to information systems hardware, software, or information
- Failure to perform services in a timely manner
- Failure to perform services accurately
- Failure to perform services professionally

Third-Party Access Countermeasures

As mentioned earlier in this section, the risks associated with a third-party service provider should be no different than if the organization were performing the service on its own. Even though new risks are introduced when transferring work to a service provider, countermeasures and compensating controls should be introduced that will keep the level of risk acceptably low.

Some of the countermeasures that can be used to mitigate risk include

- Video surveillance with video recording
- Logging all data access and associated accesses to named individuals in the third-party organization
- Access controls that prevent the third party from accessing business records that it does not need to use
- Logical access controls that limit the third party's access to only those data fields required to perform their services
- Recording of voice or data communications sessions
- Periodic audits of the service provider's activities

Generally, an organization can require that a third-party service organization that has logical access to the organization's systems or stores any of the organization's data protect this data with the same level of controls that the organization itself uses. This should result in the third-party service organization's *not* being in a situation where the organization's records are more vulnerable to theft, exposure, or compromise. For example, if your organization requires encryption of specific information when processed in your organization's systems, any service provider that processes the same information should also be required to encrypt it.

 NOTE In any situation where treatment for a specific risk associated with a third-party service provider results in unavoidable residual risk, senior management will need to be made aware of the residual risk and determine if they are willing to accept it.

When an organization is considering use of a third-party service provider, the organization should require the service provider to answer a detailed questionnaire concerning security and other aspects of its operation. The organization should also ask whether the service provider has had any external audits of its services; if so, the organization should request to see reports from those audits.

Addressing Third-Party Security in Legal Agreements

The services performed by the third-party service provider should be succinctly described in a legal agreement. This will generally include a description of the services that are performed, measures of quantity and quality for services, remedies or penalties for failures in quality or quantity, rates and payments, and roles and responsibilities for both parties.

Legal agreements with service providers need to include several security provisions, including

- A statement that all of the organization's information and knowledge of its business practices will be kept confidential
- Security- and privacy-related liabilities, roles, and responsibilities
- Security controls required to protect the organization's information

- Acceptable uses for the organization's information

- Persons who will be authorized to access the organization's information

- Background checks, nondisclosure agreements, and acceptable-use agreements for each person who is authorized to access the organization's information

- Required security training for persons authorized to access the organization's information

- Steps to be taken if a security breach should occur

- Steps to be taken to reduce the likelihood of data loss caused by a natural or manmade disaster

- Who is responsible for security and privacy in the third-party organization

- The right to inspect and audit the third-party organization's premises and operations on short notice

- Compliance with all applicable laws and regulations

- Agreement to destroy all copies of information on request or upon the termination of the agreement

Many additional security-related terms and conditions may be warranted, depending upon the nature of the services provided and the sensitivity and value of the information accessed and used by the service provider.

Addressing Third-Party Security in Security Policy

Many organizations provide commercial applications on the Web, which are as easy to set up as filling in a registration form, paying with a credit card, and uploading sensitive data right from a person's workstation. These organizations operate as application service providers (ASPs), Software-as-a-Service (SaaS), or cloud service models.

Often, the persons in an organization have little idea about the security controls that are used by service providers. Because of this, organizations can enact a security and business policy that forbids the use of any online service provider (ASP, SaaS, cloud, etc.) unless a risk assessment has first been performed for that service provider. Without such a policy, there is little to stop persons from signing up with various online service providers and potentially putting the organization's sensitive data at risk.

 NOTE An organization should have policies and processes in place to properly assess, measure, and monitor risks related to any third-party service provider.

Human Resources Security

The hearts of most organizations' business operations are not computers, machinery, or buildings, but people. People design and operate business processes; they design, build, and operate IT systems; they support processes and systems and help to improve them over time. And while people are an organization's greatest asset, they may also be a source of significant risk.

People are entrusted with access to sensitive information, and entrusted to design and create information systems to manage sensitive information properly. But an employee in a position of trust can betray that trust and cause a tremendous amount of damage to the organization's operations and long-term reputation.

Trust is the key: organizations provide access to sensitive information, trusting that their employees will honor that trust and treat information properly. The trust is reciprocal: employees also trust that their employer will treat them with respect and pay them a fair salary.

Organizations need to take several measures to mitigate human resource–related risks. These measures are described in the remainder of this section.

Screening and Background Checks

Prior to hiring each employee, an organization should verify the facts that each candidate presents on her résumé or curriculum vitae. The confirmation of these and other important facts is commonly known as a background check, and may consist of

- Verification of the candidate's identity
- Confirmation of the candidate's right to work in the employer's locale
- Verification of previous employment
- Verification of education
- Verification of professional licenses and certifications
- Investigation into the candidate's criminal history
- Investigation into the candidate's financial history
- Drug test

Irregularities in any of these areas may be a signal to the employer that further investigation is required if the employer is still intent on hiring the candidate. The organization discovering irregularities in a candidate's background may also rescind a pending offer of employment or decide not to make an offer.

In addition to a background check, an employer will usually check references. This means that the employer will contact one or more professional colleagues in order to learn more about the candidate. The employer might also make inquiries through its network of professional acquaintances to gather intelligence about the candidate from people who are not references. For example, if a security manager is hiring a security analyst and receives a résumé from an employee at a local organization, the security manager could contact other known colleagues in the organization to see if any of them are familiar with the candidate. This can be a source of valuable information, since sometimes a candidate's references may be coached to say certain things or avoid certain topics.

 CAUTION   Employers frequently search social networking sites such as MySpace and Facebook in order to gather additional intelligence on prospective employees. These and other social networking sites often reveal more about a person's character than will be found on a résumé, application for employment, or references.

Another emerging trend in organization is the practice of repeating background checks throughout an employee's tenure. This can help an employer discover certain facts about recent criminal convictions or significant financial events (such as judgments, collections, or bankruptcy) that may warrant action on the employer's part.

Job Descriptions

A job description is an employer's formal statement to an employee that says, "This is what we expect and require of you to perform this job." Employers should have formal job descriptions for each position in the organization. The main reason for this is to formally document the expectations that the organization has for each employee. These expectations should include

- **Name of the position**   (e.g., senior security auditor or database administrator)
- **Requirements**   This will include necessary education, skills, and work experience.
- **Duties and responsibilities**   This will include the tasks, projects, and other activities that the employee is expected to perform.

The duties and responsibilities section should include a statement that says the employee is required to uphold all of the organization's policies (including security policy). The job description could list the major policies by name.

Employment Agreements

In locales that permit them, organizations should utilize written employment agreements with each employee. The employment agreement should clearly specify the terms and conditions of employment, including

- **Duties**   The employment agreement should describe the employee's duties in his or her position. This may be similar to what is stated in the employee's job description.
- **Roles and responsibilities**   The employment agreement should define the employee's roles and responsibilities, as well as the responsibilities of the employer. This will be similar to what is found in the job description.
- **Confidentiality**   The employee agrees to keep all company secrets confidential, even after termination of employment.
- **Compliance**   The employee must agree to comply with all applicable laws and regulations, as well as with all organization policies. The employment agreement should state the consequences of failing to comply with laws, regulations, and policies.
- **Termination**   The employment agreement should include the conditions and circumstances by which the organization or the employee can sever the agreement.

During Employment

Organizations need to enact several safeguards during the span of employment for each employee. These safeguards ensure that each employee's behavior is appropriate and that each employee is able to do only what is required of him or her. These safeguards include

- **Periodic renewal of employment agreements**   Documents signed at the time of hire, including nondisclosure, employment, security policy, and other agreements, should be renewed periodically. Organizations that employ this practice do this annually.

- **Repeat background checks**   Occasionally, repeating background checks helps to ensure that each employee's background (criminal history in particular) is still acceptable.

- **Access changes when transferred**   Any employee who is transferred from one position to another should have their accesses for the former position removed. This helps to prevent the accumulation of privileges over time.

- **Awareness training**   Employees should undergo periodic training on important topics, including security awareness training, so that they will continue to be aware of security procedures and requirements.

Policy and Discipline   During their service, employees, contractors, temps, and other workers are expected to comply with the organization's security policy and other policies. The organization's security management program needs to include monitoring and internal auditing to ensure that policies are adhered to. When policy violations occur, human resources will need to invoke its disciplinary action process as needed.

Disciplinary action that is related to security policy violations should not be treated differently from any other disciplinary matter. IS security may be asked to provide facts about the matter, but should otherwise not be involved. Discipline is usually a matter between an employee's manager and the employee; human resources should be involved only if the matter is serious enough to warrant a letter in the employee's employment file, suspension, demotion, or termination of employment.

Equipment   The organization should keep records regarding any equipment, software, licenses, or other assets that are entrusted to the employee, particularly when the asset will be used away from company premises, such as in the employee's home. Each time an asset is issued to an employee, a simple checkout document should be completed that describes the asset, the employee's name, the date issued, and an agreement that the asset will be returned to the employer on request. The employee should be required to sign this document, and a copy placed in his or her employment file.

If the employee transfers to another position or department, or leaves the organization altogether, human resources should retrieve all equipment checkout forms and make sure that the employee returns each asset.

Transfers and Terminations

When employees are transferred from one position or department to another, they may be required to return certain assets entrusted to their care if they are no longer needed in the new role. Similarly, after transfer, an employee's access rights should be reviewed and any accesses from the old position that are not required in the new position be removed. This is covered in more detail in the earlier section, "Access Controls."

When an employee's employment is terminated, his or her access to information systems and business premises should be immediately revoked. All equipment, documents, software, and other assets in the employee's care should be returned and accounted for. The access badge and other identifying items should also be returned.

Contractors and Temporary Workers

Contractors, consultants, temps, and other workers should be required to conform to many of the same organization policies that are required of employees, including

- Nondisclosure agreement
- Security policy agreement
- Other policies

Computer Crime

Computers are involved in many criminal acts and enterprises. This section discusses the uses of computers in criminal activities.

Roles of Computers in Crime

Being the flexible, multipurpose tools that they are, computers can be used in several different ways in the commission and support of crimes. And because some computers contain valuable information, they are the targets of crimes. There are three main ways in which a computer is involved in a crime:

- **Target of a crime**   A computer or its contents are the target of a crime. Some of the types of crimes are
  - **Equipment theft**   The computer itself (or related equipment or media) is stolen.
  - **Equipment vandalism**   Computer equipment may be damaged or destroyed.
  - **Data theft**   Data that is stored on the computer or related media may be stolen. This is a more difficult crime to detect, since thieves usually steal a copy of the data, leaving the original data intact and untouched.
  - **Data vandalism**   Data that is stored on a computer may be deliberately altered, sometimes in ways that go undetected for a time.
  - **Trespass**   Someone enters the computer system without permission or authorization.
- **Instrument in a crime**   A computer is used as a weapon or tool to commit a crime. Some of the types of crimes that can be perpetrated include
  - **Trespass**   This is the unauthorized and unlawful entry into a computer or network.

- **Data theft and vandalism**   Intruders enter computers or networks and steal or destroy data and programs.

- **Sabotage**   Intruders destroy computer hardware, software, or data.

- **Child pornography**   This is the unlawful storage or distribution of child pornography content.

- **Libel and slander**   These are communications that make claims that give a subject a negative image.

- **Espionage**   An individual or group obtains information considered a military, political, or industrial secret.

- **Eavesdropping**   A computer can be used to eavesdrop on electronic messaging, such as e-mail, instant messaging, and even voice over IP (VoIP).

- **Spam**   Computers are used to generate and deliver millions of spam messages every day.

- **Support of a crime**   Computers can be used to support criminal activities. Some of the ways that this can occur include

  - **Recordkeeping**   Computers can be used to record criminal activities. For example, a petty thief who breaks into houses can track the items he steals and then resells in a spreadsheet program.

  - **Aid and abet**   Computers can be used to provide support for other criminals. For instance, a computer can be used to send helpful information and funds to a criminal in hiding.

  - **Conspiracy**   A computer can be used to document the plans for a crime. Criminals can use word processing tools, such as "track changes," to perfect their criminal schemes.

It should be easy to imagine that computers can play multiple roles in crimes: they can be used as weapons as well as recordkeeping systems, for instance.

Categories of Computer Crime

Cybercrime comes in a lot of flavors, primarily because computers are used as targets for so many purposes. It may be helpful to remember that the information stored in computers has some value—and the nature and value of that information will attract various types of criminal elements. Computer crimes are roughly analogous to crimes in the physical world: People rob banks to get the money; they deface statues in public places to embarrass government and make a political point; they attack public transportation systems in acts of terrorism; and they steal purses in order to get quick cash and maybe a few usable credit cards.

The categories of computer crime can be thought of in this way:

- **Military and intelligence**   Here, attackers are attempting to obtain military or intelligence secrets or disrupt military or intelligence operations. These attacks may occur at any time—during wartime, periods of hostility, or when there are no apparent tensions between governments. Governments as well as nongovernment-sanctioned civilian groups may carry out these attacks.

- **Political** This type of attack may be carried out by one state against another, but more typically, the attacker is a state-sponsored or independent group.

- **Terrorist** Here, attackers are attempting to induce fear and panic among a populace by damaging or disrupting critical infrastructure that is controlled or monitored by computers, including utilities, government services, financial services, health care, education, and other organizations.

- **Financial** In this type of attack, perpetrators are carrying out activities in an attempt to steal funds, credit card numbers, bank account numbers, or perpetrate fraud. Targets include financial institutions and all other organizations that store or process financial data.

- **Business** This represents a wide variety of purposes, including espionage, extortion, theft, vandalism, denial of service, and any attacks designed to weaken or embarrass a business organization.

- **Grudge** As the name implies, a grudge attack is generally motivated by feelings of revenge that an individual or group wishes to exact upon an organization.

- **Amusement** This type of attack is carried out primarily for fun. Nevertheless, these attacks can still be lethal and cause significant damage or embarrassment.

Most attacks are a blend of two or more of the categories discussed here. Understanding these categories can help an organization better understand how to prepare for possible cyberattacks.

Threats of Cybercrime on Organizations

Organizations that use computers to store information of value (whether tangible value or not) need to take steps to protect that information. The nature of the information does have a bearing on the types of threats that will be most prevalent for a given organization. In general, the threats include

- **Financial** Organizations that store financial-related information, particularly credit card numbers and bank account numbers, are more likely to be the target of crimes where criminals will attempt to steal this information. Organizations may also be the target of one or more types of financial fraud, including

  - **Transferring funds** A website that is used to send or receive funds will be the target of attackers, who will attempt to trick the application—or its other users—into transferring funds to attackers' accounts.

  - **Stealing service** Intruders may attempt to trick a website into providing free service. For instance, a flaw in a site's payment acceptance program may permit a user to receive service without paying for it.

- **Account hijacking** This can occur through malware that sniffs user IDs and passwords from existing customers, or phishing schemes that entice customers to click on links that take them to imposter sites that appear to be financial institutions.

- **Click fraud** Many online advertisers pay for clicks on their online ads. Attackers can build malware to generate clicks from victim computers in order to collect payments.

- **Social engineering** Attackers will attempt to trick people into responding to e-mails purporting to be invoices or refund requests, providing their valuable login credentials to a phony website.

- **Disclosure of sensitive information** If an organization has sensitive information, intruders will attempt to steal or deface it. Sensitive information can be almost anything of value, including bank account and credit card numbers, intellectual property, personally identifiable information, and military and government secrets. Perpetrators might try to either steal or deface this information, or simply discover how to do that and disclose that technique to others.

- **Blackmail** If hackers or organized crime enterprises are able to successfully break in to an organization's computers or networks, they may be able to encrypt or remove sensitive information and then demand payments to restore that information.

- **Sabotage** Hackers may wish to break in to computers or networks in order to damage their ability to perform their function. This kind of an attack could range from damaging operating systems, application software, or information—whatever it takes to damage or destroy a system.

- **Reputation** Intruders may be inclined to break in to an organization's computers or networks in some visible way simply for the opportunity to embarrass the organization and damage its reputation.

- **Legal** Security breaches may invite lawsuits from customers, business partners, and shareholders.

Perpetrators of Cybercrime

Many different types of individuals and groups will commit cybercrimes if they have sufficient motivation. The nature of the organization and the data that it stores on its computers will influence which groups and individuals will be more likely to attack the organization's systems. In no particular order, the perpetrators of cybercrimes include

- **Hackers** Usually lone combatants who have the skills and the tools to break in to computer systems and networks. They can steal or deface information, or plant software in an organization's computers for a variety of purposes.

- **Cybercriminal gangs and organized crime** Lured by big profits, organized crime has moved headlong into the cybercrime business with profits that exceed those from drug trafficking, according to the U.S. Treasury Department. Cybercrime organizations are well organized with investors and capital, research and development budgets, supply chains, employees on payroll, and profit sharing. Owners and employees in cybercriminal organizations network with each other and attend conferences to further their knowledge and skills.

- **Spies and intelligence agents**   People in intelligence organizations may attempt to break in to the computers or networks in target governments or industries in order to collect intelligence information. Often these agents will employ hackers to perform information-gathering activities.

- **Terrorists**   State-sponsored, privately sponsored, and just plain rogue groups of individuals perpetrate cybercrimes against populations in order to induce fear and intimidation, and eventually to precipitate changes in a nation's foreign policy. There have not been many spectacular terrorism-based cybercrimes (none that we know of anyway), but it's likely just a matter of time.

- **Script kiddies**   Inexperienced computer hackers obtain hacking tools from others. The term "script kiddies" refers to usually adolescents (kiddies) or simply inexperienced would-be hackers who obtain hacking tools (scripts) in order to break in to computers for fun or just to pass the time.

- **Social engineers**   These clever individuals will use a variety of means to gain information about an organization's inner workings that they use to exploit the organization. Social engineers frequently use pretexting (pretending to be someone they aren't) in order to get employees to give up secrets that help them break in to systems.

- **Employees**   People who work in an organization have the means and often have opportunities to steal equipment and information from their employers. Usually all they need is motivation. Employers often deliver motivation on a silver platter as a result of draconian policies and working conditions.

- **Former employees**   People who used to work in organizations know their secrets, vulnerabilities, and inner workings. Terminated and laid-off employees sometimes have sufficient motivation to steal from or embarrass their former employers as a way of getting even for losing their job.

- **Knowledgeable outsiders**   These are persons who have some knowledge about an organization's internal systems, architecture, or vulnerabilities. These individuals can gain their knowledge through espionage, social engineering, eavesdropping, or from current or former employees. The point is they know more than most outsiders.

- **Service provider employees**   Personnel employed at service providers are another class of knowledgeable outsiders; through their business relationship with the organization, they possess information about the organization's people, processes, and technology that they can use to harm the organization through criminal means.

Because cybercrime can be perpetrated by so many different types of people, it is quite a challenge to "think like a cybercriminal" in order to prepare one's defenses. While such an approach will still be helpful, it requires broad reflection on the part of security analysts and engineers who are responsible for protecting an organization's valuable assets.

Security Incident Management

A security incident is defined as any event that represents a violation of an organization's security policy. For instance, if an organization's security policy states that it is not permitted for one person to use another person's computer account, then such a use that results in the disclosure of information would be considered a security incident. There are several types of security incidents:

- **Computer account abuse** Examples include willful account abuse, such as sharing user account credentials with other insiders or outsiders, or one person stealing a password from another.

- **Computer or network trespass** Here, an unauthorized person accesses a computer network. The methods of trespass include malware, using stolen credentials, access bypass, or gaining physical access to the computer or network and connecting to it directly.

- **Interception of information** An intruder devises a means for eavesdropping on communications. The intruder may be able to intercept e-mail messages, client-server communication, file transfers, logon credentials, and network diagnostic information. Some of the methods that can be used for eavesdropping include malware, installing sniffing programs on compromised computers, or direct connection to computers or networks.

- **Malware** A worm or virus outbreak may occur in an organization's network. The outbreak may disrupt normal business operations simply through the malware's spread, or the malware may also damage infected systems in other ways, including destroying or altering information. Malware can also eavesdrop on communications and send intercepted sensitive information back to its source.

- **Denial of service (DoS) attack** An attacker can flood a target computer or network with a volume of traffic that overwhelms the target so that it is unable to carry out its regular functions. For example, an attacker can flood an online banking website with so much traffic that the bank's depositors are unable to use it.

- **Distributed denial of service (DDoS) attack** Similar to a DoS attack, a distributed denial of service attack emanates simultaneously from hundreds to thousands of computers. A DDoS attack can be difficult to withstand because of the volume of incoming messages, as well as the large number of attacking systems.

- **Equipment theft**   Here, computer or network equipment is stolen. Information contained in stolen equipment may be easy to extract unless it is encrypted.

- **Disclosure of sensitive information**   Any sensitive information that is disclosed to any unauthorized party.

The examples here should give you an idea of the nature of a security incident. Other types of incidents may be considered security incidents in some organizations.

NOTE   A vulnerability that is discovered in an organization is not an incident. However, the severity of the vulnerability may prompt a response that is similar to an actual incident. Vulnerabilities should be fixed as soon as possible to prevent future incidents.

Phases of Incident Response

An effective response to an incident is organized, documented, and rehearsed. The phases of a formal incident response plan are

- **Planning**   This step involves the development of written response procedures that are followed when an incident occurs.

- **Detection**   This is the time when an organization is first aware that a security incident is taking place or has taken place. Because of the variety of events that characterize a security incident, an organization can become aware of an incident in several ways, including

  - Application or network malfunction

  - Application or network slowdown

  - Intrusion detection system alerts

  - Logfile alerts

  - Media outlets

  - Notification from an employee or business partner

  - Anonymous tips

- **Initiation**   This is the phase where response to the incident begins. Typically, this will include notifications that are sent to response team members so that response operations may begin.

- **Evaluation**   In this phase, response team members analyze available data in order to understand the cause, scope, and impact of the incident.

- **Eradication**   In this phase of incident response, responders are taking steps to remove the source of the incident. This could involve removing malware, blocking incoming attack messages, or removing an intruder.

- **Recovery**   When the incident has been evaluated and eradicated, often there is a need to recover systems or components to their pre-incident state. This might include restoring data or configurations, or replacing damaged or stolen equipment.

- **Remediation** This activity involves any necessary changes that will reduce or eliminate the possibility of a similar incident occurring in the future. This may take the form of process or technology changes.

- **Closure** Closure occurs when eradication, recovery, and remediation are completed. Incident response operations are officially closed.

- **Post-incident review** Shortly after the incident closes, incident responders and other personnel meet to discuss the incident: its cause, impact, and the organization's response. Discussion will range from lessons learned to possible improvements in technologies and processes to further improve defense and response.

Testing Incident Response

Incident response plans should not only be documented and reviewed—they need to be periodically tested. Incident response testing helps to improve the quality of those plans, which will help the organization to better respond when an incident occurs.

Similar to disaster recovery and business continuity planning, various types of tests should be carried out:

- **Document review** In this review, individual subject matter experts (SMEs) carefully read incident response documentation to better understand the procedures and to identify any opportunities for improvement.

- **Walkthrough** This is similar to a document review, except that it is performed by a group of subject matter experts, who talk through the response plan. Discussing each step helps to stimulate new ideas, which could lead to further improvements in the plan.

- **Simulation** Here, a facilitator describes a realistic security incident scenario and participants discuss how they will actually respond. A simulation usually takes half a day or longer. It is suggested that the scenario be "scripted" with new information and updates introduced throughout the scenario. A simulation can be limited to just the technology aspects of a security incident, or it can involve corporate communications, public relations, legal, and other externally facing parts of the organization that may play a part in a security incident that is known to the public.

These tests should be performed once each year or even more often. In the walk-through and simulation tests, someone should be appointed as note-taker so that any improvements will be recorded and the plan can be updated.

If the incident response plan contains the names and contact information for response personnel, the plan should be reviewed more frequently to ensure that all contact information is up-to-date.

Incident Prevention

With the right processes and controls, many incidents can be prevented from occurring in the first place. Incident prevention is primarily accomplished through knowledge of vulnerabilities and actions to remove them. With fewer vulnerabilities, some threats are reduced or neutralized altogether.

Important elements in the prevention of security incidents include

- **Vulnerability and threat monitoring**   This involves close monitoring of security advisories published by vendor and vendor-independent services such as US-CERT, Secunia, Full Disclosure, and Bugtraq. These advisories are publications of newly discovered flaws in computer hardware and software, as well as announcements of new threats that are seen in the wild.

- **Patch management**   This is a systems management process that utilizes tools used to install security patches in operating systems, database management systems, applications, and network devices. Many threats are realized through published vulnerabilities. Sometimes hackers are able to fashion tools to exploit vulnerabilities within hours of publication. It is therefore important that an organization be prepared to quickly deploy some security patches when it is known that specific vulnerabilities are being exploited in the wild. Patch management is discussed in more detail in the section "Logical Access Controls."

- **System hardening**   This is the technique of configuring a system so that only its essential services and features are active and all others are deactivated. This helps to reduce the "attack surface" of a system to only its essential components. On a hardened system, only the essential components need to be configured to resist attack; all other components are disabled and removed, resulting in less effort and fewer vulnerabilities. System hardening is discussed in more detail in the section "Logical Access Controls."

- **Intrusion detection**   Software programs and hardware appliances known as intrusion detection systems (IDS) can give early warnings of network- or computer-based attacks. Intrusion prevention systems (IPS) go one step further by actively blocking activities that resemble attacks.

 NOTE   A relatively modest effort at incident prevention can help to prevent many otherwise-damaging security incidents.

Forensic Investigations

Forensic investigations are required when a security incident has occurred and it is necessary to gather evidence to determine the facts. Because the information gathered in an investigation may later be used in a legal proceeding, the forensic investigator must follow strict procedures when gathering, studying, and retaining information.

Chain of Custody

The key to an effective and successful forensic investigation is the establishment of a sound chain of custody. The major considerations that determine the effectiveness of a forensic investigation are

- **Identification** A description of the evidence that was acquired, and the tools and techniques used to acquire it. Evidence may include digital information acquired from computers, network devices, and mobile devices, as well as interviews of involved persons.

- **Preservation** A description of the tools and techniques used to retain evidence. This will include detailed records that establish the chain of custody, which may be presented and tested in legal proceedings.

- **Analysis** A description of the examination of the evidence gathered, which may include a reconstruction of events that are a subject of the investigation.

- **Presentation** A formal document that describes the entire investigation, evidence gathered, tools used, and findings that express the examiner's opinion of the events that occurred (or did not occur).

The entire chain of custody must be documented in precise detail and include how evidence was protected against tampering through every step of the investigation. Any "holes" in the information acquisition and analysis process will likely fail in legal proceedings, possibly resulting in the organization's failure to convince judicial authorities that the event occurred as described.

Forensic Techniques and Considerations

Computer and network forensics requires several specialized techniques that ensure the integrity of the entire forensic investigation and a sound chain of evidence. Some of these techniques are

- **Data acquisition** This is the process of acquiring data for forensic analysis. Subject data may reside on a computer hard drive, mobile device memory, or in an application's audit log. Several tools are used for forensic data acquisition, including media copiers, which are tools that acquire a copy of a computer's hard drive; USB memory stick; or removable media, such as a floppy disk or CD/DVD-ROM.

- **Data extraction** If data is being acquired from a running system or from a third party, a forensics analyst must use a secure method to acquire the data, and be able to demonstrates the integrity of the process used to acquire the data. This must be done in a way that proves the source of the data and that it was not altered during the extraction process.

- **Data protection** Once data is acquired, the forensic investigator must take every step to ensure its integrity. Computers used for forensic analysis must be physically locked so that no other persons have access to them. They must not be connected to any network that would allow for the introduction of malware or other agents that could alter acquired data and influence the investigation's outcome.

- **Analysis and transformation**   Often, tools are required to analyze acquired data and search for specific clues. Also, data must frequently be transformed from its native state into a state that is human- or tool-readable; in many cases, computers store information in a binary format that is not easily read and interpreted by humans. For example, the NTUSER.DAT file used in Windows is a binary representation of the HKEY_LOCAL_USER branch of the system's registry. This file cannot be directly read, but requires tools to transform it into human-readable form.

Logical Access Controls

Logical access controls are used to control whether and how subjects (usually persons) are able to access objects (usually data). Logical access controls work in a number of different ways, primarily:

- **Subject access**   Here, a logical access control uses some means to determine the identity of the subject that is requesting access. Once the subject's identity is known, the access control performs a function to determine if the subject should be allowed to access the object. If the access is permitted, the subject is allowed to proceed; if the access is denied, the subject is not allowed to proceed. An example of this type of access control is an application that first authenticates a user by requiring a user ID and password before permitting the user to access the application.

- **Service access**   Here, a logical access control is used to control the types of messages that are allowed to pass through a control point. The logical access control is designed to permit or deny messages of specific types (and possibly it will also permit or deny based upon origin and destination) to pass. An example of this type of access control is a firewall or screening router that makes pass/block decisions based upon the type of traffic, origin, and destination.

An analogy of these two types of access is a concert hall with a parking garage. The parking garage (the "service access") permits cars, trucks, and motorcycles to enter, but denies oversized vehicles from entering. Upstairs at the concert box office (the "subject access"), persons are admitted if they possess a photo identification that matches a list of prepaid attendees.

Access Control Concepts

In discussions about access control, security professionals often use terms that are not used in other IS disciplines. These terms are

- **Subject, object**   These are pronouns that refer to access control situations. A *subject* is usually a person, but it could also be a running program or a computer. In typical security parlance, a subject is someone (or some*thing*) that wants to access something. An *object* (which could be a computer, application, database, file, record, or other resource) is the thing that the subject wants to access.

- **Fail open, fail closed** This refers to the behaviors of automatic access control systems when they experience a failure. For instance, if power is removed from a keycard building access control system, will all doors be locked or unlocked? The term *fail closed* means that all accesses will be denied if the access control system fails; the term *fail open* means that all accesses will be permitted upon failure. Generally, security professionals like access control systems to fail closed, because it is safer to admit no one than it is to admit everyone. But there will be exceptions now and then where fail open might be better; for example, building access control systems may need to fail open in some situations to facilitate emergency evacuation of personnel or entrance of emergency services personnel.

- **Least privilege** This is the concept where an individual user should have the lowest privilege possible that will still enable them to perform their tasks.

- **Segregation of duties** This is the concept that specifies that single individuals should not have combinations of privileges that would permit them to conduct high-value operations on their own. The classic example is a business accounting department where the functions of creating a payee, requesting a payment, approving a payment, and making a payment should rest with four separate individuals. This will prevent any one person from being able to easily embezzle funds from an organization. In the context of information technology, functions such as requesting user accounts and provisioning user accounts should reside with two different persons so that no single individual could create user accounts on his own.

- **Split custody** This is the concept of splitting knowledge of a specific object or task between two persons. One example is splitting the password for an important encryption key between two parties: one has the first half and the other has the second half. Similarly, the combination to a bank vault can be split so that two persons have the first half of the combination while two others have the second half.

Access Control Models

Several access control models have been developed since the 1970s. These models are simple mechanisms that are used to understand and build access control systems. The early models include Biba, Bell-La Padula, Clark-Wilson, Lattice, Brewer and Nash, Take-Grant, and Non-Interference. The models that are of interest to the IS auditor include

- **Mandatory Access Control (MAC)** This access model is used to control access to objects (files, directories, databases, systems, networks, and so on) by subjects (persons, programs, etc.). When a subject attempts to access an object, the operating system examines the access properties of the subject and object to determine if the access should be allowed. The operating system then permits or denies the requested access. Access is administered centrally, and users cannot override it.

- **Discretionary Access Control (DAC)**   In this access model, the owner of an object is able to determine how and by whom the object may be accessed. The discretion of the owner determines which subjects will be permitted access.

NOTE   The MAC and DAC models each have their advantages and disadvantages. While DAC permits flexibility by permitting an owner to set access rights, abuse or errors could lead to exposure of sensitive information. MAC's centralized administration and inflexibility are also strengths: users cannot override MAC settings and potentially expose sensitive information to others.

Access Control Threats

Because access controls are often the only means of protection between protected assets and users, access controls are often attacked. Indeed, the majority of attacks against computers and networks containing valuable assets are against access controls in attempts to trick, defeat, or bypass them. Threats represent the intent and ability to do harm to an asset.

Threats against access controls include

- **Malware**   This includes viruses, worms, Trojan horses, rootkits, and spyware. Malware is *malicious code* that is used to perform unauthorized actions on target systems. It is often successful because of known vulnerabilities that can be exploited. Vulnerabilities are discussed in more detail in the next section.

- **Eavesdropping**   Here, attackers will install network- or system-based sniffing tools to listen to network communications in order to intercept key transmissions such as user IDs and passwords used to access sensitive or valuable information. Usually, attackers will need to use some means such as malware or social engineering to install sniffing tools on a target system. In some instances, however, attackers will have access to the physical network and can directly connect sniffing tools to the network cabling.

- **Logic bombs and back doors**   Computer instructions inserted by programmers or others in the software development process can result in an application that contains unauthorized code. A *logic bomb* is a set of instructions that is designed to perform some damaging action when a specific event occurs; a popular example is a *time bomb* that alters or destroys data on a specified date in the future. Some programmers install time bombs in code that they manage and periodically advance the date in the time bomb. If the programmer is fired from his job, the time bomb will activate after his termination, and the programmer will have gotten his revenge on his former employer. A *back door* is a section of code that permits someone to bypass access controls and access data or functions. Back doors are commonly placed in programs during development but removed before programming is complete. Sometimes, however, back doors are deliberately planted so that the developer (or someone else) can access data and functions.

- **Scanning attacks**   Here, an attacker performs active or passive scanning in an attempt to discover weak access controls. For example, an attacker can use a *port scanning tool* to discover open and possibly vulnerable ports on target systems. An attacker can search for unprotected modems through an attack known as *war dialing*. Or, an attacker can listen to Wi-Fi network traffic to look for vulnerable wireless access points in an activity known as *war driving*.

- **Race conditions**   Also known as a time-of-check/time-of-use (TOC/TOU) attack, the attacker is attempting to exploit the small window of time that sometimes exists between the time that a resource is requested and when the resource is available for use.

 NOTE   The potency and frequency of threats on a system are directly proportional to the perceived value of assets that the system contains or protects.

Access Control Vulnerabilities

Vulnerabilities are the weaknesses that may be present in a system that allow a threat to be more easily carried out.

Vulnerabilities by themselves do not bring about actual harm. Instead, threats and vulnerabilities work together. Most often, a threat exploits a vulnerability because it is easier to attack a system at its weakest point. Common vulnerabilities include

- **Unpatched systems**   Security patches are designed to remove specific vulnerabilities. A system that is not patched still has vulnerabilities, many of which are easily exploited. Attackers can easily enter and take over systems that lack important security patches.

- **Default system settings**   Default settings often include unnecessary services that increase the chances that an attacker can find a way to break in to a system. The practice of *system hardening* is used to remove all unnecessary services and to make security configuration changes on a system to make it as secure as possible.

- **Default passwords**   Some systems are shipped with default administrative passwords that make it easy for a new customer to configure the system. One problem with this arrangement is that many organizations fail to change these passwords. Hackers have access to extensive lists of default passwords for practically every kind of computer and device that can be connected to a network.

- **Incorrect permissions settings**   If the permissions that are set up for files, directories, databases, application servers, or software programs are incorrectly set, this could permit access—and even modification or damage—by persons who should not have access.

> ## Familiarity with Technology Is Key to Effective IS Audit
> The IS auditor needs to be highly familiar with information technologies to be effective. Without in-depth knowledge of security threats, vulnerabilities, and countermeasures, the IS auditor will not be able to detect any unsafe practices in a technology environment. Furthermore, without a depth of understanding, IS auditors will not be able to ask probing questions in walkthroughs or be able to correctly interpret evidence.
>
> The IS auditor must understand information technology in general, but she must also understand the technology architecture in the specific environment that she is examining. In an environment that has the appearance of being highly secure, a configuration error in a single device can betray that security like a traitor. Only an IS auditor with a thorough understanding of information technology would have a chance to detect such a weakness.

- **Application logic**   Software applications—especially those that are accessible via the Internet—that contain inadequate session management, resource management, and input testing controls can potentially permit an intruder to take over a system and steal or damage information.

Access Points and Methods of Entry

Computing and network resources must be accessed in order to provide value. The majority of information-based resources are accessed via TCP/IP networks; some resources are accessed using other technologies, such as direct hardwired connections (as in the case of some mainframe computers) and non-TCP/IP network technologies. Then there are desktop computers that sometimes themselves contain information and resources.

Modern LAN environments are protected from outside threats with firewalls. Many larger organizations also employ internal firewalls that create separate zones of trust within the organization. But generally speaking, LANs are a lot like highway systems within individual countries: once you pass a border checkpoint and show a passport or other credential, you can roam freely inside that country unhindered.

Points of Entry

The main point of entry in most organizations is the internal corporate LAN. A user who can connect to the corporate LAN is able to logically reach virtually every computing resource in the organization—subject to the access controls associated with each resource. This makes the notion of protecting corporate accesses by controlling access to the LAN an important topic.

The ease of connectivity to the corporate LAN highlights a number of important security issues. Probably the biggest issue is the ability for nonorganization-owned computers to connect to the network and access network-based resources. By permitting nonorganization-owned systems to connect to the network, the organization is essentially giving up control of the network. By letting any computer or device connect to the network, this creates risks, including

- **Exposure to malware**   Any computer that is not actively managed by centralized antivirus software could be carrying malware that would attempt to propagate itself inside the corporate network. Indeed, worms such as Nimda and Code Red were able to spread in just this way. Laptops that were the personal property of employees would become infected on home networks and then spread the infection inside the corporate LAN in "typhoid Mary" style. Many instances of malware being imported on vendor-owned computers (for "demo" purposes) are also known.

- **Eavesdropping**   While the IT department can exert some level of control over desktop and server computing by prohibiting (and even preventing) the installation of network sniffing programs, IT cannot easily control whether nonorganization-owned computers have network sniffing programs (or malware that does the same thing!).

- **Open access**   A corporate LAN that permits any device to connect will permit a wireless access point to connect to the network. This, in turn, may permit anyone with a Wi-Fi client to connect to the network. Permitting any type of device to connect could also permit the use of dial-in modems (although these would be a bit more difficult to set up, since analog phone lines would also be needed).

Technologies are now available that are used to control the systems that are permitted to connect to the corporate LAN. The NAC (network access protocol) and 802.1X protocol is used to control whether a system is permitted to connect to corporate network resources. NAC and 802.1X use an authentication mechanism to determine if each new device is permitted to connect. If the device lacks the necessary credentials, it cannot connect.

This is not the same as whether the device is able to physically connect. Rather, network switches play a role in NAC and 802.1X; if a device is not permitted onto the network, the workgroup switch will not route any packets from the denied workstation into the LAN. The workstation remains logically disconnected.

Remote Access

Remote access is defined as the means of providing remote connectivity to a corporate LAN through a data link. Remote access is provided by most organizations so that employees who are temporarily or permanently off-site can access LAN-based resources from their remote location.

Remote access was initially provided using dial-up modems that included authentication. While remote dial-up is still provided in some instances, most remote access is provided over the Internet itself, and typically uses an encrypted tunnel known as a virtual private network (VPN) to protect transmissions from any eavesdroppers. VPNs are so prevalent in remote access technology that the terms *VPN* and *remote access* have become synonymous. Remote access architectures are depicted in Figure 6-1.

Figure 6-1   Remote access architectures

The two security controls that are essential for remote access are

- **Authentication**   It is necessary to know who is requesting access to the corporate LAN. Authentication may consist of the same user ID and password that personnel use when on-site, or they may be required to provide additional credentials, such as a group or site password, token, or biometric.

- **Encryption**   Many on-site network applications do not encrypt sensitive traffic because it is all contained within the physically and logically protected corporate LAN. However, since remote access gives the same function as being on the corporate LAN, and because the applications themselves usually do not provide encryption, the remote access service itself usually provides encryption. Encryption may use SSL, IPsec, L2TP, or PPTP.

These controls are needed because they are a substitute (or *compensating control*) for the physical access controls that are usually present that control which personnel may enter the building to use the on-site corporate LAN. When personnel are on-site, their identity is confirmed through keycard or other physical access controls. When personnel are off-site using remote access, since the organization cannot see the person on the far end of the remote access connection, the authentication that is used is the next best thing.

Identification, Authentication, and Authorization

To control access, computing resources are protected by mechanisms that ensure that only authorized subjects are permitted to access protected information. Generally, these mechanisms first identify who (or what) wants to access the resource, and then they will determine if the subject is permitted to access the resource and either grant or deny the access.

This section discusses the matter of identifying the subject. Several terms are used to describe various activities, including identification, authentication, and authorization, and are explained here.

Identification

Identification is the act of asserting an identity without providing any proof of it. This is analogous to one person walking up to another and saying, "Hello, my name is _____." Because it requires no proof, identification is not usually used to protect high-value assets or functions.

Identification is often used by websites to remember someone's profile or preferences. For example, a nationwide bank's web application may use a cookie to store the city in which the customer lives. When the customer returns to the website, the application will display some photo or news that is related to the customer's location. But when the customer is ready to perform online banking, this simple identification is insufficient to prove the customer's actual identity.

Identification is just the *first* step in the process of gaining entry to a system or application. The next steps are authentication and authorization, which are discussed next.

Authentication

Authentication is similar to identification, where a subject asserts an identity. In identification, no proof of identity is requested or provided, but with authentication, some form of proof of the subject's identity is required. That proof is usually provided in the form of a secret password or some means of higher sophistication and security, such as a token, biometric, smart card, or digital certificate. Each of these is discussed later in this section.

Authorization

After a subject has been authenticated, the next step is authorization. This is the process by which the system determines whether the subject should be permitted to access the requested resource. To determine if the subject is permitted to access the resource, the system will perform some type of a lookup or other business rule. For instance, an access control table associated with the requested resource may have a list of users who are permitted to access it. The system will read through this table to see whether the subject's identity appears in the table. If so (and if the type of requested access matches the type permitted in the table), the system will permit the subject to access the resource. If the user's identity does not appear in the table, the subject will be denied access.

The preceding example is simplistic, but is often the means used to determine if a user is authorized to access something. Typically, permissions are centrally stored by the operating system and administered by system administrators, although some environments permit the owners of resources to administer user access. See the section, "Access Control Models," earlier in this chapter.

EXAM TIP   The terms *identification, authentication,* and *authorization* are often misused by IT professionals, who may not realize the differences between them. Security professionals and IS auditors need to understand the differences.

User IDs and Passwords

User IDs and passwords are the most common means for users to authenticate themselves to a resource, whether it is a network, server, or application.

User IDs   In most environments, a user's user ID will not be a secret; in fact, user IDs may be a derivation of the user's name or their identification number. Some of the common forms of a user's user ID are

- **First initial and last name**   For example, the user ID for John Toman would be jtoman. Some systems may have a limitation on the permitted length of a user ID—for instance, eight characters. If two users' user IDs would be the same (John Brown and James Brown, for example), the IT department could assign "jobrown" and "jabrown," or "jbrown" and "jbrown2."

- **First and middle initials and last name**   Similar to first initial and last name, but with fewer chances for "collisions" (two persons who would have the same user ID). User Howard W. Chang would have a user ID "hwchang."

- **First and last name together**   Systems that permit longer user IDs with special characters such as "." can adopt the common first.last form. User Rajendra Patel would have the user ID "rajendra.patel."

- **Employee ID number**   Some organizations assign unique identifying numbers to its employees, and these can be used as user IDs if those numbers are not kept secret. One advantage of using an ID number is that the user's name becomes a characteristic of the user ID and not the user ID itself; in many cultures, a woman's name changes when she marries, but in an organization that uses ID numbers, the user ID need not change or reflect a name she no longer has.

CAUTION   Confidential numbers such as social insurance (Social Security in the United States) or driver's license numbers should not be used as user IDs, as these identifying numbers are generally meant to be kept confidential.

Passwords   Whereas a user ID is not necessarily kept confidential, a password *always* is kept confidential. A password, also known as a *pass phrase*, is a secret combination of letters, numbers, and other symbols that is known only to the user who uses it. End users are typically advised the following about passwords:

- **Selecting a password**   Users should select a password that is easy for them to remember but difficult for others to guess. Passwords should not contain common words or words that are the names of their family members or pets, nor should they contain numeric combinations representing birthdays or wedding anniversaries. Many environments require passwords of a minimum length (typically eight characters), and they require that passwords contain some combination of lowercase letters, uppercase letters, numbers, and symbols. Many environments also require that passwords be changed periodically, typically every 90 days. They also forbid the use of recently used passwords, which lowers the risk of someone else using a previous password.

- **Sharing passwords**   Users should be told that they should *never* share any password with *any* other person, for *any* reason! User accounts must be used only by the person to whom they are assigned and by no one else in any situation. In many organizations, sharing passwords can result in termination of employment.

- **Transmitting passwords**   Passwords should never be sent in an e-mail message. An eavesdropper or any person who intercepts the message would then know the password and may be able to use it, compromising the integrity of the user account and possibly of some sensitive business information as well.

- **Writing down passwords**   In environments with many applications, there can be many passwords to remember. Users will be tempted to write them down or save them in a spreadsheet or text file on their workstation. It would be acceptable for users to write down their passwords, provided they keep the paper with those passwords locked away or on their person always.

- **Electronic password vaulting**   With so many complex passwords to remember, users could store their passwords in an electronic password vault; a number of good ones are available, including *Password Safe* and *KeePass*.

 CAUTION   Users should be advised to *not* store their passwords in any online password archival service.

- **Managing passwords in multiple environments**   Users are urged to *not* use the same password for every application. If anyone should discover or learn their password in one environment, they could try that same password in other applications and possibly be able to log in. Difficult as it is, users should use unique passwords in each environment.

User Account Provisioning When a user is issued a new computer or network user account, somehow they need to know the password. Generating and transmitting an initial password to a user can be tricky because passwords should never be sent in an e-mail message. A sound practice for initial user account provisioning would involve the use of a limited-time, one-time password that would be securely given to the user; upon first use, the system would require that the user change the password to a value that no one else would know.

Several factors influence how passwords are initially determined, including

- **User locations** If a user is located near the administrators who provision user accounts, one of the administrators can personally deliver the new password to the user. If the administrator and the user are not near each other, the administrator can give the password to the user by phone. In no circumstance should the password be sent via e-mail.

- **System limitations** Some environments do not support initial-use passwords that expire in a short amount of time.

- **Data sensitivity** The value of the data protected by access controls (including user accounts and their initial passwords) should be a factor in determining how user accounts are provisioned. If the data or asset being protected is of high value, more elaborate means (such as what is discussed in this section) may be needed. But if the asset value is low, then the rules for initial account provisioning may be more relaxed.

 NOTE Ideally, a user will be able to change their password as soon as they have their new user account; but some systems don't even permit this. Security analysts or IS auditors who are examining an environment's user account provisioning procedures should understand the environment's capabilities as well as the risks and value of the assets being protected. Any recommendations should reflect system capabilities and asset value.

Risks with User IDs and Passwords Password-based authentication is among the oldest in use in information systems. While still quite popular, a number of risks are associated with password authentication. The risks are all associated with the different ways in which passwords can be discovered and reused by others. Some of these risks are

- **Eavesdropping** Due to system limitations, some user account passwords are transmitted "in the clear" over networks, which permits anyone who is eavesdropping to intercept and reuse the password later on.

- **Finding a password written down** If a user neglects to protect the paper that contains written passwords, they may be discovered by a colleague or another person, who could use them or pass them on to another person for their use.

- **Finding a stored password** If an intruder (or even a trusted colleague) examines the hard drive of a user's workstation, a file containing stored user IDs and passwords could be discovered.

All of these risks follow the same theme: user IDs and passwords are static and, if discovered, can be used by others. It is for this reason that other, more secure, means for authentication have been developed. The techniques include biometrics, tokens, smart cards, and certificates.

Two-Factor Authentication

Two-factor authentication is so-called because it relies not only on "something you know" (namely, a user ID and password), but also upon "something you have." Two-factor authentication requires not only a user ID and password, but also that the user have something in their possession that is somehow used to form a part of the authentication. Several technologies are used for two-factor authentication, including

- **Tokens**   Tokens are small electronic devices that come in two forms. One form has a small display that shows a string of characters. The characters displayed are typed in during logon, and if the characters are correct, the user will be able to log in to the system or network. The advantage of these tokens is that the displayed value will change frequently, making a "replay attack" almost impossible to conduct. The other type of token authentication is the use of a small USB key that contains information associated with the authentication. This information could be a digital certificate or other value.

- **Smart cards**   A smart card is a small, credit card–sized device that contains electronic memory and is accessed with a smart card reader. Many laptop computers are equipped with smart card readers for this purpose. A smart card might contain a digital certificate or other identifying information that is difficult or impossible to reproduce.

- **Digital certificates**   A digital certificate is an electronic document that uses a digital signature to bind a public encryption key with a user's identity. The system containing the digital certificate can be hardened so that the document cannot be cloned or moved to another computer. Typically, a digital certificate will reside within the workstation's hardware or in a special computer chip, or it may be stored in a USB token.

Users of two-factor authentication systems need to be trained on their proper use. They need to be told not to store their token or smart card with their computer; otherwise, if the computer is stolen, the device will be stolen with it, entirely negating the added security of the device.

Biometrics

Biometrics refers to a number of different authentication technologies with a common theme: all use some way of measuring a unique physical characteristic of the person who is authenticating. Some of the technologies in use are

- **Fingerprint**   This is one of the most common forms of biometrics, primarily because fingerprint readers are compact and easy to manufacture, fingerprints don't change much over time, and people are generally unafraid to scan their fingers. Many notebook computers have fingerprint scanners built-in, as do some computer mice. A USB fingerprint reader is shown in Figure 6-2.

Figure 6-2
USB-connected
fingerprint reader

- **Handprint**   A handprint scanner is designed to measure the geometry of a person's hand. Since the readers are much larger than fingerprint readers, handprint scanners are generally limited to physical access settings where a user is required to enter a PIN and scan their hand in order to gain access to a controlled area. A handprint scanner is shown in Figure 6-3.

- **Palm vein**   Similar to hand scanning, the pattern of veins in a person's palm can be used as a reliable biometric. Palm vein readers resemble a computer mouse; a user places their hand a few inches above the reader so that it may read the palm vein patterns.

- **Voice recognition**   Voice recognition is designed to recognize the specific patterns in the sound of spoken words. One advantage of voice recognition is that it usually does not require additional computer hardware, since most

Figure 6-3
Biometric hand
scanner (Image
courtesy of Ingersoll
Rand Security
Technologies)

workstations have microphones built in to them. Some disadvantages of voice recognition include voice changes during head and chest colds or when angry, sad, or nervous.

- **Iris scan**   The human iris (the muscle surrounding the pupil of the eye) is similar to the human fingerprint in that they are unique among the population. A biometric iris scanner takes a high-resolution image of the human iris. This is similar to retina scanners, which required the subject to place their eye very close to a camera lens, something that many persons found discomforting.

- **Facial scan**   Facial scanning involves fine measurements of the angular dimensions of the human face. This means that computer imaging software will measure the relative distances between key features on a human face. Facial scanning, like voice recognition, can utilize built-in computer hardware (in this case, a camera) and requires only additional software. Some models of laptop computers utilize facial recognition for user authentication.

- **Handwriting**   Two main forms of handwriting recognition are available—both involve the use of a subject signing his or her name. One technology measures the dynamics of the signature as it is written on the signing surface. The other technology measures the acceleration of the pen or stylus while the subject signs their name.

Biometric technologies share a number of common operational challenges and traits that are discussed here.

Biometric Registration   Each type of biometrics requires some kind of an initial registration. Some biometric systems permit a user to self-register on their own workstation, while others require attended registration. Registration usually involves the biometric system taking several initial measurements so that it can develop an "average" reading for the subject.

Biometric Measurement Variances   Biometric measurements are not exact; instead, there will be small differences in the biometric being measured from one authentication to the next. Some of these differences are due to the gradual changes that a human body undergoes over time. The biometric system will need to incorporate these newer measurements into a user's baseline so that they will continue to authenticate properly.

Several key measurements in biometric systems are usually adjustable. These measurements are

- **False reject rate**   This is the rate at which valid subjects are rejected. This occurs when the biometric system has too small a margin of error.

- **False accept rate**   This is the rate at which invalid subjects are accepted as valid. This occurs when the biometric system has too large a margin of error.

- **Crossover error rate**   This is the point at which the false reject rate (FRR) equals the false accept rate (FAR). This is the ideal point for a well-tuned biometric system.

Biometric Usability Issues A number of issues will arise in an organization where some employees will be reluctant to use a biometric system. These issues include

- **Sanitary** For biometrics such as door entry systems, many persons will be touching the biometric system in the course of a day. Some employees will cite health-related objections to the use of biometrics on account of spreading germs and viruses.

- **Privacy** Some employees feel that scanning their fingerprints or irises constitutes an invasion of their privacy. What they need to know is that a fingerprint scanner (for instance) does not record the user's actual fingerprint, but instead a computed "hash" of the intersections in the lines in their fingerprint. Few, if any, biometric systems store actual fingerprints.

NOTE Because biometrics involves the measurement of a subject's physical characteristics, a number of employees are bound to object to its use—sometimes based on valid concerns and sometimes not.

Reduced Sign-On

Reduced sign-on refers to an environment where a centralized directory service such as LDAP (Lightweight Directory Access Protocol), RADIUS (Remote Access Dial-in User Service), Diameter, or Microsoft Active Directory is used by several applications for authentication. The term *reduced sign-on* comes from the result of changing each application's authentication from stand-alone to centralized and the resulting reduction in the number of user ID–password pairs that each user is required to remember.

EXAM TIP The terms reduced sign-on and single sign-on are often interchanged. Many times, a reduced sign-on environment is labeled as single sign-on. They are not the same.

Single Sign-On

Single sign-on refers to an interconnected environment where applications are logically connected to a centralized authentication server that is aware of the logged-in/-out status of each user. At the start of the workday, when a user logs into an application, she will be prompted for her user ID and password. When she logs into another application, the application will consult the central authentication server to see if the user is logged in and, if so, the second application will not request the user's user ID and password. The term *single sign-on* refers to the fact that a user needs to sign on only one time, even in a multiple-application environment.

Single sign-on is more complex than reduced sign-on. In a single sign-on environment, each participating application must be able to communicate with a centralized authentication controller and act accordingly by requiring a new user to log in, or not.

Access Control Lists

Access control lists (ACLs) are a common means to administer access controls. ACLs are used by many operating systems and other devices such as routers as a simple means to control access to a resource such as a server or network.

On many devices and systems, the list of packet-filtering rules (which give a router some of the characteristics of a firewall) is known as an ACL. In the Unix operating system, ACLs can control which users are permitted to access the FTP service and which users are permitted to access files and directories. ACLs in these and other contexts are usually simple text files that can be edited with a text editor.

Protecting Stored Information

Information systems store information primarily in the form of databases and flat files. Operating systems and database management systems usually provide minimum protection of databases and files by default; organizations need to determine the correct level of protection that is pursuant to the value and sensitivity of information. The controls that may need to be enacted are discussed in this section.

Access Controls

Access controls are the primary means used to protect stored information from unauthorized accesses and unauthorized users.

Operating systems access control settings (often in the form of ACLs) are used to determine which user IDs are permitted to access flat files (as well as the directories containing them). Following the principle of *least privilege,* all flat files containing sensitive information should have access restricted to only those users and processes that must be able to access them. No user or process that doesn't have a need to access specific files should be able to do so.

Access Logging

Operating systems and database management systems should be configured so that all access to files and directories is logged. This practice promotes accountability and provides a trail of evidence in the event that a forensic investigation should be conducted in the future.

Access logs themselves must be highly protected—ideally, they should be stored in a different storage system than the data whose access they are logging. Access logs should not be alterable, even by database administrators and system administrators, so that no one will be able to "erase their tracks" should they decide to tamper with sensitive information and then attempt to hide the evidence afterward.

Access logging is only effective if someone actually examines the logs. Because this can be a time-consuming activity, many organizations utilize alert-generating tools that send e-mail or pager alerts to key personnel when certain audit log entries (such as unauthorized access attempts) appear. These alerts permit personnel to act upon anomalous events when they occur.

Backup and Media Storage

Data stored on information systems can be lost or damaged. Some of the ways in which this can occur include

- **Hardware failure**   Many of the components in a storage system—particularly hard disks—are subject to failures, however rare they might be nowadays. These failures can result in data being irretrievable.

- **Administrator error**   A system or database administrator can accidentally erase or alter information in a way that is not easily undone.

- **Software bug**   An erroneous section of code in application software can inadvertently wipe out data in a database or in flat files. This can occur with an organization's own programs, or with programs that are supplied by a software vendor.

All of these possibilities should be reason enough for an IT operation to back up all-important data. Backing up data means making copies of it on other media in case the original media (or the system that it is stored on) fails. Then, after the original system is repaired, data can be copied from the backup media and processing resumed.

Backup Tools   Organizations often use backup tools that help the backup process be as efficient as possible. Some backup tools automatically manage backup media volumes and make data restoration easier than if it had to be done manually.

Protection of Backup Media   Because backup media is often transported from place to place, there are opportunities for media to be misplaced or lost in transit. For this reason, data on backup media should be encrypted so that any third party who happens to find a backup media volume will not be able to retrieve any data from it. When backup media is encrypted, a lost tape means only the loss of an inexpensive asset and not a potential compromise of sensitive information.

Offsite Backup Media Storage   In order to protect data from disasters, backup media should be stored at a location away from the original data. For example, if data from a server was backed up onto tape and the backup tapes stored near the server, both servers and backup media could be destroyed in an event such as a fire or flood. If backup media were stored in another location, however, then only the original server would be destroyed, but the system could be recovered using data on backup media at the other location.

Selecting an off-site media storage facility requires the organization to weigh several factors, including distance from the original data (too close means it may be destroyed in a regional disaster; too far away means it may take too long to obtain it when needed), security of the storage facility, security of the transportation of media back and forth between the original location and the off-site storage facility, and recordkeeping available so that it can be easily determined which media volumes are at the off-site facility at any given time. Security of the off-site storage facility should be at least as good as the security in the original location so that the protected information is not more vulnerable at the off-site facility.

Restoration Testing The organization should occasionally test backup media and data restoration software to make sure that data is actually being backed up onto the backup media and that it can be retrieved. I personally know of an organization that believed it was backing up its databases every day until it needed to restore one, only to find out that nothing was ever being written to the backup media. Clearly the organization was not testing its backup system. Restoration tests should be scheduled and their results recorded.

Media Inventory A periodic inventory of all backup media, including media at the off-site location, should be performed. This will ensure that all media volumes are being handled properly and that none have been lost or misplaced. The results of each inventory should be recorded and any anomalies corrected.

NOTE The loss of one or more backup media volumes during an inventory would be considered a security incident, unless the media was known to be encrypted.

Patch Management

Patch management is an IT operational process whereby security and functionality patches are obtained, tested, and installed on information systems. The purpose of patch management is to keep systems running on currently supported vendor software and to ensure that all known security vulnerabilities are closed and software bugs fixed.

Patch management is typically managed with tools that are able to quickly assess the "patch level" of many servers and then used to install patches en masse.

There are different points of view with regard to patches. Should all patches be installed, or just some patches? There are pros and cons to each approach. If all security patches are installed, then certainly all known vulnerabilities will be closed. However, some security patches may be unnecessary because specific components that are patched might not be used. If an organization chooses to install only the most important patches, a security analyst will need to perform a risk analysis each time a security patch is released so that a formal determination of need can be established. And even if an organization does install all available security patches, a risk analysis can help to determine how quickly each patch needs to be installed.

The argument against installing patches is that each patch can add a tiny increment of instability to the system. While the base operating system undergoes exhaustive testing, far less testing is performed on security patches before they are released. This is evidenced by the occasional security patch that breaks some other functionality—this does not happen often, but it does happen sometimes. This is another reason why organizations should first test patches (security and other) on test environments prior to installing them on production systems. Otherwise, there is a small chance that a new patch will cause unexpected problems that could be difficult to isolate.

Vulnerability Management

The purpose of vulnerability management is to identify and manage vulnerabilities in IT applications and infrastructure. Vulnerabilities can result from errors in configuration, flaws in overall architecture, or from newly discovered weaknesses reported by security researchers.

Vulnerability management requires a number of distinct but connected activities, which are

- **Subscribing to security alerts** Most manufacturers of computer hardware and software have a service whereby its customers can be made aware of new vulnerabilities, weaknesses, threats, and remedies for these. Often, the fixes for vulnerabilities, weaknesses, and threats are security patches or bulletins that advise changes in configuration. There are also some high-quality, nonvendor-related sources for security alerts, including Secunia, Bugtraq, Full Disclosure, and US-CERT.

- **Vulnerability scanning and penetration testing** This involves the use of tools that scan or examine computers, network devices, or application programs with the purpose of finding any vulnerabilities. Organizations that have any computers or applications accessed over the Internet (including simple websites) should consider performing regular scans to make sure that those computers and applications are free of any high- or medium-risk vulnerabilities. An organization that does not remediate vulnerabilities faces the very real threat of the computer or application being attacked and compromised, which could lead to a loss of sensitive information. Many commercial and open-source tools are available to inspect computers and applications for vulnerabilities; the better tools also rank findings by level of risk and include instructions on how vulnerabilities can be fixed. Organizations also need to remember that scanning a system once and removing all vulnerabilities does not mean that there will never be new vulnerabilities in the future; this is because security researchers regularly find new vulnerabilities in programs and systems. A system that is secure today will most certainly be less secure tomorrow.

- **Patch management** This is the process of responding to known vulnerabilities by installing security patches on target systems and devices. This process is described in detail in the preceding section.

- **Corrective action process** This is the process of recording vulnerabilities into an incident tracking process so that vulnerability remediation can be assigned to a person or team and be formally tracked. Corrective and preventive action processes are discussed early in this chapter.

System Hardening

System hardening is the process of changing the configuration of a system (which could be a server, subsystem, or network device) so that it is more resistant to malfunctions and attacks. The principles behind system hardening consist of the items discussed in the following sections.

Changing Systems from Multifunction to Single-Function   An individual server that performs many functions may require the presence of several services, software modules, or applications to be running at once. Consolidation may reduce the number of servers and make an environment simpler, but it also increases risk. A vulnerability on a multifunction server places all services on the server at risk.

In an environment where each server performs a single function, a vulnerability in a function will place only that function at risk. Server virtualization makes it easy to separate functions into separate OS instances while permitting them to continue to run on one physical system.

Removal of Unnecessary Services   Only the services and software features required to support a system's purpose should be installed and running; all other services and features should be disabled and, if possible, removed altogether. Removing unnecessary services reduces the "vulnerability surface" on a system to only those services that are required.

For example, the sendmail program should be disabled (prevented from running) or removed on Unix systems that do not need to send or receive e-mail. Sendmail is a large, complex program that is the subject of ongoing security research, and new vulnerabilities are discovered from time to time.

Limiting Functionality or Privilege of Necessary Services   After all unnecessary services have been removed from a server, only those that are required for the server's function will remain. The functions that any necessary service is permitted to perform should be reduced to only those that are necessary. Accomplishing this will vary, but limiting functionality should follow the principle whereby any unneeded function should be disabled if the configuration will permit this.

Each necessary service or program should be configured to run at the lowest possible privilege. In the past, it was common for all generic services (and even many applications) to run at "root," "super-user," or "administrator" level. Often this is unnecessary, and on systems where the privilege levels can be configured, each service should run at a lower service where possible. The advantage of this is that if a particular service is compromised through a vulnerability, the attacker's ability to compromise the entire system may be limited to the ability afforded by the privilege level assigned to the service.

Changing Default Passwords   One of the easiest ways for an intruder to attack a system is through known default passwords. Often, the manufacturers of systems and software utilize a documented "default" password that makes it easy for a new user or customer to begin using the system. But all too often these default credentials are never updated, which results in systems that are vulnerable to attacks that are easy to carry out.

Before being connected to a network, every system should be changed so that all accounts have nondefault passwords.

Using Nonpredictable Passwords   If an intruder is able to compromise a system, he may (if he is able) attempt to retrieve the system's encrypted user account passwords and crack them. If the intruder has been able to crack one system's passwords, he may attempt to log in to neighboring systems (those in the same organization) using the same user IDs and passwords. If many or all systems use the same passwords, particularly for administrative accounts, the intruder may be able to easily compromise all other systems in the environment. Similarly, if the intruder is able to detect a pattern in the use of passwords, he may be able to compromise many systems.

Removing Nonessential User IDs   Exploiting access privileges is one of the easiest techniques available to system hackers for breaking in to a target system. Often, a system can be compromised by attacking nonessential user IDs, such as "guest" accounts. Every user account that does not serve a specific purpose should be disabled or removed.

Some types of systems require the presence of special accounts, even though they may not be required for interactive login. System engineers should look for a way of preventing interactive logins for these types of accounts without crippling the services that use them. Some operating systems support the notion of a service account that can be used by system and application programs but will not permit interactive login.

 NOTE   The use of more advanced authentication technologies, such as two-factor authentication or biometrics, may make it far more difficult for an intruder to successfully attack target systems through user ID and password guessing.

Reducing User Privileges   The privileges required by each end user should be reduced to only those privileges necessary for each user to perform their tasks. Similar to the principle of reducing privilege levels for system services and applications, user privileges should be reduced so that the user is not permitted to perform any functions beyond what is required of them. This is similar to the principle of *least privilege* that is discussed earlier in this chapter.

Reduce or Eliminate Interserver Trust   Some operating systems, such as Unix and Linux, can be configured to trust users on other systems. Some of these trust arrangements (such as *rlogin*) assume the integrity of other systems and are vulnerable to attack. For this reason, interserver trust should be used with care.

Single sign-on (SSO), when configured properly, is considered reliable and need not be eliminated based on the principle of removing interserver trust. However, even modern SSO and other authentication services must be designed and implemented securely to avoid misuse and attack.

System and device hardening has been a topic of discussion and innovation over the past three decades. Consequently, there are many good sources for hardening standards, guidelines, and instructions, including US-CERT, NIST, SANS, and the Center for Internet Security.

Securing Virtualization Environments

Many organizations have adopted virtualization technology in order to make more efficient use of their server hardware. Virtualization permits two or more operating systems to run concurrently on a system, each with its own share of resources, and each operating as though it were running on its own physical server. Architecturally, virtualization inserts another layer of software between system hardware and the operating system in order to manage multiple copies of operating systems.

Like all other types of systems, virtualization environments must be hardened to reduce the likelihood and impact of attacks. The principles of hardening virtualization environments are

- Limit and monitor physical access to hardware.
- Restrict and periodically review administrative access.
- Remove unnecessary functions and services.
- Maintain current versions of software.
- Enable logging, and review those activity logs.
- For critical systems, monitor for availability and performance.
- Connect mechanisms that generate alerts to a centralized alerting environment.
- Back up all virtual machines, including raw VM files.
- Use only encrypted remote administration such as SSH.
- Limit or eliminate file sharing.
- Implement anti-malware software.
- Patch guest OS and VM hypervisors early and often.
- Implement file integrity monitoring, and connect it to the centralized alerting environment.
- Implement time synchronization.
- Disconnect or remove unused devices and peripherals.

If these principles sound familiar, they should. These are similar to the principles used to harden computer operating systems. However, a virtualization environment is really nothing more than a special kind of operating system, where the applications that run on it are operating systems.

Virtualization technology is discussed in detail in Chapter 5.

Managing User Access

Managing login credentials for end users (as well as for automated processes) requires that user accounts be managed in a highly consistent, organized manner. Because login credentials are often the only barrier between intruders and sensitive or valuable information, the consequences of poor security access management can be devastating.

The processes associated with user access are user access provisioning, user access termination, and user transfers. Each is discussed here.

User Access Provisioning

This is the process whereby user accounts are created for new employees or contractors. This activity should utilize a formal, documented access request and approval process that specifies who is authorized to request user accounts, who is authorized to approve access requests, and how (and which) activities are recorded.

Requests for administrative or privileged access may require additional approvals. The reason for this is that administrative and privileged accounts have higher risks associated with them (the potential for damage is directly proportional to the level of privilege).

User access provisioning occurs at the time of hire for new employees, but it also occurs when individual (or groups of) employees require additional access to applications or access to new applications. The process of vetting each account should address the following items:

- Is this person still actively employed and in good standing?
- Does this person require this access to perform their duties?
- Does the business owner of the system approve access?

A great deal of care is required in this process. The risk of errors can be devastating for an organization: the worst-case scenarios involve unauthorized insiders or outsiders having access to highly sensitive or valuable information. The practical effects of an error in user access management can be as grave as a hacking incident where an attacker is able to break in to a computer system to steal sensitive information.

The ChoicePoint Fraud Incident

In 2004, ChoicePoint suffered a major security breach where private information for more than 150,000 California residents was improperly accessed. This happened because ChoicePoint failed to properly vet a number of new business accounts that were opened expressly for the purpose of illicitly accessing private information and conducting identity theft.

ChoicePoint is in the business of acting as a private intelligence service for government and industry. It collects and stores data from many public and private sources, which is then used for personnel background checks and other purposes. ChoicePoint sells this information to businesses and governments that open business accounts.

The ChoicePoint incident should be a major lesson for organizations that protect sensitive or valuable information: the process of vetting new access requests cannot be taken lightly, for the consequences of getting it wrong can be devastating.

Employee Termination

When a worker's employment or contract ends, all logical and physical access privileges must be removed. In many situations, removing access within 24 hours is sufficient, but some situations warrant immediate removal. For example, if an employee is being terminated, the organization should arrange to have the employee's access terminated at once so that the employee does not have any opportunity to take revenge against the employer. Also, if the employee has access to high-value information, access should be removed immediately in order to protect that information from misuse.

User accounts should be locked in a way that prevents any other employees from being able to use the account. For example, if user access administrators change the password to "LOCKED," other employees who knew this could log in to the terminated employee's account and perpetrate acts that could be blamed on this person (indeed, the terminated employee himself could do this). Instead, user accounts should be locked by methods that are sophisticated or effective enough to prevent anyone from using them for any purpose. Some environments have the ability to *administratively* lock a user account; others must be *effectively* locked by changing the password to prevent anyone from logging in.

As with user access provisioning, there must be detailed and accurate recordkeeping associated with terminated users. This includes information on who initiated the termination notification process, as well as the names of user access administrators who terminated each user access account, and the date and time when user access was terminated.

Additional safeguards may be warranted, including

- **A review of the terminated employee's action prior to termination**   The employer should presume that a terminated employee might have had some suspicion about being terminated. The employee may have stolen sensitive or valuable information, or may have sabotaged systems, devices, or application source code. A thorough review of the terminated employee's activities for days or weeks prior to the incident may be needed to detect whether any inappropriate activities were performed.

- **A review of the terminated employee's actions after termination**   Access logs should be examined to make sure that there are no activities associated with the terminated employee's user accounts after the time of termination. Such activities could be an indication that the terminated employee still has access to information, or that some other employee is attempting to perform unauthorized actions that could be blamed on someone else.

- **Periodic access reviews**   Periodic access reviews should take place in all application and system environments to make sure that all users who have access still need it. These reviews should include a check to make sure that all terminated employee accounts were actually terminated properly and in a timely manner.

 CAUTION   To the extent possible, a defense-in-depth method should be used when terminating employee access. For example, in the case of building access, the employer should collect the employee's building access keycard *and* the keycard should be logically disabled so that it can no longer be used.

Employee Transfers

Employees transfer from one position to another in many organizations. These transfers may take place regularly or sparingly, depending on the type of organization.

Historically speaking, organizations are very practiced with provisioning new employees and transferring employees with new accesses that they require. Organizations are also fairly effective when handling employee terminations. However, transfers are far more difficult, because ideally an employee's old access rights should be rescinded when their new accesses are provisioned. This often does not take place, however, for a number of reasons. First, employees transferring from one job to another often have lingering responsibilities in their old position, making immediate revocation disruptive. Unless the user access management department has very good processes and recordkeeping, they are likely to forget to revoke those old accesses later on.

In organizations that do not manage user access changes that are related to employee transfers, the result is a growing number of employees who have a growing list of access privileges. This phenomenon is sometimes known as *accumulation of privileges* (or *privilege creep*).

Password Management

The management of passwords is one of the responsibilities of the user account management function. There are several activities within user account management where passwords are managed or handled in some way. These activities include

- **New user account provisioning** When users are issued new computer or network accounts, a means for transmitting the password to the user needs to be determined. The password should not be sent in e-mail, since anyone eavesdropping (or reading messages later) would be able to intercept and later reuse those passwords.

- **Account lockout** If a user tries several times to log in to their user account, their account may be administratively locked. The account may remain locked until one of the following events occurs:

  - The user calls a service desk to identify them and get their password reset.

  - A set period (usually 15 to 60 minutes) elapses.

- **Forgotten passwords** When users forget their passwords, they need to get their password reset somehow so that they can resume using their access account. Several methods are available for resetting passwords, including:

- **Self-service with secret question** Users access a "forgotten password" screen where they are asked a secret question. If they can answer the question successfully, they are taken to a screen where they create a new password.

- **Self-service with password or URL mailed to them** Users access a "forgotten password" screen where they cause a new password or one-time URL to be sent to their e-mail. If a password is sent via e-mail, the application should require the user to choose a new password on first login. If a URL is sent via e-mail, the URL will take the user to a screen where they are required to choose a new password. This method will not work if the user has forgotten their e-mail password.

- **Assisted password reset** Users call a service desk that uses a reliable means for identifying the user, usually by asking them for some information that other employees or persons would not know. When they have been successfully identified, the service desk provisions a new password and tells it to the user over the phone.

Systems and applications usually contain a number of automatic password controls that are related to the selection and use of passwords. The current practices for automatic password controls include

- **Account lockout** User accounts become automatically locked after a number of unsuccessful login attempts. This measure is used to prevent automated password attacks against a user account. The lockout threshold is usually from 4 to 10 unsuccessful attempts. If the user successfully logs in or a specific period elapses, the counter is usually reset.

- **Password length** User accounts are required to contain a minimum number of characters, usually seven or eight, but sometimes larger figures are used in highly sensitive environments. Many organizations have transitioned from using the word *password* to the term *pass phrase* to get users to begin thinking of passwords as a group of words instead of a single word. This encourages users to choose longer passwords, which are more difficult for intruders to attack.

- **Password complexity** Passwords are often required to contain more than one class of character, the classes being lowercase letters, uppercase letters, numbers, and symbols. Many systems require three or even all four types of characters in passwords.

- **Password expiration** Systems often require users to change their passwords periodically, as often as every 30 days to as seldom as every year.

- **Password reuse** Systems can require that users be unable to choose a new password that is the same as the previous password, or even the same as the previous *N* passwords. This prevents users from switching back to the same familiar password.

- **Password rechange** Systems can require that users wait a minimum period (for instance, seven days) before they can rechange their password. This is designed to prevent users from quickly cycling back to their old familiar password. For example, if a system forbids the use of the last 10 passwords and at least seven days between password changes, it would take a user 70 days to get back to their same familiar password; these settings would discourage such a practice.

NOTE Password controls should be chosen based upon the settings of other controls, as well as on system limitations, service desk processes, and the value or sensitivity of the information being protected.

Managing Tokens, Certificates, and Biometrics

Strong authentication controls that include tokens, certificates, and biometrics require support and management processes that will equip users with the knowledge and devices they require and with support processes to help them in times of trouble. Areas where support processes require additional steps include these.

Provisioning Provisioning user accounts when strong authentication is used does require more effort. Whereas user ID-and-password accounts can often be provisioned remotely, strong authentication provisioning often requires in-person presence. For instance, users need to be given a hardware token (although one could be shipped to the user); a digital certificate needs to be installed on the user's computer (although this may be possible through a remote network connection); or a user must enroll their biometric, which may or may not be possible unless the user is on-site.

Training Users will often require training in the use of their strong authentication so that they will know how to use it properly. Without adequate or effective training, users will call the service desk more frequently, raising costs even higher (the cost of implementing strong authentication is many times that of ordinary user ID-and-password authentication).

Where hardware tokens (or USB tokens or smart cards) are used, users need to be trained to carry their hardware devices separate from the computers they use. They need to understand that if their computer and hardware authentication device are kept together and stolen, an intruder may have an easier time breaking into corporate databases.

Authentication Troubles Strong authentication is more complicated, and this can trip up some end users. While digital certificates are fairly hands-off (aside from forgetting the password), tokens and biometrics have their share of support issues. Biometrics that are configured with too low a tolerance for error may lock out legitimate users (and, if configured with too high a tolerance, may admit outsiders), which could require that users re-register or their systems be looked at.

Token and smart card authentication methods use tiny electronic devices that cannot be considered absolutely trouble-free. While highly reliable, a few things can go wrong that may require their replacement.

The IT service desk will need to develop workaround procedures when users are not able to log in using their strong authentication methods. Making a user wait until they can be re-registered for their biometrics, for instance, will be unacceptable in many instances.

Replacing Devices Like keycards and other small objects, in a large enough organization, lost tokens and smart cards will be a regular occurrence. Users will lose them, damage them (spilled coffee and so on), or leave them behind in a hotel room or their other suit jacket.

The IT service desk will need to develop procedures for emergency authentication while users are awaiting replacement devices. Making them wait for replacements (even when shipped overnight) will be unacceptable in many cases. Instead, information systems need to be able to fall back to user ID-and-password authentication for emergencies.

Protecting Mobile Computing

The year 2005 was the first year that laptop computers outsold desktop computers. This development helped IT security professionals recognize that most new end-user computers were not going to be as easy to protect as they once were: there would be more and more laptop computers, containing sensitive data, away from the protection of corporate buildings and firewalls.

Corporations struggled to adjust their PC management and support, as well as policies governing the use of laptop computers. Common safeguards put in place include endpoint management software capable of communicating with laptops over slower, sporadic communication links; built-in firewalls and antivirus; whole-disk encryption; cable locks; and policies that require employees to keep their laptops safely locked away or in their custody at all times and policies that state that laptops are for business use only and for employee use only.

Management capabilities for protecting laptop computers were beginning to mature in the five years since they were outselling desktop computers. Then an even more disruptive development occurred: smart phones.

In just five more years after laptop computers outsold their desktop counterparts, smart phones are outselling laptop and desktop computers combined. Smart phones are far more disruptive than laptop computers were: for the most part, smart phones are being purchased by consumers instead of corporations, and enterprise-class management capabilities for protecting smart phones are in their infancy.

Laptop Controls

Enterprises generally enact a wide suite of policies and controls regarding the use of laptop computers. The most common are

- Whole-disk encryption.
- Firewall.
- Anti-malware.
- Restricted privileges, including limitations on the ability to change configurations and limitations on whether applications can be installed.
- Removable storage restrictions—usually limiting or prohibiting the use of USB attached storage and optical media.
- Stronger encryption, such as a smart card or biometric device.
- Policies requiring employees to keep laptops with them at all times unless they are in a locked room. Cable locks are often required for settings like hotel rooms.
- Policies permitting only assigned employees allowed to use company-issued laptop computers (no use permitted by other family members or friends).

Smart Phone Controls

The productivity gains that are realized through the use of smart phones are compelling. However, their use means that sensitive company information now resides in tiny devices that it does not own and cannot easily control. Enterprises are responding to the onslaught of employee-purchased smart phones that are being used to connect to corporate e-mail and other systems, and struggling to control them to continue protecting sensitive information.

The controls that organizations are putting into place for smart phones include

- **Authentication policies** Many enterprises are requiring employees to enact auto-lock and complex passwords on their smart phones. This helps to reduce the likelihood that an intruder who steals a smart phone will find that it is locked, and therefore difficult to unlock and access.

- **Encryption** Where possible, enterprises are enacting controls to cause any locally stored data to be encrypted.

- **Remote wipe** Enterprises are enacting controls to give them the ability to remotely wipe any smart phone that is reported lost or stolen.

- **Download restrictions** Enterprises are enacting controls to restrict which applications a user may download onto their smart phone.

Enterprises are coming to terms with new management, control, and policy issues with smart phones. Employees are buying them on their own, often with the expectation that they will be able to access corporate e-mail and other functions. Security and risk managers are cringing because they have just gotten laptops under control, which (relatively speaking) was easier since the company owns them and can more easily control whether they can connect to corporate networks.

 NOTE Security controls for mobile devices are not *additional* controls, but *compensating* controls that reduce data compromise risks since they are usually not protected by other physical and logical protections such as locked doors and firewalls.

Network Security Controls

Enterprise networks—and the network-based services that support systems and applications—require protection and control so that they will be reliable and secure. Networks carry information for virtually all applications and computing services; a compromise of network security could seriously threaten all of the applications and computing services in an organization.

Network Security

Networks are the means through which users access sensitive information. While the databases and operating systems that contain data will have controls in place to protect that information, many controls are required at the network level that protect systems and other network-based resources from various threats. Countermeasures are available to prevent or detect many threats.

Network-Based Threats

Threats are the intent and ability to cause harm. In the context of a network, a threat may have the ability to disrupt network communications, or be able to intercept communications in order to acquire sensitive information.

The most prevalent network-based threats include

- **Access by unauthorized persons** Because some network-based resources do not include authentication by their very nature, it is important to restrict network access at the point of entry. This means that users (and system-based resources) must be authenticated prior to being permitted to communicate on the network. Without that authentication, a user is not permitted to send any messages on the network, nor are they permitted to listen to any network traffic.

- **Spoofing** This is the act of changing the configuration of a device or system in an attempt to masquerade as a different, known, and trusted system. There are several reasons why someone would want to do this; primarily, the reason will be to attract incoming connections in order to steal identities that can later be used illicitly. For example, an intruder may successfully spoof an internal web server and present an authentication page where users will enter their user ID and passwords. The intruder can save these credentials and use them later to access protected resources in order to steal or alter sensitive or valuable information. Another method is to masquerade as a known, legitimate user or device in order to bypass authentication and access network resources as the other user or device.

- **Eavesdropping** Here, someone installs hardware or software to listen to other network transmissions in an attempt to intercept any available sensitive information. Or, if this is a targeted attack, the intruder will listen for the specifically desired information and then capture it for later use. The intruder could be looking for logon credentials, e-mail messages, transferred files, or communications between servers in an application.

- **Malware** While viruses, worms, Trojan horses, and so on do not directly attack networks, they do use networks to propagate from one system to another. Especially virulent malware may generate so much traffic that all legitimate network communications may cease. This may be true even if only a small number of infected systems are present and attempting to find new victim hosts to attack and infect.

- **Denial of service (DoS) attacks** This is when an attacker floods a target with such a large volume of traffic that the target is unable to function normally. Such an attack can cause the target system to either malfunction or crash, or the sheer volume of traffic may impair the target's ability to respond to legitimate messages.

- **Access bypass** Here, an individual can attach an unauthorized access device, such as a Wi-Fi access point or a dial-in modem, to the network, thereby permitting himself (or others) to access the network while bypassing security controls.

- **Man-in-the-middle (MITM) attack**   This attack is used to take over communications that are taking place between two parties. Here, an attacker intercepts communications being sent from one party to another and injects new, altered communications in their place. The attacker must be able to impersonate each party in the communication so that each party believes it is talking directly with the other party.

- **Man-in-the-browser (MITB) attack**   This attack involves the installation of a malicious "browser helper object" (BHO) onto a victim's browser. The malicious BHO alters communication between the browser and the Internet without the victim's knowledge.

There is no single detective or preventive control that is effective against all of these threats. Instead, several controls are needed to protect networks against these and other threats.

Vulnerable Network-Based Services

Many common network-based services are vulnerable to manipulation and can be used to attack other systems. Some of these services are

- **Malicious websites**   If improperly protected, websites can be attacked and loaded with malware that will be installed on site visitors' computers. This is typically called a drive-by attack, because a person was merely visiting a website, which installed malware on the victim's computer.

- **E-mail**   The darling of attackers everywhere, e-mail is used to propagate spam, phishing attacks, pharming attacks, and malware.

- **Instant messaging**   IM networks are used to propagate worms that can be used to install malware on unprotected victims' computers.

- **Message boards**   People who search the Internet for solutions to problems often find discussions about their problems on message boards. Because many message boards are operated by volunteers, they often lack security controls and do not block attackers from putting malware on them for victims to unknowingly install on their computers.

- **Social networking**   Some popular social networking sites allow for "applications" to be downloaded for subscribers' use. Some of these social networking sites do not examine these applications to see whether they are harmful or malicious in any way.

- **Peer-to-peer networking**   Peer-to-peer networks are a favorite attack vector for malware producers. Because they lack centralized servers with strong anti-malware controls, peer-to-peer networks are a great method for distributing Trojan horses and other malware.

Network Security Countermeasures

Several controls are needed to ensure the integrity and security of a network as one layer of defense in the protection of valuable or sensitive information. These controls include

- **User authentication controls**   Users can be required to authenticate to the network itself prior to accessing any network-based resources. This may be useful even if servers and other resources on the network have their own separate authentication.

- **Machine authentication controls**   Every node that attaches to the network should itself be authenticated. This can prevent nonorganization-owned assets (such as personally owned computers, unauthorized access points, sniffers, or vendor demo equipment) from being able to access the network. This helps to ensure that only organization-managed devices that have malware controls, including antivirus software, can attach to the network, thereby reducing the likelihood that malware will be introduced into the environment. The dominant technology for enforcing machine authentication is the IEEE 802.1X standard, which can also perform detailed checks on a node, including patch level and whether antivirus software is running and up-to-date.

- **Anti-malware**   Many organizations have opted to supplement workstation-based antivirus software with network-based antivirus capabilities. Centralized, network-based anti-malware may be used to filter malware and spam from incoming e-mail, or it may act as a silent or active proxy for web traffic, blocking malware that is hosted on websites. Both measures can greatly improve an organization's ability to prevent malware attacks.

- **Encryption**   Sensitive communications can be encrypted in order to reduce the threat of eavesdropping. Many methods for encryption are available, depending on the network's architecture and the specific traffic that needs to be protected. For instance, tunnels between pairs of servers can be established at the OS level using IPsec or SSH. Tunnels between networks can be established using IPsec between pairs of routers. In both cases, network-based applications and services need not be modified, as they will be completely unaware of the encryption taking place at lower layers in the IP stack.

- **Switched networks**   The use of shared-media networks (such as Ethernet through the use of hubs, repeaters, and bridges) invites eavesdroppers who can intercept some or all network transmissions. By changing to switched networks, the only traffic that a node sees are packets sent explicitly to or from the node, as well as some broadcast traffic. This greatly reduces the risk of eavesdropping, since it may not be practical to encrypt all communications.

- **Intrusion detection system (IDS)**   This is a system used to detect anomalous activities on the network, sending alerts to appropriate personnel when these anomalies occur. Like antivirus software, IDSs are typically signature-based, which requires that they be updated from time to time in order to remain effective. Some IDSs can "learn" normal network traffic behavior and generate alarms when non-normal traffic is detected. IDS systems are available in two forms: network-based (NIDS), which usually take the form of network appliances, and host-based (HIDS), which consist of software agents installed on each host and a separate management console.

- **Intrusion prevention system (IPS)**   These systems, like IDS, detect anomalies on the network. However, an IPS is also able to block an offending system by instructing a network switch to disconnect it. This can be used to block both internal as well as external threats, whether they are intruders trying to break in to a system or some malware that has been able to penetrate defenses on an organization-owned device. One drawback with IPS is that a false positive can result in the disconnection of a legitimate system or service on the network.

- **Website filtering**   These systems are designed to block users' access to categories of websites. Website filtering is often implemented with two purposes in mind: First, it is used to limit employees from visiting sites with little or no business value, thereby preventing some wasted time. Second, some categories of sites are known for hosting malware, so website filtering helps to reduce malware attacks on an organization's systems.

- **Data leakage prevention (DLP)**   These systems are designed to detect the transmission of potentially sensitive information into or out of an organization's network. DLP systems may be configured to generate alerts sent to a security incident manager, and some are able to block such transmissions altogether. These alerts can be based on general types of sensitive data such as credit card numbers, but also organization-specific data such as internal project names.

These and other network security countermeasures should be considered important controls, each of which should have complete process and procedure documentation, managed records, and periodic audits.

Securing Client-Server Applications

While no longer the platform of choice for most new applications, many client-server applications are still in use and require continued, and even improved, protection from evolving threats.

Client-server environments are subject to the same threats and have most or all of the same vulnerabilities as ordinary servers and workstations. Those threats, vulnerabilities, and countermeasures are discussed elsewhere in this chapter.

The threats and countermeasures that are specific to client-server environments include the following:

- **Access controls**   Most client-server applications were developed in an era when the prospect of impersonated client systems seemed remote. However, client-server applications that are designed today would certainly include strong authentication between client software and server software (in addition to workstation authentication using 802.1X and end-user authentication to the network). Older client-server environments may lack one or more of these authentication components. While altering the existing client-server components themselves may be infeasible, other compensating controls may be viable, including workstation-based integrity management software, anti-malware, and workstation hardening.

- **Interception of client-server communications**   Eavesdropping and interception of client-server communications can result in a compromise of sensitive or valuable information. Furthermore, an MITM attack can result in intercepted and altered communications, with consequences including compromise of sensitive information and fraud. The most effective countermeasure for traffic interception is network encryption between servers and client workstations.

- **Network failure**   See the earlier section on network security for details.

- **Change management**   When application code changes are considered, the project team making the changes needs to establish comprehensive test and implementation plans to ensure that the change will result in the correct functional changes in the environment. This is further complicated by the fact that code changes will need to be distributed to all of the client workstations in the organization. If some of those workstations are laptop computers, installation of client software updates will be logistically challenging since not all laptops will be available when the IT department intends to update them.

- **Disruption of client software updates**   If clients are unable to receive and install software updates, they may fail to operate properly. In client-server architecture, client software must be in close synchronization with server software, since part of the application's business logic is server-based and part is client-based. An update to the application that requires changes to both the server and all clients may fail for any workstations that cannot install the new updates. The purpose of attacks on the client software distribution mechanism or on client workstations themselves may be the disruption of the entire application in organization. In addition to system hardening, countermeasures include encryption, reports indicating the success rate of client updates, and tools to troubleshoot client update problems.

- **Stealing data**   Users of client-server applications will be able to steal information if their client workstations include a full operating system and access to external storage devices (this is also a viable threat to web-based applications). In environments where the information being viewed and managed is highly sensitive or valuable, additional countermeasures, such as blocking the use of external storage devices (floppy drives, CD/DVD-ROM, and USB-based storage), may be warranted.

Securing Wireless Networks

Innovations in wireless communications have produced a productivity breakthrough for many workers who no longer have to be constrained to working at their desks. Wireless network technologies have enabled workers to connect to enterprise networks, regardless of their location. However, some wireless communications technologies have significant vulnerabilities, and most are subject to serious threats.

Early wireless LAN (WLAN, or Wi-Fi) technologies did not encrypt traffic at all. This permitted other users (and outsiders—anyone within range of a wireless LAN) to use relatively simple tools to intercept and record wireless network transmissions, and they did nothing to prevent someone from joining a wireless LAN and using it for Internet access. At that time, since many internal communications, including logon sessions, were not encrypted, sniffing a wireless network from a safe location could yield as much rich information as a sniffer connected directly to the network—minus the risks related to getting a sniffer inside an office building.

Wireless networks are attractive to intruders because they provide an opportunity to easily penetrate a network without the risks associated with breaking into a physical building.

Wireless Network Threats and Vulnerabilities

Early wireless networks had significant vulnerabilities in their design and implementation that drew the attention of intruders. This attention led to research and discovery of more vulnerabilities, which have led to a proliferation of tools designed to exploit them. The threats and vulnerabilities associated with wireless networks are discussed here.

Eavesdropping This is the best-known threat identified with wireless LANs. Intruders with fairly simple tools are able to easily listen in on wireless communications, even when encrypted and protected through other means. Because wireless networks use radio frequency (RF) technology, the threat of eavesdropping will never completely disappear.

War Driving and War Chalking War driving and war chalking refer to activities where intruders will travel in dense urban areas, looking for unprotected Wi-Fi access points. The term *war driving* comes from the practice of searching from within a moving automobile.

Client-Server Applications and Data Protection Laws

Another serious issue in many client-server environments is the need to update these environments to meet new security regulations. New data protection laws and standards require protection measures in application environments that were not included in older client-server frameworks. Some of these measures include encryption of transmitted data, encryption of stored data, strong authentication, access and transaction logging, and the use of unique user accounts for each individual user. Many client-server environments are simply unable to implement one or more of these controls that are present in newer application environments. This is not to say that countermeasures are impossible; rather, each organization has to weigh the cost of implementing and supporting each required countermeasure in order to assess the long-term viability of each client-server environment.

War chalking is the practice of marking buildings (using chalk) with symbols to indicate the presence of a Wi-Fi access point, including some basic facts about it. The practice was popular in the early 2000s, but is not often used now. Figure 6-4 shows the common symbols that were used. The practice is thought to be derived from a similar practice during the Great Depression when homeless people would mark buildings that were friendly, unfriendly, and where law enforcement was located.

Weak Encryption The earliest wireless LANs used no encryption at all—not because it wasn't available, but because it required additional effort to implement. Because wireless access points can be configured to permit "wide open" (no encryption) configuration, many organizations stopped here and never implemented encryption. In addition, many Wi-Fi access points sold for home use did not have encryption enabled by default; most consumers did not bother to implement encryption because they did not know that it was important to do so.

The WEP (Wired Equivalent Privacy) encryption algorithm was developed to protect Wi-Fi networks from eavesdropping. WEP is so-named because its designers intended for WEP to provide confidentiality as effective as a traditional wired LAN. Unfortunately, WEP was soon compromised: intruders with readily available tools can completely compromise a Wi-Fi network protected with WEP within minutes. These tools can derive the WEP encryption key, enabling an intruder to easily decrypt all encrypted communications on a Wi-Fi network protected with WEP.

The WPA (Wi-Fi Protected Access) protocols were adopted as a stronger method for encryption of wireless networks. However, WPA is showing some signs of compromise as well. As of the writing of this book, WPA is still considered suitable for most commercial environments. However, organizations processing more sensitive data should consider adding layers of defense such as additional authentication and encryption.

Spoofing Intruders can use spoofing to impersonate both Wi-Fi access points and Wi-Fi network clients.

It is relatively easy for an intruder to establish a rogue access point with the same name as a legitimate access point. The intruder can use this rogue access point as a gateway to forward legitimate traffic in both directions while watching for and intercepting any sensitive information that may pass by. Or, the intruder may use the rogue access point to steal logon credentials from users trying to connect to the *real* access point.

Figure 6-4
Common war chalking symbols indicate the presence of Wi-Fi access points.

Intruders can also spoof legitimate Wi-Fi clients in an attempt to connect to Wi-Fi networks. Some Wi-Fi networks include MAC address ACLs, which means they permit only known computers (identified by their MAC addresses) to connect to the Wi-Fi network. An intruder who eavesdrops on Wi-Fi traffic can easily discern this and change his computer's MAC address to that of one of the computers that is permitted to connect.

Session Hijacking   Many popular and well-known Internet websites (including those used for social networking, blogs, and e-mail) do not force encryption in users' communications. When users' sessions are not encrypted, their session cookies are transmitted unencrypted. On public Wi-Fi hotspots, this makes those users' sessions vulnerable to session hijacking, where an intruder on the same Wi-Fi network can intercept a user's session cookie and then take over the session.

The *firesheep* tool made session hijacking a topic of discussion and debate in 2010. There are probably many other such tools available for intruders who wish to prey on and hijack users' sessions.

Wireless Network Countermeasures

Several protective countermeasures can be taken that will reduce risks associated with the use of wireless networks. These countermeasures include

- **Use an obscure SSID**   The SSID (Service Set IDentifier) should be changed from the default, but should not obviously identify the organization that operates it. Doing so would invite intruders and curious persons to try and penetrate the known network. However, in the case of "public hot spots" such as hotels, restaurants, and coffee shops, the SSID often conspicuously identifies the establishment.

- **Stop broadcast of SSID**   Except for the case of public hotspots, broadcast of the access point's SSID should be disabled. Granted, this is a weak countermeasure because determined intruders who use more advanced tools do not need to see a network's SSID to know it is there: they have tools to directly sniff packets from the airlink, whether the access point is broadcasting its SSID or not. This measure does, however, act as a mild deterrent for those who are less skilled.

- **Reduce transmit power**   The transmit strength of the Wi-Fi RF transmitter should be reduced to the lowest level that will still permit reliable use. This will prevent any distant eavesdropper from easily detecting the network.

- **Use MAC access filtering**   Wi-Fi access points can usually be configured to permit only those computers whose MAC addresses are present in a list of allowed addresses.

- **Use WPA encryption**   Because WEP has been compromised, WPA or WPA2 encryption should be used.

- **Require VPN**   Organizations that are concerned that WPA may also be compromised can configure their Wi-Fi architecture so that VPN connections must be established for users to connect to the corporate LAN.

- **Change default passwords**   Administrative user IDs and passwords on new Wi-Fi access points should be changed before they are put into use.

- **Patches and upgrades**   Before new Wi-Fi access points are put into general use, network administrators should make sure that they contain the latest firmware or software. This is especially important if any vulnerabilities have been found in older versions.

 CAUTION   Like system hardening, hardening Wi-Fi access points and supporting infrastructure is not a set-once-and-forget-it affair. Instead, making a system secure and keeping it secure requires vigilance through staying informed on the latest threats and vulnerabilities and taking action as needed.

Protecting Internet Communications

For decades, the common practice for commercial organizations that needed to establish data communication connections between locations—or between organizations—was the use of dedicated private communications links leased from telecommunications carriers. Prior to the Internet, private communications links were the *only* available method for setting up data communications.

The establishment of the Internet made it theoretically possible for organizations to connect to one another simply by connecting to the Internet backbone and letting routers do the rest. Most organizations scoffed at this idea because of the Internet's reputation for unreliable performance, as well as its lack of security. Gradually, however, Internet performance has improved in many parts of the world, and security standards have been developed that make use of the Internet for an inter- and intraorganization communications medium a practical reality.

This section describes threats, vulnerabilities, and countermeasures needed to protect Internet-based business communications.

Internet Communications Threats and Vulnerabilities

The Internet is not a safe place. Practically all of the threats against organizations' valuable and sensitive information originate from the Internet or use the Internet in their delivery. This is because the Internet is the backbone of nearly all types of data communications, like the one well in the middle of town from which all its citizens draw water—the source of life but also a source of disease when things go wrong.

Internet-related threats and vulnerabilities are discussed in the following sections.

Eavesdropping   Any data sent from one place to another over the Internet could be intercepted. While actual interception is rare, it is possible, and interception does occur from time to time. An effective analogy is the use of postcards in the mail. Most of the time, postcards are not read by anyone while in transit; nonetheless, their confidentiality cannot be assured.

Network Analysis   Similar to eavesdropping, someone who has access to an organization's data communications can perform network analysis on it. This activity would be the reconnaissance phase of some bigger effort. An eavesdropper with access to an organization's network traffic would, over time, be able to tell quite a lot about the organization's internal network by observing data coming and going.

Targeted Attack   An attacker whose objective is a specific organization's systems will probably use the Internet to transmit the attack to his target. A clever attacker will relay his attack through a series of compromised systems in order to conceal his true whereabouts, making it difficult for law enforcement to learn his true identity and location.

Malware   The Internet is the conduit through which virtually all malware travels. Whether it is transmitted in spam, hidden in downloadable software programs, or embedded in websites, the designers of malware know that the Internet is the way to travel fast and cheap. Botnets use IRC (Internet relay chat) and HTTP protocols to control their bot armies, as well as to spread spam or attack target systems.

Masquerading   An attacker can forge messages that have the appearance of originating elsewhere. The TCP/IP protocol itself does not enforce the value in the "From" IP address field in any packet, which makes it easy to send messages to a target system that have the appearance of originating from anywhere. Similarly, the SMTP (Simple Mail Transport Protocol) performs no enforcement on the "From" address in any e-mail message, a fact that has contributed to the spam problem. Many other protocols have similar weaknesses in their design.

Denial of Service   A denial of service (DoS) attack is an attack on a target system with the intent of causing it to cease functioning. There are two principal ways to perpetrate a DoS attack; first, it can be carried out by sending an enormous volume of messages to the target system in order to flood its input buffers and exhaust its available resources. The second method is to send a specially built message that is known to cause a service or application running on the target system to malfunction or stop running altogether.

Another form of a DoS attack is known as a distributed denial of service (DDoS) attack, a flooding attack that originates from a large number of systems simultaneously.

Fraud   Many kinds of fraud are perpetrated on the Internet against systems and people. In a fraud attack, the attacker is pretending to be someone or something else (a merchant, bank, or government entity, for instance) and is attempting to trick the target into performing an action, such as transferring money or providing private information.

 NOTE   One topic not covered in this section is the variety of reasons and motivations behind attacks on systems. This subject is covered in detail earlier in this chapter.

Masquerading on the Internet

The protocols at the base of the Internet, TCP/IP, were developed a generation ago by designers who assumed that TCP/IP would always be operated on controlled, closed networks. The basic design of most of the protocols and services in use on the Internet today assume that all other parties can be trusted. For this reason, the designers of TCP/IP never built in controls to prevent one system from masquerading as another. It is this design principle that has permitted the proliferation of much spam, malware, and other malevolence on the Internet.

Internet Communications Security Countermeasures

A wide variety of countermeasures are needed to protect an organization from the assortment of threats. The countermeasures described in this section should begin to look familiar if you are reading through this chapter from beginning to end; the countermeasures used to protect Internet-based threats are not much different from those protecting similar threats in other contexts.

Network- and computer-related security countermeasures discussed elsewhere in this book would often apply when any network, system, or application is opened to the Internet. The Internet represents the worst-case security scenario for any system or application, as this exposes it to the most potent threats that exist.

Firewalls   Firewalls are devices that control the flow of messages between networks. Placed at the boundary between the Internet and an organization's internal network, firewalls enforce security policy by prohibiting all inbound traffic except for the specific few types of traffic that are permitted to a select few systems. For example, a firewall will

- Permit incoming e-mail to be sent only to the organization's e-mail server.
- Permit incoming HTTP requests to be sent only to the organization's Internet-facing web server.
- Permit incoming file transfer requests to be sent only to the organization's file transfer gateway.
- Permit outbound e-mail to originate only from the organization's e-mail server.

The last item in the previous list points out that firewalls control not only what comes *in* to an organization's network, but also what *leaves* an organization's network. This last control, permitting outbound mail to originate only from the e-mail server, prevents malware from originating its own e-mail messages, thereby slowing down the spread and impact of some types of malware.

The two principal types of firewalls are

- **Screening routers**   These simpler firewalls are designed to examine each packet and compare it to an access control list (ACL) to determine if, based on its source and destination IP addresses and ports, whether it should be permitted to pass through the firewall.

- **Stateful inspection firewalls** This type of firewall is designed to record incoming packets and keep track of TCP/IP sessions between external and internal hosts. In the TCP protocol, an incoming packet is answered with an outgoing packet; a stateful inspection firewall will examine an outgoing packet and make a go/no-go decision based on whether it believes that the outgoing packet is a part of an active session. Stateful inspection firewalls are more complex and capable of more effectively protecting an organization's network.

 CAUTION Firewall rulesets should be periodically reviewed to ensure that every rule is formally approved and justified.

Application Firewalls Application firewalls are devices that are designed to protect web-based applications from application layer attacks. Some of the types of attacks that application firewalls are designed to recognize and block include

- SQL injection
- Script injection
- Cross-site scripting
- Buffer overflow
- Parameter tampering
- Denial of service

Application firewalls were developed because traditional network firewalls examine only the source and destination IP addresses as well as source and destination port numbers. Network firewalls do not examine the contents of an incoming packet, which could be harmful nonetheless if it is a part of an attack on an application server.

Application firewalls are available as stand-alone appliances (called network-based application firewalls) as well as software applications that can be installed in application servers (known as host-based application firewalls).

An application firewall is not a replacement for a network firewall. Application firewalls are designed to block application layer attacks, but not necessarily act as a general-purpose firewall.

Demilitarized Zone Network (DMZ) An organization with one or more systems that provide services to Internet users may implement a demilitarized zone (DMZ) network architecture. The DMZ is a separate network where Internet-facing systems are attached and isolated with one or more firewalls. The rules in the firewall(s) will permit specific services from the Internet to reach the DMZ servers, but will not permit access from the Internet to the internal network.

Typical DMZ architectures are shown in Figure 6-5. Organizations with large numbers of Internet-facing servers may use more complex architectures with layers of DMZ networks.

Figure 6-5 Typical DMZ networks

Intrusion Detection Systems and Intrusion Prevention Systems An intrusion detection system (IDS) is a detective control that is designed to listen to network traffic and generate alerts if it sees any messages that match a database of attack signatures. An intrusion prevention system (IPS) is a preventive control that is designed to listen to network traffic and block messages that match a database of attack signatures. IDSs and IPSs are discussed in more detail earlier in this chapter in the section "Network Security."

Honeypots and Honeynets A *honeypot* is a trap that is designed to detect unauthorized use of information systems. A honeypot will have the appearance of containing important information and of being unprotected and unmonitored. When an attacker attacks and takes over a honeypot, this provides information to the organization that will help it learn how to better protect its real production computers.

A honeypot helps an organization better understand some important facts:

- Which attackers are sufficiently interested in the organization's information to launch an attack against it
- Which available targets attract attackers
- Which tools and techniques are used by the attacker(s)

A security team in the organization can analyze this information and use it to improve defenses on the systems that actually do contain sensitive or valuable information.

CAUTION An organization that sets up a honeypot needs to take care that the honeypot cannot be used as a platform to successfully attack real production systems or to stage an attack on another organization's systems.

A *honeynet* is just what the term implies: a network of computers that are all acting as honeypots to emulate a complex production environment that consists of several computers.

There are two primary types of honeypots and honeynets:

- **High interaction** These are systems that will be partly or completely unpatched, thereby attracting attackers.
- **Low interaction** These are designed to resemble other production servers in the network. Ordinarily unused, IDS systems would trigger alarms if they are accessed, signaling that an intruder may be examining them.

Change Management and Configuration Management The protection of sensitive and valuable information—particularly that which is exposed to the Internet—depends upon the integrity of the entire environment. The environment's integrity can be assured only to the extent to which it is controlled; this means that all minor and major changes made to the environment must be managed through formal change management and configuration management processes.

These processes are described in detail in Chapter 5.

Incident Management Incident management is the two-part process of proactive and responsive activities that help to reduce the likelihood and impact of security incidents. The proactive side of incident management helps to prevent incidents from occurring at all, while the responsive side helps to quickly contain incidents and make changes to reduce the likelihood and impact of future incidents.

Incident management is discussed in detail at the beginning of this chapter in the section "Information Security Management."

Incidents can also result from manmade or natural disasters—this aspect of incident response is addressed through disaster recovery plans (covered in Chapter 5) and business continuity plans (discussed in Chapter 2).

Security Awareness Training Security awareness training helps every person in the organization be more familiar with how their tasks and responsibilities help to protect the organization's assets. Familiarity with security concepts and responsibilities helps each staff member make better decisions that help reduce risk.

This training is discussed in detail at the beginning of this chapter in the section "Information Security Management."

Encryption

Encryption is the act of hiding information in plain sight. It works by scrambling the characters in a message using a method known only to the sender and receiver, making the message useless to any party that intercepts the message.

Encryption plays a key role in the protection of sensitive and valuable information. There are some situations where it is not practical or feasible to prevent third parties from having logical access to data—for instance, data transmissions over public networks.

This technique can also be used to authenticate information that is sent from one party to another. This means that a receiving party can verify that a specific party did, in fact, originate a message and that it is authentic. This allows a receiver to know that a message is genuine and that it has not been altered in transit by any third party.

With encryption, best practices call for system designers to use well-known, robust encryption algorithms. Thus, when a third party intercepts encrypted data, the third party can know which algorithm is being used but still not be able to read the data. What the third party does not know is the *key* that is used to encrypt and decrypt the data. How this works will be explained further in this section.

 TIP Encryption can be thought of as another layer of access protection. Like user ID and password controls that restrict access to data to everyone but those with login credentials, encryption restricts access to (plaintext) data to everyone but those with encryption keys.

Terms and Concepts Used in Cryptography

Several terms and concepts used in cryptography are not used outside of the field. Security professionals and IS auditors must be familiar with these to be effective in understanding, managing, and auditing IT systems that use cryptography. Terms used in cryptography include

- **Plaintext** An original message, file, or stream of data that can be read by anyone who has access to it.
- **Ciphertext** A message, file, or stream of data that has been transformed by an encryption algorithm and rendered unreadable.
- **Hash function** A cryptographic operation on a block of data that returns a fixed-length string of characters, used to verify the integrity of a message.
- **Message digest** The result of a cryptographic hash function.
- **Encryption** The process of transforming plaintext into ciphertext. This is depicted in Figure 6-6.

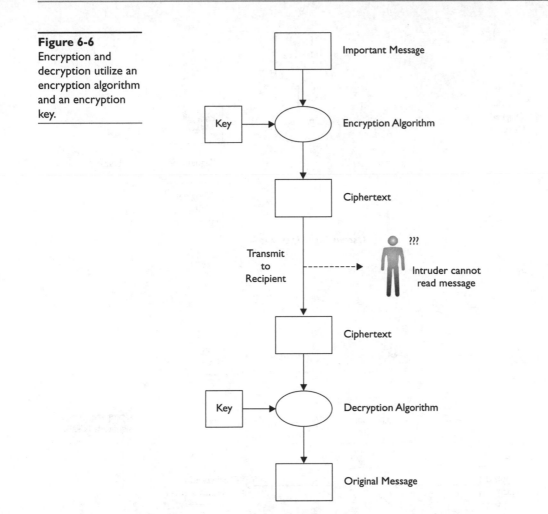

Figure 6-6
Encryption and
decryption utilize an
encryption algorithm
and an encryption
key.

- **Digital signature**   The result of encrypting the hash of a message with the originator's private encryption key, used to prove the authenticity and integrity of a message. This is depicted in Figure 6-7.

- **Algorithm**   A specific mathematical formula that is used to perform encryption, decryption, message digests, and digital signatures

- **Decryption**   The process of transforming ciphertext into plaintext so that a recipient can read it

- **Cryptanalysis**   An attack on a cryptosystem where the attacker is attempting to determine the encryption key that is used to encrypt messages

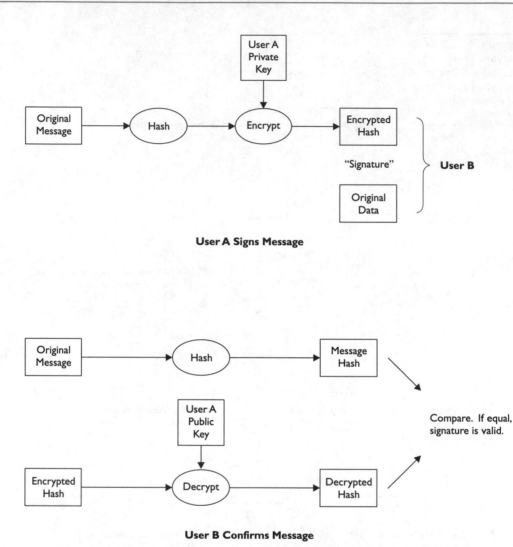

Figure 6-7   Digital signature used to verify the integrity of a message

- **Encryption key**   A block of characters, used in combination with an encryption algorithm, used to encrypt or decrypt a stream or blocks of data. An encryption key is also used to create and verify a digital signature.

- **Key length**   This refers to the size (measured in bits) of an encryption key. Longer encryption keys mean that it takes greater effort to successfully attack a cryptosystem.

- **Block cipher**   This is an encryption algorithm that operates on blocks of data.

- **Stream cipher**   This is a type of encryption algorithm that operates on a continuous stream of data such as a video or audio feed.

- **Initialization vector (IV)**   A random number that is needed by some encryption algorithms to begin the encryption process.

- **Symmetric encryption**   A method for encryption and decryption where it is necessary for both parties to possess a common encryption key.

- **Asymmetric encryption**, or **public key cryptography**   A method for encryption, decryption, and digital signatures that uses pairs of encryption keys, consisting of a *public key* and a *private key*.

- **Key exchange**   A technique that is used by two parties to establish a symmetric encryption key when there is no secure channel available.

- **Nonrepudiation**   The property of digital signatures and encryption that can make it difficult or impossible for a party to later deny having sent a digitally signed message, unless they admit to having lost control of their private encryption key.

Private Key Cryptosystems

A private key cryptosystem is based on a symmetric cryptographic algorithm. The primary characteristic of a private key cryptosystem is the necessity for both parties to possess a common encryption key that is used to encrypt and decrypt messages.

The two main challenges with private key cryptography are

- **Key exchange**   An "out of band" method for exchanging encryption keys is required before any encrypted messages can be transmitted. This key exchange must occur over a secure channel; if the encryption keys were transmitted over the main communications channel, then anyone who intercepts the encryption key will be able to read any intercepted messages, provided they can determine the encryption algorithm that is used. For instance, if two parties exchange encrypted e-mail, they would need to exchange their encryption key via telephone or fax, provided they are confident that their telephone and fax transmissions are not being intercepted.

- **Scalability**   Private key cryptosystems require that each sender-receiver pair exchange an encryption key. For a group of 4 parties, 6 encryption keys would need to be exchanged; for a group of 10 parties, 45 keys would need to be exchanged. For a large community of 1,000 parties, many thousands of keys would need to be exchanged.

Some well-known private key algorithms in use include AES, Blowfish, DES, Triple DES, Serpent, and Twofish.

Secure Key Exchange

Secure key exchange refers to methods used by two parties to securely establish a symmetric encryption key without actually transmitting the key over a channel. Secure key exchange is needed when two parties, previously unknown to each other, need to establish encrypted communications where no out-of-band channel is available.

Two parties can perform a secure key exchange if a third party intercepts their entire conversation. This is because algorithms used for secure key exchange utilize information known by both parties but not transmitted between them.

The most popular algorithm is the Diffie-Hellman Key Exchange Protocol.

Exchanging Initial Encryption Keys

Think about a private key cryptosystem. In an established cryptosystem, two users exchange messages and encrypt/decrypt them using an encryption key.

Before they can begin exchanging encrypted messages, one of the users must first get a copy of the key to the other user. They have to do this prior to the establishment of the cryptosystem, so they cannot use the cryptosystem to transmit the key.

Secure key exchange, such as Diffie-Hellman, is used to safely transmit the key from one party to the other party. Once both parties have the key, they can begin sending encrypted messages to each other.

Without secure key exchange, the two parties would have to use some other safe means for getting the encryption key across to the other user.

Public Key Cryptosystems

Public key cryptosystems are based on *asymmetric*, or *public key*, cryptographic algorithms. These algorithms use two-part encryption keys that are handled differently from encryption keys in symmetric key cryptosystems.

Key Pair The encryption keys that are used in public key cryptography are called the *public key* and the *private key*. Each user of public key cryptosystems has these two keys in his or her possession. Together, the public and private keys are known as a *key pair*. The two keys require different handling, and are used together but for different purposes that are explained in this section.

When a user generates his or her key pair (the public key and the private key), the key pair will physically exist as two separate files. The user is free to publish or distribute the public key openly; it could even be posted on a public website. This is in contrast to the private key, which must be well protected and never published or sent to any other party. Most public key cryptosystems will utilize a password mechanism to further protect the private key; without its password, the private key is inaccessible and cannot be used.

Message Security Public key cryptography is an ideal application for securing messages—e-mail in particular. The reason for this is that users do not need to establish and communicate symmetric encryption keys through a secure channel. With public key cryptography, users who have never contacted each other can immediately send secure messages to one another. Public key cryptography is depicted in Figure 6-8.

Figure 6-8 Public key cryptography used to transmit a secret message

Every user is free to publish his or her public encryption key so that it is easily retrievable. There are servers on the Internet where public keys can be published and made available to anyone in the world. Public key cryptography is designed so that open disclosure of a user's public key does not compromise the secrecy of the corresponding private key: a user's private key cannot be derived from the public key.

When User A wishes to send an encrypted message to User B, the procedure is as follows:

1. User B publishes his public key to the Internet at a convenient location.

2. User A retrieves User B's public key.

3. User A creates a message and encrypts it with User B's public key and sends the encrypted message to User B.

4. User B decrypts the message with his private key and is able to read the message.

Note that only User B's encryption key is used in this example. This method is used only to protect the message from eavesdroppers. This method is not used to verify the authenticity of the message.

Public key cryptography can also be used to verify the authenticity and integrity of a message. This is used to verify that a specific party did, in fact, create the message. The procedure is as follows:

1. User A publishes his public key to the Internet at a convenient location.

2. User B retrieves User A's public key and saves it for later use.

3. User A creates a message and digitally signs it with his private key, and then sends the signed message to User B.

4. User B verifies the digital signature using User A's public key. If the message verifies correctly, User B knows that the message originated from User A and has not been altered in transit.

In this example, only the authenticity and integrity of a message are assured. The message is not encrypted, which means that any party that intercepts the message can read it.

Public key cryptography can be used to both encrypt and digitally sign a message, which will guarantee its confidentiality as well as its authenticity. The procedure is as follows:

1. User A and User B publish their public encryption keys to convenient places.

2. User A retrieves User B's public key, and User B retrieves User A's public key.

3. User A creates a message, then signs it with his private key and encrypts it with User B's public key, and then sends the message to User B.

4. User B decrypts the message with his private key and verifies the digital signature with User A's public key.

Elliptic Curve Cryptography

A relatively new cryptography method called elliptic curve cryptography (ECC) is attracting interest for use in public key cryptography applications. ECC requires less computational power and bandwidth than other cryptographic algorithms, and is thought to be more secure as well.

Public key cryptography also supports encryption of a message with more than one user's public key. This permits a user to send a single encrypted message to several recipients that is encrypted with each of their public keys. This method does not compromise the secrecy of any user's private key, since a user's private key cannot be derived from the public key.

Verifying Public Keys It is possible for a user to claim the identity of another and even publish a public key that claims the identity of the other party. Three methods are available for verifying a user's public key as genuine:

- **Certificate authority** A public key that has been obtained from a trusted, reputable certificate authority can be considered genuine.

- **E-mail address** Public keys used for e-mail will include the user's e-mail address. If the e-mail address is a part of a corporate or government domain (for example, *adobe.com* or *seattle.gov*), then some level of credence can be attributed to the successful exchange of messages with that e-mail address. However, since e-mail addresses can be spoofed, this should be considered a weak method at best.

- **Key fingerprint** Many public key cryptosystems employ a method for verifying a key's identity, known as the key's fingerprint. If a user wishes to verify a public key, the user retrieves the public key and calculates the key's fingerprint. The user then contacts the claimed owner of the public key, who runs a function against his private key that returns a string of numbers. The user also runs a function against the owner's public key, also returning a string of numbers. If both numbers match, the public key is genuine.

 NOTE When verifying a public key, it is essential that the purported owner of the public key be authenticated, such as by viewing a government-issued ID or by contacting the owner at a publicly listed telephone number.

Hashing and Message Digests

Hashing is the process of applying a cryptographic algorithm on a block of information that results in a compact, fixed-length "digest." The purpose of hashing is to provide a unique "fingerprint" for the message or file—even if the file is very large. A message digest can be used to verify the integrity of a large file, thus assuring that the file has not been altered.

Some of the properties of message digests that make them ideally suited for verifying integrity include

- Any change made to a file—even a single bit or character—will result in a significant change in the hash.
- It is computationally infeasible to make a change to a file without changing its hash.
- It is computationally infeasible to create a message or file that will result in a given hash.
- It is infeasible to find any two messages that will have the same hash.

One common use of message digests is on software download sites, where the computed hash for a downloadable program is available so that users can verify that the software program has not been altered (provided that the posted hash has not also been compromised).

Digital Signatures

A digital signature is a cryptographic operation where a sender "seals" a message or file using his identity. The purpose of a digital signature is to authenticate a message and to guarantee its integrity. Digital signatures do not protect the confidentiality of a message, however, as encryption is not one of the operations performed.

Digital signatures work by encrypting hashes of messages; recipients verify the integrity and authenticity of messages by decrypting hashes and comparing them to original messages. In detail, a digital signature works like this:

1. Sender publishes his public key to the Internet at a location that is easily accessible to recipients.
2. Recipient retrieves sender's public key and saves it for later use.
3. Sender creates a message (or file) and computes a message digest (hash) of the message, and then encrypts the hash with his private key.
4. Then the sender sends the original file plus the encrypted hash to the recipient.
5. The recipient receives the original file and the encrypted hash. The recipient computes a message digest (hash) of the original file and sets the result aside. She then decrypts the hash with the sender's public key. The recipient compares the hash of the original file and the decrypted hash.
6. If the two hashes are identical, the recipient knows that a) the message in her possession is identical to the message that the sender sent, b) the sender is the originator, and c) the message has not been altered.

The use of digital signatures is depicted earlier in this chapter in Figure 6-6.

Digital Envelopes

One aspect of symmetric (private key) and asymmetric (public key) cryptography that has not been discussed yet is the computing requirements and performance implications of these two types of cryptosystems. It can be stated rather broadly that public key cryptography requires far more computing power than private key cryptography. The practical implication of this is that public key encryption of large sets of data can be highly compute-intensive and make its use infeasible in some occasions.

One solution to this is the use of a so-called digital envelope that utilizes the convenience of public key cryptography with the lower overhead of private key cryptography. The procedure for using digital envelopes works like this:

1. Sender and recipient agree that the sender will transmit a large message to recipient.

2. Sender selects or creates a symmetric encryption key, known as the *session key*, and encrypts the session key with recipient's public key.

3. Sender encrypts the message with the session key.

4. Sender sends the encrypted message (encrypted with the session key) and the encrypted session key (encrypted with the recipient's public key) to the recipient.

5. Recipient decrypts the session key with his private key.

6. Recipient decrypts the message with the session key.

The now-deprecated SET (secure electronic transaction, a predecessor to SSL/TLS) protocol uses digital envelopes. Digital envelopes require less computing overhead than the Diffie-Hellman key exchange, which is why digital envelopes may be preferred in some circumstances.

Public Key Infrastructures (PKI)

One of the issues related to public key cryptography is the safe storage of public encryption keys. While individuals are free to publish public keys online, doing so in a secure and controlled manner requires some central organization and control. A *public key infrastructure* (PKI) is designed to fulfill this and other functions.

A PKI is a centralized function that is used to store and publish public keys and other information. Some of the services provided by a PKI include

- **Digital certificates**   A digital certificate is a digital credential that consists of a public key and a block of information that identifies the owner of the certificate. The identification portion of a digital certificate will follow a standard, structured format and include such data as the owner's name, organization name, and other identifying information, such as e-mail address. The public key and the identifying information will reside in a document that is itself digitally signed by a trusted party, known as a certificate authority (CA).

- **Certificate authority (CA)**   A certificate authority (CA) is a business entity that issues digital certificates and publishes them in the PKI. The CA vouches for the identity of each of the digital certificates in a PKI; the CA undergoes certain safeguards to ensure that each digital certificate is genuine and really does belong to its rightful owner.

- **Registration authority (RA)**   The registration authority (RA) operates within or alongside a CA to accept requests for new digital certificates. The RA vets the request, carefully examining it, and undergoes steps to verify the authenticity of the person making the request. This verification may include viewing government-issued ID cards, passports, or taking other steps as needed to make sure that the request is originating from the genuine person. When the RA is satisfied that the requestor is indeed the person making the request, the RA will issue a digital certificate. Part of the certificate issuance will be the delivery of private encryption keys to the requesting party. This may take place in person or over a secured electronic connection.

- **Certificate revocation list (CRL)**   Some circumstances may require that a user's digital certificate be cancelled or revoked. These circumstances include termination of employment (if a person's certificate was issued expressly for employment-related purposes), or loss or compromise of a user's private key. A CRL is an electronic list of digital certificates that have been revoked prior to their expiration date. In order to be effective, any consumer of digital certificates needs to consult a CRL to be doubly sure that a certificate remains valid.

- **Certification practice statement (CPS)**   This is a published statement that describes the practices used by the CA to issue and manage digital certificates. This helps determine the relative strength and validity of digital certificates that are issued by the CA.

Key Management

The term *key management* refers to the various processes and procedures used by an organization to generate, protect, use, and dispose of encryption keys over its lifetime. Several of the major practices are described in this section.

Key Generation   The start of an encryption key life cycle is its generation. While at first glance it would appear that this process should require little scrutiny, further study shows that this is a critical process that requires safeguards.

The system on which key generation takes place must be highly protected. If keys are generated on a system that has been compromised or is of questionable integrity, it would be difficult to determine if a bystander could have electronically observed key generation. For instance, if a key logger or other process spying tool were active in the system when keys were generated, that key generation may have been observable and details about keys captured. This would mean that newly minted keys have already been compromised if an outsider knows their identities.

In many situations, it would be reasonable to require that systems used for key generation be highly protected, isolated, and used by as few persons as possible. Regular integrity checks would need to take place to make sure the system continues to be free of any problems.

Furthermore, the key generation process needs to include some randomness (or, as some put it, entropy) so that the key generation process cannot be easily duplicated elsewhere. If key generation were not a random event, it could be possible to duplicate the conditions related to a specific key and then regenerate a key with the very same value. This would instantaneously compromise the integrity and uniqueness of the original key.

Key Protection   Private keys used in public key cryptosystems and keys used in symmetric cryptosystems must be continuously and vigorously protected. At all times they must be accessible to *only* the parties that are authorized to use them. If protection measures for private encryption keys are compromised (or suspected to be), it will be possible for a key compromise to take place, enabling the attacker to be able to view messages encrypted with these keys.

A *key compromise* is any event where a private encryption key has been disclosed to any unauthorized third party. When a key compromise occurs, it will be necessary to re-encrypt all materials encrypted by the compromised key with a new encryption key.

 CAUTION   In many applications, an encryption key is protected by a password. The length, complexity, distribution, and expiration of passwords protecting encryption keys must be well designed so that the strength of the cryptosystem (based on its key length and algorithm) is not compromised by a weak password scheme protecting its keys.

Key Custody   *Key custody* refers to the policies, processes, and procedures regarding the management of keys. This is closely related to key protection, but is focused on *who* manages keys and *where* they are kept.

Key Rotation   *Key rotation* is the process of issuing a new encryption key and re-encrypting data protected with the new key. Key rotation may occur when any of the following occurs:

- **Key compromise**   When an encryption key has been compromised, a new key must be generated and used.

- **Key expiration**   This happens in situations where encryption keys are rotated on a schedule.

- **Rotation of staff**   In some organizations, if any of the persons associated with the creation or management of encryption keys transfers to another position or leaves the organization, keys must be rotated.

Key Disposal   *Key disposal* refers to the process of decommissioning encryption keys. This may be done upon receipt of an order to destroy a data set that is encrypted with a specific encryption key—destroying an encryption key can be as effective (and a whole lot easier) than destroying the encrypted data itself.

However, key disposal can present some challenges. If an encryption key is backed up to tape, for instance, disposal of the key will require that backup tapes also be destroyed.

Encryption Applications

Several applications utilize encryption algorithms. Many of these are well known and in common use.

Secure Sockets Layer/Transport Layer Security (SSL/TLS)   SSL and TLS are the encryption protocols used to encrypt webpages requested with the HTTPS (Hypertext Transfer Protocol/Secure) URL. Introduced by Netscape Communications for use in its own browser, SSL and its successor, TLS, have become de facto standards for the encryption of webpages.

SSL provides several cryptographic functions, including public key encryption, private key encryption, and hash functions. These are used for server and client authentication (although in practice, client authentication is seldom used) and session encryption. SSL supports several encryption algorithms, including AES, RC4, IDEA, DES, and triple DES, and several key lengths, from 40 bits to 256 bits and beyond.

S-HTTP (Secure Hypertext Transfer Protocol)   Not to be confused with HTTPS, S-HTTP also provides encryption of webpages between web servers and web browsers. Because Netscape and Microsoft favored HTTPS, S-HTTP never caught on and is not widely supported.

Secure Multipurpose Internet Mail Extensions (S/MIME)   S/MIME is an e-mail security protocol that provides sender and recipient authentication and encryption of message content and attachments. S/MIME is most often used for encryption of e-mail messages.

Secure Shell (SSH)   Secure shell is a multipurpose protocol that is used to create a secure channel between two systems. The most popular use of SSH is the replacement of the TELNET protocol, but it also supports tunneling of protocols such as X-Windows and FTP (File Transfer Protocol).

Secure Electronic Transaction (SET)   SET is a now-deprecated protocol designed to protect Internet-based financial transactions. SET never caught on because it required the installation of a separate client program. HTTPS became the standard for encrypting webpages, and then became the preferred method for encryption.

SET offered greater protection of credit card transactions through the substitution of tokens for actual credit card numbers. But SET never caught on, and it is no longer used.

Voice over IP

Voice over IP (VoIP) is the term that encompasses several technologies that permit telephony that is transported over IP networks. Other terms associated with VoIP include *Internet telephony* and *IP telephony*. These terms all describe services for transporting voice, video, and facsimile over IP networks, including the Internet. Organizations that implement VoIP will incorporate one or more of the following:

- **Trunking**   Here, organizations replace older-technology voice trunks with SIP (Session Initiation Protocol) trunks that have far greater capacity and lower costs. Trunks can connect an organization's private branch exchange (PBX) to telecommunications providers that offer VoIP trunking. Also, an organization can connect its digital PBXs in various locations together via MPLS (Multiprotocol Label Switching) over IP WAN connections.

- **Digital PBX**   Organizations replace older PBX systems with newer PBXs that support VoIP and SIP trunking.

- **VoIP handsets**   Digital and analog telephone sets are replaced with IP telephone sets that connect to the PBX via TCP/IP over Ethernet or Wi-Fi.

- **VoIP clients**   Here, organizations replace telephone sets with software programs on workstations that communicate over TCP/IP to the PBX. These programs eliminate the need for separate telephone handsets.

VoIP Threats and Vulnerabilities

The primary threat to VoIP systems is the fact that an organization's telephone network is connected to the TCP/IP network and thus is vulnerable to all the types of attacks that plague workstations and servers. Furthermore, many VoIP components run on devices and systems that use conventional operating systems like Unix. That means that most VoIP components are vulnerable to the same class of threats that servers and workstations are subject to. These threats include

- **Eavesdropping**   Attackers may attempt to listen in to voice, video, and facsimile transmissions.

- **Spoofing**   Attackers can send packets to VoIP devices, systems, and PBXs that impersonate other devices and systems. Possible reasons include stealing information, altering information, denial of service, toll fraud, and more.

- **Malware**   This includes viruses, worms, Trojan horses, rootkits, and so on.

- **Denial of service**   This is an attack designed to disable a target system or network by flooding it either with an enormous volume of traffic or with specially crafted traffic designed to cause the target to malfunction.

- **Toll fraud**   This is an attack designed to steal long-distance service by using another organization's telephone network for one's personal use.

These and other threats are not unique to VoIP but plague all kinds of IP and Internet-connected networks and systems. For a complete discussion on threats and vulnerabilities, see the section, "Logical Access Controls," earlier in this chapter.

CAUTION An organization that employs VoIP must now take even greater care to protect its networks. For such an organization, an attack on the network will threaten not only computer networks but also voice communications.

Protecting VoIP

Because VoIP systems communicate over TCP/IP, and because many are based on conventional operating systems, VoIP is protected through primarily the same measures that are used to protect other IT systems. The protection measures that are most effective include

- System and device hardening
- Strict access controls and access management
- Anti-malware controls
- Firewalls and session border controllers (SBCs)
- Intrusion detection systems

These and other countermeasures are discussed in detail in the section, "Logical Access Controls," earlier in this chapter.

Private Branch Exchange (PBX)

A private branch exchange, most commonly referred to as a PBX, is a private telephone switch used by an organization to manage its internal telephone calls, as well as telephone calls with parties in the public telephone network. Workers in an organization can often call one another with shortened phone numbers, such as four-digit extensions, and call "outside" numbers using a prefix such as "8" or "9."

PBXs are connected to the public-switched telephone network (PSTN) via one or more "trunks," which are telecommunications circuits designed to carry several simultaneous telephone conversations. Implemented over telephony circuits such as T-1 or E-1, trunks are leased from common-carrier telecommunications carriers.

PBX Threats and Vulnerabilities

A variety of security issues affect PBXs. IT managers and security professionals need to be aware of these threats and vulnerabilities to be able to better protect them. Some of these include

- **Default passwords on administrator console** This can permit anyone with physical access to the PBX with the ability to change the configuration of the PBX or extract data from it (including phone records and access controls). Passwords on many PBXs are left at factory default; this is an old practice still in place today.

- **Dial-in modem** Many PBXs employ an administrative dial-in modem so that the PBX administrator can perform remote administrative duties. Often, dial-in access uses either a default password or no authentication at all.

- **Toll fraud**   One of the most enticing opportunities on a PBX is the ability to commit toll fraud by using it to place long-distance telephone calls. This is done by logging into the PBX (when passwords are weak or nonexistent) and changing its configuration to permit the attacker to place long-distance calls at the PBX owner's expense.

- **Espionage**   PBXs are also the target of attempts to eavesdrop on telephone conversations as well as retrieve phone records.

Many PBXs have IP connections to facilitate remote administrative access. PBXs with IP connectivity are subject to the broader scope of IP-related threats and vulnerabilities that are discussed in detail earlier in this chapter in the section, "Logical Access Controls."

PBX Countermeasures

PBXs without IP connectivity are fairly easy to protect. Some of the most effective countermeasures include

- **Administrative access control**   Console and modem access should be configured with the strongest reasonable controls, including strong, complex passwords; administrative access logging; and dial-back modems.

- **Physical access control**   Be sure that only authorized personnel have physical access to the PBX. A PBX should be protected with keycard and/or video surveillance so that the organization can positively identify individual personnel who access it.

- **Regular log reviews**   Administrative personnel should regularly review access logs to verify that only authorized personnel are accessing administrative consoles and functions. Furthermore, toll records should be reviewed frequently to ensure that no toll fraud is taking place.

- **Calling restrictions**   Administrative personnel should configure a PBX to block outbound calling to countries that the organization does not call. This will help to combat toll fraud should an intruder gain access to an outbound call trunk.

PBXs with IP connectivity will require additional IP-centric countermeasures that are similar to those required for servers and other network-connected devices.

Malware

Malware is the inclusive term that includes many types of malicious code, including viruses, worms, Trojan horses, rootkits, and more. Malware is increasingly stealthy and potent, and if the past 20 years is any indication, malware will always be one step ahead of the measures that try to keep it at bay.

Blocking malware is rarely a matter for discussion, any more than locks on the outside doors. The malware threat is just too real, and the consequences can be devastating.

Malware has many "attack vectors," meaning it has many ways to get into an organization, which requires a variety of defenses operating simultaneously. It is no longer sufficient to just run antivirus software on end-user workstations; instead, it is necessary to employ several means for detecting and filtering malware.

Malware Threats and Vulnerabilities

Malware is capable of making a wide variety of mischief, as well as serious trouble, for organizations. The earliest viruses were relatively benign, whereas contemporary malware is able to produce a wide range of economic damage.

There are several classes of malware:

- **Viruses** These are fragments of code that attach themselves to .exe files (executable programs) and are activated when the program they are attached to is run.

- **Worms** These are stand-alone programs capable of human-assisted and automatic propagation.

- **Trojan horses** As the name suggests, these are programs that are purported to perform one function, but which actually perform other (or additional) undesired functions. For example, something might be advertised as a game that actually erases files (or does both).

- **Spyware** This type of software performs one or more surveillance-type actions on a computer, reporting back to the spyware owner. The most insidious form of spyware is the key logger, a software program (and also an implantable hardware device) that records user keystrokes and transmits them back to a central location.

- **Rootkits** These are malware programs that are designed to hide themselves from the operating system as well as evade detection by antivirus software. Some rootkits are also able to run "underneath" the operating system so that they are undetectable.

- **Bots** These are agents implanted by other forms of malware and which are programmed to obey remotely issued instructions. Collections of bots are called *bot armies*. These are built to create spam, propagate malware, attack target systems and networks, and host phishing sites.

 CAUTION Security managers and architects need to thoroughly understand the different types of malware—how they are made, how they propagate, and how they attack systems. But security professionals can't forget the forest for the trees: it is essential to establish a defense-in-depth set of controls to block all types of known and unknown malware, and not simply rely on antivirus software on end-user workstations.

The types of damage that malware can cause include

- Computer slowdowns and crashes
- Alteration or destruction of data
- Eavesdropping on communications
- Stolen data
- Attack or damage to other systems

Malware infiltrates an organization through avenues of opportunity. The vulnerabilities that malware is able to exploit include

- **Missing patches**   Many malware programs are designed to exploit known vulnerabilities that remain on many computers that do not have security patches installed.

- **Software flaws**   Malware designers will use various tools to discover and exploit flaws in applications, operating systems, tools, and other programs. Some of these flaws may be known and have patches available, but others may be relatively unknown.

- **Unsecure configuration**   Old, outdated, or incorrectly set configuration settings can leave a computer vulnerable to attack.

- **Faulty architecture**   Mistakes in a network's architecture (for example, incorrect placement of a firewall that exposes too many systems) or errors in implementation can leave systems open to attack.

- **Faulty judgment**   Mistakes and decisions that are based on incomplete knowledge can lead to configuration or architecture errors that introduce vulnerabilities.

- **Gullibility**   Often, the target of malware is end-users' gullibility and curiosity. They are inclined to click on links in spam e-mail messages, open attachments, and visit unknown sites—all of which are nowadays the primary means for injecting malware into their computers.

Malwares' most common threat vectors to organizations include

- **Spam**   Junk e-mail either often contains malware or entices users to connect to websites that contain malware. Spam also includes e-mail messages that advertise both legitimate goods and services as well as fakes; prescription medication is a good example of the phony merchandise that many people buy in the hopes of saving money.

- **Phishing**   Some spam impersonates real government and private institutions, pretending to communicate urgent news to customers, who need to act quickly. A common ploy is an e-mail message from a bank telling customers that their bank accounts will be locked unless they respond by logging in to an imposter site. People who fall for these schemes inadvertently provide login credentials to thieves, who use them to transfer funds out of their victims' accounts. Many similar schemes exist that attempt to steal money or other valuables from victims.

- **Denial of service** Some malware deliberately causes computers to malfunction. Plus, malware that is designed to rapidly spread from computer to computer over networks will cause high volumes of network traffic that make the networks, as well as computers, unusable.

- **Recording keystrokes** Some malware is designed to intercept keystrokes and displayed information and relay that data back to a central location. The information of greatest interest is credit card numbers, bank account numbers, and user ID-and-password combinations for high-value sites such as online banking.

Anti-Malware Administrative Controls

Organizations' anti-malware controls need to include several administrative controls to stop the introduction and spread of malware. These controls include policies such as

- **Spam policy** Security policy and awareness training needs to include "don't open strange or unusual e-mail messages, even from people you know" guidance to workers. Even in an environment with effective spam filters, some spam does get through, so this policy helps users think twice before opening them.

- **Only business-related Internet access** Because some malware spreads through malicious code implanted on websites (and for other reasons like lost productivity), organizations may forbid its employees from visiting websites with no direct business purpose.

- **No removable media** Malware can be introduced via removable media. In fact, the earliest viruses were spread via floppy disk. Today, many organizations forbid, and even actively block, the use of removable media such as USB drives and memory sticks.

The Malware Industry

The face of malware is rapidly changing. Once the purview of hacker-hobbyists and script kiddies, malware is now the domain of large organized crime syndicates and cybercrime gangs. These are businesses with investors, research and development, profit sharing, and benefits. The only thing fundamentally different from legitimate businesses is that organized crime is in the business of conducting illegal operations, such as financial fraud.

The U.S. Treasury Department published a report in 2006 that claimed that, on a worldwide scale, organized crime is now making more profits from Internet-based fraud than from drug trafficking. And they are just getting better at it.

- **No downloading** Because some malware is implanted in downloadable software, many organizations have enacted policies that forbid the practice of downloading software. Instead, requests are made to the IT service desk if additional software or tools are needed.

- **Restricted privileges** A popular operating system from Redmond, Washington, configured end-user accounts at the same level of privilege as system administrators. The harmful result of this is that malware, introduced by end users, will execute on the computer with administrative privileges and cause significant damage. The new norm is to restrict end-user workstation privileges to the lowest access level, thereby reducing malware potency.

- **No personally owned computers** In many organizations, it was once okay to access the corporate network remotely using personally owned computers. Because the organization is unable to control the spread of malware on computers it does not own or control, the right place to draw the line is to enact a policy that forbids all but company-owned computers from connecting to any network, local or remote.

- **Restricted smart phone access** Organizations that don't take the hard line of "no personally owned computers will connect to the network, including smart phones" may take a softer line and permit limited access for smart phones, such as e-mail access only.

Anti-Malware Management Controls

Several procedural controls are needed to ensure that systems remain free of malware:

- Include anti-malware procedures in employee security awareness training.
- Build servers only from original read-only media.
- Scan all new software (regardless of source) for malware on nonproduction systems prior to use.
- Prohibit any use of personally owned computers for any business purpose, on or off work premises.

Malware: Avoiding Repeats of History

For the most part, organizations are serious about stopping malware at the network boundary. This is because they remember malware attacks of the past 10 years that completely incapacitated corporate networks for days at a time. Malware with names like *I Love You*, *Code Red*, *Blaster*, and *SQL Slammer* evoke memories of battles to keep corporate networks running.

Those were painful events that resulted in serious business disruption, sometimes enough to affect financial results. Pointed questions from senior executives, who often did not understand the rules of the new cyberwars, distracted IT managers from their primary objective: keep the malware out of the network!

- Scan all incoming files for malware prior to releasing them for use.

- Verify all network equipment software releases as genuine and free of malware prior to use.

Anti-Malware Technical Controls

Because malware is so potent, and because some kinds of malware are able to spread without any human interaction or assistance, a defense-in-depth strategy for blocking it is needed in most organizations to make sure that malware has few opportunities to enter the network:

- **Anti-malware on all servers and workstations** Every workstation should have current anti-malware software. It should be configured to perform real-time malware detection, plus regular scans (daily in high-risk environments, weekly in others). Users should not be able to remove or tamper with anti-malware software, even if they are local administrators for their workstations. However, users should be able to perform scans on demand if they sense that their system may be infected.

- **Anti-malware on e-mail servers** E-mail servers should have anti-malware programs designed to block malware on incoming and outgoing e-mail. This cannot be ordinary anti-malware software, but a type designed to run on an e-mail server and interoperate with the e-mail server programs.

- **Anti-malware on web proxy servers/filters** Organizations should have active or passive web proxy servers that have anti-malware software on board. This will prevent malware from entering an organization from websites that users are visiting.

- **Centralized anti-malware console** Organizations should consider using enterprise versions of anti-malware software that provide central monitoring and configuration consoles. This gives the organization the ability to instantly see the "big picture" with regard to anti-malware controls. For instance, a console will show which workstations' anti-malware programs are having trouble running or getting new updates and where infections are occurring. Centralized consoles can also be used to force selected systems to perform immediate malware signature updates and perform scans if management believes that a malware outbreak is imminent or in progress.

- **Intrusion prevention systems** Organizations can employ agented or agentless intrusion prevention systems (IPSs) that will automatically sense activities typical of malware. An IPS has the ability to immediately disconnect an infected system from the network so that it cannot infect other systems or disrupt network traffic.

- **Spam filters** A lot of malware (not to mention phishing schemes and fraud) enters an organization through e-mail. Centralized spam filters can intercept and block spam before it even reaches the e-mail server. Many spam filters also have antivirus programs on them to scrub viruses from incoming e-mail—even when it comes from legitimate, known persons.

- **Blocking use of removable media**   While external memory devices such as USB sticks and external hard drives are popular, they do represent a number of threats, including malware. Blocking removable media is also one measure that is effective against information leakage.

- **Block outbound network services on servers**   It is rare that a server should need to initiate communications over the Internet, except for specific business connections that may be a part of distributed applications. All other accesses should be blocked. This would effectively block any malware's attempt to communicate information back to its source.

- **Boot servers from protected images**   In virtual environments, it is possible to boot servers from read-only images stored on a centralized storage system. This would prevent malware from being able to permanently install itself on a server, since the next reboot from a clean image would effectively remove it.

- **Block read-only objects**   Except in rare and well-controlled circumstances, software should not be able to write to a hard drive's boot sector or the system's CMOS (complementary metal oxide semiconductor, the technology used to store a computer's hardware configuration). These and possibly other portions of a system should be protected so that malware cannot alter or destroy them.

 CAUTION   Blocking malware is not a one-time effort of procuring and configuring tools. Rather, this should be thought of as the "malware wars" that continue indefinitely and require constant vigilance.

Information Leakage

Information leakage refers to the tendency for sensitive information to leak out of an organization's systems through various means. Blocking opportunities for information leakage is a developing area in information technology today.

There are fundamentally two forms of information leakage: accidental and malicious. Accidental leakage occurs when, for instance, an employee selects the wrong recipients in an outgoing e-mail that contains sensitive information and mistakenly sends sensitive information to the wrong external party, resulting in a potential security breach.

Deliberate information leakage occurs when an employee chooses to acquire sensitive data with the intention of taking it out of the organization. There are two primary reasons and motivations for this:

- **Profit**   Some sensitive information such as credit card and bank account numbers are easily sold on the black market.

- **Revenge**   If the employee senses that injustice has occurred—or will occur—in the organization, the employee may exact a form of revenge by taking copies of sensitive information for later use, whether extortion, exposure, or profit.

Leakage also occurs when malware intercepts logon credentials, resulting in a hacker's ability to log in and steal sensitive information. Leakage is multifaceted and extends into other areas, including social engineering, malware, proper HR hiring procedures, and more.

Because of the numerous means available for users to deliberately remove data from the organization, several measures should be taken to limit those opportunities, including

- **Outbound e-mail filtering** Outbound e-mail filters that check for information leakage can be used to observe and even block sensitive information that is leaving the organization.

- **Control removable media** Through centralized automatic policies, organizations can prevent the use of USB media, writing to CD-ROM discs, and other actions contributing to information leakage.

- **Blocking Internet access** Users in the most sensitive functions (those with access to the most sensitive information) should be prevented from accessing any computer or network outside of the organization. This not only reduces the likelihood of malware infecting a sensitive system, but also reduces the opportunity for leakage.

- **Tighter access controls** Organizations should periodically examine their access controls for the most sensitive information, looking for ways to further reduce the ability for people to access that data, except in situations where they must for business purposes. When fewer people have access, there will be fewer opportunities for leakage.

- **Access logging** The organization should improve access logging so that all accesses (not just updates) to information are logged. This can be an effective detective control, since this would tell the organization who is accessing which data records. If the organization discloses the logging to its workers, this also becomes a deterrent control, not unlike video surveillance.

- **Job rotation** Staff members should be periodically shifted into other positions so that their opportunities for covertly extracting information are fewer. When organizations shift their employees on short notice and on sporadic schedules, employees are less likely to engage in information-pilfering schemes since they do not want to get caught.

- **Periodic background checks** Organizations should consider periodic background checks for employees in positions of access to sensitive information. Changes in an employee's current background may provide additional incentives for employees to engage in unauthorized or illegal acts. For instance, an employee whose credit background has gone from good to terrible may be tempted to find ways to supplement his income, such as embezzlement or selling information on the black market. Also, an employee who started employment with a clean criminal record may, over time, turn to the dark side and enter a lifestyle of crime. That two-week vacation last year could actually have been a jail sentence.

- **Implement a data leakage prevention (DLP) system** Organizations can implement a DLP system that will observe all inbound and outbound network traffic and create alerts when sensitive information is believed to be leaving or entering. Some DLP systems can also block these transmissions, thereby blocking illegitimate attempts to steal information and forcing legitimate activities to use more prudent means such as encryption.

 NOTE Employers should understand that a patient employee who is determined to remove information from the organization would probably be able to do so, despite many controls to detect or prevent it. For systems containing the most sensitive information, security specialists should perform a detailed risk analysis to understand exactly how data leakage can be controlled in their organization.

Environmental Controls

Computers and networks operate in the physical world. Networks consist of devices like routers, switches, and firewalls, plus cabling within and between buildings. Computer systems and network devices are designed to operate within a narrow band of temperature, humidity, moisture, and cleanliness. When they operate within these bounds, they are likely to provide years of service, but even brief periods outside these bounds can significantly shorten the life of many components.

Organizations that employ computers and networks to support vital business processes need to provide suitable environments for them. Failure to do so can result in higher operating costs and business disruptions due to frequent downtime. This section discusses the environmental systems and controls required to maintain a suitable environment for computers and networks.

Environmental Threats and Vulnerabilities

Computer systems require special facilities that include reliable electric power, environmental controls, and physical security. By their very nature, the controls that support and protect computer systems are complex and require periodic maintenance in order to provide reliable service. Redundant controls or systems are often needed for organizations intolerant of downtime.

This section discusses electric power, cooling and humidity controls, fire detection and suppression, and physical security.

Electric Power Vulnerabilities

Computer systems require a steady diet of clean electric power. The quality and delivery of electric power from virtually every public utility falls far short of the needs required by IT systems. Several power-related events threaten the health of computer equipment, including

- **Spike or surge** This is a sharp increase in voltage that lasts for only a fraction of a second.

- **Inrush**   A sudden increase in current flowing to a device, usually associated with the startup of a large motor. This can cause a voltage drop that lasts several seconds.

- **Noise**   This is the presence of other electromagnetic signals within incoming power.

- **Dropout**   This is a momentary loss of power that lasts from a few milliseconds to a few seconds.

- **Brownout**   This is a sustained drop in voltage that can last from several seconds to several hours.

- **Blackout**   A complete loss of electric power for more than a few seconds.

All of these phenomena can damage computer and network equipment by damaging internal components that make them fail outright or through latent damage that may shorten the life of a component.

Physical Environment Vulnerabilities

Computer and network equipment is sensitive to changes in environmental conditions. The conditions that warrant discussion here are

- **Temperature**   Computer and network equipment generate potentially large volumes of waste heat that must be continuously siphoned away. Even a brief interruption in environmental systems can cause sharp rises in temperature that can damage equipment. Temperature that is too low can cause condensation on equipment, which can invite corrosion and even cause short circuits when it occurs on electrical components.

- **Humidity**   Computer and network equipment must operate within a narrow band of humidity, usually 40 to 55 percent. When humidity drops below 40 percent, static buildup can occur that can damage sensitive electronics. Excessively high humidity can result in condensation, inviting corrosion and short circuits.

- **Dust and dirt**   Computer and network equipment is designed to be used in clean environments that are reasonably free of dust and dirt. Dust and dirt can accelerate wear in mechanical components and clog air filters, causing heat buildup.

- **Smoke and fire**   A fire that is in or near a data center can introduce smoke, which can damage computer and network equipment. Fire extinguishing agents such as water can also damage sensitive equipment. Fire departments often cut electric power to a building when there is a fire, so even equipment that is not threatened by the fire will suffer the effects of a blackout.

- **Sudden unexpected movement**   Earthquakes and landslides can violently shake equipment, pulling it away from its fastenings. Personnel moving equipment may accidentally bump into other devices or snag or damage loose cabling.

Environmental Controls and Countermeasures

Several environmental control systems are required to counteract the threats and vulnerabilities discussed in this section. When designed and operated properly, these controls will contribute to high reliability and a good service record for IT equipment, which is sensitive to environmental conditions.

Electric Power

Because the quality of commercial utility electric power is usually insufficient for sensitive and critical computing equipment, several additional controls may be needed to improve the quality and/or quantity of available electric power. These controls are described in the following sections and depicted in Figure 6-9.

Uninterruptible Power Supply (UPS)   This is a system that filters incoming power from spikes and other noise, and supplies power for short periods through a bank of batteries. A UPS is sufficient for power outages that last from a few minutes to as long as a few hours (provided there is sufficient battery capacity). A UPS provides a continuous supply of electricity; when there is a brownout or blackout, power delivered to computer systems is unaffected.

Electric Generator   This is a system consisting of an internal combustion engine powered by gasoline, diesel fuel, or natural gas that spins an electric generator. A generator can supply electricity for as long as several days, depending on the size of its fuel supply and whether it can be refueled.

Figure 6-9   Components in a facility power system

Dual Power Feeds   An organization that is especially dependent on reliable electric power can consider using two separate power feeds that would ideally originate from separate utility substations.

Power Distribution Unit (PDU)   A power distribution unit is a device that distributes electric power to a computer room or data center. A PDU may be large and supply dozens of separate power circuits or be as small as a power strip. Some PDUs also have voltage step-down capabilities, converting higher-input voltages into voltage levels used by computer equipment.

It is important to understand present and future electric power requirements so that the components discussed here can be appropriately sized. Some organizations with high reliability requirements may build fully redundant power systems consisting of dual power feeds, dual switchgears, generators, UPSs, and PDUs, delivering fully redundant power to each computer. Organizations that utilize redundant power systems usually refer to their power systems as "A side" and "B side" systems. Computer and network equipment that utilizes dual power supplies can take advantage of redundant power systems by connecting one power supply to the A side and one to the B side. This permits systems to continue functioning, even in the event of a complete failure of any single component in the facility's power system.

Temperature and Humidity Controls

Because computing and network equipment sheds a large volume of waste heat, highly reliable and adequately sized HVAC (heating, ventilation, and air conditioning) systems are required.

The temperature in rooms containing computer and network equipment should range from 68° to 75°F, and humidity should range from 40 to 55 percent. In facilities with a considerable number of computer systems, this will require highly reliable and high-capacity HVAC systems.

It is recommended that facilities utilize an "N + 1" design, which means that there should be at least one additional HVAC system than is required to continuously cool the facility. For example, if a facility requires four HVAC systems for cooling, then at least five HVAC systems should be used. This permits adequate cooling to continue in the event one system fails or is being maintained.

Computer facilities should employ continuous temperature and humidity monitoring that regularly records readings and alerts personnel when readings exceed safe levels. Sensitive equipment should also have internal temperature monitoring capabilities that alert support personnel when readings exceed tolerance. Systems that are sensitive to variations in temperature should have auto-shutdown capabilities in the event that support personnel are unable to respond in time.

Many computer rooms and data centers employ a raised floor system consisting of removable tiles. The space under the tiles acts as an air plenum for air conditioning systems; tiles with holes in them are strategically placed to direct cold air into areas requiring it. Tiled floors are typically 80 to 100 cm above the floor beneath.

Fire Prevention, Detection, and Suppression Controls

Virtually every local government authority requires fire detection, prevention, and suppression controls. However, the minimum controls may be considered inadequate for facilities containing expensive computer and network equipment. For example, regulations requiring water sprinkler suppression systems would certainly extinguish a fire in a data center, but the water would also cause considerable damage. For this reason, different types of detection and suppression systems are often used to protect valuable equipment from fire and suppression agent damage.

Fire Prevention   Measures that help to prevent fires in the first place contribute to a safer environment. Some measures include

- **Combustibles**   Materials such as packing boxes and manuals should be stored away from computer equipment. Reductions in combustible materials make fires less likely to start or spread.

- **Cleanliness**   Dust can sometimes trigger highly sensitive smoke detectors; this is another reason to practice good cleanliness measures in data centers.

- **Electrical equipment maintenance**   Maintenance activities such as soldering should not be done near computer equipment. Smoke from soldering can trigger smoke detectors and cause a discharge in fire suppression agents.

Fire Detection   Facilities can be equipped with more than the minimum required capabilities for smoke detection. Highly sensitive smoke and heat detection systems are available that can provide earlier warning. This gives personnel an added opportunity to identify the cause of the fire and suppress it with limited-impact means such as fire extinguishers. Such measures help to avoid a larger fire that would require more aggressive suppression measures.

Commercial buildings also employ many manually operated fire alarms, often called "pull stations," where someone who sees a fire can pull the lever to set the alarm manually. In most cases, this causes fire alarms and bells to ring but does not trigger fire suppression.

Fire Suppression   Most commercial facilities are required to have automatic or semi-automatic fire suppression systems. While the minimum is usually water-based sprinkler systems and a complement of hand-operated fire extinguishers, often an organization will make an investment in more sophisticated suppression systems that have less of an impact on computing equipment. But in some locations, even where advanced suppression systems are permitted, sometimes water-based systems are still required as a backup.

The types of centralized fire suppression systems include

- **Wet pipe**   In this type of system, all sprinkler pipes are filled with water. Each sprinkler head is equipped with a fuse—a heat-sensitive glass bulb—that breaks upon reaching a preset temperature. When this occurs, water is discharged from just that sprinkler head, which is presumably located near a fire. When water begins to flow, an automatic sensor trips a fire alarm. This is the most common type of sprinkler system.

- **Dry pipe** This type of system is used where ambient temperatures often drop below freezing. In this type of system, pipes are filled with compressed air. When sufficient heat causes one of the sprinkler head fuses to break, a control valve releases water into the piping. A delay of up to one minute occurs as water flows from the control valve to the sprinkler head.

- **Pre-action** This type of system is used in areas with high-value contents such as data centers. A pre-action system is essentially a dry pipe system until a "preceding" event, such as a smoke detector alarm, occurs; at this time, the system is filled with water and essentially converted in real time to a wet pipe system. Then, if the ambient temperature at any of the sprinkler heads is high enough, those fuses break, releasing water to extinguish the fire. Pre-action systems are more expensive and complicated than wet pipe or dry pipe systems.

- **Deluge** This type of system has dry pipes and all of the sprinkler heads are open. When the system is operated (for instance, when an alarm is triggered), water flows into the pipes and out of all of the sprinkler heads.

- **Inert gas** Often the choice for use in computer centers because of its low impact on computing equipment and high effectiveness in fire suppression. Inert gas systems work by displacing oxygen from the room by bringing down the concentration of oxygen from the usual 21 percent to a lower figure, which slows the advancement of a fire. Through the 1980s, Halon 1301 was the substance of choice for inert gas systems. Declared a greenhouse gas in 1987, Halon 1301 has been replaced by other substances, such as FM-200.

In addition to centralized fire suppression systems, many commercial buildings are required to have hand-operated fire extinguishers. These come in a range of sizes, from 1 to 30 pounds, and have fire retardants of several types, including

- Class A: Suitable for ordinary solid combustibles such as wood and paper
- Class B: Suitable for flammable liquids and gases
- Class C: Suitable for energized electrical equipment
- Class D: Suitable for combustible metals
- Class K: Suitable for cooking oils and fats

The types listed here are U.S. standards. Different classifications are used in other countries.

Larger fire extinguishers are used in some facilities that have 50 pounds or more fire retardant. These larger units are mounted on large-wheeled carts that can be pulled to the site of a fire.

> ## Classification of Data Center Reliability
>
> The Telecommunications Industry Association (TIA) released the TIA-942 Tele-communications Infrastructure Standards for Data Centers standard in 2005. The standard describes various aspects of data center design, including reliability. The standard describes four levels of reliability:
>
> - **Tier I–Basic Reliability**   Power and cooling distribution are in a single path. There may or may not be a raised floor, UPS, or generator. All maintenance requires downtime.
> - **Tier II–Redundant Components**   Power is in a single path; there may be redundant components for cooling. Includes raised floor, UPS, and generator. Most maintenance requires downtime.
> - **Tier III–Concurrently Maintainable**   Includes multiple power and cooling paths, but with only one path active. Includes sufficient capacity to carry power and cooling load on one path while performing maintenance on the other path. Includes raised floor, UPS, and generator.
> - **Tier IV–Fault Tolerant**   Includes multiple active power and cooling distribution paths. Includes redundant components, including UPS and generator. Includes raised floor.

Cleaning

Facilities containing computing and network equipment need to be kept clean, with dirt, dust, and debris kept to a minimum. While computer rooms do not need to be kept clean to the same extent as "clean rooms" (facilities that manufacture disk drives and computer chips), they do need to be regularly cleaned to prevent the buildup of dust, dirt, and other particles that will clog filters and get inside computers and network devices, shortening their life span.

Physical Security Controls

Physical security controls are primarily concerned with the protection of valuable or sensitive facilities (including those with computers and network devices) from unauthorized personnel. Controls are used to detect or prevent the entry of unwanted persons at these facilities. This section describes typical threats and vulnerabilities related to physical security and the controls and countermeasures that can be employed to protect a facility.

Physical Access Threats and Vulnerabilities

The threats and vulnerabilities in the realm of physical security are all associated with unwanted persons at business premises. A site without proper security controls may be subject to one or more threats, including these:

- **Theft**   Persons who are able to enter a building may be able to steal equipment, records, or other valuable items.

- **Sabotage**   Persons who may enter a building or work site may be able to damage or destroy valuable equipment or records.

- **Espionage**   Persons may wish to conduct espionage in order to acquire information about the organization.

- **Covert listening devices**   These are listening devices that can be placed in a building to overhear conversations and transmit them to a receiver located in a remote location. Covert listening devices are commonly known as *bugs*. Sometimes intruders plant bugs; bugs can also be hidden in articles that are delivered to a building (for example, in flower bouquets or gift baskets).

- **Tailgating**   This is a specific technique that intruders may use when attempting to enter a building; they may follow an employee into a building without showing their own security credentials (for example, a keycard). This practice is also known as *piggybacking*.

- **Propped doors**   Sometimes a front, rear, or side door that is equipped with security controls will be propped open for various reasons, including hot weather (to permit a cooling breeze to enter and cool the building), frequent traffic moving in or out, or persons going out for a quick smoke who don't want the hassle of having to return to the building through another door.

- **Poor visibility**   A facility may have exterior features that permit an unauthorized person to lurk about without being noticed. The person may be able to gain entry if he can discover a weakness before he is noticed himself.

Physical Access Controls and Countermeasures

Several controls can be used to improve the physical security of a worksite, reducing the threat of intruders and resultant theft or damage. Some of these controls are

- **Keycard systems**   Authorized persons are issued electronically activated ID cards that can be used to momentarily activate entry doors that are usually locked. These systems record the date and time that persons entered each door. Some keycard systems are also equipped with a "PIN pad" that requires the person to enter a numeric PIN before the door will unlock. This helps to prevent someone who finds a keycard from entering a facility. Keycard systems can also utilize biometrics such as palm scan, fingerprint scan, or iris scan.

- **Cipher locks**   These are electronic or mechanical doors equipped with combination locks. Only persons who know the combination may unlock the door. Some cipher locks can be equipped with different combinations for each person and also record each entry.

- **Fences, walls, and barbed wire**   These barriers are used to prevent unauthorized persons from approaching a building, keeping them at a safe distance.

- **Bollards and crash gates**   These barriers prevent the entry of vehicles into protected areas. Some bollards can be retracted or removed when needed. Crash gates are hard barriers that lift into position, preventing the entry (or exit) of unauthorized vehicles, and can be lowered to permit authorized vehicles.

- **Video surveillance**   The use of video cameras, monitors, and recording systems can be used to record the movement of persons in or near sensitive areas.

- **Visual notices**   This includes signs and placards that warn intruders that premises are monitored and protected.

- **Bug sweeping**   Because most covert listening devices emit radio frequency radiation, it is possible to detect them through the use of a bug sweeper.

- **Security guards**   These are personnel who control passage at entry points or roam building premises looking for security issues such as unescorted visitors.

- **Guard dogs**   These assist security guards and can be used to apprehend and control trespassers.

 NOTE   A detailed risk analysis, including a study of physical facilities and access controls, should be used to determine which controls are appropriate for a facility.

Auditing Asset Protection

Auditing asset protection requires substantial knowledge about information technology, threats, vulnerabilities, countermeasures, and common asset protection practices. The IS auditor who lacks this knowledge will likely overlook threats or vulnerabilities that might be obvious to more knowledgeable auditors.

Auditing Security Management

Auditing security management activities requires attention to several key activities, including

- **Policies, processes, procedures, and standards**   The auditor should request and examine information security policies to see what processes are required. This should be followed by requests to examine process and procedure documentation for key processes that are cited in security policies. The IS auditor should review the entire body of information security policy to determine if there is adequate coverage on every topic. Rather than examine the organization's security policy in a vacuum, it should be compared to an industry standard, such as ISO 27001, to ensure that the organization has not omitted any topic that should be included in its security policy.

- **Records**   For those security management processes that usually have associated recordkeeping, the auditor should examine business records to see whether processes are active.

- **Security awareness training** The auditor should examine training materials, training procedures, and training records to determine the effectiveness of the organization's security awareness training program. In various walkthroughs on this and other topics, the IS auditor should ask questions related to security awareness training, such as, "Have you received security awareness training?", "Does your organization have a security policy?", or "What security procedures are required for laptop computers?" to see whether employees can corroborate the effectiveness of the security awareness program.

- **Data ownership and management** The IS auditor should inquire about the methodology used to determine ownership and management of business data. The key point with data ownership and management is accountability: When someone is responsible for management of a given data set, that person will ensure that only authorized parties have access to it and will take steps to ensure the continuing integrity of the data. The auditor should determine if there are company-wide policies and procedures on data management, or whether this is a disorganized or undocumented activity.

- **Data custodians** Often, business owners of information and systems delegate management to the IT department, who will manage access on their behalf. If an organization manages data in this way, the IS auditor should identify whether data custodians effectively carry out the wishes of the data owner, or whether data custodians act on their own *as if* they are the owner.

- **Security administrators** Often, an IT department will handle the day-to-day responsibilities of managing access to, and integrity of, business data. The IS auditor should determine if IT staff are knowledgeable about these duties and qualified to carry them out.

- **New and existing employees** Data management is implicitly every employee's responsibility. As individuals who are entrusted to properly access and use company data, individual employees are obligated to handle data properly, to keep data confidential, and to be alert for any misuse of data. The IS auditor should determine if any policies exist on this topic and whether security awareness training covers this theme.

Auditing Logical Access Controls

Auditing logical access controls requires attention to several key areas, including

- Network access paths
- User access controls
- User access logs
- Investigative procedures
- Internet points of presence

These topics are discussed in depth in this section.

Network Access Paths

The IS auditor should conduct an independent review of the IT infrastructure to map out the organization's logical access paths. This will require considerable effort and may require the use of investigative and technical tools, as well as specialized experts on IT network architecture. The reason for this is that the IT network may have undocumented access paths that are deliberately hidden from most personnel, or the network may have unexpected access paths due to incorrect configuration of even a single device. For instance, the IS auditor or a security specialist may discover a hidden, unauthorized Wi-Fi access point in an office or data center network or a network back door in the form of a dial-in modem. The presence of deliberate or accidental back doors is a particular problem in larger organizations with highly complex network infrastructures that have many interconnections within the network and with external parties. Any of those connections could be a wide-open back door. Proving the absence of such a path is similar to the analogy of proving that there is no spider in the room where you are now.

The IS auditor should request network architecture and access documentation to compare what was discovered independently against existing documentation. The auditor will need to determine why any discrepancies exist.

Similar investigations should take place for each application to determine all of the documented and undocumented access paths to functions and data. This topic is explored in Chapter 4.

Auditing User Access Controls

User access controls are often the only barrier between unauthorized parties and sensitive or valuable information. This makes the audit of user access controls particularly significant. Auditing user access controls requires keen attention to several key factors and activities in four areas:

- User access controls, to determine if the controls themselves work as designed
- User access provisioning, to determine if provisioning processes are effective
- Password management, to determine if passwords are effectively managed
- Employee transfers and terminations, to determine if accesses are managed and removed effectively

---

 NOTE   The IS auditor should not become so entrenched in the details of user access controls as to lose sight of the big picture. One of the responsibilities of the IS auditor is to continue to observe user access controls from the "big picture" perspective to determine if the entire set of controls *works together* to effectively manage this important process.

Auditing User Access Controls   Auditing user access controls requires attention to several factors, including

- **Authentication**   The auditor should examine network and system resources to determine if they require authentication, or whether any resources can be accessed without first authenticating.

- **Authentication bypass**   The auditor should examine network and system resources to determine if it is possible to bypass user authentication methods. This may require the use of specialized tools or techniques. This needs to include penetration testing tools and application scanning tools to determine the presence of vulnerabilities that can be exploited to bypass authentication. For highly valued or sensitive data and applications that are Internet-accessible, hackers will certainly try these techniques in attempts to access and steal this information; the organization's security staff should regularly attempt to determine the presence of any such vulnerabilities.

- **Access violations**   The auditor should determine if systems, networks, and authentication mechanisms have the ability to log access violations. These usually exist in the form of system logs showing invalid login attempts, which may indicate intruders who are trying to log in to employee user accounts.

- **User account lockout**   The auditor should determine if systems and networks have the ability to automatically lock user accounts that are the target of attacks. A typical system configuration is one that will lock a user account after five unsuccessful login attempts within a short period. Such a control helps to prevent automated password-guessing attacks. Without such detective and preventive controls, intruders could write scripts to guess every possible password until a user's correct password was guessed correctly, thereby enabling an intruder to log in to a user account. Systems use different methods for unlocking such locked accounts: some will automatically unlock after a "cooling off period" (usually 30 minutes), or the user is required to contact the IT service desk and, after properly identifying themselves, get the account manually unlocked. The IS auditor should obtain policies, procedures, and records for this activity.

- **Intrusion detection and prevention**   The auditor should determine if there are any IDSs or IPSs that would detect authentication-bypass attempts. The auditor should examine these systems to see whether they have up-to-date configurations and signatures, whether they generate alerts, and whether the recipients of alerts act upon them.

- **Dormant accounts**   The IS auditor should determine if any automated or manual process exists to identify and close dormant accounts. Dormant accounts are user (or system) accounts that exist but are unused. These accounts represent a risk to the environment, as they represent an additional path between intruders and valuable or sensitive data. A dormant account could also be a back door, deliberately planted for future use. But chances are that most dormant accounts are user accounts that were assigned to persons who ended up not needing to access the environment, or terminated employees whose accounts were never cleaned up.

- **Shared accounts** The IS auditor should determine if there are any shared user accounts; these are user accounts that are routinely (or even infrequently) used by more than one person. The principal risk with shared accounts is the inability to determine accountability for actions performed with the account. Through the 1990s, information systems were routinely designed with shared user accounts, and many such systems continue to use shared accounts. To the greatest extent possible, shared user accounts should be identified as audit exceptions and be replaced with individual user accounts.

- **System accounts** The IS auditor should identify all system-level accounts on networks, systems, and applications. The purpose of each system account should be identified, and it should be determined if each system account is still required (some may be artifacts of the initial implementation or of an upgrade or migration). The IS auditor should determine who has the password for each system account, whether accesses by system accounts are logged, and who monitors those logs.

Auditing Password Management Auditing password management requires attention to several key technologies and activities, including

- **Password standards** The IS auditor needs to examine password configuration settings on information systems to determine how passwords are controlled. Some of the areas requiring examination are

  - **Minimum length** How many characters must a password have and whether there is a maximum length.

  - **Complexity** Whether passwords must contain various types of characters (lowercase alphabetic, uppercase alphabetic, numeric, symbols), whether dictionary words are permitted, and whether permutations of the user ID are permitted.

  - **Expiration** How frequently must passwords be changed.

  - **History** Whether former passwords may be used again.

  - **Minimum time between changes** Whether users are permitted to change their passwords frequently (for instance, to cycle back to the familiar password they are used to).

  - **Display** Whether the password is displayed when logging in or when creating a new password.

  - **Transmission** Whether the password is encrypted when transmitted over the network or if it is transmitted in plaintext.

  - **Storage** Whether the password is stored encrypted or hashed, or if it is stored in plaintext. If it is stored encrypted or in plaintext, the IS auditor needs to determine who has access to it.

- **Account lockout** The IS auditor should determine if systems automatically lock user accounts after a series of unsuccessful login attempts. The auditor should determine how locked user accounts are unlocked—whether automatically or manually—and whether these events are logged.

- **Access to encrypted passwords**   The IS auditor should determine if end users are able to access encrypted/hashed passwords, which would enable them to use password-cracking tools to discover other users' and administrative passwords.

- **Password vaulting**   The IS auditor should determine if users are encouraged or required to use password vaulting tools for the safe storage of passwords and if administrative passwords are vaulted for emergency use.

Auditing User Access Provisioning   Auditing the user access provisioning process requires attention to several key activities, including

- **Access request processes**   The IS auditor should identify all user access request processes and determine if these processes are used consistently throughout the organization. The auditor should determine if there is one central user access request process or if each environment has a separate process. The auditor should identify what data elements are required in a user access request—for instance, if the request specifies *why* and for *how long* the user needs this access. The auditor should examine business records to determine how access requests are documented.

- **Access approvals**   When studying the user access process, the IS auditor needs to determine how requests are approved and by what authority they are approved. The auditor should determine if system or data owners approve access requests, or if any accesses are ever denied (if no access requests are denied, the IS auditor should see if all requests are merely "rubber stamped" without any real scrutiny). The auditor should examine business records to look for evidence of access approvals.

- **New employee provisioning**   The IS auditor should examine the new employee provisioning process to see how a new employee's user accounts are initially set up. The auditor should determine how a new employee's initial roles are determined: Does a new user have an established "template" of accesses, or do requests simply state, "Make John's access just like Susan's"? The auditor should determine if new employees' managers are aware of the access requests that their employees are given and if they are excessive. Furthermore, the IS auditor should determine if access to applications requires any initial training of the user of the application, or if the organization just "turns them loose" to figure out how the application is supposed to be used. The IS auditor also needs to determine how initial user credentials are communicated to the new employee and if the method is secure and reasonable.

- **Segregation of duties (SOD)**   The IS auditor should determine if the organization makes any effort to identify segregation of duties. This may include whether there are any SOD matrices in existence and if they are actively used to make user access request decisions. Furthermore, the IS auditor should determine if the organization performs SOD reviews to identify persons who have access privileges within or among applications that would constitute SOD violations. The auditor should determine how violations are managed when they are found.

- **Access reviews**   The IS auditor should determine if there are any periodic access reviews and what aspects of user accounts are reviewed; this may include termination reviews, internal transfer reviews, SOD reviews, and dormant account reviews.

Auditing Employee Terminations   Auditing employee terminations requires attention to several key factors, including

- **Termination process**   The IS auditor should examine the employee termination process and determine its effectiveness. This examination should include understanding how terminations are performed and how user account management personnel are notified of terminations. The auditor should identify specific security policies to determine how quickly user accounts should be terminated. The auditor should examine HR records to see if all employee terminations correspond to user account management termination records.

- **Timeliness**   The IS auditor should examine employee termination records and the records on individual information systems to determine if user accounts are locked or removed in a timely manner. Typically, user accounts should be locked or removed within one business day, but in environments with particularly valuable or sensitive information, employee terminations should be processed within minutes or hours to ensure that a departing employee cannot access systems immediately afterward (when passions often run high).

- **Access reviews**   The IS auditor should determine if any internal reviews of terminated accounts are performed, which would indicate a pattern of concern for effectiveness in this important activity. If such reviews are performed, the auditor should determine if any missed terminations are identified and if any process improvements are undertaken.

- **Contractor access and terminations**   In most organizations, a contractor's tenure is not managed by HR, so the IS auditor needs to determine how contractor access and termination is managed and if such management is effective. The classic problem with contractors is that it's sometimes difficult to precisely determine when a contractor no longer requires access to a system or network. The reason for this uncertainty lies in the nature of the contracted work: sometimes the contractor performs services sporadically or on request, and sometimes months or even years pass between these events. Furthermore, contractors are often hired and fired by internal managers without any notification to or tracking by HR. In light of these aspects, it can be difficult to determine the effectiveness of contractor-related access management.

Auditing Access Logs

Auditing access logs requires attention to several key points, including

- **Access log contents**   The IS auditor needs to determine what events are recorded in access logs. Events may include every user login and granular information, such as every program run and file accessed, or logs may include only invalid logon attempts (or not even that). The IS auditor needs to understand the capabilities of the system being audited and determine if the right events are being logged, or if logging is suppressed on events that should be logged.

- **Centralized access logs**   The IS auditor should determine if the organization's access logs are aggregated or if they are stored on individual systems.

- **Access log protection**   The IS auditor needs to understand access log protection mechanisms. Primarily, the auditor needs to determine if access logs can be altered, destroyed, or attacked to cause the system to stop logging events. For especially high-value and high-sensitivity environments, the IS auditor needs to determine if logs should be written to digital media that is unalterable, such as optical WORM (write once read many) media.

- **Access log review**   The IS auditor needs to determine if there are policies, processes, or procedures regarding access log review. The auditor should determine if access log reviews take place, who performs them, how issues requiring attention are identified, and what actions are taken when necessary.

- **Access log retention**   The IS auditor should determine how long access logs are retained by the organization and if they are backed up.

Auditing Investigative Procedures

Auditing investigative procedures requires attention to several key activities, including

- **Investigation policies and procedures**   The IS auditor should determine if there are any policies or procedures regarding security investigations. This would include who is responsible for performing investigations, where information about investigations is stored, and to whom the results of investigations are reported.

- **Computer crime investigations**   The IS auditor should determine if there are policies, processes, procedures, and records regarding computer crime investigations. The IS auditor should understand how internal investigations are transitioned to law enforcement.

- **Computer forensics**   The IS auditor should determine if there are procedures for conducting computer forensics. The auditor should also identify tools and techniques that are available to the organization for the acquisition and custody of forensic data. The auditor should identify whether any employees in the organization have received computer forensics training and are qualified to perform forensic investigations.

Auditing Internet Points of Presence

The IS auditor who is performing a comprehensive audit of an organization's system and network system needs to perform a "points of presence" audit to discover what technical information is available about the organization's Internet presence. Some of the aspects of this intelligence gathering include

- **Search engines**   Google, Yahoo!, and other search engines should be consulted to see what information about the organization is available. Searches should include the names of company officers and management, key technologists, and any internal-only nomenclature such as the names of projects.

- **Social networking sites**   Social networking sites such as Facebook, LinkedIn, MySpace, and Twitter should be searched to see what employees, former employees, and others are saying about the organization. Any authorized or unauthorized "fan pages" should be searched as well.

- **Online sales sites**   Sites such as Craigslist and eBay should be searched to see if anything related to the organization is sold online.

- **Domain names**   The IS auditor should verify contact information for known domain names, as well as related domain names. For instance, for the organization *mycompany.com*, organizations should search for domain names such as *mycompany.net*, *mycompany.info*, and *mycompany.biz* to see if they are registered and what contents are available.

Justification of Online Presence   The IS auditor should examine business records to determine on what basis the organization established online capabilities such as e-mail, Internet-facing websites, Internet e-commerce, Internet access for employees, and so on. These services add risk to the business and consume resources. The auditor should determine if a viable business case exists to support these services or if they exist as a "benefit" for employees.

Auditing Network Security Controls

Auditing network security controls requires a thorough understanding of network technologies, network security techniques, and the architecture of the organization's network being audited. Any gaps in understanding may lead to insufficient scrutiny of the network, possibly resulting in a failure to identify serious deficiencies.

Performing an Architecture Review

The IS auditor needs to conduct a meticulous review of the organization's network architecture. This will require an examination of architecture diagrams and documents, walkthroughs with key systems and network staff, and inspection of many system and network device configuration files.

 NOTE   The IS auditor needs to conduct an investigation into the available network paths, independent of any examination of documents, in order to discover any undocumented or unintended paths. This process is explained in more detail earlier in this section.

Auditing architecture requires attention to several key details, including

- **Architecture diagrams**   The IS auditor should obtain and become familiar with high-level and detailed architecture diagrams that show the logical relationships between key network and system features.

- **Architecture documents**   Visual diagrams are usually accompanied by written documents that describe the purpose of various architectural features. The IS auditor should use these documents to supplement diagrams to get a more complete picture of the network architecture.

- **Support of business objectives**   The IS auditor should determine if the network's architecture supports key business objectives.

- **Compliance with security policy**   The IS auditor should determine if the network's architecture is compliant with the organization's security policy. This may include the logical segregation of business functions, protection of key assets, and separation of responsibilities between departments.

- **Comparisons of documented versus actual**   The IS auditor should examine several key points in the documented network architecture to see if the network's configuration actually reflects its documented design. The IS auditor should seek to understand any discrepancies found.

- **Change and review process**   The IS auditor should determine if the organization has any processes used to identify, review, and approve any network architecture changes. This is described more fully in the next section.

Auditing Network Access Controls

Auditing network access controls requires attention to several key factors and activities, including

- **User authentication**   In environments that employ network-centric user authentication (such as Microsoft Active Directory or LDAP), IS auditors need to apply the full range of user access control audit. See the section, "Auditing User Access Controls," earlier in this chapter for a detailed discussion on this topic.

- **Firewalls**   The IS auditor should examine network architecture (described earlier in this section) and understand the role of firewalls in the network. With this understanding, the auditor should carefully examine network security policies, firewall access control lists, and configurations to determine if firewalls support security policy. The auditor should also examine change control records and firewall change records to determine if all firewall changes are approved and applied properly.

- **Intrusion detection and prevention system (IDS/IPS)**   The IS auditor should examine network security policy and IDS/IPS settings and logs to see if they detect violations of security policy.

- **Data leakage prevention (DLP)** The IS auditor should examine the DLP system to see whether it is properly configured to detect outgoing sensitive data, and whether there are procedures and records indicating that people do respond to alerts.

- **Remote access** The IS auditor should examine remote access policy to determine acceptable remote access scenarios. The auditor should then examine remote access servers and some workstations to determine if remote access infrastructure supports and enforces policy. Some issues to consider when auditing remote access include

  - Whether user authentication is any more difficult over remote access than on the physical network

  - Whether remote access clients allow split tunneling

  - Whether remote access permits noncompany-owned computers to remotely access network resources

  - Whether workstations missing security patches are permitted to connect via remote access

  - Whether workstations with nonfunctioning or out-of-date antivirus software are permitted to connect

- **Dial-up modems** The IS auditor should determine if dial-up modems are permitted in the infrastructure. The auditor should use tools to independently verify if any dial-up modems exist in the infrastructure and if they permit access to the network.

- **Wi-Fi access points** The IS auditor should determine whether Wi-Fi access points are used and, if so, how they are controlled. The IS auditor should determine whether there are any rogue (unapproved) access points in use and whether the organization routinely scans for them and takes action.

Auditing Network Change Management

Auditing network change management requires attention to several key factors and activities, including

- **Change control policy** The IS auditor should examine the organization's change control policy to understand how change is supposed to be controlled and managed.

- **Change logs** The IS auditor should determine if information systems contain automatic logs that contain all changes to systems and if these logs are reviewed by IT staff to ensure that only approved changes are being made to systems. The auditor should examine procedures and records to determine what actions are taken when unapproved changes are discovered.

- **Change control procedures** The IS auditor needs to examine change control procedures and examine records to determine if procedures are effective and are being followed.

- **Emergency changes** The IS auditor should examine change control policy, procedures, and records to see how emergency changes are handled and how they are approved.

- **Rolled-back changes** The IS auditor should examine change control records to see what changes needed to be rolled back because of problems. The auditor should determine how these situations were handled.

- **Linkage to software development life cycle (SDLC)** The IS auditor should understand how the organization's software development life cycle is integrated with its change management processes to ensure that only completed and properly functioning software changes are proposed for promotion into production.

NOTE The IS auditor should examine all of these aspects of change management to understand whether the organization is really in control of its environment.

Auditing Vulnerability Management

Auditing vulnerability management requires attention to several key factors and activities, including

- **Alert management** The IS auditor should determine if the organization actively searches for or subscribes to security alert bulletins. The auditor should examine procedures and records to see if any alert bulletins result in responsive actions such as applied security patches or configuration changes.

- **Penetration testing** The IS auditor should determine if the organization performs any penetration testing on its own network and system infrastructure. The auditor should examine procedures and records to determine if the organization's penetration testing program is effective. The auditor should see if vulnerabilities are mitigated and confirmed.

- **Application scanning** The IS auditor should determine if the organization performs any application vulnerability scanning on its software applications to identify vulnerabilities. He or she should examine procedures and records to determine if the organization's application scanning process is effective.

- **Patch management** The IS auditor should examine procedures and records to determine if the organization performs any patch management activities. These activities might consist of a periodic review of available security and functionality patches and whether any patches are applied to production systems. The auditor should determine if patches are tested on nonproduction environment systems to understand their impact.

Complementary Penetration Testing The IS auditor should consider the use of penetration testing during a network security audit. The purpose of penetration testing is to identify active systems on a network and to discover the services that are active on those systems. Many penetration testing tools go a step further and identify vulnerabilities on systems.

Auditing Environmental Controls

Auditing environmental controls requires knowledge of building mechanical and electrical systems as well as fire codes. The IS auditor needs to be able to determine if such controls are effective and if they are *cost*-effective. Auditing environmental controls requires attention to these and other factors and activities, including

- **Power conditioning**   The IS auditor should determine if power conditioning equipment, such as UPS, line conditioners, surge protectors, or motor generators, are used to clean electrical anomalies such as noise, surges, sags, and so on. He or she should examine procedures and records to see how frequently this equipment is inspected and maintained and if this is performed by qualified personnel.

- **Backup power**   The IS auditor should determine if backup power is available via electric generators or UPS and how frequently they are tested. He or she should examine maintenance records to see how frequently these components are maintained and if this is done by qualified personnel.

- **Heating, ventilation, and air conditioning (HVAC)**   The IS auditor should determine if HVAC systems are providing adequate temperature and humidity levels, and if they are monitored. Also, the auditor should determine if HVAC systems are properly maintained and if qualified persons do this.

- **Water detection**   The IS auditor should determine if any water detectors are used in rooms where computers are used. He or she should determine how frequently these are tested and if they are monitored.

- **Fire detection and suppression**   The IS auditor should determine if fire detection equipment is adequate, if staff members understand their function, and if they are tested. He or she should determine how frequently fire suppression systems are inspected and tested, and if the organization has emergency evacuation plans and conducts fire drills. The auditor should examine the inspection tags on fire suppression equipment, including sprinkler valves and fire extinguishers, to see if their inspections are up-to-date. He or she should check the walls in data centers to ensure that they extend all the way to the real floor and ceiling, and not merely to the raised floor and dropped ceiling.

- **Cleanliness**   The IS auditor should examine data centers to see how clean they are. IT equipment air filters and the inside of some IT components should be examined to see if there is an accumulation of dust and dirt.

 NOTE   The IS auditor may need to consult with electrical and mechanical engineers to determine if power conditioning, backup power, HVAC systems, and fire detection and suppression equipment are in good working order and are adequately sized to meet the organization's needs.

Auditing Physical Security Controls

Auditing physical security controls requires knowledge of natural and manmade hazards, physical security controls, and access control systems.

Auditing Siting and Marking

Auditing building siting and marking requires attention to several key factors and features, including

- **Proximity to hazards** The IS auditor should estimate the building's distance to natural and manmade hazards, such as:
  - Dams
  - Rivers, lakes, and canals
  - Natural gas and petroleum pipelines
  - Water mains and pipelines
  - Earthquake faults
  - Areas prone to landslides
  - Volcanoes
  - Severe weather such as hurricanes, cyclones, and tornadoes
  - Flood zones
  - Military bases
  - Airports
  - Railroads
  - Freeways

    The IS auditor should determine if any risk assessment regarding hazards has been performed and if any compensating controls that were recommended have been carried out.

- **Marking** The IS auditor should inspect the building and surrounding area to see if building(s) containing information-processing equipment identify the organization. Marking may be visible on the building itself, but also on signs or parking stickers on vehicles.

Auditing Physical Access Controls

Auditing physical access controls requires attention to several key factors, including

- **Physical barriers** This includes fencing, walls, barbed/razor wire, bollards, and crash gates. The IS auditor needs to understand how these are used to control access to the facility and determine their effectiveness.

- **Surveillance** The IS auditor needs to understand how video and human surveillance are used to control and monitor access. He or she needs to understand how (and if) video is recorded and reviewed, and if it is effective in preventing or detecting incidents.

- **Guards and dogs** The IS auditor needs to understand the use and effectiveness of security guards and guard dogs. Processes, policies, procedures, and records should be examined to understand required activities and how they are carried out.

- **Keycard systems** The IS auditor needs to understand how keycard systems are used to control access to the facility. Some points to consider include

  - **Work zones** Whether the facility is divided into security zones and which persons are permitted to access which zones.

  - **Records** Whether keycard systems record personnel movement.

  - **Provisioning** What processes and procedures are used to issue keycards to employees. See the earlier section, "Auditing Logical Access Controls," for more details.

  - **Access reviews** Whether the organization performs reviews of access logs and user access lists.

  - **Visitors** How visitors are handled in terms of building access.

  - **Incidents** What procedures are in place to respond to access incidents.

Summary

Information security management is concerned with the identification and protection of valuable and sensitive assets. Security management begins with executive support of the organization's information security program, including the development and enforcement of an organization-wide information security policy. Several processes also support security management, including security monitoring, auditing, security awareness training, incident response procedures, information classification, vulnerability management, service provider management, and corrective and preventive action processes.

Security roles and responsibilities need to be explicitly developed and communicated. Managers and staff need to demonstrate knowledge of their roles and responsibilities through proper decisions and actions.

Access management is a critical activity in a security management program. Access controls are often the only thing standing between valuable or sensitive information and parties who wish to access it. Access management consists of several separate but related processes, including user access management, network access management, and access log review.

Computers are used as instruments of crimes, can be used to support criminal activity, and are the target of crimes. Criminal activities are a threat to organizations, whether the activity is espionage, data theft, fraud, or sabotage.

Several techniques are used to protect sensitive and valuable information from disclosure to unauthorized parties. These techniques include user access controls, network access controls, anti-malware, system and network hardening, and encryption. Many threats exist that require a variety of countermeasures, many of which require continuous vigilance and effort.

Physical and environmental controls are required to safeguard the physical safety and reliability of computing and network equipment. These controls include power system improvements; heating, cooling, and humidity controls; fire control systems; and physical access controls, such as keycard systems, fences, walls, and video surveillance.

Notes

- The foundation of an effective information security program is an information security policy that includes executive support and well-defined roles and responsibilities.

- A security awareness program is used to communicate security policy, procedures, and other security-related information to an organization's employees. Security training should be administered upon hire and regularly thereafter.

- An organization needs to continuously monitor and periodically audit its processes and systems to ensure that security controls effectively protect information systems and assets.

- An information classification program defines levels of sensitivity and handling procedures for each classification level.

- Access controls are used to control access to programs and data. Access control methods include authentication, authorization, access control lists, and encryption, as well as physical access controls. Access controls are usually implemented in several technology layers, including physical, operating system, database, and application. Because access controls are subject to a variety of threats, they should be regularly tested to ensure that they remain effective.

- Third-party service organizations that store, transmit, or process an organization's information should be required to implement controls that result in a level of risk that is the same or lower than if the organization managed it themselves.

- An organization should implement controls to ensure that its personnel have an appropriate background prior to employment and that their behavior is monitored and controlled during employment.

- Organizations need to implement controls to prevent and processes to respond to computer crimes and security incidents. Response processes should be periodically tested. Some personnel should be trained in forensic investigation techniques.

- Stored information needs to be protected through several controls, including access controls and logging, sound user access management processes, patch management, vulnerability management, anti-malware, system hardening, and backup.

- Organizations need to implement effective network security controls, including firewalls and other access controls, protection of mobile devices, encryption of sensitive communications, protection of wireless networks, and prevention of information leakage, all to control access and prevent security incidents.

- Organizations need to implement effective controls to assure high-integrity environments for their computer systems and networks. These controls include power conditioning and backup power systems, temperature and humidity control, and fire detection and suppression systems.

Questions

1. A fire sprinkler system has water in its pipes, and sprinkler heads emit water only if the ambient temperature reaches $220°$ F. What type of system is this?

   A. Deluge

   B. Post-action

   C. Wet pipe

   D. Pre-action

2. An organization is building a data center in an area frequented by power outages. The organization cannot tolerate power outages. What power system controls should be selected?

   A. Uninterruptible power supply and electric generator

   B. Uninterruptible power supply and batteries

   C. Electric generator

   D. Electric generator and line conditioning

3. An auditor has discovered several errors in user account management: many terminated employees' computer accounts are still active. What is the best course of action?

   A. Improve the employee termination process.

   B. Shift responsibility for employee terminations to another group.

   C. Audit the process more frequently.

   D. Improve the employee termination process and audit the process more frequently.

4. An auditor has discovered that several administrators in an application share an administrative account. What course of action should the auditor recommend?

   A. Implement activity logging on the administrative account.

   B. Use several named administrative accounts that are not shared.

   C. Implement a host-based intrusion detection system.

   D. Require each administrator to sign nondisclosure and acceptable-use agreements.

5. An organization that has experienced a sudden increase in its long-distance charges has asked an auditor to investigate. What activity is the auditor likely to suspect is responsible for this?

   A. Employees making more long-distance calls

   B. Toll fraud

   C. PBX malfunction

   D. Malware in the PBX

6. An auditor is examining a key management process and has found that the IT department is not following its split-custody procedure. What is the likely result of this failure?

   A. One or more individuals are in possession of the entire password for an encryption key.

   B. One or more individuals are in possession of encrypted files.

   C. Backup tapes are not being stored at an off-site facility.

   D. Two or more employees are sharing an administrative account.

7. A programmer is updating an application that saves passwords in plaintext. What is the best method for securely storing passwords?

   A. Encrypted with each user's public key

   B. Encrypted with a public key

   C. Encrypted with a private key

   D. Hashed

8. An organization experiences frequent malware infections on end-user workstations that are received through e-mail, despite the fact that workstations have antivirus software. What is the best measure for reducing malware?

   A. Antivirus software on web proxy servers

   B. Firewalls

   C. Antivirus software on e-mail servers

   D. Intrusion prevention systems

9. An auditor has reviewed the access privileges of some employees and has discovered that employees with longer terms of service have excessive privileges. What can the auditor conclude from this?

   A. Employee privileges are not being removed when they transfer from one position to another.

   B. Long-time employees are able to successfully guess other users' passwords and add to their privileges.

   C. Long-time employees' passwords should be set to expire more frequently.

   D. The organization's termination process is ineffective.

10. An organization wants to reduce the number of user IDs and passwords that its employees need to remember. What is the best available solution to this problem?

    A. Password vaults for storing user IDs and passwords

    B. Token authentication

    C. Single sign-on

    D. Reduced sign-on

11. An IS auditor has discovered that an employee has installed a Wi-Fi access point in his cube. What action should the IS auditor take?

    A. The IS auditor should include this in his audit report.

    B. The IS auditor should immediately report this as a high-risk situation.

    C. The IS auditor should ask the employee to turn off the Wi-Fi access point when it is not being used.

    D. The IS auditor should test the Wi-Fi access point to see whether it properly authenticates users.

12. An auditor is examining an organization's data leakage prevention (DLP) system. The DLP system is recording instances of sensitive information that is leaving the organization. There are no records of actions taken. What should the IS auditor recommend?

    A. That management appoint a party responsible for taking action when the DLP system detects that sensitive information is leaving the organization

    B. That management develop procedures for responding to DLP alerts

    C. That management discontinue use of the DLP system since no one is taking action

    D. That the DLP system be reconfigured to stop issuing alerts

13. An organization's remote access requires a user ID and one-time password token. What weakness does this scheme have?

    A. Someone who finds a one-time password token could log in as the user by guessing the password.

    B. Someone who finds a one-time password token could log in as the user by guessing the user ID.

    C. Someone who knows the user ID could derive the password.

    D. Someone who is able to eavesdrop on the authentication can log in later using a replay attack.

14. An organization has configured its applications to utilize an LDAP server for authentication. The organization has set up:

    A. Automatic sign-on

    B. LDAP sign-on

    C. Single sign-on

    D. Reduced sign-on

15. An organization has hundreds of remote locations containing valuable equipment and needs to enact a secure access control system. The locations do not have electricity. What is the best choice for an access control method that can be implemented at these locations?

    A. Key cards

    B. Metal keys

    C. Cipher locks

    D. Video surveillance

Answers

1. **C.** A wet pipe fire sprinkler system is charged with water and will discharge water out of any sprinkler head whose fuse has reached a preset temperature.

2. **A.** The best solution is an electric generator and an uninterruptible power supply (UPS). A UPS responds to a power outage by providing continuous electric power without interruption. An electric generator provides backup power for extended periods.

3. **D.** The best course of action is to improve the employee termination process to reduce the number of exceptions. For a time, the process should be audited more frequently to make sure that the improvement is effective.

4. **B.** Several separate administrative accounts should be used. This will enforce accountability for each administrator's actions.

5. **B.** The auditor is most likely to suspect that intruders have discovered a vulnerability in the organization's PBX and is committing toll fraud.

6. **A.** Someone may be in possession of the entire password for an encryption key. For instance, split custody requires that a password be broken into two or more parts, where each part is in possession of a unique individual. This prevents any one individual from having an entire password.

7. **D.** Passwords should be stored as a hash. This makes it impossible for any person to retrieve a password, which could lead to account compromise.

8. **C.** Implementing antivirus software on e-mail servers will provide an effective defense-in-depth, which should help to reduce the number of viruses encountered on end-user workstations.

9. **A.** User privileges are not being removed from their old position when they transfer to a new position. This results in employees with excessive privileges.

10. **D.** The most direct solution to the problem of too many user credentials is reduced sign-on. This provides a single authentication service (such as LDAP or Active Directory) that many applications can use for centralized user authentication.

11. **B.** Finding an unauthorized access point is a high-risk situation that the IS auditor should report immediately to management.

12. **A.** An organization using a DLP should be acting on alerts that the DLP system generates in order to curb employee and system behavior.

13. **B.** Someone who finds a one-time password token and then tries to log in to a VPN and discovers that the site does not request a password could guess the user ID and possibly be able to log in to the network.

14. **D.** Reduced sign-on is the term used to describe an environment where many different systems use a centralized authentication server (such as LDAP).

15. **C.** The best choice for an access control system for many remote locations is cipher locks. They do not require a power supply or remote connectivity, but they can be configured with a different combination for each user, and some retain a memory of which persons used them.

Conducting a Professional Audit

This appendix discusses the following topics
- Auditing in the real world
- Carrying out the IS audit cycle
- Internal audits versus external audits
- Ethics and independence
- Writing audit reports

The goals and structure of this appendix are slightly different from the rest of this book. Whereas Chapters 1 through 6 convey information to the CISA candidate, here, the focus shifts to the professional world of the information systems (IS) auditor. It addresses the nature of different professional engagements common to information systems auditors. I review the stages of and responsibilities involved in performing a risk-based information systems audit for both internal and external auditors. This appendix also serves to introduce and frame examples of professional situations that may challenge an auditor.

This appendix reviews the process of performing an information systems audit, and in doing so, identifies how sections of the study materials in this book can be applied in the "real world." By bringing the subject of conducting an IS audit "up a level," I provide associations between concepts found in the main chapters in this book so you have real-life examples of a number of these concepts. This should help solidify material you learned from the rest of the book, and hopefully assist in recalling information while sitting for the test.

In addition, this appendix can be employed as a guide (or adapted to create a checklist) for the reader who is executing or participating in an information systems audit. The material here is based on methods used in professional environments that have succeeded in achieving high client satisfaction ratings and delivering quality audits.

To employ an automotive metaphor, the study material in the main chapters of this book may teach the reader about how a vehicle functions and relates to the road, while this appendix teaches the reader about driving.

Understanding the Audit Cycle

The information systems audit cycle is central to the profession of an IS auditor. The cycle itself could be executed by a single auditor, or the responsibilities could be distributed to many team members. In some professional situations, one or more sections discussed here may be unnecessary. The IS audit cycle described here is not the *only* cycle an IS auditor may perform, as the needs of different situations may require alternate procedures or approaches.

Candidates for the CISA exam will have had some experience with information systems auditing, but not all candidates will have had visibility into the whole end-to-end business process. Here, the stages of the cycle are illustrated as they would be considered by someone managing a professional audit.

For persons early in their professional career, this appendix unveils some of the stages that their supervisors may perform. Understanding these phases will help early career professionals see the big picture, deliver meaningful work, and hopefully hasten their advancement.

How the Information Systems Audit Cycle Is Discussed

Some components of an information systems audit cycle are uniform, regardless of the size of the client and the scope of the audit. Each stage discussed is a valid consideration during the course of performing a mildly complex audit project. This appendix provides a relevant audit skeleton, regardless of whether the auditor serves as an internal auditor within an organization or is brought in from outside the organization being audited. This is relevant for working on a variety of audit services, including SSAE16, SOX, OMB Circular A-123 auditing, financial audits, internal audit report writing, compliance audits, and other services.

Although the focus is on executing an audit involving controls testing, many project stages will apply when performing other projects where an information systems auditor's skills are required. It is not meant to be a complete reference when a project's needs go beyond the scope of this appendix. Additional procedures will be required to deliver services supporting other functions, such as enterprise-wide risk assessments, project life cycle evaluations, and disaster recovery planning.

For the sake of "telling the story," terms are introduced from outside of the CISA exam terminology.

 NOTE I will most often use the term "control testing," which is synonymous with auditing. "Testing" is the IS auditor's vernacular for auditing. It simply means to put a control to the test to see whether it is "effective." The effectiveness of a control is the opinion that the IS auditor develops after performing a test. The outcome of the test of a control will help the auditor know whether the control is being operated properly and that it contributes to the integrity of the control objective.

"Client" and Other Terms in This Appendix

This section explains how an experienced auditor's vernacular employs the versatile term "client" contextually so examples in this appendix are clear to the reader. In this appendix, the terms "client" and "client organization" refer to the business entity or departments within a project's scope.

- **Client** The organization, department(s), and individual persons being audited.
- **Client organization** The broader legal entity being audited. In some cases, this can be defined as subdepartments within a larger organization.

To say "in front of the client" can refer to being outside the building, in a meeting, or sitting with a control owner.

More specific terms are employed for parties encountered within client organizations. This will assist in this discussion of the information systems auditing process. In this appendix, I use the following definitions to categorize client personnel as having the following roles:

- **Audit sponsor** The person or committee within the client organization that has determined that the audit needs be performed. When audits are required by regulation, the lead executive (commonly the CFO or CIO) over the group being audited is most often the audit sponsor.
- **Audit audience** The party that will review and employ the information contained in a report.
- **Primary contact** The person who serves as the initial point of communication between the audit team and client organization's control managers and owners. They have the ability to schedule meetings and address issues, and may be provided regular status reports.
- **Control owners** The person(s) performing manual control activities or maintaining the successful performance of automated controls.
- **Control managers** The members of management who oversee control owners. They are ultimately responsible for ensuring the successful execution of control activities, and have a role in remediating issues discovered during testing.

"Client" as a Term for Internal Auditors

The term "client" usually implies parties are not under the same roof. In this appendix, "client" means the auditee—whether an audit is an external or internal audit. A department within a larger organization may be the audit "client." Audit reviewing procurement practices view the procurement department as the client.

With internal auditing, while the audit cycle will lack a bidding process, contract negotiation, and engagement letters, an auditor within an organization is still an independent party. Within this appendix, if there are points in the auditing process where there is a recognizable difference between performing work internally as opposed to externally, the difference is noted.

Overview of the IS Audit Cycle

This section describes the IS cycle, and covers background information that may be pertinent to an auditor's engagement. Included is a discussion on where audits originate and some of the particularities of different engagement types. Different reasons are addressed regarding why a client organization may initiate a project requiring the assistance of an IS auditor.

The IS audit cycle is a fairly standardized procedure, in that established steps are agreed upon as providing the basic structure for performing an information systems audit. Common milestones have been established. IS audit projects will involve some, if not all, of these milestones. This appendix explores the details of these milestones, but at a high level, they can be viewed as:

- Project origination
- Engagement letter or audit charter
- Risk-based planning
- Test plan development
- Performing testing
- Evaluating the results of testing
- Reporting audit findings
- Audit close and follow-up

Each of these stages is covered in more detail within this section.

Project Origination

This section addresses the origination of information systems audit projects. This is the beginning of the information systems audit cycle. The following service areas are included in this discussion, although some of these service areas are not fully covered in this appendix:

- External attestations
- Internal audits
- Incident response
- Disaster recovery planning
- Life cycle reviews
- Governance reviews
- Staffing arrangements

This appendix surveys how the need for audit work in each service area is identified and originates as a project. This continues with a discussion of how an auditor's help is solicited and their common roles in supporting certain projects.

NOTE   Central to the risk-based audit approach is the determination of audit objectives, performance of a risk assessment, and determination of audit scope. In some situations, part or all of these stages are performed before an audit project is launched. If the audit project is being performed by persons outside of this process, audit team members should have a clear understanding of how these stages lead to the audit.

External Attestations

An attestation is simply a statement made by an auditor that summarizes the results of the audit. Often, an attestation takes the form of a memo that is signed by an owner or partner in an auditing firm, or by the head of the audit department in the case of an internal audit.

Many organizations are required to have an audit by government regulation or contractual obligations. External auditors provide results free from the pressures of a management reporting relationship. Strict ethical, and sometimes legal, guidelines prohibit relationships that can impair independence, even in appearance. These measures seek to remove obstacles to an auditor's objectivity when confirming the existence of practices and assessing the operation of controls within their organization. Examples of these services include

- Financial audits
- Bank system controls testing
- Lending or equity arrangements
- SSAE16 and other specialized audits
- Certifications such as ISO and PCI

For external attestations services, a bid solicitation process is most commonly followed. The client organization issues a request for proposals (RFP) from external parties. The RFP will identify, at a high level, the scope of the work and some of the technologies involved. Proposals are collected and reviewed by the client organization, often including the audit sponsor and/or the primary contact. Proposals are vetted for approach, skills, terms, fees, expenses, and other considerations. The party selected by this process is then brought in to negotiate a contract (discussed further in the section, "Engagement Letters and Audit Charters").

Management's Need for an Independent Third Party

In addition to externally required attestations, the executive management of an organization can initiate projects for outside auditors. It is not uncommon for management to decide that a task should be handled by an independent third party. Management may have many reasons for hiring independent third parties to perform reviews, some of which include

- Unbiased
- Fresh perspective ("a new set of eyes")

- Professional perspective, if a certified or accredited auditor is employed
- Not employing the necessary skills in-house
- Answering inquiries by external parties (i.e., performing agreed-upon procedures)
- Support management decision-making (such as "buy versus build" and system selection decisions)
- Gain access to advice from outside professionals with deep industry experience

Projects at the request of management are likely to report to a CFO or CIO, as well as an internal audit director. Such projects may involve testing that supports goals that are not standard audit goals. It is important for auditors to be clear with a client regarding objectives and scope, and how to address requests for additional work.

Internal Audits

Internal audit (IA) departments usually report to the organization's audit committee or board of directors (or a similar "governing entity"). The IA department usually has close ties with (and possibly a "dotted line" reporting relationship to) finance leadership. This department will launch projects at the request of the governing entity and, to a degree, members of executive management.

Regulation plays a large role in internal audit work. For example, public companies, banks, and government organizations are all subject to a great deal of regulation, much of which requires regular information systems controls testing. Management, as part of their risk management strategy, also requires this testing. External reporting of the results of internal auditing is sometimes necessary.

A common internal audit cycle consists of several categories of projects:

- Risk assessments and audit planning
- Cyclical controls testing (SOX and A-123, for example)
- Review of existing control structures
- Operational and IS audits

The central function of an internal audit department is the entity-wide risk assessment process. Annually, an attempt is made to identify and weigh all risks to an organization. This process results in ranking the organization's "areas of greatest risk." This is provided to the governing entity (commonly the audit committee) to review and determine the scope of the organization's internal audit function. Areas of greater risk command more attention by the governing entity. They may choose to have the scope of the IA department's work address these areas.

It is common for the IA department to maintain a multiyear plan (as discussed in Chapter 3), in which it maintains a schedule of audits. The audit plan is shared with the governing entity, along with the risk assessment document, and the governing entity is asked to approve the IA department's plan. The governing entity may seek to include specific reviews in the IA department's audit plan at this point. When an audit plan is approved, the IA department's tasks for the year (and tentative tasks for future years) are now determined.

NOTE The IIA (Institute of Internal Auditors) has excellent guidance for audit planning at www.theiia.org.

Even if the risk assessment is carried out by other personnel, IS auditors are often included in a formal risk assessment process. Specific skills are needed to communicate with an organization's IT personnel regarding technology risks. IS auditors will use information from management to identify, evaluate, and rank an organization's main technology risks. The outcome of this process may result in IT-related specific audits within the IA department's audit plan. The governing entity may select areas that are financial or operational and that are heavily supported by information systems.

Internal audits may be launched using a project charter, which formalizes the project to audit sponsors, the auditors, and the managers of the department(s) subject to the audit.

NOTE Some governing entities may not have staff that understands technology risks. IS auditors may find they are educating governing entities on the natures of the risks they face.

Cyclical Controls Testing A great deal of effort has recently been expended getting organizations to execute a control testing cycle. Most frequently, these practices are supporting the integrity of controls in financially relevant processes. Public corporations have needed to comply with Sarbanes-Oxley Section 404 requirements, and U.S. government organizations have been subject to OMB Circular A-123, compliance with the Federal Information Security Management Act (FISMA), and other similar requirements. Countries outside of the United States have instituted similar controls testing requirements for publicly traded companies and governmental organizations. Many industries, such as banking, insurance, and health care, are likewise required to perform control testing.

Financial leadership is required to affirm that control testing cycles are operating successfully and that controls surrounding financial reporting are operating effectively. This includes control testing by qualified and independent auditors (common regulations require that a portion of the control testing require using an external IS auditor).

Organizations employ software tools to assist with tracking controls testing. These systems track the execution and success of control tests performed as part of a testing cycle, and can frequently manage archiving supporting evidence. Organizations may employ IS auditors to implement a system for tracking controls testing.

Many organizations have functioning internal audit departments. Most internal auditors come from a financial background and have limited knowledge of the practice of information systems auditing. Organizations that lack an existing internal audit department may outsource their whole internal audit function via the RFP process. IA departments may seek to augment their staff with IS auditors to cover internal shortcomings.

Establishing Control Testing Cycles   Young or growing organizations may not have established controls testing cycles. IS auditors will participate in the establishment of controls testing. The auditor produces documentation of controls through a series of meetings with management. During the process, auditors will develop process and controls documentation and confirm their accuracy with control owners.

These engagements are most likely to occur when companies prepare to go public. Such companies need to comply with Sarbanes-Oxley Section 302 requirements, which involve documenting controls and performing a test of existence, also known as a "test set of 1," for each identified key control.

Private companies will maintain SOX-equivalent documentation to retain the option of seeking public financing, or when lenders or private investors require it. Many organizations will find external resources for these tasks.

When auditors are bidding on engagements for establishing control testing cycles, there are uncertainties regarding the amount of time this process will take. Factors that can take unexpected amounts of time include

- Functions prove complex or disorganized.
- Documentation provided by management could be out of date.
- Control owners may be impatient with an auditor documenting their procedures.
- Control weaknesses and failures may be uncovered, requiring unplanned remediation.
- Fraud may be uncovered, resulting in project interruptions and turnover of control owners.

If management has documented procedures or experience with controls testing, this process will take less effort on the part of auditors.

 NOTE   Budgets and fee arrangements for these engagements should keep in mind how the degree of effort required may not be uncovered until auditors are in the field.

Reviewing Existing Controls   Control structures change as an organization and the regulatory landscape change. Outside the organization, a change in regulations may change the focus of certain processes and controls testing. Guidance covering SOX and A-123 auditing has changed over time. For example, recent changes by the American Institute of Certified Public Accountants (AICPA) and other organizations have shifted a greater degree of reliance upon monitoring controls. Within an organization, objectives may change, and with them the technologies and procedures. New systems or new lines of business may change which controls are most material. IS auditors are often asked to review and update the individual controls within a controls testing cycle. They will update wording and may advise management on how to bring the controls testing closer in line with external guidance.

Early SOX compliance efforts often led to long lists of control activities that would be considered excessive by today's standards. Older control structures predate more recent directives, causing an excessive testing burden for the organization. Business, process, and technology changes may have left parts of a control structure obsolete or not yet included. Organizations often seek assistance updating and "streamlining" their list of key control activities to realign their controls with both current regulatory directives and recent risk assessments. IS auditors may be tasked with updating controls documentation as an additional service while performing control tests.

Operational Audits   Operational audits are typically internal audits. These are internal reporting to management and/or an organization's governing committees, and can cover any area of the business. These reports are done at the request of a member of executive management or the governing entity, and may originate from the annual risk assessment and audit planning cycle. These audits often will be performed over a limited period, have a clearly specified scope, and result in issuing an internal audit report.

Operational audits require an auditor with experience in the function being audited. Many organizations will want to grow out their internal audit function from within their ranks so their auditors have a functional knowledge of the departments they audit. If an organization lacks an internal auditor, they will seek audit professionals with experience in their industry.

Such audits will employ whatever methods of testing or analysis support the audit's objectives, and may not include controls testing. Some examples of the objectives for operational and IS audits could include the following:

- Evaluate procedures within a department.
- Process reengineering within a complex function.
- Test compliance with policies.
- Prepare for a system implementation.
- Uncover internal inefficiencies.
- Perform data analysis for management decision-making.
- Identify improvement opportunities to existing systems.
- Detect fraud and the risk of fraud.

When an operational area relies heavily on supporting systems, it is common for a CISA to own part or all of the cycle of performing operational audits. For certain operational audits, a CISA's background with the operation is important. Familiarity with the business of the department and the procedures performed is often required. A project could require a CISA with a financial background or experience with certain financial business processes.

NOTE Operational audits requested by management are more likely to experience scope expansion during the course of the audit than other audits. The audit sponsor may determine that there is a need for more thorough analysis as preliminary test results are received. Both client and audit management may need to be made aware of resource constraints or competing priorities that may be deferred as a result of including additional work in the audit's scope.

Auditing Incident Response

Incidents can take many forms, and can include but are not limited to

- Internal and external hacking
- Network traffic failures
- Post-implementation problems
- Misuse of information systems
- Failure of key equipment
- Natural disasters

Many occurrences might lead to the formation of a "response team," sometimes referred to as a computer incident response team (CIRT). This team is assembled to involve the appropriate parties from within an organization to handle the issue. Internal auditors are often included in a CIRT.

An organization that has experienced an "incident" is unlikely to have a clear approach to how IS auditors can assist, but auditors often have a role to play in the aftermath of an incident. An unplanned damaging event often leads an organization to gather special teams. These teams will seek to assess, contain, and recover from the incident, as well as design and implement changes that will prevent future occurrences.

An IS auditor has skills that are useful in these situations, but it is important to recognize that some of the skills needed are beyond the scope of the CISA study materials. A CISA certification does not by itself provide the preparation needed for gathering forensic evidence or performing technological remediation. A person with a CISA certification may, with appropriate oversight, prove a useful assistant to a forensic auditor or other expert. An IS auditor does have the skills to assess where control structures broke down or were insufficient, and can assist in or advise while developing controls as part of remediation. Independence, however, must always be considered, even during an investigation. Once remediation has been implemented, the auditor can confirm controls are operating effectively.

Incidents can be embarrassing for an organization, and can affect their reputation and relationship with a customer base and with other organizations. During the course of remediation from an incident, it is not uncommon for executive management to hire external IS auditors to provide independent verification of the progress of remediation plans. Executive management can see this service as providing assurance to their customers and/or partners that they should be protected from the incident recurring.

Some "incidents" may be understood by executive management, but the necessary skills to perform remediation are in short supply—for example, a system implementation with faults requires an assessment independent of management responsible for the project, or an acquiring company has problems related to data migrated onto their systems from companies they acquired. It is not uncommon for a CISA to be contacted for these jobs. Some of these tasks can be handled by information systems auditing techniques; however, the more the task involves a consulting solution, the more it is likely to stray from the standard information systems auditing process. When an IS auditor is brought into these situations, they should be very clear about the scope of the work to be performed and ensure they have the appropriate skills at their disposal.

Project Life Cycle Reviews

Project life cycles are a central function of an IT department, and project management practices can come under review as part of risk assessments and other projects. Areas frequently addressed in project life cycle reviews include

- Tasks supporting implementing or upgrading existing software
- Software development life cycle (SDLC) methodology
- Asset management
- Change management
- Patch management of critical systems
- Configuration management

IT projects often involve a great investment on the part of an organization. The success of these projects can be critical to an organization's future well-being and may have a bearing on members of management's future with an organization. Management has a strong interest in ensuring that their investment in the project goes well.

An IS auditor can assess life cycle reviews to cover an IT department from a number of different angles. SDLC reviews can cover segregation of duties of project personnel, quality assurance measures, or a review of issues tracking tools and associated controls. Reviews may hope to learn whether certain project management "best practices" are followed, such as maintaining project plans and meeting minutes and capturing approvals on customization design documents. These audits may assess compliance with management's policies.

Examples of possible life cycle projects include the following:

- An organization has just implemented new financial accounting software. Financial auditors determine the change to systems is material and seek to gain an understanding of controls in the process of implementation. An IS auditor is called in to review project documentation and speak with key project personnel. The auditor will review scope documents, approvals for customizations, test plan records, issues tracking, and other key records from the process. The IS auditor reports to the financial audit team whether the process is well controlled, and the audit team incorporates this information into their test plan development.

- Internal audit may perform an IS review that addresses the controls in an organization's SDLC to ensure that proper review, approvals, version retention, and segregation of duties are performed in accordance with controls documentation.

- An organization is experiencing delays on an implementation project. Management is not sure whether this is due to the performance of the project manager or because of an underestimation of the project requirements. An independent reviewer is asked to speak with persons involved in the project and review project documents to provide feedback.

- A government agency is preparing to comply with new legislation and is hoping to clarify the scope of compliance projects. The new legislation will result in increased traffic through their agency. Agency management seeks to learn whether procedures and technology are prepared for the increased traffic. They don't have the bandwidth to task their own people with the review, so they hire outside reviewers to report on what changes are necessary and what changes may be desired.

- An organization's network security has been successfully compromised by ethical hackers ("ethical hackers" is a term signifying a professional services firm hired to test an organization's security controls). Management has committed to performing remediation activities to prevent future intrusions. IT management is strengthening existing controls and pursuing projects that aim to institute new control measures. IS auditors are brought in at the request of executive management to validate IT management's claims regarding the successful implementation of controls measures.

Life cycle reviews may be covered in part by methods discussed in this appendix, but some reviews may require procedures not addressed here.

Implementation Problems   Problems from system implementations and data conversions are common, and management may be strapped to remediate the issues. Client management may seek the help of IS auditors as additional bandwidth.

Here is an example: A company is acquiring smaller competitors and migrating their information systems into one consolidated system. Attempts to report using migrated data show problems in the underlying data. Auditors are tasked with learning about the process and controls related to correctly loading data sets onto the system. The auditor will then test report data and attempt to identify the specific problems.

These tasks can be handled by information systems auditing techniques. The more the task involves a consulting-style solution, the more the project is likely to stray from the standard information systems audit process. When an IS auditor is brought into these situations, the auditor should be very clear about the scope of the work to be performed and ensure they have the appropriate skills to deliver on the task at hand.

IT and IS Governance Reviews

Often, IT and IS governance reviews are required by external regulations. Governance reviews are usually focused on management's risk management and performance measurement responsibilities. Financial auditing procedures require governance evaluations. An auditor's risk analysis could identify information systems as an area material to an organization's control structure, such as within an e-commerce company.

Management's risk analysis could also identify areas of IT governance to review. Management could request that an internal audit department or external reviewers be requested to assess whether an IT department is aligned with a company's strategies or is delivering appropriate value for an organization's investment in IT.

A few examples of IT governance projects include the following:

- Management is facing some long-term budgeting decisions, possibly including eliminating positions. Rather than determining which positions to eliminate, management finds an independent party to provide an impartial perspective on the value each of the groups within the IT department provides. They want IS auditors to provide feedback on whether each group within IT is efficiently delivering value to the organization and is appropriately sized.

- A manufacturing company is preparing for growth. The IT department has not changed much since the company was small. Management wants an outside reviewer to recommend ways to "tune up" the IT department ahead of the expansion. Management hopes IS auditors will identify key IT risks facing expansion and work on developing an IT governance structure appropriate for a larger organization.

- Auditors are asked to review management's security policies and offer recommendations for improvement.

Organizations may seek the help of IS auditors to provide recommendations to strengthen their governance function.

Staff Augmentation

When an organization has the ability to oversee the work of an IS auditor but needs "hands on deck" to get work accomplished, they may opt for outsourced staffing arrangements. It is not uncommon to temporarily requisition the help of a skilled IS auditor to support controls testing or to serve on special teams (such as a CIRT). In this situation, the IS auditor reports directly to management in a client organization. In these situations, the auditor may perform a limited part of the information systems auditing cycle.

 NOTE Information systems audit services will change over time. New audit practices are sure to be introduced with changes in technology, business, regulation, and the economy as other practices become obsolete or dated. Recent history includes the rapid emergence of Sarbanes-Oxley work as companies implement SOX compliance. There is still considerable work in this subject area, though it has decreased.

Engagement Letters and Audit Charters

Engagement letters govern the terms of the audit engagement when external auditors are used. This section lists a few of the general terms and goes into more detail on a few subjects of interest to auditors. General subject areas addressed within the engagement letter include

- Distribution of the report
- Rates, time estimates, and fees
- Ownership of workpapers
- Terms for addendums
- Nondisclosure agreements
- Audit charters

Audit organizations and client organizations will both review a contract, and each party may require specific wording. Some contract negotiations can prove lengthy.

When audits are externally required, the party serving as audit sponsor may not be supportive of the audit. In these situations, the audit may not be welcomed by the primary contact or the control managers. Thus, it can be beneficial to give extra attention to

- Audit terms on turn-around time for requests
- Availability of control owners and other key personnel
- The relationship with the primary contact

 NOTE This is not a legal discussion and makes no claim to be legal advice, but is rather a general discussion about the contents and nature of standard engagement letters. Additional legal clauses that may be required in an engagement letter are not discussed in this book.

Distribution of the Audit Report

The outcome of an audit is an audit report, a written explanation of the audit project, including the project's objectives, the controls tested, and the auditor's opinion of the effectiveness of each control. Most audit reports are solely for use by an organization's management and governing entities. Reports will contain language reflecting the limited distribution and use of the report. The audit organization will only reply to inquiries regarding the report with members of management and no other parties. For example, the cover sheet and the footer on each page of the report can include the following phrase:

> "This report is restricted to business use by management of XYZ Corporation and is not to be relied upon by any other party for any purpose."

Certain reports, such as an SSAE16 (formerly SAS70) report, *are* for distribution to third parties. The engagement letter will state clearly the terms under which parties are permitted to receive these reports, and will provide a process for getting permission from the audit organization if they seek to provide the report to another party.

As an example of contract terms surrounding a report, SSAE16 clients are forbidden from distributing a report to parties other than those using the control information in the SSAE16 report for management's review and to provide to their financial auditors. This means client organizations are not permitted to share this report with a potential client as a marketing tool without express written permission from the audit organization. If management does distribute a report beyond the terms of the engagement letter, the audit organization is no longer responsible for the content of that report if relied upon by a nonpermitted third party.

Rates, Time Estimates, and Fees

Part of an engagement letter will address the billing for services. Many attestation engagements are fixed-fee engagements, although additional billings may be agreed upon with time budget overruns. Many nonattestation (in other words, professional services instead of audit) engagements will bill based on hourly rates. Rates could be blended across teams, or could identify individual rates for specific resources. The contract could identify the degree of detail the client will receive on their statement.

Expenses are usually addressed in this section. Any conditions on expenses will be spelled out here. Clients may only permit certain kinds of expenses, or may ask for invoices with itemizations. Clients often select nearby audit firms that can provide resources without incurring travel or lodging expenses. Larger audits may draw resources from all over the country, and may not flinch at sizeable expense bills.

Ownership of Workpapers

For external auditors, ownership of workpapers is different in attestation and internal audit engagements.

When a certified professional is signing off on an audit, they retain ownership of workpapers because they may be asked to defend their opinion with evidence. In some engagements, auditors may not have a problem providing a copy of part or all of the workpapers to management. Audit documentation of procedures is sometimes shared with management, and the documentation of test results beyond the report may be shared with management to support remediation efforts. In some external audits, no audit workpapers are shared, such as a bank requiring compliance testing from service providers.

Internal audit engagements are services done on behalf of management, and management retains ownership of audit documentation. Traditional audit practices keep paper records, although increasingly IA departments keep only electronic copies of workpapers.

The ownership and sharing of workpapers will be addressed in the engagement letter.

Terms for Addendums

Most contracts prepare for the possibility that they can be extended with an addendum. The addendum can increase or remove scope, extend deadlines, and add audit cycles based on the terms of the original engagement letter.

Nondisclosure Agreements

Because auditors gain access to proprietary information during the course of the audit, they are almost always bound by nondisclosure agreements (NDAs). These may be signed by the individual auditors, or for auditing firms, and they may be signed at an engagement level covering all team members. It is worth noting that NDAs usually do not cover disclosure to legal authorities if fraud or other illegal activities are discovered during an audit.

NOTE Audit firms often sign blanket NDAs for their personnel. Audit firms using these often do not permit their auditors to sign individual nondisclosure forms. When auditors arrive at a client for the first time and are provided contracts to sign, they may need to address the requirement with audit management. Audit firm lawyers may wish to avoid nonapproved language, as well as avoid having their auditors signing individual contracts with a client.

Audit Charters

Audit charters are used for projects internal to an organization. Internal audit projects will often employ an audit charter. They prove useful to ensure management's buy-in within an organization. Audit charters provide assistance to the project by communicating and formalizing the following:

- Sponsorship by executive management
- The goals of the project
- The planned time frame for audit activities
- Obligations of team members
- Expectations of team members

Chartered projects will often be kicked off with a meeting or a social event. This will help the team by allowing introductions to be made between team members in different departments. The event also serves to promote teamwork and reinforce the goals, obligations, and expectations of the project.

When an outsourced IS audit resource is brought in to a chartered audit project, it is important that the auditor become familiar with the audit charter. This will allow the auditor to understand what has been communicated to client management and control owners.

NOTE Software implementation projects involving multiple departments may also employ a similar project charter. IS auditors may be brought into projects working under a project charter as well.

Ethics and Independence

It is important that the auditor maintain independence from the client organization in both fact and appearance. This appendix will provide a few examples, but to comprehensively address the subject, refer to the discussion on ethics, independence, and the ISACA Code of Ethics in Chapter 3.

Independence in Fact

Avoiding issues of independence in "fact" is rather straightforward. An auditor may not audit their own work, and may not report on testing if the subject of testing is a function owned or managed within their reporting relationship. The auditor may not design or be part of implementing controls and be called on to test those controls. Some examples of this include the following:

- An auditor has had the responsibility of implementing the new AR (accounts receivable) module as part of the ERP (enterprise resource planning) implementation team; the auditor should not be performing control reviews on this system.

- An auditor has been tasked with the daily monitoring of the firewall log. They may not perform testing as to whether the firewall log is regularly monitored.

- An auditor has a reporting relationship with a control manager. The auditor may not test controls managed by that control manager.

In addition, one should avoid testing the work of control owners or control managers when the auditor has family, intimate personal relationships, or external business relationships involved.

Independence in Appearance

Avoiding issues of independence in "appearance" is where an auditor faces more challenges. Gifts from the client are one area where judgment can be required. Fortunately, an auditor often is able to lean upon workplace policies in such situations. Common workplace policies include forbidding gifts over certain values and getting permission to accept certain gifts (such as tickets to a baseball game). Regardless of policies, an auditor must exhibit care when accepting gifts. A few examples are discussed here.

- The client organization's CFO offers the team coffee mugs with the company's new logo. Since this item has a limited cost and has marginal value, and is also a promotional tool for the company, there should not be an issue of independence in appearance.

- A control manager at the company offering to pay for a coffee may be a limited and acceptable gift.

- The CFO met the audit team for dinner and covered the bill. This can be acceptable as team building. The CFO then seeks to fund a night on the town with drinks and entertainment; this may be perceived as crossing the line.

- Small talk with a control owner about their office decorations leads to them offering you a gift from their collection of sports memorabilia. This could be perceived by the client as impairing independence.

 NOTE   This is a subject of broad debate. An auditor should be aware of his or her audit organization's rules and guidelines regarding ethics, independence, and acceptable behavior.

Launching a New Project: Planning an Audit

A new project is on the table. The client wants auditors to start work soon, and so the process begins. Often in external audits, clients will limit the information provided until engagement letters and nondisclosure agreements have been signed. Most external audit organizations severely limit the amount of work auditors are permitted to perform on a project before the client has signed the engagement letter. So valuable time is not wasted, management waits until both the audit firm and the client have a clear and formal understanding on the scope and purpose of the audit.

 NOTE   Planning for an internal audit with internal resources is similar to an external audit without needing to address cost and payment terms. Otherwise, most of the planning elements are nearly the same.

Understanding the Client's Needs

When a client organization decides that an audit is needed, they will usually describe their needs in writing and use a formal or informal selection process to choose an auditor. This selection process is centered on communication between the audit organization and the client about the client's needs. A client needing a signed attestation still looks for the best audit firm for their "needs." A client has reasons in addition to price to consider when selecting an audit firm. If an audit firm does not have experience in their industry or technologies, the auditors may not work effectively with management. If a client is the smallest in an auditor's book of business, they might be concerned about the level of service they will receive. A firm may be selected because of experience with an area of a client's needs that are peripheral to the audit scope, and management's decision to perform such an audit could relate to these needs. Understanding the reasons behind an audit can be important to successful planning and meeting client expectations.

A client organization may open up with more detailed reasons once auditors are selected and nondisclosure agreements are signed. Having such conversations with the primary contact or the audit sponsor early in the audit can provide valuable information to the audit team.

Some examples of a client organization's needs that may factor into an audit include

- Augment documentation of new or changed procedures.
- Get an internal audit function operating.
- Update an outdated controls infrastructure.
- Assist in the education of a new executive.
- Support a financing relationship.
- Repair relationships damaged by a previous control failure.
- Meet contract conditions by providing an audit report by a certain date.

Knowing the reason behind management's decision to perform an audit will allow audit personnel to

- Better understand the client's risk environment.
- Provide more useful feedback on their controls structure.
- More accurately plan for the audit.
- Focus extra testing on the most critical control objectives.
- Meet client expectations and deadlines.

IT managers frequently ask their auditor about how they compare with their peers.

Preliminary Discussions

Preliminary discussions between audit management and client management will set the stage for how well the parties will work together. It is important at this phase to anticipate challenges that may be faced during the audit. Common things to address in these initial discussions are

- Clarifying scope by confirming an understanding of client needs and their risk environment
- Acquiring more detailed information on employed technology and a deeper understanding of how it supports the organization's objectives
- Establishing engagement procedures, such as scheduling control owner time and requesting documentation
- Setting expectations, such as frequency and depth of status reports and review of testing exceptions

Both the client and the audit manager have an important investment in the success of this phase. The client organization is hoping to maximize the benefit of the service, so they may identify areas where they would seek professional advice. The client representative may aim to minimize internal disruptions and ask the auditor to observe certain practices.

Understand the Technologies Employed

The audit manager uses information on employed technologies when developing the audit plan and when assigning resources to test controls.

When involving an external auditor, a client's selection process will limit the amount of information they share publicly about their systems. If there is a bidding process, it may permit formal or informal Q&A, where answers will be provided in response to vendor inquiries for the purposes of estimating effort. When the audit is launched and NDAs are signed, the client should be willing to share relevant documentation and information freely.

An audit manager also will be gathering information on the nature of testing that will be performed. Some questions an audit manager may consider include

- What kind of security testing is required
- What kind of process evaluation is required
- What kind of application testing is required

- What relevant customizations exist
- Are any in-house developed technologies employed

In these preliminary discussions, the audit manager needs to gather more specific information on the technologies involved and the testing to be performed. The version numbers, implementation dates, and an idea of the transaction volumes are useful information. The audit manager will use such information during audit planning.

Performing a Risk Assessment

A risk assessment process takes into account the innate risks of a certain operation and considers information from within the organization. Auditors will weigh information from several sources when performing a risk assessment, as illustrated in Figure A-1.

It is common to have financial information available for the purpose of assessing the materiality of certain activities. Here are some examples:

- An organization may have extensive automated transactions in revenue and have very few assets tracked within their asset management system. Therefore, there is less innate risk surrounding asset tracking, but thorough attention needs to be given to the systems supporting the revenue cycle. There could be a high-risk of data redundancy or incomplete capture of information in the event of system failure.

- A debt collection service outsources the software maintenance for their core collections-processing software to a software vendor. Therefore, risks relating to change management controls surrounding their core systems are reduced. However, because it is a high-transaction environment, data backup and restoration controls are elevated in criticality.

A risk assessment is arguably the most important aspect of an audit. Without a risk assessment, high-risk situations may not be addressed sufficiently during an audit. Management may not realize the opportunity to reduce serious risks.

Figure A-1
Different
considerations in a
risk assessment

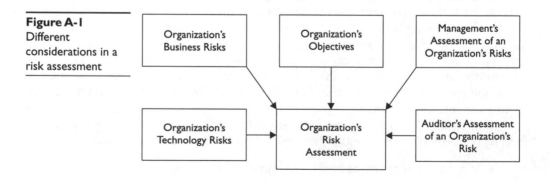

> **NOTE** In certain situations, it may be necessary for a financial auditor to participate in the risk assessment so that certain business risks that may not be obvious to the IS auditor can be identified. In addition, a financial auditor can help an IS auditor determine which systems controls are most material in a financially based risk assessment.

Audit Methodology

Audit methodologies are designed by audit management and standardize how parts of audits are performed. Methodologies are the procedures used by the audit team to perform an audit. They can be as simple as requiring scope to be documented and approved, to employing audit software and detailed procedures that govern the entire audit process.

ISACA considers the following items so central to the audit process that all audits will at least generate documented statements addressing

- Audit charter
- Audit scope
- Audit objectives
- Audit testing program

Audit organizations that regularly provide certain services will standardize methodologies for performing their audits. These methodologies can assist an organization in ensuring completeness, maintaining standards, and streamlining the process of management's review of audit work that is done.

Methodologies can include policies, procedures, software tools, templates, checklists, and other means of providing uniformity across the audit process. These methodologies are documented and taught to new members of the organization.

Documented methodologies can serve to govern many stages of the process, such as

- Bidding on RFPs
- Risk assessments
- Scope
- Objectives
- Resource allocations
- Comprehensiveness of testing
- Sample size guidelines for testing
- Report templates
- Completion checklists

Methodologies will provide a structure for achieving milestones within the audit process. For example:

- **Risk assessment**   An audit firm's risk assessment approach involves employing a spreadsheet predesigned to compute an aggregate score from several different risk measurements. Form letters may be used to communicate with management and collect their feedback on the client organization's risks. Management's feedback can be populated into the spreadsheet along with auditors' assessments, and the risks are ranked.

- **Budget**   A budget tracks time and rates incurred by auditors. This will be developed initially in the RFP process and updated in the planning process. Actual time incurred will be compared with the budget so audit management can better understand how to plan for future engagements.

- **Lead sheets**   Lead sheets are intake forms used by auditors to capture and organize test information. They provide a uniform method to represent test results and enable audit management to perform a formulaic review of test results.

- **Testing standards**   In order to maintain a rigorous standard of testing to support their reputation, an audit organization institutes testing standards. These standards require different methods of testing in order to pass a control test. Testing methods are identified as follows: collaborative inquiry, observation, inspection, and reperformance. In addition, each control objective must be supported by one form of substantive testing.

- **Auditing software**   Large audit organizations frequently enforce their audit methodology with software that attempts to accommodate as much of the audit process as possible. These programs may accommodate most audit possibilities and enforce that certain procedures be executed by the audit team. They may even manage images of workpapers so that the software captures all audit documentation.

Methodologies used by audit firms may be designed to meet requirements published by regulatory organizations, such as the AICPA or the U.S. government's Office of Management and Budget.

Developing the Audit Plan

An audit plan is a project plan designed for performing an IS audit. The audit plan, like a project plan, is a tool for tracking tasks and forecasting the time and resource needs of the audit process. It will describe the audit methodology to be used and lay out milestones and the sequential dependencies for the different tasks within the audit. The plan is updated with progress milestones, and may be adjusted with certain audit changes.

In addition to serving as a high-level audit plan, in the beginning, the audit plan serves to organize the stages of risk assessment, audit objectives, and the initial assessment of client procedures.

The audit plan does not track the detail of audit testing—this is tracked in the audit testing matrix and the lead sheets.

Gathering Information—"PBC" Lists

A "Provided by Client" (PBC) list is a common tool used by auditors for managing information requested from the client. It provides a consolidated list that the auditor can use as a record of request for process documents and records, and provides an effective checklist for tracking receipt of information. It will also help a primary contact manage fulfillment of auditor information requests. Several PBC lists may be needed during an audit. PBC lists should be dated when they are delivered, and, if possible, they should document an agreed-upon delivery date.

Initial Information Requests

At the beginning of an audit, the auditor will require information about the organization. Common requests include

- Organizational charts
- Company directory
- Controls documentation
- System documentation
- Relevant reports or other information

This information will be used to prepare for and execute the audit. The list may also identify documents that a client has indicated exist, such as an information security policy document.

A Client's Preparedness for an Audit

When an organization is facing their first audit, auditors frequently include in their plans an evaluation of the client's preparedness. A client may have a need for an audit, but may not be prepared. In attestation situations, the client organization may not yet be ready for an audit. A few possible examples of this include the following:

- A company hopes to undergo an initial SSAE16 audit, but the control infrastructure is not yet documented or in place.
- A company has experienced significant growth. New ways have been devised to perform key processes. Procedures are inconsistent, and documentation is incomplete.
- Changes to business products, processes, and supporting technologies have left controls documentation out-of-date.
- New control procedures have been only partly implemented.
- Logging in key systems hasn't been configured correctly, so there is inadequate capture or retention of audit information.
- There has been turnover of key control owners or control managers.

If a client organization's support for an audit is below par, the first order of business is housekeeping. If the engagement letter does not account for providing services to help the client prepare, it may be necessary to delay the launch of an audit. Some challenges may be addressed by expanding the scope of the engagement letter to include the auditors providing assistance (such as with updating procedures) ahead of an audit. This is, however, a tricky issue: in an attestation or external audit, this is most frequently not possible or desirable due to independence or regulatory issues—auditors can't audit the structures they help to develop.

Developing Audit Objectives

An audit's objectives clarify the goals of the audit. Audit objectives also ensure the audit complies with applicable standards, laws, or regulations. Objectives are clarified in a formal document and retained in project workpapers. The objectives provide a basis for measuring the success of testing, and are central to an audit report's opinion.

Objectives are developed by giving consideration to several different sources:

- The engagement letter or audit charter will address the nature of the subject of testing and the expectations of reporting, and provides a central pillar to an audit's objectives. This may focus on external security, operating effectiveness, or the correctness of transactions and processing.

- At this point, auditors will understand the nature of the client organization's business and have discussed the key processes at a high level.

- An overall understanding of the organization's risks from the risk assessment process will be incorporated.

- An understanding of a client's needs for launching the audit will also be considered. This may reveal the goals of management in conducting the audit or clarify the nature of a third-party's interests in the outcome of the report.

Statements of audit objectives may incorporate additional perspectives. Figure A-2 illustrates how an audit objective is developed through the consideration of many information sources.

For example, an audit engagement letter identifies a client as needing controls documentation and limited financial controls testing. Auditors are aware of new financial systems. The risk assessment shows that financial auditors annually perform test proce-

Figure A-2 Audit objectives are developed using information from several sources.

dures on manual and automatic controls within the financial software of an organization. Conversations with management reveal that they hope to update documentation, confirm the success of their system implementation, and provide financial auditors with a report that shows system controls are operating effectively so that they can reduce the scope and cost of the financial audit. The objectives of the audit will be focused on updating procedure and controls documentation for the new system and testing new software controls.

Developing the Scope of an Audit

An audit's scope is documented in a series of statements addressing the processes and/or systems to be reviewed and to what depth. It will address how to enact the audit's objectives. The stages leading to the development of an audit's scope are illustrated in Figure A-3.

A risk assessment has identified the areas with the greatest risk, so an audit scope will be constructed to address areas of greater risk. For example, testing of low-risk areas may focus on a small number of key controls when more robust testing is called for in areas with greater risk.

Similar to casting a net, the scope statement will identify what is included under the net and set the boundaries of what is outside it. A well-defined scope will assist in the development of focused test plans.

Examples of project scope statements include

- Testing addresses internal and external access to key systems, including procedures to set up accounts within Active Directory, password controls, VPN administration, and reviewing the network configuration and the firewall rule base. Not included in the scope are inquiries into firewall rule-base areas beyond those controlling external access, application access beyond network connectivity, or network penetration tests.

- Controls surrounding files feeding financial information into the financial system are the focus of testing. This includes testing controls and validating report values from systems in the revenue cycle, billing, and AP, which are managed outside of the financial system. Excluded will be any testing of data once it is within the financial system.

If, for some reason, testing issues reveal a need to go beyond the scope of an audit, auditors and the client will need to discuss the expansion of scope. This can happen when controls fail and compensating controls need to be tested. When auditors are externally sourced, any augmentation of scope will need to be formalized through a signed addendum to the engagement letter.

Figure A-3 Audit objective and risk assessment help to determine audit scope.

NOTE A client organization may set scope rather than let it be determined by an IS auditor. An example of this is when auditors are brought in to perform an already determined set of tests.

Prior Period Issues

When an audit fails a test, succeeding audits will retest the failed test. When developing scope, audit reports from a prior period must be reviewed so auditors understand which issues require revisiting. An exception from a prior period may have been fixed, in which case audit documentation and testing plans may need to adjust to changes. Projects remediating issues to primary controls may be in-process, so only secondary controls are available for testing.

Expanding Scope

In certain audits, such as internal audit reports, management may have some leeway in changing the scope during the reporting period. Understanding procedures or testing exceptions may reveal an area where management needs to dig deeper. It may be more economical to augment the current audit than to perform a procedure as part of a subsequent, currently unscheduled audit. Auditors are most likely available and are currently immersed in the procedures. Management may wish to push deeper to get to the root of an issue immediately.

Developing a Test Plan

When an audit's scope has been approved, it's time to develop a test plan. This section covers stages that go into developing the test plan. The test plan involves the following stages:

- Understand the controls environment.
- Identify control objectives and the client's supporting controls to be tested.
- Confirm an understanding of controls and identify test evidence.
- Prepare the testing program document for testing.

Audits that are performed on a cycle may base much of their test plan work on plans used in prior audits. However, auditors must avoid any temptation to simply reuse an audit plan. It is very important that an auditor revisit audit objectives and reevaluate the scope of an audit for each audit cycle. Failure to do so can lead to serious audit problems when testing performed fails to satisfy audit objectives.

Understanding the Controls Environment

When an auditor is preparing the test plan, information is drawn from several sources. If the audit is not in its initial year, documentation will be available from previous audits. Auditors who have performed the same audit in prior periods will have historical knowledge. Client management is consulted to update procedure and controls documentation as well as identify the control owners.

When auditors collect information on the controls environment, they often use PBC lists. Upon review, auditors may find provided information falls short of an auditor's needs, requiring additional information requests. Shortfalls might be due to procedures that are new to the control structure or that have not been previously tested. It is common for auditors to meet with client management during this process.

Understanding the Client's Procedures

An auditor must understand a procedure before she can effectively plan and perform testing. Auditors begin by reviewing information provided by the client. Procedure documentation may be provided in a number of different forms:

- **Financial audit write-ups** CFOs usually keep copies of the process documentation generated by financial auditors. It is common for a CFO to make these available to audit teams when areas are in scope. These could also include written procedures and systems-level documentation.

- **Internal audit documentation** If the internal audit department tests controls on a cycle, the department keeps procedure documentation regarding the controls they test. Other auditors can benefit greatly from this documentation when it is within an audit's scope.

- **Management procedure documentation** Management may have procedure documentation, such as instructional or reference material for employees. A department's policies may contain procedure documentation. Management may also retain procedure documentation from previous auditors.

- **Instruction manuals** When management trains many people to perform the same procedures, a training department may provide instruction to employees. Training material may provide instruction on control procedures that are within the scope of the audit.

- **Checklists** Management may oversee a process with a checklist. If these are provided, they will offer a high-level understanding to auditors (as well as provide evidence of a controlled environment), but follow-up is likely to be required.

Other sources may provide information on procedures as well.

An auditor must understand a procedure in the context of the audit. The impact of a procedure in relation to the audit objectives is important when understanding controls within the procedure. This will affect the degree or depth of testing that should be employed.

Many auditors bring to the table experience with procedures performed (or technologies employed) at other organizations. An auditor who has experience elsewhere can often more quickly understand a similar procedure (or technology) in a new environment. Such experience can also assist by being available to a junior auditor who is responsible for a subject for the first time.

Understanding the Technology Environment

With an understanding of a business procedure, an auditor can then understand how technology is employed to support it. Procedure documentation will often identify existing systems at a high level. To develop an audit program, the audit team needs to "look under the hood." A PBC list may have been sent to the IT department. Conversations with IT may be required to identify what kind of information they keep on their systems. Possible sources of information include

- **Audit documentation**   Previous audits of different kinds may have documented certain processes within IT. Because of the speed at which many IT environments change, information from an audit a few years back may no longer be relevant.

- **Network and system diagrams**   Information about network and data security can be provided in network diagrams. All network documentation should be dated, and auditors should be sure to inquire about its accuracy and completeness. Diagrams can help an auditor quickly identify areas where they will need a greater depth of information.

- **System inventories**   An IT department may keep a consolidated list of the systems they support. System inventories are performed to different depths and may not contain exactly the information an auditor seeks, but they are often useful tools for drilling into that information. One can review items on the list and inquire as to their relevance to procedures, or identify where a system's data resides, or whether it is on a standard backup schedule.

- **Management's procedure documentation**   Management may have formalized certain procedures as part of developing a controlled environment. This information, when available, is often quite useful.

- **Disaster recovery plans**   IT departments may have formalized within disaster recovery plans certain procedures to be performed in the event of an incident. At times these reflect common procedures performed by management. An auditor may find relevant procedure, technology, and controls information from reviewing a disaster recovery plan.

It is important for an auditor to validate understandings based on documentation received from IT personnel.

In addition to being outdated, it is not uncommon for IT documentation to come up short of auditors' needs. A few examples include the following:

- Documentation may reveal that data entry and processing controls are employed within PeopleSoft, but it might not identify the Linux-hosted Oracle database on the back end, which should be included when testing data security.

- A written description of network security controls might identify the Cisco PIX firewall, but might omit it being used in series with an intrusion prevention system.

These clarifications are important for a test plan to be well designed. It is not uncommon for auditors to sit down with members of IT leadership at this phase to confirm the understanding of key systems and how they are managed.

Changes to IT Environments

Technologies and technological procedures change with some regularity. If the auditors learn of changes, they should be sure to address them with client IT personnel. Conversations with IT should address the landscape of current IT projects and review whether they will have an impact on testing controls.

New system implementations must be considered carefully when designing test procedures. When new systems are employed, there are many questions regarding the success of the deployment. Auditors may seek to review life cycle controls employed during a development process to determine if the system's implementation method introduces control risks. With new systems, there is a risk that documentation was not updated to reflect the use of a new system, or that management shared documentation produced ahead of the system going live. "To-be" documentation could contain claims that certain controls exist that were actually omitted from the production launch.

In addition, it is important to know of systems that are due to be implemented before or during a testing period. These can prove problematic to testing plans, as there could be an interruption or a change in control structures with a new system. For example: An SSAE16 engagement is testing controls over a long period, typically 12 months. Control objectives are signed off by management ahead of the testing period, and they include performing weekly backups. Four months into the testing period, the IT department upgrades their backup software. In doing so, they change the cycle of backups. This introduces a number of problems:

- **Lack of testing evidence**   The old backup system may have housed records on success and failure of backup jobs. If the system has been retired, records of backup success and failure might no longer be available when auditors request evidence.

- **Outdated control objectives**   Control objectives and control activities might be outdated as documented. The control objective reads that full backups are performed weekly, but the newly implemented practice performs daily incremental backups and full backups only every two weeks. This new practice could fail the stated control objective.

- **Outdated controls and control failures**   The IT department may have encountered problems with the new software performing backups on certain technologies, and may, for a period, fail to perform backups of systems hosted on certain critical servers.

An auditor is now challenged with how to report on the failure, and client management disputes that they should fail a control objective when they have a reasonable controls structure in place. With a full understanding of IT plans, auditors might have worked with the client to accommodate the changes. Appropriate controls language could have been used, and coordination with management might have ensured the transition did not interfere with the audit.

Controls and Control Objectives

Controls are selected for testing because they support a control objective. The control objective is achieved when testing shows tested controls are operating effectively. When building a test plan, auditors organize controls they will test by their support of control objectives.

Controls are implemented to mitigate risks within an organization. Multiple controls often work together to mitigate risks within a process or procedure. The control objective statement summarizes the risk-mitigation goals of controls within a procedure. The control objectives will collectively support the audit's objectives.

For use in the test plan, control objectives are listed with their supporting controls. This is depicted in the example in Table A-1.

Though not all engagements will involve auditors developing lists of control objectives and control activities, many will involve auditors reviewing and providing the client organization feedback on existing controls.

Developing Control Objectives and Supporting Controls When an auditor is tasked with developing the control objectives and the list of controls to test, they must keep the audit's objectives and scope in mind. It is important that control objectives be properly phrased to both reflect the actual control activities performed by management and support the audit objectives.

When examining existing control objectives and control activities, the auditor should determine if each control activity actually supports the control objective. Control activities can exist within procedures that do not support, or poorly support, the control objective. Any such control activities should be removed from the list. A replacement control may need to be identified so an objective is effectively supported. If an auditor experiences trouble in this area, they should consult upward within their organization.

CO #	Control Objective	Control #	Control Description
1	Full data backups are performed weekly and securely stored off-site.	1.1	Backup e-mails alerts to the backup administrator when jobs are not successful. The backup administrator follows up on issues and records them in the issues tracking system.
		1.2	Backup tapes are numbered and numbers are kept in the tape log. The location of backup tapes is tracked in the tape log.
		1.3	Backup tapes are kept physically secure behind locked doors with limited access. When transferred to storage, they are locked in metal boxes.
		1.4	Tapes are stored securely off-site.

Table A-1 Control Objectives and Their Supporting Controls

With the list of supporting controls, the auditor should determine if any of these controls ultimately perform the same function. If two control activities protect against the same problem, the auditor should determine which one should be selected as the key control and remove the other one from the list. An auditor may wish to learn which of these controls can be more efficiently tested before selecting equal controls as key. Management may agree that one of the controls is redundant and elect to cease performing one of them.

 NOTE There are different methods one can follow to arrive at sets of control objectives and control activities. Only one approach is conveyed here.

Key Controls and Compensating Controls

Compensating controls are valuable to identify during this phase of audit planning. When a control failure occurs, the organization relies on a compensating control, which is a secondary measure that mitigates the same risks addressed by the key control. A good test to determine if a control is a compensating control is whether a failure of the key control is caught by the compensating control.

An example of a key control is an access card that is required to enter the data center. The access card is a key control for securing the data center. In the event a person is able to follow someone through a door and gain access to the data center, locked doors on server racks within the data center may be an effective compensating control that can still provide a degree of physical security.

In the event of a control failure of a key control, a compensating control can be considered for testing to determine the materiality of the failure of the key control.

Reviewing Control Objectives and Supporting Controls

Over time an organization will change elements of its controls infrastructure. Control structures may evolve due to changes in the organization's business model, changes in management, or possibly in response to guidance from governing entities, such as how guidance on SOX controls testing now emphasizes a greater focus on governance and monitoring.

When an auditor is tasked with reviewing a control structure, her goal is to make three key determinations:

- Do control activities correctly support management's activities
- Do control activities support the control objectives
- Do the control objectives effectively mitigate risks

Auditors usually provide feedback to management on how the client can improve the wording of certain controls. Problems with the control structure could be identified, and management may need to institute additional control measures. Occasionally, auditors will determine that two controls mitigate the same risk and one of them can be relegated to the level of compensating control, be omitted from testing, or even be eliminated from management's control structure altogether.

Helping a Client Understand and Identify Controls Client management often has the obligation of writing and maintaining their control objectives and control activities. In these situations, auditors often still need to evaluate whether the provided control structure is sound and pertinent to the goals of the audit.

An IS auditor coming in to audit a new organization must keep in mind that not all organizations employ the skills to understand, identify, and document controls. Client organizations may be seeking the assistance of outside auditors to update or even write their controls documentation. If this is the case, auditors should make sure the engagement letter identifies this service.

Certain engagements, such as SSASE16, agreed-upon procedures (AUPs), and external (outsourced) SOX testing, presume management owns and maintains controls documentation. If a client is seeking these services, the burden is upon client management to have controls identified and documented. These engagements involve testing "management's controls." If management does not have a control structure (which happens), these engagements can run into problems. Consider the following examples:

- A company is undergoing its first SSAE16 audit. They are responsible for providing the controls structure for testing, as well as writing "Section 2," which is management's description of controls. This is a smaller, growing company that doesn't have controls experience in-house. They have agreed with a partner, acquiring company, or a potential client that they will perform an SSAE16 audit. They figure the auditors they have hired will help them get through a process they have yet to understand.

- A bank has had trouble with an information system conversion. They have data problems, and outside parties have concerns. The bank hires a third-party auditor to perform agreed-upon procedures on converted data, but the auditor is not sure what they need to test.

- An internal audit department has relied upon external IS auditors. Since their last testing, a new ERP system has recently been implemented, but controls documentation has not been updated to reflect current controls. Deadlines require testing be completed soon, so they line up auditors to perform the testing, though their controls are not current.

In these situations, the client may presume that the auditors will write the controls that will help them through the process. In the internal audit example, the burden of working with outdated controls may introduce problems meeting the deadline and may introduce problems when attesting to controls over a defined period. Moreover, in the SSAE16 and agreed-upon procedures examples, there is a line an auditor must not cross. Auditors are not permitted to test controls they have designed. Feedback that does not involve writing controls language can be provided.

Documenting Procedures

Certain projects call for the IS auditor to generate systems and procedure documentation. When an auditor must draft these documents, it may take several meetings with client personnel before documentation goals can be achieved. Providing draft documentation allows an auditor to more effectively communicate with control owners and control managers to confirm an understanding of the subject matter.

The following are examples of documentation formats an auditor may use:

- Written text and lists
- Flowcharts
- Network diagrams
- Spreadsheets
- Data structure and data flow diagrams
- Screenshots
- Text files of command output

The task of documentation faces several challenges. When dealing with information systems, an auditor is often attempting to abstract complex concepts in an organized manner to the correct audience. It is common to rely on multiple visual tools to fully communicate processes and the systems that support them (see Figure A-4).

When developing documentation, it is useful to share documentation with control owners and managers. Control owners are often helpful when their area of expertise is being represented in new ways. It is also important for the success of testing that the auditor and control owner agree closely on what is being tested. Draft documentation proves a convenient tool for capturing accurate feedback, as notes and corrections can be written on the draft documentation.

Procedure Flow Diagram

Procedure Step 1	Procedure Step 2	Procedure Step 3
Personnel enter hours worked	Billing DB pulls hours worked and computes bills	Billing department reconciles database reports

Data Flow Diagram

Figure A-4 Different methods of diagramming can support information systems auditing.

Documentation frequently reflects a version number, the date of latest update, and the name of the person who created the document.

CAUTION   Before a document's review is complete, an auditor should take care to always write "DRAFT" on any documentation that is not in final condition. "Final condition" would mean reviewed and accepted (and approved, if possible) by management and ready for inclusion in the audit workpapers. If an auditor has neglected to insert "DRAFT" onto a document before printing, one can simply write it with a pen before presenting it.

Mapping Controls to Documentation   For an auditor's purposes, individual control activities are often included in the procedure documentation. These may be cited within text and repeated at the end of a section of writing, or they could be identified on a process or data flow diagram. This technique of mapping controls to process diagrams is shown in Figure A-5.

One way to confirm that controls documentation is complete is to examine a list of controls and verify that each control is reflected in supporting documentation.

Figure A-5   Diagrammatic process mappings can visually overlay controls and tie them to controls listings.

NOTE   If an IS auditor is doing documentation on behalf of a client, the client may have preferences regarding the technologies employed in documentation. For example, a client may prefer the auditor not use certain software out of concerns about their ability to maintain the documentation. For example, a client may prefer the documentation not employ certain flowcharting software, as the client may not have knowledge of the software in-house and prefers to avoid purchasing a license.

Perform a Pre-audit (or "Readiness Assessment")

When audit management is unsure as to whether an audit program will be successful, they will often perform a preliminary review, which may be called a "pre-audit" or a "readiness assessment." This is frequently employed when an organization is facing its initial audit, but may be performed when employing new auditors or after significant changes to business processes or information systems.

The goals of a readiness assessment are to confirm that the control structure is correctly documented and that control activities are correctly represented. The readiness assessment should serve to avoid the embarrassment and disappointment of failed testing because of misunderstandings. It will determine if control procedures are implemented as documented and hopes to confirm that documentary evidence needed for testing is available. The process involves auditors reviewing controls documentation and conducting meetings with control owners. Auditors may perform some testing to the level of compliance, such as observing controls in walkthroughs, to confirm the existence of key controls.

If the engagement plans to test controls over a defined period, the pre-audit must be performed before the beginning of the test period. Adequate time after a pre-audit permits the client time to remediate issues discovered in the pre-audit. It may take time to remediate a control issue.

An example of this would be a company's first SSAE16 audit, when the client owns the audit program and external auditors are to perform testing on management's stated controls. The auditor will confirm that they have learned management's procedures and controls, and will determine if the client is prepared for testing to begin.

This phase is in addition to procedures performed to generate an audit report, and no testing burden or required documentation is generated. Auditors will outline their observations and recommendations to management. Documentation gathered during this phase may contribute to procedure documentation in the audit workpapers, but may never be used as documentation in support of testing. It will not serve to reduce any testing to be performed during the testing period because it is collected outside of the testing period.

NOTE   If it has not been thoroughly explained to client personnel, control owners and managers may question why auditors hope to perform a confirmation of certain controls twice. It is important to communicate to management how a pre-audit is different from testing.

Presenting Pre-audit Results

Any deficiencies identified are often presented in letter form to management. Any controls not in place also will be reported to management. The letter can address concerns at a number of different levels. Some examples of feedback that might be delivered on a readiness assessment include

- Control language requires updating or is inaccurate.
- Evidence of control activities is not captured.
- Certain transactional records are moved off-site monthly, but testing will require this information to be retained on-site for testing purposes.
- Control practices are not uniform in certain situations.
- Planned system changes will affect the performance or relevance of a control activity during a given period.

Some methodologies involve management agreeing in writing that they understand and will address any deficiencies in controls descriptions or performance before the attestation period begins. If management lacks time for remediation, findings are likely. Management may accept an audit despite problems, perhaps citing that they accept the findings in a report, and intend to have the issue fixed by the succeeding audit cycle.

Correcting Control Language

Most IS auditors are skilled at writing controls language. When an auditor stumbles upon control wording that is incorrect, there are specific situations where an auditor should exhibit caution. Control language is the responsibility of management, and an auditor testing controls is forbidden from writing controls language. This would amount to auditors performing management's function and testing their own work. An auditor can report why a control statement is not accurate and can suggest that management reword the control to correctly reflect the control activity.

Client personnel may be unsure what the audit team is seeking, especially when management currently has limited experience with proper control language. This scenario has the potential to become frustrating for the client. The client is likely looking to expedite the audit progress. Audit management should clearly express to management why this separation of duties is important, and can perhaps provide limited advice on what makes effective control language.

Organize a Testing Plan

The audit team now has a sense of the control landscape. They have reviewed system and procedure documentation, and have spoken with control owners about the control environment. Once control wording is in its final form, the team is ready to assemble the audit's test program, sometimes referred to as the "test plan," "testing matrix," or abbreviated as the "matrix."

The test program is often in a spreadsheet. Control activities are listed in the document, and auditors design a set of tests for each control. Depending on the control, there could be one to several test actions to perform, which could range from performing inquiries with control owners to complex substantive testing. Certain methodologies may require multiple types of testing to support the passing of each control. The degree of testing required for each control may consider the risk assessment, the audit objectives, and the project's budget.

A test plan outlines the testing down to the individual task level and provides a structure for capturing test results in a central document. The document serves to ensure that the auditors perform testing completely. A test plan is an audit team's internal document. It helps auditors manage the process of testing and serves to track their progress.

> **NOTE**   If one is working closely with financial auditors, the term "matrix" may refer to a central document in the joint financial-IT audit process.

Contents of a Test Plan

A test plan organizes a set of control objectives and controls within a spreadsheet. The test plan is designed to assist auditors in performing complete testing and tracking their progress, and will contain many fields that will be populated later during the course of testing. In order to prepare for testing, certain fields will need to be populated before an auditor is ready to start testing. Fields required to be populated include

- Control number and name
- Control description
- Control objective supported
- Method of testing
- Date that testing will take place
- Test description
- Control owner
- Auditor resource assigned to test the control

Fields that are prepared by an auditor when developing a test plan include test results in narrative form. This part should provide an answer to a reviewer's question, "Was testing adequately performed?" and may include

- Dates and names of people interviewed
- Short responses to inquiries when a full memo is not required
- Short description of the testing process
- Discussion of determinations made during testing
- References to supporting documentation
- Summary of test results
- Testing status
- Test results
- Residual risk
- Recommendations to management

An example test plan, shown here in Figure A-6, illustrates how a control may be documented as an entry in a testing plan.

Control objective #	2
Control objective	Accurate import of data files into system
Control #	2.3
Control activity	Reconciliation of validation totals upon file import
Description and control process	Users receive the file from the vendor and record key metrics relating to…
Risk	Data import results in inaccurate, incomplete, or improper transactions
Location performed	IT Department, Seattle, WA
Control validates for:	
Completeness	X
Existence	X
Accuracy	X
Presentation	
Validity	
Rights and obligations	
Cutoff	
Control type	Reconciliation
Control attribute	Preventative
Auto or manual	Manual
Documentary evidence generated	Initials on report
Testing	
Resource assigned to task	Michael, the auditor
Control tests	Manual
1.1	Existence of evidence containing initials
Test 1.1 result	TBD
1.2	Sample testing on population of initialed reports
Test 1.2 result	TBD
1.3	Corroborative inquiry regarding procedures being followed correctly
Test 1.3 result	TBD
1.4	Inquire regarding availability of procedure documentation
Test 1.4 result	TBD
Documentary evidence collected	TBD

Figure A-6 A testing plan helps to organize the details of an IS audit.

The testing section of the test plan in Figure A-6 is developed to capture test results even though testing has not yet occurred. Auditors could choose to expand this with sections for capturing residual risk and recommendations.

Review of Test Plans

Before testing is to launch, audit management will approve the test plan. The review will consider the following:

- Do planned test procedures support a valid test of the control?
- Is the degree of testing appropriate to support each control objective? The audit's objective?
- Are all scope areas covered by testing?
- Do planned test procedures appear to fit in the planned time frame?
- Are auditors appropriately skilled to test their assigned controls?

The approved test plan document is placed in the audit's workpapers. Audit management may share this plan (or parts of it) with client personnel, or it may be kept internal to the audit team to protect the integrity of testing. If management knew precisely how each control was going to be tested, control owners could manipulate their controls to pass the audit even if they were not effective controls.

Estimating Effort

Evaluating the time required for testing is important. In the course of designing testing, the time it would take for an auditor to perform the task should be estimated and tracked. Estimates should include the amount of time to schedule meetings, perform interviews, review test materials, document testing results, update the test plan, and file documents. Experience is the best guide to estimating the amount of effort necessary to perform testing.

When reviewing a draft test plan, it can be helpful to review how many hours are estimated for each test, each control objective, and the plan as a whole. Plans should avoid spending too much time on less important controls or control objectives, and ensure that testing for the most material control objectives is thorough.

It is important to compare test plan time estimates with the planned time budgets in the audit plan. If the testing plan is much larger than the time allotted, several issues could arise, such as

- Testing is too ambitious, and there may need to be a reduction in test activities, control tests, or even control objectives.
- The scope of testing is appropriate and individual controls tests are appropriately sized; however, testing time estimates were inaccurate. The client may agree to pay for the testing or may wish to work with auditors to trim the scope.

NOTE Time budgets for testing should build in some buffer time. Some technology tests sometimes don't reveal their magnitude until testing is performed. There could be issues with evidence delivered, unexpected test values, remediation of possible exceptions, and other interruptions.

Resource Planning for the Audit Team

Depending on how many audit professionals are available, resource planning will be more or less complex. For external engagements, the selection and bid solicitation process is the first place where an audit team assesses whether they have the skills available to perform an audit. Once more detailed information is gathered from the primary contact, it is time to determine who will perform what work. The most efficient work will be performed by persons who have done testing on that technology (and the supported procedure) in the past. A project will be managed more efficiently with fewer persons involved; however, more hands on deck (with skilled supervision) can accelerate completion—to a point.

An auditor may find it useful to list the technologies in-scope and assign audit resources to the technologies on the list.

If the audit organization has resources with "deep skills" in specific areas, those resources might not need to be included on the team in the field. A skilled auditor can meet with management to gather test materials and then "push down" specific testing tasks to persons with deeper skills. Without bringing them into the field, they can still contribute their skills, perhaps without requiring them to travel or meet with auditors. Here is an example situation:

> You have Auditor A ("Anne"), who is reasonably familiar with Unix and available to the audit team, and Auditor X ("Xavier"), who is a Unix expert with limited availability. Auditor A can own several responsibilities on the audit team, including working with the Unix control owners. When information is gathered for the purposes of testing, Anne can pass the test materials, with detailed testing instructions, to Xavier. Xavier returns test results to Anne, identifying the nature of any exceptions found. Anne is then able to address testing exceptions with the control owner and control manager. Anne has been freed up for other meetings, the testing has been performed by the most capable resource, and the audit has been expedited. Anne also gains valuable Unix testing experience.

In a situation where younger auditors are mentored, developing the technology skills and expanding the experience base of the audit team is a forward-thinking consideration. Exposure to new processes or technologies is best done when a more senior person is guiding them and able to serve as backup. By doing so, an organization grows its skills from the inside.

Preparing Staff

Staff members are usually informed of the project when an engagement letter is signed. Details on a project's requirements may be scarce at the time, but management may share with staff a high-level summary of the engagement, the intended roles, and the planned hours per their proposal.

Once resource planning has been completed, it will be clear which personnel will be performing which tasks within an audit. When this occurs, it is important to meet with audit personnel to explain the project and define the roles of auditors during the project. During this meeting, audit management may provide resources or web links for auditors to use when researching the company, and perhaps update their knowledge on technologies they will review. If audit team members will be tasked with technologies with which they have limited or outdated experience, this is the time to consider providing training.

Once schedules are set for resources visiting the client site, guidelines should be provided to audit staff on the logistics of traveling to their location and, if possible, finding acceptable lodging in the area. This is also a chance for audit personnel to raise questions about the audit. Frequently, dress code and other auditee office norms are communicated at this time.

Performing Control Testing

Thorough preparation for testing will reap benefits when the audit team enters the testing phase. It may appear that effort spent preparing is excessive compared to the task still at hand. Preparation's greatest benefit will be avoiding problems during testing, review, and developing reports. Failure to include a few needed tests may set a team back several days. An error in objectives, scope, or an understanding of the test environment can cause greater problems.

A test plan developed with proper care will provide the audit team with a structure that facilitates effective and efficient testing. Testing is busy enough when it all goes well.

Project Planning with the Client

The readiness assessment is now complete, the client has addressed any preparedness issues, and the attestation period is approaching. The primary contact will help the audit team plan and schedule testing. Table A-2 is a quick summary of topics to address at this phase.

Gathering Testing Evidence

The process of gathering evidence should be orderly. Several common ways of requesting evidence are

- Requesting information in person
- E-mail
- PBC lists

Subjects	Common Consideration
Dates	What schedule works for the client and the auditors? This will center on the availability of key resources, and may consider busy periods in the client's cycle, such as financial closing cycles.
Availability of key resources	When will key control owners be away on training or vacation? Are there events or time periods to schedule around? Control managers are often asked to provide availability information on control owners.
Opening meetings	An audit traditionally starts with an opening meeting. In addition to audit management and the primary contact, it may include the audit sponsor, control managers, control owners, and staff auditors. Audit scope, schedules, procedures, permissions, and other subjects are discussed at this time.
Permission to access information	It should be clear to control owners what information they are permitted to provide to auditors and how they may provide it. Clients who manage sensitive information may follow risk-averse practices. For example, the client may forbid the use of flash drives or e-mail to deliver audit evidence. They may require approval prior to the sharing certain documents, or deliver information on a CD-ROM of which they later oversee the destruction.
Turn-around time guarantees	The time between when information is requested and when it is provided is sometimes an issue. Turn-around times can cause work bottlenecks within a client and can affect how quickly an auditor completes their work.
Learning procedures	How will an auditor get up to speed with the client's procedures? Are meetings with control owners required to confirm documentation is up-to-date? Is there a need to perform a walkthrough of the controls before testing?
Scheduling testing	Do auditors coordinate with the control owners directly, or does the control manager want to manage their schedules? Also, remember the need for lead time, absences, and vacations.
Auditor workspace and Internet access	Where will auditors set up to do work? What hours is the workspace accessible? Do auditors require the workspace to be locked? Do auditors require keycards or other means for accessing the client work site? Is Internet access available? Will gaining access require accounts or passwords? Or training on client policies?

Table A-2   Project Planning to Audit Project Planning

It is common when interviewing personnel to make in-person requests while discussing the control being tested. Direct requests may involve an auditor sitting with a control owner observing software controls and gathering screen-prints and other electronic information as evidence. An auditor may confirm the availability of policies, procedures, and disaster recovery plans by asking a person to show them where they are located. Direct requests may be made for information to be supplied later. An auditor might follow up a meeting with an e-mail summarizing requested information and what is to be expected.

PBC lists are a tool that brings order to the process of gathering test information, but are best employed when an auditor does not have a need to observe an activity directly. Concise and easy to understand, PBC lists are a tool for client management to track information they are providing to auditors, and for auditors to track what information they have requested and received. PBC lists are ideal for requesting transaction records, data, and process documents.

Depending on the testing being performed, there can be several phases of requests for information supporting testing. The audit team should be orderly regarding requests. If requests are made directly of control owners, the requests should be tracked.

Testing can demand a great deal of time from client personnel, and a client may seek to minimize the impact. When gathering test evidence, the client contact may request the team limit the frequency of information requests to their staff. Some requests may need to be made through the primary contact or their designee. Clients also may request liberal turn-around times so as not to overburden their personnel.

Sample Testing   Sample testing usually requires multiple rounds of requests. Initial requests are made by auditors for sampling populations, from which auditors will select their test populations. Assuming the sample population information is correctly delivered and understandable, auditors then submit a request for test evidence for the selected sample. Unless test results are extremely successful, there could be requests for follow-up information. Unclear sample test results may require further investigation, resulting in requests of additional records or a live discussion with the control owner.

Security and HR Procedure Testing   Testing of information security often covers setup and removal of user account permissions. To determine if access granting and removal procedures are operating, auditors will involve two key lists:

- Current employee listing
- List of employees terminated within a given period

These lists must be dated and should be provided at the same time. Lists should include (at a minimum) employee name; manager's name, department, or title; hire date; and termination date. Testing surrounding HR procedures (such as approvals) may require these lists as well. They may be requested early during testing or, in some cases (such as for an SSAE16), after some time has passed within a test period. These lists may also help auditors determine if user account permissions are granted appropriately for their role.

NOTE It may be necessary to explain to a client why an IS audit requires auditors to speak with or make requests of HR personnel.

Requests for Follow-up Information

Often, testing doesn't go precisely as planned. Certain information may be lacking from provided evidence. This may occur when the course of business requires exceptions to standard procedures. An auditor may not learn of all of these possibilities when meeting with a control owner, but instead the auditor finds out later while examining evidence. Auditors usually need to make follow-up requests to determine if a notable occurrence during testing is an exception or is acceptable.

Launching the Testing Phase

The audit team and client personnel are ready for testing, so it is time for auditors to begin. The availability of client personnel may determine the schedule of certain tests. Planning meetings will set expectations as to when auditors are expected to complete their work. Once schedules are set, logistics should be set for getting auditors into the field (such as securing transportation and lodging).

A testing period often starts with a series of kickoff meetings before interviews are scheduled with individual control owners. These meetings serve the purpose of introducing auditors to the control managers and their team of control owners. This forum allows for

- Auditors to meet personnel in person before testing launches
- Auditors to explain the scope of their audit and clarify testing expectations
- Control managers to frame the event for their personnel and to set rules and expectations
- Control owners to raise questions they may have about the process

Control owners may be experiencing some degree of nervousness, especially if they have not spoken with auditors before. Auditors will often find testing interviews work more smoothly when control owners have already met the auditor. Gathering evidence will work more smoothly when control owners have had expectations set by management as to what they can expect during interviews and what they are permitted to provide auditors. In addition, explaining to control owners that results of testing will be reviewed with them before they are reported will often help control owners relax when communicating with auditors.

Performing Tests of Control Existence

Tests of control existence determine if a control is in place and operating effectively. They also determine if the control activity occurs. Many controls will pass if a document simply exists or a software configuration setting is confirmed.

Control existence does not imply that a control is operating effectively over time, but whether or not it works when successfully operated. Existence tests are often performed using the following testing methods:

- **Inquiry and corroboration** Auditor questions control owners about controls.
- **Observation** Auditor views a control being performed.
- **Inspection** Auditor reviews material evidencing compliance with stated control.
- **Reperformance** Auditor performs control activity himself.

Many existence tests are performed when accompanying the control owner. Existence testing is a leading method of testing automated controls enforced by software.

Certain controls testing engagements, such as SOX 302 testing and a SSAE16 Type I, test for a control's existence. An SSAE16 reports that at one moment in time these controls are in place. SOX 302 requirements also verify that the controls environment is documented and that the controls have been tested once. In contrast, when the burden of controls testing involves confirming operation over a given period, such as SOX 404 or a SSAE16 Type II report, control tests for existence may be performed multiple times during the test period.

Automated Controls

Automated controls are tested for existence. Many tests involve confirming that software configurations are set to specific values or observing whether systems enforce a rule.

Automated controls are most often observed in person by an auditor, and the auditor documents the occurrence for testing workpapers. Screen-prints or other captured images provide evidence of software configurations. These images can be accompanied with an auditor's descriptive text for use as documentary evidence of the control test.

CAUTION In certain client situations, a control owner may ask to generate documentation of controls on their own. If at all possible, documentation of controls settings should be gathered in the presence of the auditor, and preferably the first time an auditor asks to see it. Allowing a control owner to prepare evidence of controls can present certain issues, such as the control owner cutting corners and using images provided to previous auditors.

Governance Controls

Governance controls are often tested for existence—for example, policies, procedure documentation, committee meeting minutes, approvals, and other documents can be tested for existence. The provided documents may be subject to additional review per the test plan. If the evidence does not exist, additional test procedures will not be performed and tests will likely fail.

Testing Existence via Observation

Tests by observation are performed by an auditor witnessing whether a control activity is performed. This can involve the auditor looking over the shoulder of the control owner and requesting they perform certain tasks as they demonstrate a procedure, or by viewing software settings within applications. Examples of observation testing include

- Confirming that software requires and tracks approvals
- Observing physical and environmental controls for a server room
- Noting the existence of signed policies and a background report in an HR file
- Viewing system-generated alerts reaching a pager
- Reviewing a firewall rule base to confirm settings

Control tests by observation are recorded in writing in testing workpapers. Recording observations should be sure to include the date and time, as well as the full name and title of the control owner. If observations can be supported by documentation beyond an auditor's recorded observations, this is preferable. Not all client or technology situations will provide such evidence.

 NOTE Client organizations may not permit their firewall rule base to be printed or carried off the premises. An auditor may have to observe the rule base and document their review as a test by observation.

Testing by Inquiry and Corroborative Inquiry

Testing by inquiry involves asking questions of control owners. Inquiry is most commonly performed in person, over the phone, or via e-mail. Some standards of testing require corroborative inquiry, meaning two persons with knowledge of a control must make agreeing statements. Discussions are documented, often in memos, and placed in the workpapers.

When documenting inquiry in workpapers or reports, the auditor must take care to phrase any statements by management as "representations" made by the client rather than facts. Wording might read: "Per the Unix system administrator, security logs are reviewed on a weekly basis," or "The CIO represented that spending is reviewed monthly."

The audit workpapers will include the record of the conversation and a memo addressing the result of the test.

Testing Existence by Inspection

Inspection is performed by a reviewing of the content of client-provided evidence. Testing may seek to analyze the nature of information discovered within the material being tested, which could be a report, policies, meeting minutes, or other document. Testing by inspection might seek to determine whether

- Forms reflect the proper approvals signatures
- Data backup software schedules match documented schedules

- Committee meeting minutes reflect management's discussion of the log file review
- Network and data flow diagrams are dated and current

The audit workpapers should include a memo addressing the results of testing, which identifies the inspected documents and copies of the documents. Any exceptions should be marked in the document and addressed in the memo.

Testing Existence Through Reperformance

Auditors may test security controls and automated controls via reperformance. In this type of test, auditors are taking information that is input to a control and performing tasks or calculations on their own to see if they achieve the same results that the control does. Examples of reperformance testing include

- Attempting to set a password that is noncompliant with policies
- Confirming VPN authorization is required and no guest account is enabled
- Seeing whether specific employee key cards permit access to a restricted area
- Reproducing report values from business rules and raw data

 NOTE   Reperformance can be used to perform substantive testing. Recomputing batch totals is a common audit procedure in financial audits.

The audit workpapers should include a description of the reperformance test. Workpapers for a reperformance test may then resemble other forms of testing, such as observation (VPN example) or sample testing (transaction records example).

Control Existence Failures

One possible result of testing is that a control being tested is not implemented. This is often discovered during initial discussions with control owners or during a procedure walkthrough. This can occur for several reasons:

- Documentation of controls has not been updated for new procedures. Effective controls may exist, but they are not included in testing programs.
- Changes in personnel resulted in a lack of ownership of the control process.
- Controls were documented as "to be implemented," or implementation was not successful.

When controls are found not to exist, they should be brought quickly to the client's attention. If it is possible (or prudent), validate the absence with a control manager before elevating the issue to the primary contact. A control manager may be able to clear up the confusion and prevent embarrassment, such as identifying a compensating control that could be tested to support audit objectives.

Perform Testing of Control Operating Effectiveness

Tests of control effectiveness confirm that the performance of a control activity has been successful. Audits most often test control effectiveness over a defined period. In order to test for successful operation, evidence needs to indicate that a control repeatedly occurs correctly or appears to occur without interruption.

There are several methods of testing operating effectiveness, including inspection, reperformance, sample testing, and automated testing methods (not to be confused with testing of automated controls).

Testing Effectiveness by Inspection

Inspection can be used as a test of effectiveness as well as existence. Inspection can reveal that evidence indicates continued operation of a control activity. To test for control effectiveness, inspection is often used to review system log files or similar reports. Some examples of how inspection methods are employed effectively for testing of reports or log files include

- Confirming log entries were captured without interruption
- Reviewing changes to administrator passwords, confirming they are periodically changed in accordance with policy
- Changes to key settings, confirming that logs were not turned off and that settings were not changed at times during the testing period

Inspection may be employed as a method within sample testing as well. Testing may produce documents that are then tested by inspection.

 NOTE Gathering log file information for testing can be a challenge, as log files can be quite large and reviewing them can take special tools. A client may need to assist an auditor in interpreting the contents of the logs. If filtering is performed on a file before an auditor's inspection, it is best if the auditor observes the filtering operation and documents her observations. Some log files are overwritten on a periodic basis, limiting the availability of evidence.

Testing Effectiveness Through Reperformance

Effectiveness testing using reperformance can involve an auditor reproducing control activities performed by clients. This method can allow an auditor to confirm that controls have been operating correctly because they can re-create the control activity themselves. Reperformance can involve recomputing figures or confirming the reported values from source data. Some examples of testing by reperformance include

- Comparing a list of active system users against a list of terminated employees to see whether terminated employees' accounts were removed.
- The control owner performs a reconciliation on reports provided by two different systems and initials the documents before processing. To test that the reconciliation was performed correctly, an auditor reviews whether the figures match on a sample of initialed documents.

- A billing application generates reports on hours worked by querying a database of hours worked on each project. An auditor seeks to validate that report totals are accurate. This data is imported into a database, and the auditor runs queries to attempt to reproduce the values generated by the billing application.

If the auditor is using a database or spreadsheet application to manipulate the data, workpapers may include evidence in electronic form. A standard, noneditable format (such as a CD-ROM) is preferable to rewriteable media. Workpapers should contain a memo discussing the testing methodology and identifying how and where (in the workpapers) the information is stored digitally.

Sample Testing

Sample testing is conducted when a control is performed on a regular basis and a record of the control activity exists. An auditor will select a population of control activity records to confirm that the control is being performed correctly. An auditor must review the population of control tests and then request the evidence supporting elements of that population. This often involves two rounds of requests from a control owner to gather a sample population and test evidence.

Auditors may select sample populations by random test sets, or they can judgmentally select a population from the test set. Judgmental selection is often helpful when the materiality or criticality of transactions varies. Auditors might select transactions that relate to a company's largest clients or most critical systems. Judgmental selections may also seek to test a variety of transactions. Auditors might include different kinds of clients, or from applications hosted on different systems.

When an auditor performs sample testing, the audit workpapers should include

- A written description of the testing process, including a discussion of how sample selection was performed
- A record of the sampling population
- List of the test set population
- Test results
- At least one example of a successful test and each exception (if all test materials are not retained)

An auditor's workplace may have policies covering workpaper documentation requirements. Testing sometimes includes lengthy printed reports, and some places permit audit management to use their judgment regarding when retaining a sample of the report is sufficient evidence.

Automated Testing

Automated testing can quickly provide an auditor with large amounts of critical system information. It often involves the use of testing programs (sometimes off-the-shelf) or test scripts. Test scripts may be designed by the audit organization, the software's manufacturer, or a third party. Running scripts should only be done in close cooperation with a control owner, such as a database administrator or operating system administrator, and approved.

Testing programs and scripts may need to be run on a client's system. Many organizations will require that a script or testing program be reviewed before auditors are permitted to run it on their system. A client's review will usually confirm that a script is only executing inquiry commands. Special user accounts may be enabled temporarily for test programs to run. The use of automated testing should be brought up early in conversations with the client, as approval for their use may take some time.

Testing Programs   Testing programs will often be developed by a software vendor. To assist a client's review of a software program, the client can be provided with the software make and version number, and, if possible, the auditor can provide software documentation.

Examples of automated testing programs include

- Penetration testing
- A program that runs on a network to identify all workstations connected to the domain and to confirm that antivirus definitions are current on all workstations
- Network analysis programs that review network components and the protocols enabled on network devices

Testing programs often provide organized reporting of the results of testing. An auditor's test consists of reviewing output reports from the test and recording the observations in a document. In addition to the output report and a record of an auditor's testing, the workpapers should include details on the testing program used, including name, manufacturer, version number, and relevant configuration settings used. The results of analysis are then recorded in the testing matrix.

Test Scripts   Scripts are programs that are run on systems and that usually generate a file showing the commands executed and the results. Scripts are written in scripting languages (such as SQL), which execute commands sequentially. They can run a query and write query results into an output file. Test procedures will involve reviewing scripts' output files.

When a script is employed, an auditor should observe management running the script and collect the evidence without delay. The audit workpapers should include

- Information on the system being tested, including version, current patches, and relevant configuration settings
- Text of the script itself, plus any information on the publisher, name of the product, and version number
- Output report from running the script
- Results of the auditor's review of the output report

Scripts designed for certain technologies have the issue of expiring as the technology becomes obsolete, so infrastructure is required to keep them current. Unless an auditor is an expert in a given scripting language, he should avoid writing or editing scripts. Automated tools are more common with large audit organizations and cutting-edge audit shops.

Discovering Testing Exceptions

Auditors will face problematic test results, and will need to determine the nature of any exception. It may not be clear whether an unexpected result equates to a test failure. Despite preparation, an auditor may not immediately understand test results. A clear understanding of the procedure, and the role of the control within that procedure, is needed so that the auditor can determine if a nonstandard test result amounts to an exception, or simply a test that was run incorrectly. If an auditor reports prematurely on findings, it can lead to challenges with the client relationship and loss of professional integrity for the auditor. Auditors should attempt to confirm an understanding of how the test results amount to an exception.

An auditor should communicate an exception with audit management first. Audit managers will confirm their understanding as to why it appears to be an exception. Then the control manager and primary contact will be informed—perhaps at regular update meetings, or more immediately if the finding is highly material.

When an exception is confirmed, it is documented in test matrices and the workpapers. If possible, the description of the exception should accompany the source document, including where it was identified. If the test was discovered in data testing or images of a screen, the evidence should be captured electronically (and perhaps printed), and a written description should be included.

Reporting exceptions in audit reports usually includes reporting to the client the residual risk and making recommendations.

Issues Requiring Follow-up

There can be several reasons why an auditor must return to the control owner for a clear understanding of test results and exceptions. Most often, this will be because a procedure or a control is not completely understood, possibly because control documentation is insufficient or outdated.

When following up with a control owner, if e-mail or a short conversation is not possible, it is often best to inform the primary contact and control manager that you will require more time with control owners.

After completing follow-up with control owners, any clarifications the auditor acquires should be documented in the workpapers as support for the results of testing. In addition, procedure and controls documentation could require updating. If follow-up confirms the exception is valid, it must be documented as such.

Confirming an exception with the control owner and control manager should prevent disagreements when an audit report is presented to a client organization.

An example requiring follow-up involves network security. Upon an initial review of the client's firewall rule base, the firewall appears to permit traffic that includes less secure protocols. The auditor does not yet know if this is an exception. Further inquiry is required for the auditor to learn whether compensating controls address the residual risk:

- Traffic could additionally be managed by a router, isolating it to specific servers.
- An intrusion prevention system (IPS) may be employed to isolate traffic that introduces security issues into the network.
- Valid business reasons may have led to management accepting the risk of permitting this protocol. Staff may regularly monitor the activity.

Auditors may be told that management is aware of and accepts the risk of these protocols. Auditors would document management's communication in the workpapers, perhaps with an e-mail printout or a memo recounting the conversation.

Discovering Incidents Requiring Immediate Attention

During the course of testing, an auditor could discover information that requires immediate attention by the audit team, client management, or both. An auditor has a professional duty to be aware of possible indicators of illegal activities, fraud, hacking, or other improper actions. Situations that could require immediate attention include

- Fraudulent evidence provided by client personnel
- Discovery of critical vulnerabilities that compromise the computing or network infrastructure
- Improper or fraudulent actions on the part of client personnel
- Manipulation of financial figures reported to internal or external parties
- Requests made to auditors that could compromise the integrity of the audit process

An auditor must make sure they correctly understand the nature of the discovery. In many instances, auditors will not have a problem consulting with control owners to confirm their understanding; however, situations such as fraud could require a high degree of confidentiality if a proper investigation is required. If the audit team together is still unclear on how to handle a situation, it is best to consult certified professionals on how best to proceed.

Discovery of Fraud

If an auditor uncovers evidence of possible fraudulent or criminal activity, it is urgent that they address this with audit management. They must begin thoroughly documenting all communications and should write a description of how they made their discovery. The auditor should confidentially consult with fellow auditors to confirm their interpretation of the evidence. If the team suspects a possible issue, they must then decide how to proceed.

If there is agreement among auditors that evidence appears to show fraudulent or criminal activity, the audit team will need to notify client personnel of the incident. The audit team should consider the nature of the incident and carefully consider which members of client management are the most appropriate to inform.

In small to middle-sized organizations, the audit team may consider informing the CIO, CFO, legal counsel, internal audit director, or other members of executive management. In larger organizations, a level below executive management may prove more appropriate. In extreme situations, the chair of the audit committee or other governing board might need to be informed first. A meeting should be set up to discuss the evidence and see how the client would like to proceed.

Handling Evidence of Fraud or Criminal Activity   If the auditor possesses documentary evidence of a potentially fraudulent activity, they will need to isolate the document and establish a chain of custody for the potential evidence should criminal investigation proceedings occur. This appendix does not claim to be an authoritative resource on procedures to follow in the event of discovering fraud. If fraud is discovered, the advice of a professional investigator should be consulted immediately for guidance in these situations. This person will advise the audit team on how to act until an investigator is able to take over the chain of custody for evidence and continue the investigation.

An auditor may be required to handle evidence relating to the discovery of fraud or criminal activity. In these situations, evidence is secured and a chain of custody must be established. It is preferable to establish the custody of evidence following the instructions of a certified professional. A certified professional may not be able to assume the chain of custody of evidence the day it is identified, so an auditor may be required to perform certain actions. The following points are important to consider when developing a chain of custody of evidence:

- Do not make any marks or additional marks on the evidence or disfigure it in any way (for example, don't punch any holes in it to insert it into a binder).
- Begin an evidence log spreadsheet that will track the location and possession of the evidence. The spreadsheet should be constructed to track the following information:
  - Evidence log number
  - Date and time evidence was received from the source
  - Information on the source of the evidence, including person, source system, report names, and other details
  - Name of person submitting evidence to custody
  - Date and time evidence is entered into the evidence log
  - A discussion of the information located within the documentary evidence that may indicate fraud
  - The method of storage of the documentary evidence. Evidence should be stored behind locked doors or in locked cabinets when not in the custodian's direct possession.

- Identify the person responsible for keeping documentary evidence secure and in their possession, and the time and date when they accepted possession of the evidence. If the security of the evidence is transferred between members of the audit team, be sure to record the date and time when this transfer of ownership occurs.

- If the evidence is a piece of paper that has information on only one side, some parties advise that one may write the following on the back of the page: document number, date, and the source of the document, and sign and date it.

- Place the evidence into a tamper-evident envelope.

- Lock the evidence in a locking cabinet or safe.

If anyone on the audit team has experience with fraud investigations, they should oversee this process, and as soon as possible a certified fraud investigator should be consulted. When a certified fraud investigator arrives, auditors will formally hand over custody of any documentary evidence and the evidence log to the investigator, and record the transfer of custody in the evidence log.

 CAUTION When collecting evidence that may later be used in a legal proceeding, strict forensic rules for collecting and protecting evidence must be followed. This often requires the services of a trained forensic specialist, who will follow these procedures in order to protect the evidence and its chain of custody.

Improper Actions by Management

Management may behave improperly during the course of the audit, and client personnel may fear for their reputation with client management when auditors are around. Client personnel may not act appropriately. It is important for an auditor to maintain professional composure when client personnel act inappropriately. Less serious issues of inappropriate behavior can be addressed between audit management and the primary contact. More serious issues may require a meeting between control managers and audit sponsors.

Certain improper actions may be severe enough to interfere with the execution of the audit, such as

- Refusing to provide test evidence

- Providing fraudulent or "doctored" evidence

- Requesting audit personnel act inappropriately

- Threatening audit personnel

Violations at this level will require action by the audit team. Auditors should document and communicate the incident immediately to audit management. Audit management and client management should then meet and address the issue.

Certain improper actions by management could strongly affect the audit execution and the final report. In some situations, refusal to provide evidence or providing fraudulent evidence can be reason for the audit team to cease performing an audit.

Materiality of Exceptions

The auditor employs judgment to assess the materiality of exceptions. During testing, an auditor will determine if the exception is serious enough to warrant the immediate attention of management or is a discrepancy of limited consequence. The question of materiality is addressed partly in the testing matrix, when an auditor assesses residual risk for a control that did not pass.

The materiality of controls and control failures is discussed in more detail in Chapter 3.

 CAUTION   Audit management may not always agree with an auditor's assessment of materiality. Hopefully, this situation is resolved quickly and a final determination can be made. A staff auditor may have a client-specific perspective, and management may have more insight on the nature of certain risks.

Assessing Residual Risk

After the nature of a control failure is confirmed, the auditor can assess its residual risk. Certain failures will introduce a relatively limited amount of risk, such as identifying low-access accounts that are not compliant with a password policy. Other failures can be highly material and require immediate attention. An example of a material failure could be the following:

> Auditors are performing tests of network security controls. When testing a requirement that employees use VPN for external access, auditors learn that RDP (Remote Desktop Protocol) traffic is permitted through the firewall and enabled on workstations. Inquiry reveals that a number of IT personnel work from home and that they access their workstations remotely using RDP. The residual risk is that unencrypted traffic, including authentications, is permitted through the firewall and is potentially visible to third parties. This is clearly a material breach of compliance with policies and compromises network security controls.

Examples of how different exceptions from the same test could result in different levels of residual risk are depicted in Table A-3.

In Table A-3, the high-risk example would definitely be brought to the attention of the report's audience; however, it would be up to the auditor whether to bring medium- and low-risk exceptions to the attention of management.

Risk Level	Exception	Residual Risk
Low	No password policy is enforced on a shared account used in a lab for Internet access only.	Inappropriate persons may gain Internet access.
Medium	No password policy is applied to several user accounts with mid-level permissions.	Inappropriate persons may be able to compromise certain tasks within a procedure.
High	No password policy is applied to security administrator and executive-level accounts.	Inappropriate persons may gain access to executive-level accounts and perform inappropriate authorizations or access administrative accounts and compromise security administration.

Table A-3 Different Kinds of Exceptions and How Residual Risk Is Evaluated

Categorizing or Ranking Exceptions

In some reports, such as internal audit reports, the severity of exceptions may be weighed. Categorizations of materiality can be selected, such as

- Ranked most to least important
- Linear, such as low, medium, and high, or on a scale of 1 through 10
- Stoplight: Green (controls operating or compliant), yellow (requiring attention), red (controls not operating or noncompliant)

Several parties can use weighted exceptions:

- Auditors may choose to present only the most material exceptions to the governing entity. These exceptions are again ranked by importance to the governing entity. Exceptions of lesser materiality are addressed with management.
- The IA department can use the ranking when scheduling retesting of failed controls.
- Management may use the ranking to prioritize their remediation plans.

Weighted results lend effectively to diagrammatic representations of the residual risk. This helps management better understand which residual risks are the most important.

Developing Audit Opinions

Auditors will develop opinions on individual control tests, control objectives, and at times, an audit as a whole. Reviewing test results and developing an opinion can be performed after all testing is complete, any follow-up with the control owner has been performed, and the test evidence is ready to be documented in the workpapers. In the event testing revealed exceptions, the control owner and the auditor will have already agreed to the facts relating to a performed test. An audit opinion is entered into the audit testing matrix.

NOTE   Agreeing on facts ahead of an opinion will reduce disagreements when reporting reveals the exceptions to management.

An auditor will conclude his opinions on all controls supporting a control objective before developing an opinion on a control objective.

Management Representation Letter

When certain licensed professionals are performing an external attestation, it is sometimes the practice to have client management sign a "Management Representation Letter." A Management Representation Letter states that client personnel have provided truthful information throughout the audit process. By signing, management takes responsibility for information provided to auditors. This provides an auditor with a degree of legal protection in the event the report's contents are subject to litigation. When this practice is followed, audit checklists require this letter before delivery of a signed report to the audit client.

Control Activities

Developing opinions involves weighing the materiality of the exception, the residual risk, and the impact on control or audit objectives. Opinions on control activities will most often take the form of

- Control passes
- Control passes with observations
- Control passes with notable but not material exceptions
- Control fails due to exceptions
- Control fails because the control activity is not performed

Tests that merely "pass" the planned test procedures are easy to handle. Passing controls are entered into the testing matrix and reflect simply that the test passed. There is no burden for the auditor to develop statements of residual risk or recommendations.

Testing observations are generated when a situation is uncovered during the course of testing that relates to the control environment. Inquiry, for example, may reveal controls weaknesses outside of the test plan scope. An auditor might also identify possible improvements to the control structure, or note that certain procedures are not always performed consistently.

When an audit test does identify exceptions but the audit team considers the materiality of the exceptions to not constitute a control failure, the control may pass, but the exceptions may be brought to the attention of management. For example, an Active Directory control states that no shared accounts are permitted on the network. Inquiry confirms that setup of shared accounts is not permitted, but a review of accounts identifies several old shared accounts, though follow-up reveals the access granted to these accounts is appropriately limited and that the accounts were not used by personnel.

Testing a control activity could result in failure before all supporting tests are performed. In these situations, an auditor will need to decide whether to curtail any more testing of that control and conserve effort. An auditor decides whether additional tests of that control will provide any benefit to the client and whether the opinion of the control objective or the audit as a whole is influenced by these control activity test results.

Control Objectives

An auditor opines on control objectives once the opinions of all its supporting controls activities are complete. Auditors will determine how the results of controls testing support the control objective. Opinions on control objectives will state that controls pass with notable observations, or fail. An audit's methodology may provide guidance in determining if a control objective passes or fails. Audit methodologies might provide guidance such as

- Each passed control objective must be supported by at least one substantive test confirming the effectiveness of supporting controls.
- A single control failure shouldn't fail a control objective unless the control is a key control or the auditor documents a clear justification.
- A failure of two or more control activities should fail a control objective, unless an auditor documents a clear justification of their determination.

If auditors are weighing a control objective, when testing failures exist, auditors must consider how the control objective supports the audit's objectives. In the course of developing an opinion on a control objective, auditors may determine that evidence is inconclusive and that additional testing is needed before a determination can be finalized.

Final determinations on control objectives should be documented in the workpapers and approved by audit management.

Audit Opinions

Certain reports will deliver an opinion on the audit's results. An SSAE16 type II report will attest to whether controls appear to be operating effectively. To develop an audit opinion based on control objectives, the opinions on control objectives will be weighed against the audit's objectives. Audit opinions typically pass, pass with qualifying conditions, or fail. A statement supporting this determination should be approved and entered into the workpapers.

Developing Audit Recommendations

At the conclusion of an audit, it is common for an auditor to provide recommendations on improvements to a client's control environment. This can be done formally or informally.

Formal Recommendations

Auditors can provide formal recommendations to the client. This could take the form of internal audit reports or a letter accompanying the audit report. Recommendations included in a report are frequently accompanied by management's responses and possibly remediation plans.

Formal recommendations are often carefully worded. Auditors must be careful to advise that management take action to remediate a weakness, avoiding statements that may appear that auditors are making decisions on the part of management. Wording is commonly along the lines of "management should consider" performing a certain action. Auditors may avoid highly specific recommendations, because there are often several options on how a control weakness can be mitigated and clients may argue specific methods rather than agree on a need to fix controls.

Informal Recommendations

Auditors often discuss informal recommendations with control managers during the course of testing. It is constructive for both the auditor and control managers to discuss improving an organization's controls. Executive management, such as an audit sponsor, may have some pointed questions they would like to ask auditors at the close of an audit. Similar to formal recommendations, auditors should phrase responses with care and maintain impartiality and professionalism in their answer.

Managing Supporting Documentation

In the process of auditing, an auditor will handle a significant volume of audit documents, process documentation, and testing evidence. Having a complete set of documentation is necessary to ensure integrity of the audit process. In addition, having clear and organized documentation will benefit the execution of the audit. Some of these benefits include the following:

- Auditors will be able to answer detailed questions about test results.
- Audit managers will be able to confirm work is being done to expected standards.
- For auditors in accounting firms, the audit may be subject to a peer review, where other firms review a project's report and its workpapers and scrutinize the audit. An accounting firm may also be audited by the Public Company Accounting Oversight Board (PCAOB), in which case the auditor will be required to show all of the documentation that has been collected during the audit.

It is important that the format of testing documentation be clear when staff auditors begin testing. Auditors also need to make sure that documentation keeps up with the progress of testing. Memos recording conversations should be inserted promptly into workpapers.

During the course of the audit, it is often convenient to manage testing evidence in binders that are separate from audit documents.

Complete audit documentation will often have most or all of the following sections:

- Table of contents
- Engagement documentation, such as the signed engagement letter
- Memos providing direction on understanding documentation
- Meeting minutes and memos from meetings between auditors and client personnel

- Procedure documentation and background information on key systems
- Testing matrices and lead sheets
- Supporting documentation generated during testing
- Checklists for audit completion
- Testing methods used
- Sample guidance
- Document review

Storing Electronic Documentation

It is becoming increasingly common to retain electronic versions of documentation. Electronic documentation can be stored as files within a file system, such as on a shared network, but it is sometimes managed by supporting software.

In some engagements, outside auditors provide a copy of audit workpapers to the client. Sharing electronic versions of documentation can make this easy to do. When delivering electronic documentation, the auditor must confirm the preferred media and schedule of delivery with the client.

Electronic storage can introduce challenges if it is to be archived for a specific period. Storage media preferences evolve and could render documentation difficult to access if it is stored on outdated media. Another consideration is that certain media has a limited shelf life. Data that is to be stored for extended periods (generally, for more than five to ten years) may need to be periodically rearchived onto newer media to ensure that the data can be retrieved if needed.

Storage of data used within audit management software runs the risk of becoming difficult to access in the distant future. Using software can be expensive, and an organization could face the risk of software compatibility issues once the systems that generated the archive files have been upgraded or replaced, or are no longer supported.

Lead Sheets

One common practice for organizing testing documentation is to begin a documentation section for each control with a "lead sheet." Lead sheets often contain similar information to what information was tracked in the testing matrix. Lead sheets provide the reviewer with a tool for following the testing process and understanding the accompanying documentation. Lead sheets can also capture a reviewer's sign-off.

NOTE Within most spreadsheet software, it is possible to populate information into lead sheets from the testing matrix.

Lead sheets typically end with the result of testing clearly stated, as in Figure A-7. Evaluations of residual risk, auditor opinions, and recommendations will often be tracked in separate tools, but this is not necessary.

Testing Lead Sheet
Company ABC, Inc.

Control ID	2.3
Tested by	Michael, the auditor
Date completed	3/29/2010
Reviewed by	

Control ID	2.3

Control Objective

Accurate import of data files into system

Control Activity

Reconciliation of validation totals upon file import

Tests Performed

Inquiry	X
Inspection	
Observation	
Re-performance	
Sample testing	X

Control Owner

Michael, the auditor

Sample Size

Approximately 440 file imports over the 6-month test period

Test Procedures Performed

1) Inquiry—Corroborate between two different department personnel

2) Sample testing—From a sample of reports, verify that the batch number of the import was recorded on the report and that import totals have been initialed and dated.

Workpaper Reference

2.3a—Memo describing sample selection process
2.3b—Test population
2.3c—Memo describing test results

Test Results

Inquiry
Inquired of file import manager Jane...

Sample Testing
Reviewed 40 out of 440 reviewed import reports and found initials

Conclusion

No exceptions noted

Figure A-7 A testing lead sheet contains comprehensive information on the control and the testing performed.

Delivering Audit Results

An audit's fieldwork has been completed, and control owners and managers have agreed to the facts of testing. Before delivering audit results, the auditor updates all matrices with test results, residual risks evaluated, and draft versions of audit opinions written. The next task is to compose results into presentable form.

Typical presentations of audit results can include

- Delivery of a formal report for review by the audit sponsors and other management
- Presentation of the report to the organization's audit committee of the board
- Publication for distribution to and review by third parties (such as SSAE16 audits)
- Memo or letter summarizing audit results and reporting issues to control managers and/or audit management
- If IS audit procedures are a subset of a larger audit, IS audit results are communicated to audit management for inclusion in their report

Discussions with audit sponsors and the primary contact will have clarified what a client expects for their deliverable at the beginning of the audit. The degree of formality will vary depending on what client needs and the company culture.

NOTE In the event of cyclical testing, such as SOX 404 or OMB A-123, the completed tests are entered into a tracking system. After test completion, depending on the structure of testing and review, a limited amount of additional reporting may be requested. Internal audit management will prepare internal reporting for financial leadership so that they are comfortable signing off on controls supporting financial figures. This process includes a review of exceptions and their remediation projects.

Contributing to Larger Audit Reports

When an IS auditor is working for a team that includes non-IS auditors, it is frequently the case that audit management does not have an IS audit background. In this situation, the IS auditor may have a stronger understanding of the materiality of certain test results and the residual risks than does the audit manager responsible for writing and delivering the report. This will require close coordination between the IS and non-IS auditors, which can be a challenge toward the end of an audit when time schedules are tight and several tasks are being pushed to completion. Ensuring that audit results are communicated correctly in final reports and during presentations can be a challenge. If audit reporting over- or under-represents the materiality of information systems risks, it could have consequences to the audit relationship and the reputations of control managers or auditors.

IS auditors should make sure they participate in reviewing the report's representations. The audit manager should be receptive and allow this participation. This situation may be delicate, because the audit team is balancing the success of its relationship with the audit manager with the needs of the audit organization and the client.

Audit Report Contents

Frequently, either the audit organization or the client organization will provide an audit report template. At a high level, a report communicates scope, procedures, and conclusions. In audits involving numerous auditors, several parties may contribute content. Coordination between the report writer (frequently the audit manager or senior) and auditors who performed testing is standard during this time. The report writer will confirm with the field auditors that their statements correctly represent audit activities.

An audit report often includes the following:

- Standard language addressing the parties involved, audit scope, and auditing standards invoked during the audit
- Rules regarding the distribution of the report
- If applicable, the audit opinion
- If applicable, statements by client management regarding company history, financial activities, processing activities, and related controls
- Audit objectives
- Controls to be tested and how they support control objectives
- Test results and conclusions from testing, including exceptions, and evaluations of materiality and residual risk
- Auditor recommendations
- Client-provided feedback on exceptions, conclusions, or recommendations

During this process, audit staff and management review how to appropriately present the audit results. Younger auditors stand to experience mentoring, corrections, and rework during this phase.

Audit Management and Staff Disagreements

A staff auditor and an audit manager may draw different conclusions from test results. For an audit opinion to be defensible by audit management, the report and supporting detail must agree. During report writing and review, as audit management becomes familiar with test result detail, the practices and judgment of a staff auditor face criticism. Disagreements can arise surrounding the assessments of the nature of an exception and the residual risks.

When a staff auditor concludes differently about an exception's residual risks than does audit management, a discussion must follow. The following are several scenarios where disagreements may occur:

- A staff auditor may lack a thorough understanding of specific technologies or client procedures, and may draw incorrect conclusions from test results.

- Staff auditors frequently have more familiarity with a procedure than does audit management, so their conclusions may consider as-of-yet-undocumented knowledge of the situation. If an audit staff person does not thoroughly articulate the reasons for their conclusion, they may omit information critical to audit management's review. Audit management may require augmenting documentation when they come to understand the reasons behind their judgment.

- A staff auditor can be younger and less experienced with a technology than the control owner, and may prove impressionable in the presence of an "expert." A young staff auditor's judgment may be affected by representations of the control owner that an exception is not serious. Staff auditors may require mentoring on the nature of the exception and related risks.

Audit management may need to engage in discussions with the client regarding the exception. Additional procedures may be required, such as increasing test set size or testing a compensating control. This may prove frustrating to the client and audit team, as both client and audit team personnel are not expecting additional burdens on their schedules. This situation should be preventable through clear communication during audit procedures and the regular oversight by management.

Writing the Report

Once test results are clear, writing the report should be a rather straightforward process. Most audit firms or IA departments have developed reporting templates, though in some cases clients will provide a report template. When no standard template is provided (or expected), it is common to select a report from a similar engagement and benchmark. When developing the shell of a report, it is common to identify within the shell the parties responsible for providing content for the different sections.

A report can be drafted in sections, even as testing progresses. As soon as a test has been captured fully in the workpapers, the section of a report relating to that test can be drafted for inclusion. It is common for the greatest amount of writing to be done to account for exceptions.

Attention to these few practices will deliver effective audit reports:

- Say things in the clearest way possible. This can mean breaking up run-on sentences into single statements and saying things with the fewest words.

- It is often preferable to refer to control owners by their title. The person can be listed with their title as a participant. A report will be meaningful to more people when individual names are avoided, and it will serve as a more effective tool for future management and reviewers.

- If multiple writers are contributing report sections, employing uniform language throughout the report is essential, but can prove challenging. If dissimilar language is used, more time may be required during review. It is handy to provide writing examples upon which the auditors writing each section can benchmark.

The testing matrix plays an important role when writing the report. Some reports will present results from the full testing matrix, such as SSAE16 reports. Internal audits may focus reporting on the most material exceptions.

The report is not complete until the workpapers and testing matrix have been reconciled to the report detail. This means evidence in the workpapers is organized and supports the content of the report.

Solicitation of Management's Response

When the conclusions of the audit report are clear to the audit team, the team sits down with the primary auditee contact, and possibly control managers, and delivers the results of testing. Presentations should share draft language of exceptions wording and audit opinions from testing, which will be included in the final report.

Some report formats seek management's responses to the results of testing. Client management will review the wording and the nature of the audit findings and compose responses. The auditor will include these responses in the final report.

Discussing the Auditor's Wording

Client management may wish to discuss the wording of exceptions or opinions. There may be situations where the wording of the audit opinion could trigger confusion for the auditee organization. So long as a rewording doesn't affect the message or the nature of the opinion, audit management might concede to adjust certain wording.

Examples of word changes include the following:

- Data backups have been a persistent problem, and the control objective of "daily incremental, weekly full" backups is not being met. Configuration problems existed within the backup software. Because resources were busy on other critical projects, the configuration problems were not addressed. IT management argues the successful weekly full backup is a mitigating factor not mentioned in test results or the opinion, though they agree the control failed as worded.

- Partway through the audit period, an organization replaced a system that had been problematic from a controls issue. Per testing guidance, testing at different points during the period reveals material exceptions. Management impresses the point that the situation is now controlled effectively and argues test wording does not fully reflect the effectiveness of their current and ongoing controls.

Auditors will have to consider these situations carefully. Client management may be seeking to avoid embarrassment for any exceptions, and an auditor must take special care not to give in to pressure or suggestions that result in misrepresenting exceptions or residual risks. If an auditor is unsure whether a change is appropriate, they should consult with higher levels of audit management regarding management's requests.

Management's Responses to Auditor Recommendations

Reponses from client management about audit recommendations usually involve one of three responses:

- Management will perform auditor-suggested remediation.
- Management will seek an alternate solution to their control weakness.
- Management believes no remediation action is necessary and assumes the risk of control failure.

Management may address the audit opinion in their written response to defend their position.

The auditor will then review management's responses and develop his own opinion on management's action plans. The auditor may believe that the response is appropriate and agree with management about the plans, but this is not always the case. When management responds saying no action is necessary, an auditor may be compelled to report this inaction to regulators or governing entities, or include in the report that management's responses do not satisfy their own concerns about the risks involved.

Report Audiences

The audience of an audit report will be defined at the beginning of the audit engagement. The report should be written with language and at a level of depth appropriate to that audience.

Reports to Audit Committees

Reports presented to audit committees are written to communicate at a high level. Audit committees consist of members of the board of directors, who are usually removed from the day-to-day operations of an organization. Their main concern is whether there are problems that they need to be aware of.

Frequently a report will start with a high-level "executive summary." Language in the executive summary must be clear and direct without diving into details. For subjects warranting more thorough attention, additional pages provide supporting detail so interested members can "drill down" further into a subject. Auditors will make sure that the issues of greatest concern get the attention of the committee.

Audit committee reports often make a point of

- Clarifying the scope of the audit
- Drawing attention to significant issues
- Communicating management's response to issues

Reports attempting to describe mid-to-low-level operations are likely to lose the attention of the audit committee or, in the worst case, confuse members. Care must be taken not to introduce confusion, as this will waste valuable time and might complicate the auditor/client relationship.

Audit management will frequently attend the meeting to present results and field any questions the committee may have about the report.

The report will be provided to committee members several days in advance of an audit committee meeting. Auditors will need to be aware of the committee's deadlines and procedures for submitting reports on time.

Reports to Client Management

Client management has a high level of interest in the detailed results of an audit. Reports written for management will contain operational-level information with which they are familiar. The report's audience will include control managers and their directors. It is important that information in the report be accurate to ensure the report is deemed credible. Within the client organization, there may be parties with motives to discredit a report or the audit organization, so an auditor's diligence in presenting undisputable facts will protect their reputation.

Reports to management will often contain information on the results of each test performed. Exceptions will be addressed with more detail, and auditors will present their assessment of residual risk and will include recommendations.

In audit situations where management is tasked with providing their own responses addressing exceptions and recommendations, a report's completion can be held up by management delaying in providing their response to the audit. Auditors may need to engage their primary contact and perhaps their audit sponsor to ensure management delivers timely responses.

Frequently, when an audit is being presented to an audit committee, a second, more detailed report is issued to client management. Composing a report to management before drafting the report to the audit committee will ensure that all communications with management are complete.

Depending on the organization, a senior executive may ask to sit with auditors and control managers to discuss the detailed report's findings.

Reports to Third Parties

Certain engagements involve presenting testing results to parties outside of the client organization. A few examples of such audits are the following:

- Organizations that provide services to third parties will hire their own auditors to publish an audit report. A service organization thus avoids opening their doors to auditors hired by their customers. The final report is provided to customers and their auditors. An example of this is the transaction-based SSAE16 reports that are governed by the American Institute of Certified Public Accountants (AICPA).

- When two organizations agree to a partnering relationship or are considering a merger or acquisition, one party may request the results of an audit of the second party.

- Banks and other parties extending credit to an organization may require a set of procedures be performed by auditors as terms of lending.

NOTE   Terms of an audit engagement should clarify what parties are permitted to review the report.

Reviewing the Draft Report

Once the report is a final draft form, it is subject to review by the head of audit management. They will proofread the report for correct language and will tie the report back to the testing matrix and supporting workpapers. When a certified professional is signing a report, they will go through this process with great care before putting their name on the report. Reviews often include reviewers initialing sections as complete during the review, such as initialing lead sheets when review of testing documentation has been completed.

Ideally, a review will go well; certain points of feedback will be delivered to improve the report, testing matrix, and workpapers; and the audit team will have a limited number of points of clean up: opportunities for feedback and retesting may be required.

In lengthy audit projects, it may also be appropriate for auditors to conduct periodic reviews of audit results throughout the audit, instead of waiting until the end of the audit.

 NOTE Some situations will lead to the testing workpapers not following the same structure as a report. If this occurs, it is important to include a description in the workpapers describing how they can be navigated to support the report.

Signed Reports

Certain reports must be signed by a certified professional. For example, an SSAE16 audit report must be signed by a CPA. The certified professional will have taken care to make sure the audit process has complied with the standards set out by the certifying organization. The audit will have followed guidelines for documentation, review, sample size, internal review, and perhaps other areas. Checklists may be employed that must be completed before an audit may be signed.

Internal audits performed by outside parties may request that the audit report be signed by a certified professional. Client management can have reasons to seek a certified professional's sign-off on specific testing or internal audit reports.

For example, a company has had challenges with their fledgling internal audit department. Another company is seeking to partner with the company, but has concerns, and places conditions on their partnership agreement that an outsourced certified internal audit firm provide a signed report.

Delivery of the Report

Audit management will clarify with the client how they would prefer to have the report delivered. Depending on the engagement, a report may be delivered during a closing meeting. Some clients expect a bound hardcopy report, while others will be happy with a printout or electronic file. Reports may be delivered at a formal occasion, such as a closing meeting or an audit committee meeting.

Reports delivered to management often will be provided to specific personnel. Audit management will get a distribution list from the primary contact and provide sufficient copies.

Service providers often need to make their audit reports available to their customers' auditors. Usually this is achieved by mailing hardcopy reports, sending electronic copies via e-mail or posting audit reports on a website.

Delivering Electronic Reports

If reports are delivered in electronic form, they should be prepared so that they cannot be altered. Additional controls, such as preventing text or figures from being copied out of the report or preventing the report from being printed, may also be appropriate in some circumstances. These controls will help to prevent the original audit report from being misrepresented or abused.

Additional Engagement Deliverables

A client organization, or the department being tested, could request additional information from an audit process. Examples of this include

- Feedback on policies
- Suggestions for improving the control environment
- Test results information in greater detail than in the report
- The feasibility of mitigating controls

The client organization may have selected the contracted audit party because of the experience of team members. Certain audit projects give an auditor a significant understanding of a client organization's environment. After testing, it is not uncommon for clients to ask the auditor how their systems compare to their peers' systems.

Auditors can be helpful when asked questions, but ought to be cautious in their responses. There are several potential pitfalls to avoid:

- Auditors should avoid making statements that go beyond their experience with the client and their personal areas of expertise.

- It would be problematic if a manager justifies a decision based on the fact that "the auditor told me we should do it." An audit is usually not a consulting arrangement, and engagement letters often are not written with disclaimers used by business advisors.

- An auditor should exhibit prudence when performing assessments at clients that are business competitors. An auditor should be careful not to reveal details of a competitor's systems. Even without identifying the party, providing certain information could be perceived as unethical. If a client believes an auditor is overly liberal regarding sharing business information, they may fear that the auditor will treat their sensitive information similarly.

An auditor is in no way discouraged from providing advice to management, but must do so in accordance with an engagement's requirements and in accordance with ethical and professional standards. Auditors may seek to avoid putting certain comments or advice in writing to protect them from exposure to liability or professional criticisms.

Audit Closing Procedures

The audit process comes to a conclusion when reporting is finalized and workpapers are ready for storage. Methodologies may require certain checklists and that approvals are followed when wrapping up an audit.

Audit Checklists

Audit management may follow checklists for certain milestones during the audit. These may include requirements during the bidding and launching cycle, as well as closing procedures that make sure the audit is complete. Audit closing procedures may include the following:

- The report and workpapers have been reviewed.
- The report has been delivered.
- The signed management representation letter is in the workpapers.
- Workpapers are signed off on and archived.
- Final invoices have been sent.

Audit checklists are typically filed along with the engagement workpapers.

Closing Meetings

At some point after the delivery of reports, audit management and the client will discuss the performance of the audit. In situations where the audit organization plans to continue performing audits for the client in the future, these inquiries help to develop business relationships as well as refine the performance of the audit. It is common to identify points of friction in the audit and seek ways to improve interactions. Clients might prefer to perform testing within certain calendar periods, or want to centralize requests for information. This occasion is a good opportunity to address changes in personnel. A client may choose to have another person serve as the primary contact, or the audit team may announce a change in staffing or management.

When delivering reports to management, these discussions frequently append the meeting where reports are delivered. Auditors should be prepared to discuss such points at the end of the audit. It may prove best to address certain issues at a later time.

Final Sign-off with the Client

Audit methodologies may involve formalizing the closing of an audit with a client. Audit organization management may seek closure to know that they can close the book on an audit. Auditors will know all work on a project is complete and no more hours will go against project budgets. Final billings can be processed, and the auditor can send a final invoice for audit services to the client.

One way of formalizing the end of an audit is to have management sign a letter accepting its completion. A final document is often signed by the client that states the auditor has provided all services as contracted under the engagement letter. Such letters are placed in the engagement files.

Client Feedback and Evaluations

After an engagement is completed, the audit organization frequently will ask for feedback from client management. Some audit organizations track a complex set of feedback metrics. It is common to use this information for internal performance evaluations and bonuses.

An audit firm may follow up with clients with surveys. These surveys will solicit feedback on different parts of the audit. The client will provide the audit team with different "grades," which the audit firms may consider when seeking to improve service quality in the future. If a client is pleased with the service, this proves an opportunity for the audit firm to ask a client if they may serve as a referral when the audit firm is bidding on services to a new client.

Some audit firms will bring the audit team together to review the feedback from the client.

Audit Follow-up

From a company's perspective, an audit is a part of an on-going cycle. After the initial growing pains of the "first time through," an organization usually experiences audits on a regular cycle. Control managers and owners are often familiar with the audit process, though specific testing practices may evolve to fit changes in business, technology, and regulation.

A mature audit function will track issues over successive audit periods. The results of testing cycles or prior audit reports will have identified areas of improvement. Management will have agreed to certain remediation measures. The audit cycle provides an auditor with an opportunity to revisit controls that have failed in previous periods.

Follow-up on Management's Action Plans to Remediate Control Failures

Internal audit cycles will suggest improvements to control activities, and management will reply to these recommendations. Sometimes, management implements the auditor's recommendations; sometimes, they reply with alternate approaches to the issue. Often, a project is started by management as remediation and the planned completion date is provided with management's reply. Internal audit departments will track management's remediation plans on the calendar and will follow up with the project owner regarding completion. Testing will be reperformed on failed controls, and may be performed on controls newly introduced by a project as well.

Retesting Issues in Succeeding Periods

Controls with audit exceptions will be retested either until improvements are made and the control passes or the control is replaced with a new control activity. A test with repeated control failures will be shared with appropriate executive management and, depending on materiality, may be reported to a governing entity.

External Audit

External audit agreements often approve performing audits over several periods. The audit organization develops in-house knowledge of the client organization's issues. Audit recommendations aim to work with management to improve the controls environment so testing failures in previous periods are avoided. It is standard to retest areas where previous tests have failed.

In the event that tests continue to fail over successive periods, auditors will draw attention to the issues in their reports; audit reports will draw attention to issues that persist. In high-risk areas, audit management may deem the issue material enough to issue a qualified or adverse audit opinion.

When an audit organization is performing their first audit of a client, they will review previous periods' audit reports. These help the auditors evaluate the risk of different areas, and include in-scope failed tests and management's remediation plans.

Internal Audit

Internal audit departments frequently track controls to be tested over cycles. Certain controls testing cycles, OMB A-123, for example, will permit less critical controls testing on a less frequent basis. If a control has passed in previous testing, a risk evaluation may deem the control need only be tested on a two- or three-year cycle. However, control tests that have experienced exceptions in previous periods probably will need to be retested on a more frequent basis.

Cyclical control testing is only a portion of internal audit work. An internal audit will, at the direction of the board of directors, pursue audits of different functions within an organization. Unlike internal audit testing cycles or external audits, audits of specific functions may be a one-time event. Issues discovered in these reports are tracked within the internal audit department. Internal audit management and the audit committee should allocate time each year to revisit the status of different issues uncovered in these audits.

Management Projects

Frequently, management will agree to remediate issues by initiating a project to solve the problem. Information systems projects end up in a priority queue, where they are allocated time based on available resources as well as complexity, relative importance, and other factors. Management is frequently cooperative in understanding the importance of a remediation project, but these are evaluated and prioritized among dozens, if not hundreds, of other IT projects. Auditors may find themselves pressing management on delayed projects relating to on-going control issues.

Summary

This appendix has provided the reader with an in-depth study of the IS audit cycle, with the goal of providing a link between CISA study materials and the discipline of professional information systems auditing. By providing real-world associations for the subject materials addressed in this book, your memory will benefit from this material. After all, successfully passing the CISA audit exam requires more than being able to recite facts, but to understand all aspects of IS auditing and many aspects of IT management and security.

An additional goal of this appendix has been to portray the "organic" challenges that auditors face in the field. Examples have illustrated scenarios that experience has shown are reasonable considerations during an audit.

Hopefully you feel you have a better grasp of the process of information systems auditing and an awareness of the challenges encountered in the field. To the experienced auditor, it is frequently the case that as soon as one audit cycle ends, planning for the next period's audit is just around the corner. There are always opportunities to improve a current process, and experience will unveil more perspectives and stories.

Popular Methodologies, Frameworks, and Guidance

This appendix discusses the following topics
- Common terms and concepts utilized in methodologies, frameworks, and guidance
- Demystifying the various resources available and their value to the CISA

Are you getting ready to develop, document, or audit IT controls? Several methodologies, frameworks, and guides contain detailed information on processes, control objectives, and controls that may assist you in your efforts. This appendix is dedicated to helping you make sense of these available resources and the terminology used within each of them.

The appendix is divided into two main sections. The first section focuses on common terms and concepts, while the second section describes the various methodologies, frameworks, and guides available and provides background information, high points, and a summary of why the resource may be helpful to a CISA-certified professional.

If you are reading this for the first time, it is recommended that you pay close attention to the first section ("Common Terms and Concepts"), which provides you with a foundation from which to view the resources. Once you are familiar with the terminology, you can skip to the second section ("Frameworks, Methodologies, and Guidance") and find the resources that most directly apply to you and your organization's objectives. A table is provided at the end of the appendix as guidance for which frameworks may be most relevant to you.

 EXAM TIP   You are not going to be tested on details of the various frameworks discussed in the second section of this appendix. The purpose of this appendix is to provide the professional IS auditor with additional tools and techniques that may be required in an organization.

Common Terms and Concepts

This section was created with the intention that it be used for reference when you are working with one of the frameworks discussed in the second section (or another that is not discussed in this book). At some point, you may hear someone refer to one of the frameworks or methodologies described in this appendix or find yourself wondering if a particular framework or methodology may be valuable to you.

When looking for resources, consider the level and type of information you are looking for. Are you looking for information on implementing processes, control objective statements, or detailed guidance on specific controls? Are you developing a set of general IT controls, assessing a process, or writing particular policies? Each of these activities may be covered in complementary resources; however, if you are in a time crunch, it is recommended that you first determine what you are looking for. Using the following common terms and concepts, we're hoping you'll be on your way to narrowing down the type of information you are on an adventure to find.

Governance

Enterprise governance is defined as the responsibilities and practices followed by executive management and the board of directors to ensure that the enterprise's strategic goals and objectives are met, risks are managed, and resources are used responsibly. Examples of enterprise governance practices would be that of senior management providing direction and oversight, clearly identifying roles and responsibilities, coordinating initiatives, managing resources, and enforcing compliance. Integrity, ethical behavior, transparency, and accountability are just a few principles of enterprise governance. Enterprise governance is critical for increasing investor confidence and ensuring compliance and profitability.

IT governance is a vital part of enterprise governance and aims to ensure that IT is meeting strategic goals and managing risks, and that IT investments are generating business value. IT governance is the foundation for all IT strategic and tactical activities. It helps ensure that strategic goals and objectives are set and measured against; activities, resources, and investments are managed and prioritized; and IT risks are identified and managed.

The IT Governance Institute (ITGI) and ISACA have developed an IT governance framework that focuses on strategic alignment of IT with the business strategy, value delivery of IT, IT resource management, IT performance management, and IT risk management. More information on this can be found online in the ITGI publication, *Board Briefing on IT Governance: 2nd Edition*.

Although governance is the focus of the new *Certified in the Governance of Enterprise IT* (CGEIT) certification, it is important to understand that IT governance is the foundation of IT and may affect which processes and controls are prioritized or assessed at any given time.

Goals, Objectives, and Strategies

Often, the terms "goals" and "objectives" are used synonymously in documentation and planning. Both are used to describe a desired end state, or what an organization intends to achieve. Strategies are the means, or actions, by which an organization intends to realize these goals.

One of the most popular terms in the IS world and control and process frameworks is "objective." Keep in mind that an objective is what the enterprise is trying to achieve. It is always set within a context. For example, the Control Objectives for Information and related Technology (COBIT) framework describes several IT processes and related objectives. In addition, the framework describes specific control objectives. COBIT is not an objective, but aligning IT processes to COBIT may help to achieve objectives.

Business objectives, process objectives, and *control objectives* are different from each other. Business objectives are higher-level statements that guide the organization. Process objectives describe what the process activities intend to achieve, while control objectives describe what the implemented controls are trying to achieve. It is important to understand that the concept of objectives is widely used and they need to be kept in proper context. Some examples of different objectives are shown in Table B-1.

Detailed definitions of goals and objectives can be found in the *Business Motivation Model*, which is published by the Business Rules Group. In this publication, *goals* are seen as general statements that are on-going, longer-term, and qualitative, whereas *objectives* are intended to be more specific, shorter-term, time-specific, and quantitative. In the same model, strategies are said to be the activities that are planned to channel efforts toward goals. The model provides an entire framework for developing mission, vision, goal, objective, strategy, tactic, and directive statements, just to name a few, for an organization.

Type of Objective	Context	Example Objective
Business Objective	Supports Business Goal of Managing IT-Related Business Risks	Implement IT risk quarterly reporting by Q4
Process Objective	Risk Assessment and Management Process	Ensure all risk mitigation plans are updated by risk owners on a quarterly basis.
Control Objective	Risk Response	Ensure the risk response process identifies risk strategies such as avoidance, reduction, acceptance, or sharing; determines risk responsibilities; and considers risk tolerance levels.

Table B-1 Examples of Objectives

Processes

Simply stated, processes are used to manage and organize a set of activities and to help ensure that organizational goals are being met.

Each process represents a series of steps or activities that are designed to take input(s) and create some sort of output(s) that deliver a service or product in order to meet specific expectations or desired objectives/goals for a particular group of customer(s). Usually a process consists of one or more written procedures that describe the actions that people (and/or systems) perform. In summary, processes are put into place to guide how an organization does work in order to produce value for customers.

Example Process

An example of a process would be the assessment and management of IT risks.

The process would represent a set of activities and may look like this: Determine the Context > Identify Risks > Assess Risks > Prioritize > Respond > Monitor

- Potential Inputs: Internal and external audit reports, vendor assessments, vulnerability scans
- Potential Outputs: Risk registers, risk reports, mitigation tracking reports
- What business goal does this process meet? Manage IT-related business risks

Several frameworks describe the various IT processes, interdependencies, inputs, outputs, and metrics, most notably COBIT and IT Infrastructure Library (ITIL). These frameworks are discussed later in this appendix. For more detailed information on business process design or improvement, you may want to research business process modeling or methodologies and toolkits on the Web, such as Rummler-Brache (www.rummler-brache.com/toolkit).

Capability Maturity Models

Initially developed by the Carnegie Mellon Software Engineering Institute as a software evaluation model, capability maturity models (CMMs) are used in several frameworks to determine and describe incremental maturity levels of business process and engineering capabilities.

The maturity of a process or system is rated on a scale from 0 to 5, with a level of 0 referring to a nonexistent process and a 5 equating to the greatest maturity in capability. The ideal maturity rating differs for each organization.

CMMs can be used to assist organizations with developing process maturity baselines, benchmarking, prioritizing activities, and defining improvement. They can be useful in conjunction with any process framework adopted. An example of a CMM is that which is used in the COBIT framework to describe the maturity of COBIT-identified processes.

Table B-2 provides an example of a maturity model and the ratings used to measure those processes outlined in COBIT. Figure B-1 represents how this maturity model can be used to show current and future desirable states and for benchmarking against competitors or industry standards.

Level	Label	Description
0	Nonexistent	Complete lack of any recognizable processes. The enterprise has not even recognized that there is an issue to be addressed.
1	Initial/ad hoc	There is evidence that the enterprise has recognized that the issues exist and need to be addressed. There are, however, no standardized processes; instead, there are ad hoc approaches that tend to be applied on an individual or case-by-case basis. The overall approach to management is disorganized.
2	Repeatable but intuitive	Processes have developed to the stage where similar procedures are followed by different people undertaking the same task. There is no formal training or communication of standard procedures, and responsibility is left to the individual. There is a high degree of reliance on the knowledge of individuals and, therefore, errors are likely.
3	Defined process	Procedures have been defined and documented and communicated through training. It is mandated that these processes should be followed; however, it is unlikely that deviations will be detected. The procedures themselves are not sophisticated but are the formalization of existing practices.
4	Managed and measurable	Management monitors and measures compliance with procedures and takes action when processes appear not to be working effectively. Processes are under constant improvement and provide good practice. Automation and tools are used in a limited or fragmented way.
5	Optimized	Processes have been refined to a level of good practice, based on the results of continuous improvement and maturity modeling with other enterprises. IT is used in an integrated way to automate the workflow, providing tools to improve quality and effectiveness, and making the enterprise quick to adapt.

Table B-2   Example Process Maturity Model

Figure B-1
Rating scale for
process maturity

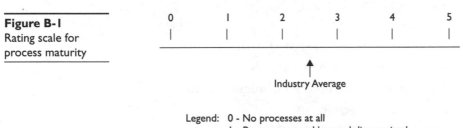

Legend: 0 - No processes at all
1 - Processes are ad hoc and disorganized
2 - Consistent processes
3 - Documented processes
4 - Measured and managed processes
5 - Processes are continuously improved

Controls

Controls are the means by which management establishes and measures processes by which organizational objectives are achieved. Controls may be established in order to improve effectiveness, efficiency, integrity of operations, and compliance with laws and regulations.

Frameworks may represent collections of controls that work together to achieve an entire range of an organization's objectives. Because many organizations operate similarly, standard frameworks of controls have been established, which can be adopted in whole or in part. These frameworks are discussed later in this appendix.

There are many ways in which the frameworks discuss controls:

- **Internal control** The aggregate system that is put into place in an organization to provide management with reasonable assurance that objectives are met. It refers to the many control objectives and related control activities in place to meet business objectives.

- **Control objectives** Control objectives ensure that business objectives are achieved and that undesirable events are prevented or detected and corrected.

- **Control activities/controls** These are the specific policies, procedures, and activities in place to meet the control objectives. Controls may be put into place to help prevent or detect and correct undesired events in the organization.

There are two main types of controls: general controls and application controls. General controls support the functioning of the application controls—both are needed for complete and accurate information processing. General controls apply to all systems and the computing environment, while application controls handle application processing.

Some examples of IT general controls include

- Access controls
- Change management
- Security controls
- Incident management
- Software development life cycle (SDLC)
- Source code and versioning controls
- Disaster recovery and business continuity plans
- Monitoring and logging
- Event management

Examples of application controls include

- Authentication

- Authorization
- Completeness checks
- Validation checks
- Input controls
- Output controls
- Identification/access controls

Tips for identifying and documenting controls include the following:

- When looking at processes, define potential risks/points of failure.
- Identify controls and examine whether they are adequate in preventing or detecting errors and irregularities.
- Check to see if the control's strength is commensurate with the level of risk the control is mitigating.
- The cost of implementing a control should not exceed the expected benefit.
- Well-designed internal controls can lead to operating efficiencies and sometimes reduction in costs and risks.
- Effective controls reduce risk, increase the likelihood of value delivery, and improve efficiency because of fewer errors and a consistent management approach.
- Auditors are responsible for the independent evaluation of internal controls and whether they are adequate.

The Deming Cycle

Dr. W. Edward Deming developed a four-step quality control process known around the world as the Deming Cycle, PDSA (Plan-Do-Study-Act) or PDCA (Plan-Do-Check-Act). The steps in the Deming Cycle are

- **Plan**   Establish objectives to align with desired outcomes and predict results.
- **Do**   Execute the plan in a controlled manner.
- **Check/Study**   Check the results on a regular basis and compare with expectations.
- **Act**   Analyze the results and take corrective actions.

Many of the frameworks described in this appendix are based on this concept, which supports continuous quality monitoring and business process improvement. Each framework defines the set of processes and how they support the different steps. For example, in the project management frameworks, specific processes are necessary for properly planning, executing, and monitoring a project. Although each of the processes is unique, they collectively contribute to continuous quality and improvement.

Projects

Virtually all technology professionals participate in projects. Projects are organized activities intended to bring about a new process or system, or a change to a process or system. Projects are generally thought of as unique, one-time, nonrepeated efforts. Examples of projects include

- Design and development of a new software application
- A migration of an application from Windows to Linux
- Development of a new accounts payable process

Most of the time, formal project management techniques will be implemented in conjunction with software or system acquisition and implementation processes.

A few things to keep in mind about projects and project management:

- Projects are a means to organize activities that are not addressed within normal operational limits. Often, projects are used as a means to achieve an organization's strategic objectives.
- Project management consists of a set of processes.
- Projects are similar to operations in that they are performed by people, constrained by resources, planned, executed, and controlled.
- Operations are on-going, while projects are temporary and unique.
- Project and operational objectives are different. Once project objectives are met, the project is considered complete. Operational objectives are on-going and are in place to sustain business activities and goals. Once operational objectives are met, new ones are adopted and things keep moving forward.
- Controls exist in projects. Examples include comparing actual with planned budgets and time, analysis of variances, assessment of trends to effect process improvements, evaluation of alternatives, and recommendation of corrective actions.

There are frameworks to assist you, should you be responsible for planning or managing a project. In addition, the information provided within these frameworks may help should you be responsible for auditing the software delivery life cycle or assessing any related project documentation.

Frameworks, Methodologies, and Guidance

Creating appropriate processes and controls can be daunting. This is where frameworks, methodologies, and guidance can become valuable. Many internationally recognized organizations have already conducted the research and documented their conclusions, resulting in the publication of several high-quality frameworks and methodologies.

Before re-creating the wheel, consider utilizing these existing resources as a basis for your process and control discussions, audits, or project planning. Many of the documents available today are quite comprehensive, and can save you a great deal of time and heartache. They often outline key processes and controls that can be implemented to meet specific business goals and objectives.

The following sections identify the most renowned and respected resources with regard to managing IT governance, controls, processes, information security, and projects. The background and high points of each resource will be described, as well as how each may be useful for a CISA-certified professional.

Keep in mind that the following resources are merely structures of ideas formulated to solve or address complex issues, or outline possible courses of action to represent a preferred and reliable approach to an idea. They are not intended to be the sole source for your efforts.

Business Model for Information Security (BMIS)

Based on research conducted by the University of Southern California's Marshall School of Business Institute for Critical Information Infrastructure Protection, the Business Model for Information Security (BMIS) was developed in 2009 by ISACA mainly for use by security professionals. Primarily built on a foundation of systems theory, the business model is unique in that it tackles security issues from a systems perspective. The model is not intended to replace security program best practices, but should be used to integrate security program components into one complete functioning system.

BMIS Highlights

BMIS is a three-dimensional model, similar to a pyramid, composed of four elements and six dynamic connections, shown in Figure B-2. The model requires balance and can be distorted should one of the elements not be addressed or appropriately managed. Using a business-oriented approach, the model explores the elements and the relationships between them in great detail.

The model's primary objective is to create an "intentional" security culture through instituting awareness campaigns, cross-functional teams (i.e., risk councils and steering committees), and obtain management support and commitment. In addition, this intentional culture should aim to fulfill enterprise governance needs by ensuring the alignment of information security objectives to business objectives; instituting a risk-based approach to controls; instilling balance among the organization, people, process, and technology; and aligning security strategies across the enterprise.

BMIS Value for the CISA

The model is useful for senior executives; information security managers; those responsible for managing business risk; and those responsible for designing, implementing, monitoring, or improving an information security management system.

In addition, the model is useful if you are looking for ways to align information security to privacy, risk, physical security, and compliance. It also provides a common language to talk to business management about information security.

COSO Internal Control Integrated Framework

Authored in 1992 by Coopers & Lybrand (now PricewaterhouseCoopers) for the Committee of Sponsoring Organizations of the Treadway Commission (COSO), the COSO Internal Control Integrated Framework is by far one of the most fundamental

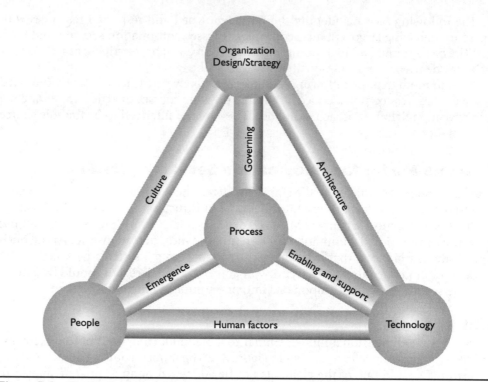

Figure B-2 The Business Model for Information Security

frameworks available to an IS auditor. The framework defines internal control and provides guidance for assessing and improving internal control systems. The term "internal control" stems from senior management's need to "control" and be "in control."

Formed in 1985, COSO is a private-sector group in the United States sponsored by the American Institute of Certified Public Accountants (AICPA), American Accounting Association (AAA), Financial Executives International (FEI), The Institute of Internal Auditors (IIA), and The Institute of Management Accountants (IMA).

It is highly recommended that those who are CISA-certified take the time to become familiar with this framework. It is the basis of internal control descriptions and is fundamental to successfully understanding, assessing, and making improvements to an internal control environment.

COSO Highlights

The COSO framework is composed of four volumes, the framework volume being the most widely used, which contains these sections:

- Executive summary
- Framework
- Reporting to external parties
- Evaluation tools

Figure B-3
The COSO pyramid

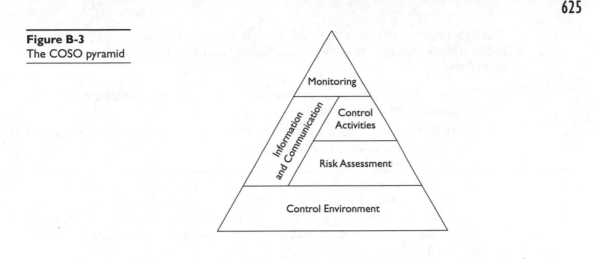

The framework focuses on one main concept and five interrelated internal control components. This concept and components comprise what many call the COSO "pyramid" (Figure B-3) and the COSO "cube" (Figure B-4).

The COSO pyramid consists of four elements:

- **Monitoring**   At the top of the pyramid
- **Control environment**   At the base of the pyramid
- **Risk assessment and control**   Stacked in the middle of the pyramid
- **Information and communication**   On the edges

The COSO cube consists of three dimensions:

- Objectives
- Components
- Business units/areas

Figure B-4
The COSO cube

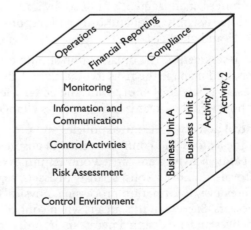

The main concept of the COSO framework is that internal control is a **process, affected by people**, designed to provide **reasonable assurance** that the entity is meeting its **objectives**.

- **Process**   A process is not one event, but a series of activities that are integrated in an organization.

- **Affected by people**   People across the organization establish objectives and ensure that controls are in place. At the same time, internal controls affect people's actions.

- **Reasonable assurance**   Internal control can only provide reasonable, not absolute, assurance that the organization is meeting its objectives. This is due to limitations such as human judgment and error, potential for controls to be circumvented through collusion, or controls being overridden by management.

- **Objectives**   Internal control helps organizations meet the following objectives, all of which are separate but may overlap:
  - Effectiveness and efficiency of operations: Performance, profitability goals, safeguarding assets
  - Reliability of financial reporting: Prepare reliable financial reports while preventing financial misstatements
  - Compliance with applicable laws and regulations

In addition, the framework describes the five interrelated components of internal control: control environment, risk assessment, control activities, information and communication, and monitoring.

- **Control environment**   This is the foundation of how the business operates, where individuals know that they are to conduct activities and carry out control responsibilities. A solid control environment is exhibited by integrity and ethical values, commitment to competence, dedicated board and audit committees, management's philosophy and operating style, the organizational structure, assignment of authority and responsibility, and human resources policies and practices.

- **Risk assessment**   The organization should establish mechanisms to identify, assess, and manage the risks to objectives. This component is evident through the establishment of entity-wide and activity-level objectives, risks identified, and how well the organization manages change.

- **Control activities**   Control policies and procedures are in place to ensure that the actions and controls needed to ensure objectives are met and that mitigating activities are carried out. Examples of control activities include approvals, authorizations, security of assets, segregation of duties, top-level reviews, information processing, physical controls, and performance indicators. Success in this area is when control activities are linked to meeting objectives and are deemed necessary in order to mitigate risks in meeting the objectives.

- **Information and communication** Information pertaining to control activities should flow through the organization. This enables management to know if its objectives are being met, and should be in a form and time frame to ensure that people can carry out responses. Information and communication can be considered successful when they are flowing up to management and down to employees in sufficient detail and in a timely manner, established communication channels exist internally and with external parties, and management is open and receptive to suggestions.

- **Monitoring** The process should be monitored and modified as necessary through on-going monitoring activities, separate evaluations, or a combination of both. Control deficiencies should be reported upstream, with important issues being communicated to the board or senior management. Management needs information in order to ensure that the internal control system is effective, identify whether new risks have developed, and determine if internal controls are still relevant. Monitoring is considered successful when it is on-going and built into operations, separate evaluations are conducted, and deficiencies are reported on an open and timely basis.

When is an internal control system effective? When you've assessed and concluded that the five components are functioning successfully and the organization's objectives are being met:

- The board of directors and management understand operational objectives and whether they are being achieved.

- Financial reporting is prepared reliably.

- Laws and regulations are being complied with.

Making Sense of the COSO "Cube" and the COSO "Pyramid"

Each organization has three main types of objectives that span across all divisions and groups. In order to ensure that these objectives are met, the five interrelated internal control components must be in place. There must be a solid control environment, with risk assessments to confirm that adequate control activities are in place to mitigate risk and that risks to objectives are properly managed. In addition, information regarding risk, activities, and deficiencies should be reported through the organization and in a timely manner and responded to. Evaluation and monitoring of activities to ensure that objectives are met should be done on a continual basis, with corrective actions being taken when necessary.

COSO Value for the CISA

COSO is the basis for the majority of all internal control discussions and process and control frameworks. Whether you are educating others on internal controls, as outlined in the Professional Code of Ethics, or evaluating or testing internal control effectiveness, COSO provides a foundation with which the CISA should be familiar. COSO is a great source for definitions and explanations. Due to the enterprise basis by which COSO has been developed, it is highly recommended that it serve as the foundation, and other frameworks, such as COBIT, ISO 27001, and ITIL, build upon this knowledge.

COSO is currently reviewing the Internal Control framework and planning to publish an update in 2012. Other COSO products include 2004 Enterprise Risk Management (COSO ERM) and Guidance on Monitoring Internal Control Systems, published in 2009.

COBIT

The Control Objectives for Information and related Technology (COBIT) framework was created in 1992 by the Information Systems Audit and Control Association (ISACA) and the IT Governance Institute (ITGI). In 1996, the first edition of COBIT was released to the public. Version 4.1 was released in May 2007 and is, at the time of this writing, the most current version available. COBIT aligns with and meets COSO internal control requirements. COBIT v5 is being developed and is expected to be released in late 2011. For an overview of this new version please see the section "COBIT Value for the CISA."

COBIT was developed in order to assist companies in maximizing the benefits derived through the strategic use of IT. Broad yet detailed, the COBIT framework was designed for use by managers, auditors, and IT personnel, and contains IT governance guidance. The framework aligns IT goals with general business goals; contains a comprehensive list of IT processes; and links related control objectives, metrics, and roles and responsibilities for carrying out process activities.

COBIT Highlights

The COBIT framework is composed of six elements, covered in multiple documents:

- Executive summary
- Governance and control framework
- Control objectives
- Management guidelines
- Implementation guide
- IT assurance guide

The framework is complex and requires dedicated individuals to implement and compile the elements. It is composed of 34 processes in four domains, with 318 control objectives. The framework is based upon the notion of strong IT governance, stressing alignment to business strategy and goals.

As with many frameworks, COBIT is based on the Deming Cycle, with 34 IT processes falling into the following four domains:

- **Planning and organization** Processes in this domain are dedicated to ensuring that IT goals are strategically aligned with the business strategy and goals.
- **Acquisition and implementation** Processes for acquiring software, personnel, and external resources are covered in this domain, along with those processes needed to implement them.

- **Delivery and support** Operational managers can focus on these processes for delivering and supporting the resources utilized, including people, infrastructure, software, and third-party services.

- **Monitor** Processes ensure that the outcome is delivered and measured against initial expectations and that deviations are investigated and result in corrective actions.

Figure B-5 provides an overview of the COBIT framework. Note how the 34 process categories coincide with a cycle similar to that of the Deming Cycle (Plan-Do-Check-Act).

Each process is outlined in the framework and details the associated process objectives, control objectives, roles and responsibilities charts, metrics, and process maturity levels.

COBIT Value for the CISA

The COBIT framework is ideal for those looking for a comprehensive framework to outline how IT goals and processes align with business goals, what processes IT should consider implementing, and related control objectives.

COBIT nicely ties general business goals to IT goals with the use of a balanced scorecard. This allows one to see which IT processes are key in supporting specific IT goals and, ultimately, business goals.

For personnel who are implementing or evaluating a process, the COBIT framework provides an overview of general processes utilized to manage IT. Each process in COBIT includes key activities, control objectives, and metrics that should be in place.

COBIT is one of the most comprehensive and widely used frameworks available, which equates to the development of additional research and documentation being

Figure B-5
The COBIT
framework

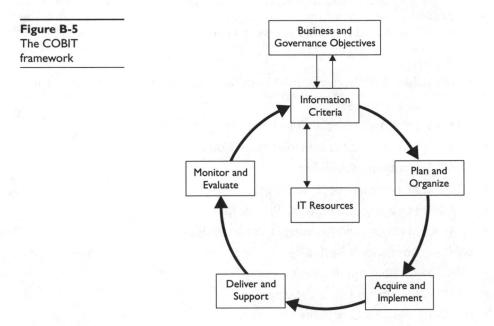

available. See the ISACA website for an extensive line of COBIT and COBIT-related documents. Not only will you find COBIT translated into more than eight foreign languages, you also will find documents mapping popular frameworks with COBIT, a "quickstart" guide to implementing COBIT, and guides for utilizing COBIT within various focus areas (i.e., security, Sarbanes-Oxley, IT assurance and service management).

COBIT v5 is scheduled to be released in late 2011. This new version will consolidate three major frameworks into one: COBIT v4.1, VAL IT, and RISK IT. It will also integrate much of the information within the Business Model for Information Security (BMIS) and ITAF. Each of these frameworks is described in more detail later. When COBIT v5 is complete and published, it is expected that a CISA will be able to more effectively and efficiently align governance, value delivery, and risk management using this single enterprise-wide framework.

GTAG

Global Technology Audit Guide (GTAG) represents a series of documents developed by the Institute of Internal Auditors (IIA) to help organizations with their IT control framework and audit practices. The guides are developed to assist with describing the importance of IT controls as part of the internal controls environment, establishing the roles and responsibilities required for ensuring controls are in place and assessed, and addressing the risks inherent in using and managing IT. The first GTAG guide was published in 2005.

Several groups aid in the development of the guides, including an advanced technology committee and other professional organizations (i.e., ACIPA, FEI, ISSA, Sans Institute, and Carnegie Mellon SEI).

The GTAG guides are geared toward chief audit executives and other executives needing a high-level overview of the latest technology issues and how they affect the organization, the associated risks, and necessary IT controls.

GTAG Highlights

Several GTAG guides have been published and are available through the IIA. These guides are

- GTAG-1, Information Technology Controls
- GTAG-2, Change and Patch Management Controls
- GTAG-3, Continuous Auditing
- GTAG-4, Management of IT Auditing
- GTAG-5, Managing and Auditing Privacy Risks
- GTAG-6, Managing and Auditing IT Vulnerabilities
- GTAG-7, Information Technology Outsourcing
- GTAG-8, Auditing Application Controls
- GTAG-9, Identity and Access Management
- GTAG-10, Business Continuity Management

- GTAG-11, Developing the IT Audit Plan
- GTAG-12, Auditing IT Projects
- GTAG-13, Fraud Detection and Prevention in an Automated World
- GTAG-14, Auditing User-developed Applications
- GTAG-15, Information Security Governance

GTAG Value for the CISA

Although primarily targeting the chief audit executive, IS auditors can utilize GTAG documents to learn more about controls and for assistance with describing IT risk and controls in executive terms.

GTAG can be downloaded by IIA members free of charge, or for a reasonable price for nonmembers, from the IIA. Hard copies of some guides can also be purchased should you choose to add the publications to your library.

GAIT

The Guide to the Assessment of IT Risk (GAIT) was developed by the Institute of Internal Auditors to assist with IT general-control risk assessment and scoping for Sarbanes-Oxley Section 404 (SOX 404). The GAIT series provides guidance on assessing risk to the financial statements and key controls that could be implemented within the business and IT sectors, including IT general controls (IT GC) and automated controls.

GAIT Highlights

The methodology provides guidance on identifying risks and related controls needed to protect financially significant applications and related processes and data.

Currently, three practice guides are available:

- The GAIT Methodology uses a risk-based approach to scope IT GCs
- GAIT for IT General Controls Deficiency Assessment
- GAIT for Business and IT Risk

GAIT does not specify key controls, but does describe the IT GC processes and control objectives that should be addressed.

GAIT is based on four principles:

- A top-down, risk-based approach should be used to identify significant accounts and key controls needed to mitigate risk.
- Risks that are identified in IT GC processes are those that affect critical IT functionality in financially significant applications and related data.
- When assessing IT GC process risk, risks that exist within multiple IT layers, from the database to the application and network, need to be identified.
- Risks identified in IT GC processes are mitigated through the achievement of control objectives, not specific controls.

GAIT Value for the CISA

If you are asked to scope and identify key IT general controls for SOX 404 compliance or general prevention of financial reporting misstatements, GAIT can help you determine which control objectives and controls are key through the use of a risk assessment. GAIT can be downloaded by IIA members free of charge, or for a reasonable price for nonmembers, from the IIA.

ISF Standard of Good Practice

The Standard of Good Practice was first published in 1996 by the Information Security Forum (ISF). The ISF is a nonprofit organization dedicated to the development of information security good practices. Like ISACA, ISF is a paid membership organization with chapters throughout the world. The standard was last updated in February 2007.

ISF Highlights

The Standard of Good Practice contains guidance on security principles, control objectives, and controls in the following areas:

- Enterprise security management
- Critical business applications
- Computer installations
- Networks
- Systems development
- End-user environment

Although the document is primarily divided into these main areas, there are reference tables so that specific control areas that may be present in more than one area can be found easily.

Standard of Good Practice Value for the CISA

The Standard of Good Practice document can provide you with information security control objective statements and describes the controls that should be in place. If you are looking for specific controls, such as access controls or controls around firewalls or e-mails, a reference guide can help point you to the proper section within each area.

ISO/IEC 27001 and 27002

Organizations faced with privacy and information security concerns may decide that they need to implement a formal information security management system (ISMS) to ensure that information security is managed, risks are assessed, and appropriate controls are put in place to mitigate risk to information security. Published in October 2005 by the International Organization for Standardization (ISO) and the International Electrotechnical Commission (IEC), and based on British Standard (BS) 7799

Part 2, ISO/IEC 27001 is a standard that organizations can use for developing, implementing, controlling, and improving an ISMS. ISO/IEC 27001 provides the general framework for the ISMS, while ISO/IEC 27002, formally known as ISO 17799, provides a more detailed list of control objectives and recommended controls. The controls presented within the document act as a guide for those who are responsible for initiating, implementing, or maintaining information security management systems.

Organizations may choose to be certified as compliant with ISO/IEC 27001 by an accredited certification body. Similar to other ISO management system certifications, there is a three-stage audit process.

In addition to the Standard of Good Practice guide, there is an entire series of ISO/IEC 27000 documents, including a glossary, ISMS auditing guidelines for the management system and controls, implementation guide, and guides on IT network security and application security, to name a few.

ISO/IEC 27001/27002 Highlights

The concept of ISMS centers on the preservation of

- **Confidentiality**   Ensuring that information is accessible only to those authorized to have access
- **Integrity**   Safeguarding the accuracy and completeness of information and processing methods
- **Availability**   Ensuring that authorized users have access to information and associated assets when required

The standard contains an introductory section and a description of the risk management process framework needed around information security controls. Each organization is expected to perform an information security risk assessment process to determine which regulatory requirements must be satisfied before selecting appropriate controls.

The 11 main domains in ISO 27001 and 27002 are

- Security policy
- Organization of information security
- Asset management
- Human resources security
- Physical and environmental security
- Communications and operations management
- Access control
- Information systems acquisition, development, and maintenance
- Information security incident management
- Business continuity management
- Compliance

Control objectives and controls for each section are listed in the standards and code of practice. ISO 27001 focuses on the implementation of controls throughout the Deming Cycle, while ISO 27002 lists the good practice controls an organization can implement.

ISO/IEC 27001 and 27002 Value for the CISA

Those involved with implementing or assessing information security controls or the management of information security risk may find it helpful to look more closely into these standards. ISO standards documents can be purchased from the International Standards Organization.

ITAF

In 2006 the ISACA board of directors approved the IT Assurance Framework (ITAF) project to address the need for audit and assurance standards. As the project matured, additional needs, such as taxonomy and guidelines, were identified and addressed. In 2008 ISACA published the first and current version of the ITAF: A Professional Practices Framework for IT Assurance.

ITAF is a framework that establishes mandatory standards that address IT audit and assurance professionals' roles and responsibilities, knowledge, skills and diligence, conduct, and reporting requirements. The framework also provides nonmandatory guidance on design, conduct, and reporting on IT audit and assurance engagements and defines common IT assurance terms and concepts.

ITAF Highlights

There are three categories of standards in the document: general, performance and reporting.

General Standards   These are the guiding principles by which the profession operates. These standards deal with all IT audit and assurance activities conducted, and include

- Independence and objectivity
- Reasonable expectation
- Management's acknowledgement
- Training and proficiency
- Knowledge of the subject matter
- Due professional care
- Suitable criteria
- Available criteria
- Selection of criteria

Performance Standards These focus on the IT audit or assurance professional's conduct of assurance activities such as the design of audit and assurance activities, evidence, findings, and conclusions. ISACA IS Auditing Standards are performance standards (current IS Auditing Standards are listed in more detail in Chapter 3). These standards include topics such as

- Planning and supervision
- Obtaining sufficient evidence
- Assignment performance
- Representations

Reporting Standards These standards cover the report produced by the IT audit or assurance professional and address

- Types of reports
- The means of communication
- Information to be communicated

The ITAF documentation also outlines guidelines for applying the standards. Guidelines assist the IT audit or assurance professional with understanding enterprise-wide issues and IT management processes, as well as processes, procedures, methodologies, and approaches for conducting an IT audit and assurance engagement.

ITAF incorporates ISACA's IS auditing standards and the ISACA Code of Professional Ethics. In addition, all of the ISACA guidance is mapped to the framework. For more detailed information, please see the ITAF framework at the ISACA website.

ITAF Value for the CISA

The standards within ITAF are mandatory for all CISAs. It is recommended that all CISAs review the standards prior to certification and formulate good habits to ensure standards are applied to any assurance work conducted. Although not mandatory, the guidelines, tools, and techniques can assist anyone needing to conduct IT audits or assurance activities, and even those on the receiving end of IT audit or assurance reports.

ITIL

In the 1980s, when the British government determined that the level of IT service quality provided to them was insufficient, it was clear that an IT control framework was needed. The Central Computer and Telecommunications Agency (CCTA), now the Office of Government Commerce (OGC), developed the Information Technology Infrastructure Library (ITIL, pronounced *EYE-till*), which began guiding organizations on the efficient and financially responsible use of IT resources within public and private entities worldwide.

The current version of ITIL, ITIL v3, consists of a collection of books that contain guidelines for different aspects of good practice around IT service management (ITSM) and aligning IT services to business needs. The subjects of the books are referred to as *sets*; currently there are five. The sets are further divided into *disciplines*, with each focusing on a specific subject. When all volumes are combined, ITIL presents a comprehensive view of proper provisioning and management of IT services.

ITIL Highlights

ITIL v3 is a high-level, user-focused framework that defines a common language for IT service management processes. The framework describes the IT service organization that delivers agreed-upon services and maintains the infrastructure on which the services are delivered. One of the critical components of ITIL is that the services and maintenance must be aligned and realigned according to business needs. In order to do this, the framework closely aligns its five volumes with the Deming Cycle:

- **Service strategy** Focuses on determining potential market opportunities with regard to delivering IT services, with sections dedicated to service portfolio management and financial management.

- **Service design** Determines how to design proposed services with adequate processes and resources to support them. Availability management, capacity management, continuity management, and security management are key areas of service design.

- **Service transition** Describes the implementation of the design and creation or modification of the IT services. Key areas identified are change management, release management, configuration management, and service knowledge management.

- **Service operation** Provides guidance on the activities needed to operate IT services and maintain them according to service-level agreements. This volume focuses on the key areas of incident management, problem management, event management, and request fulfillment.

- **Continual service improvement** Focuses on how to ensure that the IT services delivered to the business are continually improved through service reporting, service measurement, and service-level management.

ITIL outlines the general IT processes needed to manage IT; the resources, outputs, and inputs utilized; and the controls that must be implemented to ensure business goals are met (i.e., policies, budgets).

ITIL Value for the CISA

Whether documenting, implementing, or assessing processes, the IS auditor can utilize the volumes for additional information on specific IT processes, such as change management or incident management. The framework outlines recommended controls to ensure that IT services are delivered as promised.

The volumes of ITIL v3 can be purchased online from the OGC.

PMBOK

A Guide to the Project Management Body of Knowledge (PMBOK) is a guide on project management fundamentals and practices. The guide is published by the Project Management Institute (PMI). It began as a whitepaper in 1987 and was published as a guide in 1996. The fourth edition was released in December 2008.

Not only is PMBOK a guide to project management, it also is an internationally recognized standard on project management practices. Those with an interest in obtaining certification in this area may want to look into becoming certified as a Project Management Professional (PMP) through the PMI.

PMBOK Highlights

The PMBOK Guide describes the many processes that are often used in managing projects. It consists of three main sections:

- **Section 1: The Project Management Framework**   Describes key terms and provides an overview of the basic structure of project management, including the project life cycle.

- **Section 2: The Standard for Project Management of a Project**   Describes the 44 processes that are used by project teams. These processes fall into five groups, which are consistent with the Plan-Do-Check-Act activities as seen in the Deming Cycle:

  - **Initiating process group**   Defines the project/phase and gathers authorization.

  - **Planning process group**   Defines objectives and courses of actions required to meet objectives and scope.

  - **Executing process group**   The processes in this group correspond to carrying out the project management plan.

  - **Monitoring and controlling process group**   Regularly monitors progress and identifies variances from the plan; takes corrective actions.

  - **Closing process group**   Concludes that all objectives are met and the service, product, or result is accepted by the customer/sponsor. End of the project.

- **Section 3: The Project Management Knowledge Areas**   Outlines the nine knowledge areas that are needed for an effective project management program and the processes involved, as well as inputs, outputs, tools, and techniques for each. Each process belongs to a process group and is associated with a knowledge area. This section represents the bulk of the guide and details how the 44 processes interrelate. The nine knowledge areas are

  - Project integration management

  - Project scope management

  - Project time management

- Project cost management
- Project quality management
- Project human resource management
- Project communications management
- Project risk management
- Project procurement management

PMBOK Value for the CISA

As an IS auditor, you may be asked to take a closer look at the process for introducing new applications or systems to your organization. Many times, new applications and systems are delivered via a system/software/solution delivery life cycle and coupled with project management. Solutions are scoped and assessed, projects ensue, and there is a great deal of activity and documentation throughout the process. Project management methodologies and frameworks can help one make sense of this madness.

In addition, project management skills can be valuable for an IS auditor. Being well versed in project management can help ensure that your IS audit work remains in scope and on budget and that you are planning your time adequately. For example, you will want to ensure that you are giving yourself enough time for audit planning, documentation, and taking into account complex interview schedules.

PMBOK can be purchased from booksellers worldwide or from the PMI.

PRINCE2

PRojects IN Controlled Environments (PRINCE) is a structured project management standard covering project management fundamentals. The original standard was developed in 1989 by the UK's Office of Government Commerce (OGC) specifically for IT project management. In 1996, PRINCE2 was released, representing a change in focus from beyond IT to general project management. In addition to becoming the de facto standard for project management in the UK, the standard has been adopted by organizations worldwide. As with ITIL, an individual may pass an exam to become accredited.

PRINCE2 Highlights

PRINCE2 consists of one main manual: *Managing Successful Projects with PRINCE2*. It is similar to PMBOK in that it consists of processes and components, but is different in that it fully describes the methodology and implementation techniques. The main concept behind PRINCE2 is that projects should have an organized and controlled start, middle, and end. Although it is not as comprehensive as PMBOK, PRINCE2 supplements general project management knowledge by specifically describing how to manage projects in a controlled and organized manner.

PRINCE2 is a process-driven framework and integrates well with other processes and practices, such as Agile Scrum. The framework details 45 processes categorized in eight process groups. The process groups lead one through the project life cycle, similar to the Deming Cycle:

- Starting up a project
- Planning
- Initiating a project
- Directing a project
- Controlling a stage
- Managing product delivery
- Managing stage boundaries
- Closing a project

Key inputs, outputs, goals, and activities are defined for each process. In addition, a maturity model is available to measure project management capability maturity. Another bonus is that the entire framework can be tailored for each project, as every process has guidance on how to scale it for small or large projects. This results in a flexible, scalable, and fully described framework.

Similar to PMBOK knowledge areas, PRINCE2 details eight "components" that are deemed critical for project success:

- Business case
- Organization
- Plans
- Controls
- Management of risk
- Quality in a project environment
- Configuration management
- Change control

PRINCE2 offers three different techniques for managing projects:

- Product-based planning
- Quality review
- Change control

PRINCE2 Value for the CISA

An IS auditor may be asked to take a closer look at the process for introducing new applications or systems to your organization, including the software/system/solution delivery cycle and associated project management methodology and documentation. In addition, project management skills can be valuable for an IS auditor.

Similar to PMBOK, PRINCE2 will provide you with general guidance on project management processes and controls. PRINCE2 is complementary to PMBOK in that it helps shape and direct the use of PMBOK through the introduction of certain techniques. PMBOK will lay a more comprehensive foundation, whereas PRINCE2 will help describe how to start managing projects and put the pieces together.

Risk IT

Published in 2009 by ISACA, Risk IT is the first comprehensive IT-specific risk framework that has been developed. The framework is based upon enterprise risk management frameworks such as COSO ERM and ISO 31000, making it much easier to integrate the management of IT risks into overall enterprise risk management. Risk IT also complements COBIT. Risk IT provides guidance for managing all aspects of IT-related risks, including project, value delivery, compliance, security, availability, service delivery, and recovery risks.

Risk IT Highlights

Two major documents have been published by ISACA: The Risk IT Framework, containing the principles, process details, management guidelines, and domain maturity models, and the Risk IT Practitioner Guide, which provides an overview of the Risk IT process model, describes how Risk IT links to COBIT and Val IT, and describes in detail how to use the model.

To ensure the effective enterprise governance and management of IT risk, The Risk IT Framework is based upon the following principles:

- Always align with business objectives.
- Align IT risk management with enterprise risk management.
- Balance the costs and benefits of IT risk management.
- Promote fair and open communication of IT risks.
- Establish the right tone from the top, while defining and enforcing accountability.
- Ensure a continuous process that is a part of daily activities.

There are three main domains in the framework: risk governance, risk evaluation, and risk response. Each of these domains is supported by three processes with various activities. Similar to COBIT, the guidance will provide a list of components, inputs and outputs, RACI charts, goals, and metrics for each process. The framework is depicted as a pyramid as seen in Figure B-6.

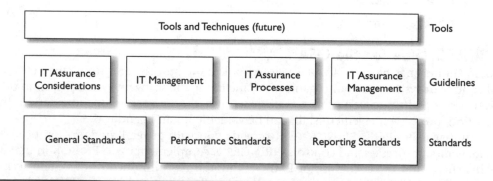

Figure B-6 The Risk IT Framework

In addition to the guiding principles and process model mentioned earlier, The Risk IT Framework contains good practice guidance, domain maturity models, reference materials, and a high-level comparison of risk frameworks.

For more detailed guidance on governing and managing risk, The Practitioner Guide walks you through the entire process from defining a risk universe, developing risk appetite and risk tolerance, to setting up risk scenarios, responding to, and prioritizing risks. More information can be found, and both documents downloaded or purchased, at the ISACA website.

Risk IT Practice Value for the CISA

If you are being asked to audit an IT risk program or identify, govern, or manage IT-related risks, The Risk IT Framework and the Practitioner's Guide will be of great value to you. These can also help with assessing risk and comparing it against the organization's risk appetite and risk tolerance, or assist with the integration of IT risk management within an existing enterprise risk management program.

Val IT

Developed in 2006 by the ITGI, Val IT is a governance framework focused on the management of the IT-related business investments and portfolios. It is based on and attempts to address the "Four Areas" as described in John Thorp's book *The Information Paradox: Realizing the Business Benefits of Information Technology*:

- Are we doing the right things?
- Are we doing them the right way?
- Are we getting them done well?
- Are we getting the benefits?

Val IT complements COBIT, adding best practices for measuring, monitoring, and maximizing the realization of business value from IT investments. Val IT focuses on the IT investment decision processes and the realization of benefits, whereas COBIT focuses on the execution of IT processes.

Val IT Highlights

There are four Val IT publications: The Val IT Framework v2.0, Getting Started with Value Management, The Business Case Guide: Using Val IT 2.0, and Guidance for Assurance Professionals Using Val IT 2.0.

The Val IT Framework v2.0 contains information on the framework's seven key principles, three domains, key processes, and related practices.

VAL IT is based upon the following seven principles:

1. IT-enabled investments will be managed as a portfolio of investments.
2. IT-enabled investments will include the full scope of activities required to achieve business value.
3. IT-enabled investments will be managed through their full economic life cycle.

4. Value delivery practices will recognize different categories of investments to be evaluated and managed differently.

5. Value delivery practices will define and monitor key metrics and respond quickly to any changes or deviations.

6. Value delivery practices will engage all stakeholders and assign appropriate accountability for delivery of capabilities and realization of business benefits.

7. Value delivery practices will be continually monitored, evaluated, and improved.

The principles are applied to three Val IT domains: value governance, portfolio management, and investment management. Each of these domains contains various processes, each enabled by a number of key management practices. Similar to COBIT, for each process identified in Val IT one can find associated inputs and outputs, RACI charts, goals, and metrics.

The Getting Started with Value Management publication provides various approaches for implementing Val IT. Documentation includes assessment templates, maturity models, and approaches for managing and sustaining change.

The Business Case Guide: Using Val IT 2.0 provides guidance for developing an effective business case. Business cases are developed for IT-enabled investments and take into consideration the following:

- Resources are needed for development
- A technology/IT service that will be supported
- An operational capability that will be enabled
- A business capability that will be created
- Stakeholder value that will be realized

This publication outlines an eight-step process for developing the business case that involves building a fact sheet, analyzing various data and risk, appraising the risk and/or return of the investment, documentation, and review.

Guidance for Assurance Professionals Using Val IT 2.0 describes how to use Val IT to support an assurance review of IT investment governance for all three Val IT domains. Included is a set of assurance tests covering the full scope of Val IT as well as guidance for planning and scoping assurance activities.

Val IT Value for the CISA

Val IT publications, especially The Guidance for Assurance Professionals Using Val IT 2.0, can be a useful tool should you need to audit or assess how IT investments and the IT portfolio are managed and governed. More information about Val IT can be obtained from ISACA.

Summary of Frameworks

Table B-3 contains a summary of the frameworks discussed in this appendix. The table indicates whether the framework is available for a fee, the primary focus of the framework, and best uses for the framework.

Title	Summary	Free Online/Hardcopy Cost	Primary Focus				Cont	Gov	Best Use
			DemCyc	MatMod	Proc	ContObj			
COSO Internal Control Integrated Framework	Provides general overview of enterprise internal control	NO/$				X	X	X	To get an overview of what internal control is. Foundational. Can use Evaluation Tools volume to assist with risk, controls, and objectives.
COBIT v4.1	Provides detailed framework of IT processes and controls	YES*/$$	X	X	X	X	X	X	Details on processes, RACI, control objectives, and audit foundation. Links all other frameworks to it; most comprehensive/detailed. Audit and implementation.
GAIT	Assess scope of IT general controls	YES*/$			X	X			Determine/assess risk and scope IT general controls. Assists with SOX 404 planning.
GTAG	High-level overview of IT audit and controls	YES*/$			X	X			Foundational: provides overviews of IT controls in business terminology.
ISF	Overview of information security controls/domains	YES/N/A			X	X			Excellent resource when implementing information security controls.
ISO 27001	Overview of information security controls/domains	NO/$$	X			X	X		Overview, details on information systems. Control/activities. Use for audit and implementation of information security controls.
ITAF	Standards and guidance for conducting IT audit and assurance activities	YES*/$							Fundamental framework for every CISA as it contains mandatory standards and several guidelines to assist with conducting IT audit and assurance activities.
ITGI Boardroom Briefing	Overview of IT governance	YES*/$		X		X			Overview of the five main components of IT governance.
ITIL	Service delivery standards	NO/$$	X		X				Overview. Use for guidance in improving service delivery processes.
PMBOK	Enterprise project management	NO/$	X		X				Provides thorough guidance on managing projects: what to do.
PRINCE2	IT project management	NO/$$	X	X	X				Guidance on managing projects: how to do it.
RISK IT	IT-related business risk governance and management Complements COBIT.	YES*/$		X	X			X	Best used for developing or auditing IT risk processes and/or programs.
Val IT	Governance of IT-enabled business investments and the portfolio Complements COBIT.	YES*/$		X	X	X		X	Useful for CISAs needing to audit the IT-enabled business investment or portfolio management processes.

* Must be an ISACA or IIA member to download the documents free of charge

$ Denotes materials that can be purchased for <$100US

$$ Denotes materials that can be purchased directly or through membership > $100US

Table B-3 Summary of Frameworks

Pointers for Successful Use of Frameworks

- Take time to learn the fundamentals of governance, controls, and processes. Become familiar with COSO, COBIT, and fundamental GTAG documents.
- Not one single framework is the "right" framework.
- There has been a great deal of research on governance, controls, and frameworks. Start here—don't reinvent the wheel.
- Use frameworks for guidance and tailor them to your unique organization.

Notes

- Goals and objectives define what the organization is trying to achieve.
- Governance is what organizations put in place to identify and ensure achievement of goals, objectives, and strategies.
- A process is a set of activities that is put in place to maximize effectiveness and efficiency of operations. Organizations can manage operations through processes.
- Maturity models are often used to measure the maturity of process capabilities.
- The Deming Cycle focuses on continuous improvement through the implementation of a range of processes that address planning, execution, monitoring, and taking corrective actions.
- Control objectives are developed to ensure that business objectives are achieved.
- Control activities support control objectives and can be implemented within processes.
- Projects are temporary, unique, and have specific objectives and controls implemented.

In this appendix, we focused on processes and internal controls, and learned about the various frameworks, methodologies, and guides available as resources. Now that we have examined the available resources, it's time to put all of this to use. For an overview of conducting professional audits, see Appendix A.

References

- *Board Briefing on IT Governance: 2nd Edition*; IT Governance Institute. www.itgi.org
- *Certified in the Governance of Enterprise IT (CGEIT)* certification; ISACA. www.isaca.org/cgeit
- *Business Motivation Model*; Business Rules Group. www.businessrulesgroup.org/bmm.shtml
- *The RummlerBrache Toolkit*; RummelerBrache. www.rummler-brache.com/toolkit

- *Business Model for Information Security (BMIS)*; ISACA. https://www.isaca.org/BMIS
- *COSO Internal Control Integrated Framework*; Committee of Sponsoring Organizations of the Treadway Commission (COSO). www.coso.org/IC-IntegratedFramework-summary.htm
- *2004 Enterprise Risk Management (COSO ERM)*; Committee of Sponsoring Organizations of the Treadway Commission (COSO). www.coso.org/-ERM.htm
- *Guidance on Monitoring Internal Control Systems*; Committee of Sponsoring Organizations of the Treadway Commission (COSO). www.coso.org/guidance.htm
- *Control Objectives for Information and related Technology (COBIT)* framework version 5; (ISACA) and the IT Governance Institute (ITGI). www.isaca.org/COBIT5
- *Global Technology Audit Guide (GTAG)*; Institute of Internal Auditors. www.theiia.org
- *Guide to the Assessment of IT Risk (GAIT)*; Institute of Internal Auditors. www.theiia.org
- *The Standard of Good Practice*; the Information Security Forum (ISF). https://www.isfsecuritystandard.com
- *Information technology – Security techniques – Information security management systems – Requirements* (ISO 27001:2005); ISO. www.iso.org
- *Information technology – Security techniques – Code of practice for information security management* (ISO 27002:2005); ISO. www.iso.org
- *Information Technology Assurance Framework (ITAF): A Professional Practices Framework for IT Assurance*; ISACA. www.isaca.org/itaf
- *Information Technology Infrastructure Library (ITIL)* version 3; Office of Government Commerce (OGC). www.itil-officialsite.com/
- *A Guide to the Project Management Body of Knowledge (PMBOK)*; Project Management Institute (PMI). www.pmi.org
- *Managing Successful Projects with PRINCE2*; Office of Government Commerce (OGC). www.prince-officialsite.com
- *The Risk IT Framework and Risk IT Practitioner Guide*; ISACA. www.isaca.org/riskit
- *Val IT Framework for Business Technology Management*; ISACA. www.isaca.org
- *Guidance for Assurance Professionals Using Val IT 2.0*; ISACA. www.isaca.org

About the CD-ROM

The CD-ROM included with this book comes complete with MasterExam and the electronic version of the book. The software is easy to install on any Windows 2000/XP/Vista/7 computer and must be installed to access the MasterExam feature. You may, however, browse the electronic book directly from the CD without installation. To register for the bonus MasterExam, simply click the Bonus MasterExam link on the main launch page and follow the directions to the free online registration.

System Requirements

Software requires Windows 2000 or higher, Internet Explorer 6.0 or above, and 20MB of available hard disk space for full installation. The electronic book requires Adobe Acrobat Reader.

Installing and Running MasterExam

If your computer CD-ROM drive is configured to auto-run, the CD-ROM will automatically start up upon inserting the disk. From the opening screen you may install MasterExam by clicking the MasterExam link. This will begin the installation process and create a program group named LearnKey. To run MasterExam, select Start | All Programs | LearnKey | MasterExam. If the auto-run feature did not launch your CD, browse to the CD and double-click on the LaunchTraining.exe icon.

MasterExam

MasterExam provides you with a simulation of the actual exam. The number of questions, the type of questions, and the time allowed are intended to be an accurate representation of the exam environment. You have the option to take an open-book exam, including hints, references, and answers; a closed-book exam; or the timed MasterExam simulation.

When you launch MasterExam, a digital clock display will appear in the bottom-right corner of your screen. The clock will continue to count down to zero unless you choose to end the exam before the time expires.

Electronic Book

The entire contents of the All-in-One Exam Guide are provided as a PDF. Adobe's Acrobat Reader has been included on the CD.

Help

A help file is provided through the help button on the main page in the lower-left corner. An individual help feature is also available through MasterExam.

Removing Installation(s)

MasterExam is installed to your hard drive. For best results removing programs, select Start | All Programs | LearnKey| Uninstall to remove MasterExam.

Technical Support

For questions regarding the content of the electronic book or MasterExam, please visit www.mhprofessional.com/techsupport. For customers outside the United States, e-mail international_cs@mcgraw-hill.com.

LearnKey Technical Support

For technical problems with the software (installation, operation, removing installations), please visit www.learnkey.com, e-mail techsupport@learnkey.com, or call toll-free at 1-800-482-8244.

802.11 The wireless network standard commonly known as "Wi-Fi" that can transport data up to 108 Mbit/sec up to a distance of 300 m.

802.1X A standard for network authentication and access control for devices that wish to attach to a LAN or wireless LAN.

acceptable use Security policy that defines the types of activities that are acceptable and those that are not acceptable.

access bypass Any attempt by an intruder to bypass access controls in order to gain entry into a system.

access control Any means that detects or prevents unauthorized access and that permits authorized access.

access control list (ACL) An access control method where a list of permitted or denied users (or systems, or services, as the case may be) is used to control access.

access control log A record of attempted accesses.

access control policy Statement that defines the policy for the granting, review, and revocation of access to systems and work areas.

access management A formal business process that is used to control access to networks and information systems.

access point A device that provides communication services using the 802.11 (Wi-Fi) protocol standard.

access review A review of the users, systems, or other subjects that are permitted to access protected objects. The purpose of a review is to ensure that all subjects should still be authorized to have access.

account lockout An administrative lock that is placed on a user account when a predetermined event occurs, such as reaching an expiration date, or when there have been several unsuccessful attempts to access the user account.

address resolution protocol (ARP) A standard network protocol used to obtain the address for another station on a local area network (LAN).

administrative audit An audit of operational efficiency.

administrative control Controls in the form of policies, processes, procedures, and standards.

agile development Software development process where a large project team is broken up into smaller teams, and project deliverables are broken up into smaller pieces, each of which can be attained in a few weeks.

algorithm In cryptography, a specific mathematical formula that is used to perform encryption, decryption, message digests, and digital signatures.

annualized loss expectancy (ALE) The expected loss of asset value due to threat realization. ALE is defined as SLE × ARO.

annualized rate of occurrence (ARO) An estimate of the number of times that a threat will occur every year.

anti-malware See *antivirus software.*

antivirus software Software that is designed to detect and remove viruses and other forms of malware.

AppleTalk The suite of protocols used to transmit packets from one station to another over a network.

appliance A type of computer with preinstalled software that requires little or no maintenance.

application Layer 7 of the OSI network model. See also *OSI network model.*

application Layer 4 of the TCP/IP network model. The purpose of the application layer is the delivery of messages from one process to another on the same network or on different networks. See also *TCP/IP network model.*

application firewall A device used to control packets being sent to an application server, primarily to block unwanted or malicious content.

application programming language See *programming language.*

application server A server that runs application software.

architecture standard A standard that defines technology architecture at the database, system, or network level.

arithmetic logic unit (ALU) The part of a central processing unit that performs arithmetic computations. See *central processing unit.*

asset inventory The process of confirming the existence, location, and condition of assets; also, the results of such a process.

asset management The processes used to manage the inventory, classification, use, and disposal of assets.

assets The collection of property that is owned by an organization.

asset value (AV) The value of an IT asset, which is usually (but not necessarily) the asset's replacement value.

asymmetric encryption A method for encryption, decryption, and digital signatures that uses pairs of encryption keys, consisting of a public key and a private key.

asynchronous replication A type of replication where writing data to the remote storage system is not kept in sync with updates on the local storage system. Instead, there may be a time lag, and there is no guarantee that data on the remote system is identical to that on the local storage system. See also *replication*.

asynchronous transfer mode (ATM)   A LAN and WAN protocol standard for sending messages in the form of cells over networks. On an ATM network, all messages are transmitted in synchronization with a network-based time clock. A station that wishes to send a message to another station must wait for the time clock.

atomicity   The characteristic of a complex transaction whereby it is either performed completely as a single unit or not at all.

attribute sampling   A sampling technique used to study the characteristics of a population to determine how many samples possess a specific characteristic. See also *sampling*.

audit charter   A written document that defines the mission and goals of the audit program as well as roles and responsibilities.

audit logging   A feature in an application, operating system, or database management system where events are recorded in a separate log.

audit methodology   A set of audit procedures that is used to accomplish a set of audit objectives.

audit objective   The purpose or goals of an audit. Generally, the objective of an audit is to determine if controls exist and are effective in some specific aspect of business operations in an organization.

audit procedures   The step-by-step instructions and checklists required to perform specific audit activities. Procedures may include a list of people to interview and questions to ask them, evidence to request, audit tools to use, sampling rates, where and how evidence will be archived, and how evidence will be evaluated.

audit program   The plan for conducting audits over a long period.

audit report   The final, written product of an audit. An audit report will include a description of the purpose, scope, and type of audit performed; persons interviewed; evidence collected; rates and methods of sampling; and findings on the existence and effectiveness of each control.

audit scope   The process, procedures, systems, and applications that are the subject of an audit.

authentication   The process of asserting one's identity and providing proof of that identity. Typically, authentication requires a user ID (the assertion) and a password (the proof). However, authentication can also require stronger means of proof, such as a digital certificate, token, smart card, or biometric.

authorization   The process whereby a system determines what rights and privileges a user has.

automated workpapers   Data that has been captured by computer-assisted audit techniques. See also *computer-assisted audit technique (CAAT)*.

automatic control   A control that is enacted through some automatic mechanism that requires little or no human intervention.

availability management   The IT function that consists of activities concerned with the availability of IT applications and services. See also *IT service management.*

back door   A section of code that permits someone to bypass access controls and access data or functions. Back doors are commonly placed in programs during development but are removed before programming is complete.

background check   The process of verifying an employment candidate's employment history, education records, professional licenses and certifications, criminal background, and financial background.

background verification   See *background check.*

back-out plan   A procedure used to reverse the effect of a change that was not successful.

backup   The process of copying important data to another media device in the event of a hardware failure, error, or software bug that causes damage to data.

backup media rotation   Any scheme used to determine how backup media is to be reused.

balanced scorecard   A management tool that is used to measure the performance and effectiveness of an organization.

barbed wire   Coiled or straight wire with sharp barbs that may be placed along the top of a fence or wall to prevent or deter passage by unauthorized personnel.

benchmark   The practice of measuring a process in order to compare its performance and quality with the same process as performed by another firm. The purpose is to discover opportunities for improvement that may result in lower cost, fewer resources, and higher quality.

biometrics   Any use of a machine-readable characteristic of a user's body that uniquely identifies the user. Biometrics can be used for strong authentication. Types of biometrics include voice recognition, fingerprint, hand scan, palm vein scan, iris scan, retina scan, facial scan, and handwriting. See also *authentication, strong authentication.*

blackmail   An attempt to extort money from an individual or organization through a threat of exposure.

blackout   A complete loss of electric power for more than a few seconds.

blade server   A type of computer architecture where a main chassis equipped with a power supply, cooling, network, and console connectors contains several slots that are fitted with individual computer modules called blades. Each blade is an independent computer system.

block cipher   This is an encryption algorithm that operates on blocks of data.

Bluetooth   A short-range airlink standard for data communications between peripherals and low-power consumption devices.

bollard   A barrier that prevents the entry of vehicles into protected areas.

border gateway protocol (BGP)   A TCP/IP routing protocol that is used to transmit network routing information from one network router to another in order to determine the most efficient path through a large network.

bot   A type of malware in which agents are implanted by other forms of malware and which are programmed to obey remotely issued instructions. See also *bot army*.

bot army   A collection of bots that are under the control of an individual. See also *bot*.

bridge   An Ethernet network device that is used to interconnect two or more Ethernet networks.

broadcast address   The highest numeric IP address in an IP subnet. When a packet is sent to the network's broadcast address, all active stations on the network will receive it.

brownout   A sustained drop in voltage that can last from several seconds to several hours.

budget   A plan for allocating resources over a certain time period.

bug sweeping   The practice of electronically searching for covert listening devices.

bus   A component in a computer that provides the means for the different components of the computer to communicate with each other.

bus topology   A network topology where each station is connected to a central cable.

business case   An explanation of the expected benefits to the business that will be realized as a result of a program or project.

business continuity planning (BCP)   The activities required to ensure the continuation of critical business processes.

business functional requirements   Formal statements that describe required business functions that a system must support.

business impact analysis (BIA)   A study that is used to identify the impact that different disaster scenarios will have on on-going business operations.

business realization   The result of strategic planning, process development, and systems development, which all contribute toward a launch of business operations to reach a set of business objectives.

business process reengineering   The set of activities related to the process of making changes to business processes.

business recovery plan   The activities required to recover and resume critical business processes and activities. See also *response document*.

call tree   A method for ensuring the timely notification of key personnel, such as after a disaster.

campus area network (CAN)   The interconnection of LANs for an organization that has buildings in close proximity.

capability maturity model   A model that is used to measure the relative maturity of an organization or of its processes.

capability maturity model integration (CMMI)   A maturity model that represents the aggregation of other maturity models.

capacity management   The IT function that consists of activities that confirm there is sufficient capacity in IT systems and IT processes to meet service needs. Primarily, an IT system or process has sufficient capacity if its performance falls within an acceptable range, as specified in service-level agreements (SLAs). See also *IT service management, service-level agreement*.

Category 3   A twisted-pair cabling standard that is capable of transporting 10MB Ethernet up to 100 m (328 ft). See also *twisted-pair cable*.

Category 5   A twisted-pair cabling standard that is capable of transporting 10MB, 100MB, and 1000MB (1GB) Ethernet up to 100 m (328 ft). See also *twisted-pair cable*.

Category 6   A twisted-pair cabling standard that is capable of transporting 10MB, 100MB, and 1000MB (1GB) Ethernet up to 100 m (328 ft). Category 6 has the same transport capability as Category 5, but has better noise resistance. See also *twisted-pair cable*.

Category 7   A twisted-pair cabling standard that is capable of transporting 10GB Ethernet over 100 m (328 ft). See also *twisted-pair cable*.

Category 8   A new cable standard, still under development, designed for high-speed networking. See also *twisted-pair cable*.

central processing unit (CPU)   The main hardware component of a computer that executes program instructions.

certificate authority (CA)   A trusted party that stores digital certificates and public encryption keys.

certificate revocation list (CRL)   An electronic list of digital certificates that have been revoked prior to their expiration date.

certification practice statement (CPS)   A published statement that describes the practices used by the CA to issue and manage digital certificates.

chain of custody   Documentation that shows the acquisition, storage, control, and analysis of evidence. The chain of custody may be needed if the evidence is to be used in a legal proceeding.

change control   See *change management*.

change management   The IT function that is used to control changes made to an IT environment. See also *IT service management*.

change request   A formal request for a change to be made in an environment. See also *change management.*

change review   A formal review of a requested change. See also *change request, change management.*

channel service unit/data service unit (CSU/DSU)   A device used to connect a telecommunications circuit to a local device such as a router.

cipher lock   An electronic or mechanical door equipped with combination locks. Only persons who know the combination may unlock the door.

ciphertext   A message, file, or stream of data that has been transformed by an encryption algorithm and rendered unreadable.

circuit switched   A WAN technology where a dedicated, end-to-end communications channel is established that lasts for the duration of the connection.

CISC (complex instruction set computer)   A central processing unit design that uses a comprehensive instruction set. See also *central processing unit.*

class   The characteristics of an object, including its attributes, properties, fields, and the methods it can perform. See also *object, method.*

class library   A repository where classes are stored. See also *class.*

classful network   A TCP/IP network whose addressing fits into one of the classes of networks: Class A, Class B, or Class C. A classful network will have a predetermined address range and subnet mask.

classless network   A TCP/IP network whose addressing does not fit the classful network scheme, but instead uses an arbitrary subnet mask, as determined by the network's physical and logical design.

client-server application   An application design where the database and some business logic are stored on a central server and where some business logic plus display logic are stored on each user's workstation.

cloud computing   A technique of providing a dynamically scalable and usually virtualized computing resource as a service.

cluster   A tightly coupled collection of computers that are used to solve a common task. In a cluster, one or more servers actively perform tasks, while zero or more computers may be in a "standby" state, ready to assume active duty should the need arise.

coaxial   A type of network cable that consists of a solid inner conductor surrounded by an insulating jacket, which is surrounded by a metallic shield, which in turn is surrounded by a plastic jacket.

code division multiple access (CDMA)   An airlink standard for wireless communications between mobile devices and base stations.

code division multiple access 2000 (CDMA2000) An airlink standard for wireless communications between mobile devices and base stations.

code of ethics A statement that defines acceptable and unacceptable professional conduct.

codec A device or program that encodes or decodes a data stream.

cold site An alternate processing center where the degree of readiness for recovery systems is low. At the very least, a cold site is nothing more than an empty rack, or just allocated space on a computer room floor.

compensating control A control that is implemented because another control cannot be implemented or is ineffective.

compliance audit An audit to determine the level and degree of compliance to a law, regulation, standard, contract provision, or internal control.

compliance testing A type of testing that is used to determine if control procedures have been properly designed and implemented, and are operating properly.

component-based development A software development life cycle process where various components of a larger system are developed separately.

computer-aided software engineering (CASE) A broad variety of tools that are used to automate various aspects of application software development.

computer-assisted audit technique (CAAT) Any technique where computers are used to automate or simplify the audit process.

computer trespass Unlawful entry into a computer or application.

confidence coefficient The probability that a sample selected actually represents the entire population. This is usually expressed as a percentage.

configuration management The IT function where the configuration of components in an IT environment is independently recorded. Configuration management is usually supported by the use of automated tools used to inventory and control system configurations. See also *IT service management.*

configuration management database (CMDB) A repository for every component in an environment that contains information on every configuration change made on those components.

configuration standard A standard that defines the detailed configurations that are used in servers, workstations, operating systems, database management systems, applications, network devices, and other systems.

conspiracy A plan by two or more persons to commit an illegal act.

constructive cost model (COCOMO) A method for estimating software development projects based on the number of lines of code and the complexity of the software being developed.

contact list   A list of key personnel and various methods used to contact them. See also *response document*.

continuity of operations plan (COOP)   The activities required to continue critical and strategic business functions at an alternate site. See also *response document*.

continuous and intermittent simulation (CIS)   A continuous auditing technique where flagged transactions are processed in a parallel simulation and the results compared to production processing results.

continuous auditing   An auditing technique where sampling and testing are automated and occur continuously.

contract   A binding legal agreement between two parties that may be enforceable in a court of law.

control   Policies, processes, and procedures that are created to achieve desired events or to avoid unwanted events.

control failure   The result of an audit of a control where the control is determined to be ineffective.

control objective   A foundational statement that describes desired states or outcomes from business operations.

Control Objectives for Information and related Technology (COBIT)   A control framework for managing information systems and security. COBIT is published by ISACA.

control risk   The risk that a material error exists that will not be prevented or detected by the organization's control framework.

control self-assessment (CSA)   A methodology used by an organization to review key business objectives, risks, and controls. Control self-assessment is a self-regulation activity.

corrective action   An action that is initiated to correct an undesired condition.

corrective control   A control that is used after an unwanted event has occurred.

corroboration   An audit technique where an IS auditor interviews additional personnel to confirm the validity of evidence obtained from others who were interviewed previously.

countermeasure   Any activity or mechanism that is designed to reduce risk.

crash gate   Hard barriers that lift into position, preventing the entry (or exit) of unauthorized vehicles, and that can be lowered to permit authorized vehicles.

critical path methodology (CPM)   A technique that is used to identify the most critical path in a project to understand which tasks are most likely to affect the project schedule.

criticality analysis (CA)   A study of each system and process, a consideration of the impact on the organization if it is incapacitated, the likelihood of incapacitation, and the estimated cost of mitigating the risk or impact of incapacitation.

cross-over error rate   The point at which the false reject rate (FRR) equals the false accept rate (FAR). This is the ideal point for a well-tuned biometric system. See also *biometrics, false reject rate,* and *false accept rate.*

cryptanalysis   An attack on a cryptosystem where the attacker is attempting to determine the encryption key that is used to encrypt messages.

cryptography   The practice of hiding information from unwanted persons.

cryptosystem   A set of algorithms used to generate an encryption key, to perform encryption, and to perform decryption.

custodian   A person or group delegated to operate or maintain an asset.

customer relationship management (CRM)   An IS application that is used to track the details of the relationships with each of an organization's customers.

customization   A unique change that is made to a computer program or system.

cutover   The step in the software development life cycle where an old replaced system is shut down and a new replacement system is started.

cutover test   An actual test of disaster recovery (DR) and/or business continuity response plans. The purpose of a parallel test is to evaluate the ability of personnel to follow directives in emergency response plans—to actually set up the DR business processing or data processing capability. In a cutover test, personnel shut down production systems and operate recovery systems to assume actual business workload. See also *disaster recovery plan.*

cyclical redundancy check (CRC)   A hash function used to create a checksum that is used to detect errors in network transmissions. The Ethernet standard uses a CRC to detect errors.

damage assessment   The process of examining assets after a disaster to determine the extent of damage.

data acquisition   The act of obtaining data for later use in a forensic investigation.

data classification policy   Policy that defines sensitivity levels and handling procedures for information.

data control language   A procedural language used to control access to a database.

data definition language (DDL)   A procedural language used to describe the structure of data contained in a database.

data dictionary (DD)   A set of data in a database management system that describes the structure of databases stored there.

data file controls   Controls that ensure the security and integrity of data files and their contents.

data flow architecture   The part of network architecture that is closely related to application and data architecture. See also *data flow diagram*.

data flow diagram   A diagram that illustrates the flow of data within and between systems.

data link   Layer 2 of the OSI network model. See also *OSI network model*.

data management utility   A type of utility software used to manipulate, list, transform, query, compare, encrypt, decrypt, import, or export data. See also *utility software*.

data manipulation language (DML)   A procedural language used to insert, delete, and modify data in a database.

data-oriented system development (DOSD)   A software development life cycle process that starts with a design of data and interfaces to databases and then moves on to program design.

data restore   The process of copying data from backup media to a target system for the purpose of restoring lost or damaged data.

database management system (DBMS)   A software program that facilitates the storage and retrieval of potentially large amounts of structured or unstructured information.

database   A collection of structured or unstructured information.

database server   A server that contains and facilitates access to one or more databases.

debugging   The activity of searching for the cause of malfunctions in programs or systems.

decryption   The process of transforming ciphertext into plaintext so that a recipient can read it.

default gateway   A station on a network (usually a router) that is used to forward messages to stations on distant networks.

default password   A password associated with a user account or system account that retains its factory default setting.

deluge   A fire sprinkler system that has dry pipes and all of the sprinkler heads are open. When the system is operated (for instance, when an alarm is triggered), water flows into the pipes and out of all of the sprinkler heads. See also *fire sprinkler system*.

denial of service (DoS)   An attack on a computer or network with the intention of causing disruption or malfunction of the target.

desktop computer   A computer used by an individual end user and located at the user's workspace.

detection risk The risk that an IS auditor will overlook errors or exceptions during an audit.

detective control A control that is used to detect events.

deterrent control A control that is designed to deter people from performing unwanted activities.

development The process where software code is created.

diameter An authentication standard that is the successor to RADIUS. See also *RADIUS*.

Diffie-Hellman A popular key exchange algorithm. See also *key exchange*.

digital certificate An electronic document that contains an identity that is signed with the public key of a certificate authority (CA).

digital envelope A method that uses two layers of encryption. A symmetric key is used to encrypt a message; then a public or private key is used to encrypt the symmetric key.

digital private branch exchange (DPBX) A private branch exchange (PBX) that supports digital technologies such as Voice over IP (VoIP) and Session Initiation Protocol (SIP). See also *private branch exchange (PBX)*, *Voice over IP (VoIP)*, and *Session Initiation Protocol (SIP)*.

digital rights management (DRM) Any technology used to control the distribution and use of electronic content.

digital signature The result of encrypting the hash of a message with the originator's private encryption key, used to prove the authenticity and integrity of a message.

digital subscriber line (DSL) A common carrier standard for transporting data from the Internet to homes and businesses.

directory A structure in a file system that is used to store files and, optionally, other directories. See also *file system*.

directory system (DS) See *data dictionary*.

disaster An unexpected and unplanned event that results in the disruption of business operations.

disaster declaration criteria The conditions that must be present to declare a disaster, triggering response and recovery operations.

disaster declaration procedure Instructions to determine whether to declare a disaster and trigger response and recovery operations. See also *disaster declaration criteria*.

disaster recovery and business continuity requirements Formal statements that describe required recoverability and continuity characteristics that a system must support.

disaster recovery plan   The activities required to restore critical IT systems and other critical assets, whether in alternate or primary locations. See also *response document*.

disaster recovery planning (DRP)   Activities related to the assessment, salvage, repair, and restoration of facilities and assets.

discovery sampling   A sampling technique where at least one exception is sought in a population. See also *sampling*.

discretionary access control (DAC)   An access model where the owner of an object is able to determine how and by whom the object may be accessed. The discretion of the owner determines permitted accesses by subjects.

disk array   A chassis in which several hard disks can be installed and connected to a server. The individual disk drives can be "hot swapped" in the chassis while the array is still operating.

disk management system (DMS)   An information system that is used to manage disk media, usually for the purpose of performing information backup. See also *backup*.

distributed denial of service (DDoS)   A denial of service (DoS) attack that originates from many computers. See also *denial of service (DoS)*.

document review   A review of some or all disaster recovery and business continuity plans, procedures, and other documentation. Individuals typically review these documents on their own, at their own pace, but within whatever time constraints or deadlines that may have been established.

documentation   The inclusive term that describes charters, processes, procedures, standards, requirements, and other written documents.

domain name service (DNS)   A TCP/IP application layer protocol used to translate domain names (such as www.isecbooks.com) into IP addresses.

dropout   A momentary loss of power that lasts from a few milliseconds to a few seconds.

dry pipe   A fire sprinkler system used where ambient temperatures often drop below freezing. In this type of system, pipes are filled with compressed air. When sufficient heat causes one of the sprinkler head fuses to break, a control valve releases water into the piping. See also *fire sprinkler system*.

dual power feeds   The use of two physically separate electric power feeds into a facility.

dynamic host configuration protocol (DHCP)   A TCP/IP application layer protocol used to assign an IP address, subnet mask, default gateway, IP address of DNS servers, and other information to a workstation that has joined the network.

dynamic random access memory (DRAM)   The most common form of semiconductor memory, where data is stored in capacitors that require periodic refreshing.

E-1 A common carrier standard protocol for transporting voice and data. E-1 can support up to 32 separate voice channels of 64 kbit/sec each and is used primarily in Europe.

E-3 A common carrier standard protocol for transporting voice and data. E-3 can support up to 512 separate voice channels of 64 kbit/sec each and is used primarily in Europe.

e-mail A network-based service used to transmit messages between individuals and groups.

eavesdropping The act of secretly intercepting and recording a voice or data transmission.

electric generator A system consisting of an internal combustion engine powered by gasoline, diesel fuel, or natural gas that spins an electric generator. A generator can supply electricity for as long as several days, depending upon the size of its fuel supply and whether it can be refueled.

electrically erasable programmable read-only memory (EEPROM) A form of permanent memory that can be rewritten using a special program on the computer that it is installed on.

elliptic curve A public key cryptography algorithm.

embedded audit module (EAM) A continuous auditing technique that consists of a special software module embedded within a system that is designed to detect processing anomalies.

emergency communications plan The communications that are required during a disaster. See also *response document.*

emergency response The urgent activities that immediately follow a disaster, including evacuation of personnel, first aid, triage of injured personnel, and possibly firefighting.

employee handbook See *employee policy manual.*

employee policy manual A formal statement of the terms of employment, facts about the organization, benefits, compensation, conduct, and policies.

employment agreement A legal contract between an organization and an employee, which may include a description of duties, roles and responsibilities, confidentiality, compliance, and termination.

encapsulation A practice where a method can call on another method to help perform its work. See also *method.*

encryption The act of hiding sensitive information in plain sight. Encryption works by scrambling the characters in a message, using a method known only to the sender and receiver, making the message useless to anyone who intercepts the message.

encryption key A block of characters, used in combination with an encryption algorithm, to encrypt or decrypt a stream or block of data.

enhanced interior gateway routing protocol (EIGRP)   A TCP/IP routing protocol that is used to transmit network routing information from one network router to another in order to determine the most efficient path through a large network.

enterprise architecture   Activities that ensure important business needs are met by IT systems; the model that is used to map business functions into the IT environment and IT systems in increasing levels of detail.

erasable programmable read-only memory (EPROM)   A form of permanent memory that can be erased by shining ultraviolet (UV) light through a quartz window on the top of the chip.

error handling   Functions that are performed when errors in processing are encountered.

espionage   The act of spying on an organization.

Ethernet   A standard protocol for assembling a stream of data into frames for transport over a physical medium from one station to another on a local area network. On an Ethernet network, any station is free to transmit a packet at any time, provided that another station is not already doing so.

evacuation procedure   Instructions to safely evacuate a work facility in the event of a fire, earthquake, or other disaster.

evidence   Information gathered by the auditor that provides proof that a control exists and is being operated.

expected error rate   An estimate that expresses the percent of errors or exceptions that may exist in an entire population.

exposure factor (EF)   The financial loss that results from the realization of a threat, expressed as a percentage of the asset's total value.

false accept rate (FAR)   The rate at which invalid subjects are accepted as valid. This occurs when the biometric system has too large a margin of error. See also *biometrics*.

false reject rate (FRR)   The rate at which valid subjects are rejected. This occurs when the biometric system has too small a margin of error. See also *biometrics*.

feasibility study   An activity that seeks to determine the expected benefits of a program or project.

fence   A structure that prevents or deters passage by unauthorized personnel.

fiber distributed data interface (FDDI)   A local area network technology that consists of a "dual ring" with redundant network cabling and counter-rotating logical tokens.

fiber optics   A cabling standard that uses optical fiber instead of metal conductors.

Fibre Channel A standard protocol for assembling a stream of data into frames for transport over a physical medium from one station to another on a local area network. Fibre Channel is most often found in storage area networks. See also *storage area network*.

field A unit of storage in a relational database management system (rDBMS) that consists of a single data item within a row. See also *relational database management system*, *table*, and *row*.

file A sequence of zero or more characters that is stored as a whole in a file system. A file may be a document, spreadsheet, image, sound file, computer program, or data that is used by a program. See also *file system*.

file allocation table (FAT) A file system used by the MS-DOS operating system as well as by early versions of the Microsoft Windows operating system.

file server A server that is used to store files in a central location, usually to make them available to many users.

file system A logical structure that facilitates the storage of data on a digital storage medium such as a hard drive, CD/DVD-ROM, or flash memory device.

file transfer protocol (FTP) An early and still widely used TCP/IP application layer protocol that is used for the batch transfer of files or entire directories from one system to another.

file transfer protocol secure (FTPS) A TCP/IP application layer protocol that is an extension of the FTP protocol where authentication and transport are encrypted using SSL or TLS. See also *File Transfer Protocol (FTP)*, *Secure Sockets Layer (SSL)*, and *Transport Layer Security (TLS)*.

financial audit An audit of an accounting system, accounting department processes, and procedures to determine if business controls are sufficient to ensure the integrity of financial statements.

financial management Management for IT services that consists of several activities, including budgeting, capital investment, expense management, project accounting, and project ROI. See also *IT service management, return on investment*.

fire extinguisher A hand-operated fire suppression device used for fighting small fires.

fire sprinkler system A fire suppression system that extinguishes a fire by spraying water on it.

firewall A device that controls the flow of network messages between networks. Placed at the boundary between the Internet and an organization's internal network, firewalls enforce security policy by prohibiting all inbound traffic except for the specific few types of traffic that are permitted to a select few systems.

firmware A computer's special-purpose storage that is usually used to store the instructions required to start the computer system. Firmware is usually implemented in ROM, PROM, EPROM, EEPROM, or flash.

first in first out (FIFO) A backup media rotation scheme where the oldest backup volumes are used next. See also *backup media rotation*.

flash A form of permanent memory that can be rewritten by the computer that it is installed on. Flash memory is used by several types of devices, including SD (Secure Digital) cards, Compact Flash, Memory Stick, and USB drives.

foreign key A field in a table in a relational database management system (rDBMS) that references a field in another table. See also *relational database management system, table, row,* and *field.*

forensic audit An audit that is performed in support of an anticipated or active legal proceeding.

forensics The application of procedures and tools during an investigation of a computer or network-related event.

fourth-generation language (4GL) A variety of tools that are used in the development of applications, or that are parts of the applications themselves.

Frame Relay A common carrier standard for transporting packets from one network to another. Frame Relay is being replaced by MPLS. See also *multiprotocol label switching (MPLS).*

fraud The intentional deception made for personal gain or for damage to another party.

function point analysis (FPA) A method for estimating software development projects based on the number of user inputs, outputs, queries, files, and external interfaces.

functional testing The portion of software testing where functional requirements are verified.

gateway A device that acts as a protocol converter or that performs some other type of transformation of messages.

general computing controls (GCC) Controls that are general in nature and implemented across most or all information systems and applications.

generalized audit software (GAS) Audit software that is designed to read data directly from database platforms and flat files.

general packet radio service (GPRS) An airlink standard for wireless communications between mobile devices and base stations.

governance Management's control over policy and processes.

grandfather-father-son A hierarchical backup media rotation scheme that provides for longer retention of some backups. See also *backup media rotation.*

grid computing A large number of loosely coupled computers that are used to solve a common task.

guard dogs Dogs that assist security guards and that can be used to apprehend and control trespassers.

guest A virtual machine running under a hypervisor.

hacker Someone who interferes with or accesses another's computer without authorization.

hardening The technique of configuring a system so that only its essential services and features are active and all others are deactivated. This helps to reduce the "attack surface" of a system to only its essential components.

hardware monitoring Tools and processes used to continuously observe the health, performance, and capacity of one or more computers.

hash function A cryptographic operation on a block of data that returns a fixed-length string of characters, used to verify the integrity of a message.

heating, ventilation, and air conditioning (HVAC) A system that controls temperature and humidity in a facility.

hierarchical file system (HFS) A file system used on computers running the Mac OS operating system. See also *file system.*

honeynet A network of computers that is acting as a honeypot. See also *honeypot.*

honeypot A trap that is designed to detect unauthorized use of information systems.

host-based intrusion detection system (HIDS) An intrusion detection system (IDS) that is installed on a system and watches for anomalies that could be signs of intrusion. See also *intrusion detection system (IDS).*

hot site An alternate processing center where backup systems are already running and in some state of near-readiness to assume production workload. The systems at a hot site most likely have application software and database management software already loaded and running, perhaps even at the same patch levels as the systems in the primary processing center.

hub An Ethernet network device that is used to connect devices to the network. A hub can be thought of as a multiport repeater.

humidity The amount of water moisture in the air.

Hypertext Transfer Protocol (HTTP) A TCP/IP application layer protocol used to transmit webpage contents from web servers to users who are using web browsers.

Hypertext Transfer Protocol Secure (HTTPS)   A TCP/IP application layer protocol that is similar to HTTP in its use for transporting data between web servers and browsers. HTTPS is not a separate protocol, but instead is the instance where HTTP is encrypted with SSL or TLS. See also *Hypertext Transfer Protocol (HTTP)*, *Secure Sockets Layer (SSL)*, and *Transport Layer Security (TLS)*.

hypervisor   Virtualization software that facilitates the operation of one or more virtual machines.

identification   The process of asserting one's identity without providing proof of that identity. See also *authentication*.

identity management   The activity of managing the identity of each employee, contractor, temporary worker, and, optionally, customer, for use in a single environment or multiple environments.

impact   The actual or expected result from some action such as a disaster.

impact analysis   The analysis of a threat and the impact it would have if it were realized.

implementation   A step in the software development life cycle where new or updated software is placed into the production environment and started.

incident   Any event that is not part of the standard operation of a service and that causes, or may cause, interruption to, or a reduction in, the quality of that service.

incident management   The IT function that analyzes service outages, service slowdowns, security incidents, and software bugs, and seeks to resolve them to restore normal service. See also *IT service management*.

incident prevention   Proactive steps taken to reduce the probability and/or impact of security incidents.

independence   The characteristic of an auditor and his or her relationship to a party being audited. An auditor should be independent of the auditee; this permits the auditor to be objective.

index   An entity in a relational database management system (rDBMS) that facilitates rapid searching for specific rows in a table based on one of the fields other than the primary key. See also *relational database management system, table, row, field,* and *primary key.*

inert gas   A fire suppression system that floods a room with an inert gas, displacing oxygen from the room and extinguishing the fire.

information classification   The process of assigning a sensitivity classification to an information asset.

information leakage   The tendency for sensitive information to leak out of an organization's databases through various means, most of which are perpetrated by the organization's personnel.

information security management   The aggregation of policies, processes, procedures, and activities to ensure that an organization's security policy is effective.

information security policy   A statement that defines how an organization will classify and protect its important assets.

Infrared Data Association (IrDA)   The organization that has developed technical standards for point-to-point data communications using infrared light. IrDA has largely been replaced with Bluetooth and USB.

infrastructure   The collection of networks, network services, devices, facilities, and system software that facilitate access to, communications with, and protection of business applications.

infrastructure as a service   A cloud computing model where a service provider makes computers and other infrastructure components available to subscribers. See also *cloud computing.*

inherent risk   The risk that there are material weaknesses in existing business processes and no compensating controls to detect or prevent them.

inheritance   The property of a class where class attributes are passed to its children. See also *class.*

initialization vector (IV)   A random number that is needed by some encryption algorithms to begin the encryption process.

input authorization   Controls that ensure all data that is input into an information system is authorized by management.

input controls   Administrative and technical controls that determine what data is permitted to be input into an information system. These controls exist to ensure the integrity of information in a system.

input validation   Controls that ensure the type and values of information that are input into a system are appropriate and reasonable.

input/output (I/O) device   Any device that can be connected to a computer that permits the computer to send data to the device as well as receive data from the device.

inquiry and observation   An audit technique where an IS auditor asks questions of interviewees and makes observations about personnel behavior and the way they perform their tasks.

inrush   A sudden increase in current flowing to a device, usually associated with the startup of a large motor. This can cause a voltage drop that lasts several seconds.

insourcing   A form of sourcing where an employer will use its own employees to perform a function.

instant messaging (IM)   Any of several TCP/IP application layer protocols and tools used to send short text messages over a network.

integrated audit   An audit that combines an operational audit and a financial audit. See also *operational audit, financial audit.*

integrated services digital network (ISDN)   A common carrier telephone network used to carry voice and data over landlines. ISDN can be thought of as a digital version of the PSTN. See also *public-switched telephone network (PSTN).*

integrated test facility (ITF)   A type of automated test where an auditor creates fictitious transactions to trace their integrity through the system.

intellectual property   A class of assets owned by an organization; includes an organization's designs, architectures, software source code, processes, and procedures.

interior gateway routing protocol (IGRP)   A TCP/IP routing protocol that is used to transmit network routing information from one network router to another in order to determine the most efficient path through a large network.

intermediate system to intermediate system (IS-IS)   A TCP/IP routing protocol that is used to transmit network routing information from one network router to another in order to determine the most efficient path through a large network.

Internet   Layer 2 of the TCP/IP network model. The purpose of the Internet layer is the delivery of messages (called packets) from one station to another on the same network or on different networks. See also *TCP/IP network model.*

Internet   The interconnection of the world's TCP/IP networks.

Internet Control Message Protocol (ICMP)   A communications diagnostics protocol that is a part of the TCP/IP suite of protocols.

Internet Message Access Protocol (IMAP)   A TCP/IP application layer protocol used by an end-user program to retrieve e-mail messages from an e-mail server.

Internet Protocol (IP)   The network layer protocol used in the TCP/IP suite of protocols. IP is concerned with the delivery of packets from one station to another, whether the stations are on the same network or on different networks.

Internet Protocol Security (IPsec)   A suite of protocols that is used to secure IP-based communications by using authentication and encryption.

interprocess communications (IPC)   Any of several protocols used for communications between running processes on one system or between systems.

intrusion detection system (IDS)   A hardware or software system that detects anomalies that may be signs of an intrusion.

intrusion prevention system (IPS)   A hardware or software system that detects and blocks anomalies that may be signs of an intrusion.

IP address   An address assigned to a station on a TCP/IP network.

IS audit   An audit of an IS department's operations and systems.

IS operations   The day-to-day control of the information systems, applications, and infrastructure that support organizational objectives and processes.

ISACA audit guidelines   Published documents that help the IS auditor apply ISACA audit standards.

ISACA audit procedures   Published documents that provide sample procedures for performing various audit activities and for auditing various types of technologies and systems.

ISACA audit standards   The minimum standards of performance related to security, audits, and the actions that result from audits. The standards are published by ISACA and updated periodically. ISACA audit standards are considered mandatory.

ISAE 3402 (International Standard on Assurance Engagement)   An external audit of a service provider. An ISAE3402 audit is performed according to rules established by the International Auditing and Assurance Standards Board (IAASB).

ISO 15504   A world standard for evaluating the maturity of a software development process.

ISO 20000   A world standard for IT service management.

ISO 27001   A world standard for IT security management.

ISO 38500   A world standard for corporate governance of information technology.

ISO 9000   A world standard for a quality management system.

ISO 9126   A world standard for evaluating the quality of software.

ISO 9660   A file system used on CD-ROM and DVD-ROM media.

IT Assurance Framework (ITAF)   An end-to-end framework developed to guide organizations in developing and managing IT assurance and IT audit.

IT balanced scorecard   A balanced scorecard used to measure IT organization performance and results. See also *balanced scorecard*.

IT governance   Management's control over IT policy and processes.

IT Infrastructure Library (ITIL)   See *IT service management*.

IT service management   The set of activities that ensure the delivery of IT services is efficient and effective, through active management and the continuous improvement of processes.

IT steering committee   A body of senior managers or executives that discusses high-level and long-term issues in the organization.

job description   A written description of a job in an organization. A job description usually contains a job title, experience requirements, and knowledge requirements.

job rotation The practice of moving personnel from position to position, sometimes with little or no notice, as a means for deterring personnel from engaging in prohibited or illegal practices.

judgmental sampling A sampling technique where items are chosen based upon the auditor's judgment, usually based on risk or materiality. See also *sampling*.

key See *encryption key*.

keycard system A physical access control system where personnel are able to enter a workspace by waving a keycard near a reader or inserting it into a reader, activating a door lock to briefly unlock the door.

key compromise Any unauthorized disclosure or damage to an encryption key. See also *key management*.

key custody The policies, processes, and procedures regarding the management of keys. See also *key management*.

key disposal The process of decommissioning encryption keys. See also *key management*.

key exchange A technique that is used by two parties to establish a symmetric encryption key when no secure channel is available.

key fingerprint A short sequence of characters that is used to authenticate a public key.

key generation The initial generation of an encryption key. See also *key management*.

key length This refers to the size (measured in bits) of an encryption key. Longer encryption keys mean that it takes greater effort to successfully attack a cryptosystem.

key logger A hardware device or a type of malware where a user's keystrokes and, optionally, mouse movements and clicks are recorded and sent to the key logger's owner.

key management The various processes and procedures used by an organization to generate, protect, use, and dispose of encryption keys over their lifetime.

key protection All means used to protect encryption keys from unauthorized disclosure and harm. See also *key management*.

key rotation The process of issuing a new encryption key and re-encrypting data protected with the new key. See also *key management*.

known error An incident that has been seen before and its root cause is known.

laptop computer A portable computer used by an individual user.

Layer 2 Tunneling Protocol (L2TP) A TCP/IP tunneling protocol.

layer 3 switch A device that routes packets between different TCP/IP networks.

layer 4 switch A device used to route packets to destinations based on TCP and UDP port numbers.

layer 4-7 switch   A device that routes packets to destinations based on their internal content.

least privilege   The concept where an individual user should have the lowest privilege possible that will still enable them to perform their tasks.

Lightweight Directory Access Protocol (LDAP)   A TCP/IP application layer protocol used as a directory service for people and computing resources.

link   Layer 1 of the TCP/IP network model. The purpose of the link layer is the delivery of messages (usually called frames) from one station to another on a local network. See also *TCP/IP network model*.

local area network (LAN)   A network that connects computers and devices together in a small building or a residence.

logic bomb   A set of instructions that is designed to perform some damaging action when a specific event occurs; a popular example is a time bomb that alters or destroys data on a specified date in the future.

logical network architecture   The part of network architecture concerned with the depiction of network communications at a local, campus, regional, and global level.

loopback address   The IP address 127.0.0.1 (or any other address in the entire 127 address block). A packet sent to a loopback address is sent to the station that originated it.

machine authentication controls   Access controls that are used to authenticate a device to determine if it will be permitted to access resources.

main storage   A computer's short-term storage of information, usually implemented with electronic components such as random access memory (RAM).

mainframe   A large central computer capable of performing complex tasks for several users simultaneously.

malware   The broad class of programs that are designed to inflict harm on computers, networks, or information. Types of malware include viruses, worms, Trojan horses, spyware, and rootkits.

man-in-the-browser (MITB)   An attack on an end-user's browser where a malicious browser helper object interferes with the browser's operation.

man-in-the-middle (MITM) attack   An attack that is used to take over communications that are taking place between two parties. Here, an attacker intercepts communications being sent from one party to another and injects new, altered communications in their place. The attacker must be able to impersonate each party in the communication so that each party believes it is talking directly with the other party.

man-made disaster   A disaster that is directly or indirectly caused by human activity, through action or inaction. See also *disaster*.

mandatory access control (MAC)   An access model used to control access to objects (files, directories, databases, systems, networks, and so on) by subjects (persons, programs, etc.). When a subject attempts to access an object, the operating system examines the access properties of the subject and object to determine if the access should be allowed. The operating system then permits or denies the requested access.

mandatory vacation   A policy established by some organizations that requires each employee to take a vacation every year.

manual control   A control that requires a human to operate it.

marking   The act of affixing a classification label to a document.

materiality   In financial audits, a dollar-amount threshold that alters the results on an organization's financial statements. In IS audits, materiality is the threshold where serious errors, omissions, irregularities, or illegal acts could occur.

media access control (MAC)   A framing protocol used by Ethernet, DSL, MPLS, and ISDN.

media access control (MAC) address   Node addressing used on an Ethernet network where the address is expressed as a six-byte hexadecimal value. A typical address is displayed in a notation separated by colons or dashes, such as F0:E3:67:AB:98:02.

media control   A set of processes for controlling the security of storage media.

media destruction   See *media sanitization.*

media sanitization   The process of ensuring the destruction of data on digital media.

message digest   The result of a cryptographic hash function.

message server   A system in a distributed processing environment that stores and forwards transactions between systems.

message switched   A WAN communications technology where each message is switched to its destination when a communications path is available.

method   The actions that an object can perform. See also *object.*

methodology standard   A standard that specifies the practices used by the IT organization.

metropolitan area network (MAN)   An interconnection of LANs that spans a city or regional area.

middleware   A component in an application environment that is used to control or monitor transactions.

midrange computer   Large central computers capable of performing complex tasks for users.

migration   The process of transferring data from one system to a replacement system.

mitigating control   See *compensating control.*

mobile device   A portable computer in the form of a smart phone, tablet computer, or personal digital assistant (PDA).

mobile site   A portable recovery center that can be delivered to almost any location in the world.

modulator-demodulator (modem)   A device used to connect a local computer or network to a telecommunications network.

monitoring   The continuous or regular evaluation of a system or control to determine its operation or effectiveness.

multistation access unit (MAU)   A Token Ring network device used to connect stations to the network.

multiplexor   A device used to connect several separate signals and combine them into a single data stream.

multiprotocol label switching (MPLS)   A packet-switched network technology that utilizes a variable-length packet. In an MPLS network, each packet has one or more labels affixed to it that contain information that helps MPLS routers make packet-forwarding decisions without examining the contents of the packet itself (for an IP address, for instance).

N + 1   The practice of employing one more than the minimum required number of systems so that in the event of a planned or unplanned outage of one of the systems, the other systems will continue functioning and provide service. This term usually applies to HVAC, UPS, and electric generators. See also *heating, ventilation, and air conditioning (HVAC); uninterruptible power supply (UPS);* and *electric generator.*

natural disaster   A disaster that occurs in the natural world with little or no assistance from mankind. See also *disaster.*

near-field communications (NFC)   A standard for extremely short-distance radio frequency data communications.

netbook computer   A miniature laptop computer, usually with more limited storage and peripheral connectivity than a laptop computer.

network   Layer 3 of the OSI network model. See also *OSI network model.*

network access control (NAC)   An approach for network authentication and access control for devices that wish to attach to a LAN or wireless LAN.

network analysis   A reconnaissance operation on an organization's network.

network architecture   The overall design of an organization's network.

network attached storage (NAS)   A stand-alone storage system that contains one or more virtual volumes. Servers access these volumes over the network using the Network

File System (NFS) or Server Message Block/Common Internet File System (SMB/CIFS) protocols, common on Unix and Windows operating systems, respectively.

network authentication   A network-based service that is used to authenticate persons to network-based resources.

network basic input/output system (NetBIOS)   A network protocol that permits applications to communicate with one another using the legacy NetBIOS API.

Network File System (NFS)   A TCP/IP application layer protocol used to make a disk-based resource on another computer appear as a logical volume on a local computer.

network interface card (NIC)   A device that is directly connected to a computer's bus and contains one or more connectors to which a network cable may be connected.

network management   A class of software program that is used to monitor and manage devices connected to a network. Also refers to the business processes used for the same purpose.

Network News Transfer Protocol (NNTP)   A TCP/IP application layer protocol used to transport Usenet news throughout the Internet, and from news servers to end users using news reading programs. Usenet news has been largely deprecated by web-based applications.

Network Time Protocol (NTP)   A TCP/IP application layer protocol used to synchronize the time-of-day clocks on systems with time reference standards.

network-based intrusion detection system (NIDS)   An intrusion detection system (IDS) that attaches to a network and listens for network-based anomalies. See also *intrusion detection system (IDS)*.

noise   The presence of other electromagnetic signals within incoming power.

nonrepudiation   The property of digital signatures and encryption that can make it difficult or impossible for a party to later deny having sent a digitally signed message—unless they admit to having lost control of their private encryption key.

notebook computer   See *laptop computer*.

NT File System (NTFS)   A file system used by newer versions of the Microsoft Windows operating system.

object   The instantiation of a class. If a class is thought of as a design, an object can be thought of as a running example of the class. See also *class*.

object   A resource, such as a computer, application, database, file, or record. See also *subject*.

object breakdown structure (OBS)   A representation of the components of a project in graphical or tabular form.

object database   See *object database management system (ODBMS)*.

object database management system (ODBMS) A type of database management system where information is represented as objects that are used in object-oriented programming languages.

object-oriented (OO) system development Development of information systems using object-oriented languages and tools.

object request broker (ORB) gateway A system that facilitates the processing of transactions across a distributed environment that uses the CORBA (Common Object Request Broker Architecture) or Microsoft COM/DCOM standards.

objectivity The characteristic of a person that relates to his or her ability to develop an opinion that is not influenced by external pressures.

occupant emergency plan (OEP) Activities required to safely care for occupants in a business location during a disaster. See also *response document*.

off-shoring A form of sourcing where an employer will source a function with employees or contractors located in another country or continent.

off-site media storage The practice of storing media such as backup tapes at an off-site facility located away from the primary computing facility.

online inquiry An auditing technique where an auditor can log on to an application to retrieve detailed information on specific transactions.

open shortest path first (OSPF) A TCP/IP routing protocol that is used to transmit network routing information from one network router to another in order to determine the most efficient path through a large network.

operating system A large, general-purpose program that is used to control computer hardware and facilitate the use of software applications.

operational audit An audit of IS controls, security controls, or business controls to determine control existence and effectiveness.

organization chart A diagram that depicts the manager-subordinate relationships in an organization, or in a part of an organization.

OSI network model The seven-layer network model that incorporates encapsulation of messages. The OSI model has been extensively studied, but has never been entirely implemented. See also *TCP/IP network model*.

output controls Controls that ensure the accuracy and validity of final calculations and transformations.

outsourcing A form of sourcing where an employer will use contract employees to perform a function. The contract employees may be located on-site or off-site.

owner A person or group responsible for the operation of an asset.

packet switched A WAN technology where communications between endpoints takes place over a stream of packets that are routed through switches until they reach their destination.

parallel test An actual test of disaster recovery (DR) and/or business continuity response plans. The purpose of a parallel test is to evaluate the ability of personnel to follow directives in emergency response plans—to actually set up the DR business processing or data processing capability. In a parallel test, personnel operate recovery systems in parallel with production systems to compare the results between the two in order to determine the actual capabilities of recovery systems.

password An identifier that is created by a system manager or a user; a secret combination of letters, numbers, and other symbols that is known only to the user who uses it.

password complexity The characteristics required of user account passwords. For example, a password may not contain dictionary words and must contain uppercase letters, lowercase letters, numbers, and symbols.

password length The minimum and maximum number of characters permitted for a password that is associated with a computer account.

password reset The process of changing a user account password and unlocking the user account so that the user's use of the account may resume.

password reuse The act of reusing a prior password for a user account. Some information systems can prevent the use of prior passwords in case any were compromised with or without the user's knowledge.

password vaulting The process of storing a password in a secure location for later use.

patch management The process of identifying, analyzing, and applying patches (including security patches) to systems.

Payment Card Industry Data Security Standard (PCI-DSS) A security standard whose objective is the protection of credit card numbers in storage, while processed, and while transmitted. The standard was developed by the Payment Card Industry, a consortium of credit card companies, including VISA, MasterCard, American Express, Discover, and JCB.

performance evaluation A process where an employer evaluates the performance of each employee for the purpose of promotion, salary increase, bonus, or retention.

personal area network (PAN) A network that is generally used by a single individual and is usually limited to about three meters in size.

personal digital assistant (PDA) A mobile device that is similar to a smart phone in size and features, but which lacks the mobile phone component.

phishing A social engineering attack on unsuspecting individuals where e-mail messages that resemble official communications entice victims to visit imposter websites that contain malware or request credentials to sensitive or valuable assets.

physical Layer 1 of the OSI network model. See also *OSI network model*.

physical control Controls that employ physical means.

physical network architecture   The part of network architecture concerned with the physical locations of network equipment and network media.

piggybacking   See *tailgating*.

plain old telephone service (POTS)   Another name for the public-switched telephone network (PSTN). See also *public-switched telephone network (PSTN)*.

plaintext   An original message, file, or stream of data that can be read by anyone who has access to it.

point-to-point protocol (PPP)   A network protocol used to transport TCP/IP packets over point-to-point serial connections (usually RS-232 and dial-up connections).

policy   A statement that specifies what must be done (or not done) in an organization. A policy usually defines who is responsible for monitoring and enforcing it.

polymorphism   The different ways in which an object may behave, depending upon the data that is passed to it. See also *object*.

population   A complete set of entities, transactions, or events that are the subject of an audit.

Post Office Protocol (POP)   A TCP/IP application layer protocol that is used to retrieve e-mail messages from an e-mail server.

power distribution unit (PDU)   A device that distributes electric power to a computer room or data center.

pre-action   A fire sprinkler system used in areas with high-value contents such as data centers. A pre-action system is essentially a dry pipe system until a "preceding" event such as a smoke detector alarm occurs; at this time, the system is filled with water and essentially converts in real time to a wet pipe system. Then, if the ambient temperature at any of the sprinkler heads is high enough, those fuses break, releasing water to extinguish the fire. See also *fire sprinkler system*.

pre-audit   An examination of business processes, controls, and records in anticipation of an upcoming audit.

precision   A measure of how closely a sample represents the entire population.

presentation   Layer 6 of the OSI network model. See also *OSI network model*.

preventive action   An action that is initiated to prevent an undesired event or condition.

preventive control   A control that is used to prevent unwanted events from happening.

primary key   One of the fields in a table in a relational database management system (rDBMS) whose values are unique for each record (row). See also *relational database management system, table, row,* and *field*.

print server   A server that is used to coordinate printing to shared printers.

privacy   The protection of personal information from unauthorized disclosure, use, and distribution.

privacy policy   A policy statement that defines how an organization will protect, manage, and handle private information.

privacy requirements   Formal statements that describe required privacy safeguards that a system must support.

private address   An IP address that falls into one of the following ranges: 10.0.0.0–10.255.255.255, 172.16.0.0–172.31.255.255, or 192.168.0.0–192.168.255.255. Packets with a private address destination cannot be transported over the global Internet.

probability analysis   The analysis of a threat and the probability of its realization.

problem   An incident—often multiple incidents—that exhibits common symptoms and whose root cause is not known.

problem management   The IT function that analyzes chronic incidents and seeks to resolve them, and also enacts proactive measures in an effort to avoid problems. See also *IT service management*.

procedure   A written sequence of instructions used to complete a task.

process   A collection of one or more procedures used to perform a business function. See also *procedure*.

process   A logical container in an operating system in which a program executes.

process isolation   A basic feature of an operating system that prevents one process from accessing the resources used by another process.

processing controls   Controls that ensure the correct processing of information.

program   An organization of many large, complex activities; it can be thought of as a set of projects that work to fulfill one or more key business objectives or goals.

program charter   A formal definition of the objectives of a program, its main timelines, sources of funding, the names of its principal leaders and managers, and the business executive(s) who are sponsoring the program.

program management   The management of a group of projects that exist to fulfill a business goal or objective.

programmable read-only memory (PROM)   A form of permanent memory that cannot be modified.

programming language   A vocabulary and set of rules used to construct a human-readable computer program.

project   A coordinated and managed sequence of tasks that results in the realization of an objective or goal.

project change management   The process of controlling a project plan and budget through formal reviews of changes.

project evaluation and review technique (PERT)   A visual representation of a project plan that shows project tasks, timelines, and dependencies.

project management   The activities that are used to control, measure, and manage the activities in a project.

project management body of knowledge (PMBOK)   A project management guide that defines the essentials of project management.

project plan   The chart of tasks in a project, which also includes start and completion dates, resources required, and dependencies and relationships between tasks.

project planning   The activities that are related to the development and management of a project.

project schedule   The chart of tasks in a project with their expected start and completion dates.

PRojects IN Controlled Environments 2 (PRINCE2)   A project management framework.

proof of concept   A method for demonstrating the ability to build or implement complex systems through the use of simpler models.

protocol analyzer   A device that is connected to a network in order to view network communications at a detailed level.

protocol standard   A standard that specifies the protocols used by the IT organization.

prototyping   An alternative software development process where rapidly developed application prototypes are developed with user input and continuous involvement.

proxy server   A device or system used to control end-user access to Internet websites.

public key cryptography   See *asymmetric encryption*.

public key infrastructure   A centralized function that is used to store and publish public keys and other information.

public-switched telephone network (PSTN)   The common carrier-switched telephone network used to carry voice telephone calls over landlines.

qualitative risk analysis   A risk analysis methodology where risks are classified on a nonquantified scale, such as "High - Medium - Low," or on a simple numeric scale, such as 1 through 5.

quality assurance testing (QAT)   The portion of software testing where system specifications and technologies are formally tested.

quality management Methods and processes where business processes are controlled, monitored, and managed in order to bring about continuous improvement.

quantitative risk analysis A risk analysis methodology where risks are estimated in the form of actual cost amounts.

race condition A type of attack where an attacker is attempting to exploit a small window of time that may exist between the time that a resource is requested and when it is available for use.

radio resource control (RRC) A part of the UTMS WCDMA wireless telecommunications protocol that is used to facilitate the allocation of connections between mobile devices and base stations.

random access memory (RAM) A type of semiconductor memory usually used for a computer's main storage.

rapid application development (RAD) A software development life cycle process characterized by small development teams, prototypes, design sessions with end users, and development tools that integrate data design, data flow, user interface, and prototyping.

razor wire Coiled wire with razor-like barbs that may be placed along the top of a fence or wall to prevent or deter passage by unauthorized personnel.

read-only memory (ROM) An early form of permanent memory that cannot be modified.

reciprocal site A data center that is operated by another company. Two or more organizations with similar processing needs will draw up a legal contract that obligates one or more of the organizations to temporarily house another party's systems in the event of a disaster.

records Documents describing business events such as meeting minutes, contracts, financial transactions, decisions, purchase orders, logs, and reports.

recovery control A control that is used after an unwanted event to restore a system or process to its pre-event state.

recovery point objective (RPO) The time during which recent data will be irretrievably lost in a disaster. RPO is usually measured in hours or days.

recovery procedure Instructions that key personnel use to bootstrap services that support critical business functions identified in the business impact assessment (BIA).

recovery strategy A high-level plan for the resumption of business operations after a disaster.

recovery time objective (RTO) The period from the onset of an outage until the resumption of service. RTO is usually measured in hours or days.

reduced sign-on   The use of a centralized directory service (such as LDAP or Microsoft Active Directory) for authentication into systems and applications. Users will need to log in to each system and application, using one set of login credentials.

redundant array of independent disks (RAID)   A family of technologies that is used to improve the reliability, performance, or size of disk-based storage systems.

referential integrity   The characteristic of relational database management systems that requires the database management system maintain the parent-child relationships between records in different tables and prohibits activities such as deleting parent records and transforming child records into orphans.

registration authority (RA)   An entity that works within or alongside a certificate authority (CA) to accept requests for new digital certificates.

regulatory requirements   Formal statements, derived from laws and regulations, that describe the required characteristics a system must support.

relational database management system (rDBMS)   A database management system that permits the design of a database consisting of one or more tables that can contain fields that refer to rows in other tables. This is currently the most popular type of database management system.

release management   The IT function that controls the release of software programs, applications, and environments. See also *IT service management*.

remote access   A service that permits a user to establish a network connection from a remote location so that the user can access network resources remotely.

remote copy (RCP)   A TCP/IP application layer protocol that is an early file transfer protocol used to copy files or directories from system to system.

remote desktop protocol (RDP)   A proprietary protocol from Microsoft that is used to establish a graphic interface connection with another computer.

remote destruct   The act of commanding a device, such as a laptop computer or mobile device, to destroy stored data. Remote destruct is sometimes used when a device is lost or stolen to prevent anyone from being able to read data stored on the device.

remote login (rlogin)   A TCP/IP application layer protocol used to establish a command-line session on a remote system. Like TELNET, rlogin does not encrypt authentication or session contents, and has been largely replaced by secure shell (SSH). See also *TELNET, secure shell (SSH)*.

remote procedure call (RPC)   A network protocol that permits an application to execute a subroutine or procedure on another computer.

repeater   An Ethernet network device that receives and retransmits signals on the network.

reperformance   An audit technique where an IS auditor repeats actual tasks performed by auditees in order to confirm they were performed properly.

replication   An activity where data that is written to a storage system is also copied over a network to another storage system and written. The result is the presence of up-to-date data that exists on two or more storage systems, each of which could be located in a different geographic region.

request for change (RFC)   See *change request*.

request for proposal (RFP)   A formal process where an organization solicits solution proposals from one or more vendors. The process usually includes formal requirements and desired terms and conditions. It is used to formally evaluate vendor proposals in order to make a selection.

requirements   Formal statements that describe required (and desired) characteristics of a system that is to be built or acquired.

residual risk   The risk that remains after being reduced through other risk treatment options.

response document   Required action of personnel after a disaster strikes. Includes business recovery plan, occupant emergency plan, emergency communication plan, contact lists, disaster recovery plan, continuity of operations plan (COOP), and security incident response plan (SIRP).

responsibility   A stated expectation of activities and performance.

return on investment (ROI)   The ratio of money gained or lost as compared to an original investment.

reverse address resolution protocol (RARP)   A TCP/IP link layer protocol that is used by a station that needs to know the IP address that has been assigned to it. RARP has been largely superseded by DHCP. See also *Dynamic Host Configuration Protocol (DHCP)*.

reverse engineering   The process of analyzing a system to see how it functions, usually as a means for developing a similar system. Reverse engineering is usually not permitted when it is applied to commercial software programs.

right to audit   A clause in a contract where one party has the right to conduct an audit of the other party's operations.

ring topology   A network topology where connections are made from one station to the next, in a complete loop.

RISC (reduced instruction set computer)   A central processing unit design that uses a smaller instruction set, which leads to simpler microprocessor design. See also *central processing unit*.

risk   Generally, the fact that undesired events can happen that may damage property or disrupt operations; specifically, an event scenario that can result in property damage or disruption.

risk acceptance   The risk treatment option where management chooses to accept the risk as-is.

risk analysis   The process of identifying and studying risks in an organization.

risk assessment   A process where risks, in the form of threats and vulnerabilities, are identified for each asset.

risk avoidance   The risk treatment option involving a cessation of the activity that introduces identified risk.

Risk IT Framework   A risk management model that approaches risk from the enterprise perspective.

risk management   The management activities used to identify, analyze, and treat risks.

risk mitigation   The risk treatment option involving implementation of a solution that will reduce an identified risk.

risk transfer   The risk treatment option involving the act of transferring risk to another party, such as an insurance company.

risk treatment   The decision to manage an identified risk. The available choices are mitigate the risk, avoid the risk, transfer the risk, or accept the risk.

role   A set of privileges in an application. Also a formally defined set of work tasks assigned to an individual.

rollback   A step in the software development life cycle where system changes need to be reversed, returning the system to its previous state.

rootkit   A type of malware that is designed to evade detection.

router   A device that is used to interconnect two or more networks.

routing information protocol (RIP)   A TCP/IP routing protocol that is used to transmit network routing information from one network router to another in order to determine the most efficient path through a network. RIP is one of the earliest routing protocols and is not used for Internet routing.

row   A unit of storage in a relational database management system (rDBMS) that consists of a single record in a table. See also *relational database management system, table.*

RPC gateway   A system that facilitates communication through the RPC suite of protocols between components in an application environment.

RS-232   A standard protocol for sending serial data between computers.

RS-449   A standard protocol for sending serial data between network devices.

sabotage   Deliberate damage of an organization's asset.

salvage The process of recovering components or assets that still have value after a disaster.

sample A portion of a population of records that is selected for auditing.

sample mean The sum of all samples divided by the number of samples.

sample standard deviation A computation of the variance of sample values from the sample mean. This is a measurement of the "spread" of values in the sample.

sampling A technique that is used to select a portion of a population when it is not feasible to test an entire population.

sampling risk The probability that a sample selected does not represent the entire population. This is usually expressed as a percentage, as the numeric inverse of the confidence coefficient. See also *confidence coefficient*.

SAS 70 (Statement of Accounting Standards No. 70) An external audit of a service provider. An SAS 70 audit is performed according to rules established by the American Institute of Certified Public Accountants (AICPA). Deprecated by SSAE16. See also *SSAE16*.

scanning attack An attack on a computer or network with the intention of discovering potentially vulnerable computers or programs.

screened shielded twisted pair (S/STP) A type of twisted-pair cable where a thick metal shield protects each pair of conductors, plus an outer shield that protects all of the conductors together. See also *twisted-pair cable*.

screened unshielded twisted pair (S/UTP) A type of twisted-pair cable where the entire cable has a thick metal shield that protects the cables. See also *twisted-pair cable*.

screening router A network device that filters network traffic based on source and destination IP addresses and ports. See also *firewall*.

script kiddie An inexperienced computer hacker who uses tools developed by others to illegally access computers and networks.

Scrum An iterative and incremental methodology used for rapid and agile software development.

secondary storage A computer's long-term storage of information, usually implemented with hard disk drives or static random access memory (SRAM).

secure copy (SCP) A TCP/IP application layer protocol used as a file transfer protocol that is similar to remote copy (RCP), but is protected using secure shell (SSH). See *remote copy (RCP)*, *secure shell (SSH)*.

secure electronic transaction (SET) A protocol used to protect credit card transactions that uses a digital envelope. SET has been deprecated by Secure Sockets Layer (SSL) and Transport Layer Security (TLS). See also *digital envelope, Secure Sockets Layer (SSL)*, and *Transport Layer Security (TLS)*.

Secure File Transfer Protocol (SFTP)   A TCP/IP application layer protocol that is an extension of the FTP protocol, where authentication and file transfer are encrypted using SSH. Sometimes referred to as SSH File Transfer Protocol. See also *File Transfer Protocol (FTP), secure shell (SSH)*.

Secure Hypertext Transfer Protocol (SHTTP)   A protocol used to encrypt webpages between web servers and web browsers. Often confused with Hypertext Transfer Protocol Secure (HTTPS).

Secure Multipurpose Internet Mail Extensions (S/MIME)   An e-mail security protocol that provides sender and recipient authentication and encryption of message content and attachments.

secure shell (SSH)   A TCP/IP application layer protocol that provides a secure channel between two computers whereby all communications between them are encrypted. SSH can also be used as a tunnel to encapsulate and thereby protect other protocols.

Secure Sockets Layer (SSL)   An encryption protocol used to encrypt webpages requested with the HTTPS (Hypertext Transfer Protocol/Secure) URL. Deprecated by Transport Layer Security (TLS). See also *Transport Layer Security (TLS), Hypertext Transfer Protocol Secure (HTTPS)*.

security awareness   A formal program used to educate employees, users, customers, or constituents on required, acceptable, and unacceptable security-related behaviors.

security governance   Management's control over an organization's security program.

security guards   Personnel who control passage at entry points or roam building premises looking for security issues such as unescorted visitors.

security incident   An event where the confidentiality, integrity, or availability of information (or an information system) has been compromised.

security incident response   The formal, planned response that is enacted when a security incident has occurred. See also *security incident*.

security policy   See *information security policy*.

security requirements   Formal statements that describe the required security characteristics that a system must support.

segregation of duties   The concept that ensures single individuals do not possess excess privileges that could result in unauthorized activities such as fraud or the manipulation or exposure of sensitive data.

separation of duties   See *segregation of duties*.

serial line interface protocol (SLIP)   A network protocol used to transport TCP/IP packets over point-to-point serial connections (usually RS-232).

server   A centralized computer used to perform a specific task.

service continuity management The IT function that consists of activities concerned with the organization's ability to continue providing services, primarily in the event that a natural or man-made disaster has occurred. See also *IT service management, business continuity planning,* and *disaster recovery planning.*

service desk The IT function that handles incidents and service requests on behalf of customers by acting as a single point of contact. See also *IT service management.*

service-level agreement (SLA) An agreement that specifies service levels in terms of the quantity of work, quality, timeliness, and remedies for shortfalls in quality or quantity.

service-level management The IT function that confirms whether IT is providing adequate service to its customers. This is accomplished through continuous monitoring and periodic review of IT service delivery. See also *IT service management.*

service provider audit An audit of a third-party organization that provides services to other organizations.

service set identifier (SSID) A friendly name that identifies a particular 802.11 wireless network.

session Layer 5 of the OSI network model. See also *OSI network model.*

session border controller A device deployed in a VoIP network to control VoIP security, connectivity, quality of service, and metering.

session hijacking An attack on a user's browser session where the attacker intercepts the user's session cookie from an unencrypted wired or wireless network and then uses the cookie to take over the victim's browser session.

session initiation protocol (SIP) The network protocol used to set up and tear down Voice over IP (VoIP) and other communications connections. See also *Voice over IP (VoIP).*

shielded twisted pair (STP) A type of twisted-pair cable where a thin metal shield protects each pair of conductors. See also *twisted-pair cable.*

Simple Mail Transfer Protocol (SMTP) A TCP/IP application layer protocol that is used to transport e-mail messages.

Simple Network Management Protocol (SNMP) A TCP/IP application layer protocol used by network devices and systems to transmit management messages indicating a need for administrative attention.

Simple Object Access Protocol (SOAP) A protocol that is used to facilitate the exchange of structured information between systems.

simulation A test of disaster recovery, business continuity, or security incident response procedures where the participants take part in a "mock disaster" or incident to add some realism to the process of thinking their way through emergency response documents.

single loss expectancy (SLE)   The financial loss when a threat is realized one time. SLE is defined as AV × EF. See also *asset value (AV)*, *exposure factor (EF)*.

single sign-on   An interconnected environment where applications are logically connected to a centralized authentication server that is aware of the logged-in/-out status of each user. A user can log in once to the environment; each application and system is aware of a user's log-in status and will not require the user to log in to each one separately.

site classification policy   Policy that defines sensitivity levels, security controls, and security procedures for information processing sites and work centers.

smart card   A small, credit-card–sized device that contains electronic memory and is accessed with a smart card reader and used in two-factor authentication.

smart phone   A mobile phone equipped with an operating system and software applications.

snapshot   A continuous auditing technique that involves the use of special audit modules embedded in online applications that sample specific transactions. The module copies key database records that can be examined later on.

sniffer   A program that can be installed on a network-attached system to capture network traffic being transmitted to or from the system.

social engineering   The act of using deception to trick an individual into revealing secrets.

Software as a Service (SaaS)   A software delivery model where an organization obtains a software application for use by its employees and the software application is hosted by the software provider, as opposed to the customer organization.

software development life cycle (SDLC)   The life cycle process used to develop or acquire and maintain information systems. Also known as systems development life cycle.

Software Engineering Institute Capability Maturity Model Integration (SEI CMMI)   A maturity model that is used to measure the maturity of an organization's software development life cycle process.

software licensing   The process of maintaining accurate records regarding the permitted use of software programs.

software maintenance   An activity in the software development life cycle where modifications are made to the software code.

Software Process Improvement and Capability dEtermination (SPICE)   A maturity model that is based on the SEI CMM maturity model. SPICE has been made an international standard: ISO 15504.

software program library   The repository that contains program source code and that usually includes tools to manage the maintenance of source code.

source code management   The techniques and tools used to manage application source code.

source lines of code (SLOC)   A sizing technique for software development projects that represents the size of the planned program, expressed as lines of code.

sourcing   The choices that organizations make when selecting the personnel that will perform functions and where those functions will be performed.

spam   Unsolicited and unwanted e-mail.

spam filter   A central program or device that examines incoming e-mail and removes all messages identified as spam.

spike   A sharp increase in voltage that lasts for only a fraction of a second.

spiral model   A software development life cycle process where the activities of requirements definition and software design go through several cycles until the project is complete. See also *software development life cycle (SDLC)*.

split custody   The concept of splitting knowledge of a specific object or task between two persons.

spoofing   The act of changing the configuration of a device or system in an attempt to masquerade as a different, known, and trusted system or user.

spyware   A type of malware where software performs one or more surveillance-type actions on a computer, reporting back to the spyware owner.

SSAE16 (Statements on Standards for Attestation Engagements No. 16)   An external audit of a service provider. An SSAE16 audit is performed according to rules established by the American Institute of Certified Public Accountants (AICPA).

standard   A statement that defines the technologies, protocols, suppliers, and methods used by an IT organization.

standard IT balanced scorecard   A management tool that is used to measure the performance and effectiveness of an IT organization.

star topology   A network topology where a separate connection is made from a central device to each station.

stateful inspection firewall   A network device that filters network traffic based on source and destination IP addresses and ports, and keeps track of individual TCP/IP sessions to make filtering decisions, permitting established connections. See also *firewall*.

statement of impact   A description of the impact a disaster scenario will have on a business or business process.

static random access memory (SRAM) A form of semiconductor memory that does not require refreshing.

statistical sampling A sampling technique where items are chosen at random; each item has a statistically equal probability of being chosen. See also *sampling*.

stop-or-go sampling A sampling technique used to permit sampling to stop at the earliest possible time. This technique is used when the auditor feels that there is low risk or a low rate of exceptions in the population. See also *sampling*.

storage area network (SAN) A stand-alone storage system that can be configured to contain several virtual volumes and connected to many servers through fiber optic cables.

strategic planning Activities used to develop and refine long-term plans and objectives.

stratified sampling A sampling technique where a population is divided into classes or strata, based upon the value of one of the attributes. Samples are then selected from each class. See also *sampling*.

stream cipher This is a type of encryption algorithm that operates on a continuous stream of data, such as a video or audio feed.

strong authentication See *two-factor authentication*.

subject A person or a system. See also *object*.

subnet mask A numeric value that determines which portion of an IP address is used to identify the network and which portion is used to identify a station on the network. See also *IP address*.

substantive testing A type of testing that is used to determine the accuracy and integrity of transactions that flow through processes and systems.

supercomputer The largest type of computer that is capable of performing large, complex calculations such as weather forecasting and earthquake simulations.

surge See *spike*.

switch A device that is used to connect computers and other devices to a network. Unlike a hub, which sends all network packets to all stations on the network, a switch sends packets only to intended destination stations on the network.

symmetric encryption A method for encryption and decryption where it is necessary for both parties to possess a common encryption key.

synchronous optical networking (SONET) A class of common carrier telecommunications network technologies used to transport voice and data over fiber optic networks at very high speeds.

synchronous replication A type of replication where writing data to a local and to a remote storage system is performed as a single operation, guaranteeing that data on the remote storage system is identical to data on the local storage system. See also *replication*.

system classification policy   Policy that specifies levels of security for systems storing classified information.

system hardening   See *hardening.*

system testing   The portion of software testing where an entire system is tested.

T-1   A common carrier standard protocol for transporting voice and data. T-1 can support up to 24 separate voice channels of 64 kbit/sec each and is used primarily in North America.

T-3   A common carrier standard protocol for transporting voice and data. T-3 can support up to 672 separate voice channels of 64 kbit/sec each and is used primarily in North America.

table   A unit of storage in a relational database management system (rDBMS) that can be thought of as a list of records. See also *relational database management system.*

tablet   A mobile device with a touch screen interface. See also *mobile device.*

tailgating   A technique used by intruders who attempt to enter a building; they may follow an employee into a building without showing their own security credentials (for example, a keycard).

tape management system (TMS)   An information system that is used to manage tape media, usually for the purpose of performing information backup. See also *backup.*

TCP/IP network model   The four-layer network model that incorporates encapsulation of messages. The TCP/IP suite of protocols is built on the TCP/IP network model.

technical control   A control that is implemented in IT systems and applications.

technical requirements   Formal statements that describe the required technical characteristics that a system must support.

technology standard   A standard that specifies the software and hardware technologies that are used by the IT organization.

TELNET   A TCP/IP application layer protocol that is used to establish a command-line session on a remote computer. TELNET does not encrypt user credentials as they are transmitted over the network, and has been largely replaced by SSH. See also *secure shell (SSH).*

terminal emulation   A software program that runs on a workstation that emulates an older-style computer terminal.

termination   The process of discontinuing employment of an employee or contractor.

terrorist   A person or group who perpetrates violence for political or religious reasons.

test plan   The list of tests that are to be carried out during a unit test or system test. See also *unit testing, system testing.*

test server Any type of server that is used to test features; a test server does not perform production tasks.

thick client A workstation that contains a fully functional operating system and application programs.

thin client A workstation that contains a minimal operating system and little or no data storage.

threat An event that, if realized, would bring harm to an asset.

time bomb See *logic bomb*.

time division multiple access (TDMA) An airlink standard for wireless communications between mobile devices and base stations.

time of check/time of use (TOC/TOU) See *race condition*.

time synchronization A network-based service that is used to synchronize the time clocks on computers connected to a network.

timebox management A project management technique where a large project is broken down into smaller components and time periods.

token A small electronic device that is used in two-factor authentication. A token may display a number that the user types in to a login field, or it may be plugged into a workstation to complete authentication. See also *two-factor authentication*.

Token Ring A standard protocol for assembling a stream of data into frames for transport over a physical medium from one station to another on a local area network. On a Token Ring network, a three-byte token is passed from station to station over the network. A station may not transmit a packet to another station until it has first received the token.

tolerable error rate The highest number of errors that can exist without a result being materially misstated.

toll fraud An attack on a private branch exchange (PBX) that results in stolen long-distance telephone service.

Towers of Hanoi A complex backup media rotation scheme that provides for more lengthy retention of some backup media. Based on the Towers of Hanoi puzzle. See also *backup media rotation*.

training The process of educating personnel; to impart information or provide an environment where they can practice a new skill.

transaction processing (TP) monitor A system that manages transactions between application servers and database servers in a distributed processing environment.

transfer The process of changing an employee's job title, department, and/or responsibilities.

Transmission Control Protocol (TCP)   The connection-oriented protocol used in the TCP/IP suite of protocols to establish a connection and transport messages from one station to another over a network during a communication session.

transport   Layer 4 of the OSI network model. See also *OSI network model*.

transport   Layer 3 of the TCP/IP network model. The purpose of the transport layer is the controlled and ordered delivery of messages (called packets) from one application on a station to another on the same network or on different networks. See also *TCP/IP network model*.

Transport Layer Security (TLS)   An encryption protocol used to encrypt webpages requested with the HTTPS (Hypertext Transfer Protocol/Secure) URL. Replacement for Secure Sockets Layer (SSL). See also *Secure Sockets Layer (SSL)*, *Hypertext Transfer Protocol Secure (HTTPS)*.

Trojan horse   A type of malware where programs are purported to perform one function, but which actually perform other (or additional) undesired functions.

trunk   A telecommunications network technique where several communications can share a set of lines or frequencies.

tunneling   The practice of encapsulating messages within another protocol.

twinax   A type of coaxial cable that uses two inner conductors.

twisted-pair cable   A type of network cabling that consists of a thick cable containing four pairs of insulated copper conductors, all surrounded by a protective jacket.

two-factor authentication   Any means used to authenticate a user that is stronger than the use of a user ID and password. Examples of two-factor authentication include digital certificate, token, smart card, or biometric.

uninterruptible power supply (UPS)   A system that filters the incoming power of spikes and other noise and supplies power for short periods through a bank of batteries.

unit testing   The portion of software testing where individual modules are tested.

universal disk format (UDF)   A optical media file system considered a replacement for ISO 9660. See also *ISO 9660*, *file system*.

universal mobile telecommunications system (UMTS)   An airlink standard for wireless communications between mobile devices and base stations.

Universal Serial Bus (USB)   An external bus technology used to connect computers to peripherals such as mice, keyboards, storage devices, printers, scanners, cameras, and network adaptors. However, the USB specification indeed contains full networking capabilities, facilitated through the use of a USB hub.

Unix file system (UFS)   A file system used by many Unix operating systems. See also *file system*.

unshielded twisted pair (UTP)   A type of twisted-pair cable where there is no shielding—just four pairs of twisted conductors and the outer protective jacket. See also *twisted-pair cable*.

user   A business or customer who uses an information system.

user acceptance testing (UAT)   The portion of software testing where end users test software programs for correct functional operation and usability.

user datagram protocol (UDP)   The connectionless protocol used in the TCP/IP suite of protocols used to transport messages from one station to another over a network.

user ID   An identifier that is created by a system manager and issued to a user for the purpose of identification or authentication.

utility software   The broad class of programs that support the development or use of networks, systems, and applications. Utility software is most often used by IT specialists whose responsibilities include some aspect of system development, support, or operations.

V.35   A standard protocol for sending serial data between computers.

variable sampling   A sampling technique used to study the characteristics of a population to determine the numeric total of a specific attribute from the entire population. See also *sampling*.

vendor standard   A standard that specifies which suppliers and vendors are used for various types of products and services.

version control   The techniques and tools used to manage different versions of source code files.

video surveillance   The use of video cameras, monitors, and recording systems to record the movement of persons in or near sensitive areas.

virtual circuit   A logical communications channel between two endpoints on a packet-switched network.

virtual machine   A software implementation of a computer, usually an operating system or other program running within a hypervisor. See also *hypervisor*.

virtual network (VLAN)   A logical network that may share a physical medium with one or more other virtual networks.

virtual private network (VPN)   Any network encapsulation protocol that utilizes authentication and encryption; used primarily for protecting remote access traffic and for protecting traffic between two networks. See also *tunneling, encapsulation*.

virtual server   An active instantiation of a server operating system, running on a system that is designed to house two or more such virtual servers. Each virtual server is logically partitioned from every other so that each runs as though it were on its own physically separate machine.

virus   A type of malware where fragments of code attach themselves to executable programs and are activated when the program they are attached to is run.

visual notice   A sign or symbol that is used to inform personnel of security controls and/or to warn unauthorized persons.

Voice over IP (VoIP)   Several technologies that permit telephony that is transported over IP networks.

VoIP client   A computer program designed to communicate using the Voice over IP (VoIP) protocol. See also *Voice over IP (VoIP)*.

VoIP handset   A digital telephone designed to communicate using the Voice over IP (VoIP) protocol. See also *Voice over IP (VoIP)*.

vulnerability   A weakness that may be present in a system that makes the probability of one or more threats more likely.

vulnerability management   A formal business process that is used to identify and mitigate vulnerabilities in an IT environment.

walkthrough   A review of some or all disaster recovery and business continuity plans, procedures, and other documentation. A walkthrough is performed by an entire group of individuals in a live discussion.

wall   A structure that prevents or deters passage by unauthorized personnel.

WAN switch   A general term encompassing several types of wide area network switching devices, including ATM switches, Frame Relay switches, MPLS switches, and ISDN switches.

war chalking   The practice of marking buildings (using chalk) with symbols to indicate the presence of a Wi-Fi access point, including some basic facts about it. See also *war driving, Wi-Fi*.

war dialing   An attack designed to discover unprotected remote access modems by dialing phone numbers sequentially and recording those with modems.

war driving   An attack on a wireless network where attackers intercept and record information about Wi-Fi access points.

warm site   An alternate processing center where recovery systems are present, but at a lower state of readiness than recovery systems at a hot site. For example, while the same version of the operating system may be running on the warm site system, it may be a few patch levels behind primary systems.

waterfall model   A software development life cycle process where activities are sequential and are executed one time in a software project. See also *software development life cycle (SDLC)*.

web-based application   An application design where the database and all business logic are stored on central servers, and where user workstations use only web browsers to access the application.

web-based application development A software development effort where the application's user interface is based on the HTTP (Hypertext Transport Protocol) and HTML (Hypertext Markup Language) standards.

web proxy filter A central program or device that monitors and, optionally, filters web communications. A web proxy filter is often used to control the sites (or categories of sites) that users are permitted to access from the workplace. Some web proxy filters can also protect an organization from malware.

web server A server that runs specialized software that makes static and dynamic HTML pages available to users.

web services A means for system-to-system communications using the HTTP protocol.

Web Services Description Language (WSDL) An XML-based language that is used to describe web services. See also *web services*.

wet pipe A fire sprinkler system where all sprinkler pipes are filled with water. Each sprinkler head is equipped with a fuse—a heat-sensitive glass bulb—that breaks upon reaching a preset temperature. When this occurs, water is discharged from just that sprinkler head, which is presumably located near a fire. See also *fire sprinkler system*.

Wi-Fi The common name for a wireless LAN protocol. See also *802.11*.

Wi-Fi protected access (WPA) An encryption standard for 802.11 wireless networks. The final version of WPA is known as WPA-2. See also *802.11*.

wide area network (WAN) A network whose size ranges from regional to international. This term is also used to describe a single point-to-point connection between two distant locations (a "WAN connection").

wideband code division multiple access (W-CDMA) An airlink standard for wireless communications between mobile devices and base stations.

wired equivalency protocol (WEP) An encryption standard for 802.11 wireless networks. WEP has been compromised and should be replaced with WPA-2. See also *802.11, Wi-Fi Protected Access (WPA)*.

wireless USB (WUSB) A short-range, high-bandwidth standard wireless communications protocol used to connect computer peripherals.

work breakdown structure (WBS) A logical representation of the high-level and detailed tasks that must be performed to complete a project.

worm A type of malware containing stand-alone programs capable of human-assisted and automatic propagation.

X.25 A common carrier standard for transporting packets from one station to another. X.25 has been replaced by Frame Relay. See also *Frame Relay*.

Zachman framework An enterprise architecture framework used to describe an IT architecture in increasing levels of detail.

INDEX

The Best in Security Certification Prep

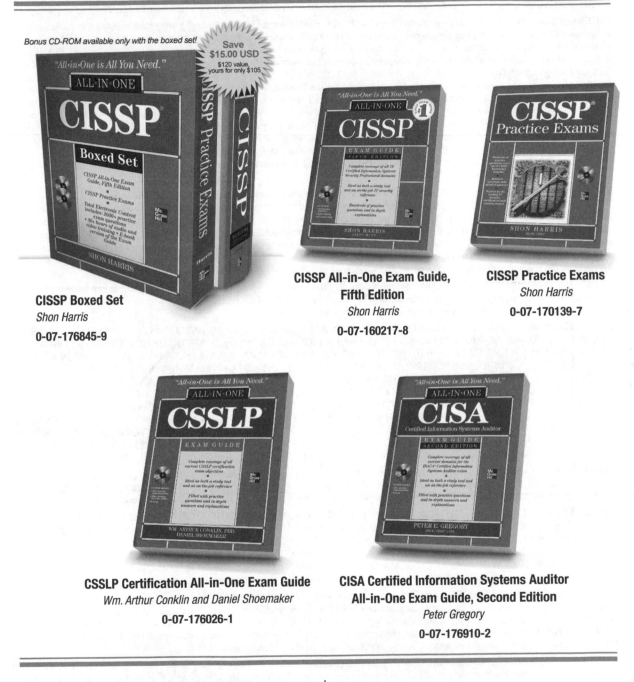

Bonus CD-ROM available only with the boxed set!

Save $15.00 USD
$120 value,
yours for only $105

CISSP Boxed Set
Shon Harris
0-07-176845-9

CISSP All-in-One Exam Guide, Fifth Edition
Shon Harris
0-07-160217-8

CISSP Practice Exams
Shon Harris
0-07-170139-7

CSSLP Certification All-in-One Exam Guide
Wm. Arthur Conklin and Daniel Shoemaker
0-07-176026-1

CISA Certified Information Systems Auditor All-in-One Exam Guide, Second Edition
Peter Gregory
0-07-176910-2

LICENSE AGREEMENT

THIS PRODUCT (THE "PRODUCT") CONTAINS PROPRIETARY SOFTWARE, DATA AND INFORMATION (INCLUDING DOCUMENTATION) OWNED BY THE McGRAW-HILL COMPANIES, INC. ("McGRAW-HILL") AND ITS LICENSORS. YOUR RIGHT TO USE THE PRODUCT IS GOVERNED BY THE TERMS AND CONDITIONS OF THIS AGREEMENT.

LICENSE: Throughout this License Agreement, "you" shall mean either the individual or the entity whose agent opens this package. You are granted a non-exclusive and non-transferable license to use the Product subject to the following terms:

(i) If you have licensed a single user version of the Product, the Product may only be used on a single computer (i.e., a single CPU). If you licensed and paid the fee applicable to a local area network or wide area network version of the Product, you are subject to the terms of the following subparagraph (ii).

(ii) If you have licensed a local area network version, you may use the Product on unlimited workstations located in one single building selected by you that is served by such local area network. If you have licensed a wide area network version, you may use the Product on unlimited workstations located in multiple buildings on the same site selected by you that is served by such wide area network; provided, however, that any building will not be considered located in the same site if it is more than five (5) miles away from any building included in such site. In addition, you may only use a local area or wide area network version of the Product on one single server. If you wish to use the Product on more than one server, you must obtain written authorization from McGraw-Hill and pay additional fees.

(iii) You may make one copy of the Product for back-up purposes only and you must maintain an accurate record as to the location of the back-up at all times.

COPYRIGHT; RESTRICTIONS ON USE AND TRANSFER: All rights (including copyright) in and to the Product are owned by McGraw-Hill and its licensors. You are the owner of the enclosed disc on which the Product is recorded. You may not use, copy, decompile, disassemble, reverse engineer, modify, reproduce, create derivative works, transmit, distribute, sublicense, store in a database or retrieval system of any kind, rent or transfer the Product, or any portion thereof, in any form or by any means (including electronically or otherwise) except as expressly provided for in this License Agreement. You must reproduce the copyright notices, trademark notices, legends and logos of McGraw-Hill and its licensors that appear on the Product on the back-up copy of the Product which you are permitted to make hereunder. All rights in the Product not expressly granted herein are reserved by McGraw-Hill and its licensors.

TERM: This License Agreement is effective until terminated. It will terminate if you fail to comply with any term or condition of this License Agreement. Upon termination, you are obligated to return to McGraw-Hill the Product together with all copies thereof and to purge all copies of the Product included in any and all servers and computer facilities.

DISCLAIMER OF WARRANTY: THE PRODUCT AND THE BACK-UP COPY ARE LICENSED "AS IS." McGRAW-HILL, ITS LICENSORS AND THE AUTHORS MAKE NO WARRANTIES, EXPRESS OR IMPLIED, AS TO THE RESULTS TO BE OBTAINED BY ANY PERSON OR ENTITY FROM USE OF THE PRODUCT, ANY INFORMATION OR DATA INCLUDED THEREIN AND/OR ANY TECHNICAL SUPPORT SERVICES PROVIDED HEREUNDER, IF ANY ("TECHNICAL SUPPORT SERVICES"). McGRAW-HILL, ITS LICENSORS AND THE AUTHORS MAKE NO EXPRESS OR IMPLIED WARRANTIES OF MERCHANTABILITY OR FITNESS FOR A PARTICULAR PURPOSE OR USE WITH RESPECT TO THE PRODUCT. McGRAW-HILL, ITS LICENSORS, AND THE AUTHORS MAKE NO GUARANTEE THAT YOU WILL PASS ANY CERTIFICATION EXAM WHATSOEVER BY USING THIS PRODUCT. NEITHER McGRAW-HILL, ANY OF ITS LICENSORS NOR THE AUTHORS WARRANT THAT THE FUNCTIONS CONTAINED IN THE PRODUCT WILL MEET YOUR REQUIREMENTS OR THAT THE OPERATION OF THE PRODUCT WILL BE UNINTERRUPTED OR ERROR FREE. YOU ASSUME THE ENTIRE RISK WITH RESPECT TO THE QUALITY AND PERFORMANCE OF THE PRODUCT.

LIMITED WARRANTY FOR DISC: To the original licensee only, McGraw-Hill warrants that the enclosed disc on which the Product is recorded is free from defects in materials and workmanship under normal use and service for a period of ninety (90) days from the date of purchase. In the event of a defect in the disc covered by the foregoing warranty, McGraw-Hill will replace the disc.

LIMITATION OF LIABILITY: NEITHER McGRAW-HILL, ITS LICENSORS NOR THE AUTHORS SHALL BE LIABLE FOR ANY INDIRECT, SPECIAL OR CONSEQUENTIAL DAMAGES, SUCH AS BUT NOT LIMITED TO, LOSS OF ANTICIPATED PROFITS OR BENEFITS, RESULTING FROM THE USE OR INABILITY TO USE THE PRODUCT EVEN IF ANY OF THEM HAS BEEN ADVISED OF THE POSSIBILITY OF SUCH DAMAGES. THIS LIMITATION OF LIABILITY SHALL APPLY TO ANY CLAIM OR CAUSE WHATSOEVER WHETHER SUCH CLAIM OR CAUSE ARISES IN CONTRACT, TORT, OR OTHERWISE. Some states do not allow the exclusion or limitation of indirect, special or consequential damages, so the above limitation may not apply to you.

U.S. GOVERNMENT RESTRICTED RIGHTS: Any software included in the Product is provided with restricted rights subject to subparagraphs (c), (1) and (2) of the Commercial Computer Software-Restricted Rights clause at 48 C.F.R. 52.227-19. The terms of this Agreement applicable to the use of the data in the Product are those under which the data are generally made available to the general public by McGraw-Hill. Except as provided herein, no reproduction, use, or disclosure rights are granted with respect to the data included in the Product and no right to modify or create derivative works from any such data is hereby granted.

GENERAL: This License Agreement constitutes the entire agreement between the parties relating to the Product. The terms of any Purchase Order shall have no effect on the terms of this License Agreement. Failure of McGraw-Hill to insist at any time on strict compliance with this License Agreement shall not constitute a waiver of any rights under this License Agreement. This License Agreement shall be construed and governed in accordance with the laws of the State of New York. If any provision of this License Agreement is held to be contrary to law, that provision will be enforced to the maximum extent permissible and the remaining provisions will remain in full force and effect.